Nixon's Vietnam War

Nixon's Vietnam War

Jeffrey Kimball

 University Press of Kansas

© 1998 by the University Press of Kansas
All rights reserved

Published by the University Press of Kansas (Lawrence, Kansas 66049), which was
organized by the Kansas Board of Regents and is operated and funded by Emporia
State University, Fort Hays State University, Kansas State University, Pittsburg State
University, the University of Kansas, and Wichita State University

Library of Congress Cataloging-in-Publication Data

Kimball, Jeffrey P.
   Nixon's Vietnam War / Jeffrey Kimball.
     p. cm. — (Modern war studies)
   Includes bibliographical references.
   ISBN 0-7006-0924-5 (alk. paper)
   1. Vietnamese Conflict, 1961–1975—United States. 2. Nixon,
Richard M. (Richard Milhous), 1913–1994. 3. Kissinger, Henry, 1923– .
4. United States—Politics and government—1969–1974. I. Title.
II. Series.
DS558.K557   1998
959.704'3373—dc21   98-19431

British Library of Cataloguing in Publication Data is available.

Printed in the United States of America

10 9 8 7 6 5 4 3 2 1

The paper used in this publication meets the minimum requirements of the American
National Standard for Permanence of Paper for Printed Library Materials Z39.48-1984.

For Pearl and Burnett

Contents

(Photo insert follows p. 212)

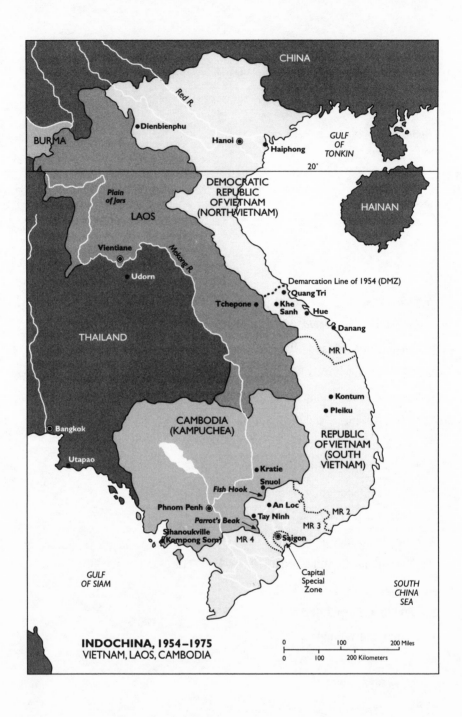

CHINA

Red R.

Dienbienphu

Hanoi ◉

Haiphong

BURMA

GULF
OF
TONKIN

20°

HAINAN

Plain
of Jars

LAOS

DEMOCRATIC
REPUBLIC
OF VIETNAM
(NORTH VIETNAM)

Vientiane ◉

Udorn

Mekong R.

THAILAND

Demarcation Line of 1954 (DMZ)

Tchepone

Quang Tri

Khe
Sanh

Hue

Danang

MR 1

Bangkok ◉

CAMBODIA
(KAMPUCHEA)

Kontum

Pleiku

REPUBLIC
OF VIETNAM
(SOUTH
VIETNAM)

Utapao

Kratie

Snuol

Fish Hook

Phnom Penh ◉

An Loc

MR 2

Parrot's Beak

Tay Ninh

MR 3

Sihanoukville
(Kampong Som)

MR 4

Saigon ◉

GULF
OF SIAM

Capital
Special
Zone

SOUTH
CHINA
SEA

INDOCHINA, 1954–1975
VIETNAM, LAOS, CAMBODIA

0   100   200 Miles

0   100   200 Kilometers

Preface

This book is about Richard Nixon's critical role in making and implementing United States policy toward Vietnam from 1953 to 1973. Following an introductory chapter about his self-conscious mythmaking and subconscious psychology, my chronological story of Nixon's Vietnam War begins with his first significant involvement in the conflict in late 1953. As a young vice president during the administration of Dwight Eisenhower and, subsequently, as a seasoned politician during the 1960s, Nixon advocated policies that drew the United States more deeply into the quagmire of Vietnam. The foreign policy lessons he learned during the fifteen years before his election in 1968 served as the basis for the policies he pursued during his own presidency, as he grappled with the dilemmas and frustrations previous presidents had faced in Vietnam. The main part of the book deals with his direction of the final climactic phase of the American war effort—from his inauguration as president in January 1969 to the signing of the Paris Agreement of January 1973, which formally terminated direct American military intervention. It concludes with a brief analysis of Nixon's own explanation of his role in waging and ending the war.

Supported by their powerful allies, the opposing Vietnamese parties continued to struggle after the Paris Agreement until late April 1975, when Saigon fell and Vietnam was reunited under a Communist government. Nixon's role in directing America's Vietnam policy progressively diminished through 1973 and up to his resignation in August 1974, as he devoted ever more attention to the unfolding Watergate scandal. A proper history of this last phase of the Vietnam War would require another, albeit smaller, volume. While it is a story well worth telling, what happened in Indochina between January 1973 and April 1975 was virtually preordained by the terms of the Paris Agreement and the circumstances of power that Nixon left behind in Southeast Asia and the United States.

The war Nixon waged during his first presidential term was only one of several phases of the thirty-year conflict in Indochina, each marked by "turning points" of de-escalation or escalation in the fighting. Yet, this Nixon phase was surely one of the most important. For the Vietnamese, Laotians, and Cambodians, it meant four more years of escalating warfare in the air and on the ground, leaving Indochina after the Paris Agreement in unresolved, violent turmoil. For American armed forces in Vietnam, the reverse was true: Nixon slowly withdrew American troops, and casualties declined. Nonetheless, American dead and wounded during the Nixon period amounted to one-half of the total during President Lyndon Johnson's Vietnam War. For Nixon himself, Vietnam became the main preoccupation of his presidency. No less significant was the legacy Nixon's war left behind. Nixon's handling of the Vietnam War, as well as his related abuses of power in what came to be known collectively as Watergate, exacerbated the complex crisis in American culture that the Vietnam War had precipitated and that he had inherited as president. The most visible manifestations of this crisis included the decline of respect for the office of the presidency and of faith in the trustworthiness of government, bitter political divisiveness, the alienation of youth, economic stagflation at home, a balance-of-payments deficit abroad, the shattering of the domestic consensus that had supported America's cold war foreign policies, and the undermining of the credibility of America's will and ability to intervene effectively against third world revolutions. Moreover, the argument Nixon made in defense of his Vietnam policies distorted the debate among Americans about the war's causes, meaning, and ending, thus hindering the process of understanding and healing. Nixon convinced many Americans that the war he waged during his four years had as one of its main purposes the release of American prisoners of war in Indochina. He further maintained that his effort to achieve "peace with honor" had been hampered by the disloyal opposition of the antiwar movement, the press, liberals, and Congress. But for their opposition, he claimed, his war would have been shorter and South Vietnam could have been saved from collapse in 1975. Despite Saigon's fall, he insisted, the war he waged not only succeeded in bringing home American POWs but also staved off revolutionary Communism long enough to make possible the emergence of "free-market" economies among the Asian Tigers of the Pacific Rim. This argument enabled future interventionists to maintain that the Vietnam War had succeeded, that it had been a noble cause, and that it had demonstrated that military power could successfully solve the global crises America faced—if only America's will were not undermined by dissenters.

But this book is not about Nixon's legacy. It is about the creation of that legacy. It is a record of Nixon's Vietnam strategies and policies and an analysis of the historical issues raised by them. The project took form in January 1988, after I had landed in Vietnam with a group of other educators and spent several weeks visiting towns and cities from Hanoi in the north to Saigon in the south. While on a trip to the Kham Thien district of Hanoi, which had been leveled on December 26, 1972, by B-52 bombings associated with Operation Linebacker II, I conceived the idea of writing a smallish monograph on these "Christmas bombings." To many Americans and Vietnamese, Linebacker II was fraught with symbolism and significance, but the operation also seemed inexplicable. Interpretations of its purpose were awash in controversy. Nixon's own explanation constituted a central element in his myth of the war's conclusion. Returning home, I came to realize, however, that I could not explain the operation without a fuller understanding of Nixon's Vietnam policies. After much reading, many trips to archives, another trek to Vietnam, and a six-month research fellowship at the Norwegian Nobel Institute in Oslo in the company of Vietnamese, Russian, Chinese, and Norwegian scholars, the once-small book about this one important event had grown into a full-scale study of Nixon's Vietnam policies and his career experiences with the Vietnam imbroglio. My task became and remained that of identifying his policy goals; relating these to the goals of previous administrations; uncovering the obscure history of his and Henry Kissinger's diplomacy; understanding Vietnamese goals, diplomacy, and strategy; assessing the events that led to the Paris Agreement; and clarifying the historical controversies that surrounded Nixon's Vietnam policy, diplomacy, strategy, and legacy.

I believe this book is the first comprehensive study devoted exclusively to Nixon's Vietnam War. It is founded on a careful analysis of the relevant memoirs, oral histories, and secondary accounts, as well as personal interviews and research into many of the most recently declassified manuscripts and documents of the Nixon period. Particularly useful have been the National Security Council files of the White House, which were opened in a major documents release in March 1998, as well as those specifically concerned with POWs and MIAs, which were previously opened in a separate release in November 1993. I also requested and obtained several declassifications of other important documents, drew on other papers in the Nixon archives, and benefited from several Soviet, East German, and Vietnamese documents that came into my possession. H. R. Haldeman's published diary, the full-text, compact disc version of which augments his original handwritten notes housed in the Nixon archives, has provided valuable perspectives and new information on the inner workings and moods of the Nixon White House. Archival documents on Vietnam issues and recently opened White House tapes on Watergate-related conversations corroborate Haldeman's notes and diary entries.

In writing the history of Nixon's Vietnam War, I chose a narrative style, occasionally interspersed by analyses of special issues or participants' accounts, in order to re-create the evolution of Nixon's policies; describe their relationship to personal, political, and international factors; and address the many controversies swirling around his policies. Imbedded in this narrative is a methodology—a scheme of investigation and argument—by which I hoped to make sense of the policies of very complex and secretive men, namely, Nixon, Kissinger, and the members of the Hanoi Politburo. I have placed the story of Nixon's Vietnam War in the context of several themes: American foreign policy constants, such as post–World War II globalism, policy makers' concerns about protecting America's credibility as a counterrevolution guarantor, and atomic diplomacy; Nixon's own "worldview," or his foreign policy ideology; Nixon's and Kissinger's psychologies; domestic political factors, such as Nixon's concerns about getting elected and reelected; the influence advisers and bureaucrats had upon his conduct of the war; the intricate connections between diplomacy and strategy, politics and war; and the international dimensions of the Indochina conflict, which include the actions and intentions of the Vietnamese, Soviets, and Chinese. These thematic elements are set up in the first three chapters.

This book is not "The Complete History of Nixon's Vietnam War," which would require fuller treatment of topics other than policy and diplomacy. It is a broadly based "diplomatic history," one that views his policy and diplomacy from the point of view of their interrelationships with the environment in which he formulated and carried them out—politics, personality, ideology, bureaucratic dynamics, economic goals, military strategy, international relations, and aspects of American and Vietnamese culture.

Throughout, I have tried to fill gaps in existing knowledge of what happened and to address as many as possible of the issues associated with Nixon's policies and strategies that have puzzled historians and other investigators. These gaps and issues are too numerous to list here, but some of the major questions include the following: Did Nixon have a personality disorder that affected his policy making? Did Nixon believe in the "madman theory," and if so, did he apply it to his Vietnam strategy? As he entered the presidency, was he seeking "victory" in South Vietnam, or was he seeking an "honorable" exit that fell short of victory? Did he have a plan to end the war? Did he and Kissinger develop a "decent-interval solution"? What was the nature of the relationship between the two men? What was the influence of the antiwar movement on Nixon's conduct of the war? What role did Nixon's "triangular" and "linkage" diplomacy vis-à-vis the Soviet Union and China play in shaping his Vietnam strategies, or vice versa? What really happened in the secret negotiations? Did Kissinger strike out on his own? Did Nixon win the war or, as he put it, win the peace?

The short answer to these questions is that Nixon's peculiar psychology and the odd relationship he had with Henry Kissinger profoundly influenced the strategy he used in seeking to achieve his globalist goals in Vietnam. The madman theory was the central element in his strategy and was even more important than Vietnamization and triangular diplomacy. The policy goals he pursued arose out of established policy currents in post–World War II American society. These were goals he had helped to define in the 1950s and 1960s, and to which he was attracted by virtue of his ideological worldview, itself rooted in his social, economic, and political background. When he entered office, he, as had previous presidents, intended to "win" in South Vietnam—that is, preserve it as a non-Communist, procapitalist, pro-Western political entity, thereby also preserving the credibility of American power. Only later, when he understood that his original strategy was failing, did he and Kissinger accept the decent-interval solution. The record of the negotiations is more difficult to summarize in a few brief sentences, but suffice it to say here that Kissinger's and Nixon's accounts, on which most histories have heretofore relied, were incomplete, disingenuous, and self-serving. The documentary record, such as it is, reveals, for example, that Nixon's goal of preserving the Saigon regime took precedence over every other issue, including the release of POWs. It was American diplomatic "intransigence," every bit as much as Vietnamese "intransigence," that served to prolong the war. In the end, however, Nixon and Kissinger, forced by political, economic, and military circumstances, agreed to a settlement that acknowledged the legitimacy of the revolutionary movement in South Vietnam and, by leaving North Vietnamese forces in place, seriously compromised the Saigon regime. Nixon's claim of victory is not supported by this negotiating record, a record he tried to obscure with his December 1972 bombing campaign and his postagreement public relations spin on the war. The antiwar movement writ large had helped to create the political circumstances that led to the withdrawal of American troops and ultimately prevented Nixon from continuing the American war beyond 1972.

I have been most fortunate in receiving the help and encouragement of many individuals and institutions. Research was made possible by grants from the Philip and Elaine Hampton Fund for Faculty International Initiatives and the College of Arts and Science of Miami University, as well as the Air Force Historical Research Agency and the Norwegian Nobel Institute. An Assigned Research Appointment in 1992 allowed me to get the project under way, and a Senior Research Fellowship from the Nobel Institute in 1995 enabled me to begin writing in an atmosphere of intellectual stimulation. The Director of the Nobel Institute, Geir Lundestad, the Research Director, Odd Arne Westad, and the Head Librarian, Anne C. Kjelling, as well as the staff of the institute and its library, were gracious in their hospitality and assistance. David Anderson of the University of Indianapolis and Stanley I. Kutler of the University of Wisconsin read the manuscript and offered helpful suggestions. Anderson also assisted me in various ways during the early stages of the project, as did Stephen E. Ambrose, Scott L. Bills, George C. Herring, Robert D. Schulzinger, and Melvin Small. Allan Winkler and Charlotte Goldy, who successively served as Chair of the Department of History at Miami University during the period of research and writing, fostered my work in numerous ways. The comments of my department colleagues on an early paper proved beneficial. Steve Delue and John Skillings, Associate Deans of the College of Arts and Science, were receptive to my requests for assistance. John McAuliff, Director of the U.S.–Indochina Reconciliation Project, led the first expedition to Vietnam in which I participated in 1987–1988. Nguyen Vu Tung, a historian at the Institute of Foreign Affairs, Hanoi, provided invaluable assistance of various kinds: helping arrange my trip to Vietnam in 1994, translating Vietnamese passages, and sharing information and ideas with me during our fellowships at the Nobel Institute. Dr. Tran Duc Cuong, Vice Director of the Institute for the History of Viet-

nam, as well as Dr. Tran Huu Dinh, Professor Vu Huy Phuc, and Mr. Doan Noi
were generous hosts, sponsoring my research in Vietnam, arranging interviews,
sharing their views on the war, and transporting me about Hanoi and the Red River
Valley. Nguyen Dinh Dung assisted with translations and travel. Interviews granted
by Daniel Ellsberg, Huong Tung, Winston Lord, Lu Van Loi, Nguyen Co Thach,
Tran Duc Cuong, Tran Tuan Mau, Nguyen Van Khanh, and Le Mau Han significantly aided my understanding of the war, as did informal conversations with other
Vietnamese citizens. Ellsberg and Thach shared documents that were most helpful. Conversations at the Nobel Institute with Ilya V. Gaiduk, a researcher with
the Moscow Institute of World History, gave me a clearer perspective on Soviet
policies during the war. Carson Clements, Michael Hebert, Jeremiah Kitunda,
Kathy Mason, and Talaat Shehata—all graduate students in the Department of
History—provided research assistance from time to time. Robert Thurston, a faculty colleague in the department, assisted with German translations, and David
Fahey, another colleague, cheered me on. Jeri Schaner and Liz Smith assisted with
secretarial matters. Historians cannot do without archives and libraries, and I am
most grateful for the courteous and efficient assistance of the staffs of the Miami
University Library, the Nixon Presidential Materials Staff, the Air Force Historical Research Agency, the National Security Archive, the Library of Congress, and
the Massachusetts Historical Society. Michael Briggs, Editor in Chief of the University Press of Kansas, was an early supporter of the project and shepherded it to
its completion. In addition to their emotional support, Leslie Kimball lent her
expertise in psychology, Daryl Kimball provided information on nuclear issues,
Sally Murray James drew the map of Indochina, and Stephen Kimball helped me
with computer issues. Linda Musmeci Kimball lovingly gave her encouragement,
engaged me patiently in many conversations about Nixon, and copyedited the
manuscript.

Abbreviations and Special Names in Text

ARVN: Army of the Republic of Vietnam (see RVNAF)

CINCPAC: Commander in Chief Pacific

COSVN: Central Office for South Vietnam

DMZ: Demilitarized Zone

DRV: Democratic Republic of Vietnam (North Vietnam)

GVN: Government of Vietnam (aka RVN)

ICCS: International Commission of Control and Supervision

Khmer Rouge: Cambodian Communists

JCS: Joint Chiefs of Staff

JMC: Joint Military Commission (representatives of the RVNAF and PLAF)

MACV: Military Assistance Command Vietnam

MIRV: Multiple Independently Targeted Reentry Vehicles

NCRC: National Council of National Reconciliation and Concord

NLF: National Liberation Front (see VC and PRG)

NSC: National Security Council

NSSM: National Security Study Memorandum

NVA: North Vietnamese Army (see PAVN)

Pathet Lao: Laotian Communists

PAVN: People's Army of Vietnam (aka NVA)

PLAF: People's Liberation Armed Forces (the military arm of the NLF; aka Viet Cong)

PRC: People's Republic of China

PRG: Provisional Revolutionary Government (representing the NLF)

RVN: Republic of Vietnam (South Vietnam; aka GVN)

RVNAF: Republic of Vietnam Armed Forces (see ARVN)

SAM: Surface-to-air missile

SVN: South Vietnam

VC: Vietcong (slang for PLAF)

VNLAF: Vietnamese Liberation Armed Forces (composite term for NVA-VC forces or PAVN-PLAF forces)

VSSG: Vietnam Special Studies Group

VVAW: Vietnam Veterans Against the War

VWP: Vietnamese Workers' Party

WSAG: Washington Special Action Group

1

Dragons of Myth and Mind

No one loves him, fears him, or hates him, and he needs to have all three.
—H. R. Haldeman, paraphrasing Richard Nixon[1]

Come not between the dragon and his wrath.
—William Shakespeare[2]

LEADERSHIP, MYTH, AND VIETNAM

President Richard M. Nixon believed that "what an individual does is irrelevant to his ability to lead; the whole point is *how* he does it." If his followers did not perceive him or his style to be great or good, then his great, good deeds would be unappreciated, and "we lose the ability to lead." In his view, John F. Kennedy "did nothing but appeared great; LBJ did everything and appeared terrible." To be effective a leader must touch the hearts of his constituency by communicating his own inner spirit, drive, and sense of destiny. A major task of presidential leadership, therefore, is to build up the "personality of the man"—to create a mystique of character. "The mystique," Nixon told Haldeman in 1970, "is more important than content." But he often complained that his staff failed in this: "The trouble with all our backgrounders," he grumbled to Harry Robbins "Bob" Haldeman, his chief of staff and faithful note taker, "was that they were all on *what* we accomplished, nothing about the man."[3]

One way of establishing a mystique, Nixon explained in a 1982 essay, is by "the creation of myths."[4] He conceived of myth in both of its senses: as invented, fictitious story, and as traditional or legendary story, involving heroes and gods, or at least large forces, that explained life, history, and cultural practice. "Legends are often an artful intertwining of fact and myth, designed to beguile, to

1

impress, to inspire, or sometimes simply to attract attention." Myths enveloped the persona of a president with an aura of meaning, mystery, drama, and mystical power, reinforcing the preexisting institutional majesty of the highest political office in the land.

Nixon attempted to apply these and other leadership maxims throughout his presidency. He had been elated, for instance on July 20, 1969, when American astronauts landed on the moon, but he became annoyed the next day when a *New York Times* editorial reproached him for "sharing the stage." In a televised direct-link conversation with the crew of *Apollo 11,* he had associated their landing on the Sea of Tranquility with his policies to achieve peace in Vietnam and the world. Smarting from this and previous criticisms of his presidency, but also inspired by the moon flight, Nixon decided to launch a new public relations campaign. On July 21 he met in the Oval Office with his "hard-core inner circle"—Haldeman, John Ehrlichman, and Henry A. Kissinger. Nixon instructed them to "build up [the] P[resident], *not* themselves"; to do this, they should acquire "a sense of history and of drama" and also employ "dirty tricks." The campaign would be called "Presidential Offensive," with the purpose of establishing "the mystique of the presidency." On that day, he spoke as he had before and would again of using the great power of the United States and the executive office "more effectively at home and abroad." He and his inner circle, he declared, must "zero in on [a] hard-nosed basis, . . . never be indecisive, get going, take risks, be exciting. . . . Boldness. . . . Go for broke now, on what's right." We have failed thus far, he felt, "where we've temporized."[5]

Five months later he was disappointed when he learned that *Time* magazine had chosen "Middle Americans" over him as "Man of the Year." Because *Time* had anointed the past four Democratic presidents after their first year in office but had not chosen Eisenhower until the second-to-last year of his administration, Nixon presumed that his own failure in achieving this coveted honor had been caused by the unwillingness of the "liberal press" to give him, a conservative, a "fair shake." His disappointment spurred him to push his inner circle to improve their public relations "operations," for he felt that while the administration had faired "pretty well," they had not succeeded in conveying the most important point about his presidency—his superior leadership—which he had demonstrated, he believed, by making "major decisions over the advice of his Cabinet, etc." He told Haldeman: "We have so little time. While you've got the power, you have to move quickly, especially now when we're up, build a mythology."[6] A week later, still complaining about their failure to develop a proper "image" of him, he returned to another theme, that of the importance of "aloofness"—a lesson he drew from observing the leadership mystique of President Charles de Gaulle, of France.

Three years later, in January 1973, Nixon's White House staff of advertising agents, speechwriters, and political campaigners fashioned a myth of Nixon's Vietnam War that incorporated his notions of mystique, leadership, and historical drama, elevating him to the status of great leader, while defending him against those who would condemn his policies. It was the eve of his second inauguration and the signing of the Paris Agreement on Ending the War and Restoring Peace in Vietnam, but Nixon was being criticized by those on the left and the center of the political spectrum for his Christmastime bombings of North Vietnam, and by those on the right for negotiating a flawed peace agreement. The Vietnam "line" he and his staff had developed asserted that despite the opposition of Congress, the press, and the antiwar movement to his policies regarding Vietnam, he had possessed sufficient political courage, diplomatic wisdom, and military forceful-ness to see the war through, thereby preserving the independence of South Viet-nam while simultaneously withdrawing American troops and gaining the release of American prisoners of war (POWs).[7] This was peace with honor.

Nixon's effort to put a positive spin on his role in the war was finally sub-sumed in his desperate postresignation battle to restore his public image from the disgrace of Watergate, which initially seemed irreversible. By late 1978, after completing the manuscript *RN: The Memoirs of Richard Nixon* and speaking to receptive audiences in Asia, Europe, and the American South, he had come to believe that he could rehabilitate his reputation by emphasizing his putative achievements in foreign affairs.[8] These, he argued, included not only his victory in Vietnam but also the opening to China; relaxing tensions with the Soviet Union while forcing its leaders to acknowledge human rights in Eastern Europe; imple-menting the Nixon Doctrine for third world security; and initiating a peace pro-cess in the Middle East. He had created a structure of global peace.[9]

To whatever degree Nixon's version of the history of his direction of the Vietnam War and of foreign policy corresponded with reality, he had not attempted to be objective. When Kissinger told him in 1974 that history would judge him one of the great presidents, the president responded, "That depends, Henry, on who writes the history."[10] Nixon "spent an inordinate amount of time," one histo-rian quipped, "trying to shape or obstruct" history.[11] He wrote at least a dozen books of autobiography and polemic, while drawing on a personal diary that no historian has seen or probably ever will see and restricting researchers' access to his presidential tape recordings and papers through vigorous litigation against the National Archives and Records Administration—as though these documents were gold to be hoarded, never to be spent.[12] Nonetheless, Nixon's history of the war would influence the way many Americans would remember it; it would influence American politics into the future; and it revealed much about how he thought about and acted upon foreign policy.[13]

There are "men of thought and men of action," Nixon argued in one of his many books, and he considered himself to be both.[14] That part of him that was the man of political action was less interested in the scholar's noble yet elusive search for dispassionate objectivity in pursuit of truth than in telling his story as he wanted it told. The objectivity he embraced was calculating, the kind he believed would enable him to be successful in the arena of political and international combat. "Geopolitics," he wrote, "is . . . the *willingness* to be objective enough to weigh the motives and actions of both sides in any conflict with an equally critical eye."[15] His opinions about opponents were not usually generous or disinterested, however, and his account of Vietnam was deliberately partisan. Richard Whalen, a speechwriter for Nixon on Vietnam issues during the 1968 campaign, believed that Nixon had an "intellectual's mind," but it was "in the service of a salesman's temperament. He did not express his ideas, he put them across—and, in the process, turned them into something else."[16]

PUBLIC IMAGE

The public relations offensive begun during his presidency was not the first campaign in which Nixon had attempted to shape his public image. To be successful, all politicians must of course influence the definition of their persona. Nixon had a well-known and deserved reputation for having excelled in this arena. Veterans of the cold war remembered how he had used the Alger Hiss hearings in 1948 to establish his credentials as a national leader and anti-Communist crusader. Defending himself in his "Checkers speech" against charges of corruption—charges that threatened his place on the Republican presidential ticket of 1952—he had pioneered the use of national television as a political tool, successfully projecting to many viewers the image of a sincere, earnest, average middle-class American who had been accused unfairly by political enemies. Many years later he would note that the great leaders of history, in whose ranks he counted himself, were "accomplished actors. . . . Like great stage performers, they played their public role so well that they virtually became the parts that they created."[17] After losing to John F. Kennedy in the 1960 presidential election and relearning previous political lessons, he concluded that he had "spent too much time in the last campaign on substance and too little time on appearance: I paid too much attention to what I was going to say and too little to how I would look."[18] Losing once again in 1962 in his bid for the governorship of California, he compounded his defeat in a petulant, self-pitying attack on the news media during a postelection press conference. But he soon rebounded, rebuilding a following among the Republican rank and file during the midsixties.[19]

When he entered the presidential race of 1968, it was as the "new Nixon"— the experienced leader, the man of peace, the champion of law and order. This was a time of crisis, a time demanding wise statesmen. The candidate needed to portray himself as the new Nixon because the "old Nixon," the image he had worked so hard to create in his prior career, or at least the image he had acquired, was in the late sixties a political liability. To his competitors and much of the public, the old Nixon was "tricky Dick," the unscrupulous, secretive, combative, chronic campaigner who had distorted facts and used devious methods to suit his own purposes. He was remembered as a perpetual office seeker who was sanctimonious in references to his own behavior but ruthless in his attack on others. He sought to slash his political opponents' jugular by accusing them of Communist ties and sympathies or of weakness, incompetence, and corruption. In foreign policy, he often appeared to have been excessively militant, even dangerous. Many on the Right doubted the sincerity of Nixon's conservative beliefs. Wanting a winner, Republicans in general worried that Nixon lacked charisma and was a loser.[20]

To win over both the extreme and moderate factions of the Republican Party and to prepare his appeal for the general election against the Democratic nominee, Nixon projected a cautious, centrist image on foreign and domestic policies. To liven and update his stodgy personal image, he surrounded himself with young, bright assistants. To avoid exposing his garrulous habits of speech and his awkward physical movements during spontaneous encounters with the electronic press, he appeared on television in mostly controlled situations—in edited clips and political commercials before selected audiences and press representatives.[21] Nevertheless, his campaign staff often had to restrain the new Nixon from lapsing into the old Nixon. To their chagrin, for example, he continued to talk publicly about how the pencil-and-paper press had "shafted" him in the past.[22] He confronted labor union crowds in Democratic districts of Detroit, where he did not even expect to receive their votes, leading one staffer to comment that "it was like Caracas," where Nixon had provoked demonstrators in 1957 while touring South America as vice president of the United States. At San Jose State University during the 1970 congressional campaign, he taunted student antiwar demonstrators he could have avoided by jumping on the hood of his limousine, waving his arms, and giving them a V sign while remarking to his aides, "These kids hate this." The old speeches and scripts, only partially erased on the palimpsest, were still visible.[23]

The core ideas in the mythology Nixon crafted during his presidency and after Watergate to create a positive mystique and counter negative perceptions had their origins in Nixon's thinking and writing during prepresidential years. His complex life acquired universal meaning, he had maintained, in the pattern of challenge, struggle, crisis, success, failure, and resurrection, which he, along with many great leaders, had experienced. In the introduction to his first book, *Six Crises* (1962), written after his two terms as vice president in the 1950s and his defeat in the presidential election of 1960, Nixon said that it had not been his idea to write a memoir in midcareer. Urged by friends, he had agreed to discuss the possibility with a publisher. "I tried to jot down some ideas which might form a basis for discussion," he remembered. "I decided that what particularly distinguished my career from that of other public figures was that I had the good (or bad) fortune to be the central figure in several crisis situations with dimensions far beyond personal consideration."[24]

The "crisis situations" Nixon chose to discuss were either those of his own making or ones posing danger mainly to himself: the Hiss case, the slush-fund controversy, President Dwight D. Eisenhower's heart attack, his own confrontation with angry demonstrators in Caracas, the debate with Nikita S. Khrushchev, and the 1960 presidential campaign. To him these were not mere personal trials.

They were tense and anxious turning points presenting both danger and opportunity and calling forth extraordinary skills of leadership and traits of character, all of which he believed he possessed: experience, selflessness, discipline, hard work, physical and moral courage, confidence, coolheadedness, boldness, tenacity, decisiveness, willpower, and dedication to great causes.[25] Crises were acutely exciting and universally meaningful events, instructive to others who must act on the historical stage: "Crisis can indeed be agony. But it is the exquisite agony which a man might not want to experience again—yet would not for the world have missed. . . . We live in an age in which individual reaction to crisis may bear on the fate of mankind for centuries to come. . . . If the record of one man's experience in meeting crises . . . can help . . . , then this book may serve a useful purpose."[26]

Thirty years later, Nixon published *In the Arena: A Memoir of Victory, Defeat, and Renewal* (1990). One of his favorite refrains, Nixon had borrowed the title from Theodore Roosevelt: "It is not the critic who counts; not the man who points out how the strong man stumbles. . . . The credit belongs to the man who is actually in the arena, . . . who strives valiantly; who errs . . . ; who spends himself in a worthy cause, who at the best knows in the end the triumphs of high achievement and. . . . at worst, if he fails, at least fails while daring greatly."[27] Using the motif of valiant struggle as the criterion, Nixon listed in one chapter his "six major foreign-policy decisions as President." Four of the six had to do with the Vietnam War. He considered these major decisions not only because they benefited the national interest but also because they were "controversial" or "difficult" or "lonely" decisions for him.[28]

Nixon's autobiographical tales of triumphant striving by a beleaguered hero against malicious villains drew on mythological and political archetypes from American as well as European culture.[29] In the vocabulary of American popular-culture success stories, Nixon cast himself as a self-made man of humble origins who became the equal of great world leaders. Appealing to the hardheaded inclinations of his conservative constituency, he was a realistic practitioner of foreign policy, but appealing to the idealism of most of the American citizenry, he was also a peacemaker. Combining these realist-idealist qualities, he hoped to be seen as the architect of a *structure* of world peace, a desired ideal built upon a hardnosed, farsighted foreign policy. He characterized himself as a courageous, innovative, tough, take-charge, nationalist champion. He was thus a virile, patriotic, capable leader in control of events, who had adroitly managed the previously mishandled Vietnam War, moved boldly toward a rapprochement with China and détente with the Soviet Union, and calmly dealt with other dangerous crises the nation faced around the globe. Although humbled by Watergate and by previous setbacks in his career, he was not a pathetic victim; he was a resilient fighter in the great arena of life's drama, who overcame adversity time and again to return, renewed for the continuing battle—an example for all those Americans who would fight against the odds to succeed. Renewal, hard work, careful planning, shrewd-

ness, perseverance, risk taking—these themes dominate the biographical orientation film shown to visitors at the Richard Nixon Library and Birthplace in Yorba
Linda, California.[30]

On the grand, romantic, mythological level rooted in European legend, Nixon
portrayed himself as a brave warrior-champion, wielding an ax of righteousness,
slaying enemy dragons at home and abroad, rescuing the kingdom from the evil
times caused by the Communist enemy and the weaknesses of Democratic Party
rulers. In time he became the wise king, bringing peace and prosperity to his and
other lands. But as fate would have it, the cycle of success and failure, good times
and bad, would recur. Richard (the name his mother had chosen for him in romantic memory of the twelfth-century crusading English king Richard the Lion-
Heart)[31] was weakened by the wounds of Watergate—"the smoke screen of false
charges that ultimately undercut my administration's ability to govern effectively."[32] Without his direction, the Vietnam victory he had won and the global
structure of peace he had erected were subsequently undermined. He was a hero
betrayed, stabbed in the back by his domestic enemies, who were, in ways only
he and a few others understood, in league with his foreign foes.[33] Aware, however, of the "phenomenon of withdrawal and return," he would once again, like
"a mythical hero who belongs to legend as much as to reality," spend his time in
the "wilderness," withdrawing temporarily to be "transfigured in a newer capacity with new powers" in a post-Watergate career dedicated to serving a "worthy
cause": furthering truth, peace, freedom, opportunity, and justice.[34]

In the discourse of classic drama, Nixon presented himself as a tragic leader
who had challenged ordinary rules and fate, and, for that, his presidency was destroyed.[35] There were times, all too rare perhaps, when he seemed to understand
that the tragedy was larger than himself, as when he told his closest congressional
supporters on the eve of his resignation: "I let down my friends. I let down the
country. I let down our system of government and the dreams of . . . young people
that ought to get into government. . . . I let the American people down." But even
sympathetic critics noted that unlike the tragic heroes we most respect, Nixon had
never truly understood or acknowledged his own responsibility in the unfolding
calamities of his life or his country's, and therefore he underwent no redeeming
transformation. He could still say after his resignation: "Well, when the President
does it, that means that it is not illegal."[36]

Nixon did sense a tragic flaw within himself; it was a flaw, however, not of
character but of tactical error in giving his enemies their chance. "I brought myself down. I gave them a sword. And they stuck it in. And they twisted it with
relish. And, I guess, if I'd been in their position, I'd have done the same thing."[37]
Nixon became a pitiable stereotype in a modern melodrama. His story was not
the classic tragedy of accountability and heroic transcendence but a lament about
human frailty, original sin, and misadventure, which in the context of twentieth-
century foreign policy serves as the justification for cynical realpolitik.

At least one observer of Nixon's political career, speechwriter Richard

Whalen, denied that he was extraordinary, and he challenged the possibility of mythologizing Nixon: "Every attempt to depict Nixon as a larger-than-life symbol, whether hero or villain, ultimately failed before the fact that he was so *un*extraordinary. . . . He seemed one of us . . . mirroring strengths and weaknesses . . . in the American grain. . . . Nixon had no mask, manner, or reputation to hide behind; no tall tale, legend, or mystique would divert attention from his performance."[38]

But Nixon did wear a mask: almost all who worked with him, including Whalen, thought him inscrutable. Even Nixon seemed incapable of penetrating the veil. When writing memos and notes to his staff, or garrulously thinking out loud in the Oval Office, for example, he sometimes referred to himself in the third person, as "Nixon" or "RN"—a stranger who followed a script written by someone else. While reading news summaries of the October 1972 cease-fire agreement Kissinger had negotiated for him, Nixon claimed credit for it, noting in the margin of the page that it was "RN's settlement."[39] Yet he had already backed away from the agreement in the face of President Nguyen Van Thieu's objections and right-wing criticism from within and without his administration.

Contrary to Whalen's observation, Nixon did possess a larger-than-life mystique, one that combined qualities Nixon had tried to project with ones he wished he could have shed. He had, for example, a distinct, extraordinary manner, part of which was involuntary, tied up with his physical appearance and psychological tendencies. His words often sounded hollow, as though they were rehearsed, which they often were. His smile seemed insincere. He was a loner. He had difficulty making small talk. He extended little or no physical affection to friends or family. He gestured awkwardly with his hands when he spoke, and he stood in a hunched posture. He had a large head, a ski-slope nose, and a five o'clock shadow, which cartoonists drew upon for caricature. He scowled, and "his heavy brows and dark, deep-set eyes," Whalen noticed, "gave him a forbidding appearance even in repose."[40] Journalist Hugh Sidey affirmed what many had thought: "Nixon looks like an evil person."[41]

A powerful national figure and an international leader, Nixon was surely also extraordinary in his achievements, behavior, and reputation. He may have been more or less ordinary—and, in Whalen's phrase, "one of us"—in his weakness of character, degree of intellectual ability, number of mistakes committed, or other such qualities, which was what he feared about himself and what he thought the intellectual and political establishment thought of him, but his fear of these things was extraordinary. Still, the public display he made of his "ordinary" strengths and weaknesses in the American grain were partly the result of his attempt to create a mystique that would appeal to the ordinary voter. Nixon described his persona as one that originated in the common man, used what was best in that background, and transcended it. Whether truly ordinary or extraordinary, he hoped and strove to become a larger-than-life symbol—for some a hero to be admired, like his nemesis, John F. Kennedy, and for others a villain to be feared, like

Machiavelli's prince. Philosophizing about his public image in 1972, Nixon told Haldeman: "All people think the P's doing an excellent job, but no one loves him, fears him, or hates him, and he needs to have all three."[42] Usually failing to attract love, he regretfully had to heed Machiavelli's advice and settle for fear and hate.[43]

Nixon's real or apparent victories during his career—political comebacks from scandal and electoral defeat, rapprochement with China, détente with the Soviet Union, post-Watergate rehabilitation, and other purported successes—lent credence to the themes he repeated so often and for so long in public relations attack plans, books, and speeches. When death came on April 22, 1994, Nixon seemed to have achieved his final, sought-after resurrection. *Time* correspondent John F. Stacks wrote: "By the time he died at 9:08 Friday evening something close to affection, born of such long familiarity, could be discerned, even from his enemies. . . . History will judge Richard Nixon as much more than the Watergate man. . . . He leaves another, brighter monument: his own superhuman determination and stamina."[44]

Eulogies at his funeral in Yorba Linda on April 27 embraced Nixon's own motifs. Spoken were the "words he long sought."[45] President Bill Clinton emphasized Nixon's self-identification with national purposes and valiant personal struggle: "His life was bound up with the striving of our whole people, with our crises and our triumphs. . . . He always seemed to believe the greatest sin was remaining passive in the face of challenges." Henry Kissinger called attention to his former chief's courage, leadership, and commitment to doing things "completely" and "properly," avoiding half measures. The essence of his eulogy echoed the inscription on the fallen president's black marble headstone in the burial garden: "The greatest honor history can bestow is the title of peacemaker." Kissinger asserted that "when Richard Nixon left office, an agreement to end the war in Vietnam had been concluded, and the main lines of all subsequent policy were established: permanent dialogue with China, readiness without illusion to ease tensions with the Soviet Union." Senator Robert Dole similarly celebrated the former president's superlatively "effective leadership," but he drew special attention to Nixon the self-made man, the Nixon who was "one of us," who was admired by Americans because he "was an American hero; a hero who shared and honored their belief in working hard, worshiping God, loving their families, and saluting the flag."[46] Eulogizers across the nation repeated this praise.

The peacemaker theme that Nixon had emphasized about his own life achievements could be found in the most unexpected places. *Nixon*, Oliver Stone's 1995 feature-length movie, for example, which otherwise painted an unflattering portrait of the former president, concluded with an epilogue in which an off-camera narrator paraphrased Nixon's version of history: "Nixon always maintained that if he had not been driven from office the North Vietnamese would not have overwhelmed the South in 1975. . . . Cambodian society was destroyed and mass genocide resulted. In his absence Russia and the United States returned to a decade of high-budget military expansion and near war." The implication was that Nixon's presidency was a portrait in tragedy, a tale of a man who was flawed but who had achieved much in foreign affairs and could have been a greater president had he not drowned in Watergate.[47]

There were Americans, however, who, like Andrew Kopkind in *The Nation,* rejected Nixon's version of foreign policy success: "He bombed and bullied his way through Cambodia and Chile and slaughtered Americans and Vietnamese. The point of his Sino-Russian gambits was to play off one against the other while keeping ultimate control. He didn't end the Cold War any more than Reagan did."[48] In this view, the view of liberals whom Nixon regarded as enemies, *Nixon* himself was the fearsome dragon that endangered others, not the reverse.

MIND

Some observers of Nixon's life, even those who conceded Nixon's constructive achievements in foreign and domestic policy, argued that the dragons he fought had been the tormenting dragons within his own mind, which, alas, he had failed to conquer: insecurity, suspicion, rage, power seeking. His life, one of battling these in the public arena, was a tale of unquiet desperation.

Nixon and members of his family occasionally acknowledged, even if obliquely, his base instincts and internal conflicts. Responding to a question about how voters could simultaneously perceive him as a discredited, evil president while honoring him for his grasp of foreign policy, Nixon said: "You've got to be a little evil to understand those people out there. You have to have known the dark side of life to understand those people."[49] His daughter Tricia, who had a different and more sympathetic view of her father's torments, seemed to believe at least that he fought something within himself. She observed in a diary entry during the last days of the Watergate crisis that "Daddy has fought alone many times, almost alone many others. But there comes a point when fighting alone must come to mean fighting against yourself."[50]

Perhaps because of Nixon's own habit of personalizing his presidency, or perhaps because he was a fascinating and powerful public figure whose reputation, even after his death, continued to influence events,[51] histories of his presidency and policies have been written mostly in terms of his personality and psychology rather than of the times or of larger forces and processes.[52] On the one hand, a few accounts similar to Nixon's own concede minor mistakes and emphasize major successes, attributing them to his strength of character. Other accounts, similar to those of Nixon's original, liberal critics, emphasize his failures, attributing them to his distorted character—to the dark pit of his mind, his "black *id.*"[53]

Negative scholarly criticism had not escaped Nixon's notice. He wrote in "Family," a chapter of *In the Arena:* "I always find it amusing when psycho-historians I have never met conclude that I have what they consider to be a warped personality. Usually they trace it to my poor, lower-middle-class family. In fact, these pseudo-biographers are telling you more about themselves than about me, because it is obvious that in their books, *lower* class equals a *lack* of class."[54] To a psychohistorian, this statement reveals the quintessential Nixon. Writing about his family, he compulsively identified what he considered to be criticism of his character and background. In characterizing his critics, he uncovered his own inner fears—in this case, his perception that his family had been poor and that others thought his family lacked dignity and status.[55]

Psychohistorians as well as "normal" biographers and memoirists have indeed traced the origins of Nixon's character to the circumstances of his family's lower-middle-class circumstance, the hard physical work he performed in youth, and his relationship with his parents, although no one knows with certainty what specific experiences troubled him so, except that the death of his younger brother, Arthur, from meningitis and that of his older brother, Harold, from tuberculosis caused him intense grief.[56] They know that his father, Frank, had been boisterous, cantankerous, aggressive, hot-tempered, argumentative, vindictive; his mother, Hannah, had been passive in comparison with his father, but also stern and unaffectionate. Unhappy for these or other reasons, young Richard sought solace in his imagination, dreaming of other worlds and future goals and determined with a grim intensity to seize opportunities when they came his way. Insecure in his social status, he was tenacious in his striving and resentful of those he considered more privileged.

Some psychohistorical biographers, as well as friends, acquaintances, and memoirists, although viewing his behavior as notably unusual, have not considered Nixon to have been "warped" in the clinical sense of being psychotic. James David Barber diagnosed him as "active-negative"; that is, he had a fundamentally aggressive character but controlled his anger, keeping his frustrations within himself.[57] Befuddled by Nixon's paradoxical personality, Haldeman thought him "weird in the sense of being inexplicable, strange, hard to understand"; nevertheless, Haldeman had "an enormous respect" for his former chief.[58] Notwithstanding his longtime admiration for Nixon, Herbert Klein, Nixon's director of communications, wrote that he was "inscrutable . . . deeply embroiled in his own ego." There was "conflict within the man, causing him to strike out at others, motivated by anxiety."[59]

Suggesting a cause for his behavior, Kissinger, who was both critic and admirer, told Hugh Sidey of *Time:* "Can you imagine what this man would have been had somebody loved him."[60] Kissinger was thinking of Nixon's parents and peers. Of his mother, even Nixon confessed to Jonathan Aitken, a biographer, that, except for one occasion, she had never kissed him; in one of his memoirs he wrote: "In her whole life, I never heard her say to me or to anyone else, 'I love you.'" Repeating this comment almost word for word to Aitken several years later, he added, "She didn't have to!" Nixon was angered by comments or speculation about his mother's love, particularly by "one of those rather pathetic Freudian psychiatrists."[61] That he would tell and retell the story suggested, however, that it bothered him and, moreover, that it influenced his running of the government. Nixon believed that staff must promote their leader, perhaps even show him affection, in order for the leader to perform with maximum efficiency.[62]

Through his vice presidency and presidency, however, Nixon did consult with a psychiatrist, Dr. Arnold Hutschnecker, for help in coping with what his friend and lawyer Leonard Garment described as "chronic, debilitating psychosomatic symptoms."[63] At least one psychohistorian has interpreted Nixon's symptoms in a way that suggests that, while he was not psychotic, he had a clinically recognizable personality disorder. Nixon was, David Abrahamsen wrote, "passive-aggressive": "Such individuals are frequently aggressive and passive—either alternately or simultaneously. They may be alcoholics. . . . They may be antisocial. They are generally impulsive, unreliable, prone to lie and to commit criminal acts. They are highly narcissistic. . . . Predominant in Nixon's character were his egocentric and paranoid feelings, which brought to the fore his secretive, manipulative, and omnipotent attitudes."[64] Given in the late 1970s, Abrahamsen's diagnosis did not conform exclusively to the criteria for the passive-aggressive personality disorder recognized by the American Psychiatric Association in the mid-1990s. The amalgam of symptoms he listed suggested instead that Nixon may have possessed a "Personality Disorder Not Otherwise Specified (NOS)": "This category is for disorders . . . that do not meet criteria for any specific Personality Disorder. An example is the presence of features of more than one specific Personality Disorder that do not meet the full criteria for any one Personality Disorder ("mixed personality"), but that together cause clinically significant distress or impairment in one or more important areas of functioning (e.g., social or occupational)."[65] Thus, Nixon's behavior may have exhibited features that were paranoid, antisocial, narcissistic, *and* passive-aggressive. For example, he manifested "pervasive patterns" of such criteria as the suspicion that others intended to harm him; exaggerated complaints of personal misfortune; the persistent bearing of grudges; deceitfulness; lack of remorse; impulsivity; irritability; reckless risk taking; a grandiose sense of self-importance; the belief that he was special; and fantasies of success and power.[66]

Nixon also often experienced mood swings—from what he and Haldeman referred to as excessive "activism" to excessive "passivity," the latter accompanied by "doldrums." It would be going too far to say that he was bipolar, but there is much evidence to suggest that he may have undergone manic or hypomanic episodes—distinct periods of "persistently elevated, expansive, or irritable mood."[67]

Although biographers disagree over whether Nixon should be regarded as having been clinically abnormal, there is a remarkable similarity in descriptions of his personality and behavior, patterns that had an important bearing on the conduct of his presidency and of foreign policy. Many commentators mention his enigmatic "complexity"—his psychological dichotomies or "ambivalences." Nixon's attitude toward strength and weakness, for example, was dichotomous:

his desire to avoid appearing weak motivated him to appear exceptionally strong—at times he downplayed his own advantages, at other times he overplayed his hand. Kissinger observed, for example: "But when suppressing his instinct for a jugular response, Nixon looked for some other place to demonstrate his mettle. There was nothing he feared more than to be thought weak."[68] Many also agree that in his insecurity he wanted to control and dominate his environment and thus sought extraordinary power—"when the President does it it is not illegal."[69]

He was ambivalent about conflict, portraying himself as calm in crisis, but also throwing frequent and legendary fits of anger. Charles Colson recollected a conversation between Nixon and the White House inner circle on board the presidential yacht *Sequoia* in 1971. Complaining about Democratic critics of his foreign policies, Nixon warned: "One day we will get them—we'll get them on the ground where we want them. And we'll stick our heels in, step on them hard and twist—right, Chuck, right?" Then, turning to Kissinger, he said, "Henry knows what I mean—just like you do it in the negotiations, Henry—get them on the floor and step on them, crush them, show no mercy."[70]

Although avoiding face-to-face confrontations with subordinates—for example, Secretary of State William Rogers and Secretary of Defense Melvin Laird—he lashed out from afar at his opponents with verbal and physical ferocity: college debating opponents, demonstrators in Caracas, Democrats, the press, the North Vietnamese. He regarded opponents as enemies, not simply as rivals in the competitive world of politics and statecraft. A major reason he treasured the political advice of John Connally, whom he appointed secretary of the treasury, was that the Texas Democrat reinforced Nixon's own inclinations: "The P[resident] should take on no enemy, but at the right time, he has to come out as a fighter, and he has to have an enemy."[71] As speechwriter William Safire observed, Nixon insisted on calling the Democratic Republic of Vietnam and the National Liberation Front the "enemy." In this time of war, they *were* the enemy, but others, including Kissinger and former secretary of state Dean Rusk, cognizant that the war was undeclared, more often used the diplomatic term "the other side."[72]

Nixon was ambivalent toward rivals and authority figures; for example, he respected but disliked or resented Communists, Congress, the bureaucracy, Kissinger, and even Eisenhower, his mentor and patron. Nixon resented having been President Eisenhower's "prat boy," always doing his dirty work as vice president; he also felt abandoned by Eisenhower's withholding of support during the slush-fund or "Checkers" crisis of the 1952 campaign, betrayed in 1956 when Eisenhower considered dumping him from the ticket, and injured by Eisenhower's grudging endorsement during the presidential race against Kennedy.[73] While generally praising Eisenhower in *RN* and indicating great satisfaction in the joining of their families with the marriage of Julie Nixon and David Eisenhower, Nixon peppered his memoirs with not-so-subtle criticisms of Eisenhower's insincerity, foreign policy mistakes, and personal aloofness—the latter symbolized by his "icy blue eyes."[74] Yet he had always sought Eisenhower's praise and approval. When

Nixon, in the presence of several top aides, learned of Eisenhower's death on March 28, 1969, he cried uncontrollably. Haldeman noted: "P then started to cry, just standing there. Then he walked slowly, still crying, into the little hall, stood there and sobbed, said "He was such a strong man," went into the little office for a few minutes. Then came back into Oval Office, others were there by then, standing awkwardly. P still had tears, and red eyes, talked with them aimlessly then sat on the edge of the desk, half crying and described in detail his last visit to DDE."[75]

There were other ambivalences. Nixon, a man who had an "iron butt," it was said, prepared intensely and at length for tasks such as debate tournaments, law school classes, and presidential speeches. Believing himself a hard worker, he resented the ease with which he thought members of the old elite such as Alger Hiss and John Kennedy seemed to move through the world. On the other hand, he spent a great deal of time during his presidency in long-winded Oval Office talk, not on substantive policy issues but in rambling, thinking-out-loud discussions about punishing his enemies and building up his own image. It was "hard," Haldeman noted in one of his many notes on White House behavior, for "P to stay on the big issues; he keeps hacking away at PR concerns." In general, Haldeman commented, "He's constitutionally unable to say he's taking time off, [and he] has to appear he's working."[76]

Many who knew him also commented on Nixon's misuse of alcohol. Leonard Garment told anecdotes in his memoirs about Nixon's formula for dealing with his chronic insomnia: a late-night combination of rambling telephone conversation, sedatives, and a stiff drink. Kissinger in particular mischievously complained to his staff that Nixon had been drunk and spoken with slurred diction during some of their meetings or phone conversations. Other aides, perhaps less inclined than Kissinger to slander their boss, acknowledged that Nixon had a "drinking problem." The problem was not one that could technically be defined as alcoholism—the continued excessive or compulsive use of alcoholic drinks—but rather one of having a low tolerance for such beverages. "One beer," Haldeman noted, "would transform his normal speech into the rambling elocution of a Bowery wino." Similarly, John Ehrlichman remarked that "one drink can knock him galley west if he is tired," or, as Ray Price, one of Nixon's speechwriters observed, if he had previously taken "a sleeping pill."[77] But one or more drinks during a foreign policy crisis could have been significant, and there appear to have been occasions, as during the Cambodian invasion of 1970, when Nixon, imbibing more than he could tolerate, fortified his truculence.

The workings of the mind of an individual occupying the American presidency are noteworthy because of the power of the office. They are even more significant when the president's personality is highly unusual, and Nixon's personality seems to have fit into this category. His slant on things was sufficiently idiosyncratic to make a difference, adding an unpredictable, chaotic element to the standard American formulas for war and diplomacy. His faith in the virtues of struggle, force, "madman" threats, and secret diplomacy, for example, encouraged him to believe that he could win the Vietnam War despite the intractable realities of a conflict that others had recognized long before. His emotions and moods influenced the tactics he chose, such as the bombing of Cambodia, the Cambodian incursion, the invasion of Laos, and the bombing of Hanoi and Haiphong.

Nixon's fundamental policies, however, were the product of large forces and broad contexts. Although his psychology led him to distrust the bureaucracy, that bureaucracy, along with the advisers surrounding him, influenced in ways he could not foresee the policies and strategies he adopted and the manner in which they would be implemented. He also operated in a political context in which the policy-making establishment and the majority of voters had become pessimistic about the prospects for success in Vietnam, and one in which there was both an influential right-wing alliance in favor of the war and a heterogeneous liberal, pacifist, and leftist coalition in opposition. Nixon was also the student of previous cold war warriors and third world interventionists such as Eisenhower, and he was the heir of America's globally hegemonic policies. He moved in a cultural milieu of capitalist values and military measures—the heir of well-established policy currents in recent American history at a time of crisis for American global leadership. He looked at American national interest and the strategies to accomplish it from a point of view that was not unusual within Establishment policy-making and political circles. Not the least of the extrapsychological circumstances impinging on Nixon's Vietnam policies were the Vietnamese enemy, his Vietnamese allies, the Soviets, the Chinese, and world opinion. He could not make his own history just as he pleased, nor could his memory of these events, his historical version of the war, match what actually happened.[78]

2

THE WORLDVIEW
OF AN IMPROBABLE PEACEMAKER:
1953-1967

Our vital interest is at stake in Vietnam.
—Richard Nixon[1]

We have understood Mr. Nixon through two Indochinese wars.
—Le Duc Tho[2]

FIRST ENCOUNTERS AND SEMINAL STRATEGIES

Richard Nixon's confrontation with the war in Vietnam began sixteen years before his inauguration as president. It was a time of crisis—a time of bitter cold war with the Soviet Union and the People's Republic of China (PRC), a time of revolutionary turmoil in the former colonies of Europe, Japan, and the United States. His long journey through the labyrinth of Indochina profoundly shaped his views about the vital goals of the United States in Asia and the strategies required to achieve a satisfactory peace in Vietnam.

The Vietnam predicament that Nixon faced as president paralleled that faced by French leaders in 1953. Their seven-year-old military effort to restore France's colonial grip over Indochina was in serious jeopardy. Military and political failure in Vietnam, the threat of greater Chinese involvement in support of the Vietminh, and war-weariness at home had driven France's leaders to consider withdrawal through a negotiated settlement. Against American opposition, in 1953 the French government managed to place the Indochina War on the agenda of the multinational, East-West conference on Asia scheduled in Geneva for late April 1954. Taking steps toward a diplomatic solution, the French believed that an honorable withdrawal required the stabilization or even improvement of their military position—a course Nixon would also follow as president. Already dependent on U.S.

16

aid, which financed 78 percent of their war effort in March 1954, the French continued to request additional American assistance in the form of money, aircraft, and technicians.[3]

To President Dwight Eisenhower and his National Security Council (NSC), a compromise agreement resulting in the partitioning of Vietnam or the participation of the Vietminh in a coalition government was unacceptable. Wanting the French to hold on and win, the administration continued to urge them to fight, but it attached political and military conditions to the granting of large amounts of supplementary aid. Hedging his bets on Indochina at the beginning of 1954, the president formed a special NSC committee to investigate "what additional measures could be undertaken to assist the French." The Joint Chiefs of Staff (JCS) conducted related contingency planning, while Washington insiders, including Nixon, debated what to do.

Matters came to a head by late March as the Vietminh began to close in on the French garrison at Dienbienphu. During the next two months, the Eisenhower administration brooded about what it considered would be the awful consequences of defeat at this remote outpost in the highlands of northwestern Vietnam. The immediate concern of the administration was that the fall of the base would further erode French resolve while strengthening the hand and determination of the Vietminh at the Geneva talks.[4] In turn, disaster at Geneva would have dire global repercussions. "My God," Eisenhower exclaimed as the crisis unfolded, "we must not lose Asia—we've got to look the thing right in the face."[5] American credibility was also on the line: "It was important that we not show a weakness at this critical time and that we not let the Russians think that we might not resist . . . in Indochina and elsewhere."[6]

In this spring of American discontent, Eisenhower publicly enunciated the "falling domino principle." At a press conference on April 7 he said: "You have a row of dominoes set up, you knock over the first one, and what will happen to the last one is the certainty that it will go over very quickly. So you could have a beginning of a disintegration that would have the most profound influences": the loss of material resources, people, and strategic military positions. Eisenhower put economics at the center of his concerns: "It takes away, in its economic aspects, that region that Japan must have as a trading area or Japan, in turn, will have only one place in the world to go—that is, toward the Communist areas in order to live. So, the possible consequences of the loss are just incalculable to the free world."[7]

Nixon had voiced this argument three months earlier, on December 23, 1953, in a radio and television report on his fact-finding, goodwill tour of Asia: "Why should Americans care what happens one-half way around the world? . . . If Indochina falls, Thailand is put in an almost impossible position. The same is true of Malaya with its rubber and tin. The same is true of Indonesia. If this whole part of Southeast Asia goes under Communist domination or Communist influence, Japan, who trades and must trade with this area in order to exist, must inevitably be oriented toward the Communist regime."[8]

These were not idiosyncratic, anomalistic ideas; they were not exaggerations designed for public consumption; they were not simply reactions to the imminent fall of Dienbienphu. They represented the positions of both the Truman and the Eisenhower administration about the importance of Southeast Asia, positions that had been agreed upon in top secret NSC meetings and papers on U.S. objectives and courses of action in that part of the world from at least 1950 to 1954. The opening statement of "General Considerations" in the Eisenhower administration's action paper NSC 5405 (January 1954), for example, was identical to that of the Truman administration's NSC 124 (February 1952): "Communist domination, by whatever means, of all Southeast Asia would seriously endanger in the short term, and critically endanger in the longer term, United States security interests." Both American administrations conceived of American "security interests" in holistic terms: security comprised an interrelated global system of military balances, geographic positions, political stability, ideological unity, national prestige, and economic resources. Although lying on the periphery of the "free world" and the "Soviet bloc," Southeast Asia was an area commanding strategic sea and air routes and possessing important military bases and economic assets. The threat in Vietnam was not from external military aggression but from "subversion." The need was to provide "internal security." Failure would create the perception in Asia that Communism was the "wave of the future." Although the threat was not seen in terms of an external Soviet or Chinese military attack, all Communist states and movements were assumed to be functionally, if not formally, allied. To these policy makers, Communism was effectively monolithic.

Some views changed over time. In 1951, for example, the Truman administration still believed it might be possible to "detach China as an effective ally of the USSR," but by 1954 the Eisenhower administration regarded China as an aggressor state that was "the immediate and major source of Viet Minh military power." Despite minor revisions, for the most part there was remarkable continuity in fundamental assumptions. Both administrations, for example, considered economic matters as integral to American security interests. NSC 48/5 (1951) and NSC 124 (1952) warned of the danger of losing access to the "material resources" of the region: rubber, tin, petroleum, rice, and other strategic commodities. Such a loss, they claimed, would be felt by the whole "free world" but in particular by Japan, India, and "free Asia." Conversely, the "Soviet bloc" would benefit by gaining access to these materials. NSC 5405 (1954) recapitulated this analysis but, in a more sophisticated appreciation that reflected changing geoeconomic conditions, added that "this area has an important potential as a market for the industrialized countries of the free world"—the people of Southeast Asia were important too. By 1959, if not before, Eisenhower, and undoubtedly Nixon, came to believe that the global struggle between capitalist and Communist models for economic growth in developing countries hung in the balance. It was a contest pitting development through free-flowing private investments and government loans and grants from the international capitalist community against development through the mobilization of wealth, labor, and resources by the developing nation's own government, which would exclude or regulate capital flows from and to the outside. It was in this context that Eisenhower and Nixon spoke of "freedom" in Vietnam, a form of freedom that the Vietnamese revolutionaries thought of as "neocolonialism."[9]

The importance of the struggle in Vietnam to American policy makers was the product of policy goals developed during a time of global turmoil, perceived threat, and international ambition that encompassed the world. The resources of Vietnam itself were not critically required for the prosperity and security of the United States. They were critical mainly in their relationship to the needs or stability of other areas: Southeast Asia, India, Japan, and Europe. The Vietnam conflict was thus primarily symbolic: defeat at the hands of revolutionaries would undermine a strategic idea—credibility—which had been put in the service of an American vision of a particular global order. It was not, as it was for the Vietnamese, a struggle for immediate, tangible, national interests—independence, unity, social change, life and death. The issues were very important, they believed, but they were not worth too many risks.

Consequently, despite his anxiety about the deterioration of the French position in Indochina in general and French military prospects at Dienbienphu in particular, Eisenhower was ambivalent about committing American forces: "While no one was more anxious . . . to keep our men out of these jungles, we could nevertheless not forget our vital interests in Indochina."[10] He thought out loud in the presence of advisers about the possibility of drastic remedies, yet he alternately cautioned them about the need for prudent responses. The president had many concerns. He was reluctant to entangle America's prestige in another war so soon after Korea, conscious of the limitations of American military power globally, aware of the complexity of the Indochinese politico-military situation, worried about expanding military budgets, uncertain about Soviet and Chinese responses, and aware of the opposition of the American public, congressional leaders, and America's allies. Some advisers, including the JCS and Secretary of State John Foster Dulles, shared some of his concerns.[11] Nevertheless, between March and early May, when Dienbienphu fell and the Geneva Conference opened, the administration's perception of crisis, the president's vacillation between extreme and cautious responses, and the momentum of military studies and contingency planning had the effect of keeping the door open to American aerial operations in Indochina. On March 24, for example, Eisenhower told Dulles that he would not "wholly exclude the possibility of a single strike, if it were almost certain this would produce decisive results."[12]

Two days earlier, Eisenhower had instructed Admiral Arthur W. Radford, the chair of the JCS, in the presence of General Paul Ely, his French counterpart, to give priority to French requests for aid to save the entrenched camp. Radford subsequently met on March 23 with Ely and considered the issue of American air strikes to relieve the siege of Dienbienphu. According to one source, they later discussed possible targets with Vice President Nixon, whose enthusiasm inspired Radford, in turn, to order the Pacific Command to make a study of the idea. One "informal" plan that emerged from these discussions was code-named *Vautour* (Vulture); it had originated with a joint American-French staff team in Saigon and been approved and named by General Henri Navarre, commander of French forces in Indochina. As the situation at Dienbienphu continued to deteriorate, Vulture evolved to include at different times proposals for attacks on Vietminh positions around the base, lines of communications to rear areas, and depots along the Chinese border. To these ends it also included a recommendation for dropping three "small" atomic bombs. Other discussions by American leaders and planners—that is, those not directly associated with Vulture—included consideration of nuclear weapons too.[13]

NUCLEAR NOTIONS

The president did not finally choose the nuclear option, but he allowed NSC and JCS studies to proceed concerning the circumstances under which nuclear bombs might be dropped, and he, Dulles, and others participated in discussions about their use. At a NATO Council meeting in Paris on April 22, for example, the secretary of state asked Foreign Minister Georges Bidault whether atomic bombs could be used effectively at Dienbienphu, informing him that the United States was prepared to offer France two of them.[14] Eisenhower was not prepared to use atomic bombs unilaterally—that is, without the concurrence of allies, whom his administration wished to organize into a coalition for united action. According to Nixon, at a meeting he attended on April 30, Eisenhower's national security adviser, Robert Cutler, "reported . . . that the NSC planning board had been discussing the possibility of telling our allies that if we went into Indochina, we might use the atom bomb." Eisenhower asked Nixon what he thought, and Nixon answered that he believed conventional bombing would be sufficient to signal the Communists that the United States "was determined to resist." Holding open the nuclear option, however, he suggested that it would not be necessary to mention the idea to allies until after they agreed on united action.[15] Nixon agreed with the tactic advocated by Admiral Radford, who believed that if the United States "could get French acceptance of the principle of the use of such weapons, the whole conception of gaining acceptance of their use [from an allied coalition] would be assisted. Furthermore, if we got French approval in principle after the coalition was formed but before we actively committed forces to Indochina, we could later use such weapons when our forces (air) were engaged."[16]

Years later, remembering the meeting with Cutler and Nixon, Eisenhower told one biographer that he had responded: "You boys must be crazy. We can't use those awful things against Asians for the second time in less than ten years. My

God."[17] Nixon had a different recollection: "To some extent Radford did believe that the early use of tactical nuclear weapons would convince the Communists that we meant business. Dulles and I both believed that if the Communists pushed too far we would have to do whatever was necessary to stop them. Eisenhower fully agreed, although I think that Dulles and I were probably prepared to stand up at an earlier point than he was."[18]

In any case, neither Eisenhower, Nixon, nor Eisenhower's key advisers seemed to have had grave moral compunctions about dropping nuclear bombs in pursuit of what they regarded the national interest.[19] Since coming to power in January 1953, Eisenhower and his administration had given serious thought to using nuclear weapons in Korea and China, just as the preceding Truman administration had. Decisions to use or not to use had been based on amoral considerations of realpolitik: domestic political conditions, world opinion, interallied relations, strategic utility, logistic feasibility, and possible enemy counteraction.[20]

Atomic strategy and diplomacy had been important elements of American policy since the Truman administration had dropped the first nuclear bombs on Hiroshima and Nagasaki. Truman and his advisers had intended these bombings as additional military measures in the war against Japan but also as indirect signals to the Soviet Union about America's will and ability to project immense destructive power. This, they expected, would give them credibility, and hence leverage, in their dealings with Moscow. Nixon's view was that the bombs had convinced the tough-minded Japanese to surrender and had saved him from being recalled to naval duty on one of the Pacific islands. He also believed they made the United States "the most powerful nation in the world," requiring America "to play a major role on the world's stage." Because the United States possessed atomic superiority over the Soviets, "the U.S. started using the Bomb as a diplomatic stick."[21]

On several other occasions between 1945 and 1954, American policy makers either had considered using atomic weapons to influence military outcomes or had threatened to use them to influence the diplomatic balance. In the first four years after the Soviets broke the U.S. nuclear monopoly in 1949, American policy makers' considerations had been predicated on making use of America's clear atomic superiority before it vanished in the face of the Soviet challenge. By 1953 the temptation to use atomic weapons militarily or diplomatically continued to seduce American policy makers, but for different reasons: the United States had succeeded in increasing its nuclear superiority while also improving the overall strategic balance in relation to Soviet and Chinese forces.[22] In January 1954, as the United States prepared to test operational prototypes of thermonuclear bombs, Hanson Baldwin, the military reporter for the *New York Times,* paraphrasing Dulles, commented enthusiastically—and paradoxically—that these tests "open an age when hydrogen weapons will be feasible in war. . . . The day of the real 'city-buster' has arrived." These weapons, of course, must be used with "discrimination and restriction." Otherwise, they "could spell the doom of the world's cities and could sound the death knell of civilization as we know it."[23]

Although both the Truman and the Eisenhower administrations had designed nuclear strategies and practiced nuclear diplomacy, there was a significant difference between the two regimes' approaches to waging the cold war. The Eisenhower administration made "massive retaliatory power" an integral part of its grand strategy—or New Look policy—which had been formally ratified in NSC 162/2 on October 29, 1953, and publicly announced on January 12, 1954. Aimed at avoiding "military expenditures so vast that they lead to [the] 'practical bankruptcy'" of the "private enterprise" economy, NSC 162/2 directed cuts in the numbers of U.S. ground forces, which under Truman administration planning would have remained at high levels over an extended period of time, producing repeated and crippling "budgetary deficits." Eisenhower's "international security system" was designed for the "long haul." To compensate for military spending reductions, it would rely on "a multiplication of means": active covert operations and propaganda, a more effective intelligence apparatus, a strengthened alliance network, and "a great capacity to retaliate, instantly, by means and at places of our choosing."[24] Relying on massive retaliation, the New Look emphasized nuclear attack. Massive retaliation was, to use a phrase common in the 1970s and 1980s, a *first-use* strategy. Or, as one scholar pointed out, massive "retaliation" was primarily a strategy of massive "preemption."[25]

The administration did not seek general war with the Soviet Union or China, but it believed a willingness to threaten and to risk war was advantageous, especially since the United States enjoyed strategic nuclear superiority. The crisis in Indochina was covered by the strategy. In fact, the crisis had contributed to the development of the strategy. NSC 162/2 explained that Indochina was "of such strategic importance . . . that an attack . . . probably would compel the United States to react with military force either locally at the point of attack or generally against the military power of the aggressor."[26] As the editors of the *New York Times* observed in January 1954, when Dulles publicly revealed the New Look policy: "There also had been earlier administration warnings that Communist aggression in Korea or open Chinese Communist aggression in Indo-China might evoke military reactions beyond those areas."[27] In April 1954 Dulles tried to win British support for threatening air and naval action against China in order to persuade Beijing to stop supporting the Vietminh. He sent a message to Foreign Secretary Anthony Eden: "We possess a military superiority in the area now which we might not have in a few years time. So if a warning was not heeded, we should now be in a position to put our threats into effect."[28] A year later, in March 1955, the *New York Times* reported that Nixon had similarly

> warned the Chinese Communists in the bluntest of terms that they would be met with atomic weapons if they embarked on any new aggression . . . [and] a war breaks out in the Pacific. . . . Tactical atomic explosives are now con-

ventional and will be used against the targets of any aggressive force. . . . He said the Administration was "convinced that despite the recognized risks involved, our policy of resisting further aggression in the long run has the best chance to attain our objective of peace without surrender."[29]

THE UNCERTAINTY PRINCIPLE

There was another but related element in the Eisenhower administration's strategy, one either unnoticed or underemphasized by historians: "The key to the success" of "massive atomic retaliation," Dulles publicly emphasized, "was to keep a potential enemy guessing about the kind of action the United States might take in any particular case."[30] Creating uncertainty in the enemy's mind and putting him off balance, unpredictability itself could operate as a coercive device. In an interview with a *Time* magazine reporter in 1985, Nixon recollected with relish how during the Berlin crisis of 1959 Eisenhower had artfully used his March 11 press conference to send a nuclear warning to the Soviets, causing them to "back down" from their own threat to recognize East German authority over the city. While acknowledging that nuclear weapons were "terrible" and could not "free *anything*," much less Berlin, Eisenhower had nevertheless affirmed that "we will do what is necessary to protect ourselves," and he made sure that the Soviets thought he was accepting the irrational, self-destructive risk of a "general war."[31]

Thinking the unthinkable about using nuclear weapons—and conveying a message of unpredictability and irrationality to the enemy—was a stratagem in which Eisenhower and other administration planners besides Dulles believed. It was well suited to Nixon's personality, and he even respected it in the enemy, or at least he projected this mentality on the enemy he feared: "Dictatorial leaders of revolutionary movements are always unpredictable. They sometimes do unreasonable things. That is why we must be prepared for the worst."[32] Unpredictability and unreasonableness were artifices he would remember when he became president, even while America's nuclear advantage was diminishing. He would call his approach the "madman theory."

Threats of or plans for atomic bombing, while in reality significantly different than threats of and plans for conventional bombing, were, nevertheless, an outgrowth of a well-established way of thinking about the use of airpower. Historian Michael S. Sherry remarked about the culture of aerial bombing: "In the nuclear age, as in the 1930s, one of the oldest temptations of air power was evident, the temptation to regard it as serving less the needs of battle than the opportunity to avoid it. . . . The aerial weapon promises to provide . . . a threat to an enemy's resolve and psychic stability, and a trump card in diplomatic crises."[33]

In this vein Nixon recalled about the Dienbienphu crisis: "We all hoped that by being prepared to fight we would never actually have to do any fighting."[34] By not fighting he meant not having to send American troops. By being prepared he meant one or more options: an American air strike or strikes using conventional or nuclear weapons to save Dienbienphu and simultaneously send a signal of determination to the Soviets and Chinese; taking political steps or providing more military aid to buttress the French militarily and diplomatically; raising and training indigenous Indochinese forces; and forming a regional defense organization to free the war from the taint of colonialism, sustain anti-Communist morale, sanction intervention, and increase American public support for greater involvement. Any or all of these measures, the administration believed, would deter "stepped-up" Communist activity. Without them, the French would falter and would rush to settle at Geneva "at any cost"; in the end, American troops might have to be sent to Vietnam.

On April 17, for example, Nixon had told the American Press Club that "if France stopped fighting in Indo-China and the situation demanded it, the United States would have to send troops to fight the Communists in that area."[35] His comments, as well as similar remarks he made at a private party for Democratic senators, caused a minor political crisis for the White House. The *New York Times* headline read, "High Aide Says Troops May Be Sent If the French Withdraw." Democratic Senator Edwin "Big Ed" Johnson reported that he had "heard the Vice President, Mr. Nixon, 'whooping it up for war' in Indochina."[36] It seemed that Nixon, the hawk, the loose cannon of the administration, was advocating American troop intervention, or at least floating a trial balloon. Democratic leaders worried about the policy implications, and Republican leaders about the political impact. In his own defense of his public statements to the press, Nixon explained that they were off-the-record responses to a hypothetical question about a possible contingency.

Nixon may have been embarrassed, but not by the import of his remarks to the press and to the Democrats, only by the confusion he had caused. Of course, confusion, which was related to unpredictability, had its useful functions, whether to keep the enemy off balance in uncertainty or to communicate a message about a possible course of action to the American public. "Public opinion," Nixon explained to the press at the time, "is not yet aware of the nature of the threat to United States interests in that part of the world."[37] Commenting on Nixon's statements, Sherman Adams, Eisenhower's assistant, said that the president believed the press incident had been beneficial because "it awakened the country to the seriousness of the situation in Indochina."[38] In his memoirs two decades later, Nixon claimed that Eisenhower had supported him during the public flap and had told him he would have responded similarly to the American Press Club questions. Nixon approvingly paraphrased a comment Eisenhower made to worried Republican congressional leaders about the incident: "It was not well to tell the Russians everything as to what we would or would not do."[39] Nixon may have been willing to intervene with American troops in Indochina, but the intent of his comments was to educate the public and threaten the various Communist states and groups he believed were conspiring to conquer Vietnam.

In the end Eisenhower decided against Vulture, the dropping of nuclear bombs, and other forms of direct military intervention. Dienbienphu had fallen before two of his key preconditions had been met: congressional approval and the formation of a united allied front.[40] French policy also contributed to his decision. Seeking to preserve their honor, their hegemony in Indochina, and the appearance of great-power status, the French had resisted American calls for the granting of greater Vietnamese political autonomy and the internationalization of the anti-Communist effort through the united action of Western and Asian allies. In 1985, as enthusiastic about airpower as he had been thirty years earlier, Nixon faulted Eisenhower and Dulles for not having intervened in the battle of Dienbienphu. In *No More Vietnams* he claimed that "by standing aside as our ally went down to defeat, the United States lost its last chance to stop the expansion of Communism in Southeast Asia at little cost to itself."[41]

The Eisenhower administration's policy was paradoxical—as would be the Nixon administration's policy fifteen years later. Although policy makers considered Vietnam to be of vital interest to the United States, they simultaneously understood that it lay on the periphery of the global struggle with Communism and the Soviet Union: it was a "non-decisive theater."[42] Although they believed U.S. national interests in Southeast Asia were too great to abandon, they did not regard them as sufficiently palpable to expend strategic and political assets—the health of the national economy, the goodwill of the public, or the lives of American soldiers—especially if a less painful strategy than direct combat appeared promising. Yet, their strategy of indirect means was open-ended; it could—and would—lead the nation into the quagmire of real war. Such a war, which the administration already suspected would be futile, could tarnish the image of the very thing it sought to protect—the credibility of its will and ability to defeat Communism and revolution.

As Dulles had put it to Ely in March 1954: "If the United States sent its flag and its own military establishment . . . we could not afford thus to . . . suffer a defeat which would have worldwide repercussions."[43] But the administration was trapped in its mind-set. The majority of senators and representatives in Congress acquiesced in these policies or were sympathetic,[44] for they as much as those in the executive branch were caught in a web of concerns about cold war and counterrevolutionary credibility.

On balance, and in the short term, the Eisenhower administration was able to stay ahead of the game despite the fall of Dienbienphu on May 7, 1954, and the opening of the Indochina phase of negotiations at Geneva on May 8. American persistence, threats of intervention, and diplomatic maneuvering during the Geneva negotiations leveraged the Soviets and Chinese into pressuring Vietminh negotiators to settle for less than they had won in battle. Dulles "felt there were some redeeming features coming out of the Geneva Conference": more nations believed

"the original proposal of the U.S. for a regional grouping . . . had been sound";
Indochina had been "purified . . . of the taint of French colonialism"; and "in losing the Tonkin Delta, the U.S. had not lost assets valuable to her, for the rice for
Japan comes from southern Indochina."[45] The Eisenhower administration intended
to make the partitioning of Vietnam permanent,[46] but holding onto the southern
half of the country would require the "establishment of a military line which could
not be crossed by the enemy," as well as the "prevention of internal and creeping
subversion." These aims could be accomplished by providing economic aid and
building up "indigenous military strength."[47]

By September 1954 the United States had formed its long-sought "regional
grouping," the Southeast Asia Treaty Organization (SEATO), a paper alliance that
offered psychological reassurance and the illusion of victory. It was also designed
to mollify Congress, mobilize allies, and serve as the basis for legitimating continued involvement in Vietnam.[48]

Nixon would draw a lesson from these events for future use: American
resolve, diplomatic machinations, and military threats had preserved South Vietnam for the struggle ahead. But there was more: the outcome would have been
better and ultimately less costly had air strikes been launched during the battle
for Dienbienphu. Nixon had not been president or secretary of state and had not
finally made the decisions, but he had been a frequent spokesman and sometime lightning rod for the administration. He had also influenced the administration's interpretation of the nature of the war and contributed to the policies
decided upon by Eisenhower and Dulles. He had opposed negotiations and had
advocated hard-line alternatives: bombing; the expanded training of indigenous
forces; stepped-up propaganda; a regional alliance to fight "subversion";[49] and
the search for a strongman to lead a viable, anti-Communist, client government
in Saigon.

By 1955, responding to army opponents of the New Look and the ideas of
civilian consultants like Henry Kissinger, and wanting to develop a full range of
capabilities for the special conditions of post-Geneva Vietnam, the NSC began to
consider the creation of "highly mobile" U.S. forces for "flexible" operations. NSC
5501 (January 6, 1955) called for units "equipped for local war, including atomic
capability, but not dependent on [the] use of atomic weapons for effective action."[50]
For the immediate future, however, the policy toward South Vietnam was "nation building," which meant shoring up the Saigon regime of Ngo Dinh Diem with
economic aid, military equipment, police and armed forces training, and advice
on politics and land reform.

In the beginning Nixon did not think highly of Diem. This Catholic, anti-
Communist, Vietnamese nationalist did not measure up to Nixon's preferred model
for Asian strongmen, South Korean leader Syngman Rhee. Nixon had met Rhee
in the fall of 1953, during a tour of Pacific Rim countries. Eisenhower had asked
him to make the trip to reassure allies, meet with neutrals, gauge the influence of
China, and deliver a letter to Rhee.

Rhee was not reconciled to the Korean War armistice agreement, which had been concluded at the end of July. In *RN* Nixon reported that Eisenhower told Rhee in his letter that "the United States would not tolerate any actions that might lead to a reopening of the war and asked for specific reassurances from Rhee."[51] The South Korean president initially resisted Nixon's solicitation on behalf of Eisenhower, but finally, as Nixon was bidding him farewell, Rhee provided the assurances Eisenhower sought. Despite the anxiety he had earlier caused the importunate American vice president, Rhee's explanation of his own apparently independent behavior resonated with Nixon's way of thinking and made a lasting impression on him. According to Nixon, Rhee told him:

> Any statements I have made about Korea acting independently were made to help America. . . . The moment the Communists are certain that the United States controls Rhee, you will have lost one of your most effective bargaining points, and we will have lost all our hope. The fear that I may start some action is a constant check on the Communists. . . . The Communists think that America wants peace so badly that you will do anything to get it. . . . But they do not think that this is true as far as I am concerned, and I believe that you would be wrong to dispel their doubts in that respect.[52]

Months later, in April 1954, as the Geneva Conference on Asia was about to begin, Nixon defended Rhee with Rhee's own argument. He told the American press: "President Rhee is a complex man, both a conspirator and a realist, who knows he could not win without United States support. But so long as the Communists fear unilateral action by President Rhee, they will be forced to act accordingly at the Geneva Conference table."[53]

In *RN* Nixon recalled how Rhee had educated him in the utility of what journalist Tom Wicker dubbed the "uncertainty principle" of foreign policy, a key element in the madman theory of his own presidency: "I left Korea impressed . . . by the strength and intelligence of Syngman Rhee. I also gave much thought to Rhee's insight about the importance of being unpredictable in dealing with the Communists. The more I traveled and the more I learned in the years that followed, the more I appreciated how wise the old man had been."[54]

In 1953 Nixon had agreed with the assessment of the British high commissioner in Kuala Lumpur, whom he also had met on his Asian trip, that Rhee was "a real SOB, but what they need there [in Indochina] is a Rhee." Lumping together three Asian strongmen, Rhee, Diem, and Nguyen Van Thieu, the vice president noted in *RN* that "until strong leaders capable of providing stability appeared in Vietnam—first Diem and later Thieu—there was no solid opposition to Communist infiltration."[55] Ironically, in late 1972 and early 1973, President Nixon would have to send his own emissaries to Saigon with arm-twisting messages for South Vietnam's President Thieu, who was as unhappy with the 1972 cease-fire agreement Nixon and Kissinger negotiated with Hanoi as President Rhee was with the Korean cease-fire negotiated in Panmunjom.

POLITICS VERSUS DIPLOMACY

Nixon, like Eisenhower, came to admire, or at least depend on, Diem. Diem survived early challenges to his rule and, with American encouragement and backing, launched a ruthless campaign against the Vietminh cadres who had stayed behind in South Vietnam after the Geneva Agreement. Nixon, who had helped to bring about renewed war in Indochina in the late fifties, continued to encourage American intervention in the early sixties when President Kennedy dramatically increased support for Diem. As was usual when Nixon complimented opponents and rivals, however, he extended backhanded praise. Concerned that Republican National Committee criticism of Kennedy's policies might undermine the "delicate military situation in South Vietnam," Nixon said in February 1962: "I don't agree at all with any partisan or other criticism of the . . . build-up in Vietnam. My only question is whether it may be too little and too late."[56] By late October 1963, while the "Viet Cong" (VC) army of the National Liberation Front (NLF) gained on the battlefield, Buddhists protested Diem's repressions, and Kennedy seemed prepared to withdraw support from Diem, Nixon declared, "In Vietnam today the choice is not between President Diem and somebody better, it is between Diem and somebody infinitely worse."[57] The "somebody worse" was either a Communist, a neutralist, or a less capable anti-Communist. Diem's military failure, corruption, authoritarian rule, and ruthlessness were overshadowed in Nixon's mind by Diem's understanding "that the first task of government is to establish order."[58]

On November 6, a few days after the South Vietnamese army generals' execution of Diem and his brother Ngo Dinh Nhu, Nixon made a public show of challenging Kennedy's policy. He apparently was angry about U.S. actions that had allowed Diem's downfall but also was seeking to maintain his credentials among right-wing hawks and the Asian lobby. Nixon informed the press that he had telephoned Mme Nhu, who had been touring the United States at the time of the coup and was now the house guest of Allen Chase, described by the *New York Times* as "a corporate financier with extensive land holdings in Asia and Australia, [who] had met . . . Diem during business trips to the Orient." The paper reported that Nixon "talked to her at length" about the refusal of U.S. consulate officials to grant asylum to Diem's two other brothers in South Vietnam and about Mme Nhu's hope that, with U.S. support, she could safely return to her homeland.[59]

Through the next three decades Nixon would cite the coup as the turning point of the war, the pivotal event from which "nothing but chaos came."[60] All the usual culprits were responsible: "To our Asian friends and allies it looked as if a combination of political expediency, public apathy, distorted reporting in the media, and partisan politics was undermining America's will to fight against Communism in Asia."[61] By their faulty strategies and their involvement in the coup, he claimed, Kennedy and his advisers were the "architects" of the mess he inherited when he became president. So obsessed was Nixon with Kennedy's role in the coup that in a convoluted series of events it became part of the Watergate scandal as Nixon's men forged documents in order to link Kennedy with the assassination.[62]

It was Johnson, however, who immediately inherited the war from Kennedy in November 1963, and it was Nixon who, among the most influential and vocal hawks outside of government, pressed the new president to continue the fight and escalate the effort. From February 1964, when he claimed Johnson was preparing Americans for "retreat or defeat," to December 1967, when he advocated retaliation against China if aircraft based there attacked U.S. armed forces, Nixon's themes were relentlessly militant. Even though he acknowledged as early as February 1965 that the "average American" favored disengagement, he supported the deployment of American troops and their participation in combat. From late 1966 and through 1967, as troop deployments became the touchstone of public unease about the war, Nixon sometimes recommended numbers lower than those proposed by the administration, although his own figures did not substantially differ from the actual deployments in the end. In September 1965 he commented that Johnson's commitment of 125,000 soldiers "would prove to be too little." A year later, as the fall 1966 congressional elections approached, he advocated an increase of 75,000 to 100,000 above the current 300,000-troop level. Although he seemed willing to accept a final deployment to a level of under 600,000, Nixon said he was "distressed" by Johnson's reputed intention to raise the total to over 600,000 after the elections. Two months later he criticized McNamara's prediction of a slowdown in deployments by the end of 1967, with the total stabilizing at 500,000; Nixon commented that 400,000 would be "sufficient." If by 1967 Nixon supported a somewhat reduced role for American ground troops, he also called for "further steps in 'pacification,'" and, in tune with other hawks, unfailingly advocated the expansion and intensification of the air and naval war from 1964 onward. Nixon pressed the administration to bomb Laos and North Vietnam more heavily day and night, to include Hanoi among the targets, and to mine and impose a naval blockade of the port of Haiphong. He also advocated trade reprisals against foreign shippers and the curtailment of foreign aid to allies supplying North Vietnam.

Although backing Johnson's commitment to the war, Nixon faulted him for "indecision." He claimed that "the president, by gradual escalation, has frittered away the advantage that massive pressure should have given us." Johnson was insufficiently "aggressive," gearing "the intensity of the war effort to the intensity of the Communist effort, letting the enemy call the shots." Joining others in complaints about the president's lack of candor, Nixon criticized Johnson not for having escalated the war but for having misled the citizenry about the pace and value of escalation. "Leadership" unwedded to past errors was needed, he asserted, to achieve "success" in Vietnam.

In his criticisms Nixon targeted not only Johnson but also the antiwar movement and dovish Democrats. He argued that the president's mismanagement of the war was the product not only of his indecision and lack of aggressiveness but also of division among the Left, liberals, and Democrats. In 1965 he advocated the firing of Marxist professor Eugene Genovese of Rutgers University, who had said that the "establishment of a Socialist regime in Vietnam would be in the best interest of the Vietnamese people and would not pose a threat to the United States." In that year and the next he censured Senator J. William Fulbright for extending "so-called peace feelers," which he charged amounted to the advocacy of a "soft line" and an "appeasement line." Calling on Democrats to halt their criticisms of the war, he charged that the "split" in the party was the chief roadblock to peace. Along with the conservative educational center Freedom House in November 1965, he called on supporters of the war to "shout" their support: "The behavior of a small segment of our population" has obscured the national "consensus" in support of the war, but supporters must end their silence in order to make it clear to the "aggressors" that they should withdraw from South Vietnam. "It is essential," Nixon repeated two years later, "that the enemy be convinced that he cannot win the war militarily, that he cannot win it through a change in public opinion in the United States." The war could be shortened "by mobilizing free world opinion and by uniting the United States."

Nixon opposed diplomatic compromise. "If the word 'negotiations' implied concessions by both sides," he told the *New York Times* in 1965, "he was opposed to any negotiations. The Communists should be given nothing at the conference table." He would only "support a settlement of the kind the Eisenhower Administration reached in Korea, in which South Vietnam retained independence and security." In February of that year he claimed that the U.S. bargaining position was "too weak" to begin talks, and from Saigon on "a private business trip" in September, he asserted that the very advocacy of negotiations by Democratic doves like Fulbright convinced North Vietnam of America's "weakness."

By the end of 1967 he came to favor "peace efforts," but he continued to approach negotiations warily and to oppose compromise. Throughout the Johnson period, he insisted on the withdrawal of the North Vietnamese army (NVA) and an end to its "infringing on the independence and territorial integrity of South Vietnam." He stood against the "neutralization" of South Vietnam, the creation of a coalition government in Saigon, and the *mutual* withdrawal of North Vietnamese *and* American troops—the latter, a position he would advocate as president. Any "concession" on these points would be tantamount to "rewarding aggression." In April 1967, on his fifth visit to Saigon since 1963, he added another reason to resist negotiations: Saigon officials did not see any "reasonable prospect of a negotiated settlement." To Nixon peace meant bringing a favorable end to the war at the "negotiating" table by virtue of having exerted sufficient military and diplomatic leverage on Hanoi, the Viet Cong, and their allies. "You can only negotiate at the conference table what you can win on the battlefield at that particular time," he said in November 1965. One year later, while critically appraising the Manila communiqué of Johnson and then South Vietnamese President Nguyen Cao Ky, which they enunciated after a meeting in the Philippines in October 1966, he said: "A strategy for the future must be devised that will increase the military, economic, and diplomatic pressure on the aggressors to end the war and will guarantee peace without surrender throughout Asia." Except for devising the details of such a strategy, he would stay with this position into his presidency.[63]

Year in and year out, Nixon urged both parties to keep war out of politics, but at the same time he warned the Johnson administration and congressional Democrats that he would make the war an issue if they pursued a diplomatically "soft line," failed to adopt a winning military strategy, or were unable to unify behind the war. Nixon's persistent attacks, which were always well reported in the press, exasperated Johnson, another consummate politician, who naturally determined Nixon was playing politics with the war. In response to Nixon's critique of the Manila communiqué in 1966, which came just before the congressional elections, he correctly if unwisely called Nixon a "chronic campaigner. . . . We oughtn't to try to get mixed up in a political campaign here . . . and have men killed because we try to fuzz up something." The president's counterattack drew more attention to his tormentor, who used the opportunity to act presidential, retorting that "Johnson was guilty of 'a shocking display of temper' and had broken the bipartisan front of support for the Vietnamese war."[64]

In his run for the presidency, which had begun after Barry Goldwater's defeat in 1964, there were two hurdles Nixon needed to surmount: the Republican Party nomination and the general election. The constituencies he needed within and without the party to clear both of these hurdles were gravely divided on a range of foreign and domestic issues, with the Vietnam War becoming the litmus test on most of them by 1967. The number of right-wingers among Republican Party operatives, activists, and voters was on the rise. Golderwaterites needed to be wooed from Ronald Reagan, and southern whites from George Wallace. Many of his own core constituency among Republican and independent voters were war hawks. But to win a presidential nomination Nixon also had to attract Republican "moderates," and to win a general election he needed to appeal to those Democrats and independents who were not hawks. From 1964 until the summer of 1967, he zigzagged between demanding the intensification of military attacks on the enemy and expressing support for keeping the door opened to negotiations—with conditions. In this first phase of his long campaign, he played the role of "unifier and regular party man, . . . staking out the middle ground and leaning slightly to the right," as one historian put it.[65]

By the fall of 1967, as he prepared to formally announce his candidacy for the Republican presidential nomination, Nixon seemed to moderate his position on the war, or at least he shifted the emphasis and altered the tone of his message. In an article published in the September issue of *Foreign Affairs,* he called for a regional security system in Asia, which, he argued, would obviate the need for future American intervention and reduce the possibility of great-power confrontations. He also proposed a long-term effort to bring China "into the world of nations." In November he expressed reservations about Eisenhower's recently televised comments, in which the former president had endorsed the "hot pursuit"

of North Vietnamese troops into Laos and Cambodia and attacks upon their artillery positions in the Demilitarized Zone (DMZ) between North and South Vietnam. "From a 'military standpoint,'" he said, "General Eisenhower was 'absolutely
right.' . . . But . . . such a move would be both diplomatically and politically unsound 'at this time.'" In December he indicated his opposition to the "extension"
of the American ground war.[66]

Nixon was beginning to position himself for the second phase of his campaign, the contest for the general election in November 1968. By the end of 1967
his nomination seemed a sure bet. His competitors, moderate governors George
Romney and Nelson Rockefeller were poorly organized, and conservative governor Ronald Reagan lacked broad support. Although Nixon still had to overcome
his image as a loser in running against Democrats, conservatives and moderates
desperate to win the presidency increasingly viewed him as the only electable
Republican candidate. The nomination was not in the bag, but Nixon was solidly
in the lead. There was, as journalist Garry Wills would later say, "a forlorn air to
arguments in favor of Nixon's leadership."[67] He could win; he could, as the campaign slogan later went, "bring us together again." Although uninspiring and
untrustworthy, the more he appeared to be in the middle—to be ordinary in extraordinary times—the more he became the most attractive choice of the field.

THE CORE OF A "HOLLOW MAN"

Nixon was an instinctive pragmatist and a skillful propagandist who knew the
importance of projecting the appropriate political image, making useful alliances,
and creating the suitable mystique of leadership. Wills remarked that he was a
"plastic man": the least "'authentic' man alive, the late mover, tester of responses,
submissive to 'the discipline of consent.'" John Osborne described him as a card-
board figure.[68] This was the familiar charge: that Nixon was an opportunistic,
hollow man who did not have a core of convictions. Psychobiographer David
Abrahamsen compared him to Henrik Ibsen's Peer Gynt: peel away layer upon
layer of his personality—defensiveness, secretiveness, passivity, "happylessness,"
aggressiveness—and nothing would be left at the core of his character.[69]

He had been the "new Nixon" so many times that opponents asked, "Who is
the real Nixon"? The real Nixon was the old Nixon, for why otherwise would he
so often feel the need to change his image? During the 1968 campaign Hubert
Humphrey quipped: "Now, I read about the new Nixon of 1968. Ladies and gentle-
men. Anyone who's had his political face lifted so many times can't be very new."
Nixon's search for consensus was in part psychological (he wanted approval) and
in part political (he wanted to win an election). But consensus was a means to an
end, not in itself his goal, and he could scuttle it when doing so served his foreign
policy objectives. When he spoke of the need for new "leadership" in 1965, for
example, he did not mean merely replacing Johnson with Nixon or Democrats

with Republicans; he also had in mind a particular kind of leadership change, one that brought about a take-charge approach. "This is no time for consensus government," he declared. "It's a time for leadership. The average citizen doesn't know what the stakes are in Vietnam."[70] At the time this was partly political rhetoric directed at conservatives, but it also revealed a mentality he would bring to the presidency four years later, when public opinion was to be molded, the cabinet and the bureaucracy bypassed, and opponents overcome.

Nixon cared about his own needs and welfare, and he probably did have a personality disorder rooted in childhood that directed his behavior, but he nonetheless had positions on policy issues that also reflected his ideology, experiences, interests, gender, class aspirations, and social milieu. The views he had voiced on the war since 1964 were consistent with his career-long views on foreign policy; they were not simply reflections of a psychology formed in childhood or of a political pragmatism adapted to meet the needs of his run for the presidency.

There was a core to Nixon's foreign policy beliefs, a center line to his apparent zigs and zags. The middle ground he had staked out in the Republican Party was hawkish compared with the middle ground of Democrats or even of the larger public. He was a practical conservative, not a practical liberal.[71] Although he had kept the door open to negotiations over Vietnam, he was unwilling to negotiate compromises on the terms for which the war was being fought. Usually thought of as a man true to his conservative principles, Barry Goldwater could endorse him in late October 1967 feeling confident that Nixon would never turn the Republican Party into the "peace-at-any-price party."[72] Although beginning to speak of opposing an "extension" of the ground war, Nixon was not in favor of the withdrawal of ground troops or of other U.S. forces from Vietnam, and in fact he continued to call for "more effective" military and diplomatic strategies. His advocacy of an Asian security system in his *Foreign Affairs* article, which some regarded as the expression of a new Nixon, was a revival of the discredited SEATO concept; its purpose was still the old goal of "containing aggression and subversion," while legitimating an American policing role through regional "cooperative action." In any event, this organization was to come about, he wrote, "after Vietnam."

Nixon's overall position on the war in 1967 was not strategically or tactically different from the Eisenhower administration's position during the Dienbienphu-Geneva crisis, except perhaps with respect to nuclear weapons. At a time when the Soviets had achieved nuclear parity, the public had become more aware of the dangers of nuclear war, and Johnson had used the public's fear to defeat Goldwater in 1964, Nixon distanced himself from more right-wing Republicans and independents who urged or hinted they favored the use of nuclear weapons in Vietnam.

On the other hand, the reasons he gave were the same expedient ones the Eisenhower administration had given in 1954: their use would be, Nixon said in 1964, "detrimental to over-all United States policy"; and, in 1967, "I am opposed . . . first, because they are not necessary, and second, because it is not wise." He did not say he was opposed to using nuclear weapons under any circumstances.

He also counterbalanced these qualified reservations by employing terms like "massive pressure" and "retaliation." In September 1965 he had recommended retaliation against China if it did not keep its "hands off" other Asian countries, and, in December 1967, retaliation if it allowed its air bases to be used by the North Vietnamese.[73] Although publicly rejecting the use of nuclear weapons, he continued to talk about them obliquely, associating the war in Vietnam with the danger of nuclear war; that is, if the war were lost, it might lead to World War III, which "would be an atomic fight because China will have nuclear weapons."[74] He did not recommend a "preventive" attack on China, but he did not rule it out either, for that was "contingent upon the degree of provocation."[75] In practice, the very discussion of the use of nuclear weapons, even in denial, served to hold them out as a *threat* of possible use. Realists among North Vietnamese and Chinese leaders might have regarded Nixon's public denials as indicators of his unpredictability—and also of his willingness to use nuclear weapons under particular circumstances. Such an interpretation of his public comments would not have been far-fetched. Not only had such action been seriously considered and communicated in the past by the Eisenhower administration, but it was at this time, in the midsixties, that the Johnson administration secretly explored the "possibilities for joint action with the Soviet Government . . . to cooperate in preventive military action . . . against Chinese nuclear installations."[76]

Nixon's policy goals, too, remained unchanged. Nothing in what he said in the late sixties revised his long-standing opposition to Communism or his support of capitalism. Biographers have rightly pointed out that the anti-Communism of his early career was political and opportunistic: Jerry Voorhis in 1946, Alger Hiss in 1948, and Helen Gahagan Douglas in 1950 were useful political targets, vulnerable to Red-baiting. But while Nixon's anti-Communism was indeed opportunistic, it was also visceral and cerebral. He had chosen to make *it,* as opposed to something else, his weapon and his badge. It was part of his socially rooted mind-set, the product not only of his opportunistic politics and antisocial, paranoid, narcissistic, passive-aggressive personality but also of his immersion in a male-dominated, capitalist culture and his acceptance of capitalist conventions. Indeed, his individualist psychology and capitalist outlook were consistent. As psychologist Dana Crowley Jack explained in her observations about the "male" versus "female" sense of self:

> Capitalism requires autonomously functioning, independent individuals making economic determinations in their own self-interest. . . . Adam Smith's legacy suggests a moral justification of this self-interested, economic self: "By pursuing his own interest he frequently promotes that of the society. . . ." The intermeshing of ideas from political theory, philosophy, and cultural legends—of the lone cowboy, the hero, the warrior—has supported the psychological theory of the separate self to make it look "right."[77]

Nixon had grown up during the Great Depression in a petit bourgeois, Republican family that had conservative economic and cultural values. He judged his family's lowly status and his father's failures in terms of the accumulation of wealth. "Struggle" in response to these economic failures was a noble, virile virtue. "My old man," he said when he resigned the presidency, "had the poorest lemon ranch in California. . . . But he was a great man because he did his job . . . up to the hilt."[78]

Nixon defined "wealth" in terms of helping oneself and others through the acquisition of power: "Wealth is the means by which an individual can afford food, housing, clothing, and leisure, which are among the essentials for a good life. It is the means to produce economic progress, opportunities, and jobs for people. It is the means by which an individual can gain power to choose the direction he believes is best for the nation. It is the means by which one can help others who are less fortunate."[79]

When his political fortunes were low, Nixon turned to the business world—a place he admired, where he could make money, and where he found independent, successful men he respected, men who became his close, personal friends and benefactors. Between 1954 and 1956, when he feared President Eisenhower would drop him from the ticket, he thought seriously about leaving politics, moving to California, and starting a lucrative practice in "foreign commerce."[80] (One of his purposes of his foreign travels during his vice presidency had been to develop a résumé in international trade.) Two years after his electoral defeat in the 1960 presidential contest against Kennedy, Nixon joined—at the suggestion of a business friend—the Wall Street law firm of Mudge, Rose, Guthrie, and Alexander as a senior partner. In 1967 the firm, now headed with Nixon's name, merged with Caldwell, Trimble, and (John N.) Mitchell—the latter his future attorney general. Nixon specialized in international economics and multinational corporations, representing several American-owned companies, including Precision Valve, owned by his friend Robert Abplanalp.[81] In 1951 he befriended Charles G. "Bebe" Rebozo—realtor, banker, and self-made millionaire—and their friendship ripened in the 1960s, during Nixon's wilderness period. By the time Nixon was elected president, Bebe had become his pal, drinking buddy, and confidant. Nixon's primary political contributors were businessmen. Mellon Scaife, the heir to the Mellon banking fortune and a major right-wing benefactor, for example, gave $1 million to Nixon's Committee to Re-Elect the President in 1973, as well as $47,000 to the Watergate "slush fund."[82]

Even though Nixon had long resented the Establishment, he had wanted to be a part of it. He had applied for and received a scholarship to Harvard but had to turn it down because his family could not afford the associated expenses of schooling in the East. Graduating from Whittier, then Duke University law school, he had applied for corporate positions in New York but was not among the chosen. He then sought entry into the FBI; he was approved but was not hired because of legislative cuts in agency appropriations. He returned to Whittier to join a local law firm and soon became involved in community and business organizations. In 1946, after a tour of duty as a naval logistics officer in the Pacific and a contract-termination officer in the East during World War II, he accepted the invitation of Twelfth District southern California Republican businessmen to run for Congress. To them he explained his view on the "two conflicting opinions about the nature of the American system. One advocated by the New Deal is government control in regulating our lives. The other calls for individual freedom and all that initiative can produce. I hold with the latter viewpoint," which he described as "practical liberalism" at a time of liberal ascendancy, but could better have labeled "practical conservatism."[83]

Much earlier, during his years as a debater at Whittier College, Nixon had concluded that "free trade" and a "free economy" were better than "protectionism" and a "managed economy." In postpresidential retirement he wrote of capitalism and democracy: "If permitted to operate, capitalism represents a tremendous natural force for generating economic growth." Although capitalism produced "tension between [economic] equality and [economic] liberty, . . . government should not guarantee equality in economic outcomes . . . , and economic liberty· should never be sacrificed to the regimentation needed to provide such security." As a form of government, "democracy, which implies both liberty and equality," should only provide equality before the law and equality of opportunity. The democracy of economic equality must take second place to "prosperity." Americans must not, moreover, impose their brand of democracy on nations that "lack the traditions and institutions to make democracy work. Democratic government does not automatically mean good government."[84]

The economic principles of Nixon's foreign policy, although not classically conservative, were solidly capitalist and internationalist. At Whittier he had studied the historical question of whether Allied war debts should have been canceled after World War I and decided that "the economic recovery of Europe was more important than our insisting on payment of war debts."[85] As a young congressman in the late 1940s, he supported the Marshall Plan when most Republicans and conservatives were against it. Speaking to the National Industrial Conference Board in September 1967, he complained about the "'lack of candor' in stating American policy objectives and a failure to see in realistic terms a world 'in ferment of change.'" He continued by warning that America's "vital interest is at stake in Vietnam," candidly explaining what he meant by "vital interest" with an observation about foreign-aid programs: "We can preserve our hard-won abundance only by bringing the have-nots within the affluent society." But, as the press paraphrased him, "This policy of self-interest can succeed only if the American private enterprise system for development is adopted in the poorer nations." Nixon continued: "It's not just seeds and fertilizer, the hungry countries need. It's the system—a system of incentives and rewards, or prices and markets."[86]

Political ideology, military strength, and international capitalism were bound together in Nixon's "realistic" formula for national security. When then-Senator Nixon visited NATO headquarters in 1951, for example, General Eisenhower congratulated him for speeches in which he had placed proper emphasis "on the need to take into account economic and ideological as well as military factors in fashioning foreign policy."[87] During his foreign travels as vice president, Nixon observed that foreign leaders seemed to know more about economics than American leaders and embassy officials, and he believed that the State Department's government-to-government economic approach was too narrow-minded. He was more broad-minded, as were Eisenhower and Dulles, and wanted "to bring economics to the foreign service," cooperating more with the private sector and becoming more assertive in promoting international commerce.[88] Nixon told one biographer in 1959, "In the next ten years, our greatest external danger will not be military but economic and ideological."[89]

Nixon, like other policy makers, saw leftism and Communism at home and abroad as a threat to the established order in America and the sought-after American order around the globe. He sometimes put that another way, as when, after two martinis, he told a New York business friend in 1964 why he would like to run for the presidency: "Because I know the fucking Commie mind. But they don't know mine. I really think I could do something. I really believe I could make a contribution to peace."[90]

Psychohistorians later determined that his concern about peace resulted from the influence of his Quaker mother. In his political biography of Nixon, Tom Wicker argued on the basis of interviews with an unidentified Nixon intimate that he sought peace to overcome "'guilt feelings' for having followed so often . . . the example of his rancorous, partisan father rather than that of his 'saintly' mother."[91] This is a very plausible argument about his psychological motives, but what is revealing is the matter of how he—and his advisers—defined "peace." Concerning Vietnam, he spoke of peace as "ending" the war, but not "at any price." The goal was a "lasting peace," which required the preservation of American credibility and the creation of an American-led "structure" of peace.[92] Nixon's peace "idealism" in the late sixties was a version of Pax Americana, one that was not fundamentally different than the one presented in NSC position papers of the Truman and Eisenhower administrations or in the *Pentagon Papers* of the Johnson administration. His desire for "peace" and order in Vietnam was probably also rooted in his personal encounters with Asia and the Pacific Rim—his California background; his Pacific tour of duty during World War II; his acquaintances with figures in the "China lobby"; his personal liking for Asians, with whom he felt comfortable, in contrast to his feelings about condescending Europeans; and his belief that the Establishment's preference for Europe was little more than racial and cultural chauvinism toward the "plain peoples" of Asia.[93]

Although American policy goals remained fundamentally the same, conditions had changed in Asia, altering American perceptions of the significance of the Pacific Rim to U.S. interests. Indochina's geoeconomic importance had evolved since 1950. Then, its resources were needed by Europe and "free Asia," but especially by Japan, which, if denied them, might have to reorient its economy toward Communist states and thus leave the American orbit. Policy makers believed or claimed that other dominoes in Southeast and South Asia would surely fall as well.

By the late 1950s and into the early 1960s, Indochina had become important as a potential market for the core industrial nations and a symbolic combat zone in the global struggle between capitalist and socialist models of development. Now, as the sixties neared an end, the emerging capitalist tigers of Southeast Asia and the rest of the Pacific Rim required continued protection against revolution and a resurgent People's Republic of China. Despite his criticisms of Johnson's "mismanagement" of the war, Nixon praised the positive role the United States was playing in Vietnam: "All around the rim of China, nations of non-Communist Asia have been growing phenomenally in wealth and achieving a new stability. . . . The American commitment in Vietnam has bought time for this to take place."[94] To Nixon, a satisfactory ending to the war in Vietnam was a prerequisite to his and others' goal of a postwar American-led economic, political, and military association of "free" Pacific Rim states, with South Vietnam at the apex of an arc curving from New Zealand to Japan.[95]

The non-Communist Asian states and the United States, however, somehow needed to come to terms with China, which, Nixon thought, must still be contained but could no longer be isolated. In late 1967 it was not yet clear to Nixon what policy he should adopt toward the PRC. Although calling in September for returning China to the family of nations, he identified "Peking" as the "common danger" to non-Communist Asian governments and only a few months earlier had ridiculed as "completely naive" Edwin O. Reischauer's suggestion that the United States remove trade barriers against the Communist giant.[96]

He was clear in his own mind about the policy goal of the United States in South Vietnam, however. Defeat would undermine America's credibility as the leader and protector of the global system it led. "If the credibility of the United States is destroyed in Vietnam, it will be destroyed in Europe as well," Nixon warned during a speech in Tokyo in April 1967.[97] In the spring of 1969, just a short time into his presidency, he favorably entertained a "capitalist blueprint" for the postwar recovery of South Vietnam that had been two years in the making and prepared by a joint U.S.-RVN "development group" headed by David E. Lilienthal. It called for $2.5 billion of U.S. foreign aid in the first decade, with matching funds provided by the South Vietnamese government; the raising of interest rates; the devaluation of the piaster; the development of South Vietnam's infrastructure; the barring of tariff walls; the export of South Vietnam's natural resources and raw materials; the encouragement of "capital intensive industries with high labor productivity and low input costs"; and the continuance of large landholdings—all policies designed to place South Vietnam in the global marketplace of investment and trade.[98] In this form, with perhaps a few exceptions, it was not a vision that appealed to Communists, socialists, many intellectuals, many peasants, or nationalists in South or North Vietnam.

For a decade and a half, Nixon had consistently taken belligerent positions on the war in Vietnam, usually advocating more militant strategies than Presidents Eisenhower, Kennedy, and Johnson. His influence on policy and politics had advanced the gathering momentum toward the Americanization and enlargement of the struggle. Now, as he began the final stage of his campaign for the presidency, he spoke increasingly of his unique ability to end the fighting and of his commitment to the role of peacemaker. His past espousal of a globalist foreign policy, his narrow conception of peace, and his long record of militancy made him, however, an improbable peacemaker.

3

WINNING ON THE HOME FRONT: 1968

Let me make one thing clear. Those who have had a chance for four years and could not produce peace should not be given another chance. We will take that chance.
—Richard Nixon[1]

THE CAMPAIGN TRAIL

Speaking to a Republican audience at the American Legion Hall in Nashua, New Hampshire, on March 5, 1968, Nixon pledged to "end the war and win the peace in the Pacific." It was a new, carefully worded formulation of his former position on the dominant issue in the first presidential primary of the 1968 campaign. As he had in the past, Nixon rejected the option of U.S. "withdrawal from Vietnam," and he urged President Johnson to "keep the pressure on" the enemy, but now he gave greater weight to the urgency of terminating the war. Directly challenging President Johnson, Nixon declared that "if in November this war is not over after all of this power has been at their disposal, then . . . the American people will be justified to elect new leadership." The president and his advisers, he claimed, had put too much emphasis on the "military side" and too little on the "non-military side." The war "can be ended," he affirmed, if "we mobilize our economic and political and diplomatic leadership." He had spoken vaguely of this strategy in 1966, but now he explained that the "key to peace" might be the application of "leverage to get the Soviet Union to use its power on the side of peace."[2]

In this and other appearances in March, the Republican front-runner trod warily on the road to the nomination, a road laid with political land mines. To counter voter apathy about the Republican race, he tried to make the New Hampshire primary a contest between him and the president. Implying by his remarks that he had a secret plan to end the war, he succeeded in attracting the attention of the press. Denying, however, that he had a surefire, "magic formula" or a "push-button technique" to achieve peace, he tried to avoid the political trap of providing a concrete plan. Needing to bridge the gap between supporters and opponents of the war, he walked a tightrope of meaning, using nuanced words and phrases to keep his balance. For doves and moderates, he spoke less of escalating military measures and protecting vital interests and more of taking *nonmilitary* steps toward *peace;* for hawks and conservatives, he continued to talk about putting on *pressure* and *winning* the peace. For all Americans, he spoke of a peace with *honor.*[3]

The political landscape had changed dramatically in recent weeks. George Romney had withdrawn from the Republican contest at the end of February, largely because of the damage done by his own political misstatements about the war. Nelson Rockefeller was disorganized and appeared indecisive, but if Nixon stumbled he might become the leading contender. Reagan had little chance of winning the nomination, but with support from hawks within the party, he could be a spoiler. The surprise of the February–March campaign season was Senator Eugene McCarthy, who in November 1967 had responded to the call of liberal antiwar Democrats to challenge President Johnson for his party's nomination. In the wake of the Vietcong offensive that began on January 30—the first day of the Vietnamese lunar new year of 1968, or Tet—he was showing unexpected strength in polls of New Hampshire voters, and he and his young, enthusiastic campaign workers were attracting most of the attention of the press. In the primary election on March 12, McCarthy drew 42.4 percent versus Johnson's 49.5 percent in the Democratic race. Four days later Bobby Kennedy announced he was entering the presidential race. Nixon won 78% of Republican vote. Damaged by his loss to Nixon, Rockefeller withdrew from the race on March 21.

PUBLIC OPINION

Below the surface of these campaign tremors, public opinion was noticeably shifting. Since early 1966, support for the war had been declining, while opposition had been rising. The changes were now more rapid. Based on responses to questions about whether "involvement" in the war was a "mistake," or whether the United States should have "stayed out" or "gotten in," polls in October 1967 indicated that for the first time in the history of America's direct military intervention, public opposition to the war surpassed support for it 46 to 44 percent. Support rebounded feebly in December after assurances by General William C. Westmoreland, the commander of Military Assistance Command Vietnam (MACV), about progress made against the enemy, and briefly again in a rally-'round-the-flag reaction to the start of the Tet offensive. But opposition to the war rose once again in February, exceeding support, 46 to 42 percent. In March the figures were 49 to 41 percent, with 10 percent having "no opinion." Questions about specific policies produced parallel results. Between December 1967 and March 1968, for example, support for stopping the bombing of Hanoi in order to encourage negotiations rose 16 points, from 24 to 40 percent.[4]

The way poll takers framed their questions influenced their findings. Respondents reacted as much to particular words and phrases and the tone in which questions were asked as they did to the substance of the issue at hand. Moreover, pollsters did not ask the same questions consistently over a long period of time, thus making it difficult for analysts to measure opinion trends and swings. In October 1967, for example, those favoring the immediate withdrawal of U.S. troops stood at 35 percent; in March 1968—responding to a differently worded question—56 percent favored halting the bombing and fighting while withdrawing gradually. When questions about a gradual U.S. withdrawal were coupled with turning the conduct of the war over to the South Vietnamese in stages, support appeared to be even higher—71 percent in October 1967 and 66 percent in June 1968. The idea of giving the Republic of Vietnam Armed Forces (RVNAF) a larger role in the war, while providing them with more training and equipment, would become known as "Vietnamization" in March 1969, when Melvin Laird, Nixon's secretary of defense, suggested the word as a preferable substitute to "de-Americanization," and Nixon approved.[5]

Perhaps indicative of a general naïveté—or indifference—about what the war was about, pollsters infrequently raised the very important issue of support for U.S. withdrawal even if it led to the Communists coming to power in South Vietnam. In one of the rare polls on the question in the spring of 1967, only 19 percent of respondents favored "a withdrawal of American troops leading to an eventual Communist takeover in Vietnam." This response seemed to uncover a fundamental contradiction between support for withdrawal and support for the goals of the war. Unknown is what the response would have been had the question been asked without the loaded phrase "Communist takeover" but, instead, in conjunction with references to a negotiated dispensation of political power in Saigon.

The opinions of an aggregate public could also be misleading, for the "public" was actually many "publics" distinguished by region, religion, race, class, education, gender, age, party affiliation, union membership, and other viable categories. Polls did not measure group differences consistently or precisely, but there was plenty of evidence that the differences existed.[6]

Despite their flaws, polls provided persuasive evidence in early 1968 of a citizenry uneasy about the war and growing more weary of it, with a majority turning against its continued prosecution. A majority favored gradual withdrawal, Vietnamization, negotiations with the enemy, and a bombing pause—whatever the qualifications. Polls influenced policy makers and politicians, who studied them carefully, comparing the data with their own personal soundings of friends, colleagues, family members, and the press. It was not just the general public's mood that had changed. The confidence of many corporate executives, Democratic policy makers, and informed officers and soldiers in the military was waning. Key Republican leaders had doubts, and rank-and-file Republican sentiment was moving away from all-out support of the war.[7] To read the memoirs of these individuals is to know that they were conscious of the antiwar movement and the divisions among Americans about the war, and realized that the movement and these divisions limited America's capacity to continue the war as it had been fought.

These shifting attitudes made Nixon's political problem even more challenging: wooing the doves while holding the hawks and clinging to his own foreign policy convictions. On the other hand, there were opportunities that the politically savvy Nixon could exploit: the diversity of opinion among the many publics about a complex, puzzling war enabled him to play both sides, as well as work the edges, without abandoning his own hawkish principles. Although the majority favored a phased withdrawal of American forces by late 1967, for example, only a small minority supported withdrawal if it led to a "Communist takeover." In early 1968 opinion was shifting toward a phased withdrawal that included Vietnamization and negotiations, but there remained strong support among many Americans for continuing the war at the "present level of military effort," the intensification of military operations, or "an all-out crash effort in the hope of winning the war quickly even at the risk of China or Russia entering the war"—as one poll phrased it. Although the majority opposed seeking victory through the use of nuclear weapons, an astounding one-quarter of those polled in March and December 1967 and March 1968 were in favor.[8] Nixon could turn these diverse opinions in his favor; that is, without abandoning his basic foreign policy goals, diplomatic tactics, and military strategies, he could propose politically appealing courses of action to particular portions of the electorate. He could advocate an end to the war, negotiations, and the withdrawal of American forces but simultaneously propose putting pressure on the enemy in support of the Saigon government, even if there were risks and costs to the nation.

Nixon's "middle-of-the-road" strategy also protected his flanks against hawks and doves. Genuine hawks (those who advocated military escalation in Vietnam) and genuine doves (those who opposed force and preferred negotiation) were in a minority. Unlike the erratic majority, who followed leaders' suggestions or responded to events and policy changes, hawks persistently advocated more forceful approaches, and doves persistently opposed them. They possessed strategic convictions. Tired of the war, however, both groups agreed that it should be ended soon—by force for hawks, and by diplomacy for doves. Nixon realized, however, as speechwriter Richard Whalen noted, that "it was not such a jump . . . from saying 'get it over with quickly' to saying 'get out and save the lives of American boys.'" This odd confluence of opinion about ending the war manifested itself in the New Hampshire Democratic primary. Hawks, angry about what they believed was Johnson's too gradual application of military power, and doves, angry about his excessive use of force, registered their protests by voting for McCarthy. Nixon's middle strategy—criticizing the president's gradualism but calling for a new diplomacy to end the war—helped him dodge the wrath of hawks and cut his losses against the doves. The aim of Nixon's "centrism," Whalen disapprovingly noted, was not to discover the most valid solution for Vietnam but "to find the least assailable middle ground."[9] To scoop up conservative support, he had stood on the political right in 1967 and before; now he was edging closer to the political center in preparation for the November elections.[10]

Driving the changes in public opinion were the war's costs and frustrations. Mounting casualties, economic burdens, social dissonance, and feelings of futility were the most palpable. Since the introduction of combat troops in 1965, U.S. battle casualties had risen slowly, in contrast to the Korean War, where the numbers of killed and wounded had been greater in the first year of fighting. But the cumulative total of U.S. casualties in Vietnam had exceeded the casualty total of the entire Korean War by the middle of 1968, which was also the year of peak per annum combat casualties in Vietnam. This turning-point year also brought more inflation, new taxes, and difficult choices between expending money for waging war and domestic programs. Other social fissures—racial division, the alienation of blue-collar and middle-class Americans from their political parties and government, and youthful "counterculture" challenges to "mainstream" values—widened with the war. It was a war that had already gone on too long, and after the Tet offensive it appeared to be irrevocably stalemated, with no end in sight.[11]

The public, especially the World War II generation, was perplexed about the causes of stalemate. How could this small, underdeveloped country of Vietnam stymie the United States, which had recently defeated Germany and Japan and contained the Soviet Union? Many Americans looked inward—at their own divisions, the mismanagement of leaders, and ineffective strategies of war. Hawks in particular blamed the allegedly restrained military strategy of President Johnson and his liberal civilian advisers for the impasse. From politicians such as Barry Goldwater to hard-line generals and admirals in the JCS, the call of hawks had been for more troops, more bombing, a naval blockade and ground attacks against North Vietnam, and even the use of nuclear weapons, regardless of the risk of war with China or the Soviet Union.[12] They argued that the pace of the administration's military escalations since 1964 had been too gradual, thereby allowing the enemy to adapt, prepare, and resist. Had more American troops been deployed in South Vietnam more rapidly, had more massive airpower been thrown against more vital targets much sooner—including dikes, Hanoi, Haiphong harbor, and enemy bases in Laos and Cambodia—the North Vietnamese and Vietcong would have been forced to capitulate or would have made requisite diplomatic concessions. Hawks also blamed the antiwar opposition—the "other" within—for having contributed to the undermining of America's will to win. The movement caused disunity at home, they maintained, encouraging the enemy to persist and discouraging American leaders from prosecuting the war more forcefully. It was assisted by the press, particularly the television press, which, they complained, excessively reported both the horrors of the war in Vietnam and the protests against it at home.

The anti–Vietnam War movement of the sixties and seventies was indeed a political force. Not simply a youth or student movement, it was an informal coalition of young, middle-aged, and elder street demonstrators, citizen-lobbyists, letter writers, draft resisters, Vietnam veterans, and vocal critics in major urban centers, grassroots America, the elite and hinterland universities, the communications industry, the military rank and file, and the halls of Congress. Politically these individuals represented radical and moderate pacifists, anti-interventionist liberals, and leftists of varying shades and degrees. Their evolving dissent at home had led Johnson to reevaluate Westmoreland's costly big-unit, search-and-destroy strategy and to consider a bombing halt in exchange for the opening of negotiations.[13]

But hawks undervalued the rapidity with which the Johnson administration had brought enormous power to bear in Indochina. Ninety-one percent of the half million U.S. troops in Vietnam by the end of 1968 had been deployed, along with their firepower, between the spring of 1965 and the end of 1967. Even Nixon had seemed to call for a slowdown in troop deployments by 1966 and 1967. The air force presence grew more rapidly, reaching 91 percent of its peak in 1966 and 97 percent in 1967. Despite the millions of tons of bombs dropped on North and South Vietnam, Laos, and Cambodia, the air campaign continued to be indecisive, prompting the JCS to call for more. There was never enough bombing. Although hard put to find genuine military targets, American airpower advocates complained of restraints and "gradualism" in the pace of escalation—disregarding the arguments of intelligence analysts, the cost-ineffectiveness of throwing high-technology airplanes and highly trained pilots against a populous preindustrial nation, and the risks of widening the war.

The antiwar movement's actual impact on the U.S. war effort was complex and hard to gauge. What few restraints the Johnson administration had imposed on their military effort had been as much, if not more than antiwar protest, the product of other concerns: the economic price and logistical feasibility of greater and more rapid escalation; the impact of a larger commitment in Vietnam upon America's global military posture; and, most of all, possible Soviet and Chinese responses to the destruction of North Vietnam.[14] The majority of the public came to dislike street-demonstration tactics more than they disliked the war itself, and in that sense vocal and organized opposition to the prosecution of the war appeared to have been counterproductive. On the other hand, by 1968 the movement had performed three vital antiwar functions. First, it had provided an alternative analysis of the war's causes, wisdom, and morality, while also proposing alternative ways of exiting Vietnam—negotiated compromises, military disengagement, and troop withdrawal. Second, by thus undermining the intellectual and ethical edifice that had supported the policy of military interventionism and the continuance of the war, it had prepared the ground for mainstream politicians and policy makers to mount viable political challenges to the war from within the executive branch and Congress and through the presidential campaign process. Finally, for those who disliked and were irritated with the protesters—including parents who worried about their children's participation in the counterculture movement, which they associated with the antiwar movement, and decision makers like Johnson and Nixon, who were disturbed by rebellion—the words and actions of the protesters contributed to their general war-weariness. "The dissidents did not stop the war," one historian of the movement argued, "but they made it stoppable."[15]

The antiwar movement on the American home front had indeed encouraged the North Vietnamese and the Vietcong, as had antiwar sentiment in countries allied to the United States. But such encouragement was not decisive, and the Vietnamese were realistic enough to know that protest could not turn the war around. After so many years of fighting, the practical-minded decision makers in Hanoi, the common soldiers in the jungles and paddies, and the northern and southern peasants in their bombed-out villages knew the war would be decided in Vietnam by their fighting skills, in the commitment and determination of *their* hearts and minds, and with the material support they received from allies. The Politburo in Hanoi had always assumed that the United States, which had global ambitions and global responsibilities, would be overextended in Asia, and that its troops and people, fighting an unjust war on foreign soil, would likely suffer low morale. Vietnamese policy makers expected that the American people would come to see that it was not in their interest to endure heavy costs and suffer high casualties in a distant war. On their side, they were confident in what they considered to be their just motives—their pursuit of independence, unity, democracy, peace, and social reform. They were convinced that the outcome of the war would be decided by this political consciousness, motivating their people fighting on the ground and enduring at home. Public opinion in Vietnam was much more important than public opinion in the United States. Communist leaders expected the American will to fight would crumble sooner than that of the Vietnamese. They were unsurprised that a peace movement had arisen from "progressive elements" in American society, and, while they were encouraged by it, they were also disappointed and realistic about its actual strength. They could plainly see that American policy makers were able to continue the war with great violence despite the doubts of the American public.[16]

It was most likely the failure of the military component of the war itself that was the main factor in producing war-weariness—impatience and frustration with losses, confusion about purpose, uncertainty about how the war could and would end, and perceptions of developing economic and social crisis. Preoccupied with their own problems and divisions, Americans underestimated the obstacles to victory presented by the nature of modern war, the special conditions of this war, and the fighting capacity and techniques of the enemy. Those who acknowledged the difficult conditions in which the war had to be waged probably understood them little. The list was long: South Vietnam's tropical climate and varied terrain; its great distance from the United States; its contiguity to Cambodia, Laos, and North Vietnam; North Vietnam's proximity to China; South and North Vietnam's large populations; these countries' rural, industrially undeveloped economies; their alien culture; Saigon's bewildering politics; Hanoi's alliance with Moscow and Beijing. Equally important were the deeply rooted nationalism of the Vietnamese, their ancient tradition of resisting foreign invaders, and the desire of many to reform the society and economy. The Vietnamese Communist Party, or Vietnamese Workers' Party (VWP), had energized patriotic nationalism during World War II but had also mobilized those intellectuals, youths, and peasants who were committed to social and economic change. The party's slogan of "independence, national unity, and democracy," although a propaganda catchphrase, was genuinely supported by countless Vietnamese, who wanted to reunify north and south, manage their own affairs, and "modernize" the country for the benefit not of foreigners but of themselves.

WAYS OF WAR

The American way of waging war in Vietnam since 1965 had been consistent with U.S. military practice in the nation's great wars of the past century. It emphasized big ground-unit campaigns of a thousand men or more and the massive application of military technology on the ground and in the air in pursuit of decisive, annihilative battles against enemy armed forces, the destruction of economic resources, and the undermining of civilian morale. The difficulty of finding and fixing enemy units for destruction very quickly led General Westmoreland to shift his strategic emphasis from annihilation to attrition.[17] Appreciating that this war was a different kind of war, one that had political, social, and psychological components, MACV also pursued parallel and subsidiary strategies of "counterinsurgency" and "pacification": programs of psychological warfare propaganda, small-unit patrols, political arrests and assassinations, and land reform. These were mainly the responsibility of the RVN's armed forces.

Although taking a heavy toll of enemy forces, both the big-unit sweeps of American forces and the pacification operations of the South Vietnamese forces were politically counterproductive. Along with subsidies to the South Vietnamese economy, counterinsurgency and pacification largely served the interests of Saigon government officials, army officers, landlords, and an urban bourgeoisie dependent on American money. Military and political operations were poorly coordinated, and arrests, torture, and assassinations were often indiscriminate. American tactics—population relocations, search-and-destroy sweeps, the bulldozing of villages, artillery barrages, and widespread bombing—alienated many in the population, whose hearts and minds were supposed to be won over or, failing that, terrorized into compliance.

Managed by military and civilian technocrats trained to manipulate weapons, nature, and statistics, this way of war was failing in the political-cultural-military environment of Vietnam and was not likely to succeed in the future—unless, Westmoreland and the JCS believed, the nation was willing to commit much larger numbers of troops and vaster amounts of ordnance, equipment, and airpower to expanded operations throughout Indochina. The public and the policy makers, however, were not so willing, particularly after Tet. In any event, although American power could destroy Vietnam even more than it had already been destroyed, it could not politically "save" Vietnam for the Pax Americana.

The Communist way of war, on the other hand, while costly for the Vietnamese, was adaptive to the conditions of the time—they fought a "people's war," or "revolutionary war." Drawing its emotional and intellectual power from the aspirations of subject peoples and the analyses of radical, nationalist intellectuals, a people's war was an organizational and strategic response to the historic problem rebels and revolutionaries had faced in countries occupied by foreign forces: how to defeat the superior military technology and organization of imperial rulers and their indigenous allies. People's war integrated ideological, political, social, and economic approaches with flexible military strategies to tap the low-technology, human resources of largely peasant populations. Its practitioners appealed to national loyalties, encouraged anti-imperial anger, advocated and carried out democratic socioeconomic reforms, systematically engaged in political-military organizing at the grassroots level, applied selective terror, and employed irregular and regular military tactics at different stages of the struggle. Materially unable to pursue a Western-style strategy aimed at destroying enemy armed forces quickly, Communist leaders in Vietnam hoped that if they could hold on through "protracted war," American soldiers, leaders, and home-front citizenry, whose tangible interests were not at stake in faraway Vietnam, would be, like the French, worn down. Through trial and error, but drawing on experience, resolve, and revolutionary war doctrine, they had guessed correctly—although at great cost. By 1968 the fighting will and ability of the Vietnamese resistance—sustained with supplies and equipment from the Soviet Union and China—had stalemated the awesome military might of the United States in Vietnam, forcing difficult choices on frustrated and disillusioned American policy makers, engendering popular warweariness and organized antiwar opposition on the American home front.[18]

Nixon had recognized as early as the French-Vietminh phase of the conflict that this was a new kind of war—different, that is, from World War II and the Korean War. He knew that the enemy was militarily weak compared with French forces and, because of its weakness, usually employed guerrilla military tactics, drawing what innate strength it possessed mainly from the political and material support of a significantly large segment of the population. The Vietminh had won their support, he explained publicly in April 1954, because they fought in the name of the aspirations of the Vietnamese: "independence from any foreign domination, recognition of equality, and peace." In a secret NSC meeting the previous January, Nixon had omitted "equality" and "peace," observing that "the French are fighting in the hope of keeping Vietnam in the French Union, whereas the

Vietnamese really want independence outside the French Union." He knew that France and its benefactor, the United States, had to win the Vietnamese population's support away from the Vietminh if they were to win their war.[19]

But Nixon's understanding of the dynamics of the struggle, like that of other counterinsurgency policy makers and theorists in America and Europe, focused on technique, not substance. To him, the support of the people had been garnered by the Vietminh through "subversion"—the *manipulation* of Vietnamese aspirations. He spoke of their methods of terror, torture, propaganda, and deception. Even their reforms—land reform, for example—were fraudulent, he insisted, for they were imported from Russia and China. They represented international "Communist colonialism," and their war was nothing but "externally supported guerrilla action." Nixon did not accept the reality that the Vietminh, while using the special techniques of revolutionary war and receiving the support of Russia and China, had come out of the people and that their revolution was an authentic manifestation of the social and national aspirations of large numbers of Vietnamese. They were homegrown. To be sure, there were other Vietnamese individuals and groups with other programs of modernization and reform and their own claims on authenticity—Nixon agreed with Diem that he, not Ho Chi Minh, was an authentic nationalist.[20] But the Vietminh were Vietnamese all the same, and their war and their motives were organically rooted in Vietnamese culture and history. That was why most observers agreed that they fought well and against the odds.

Miscomprehending the enemy's success as deriving solely from manipulative techniques, and seeking the attainment of America's own global goals, Nixon proposed not the achievement of independence, unity, and social revolution for the Vietnamese but the application of countersubversion techniques to their conversion. In public speeches he referred to the "difficult . . . problem of giving the [allied] Indo-Chinese the will to fight." The prerequisite was to keep the French in the war and, later, to maintain an American presence there. Beyond that, the way to stop "internal subversion" was "to associate" the United States with Vietnamese aspirations. While acknowledging in secret NSC meetings that "what was lacking to induce the [pro-French] Vietnamese to fight was a 'cause,'" he argued that it might be sufficient, as well as easier, to simply give them better equipment, training, and leadership.[21] He also prescribed large doses of psychological warfare and paramilitary operations.[22]

Through the years, Nixon continued to hold these views. "The Johnson Administration," he wrote in March 1968, "has tried to counter the sophisticated techniques of revolutionary warfare with means appropriate to the two World Wars and the Korean War." What was needed, he maintained, was "a full array of . . . political and economic development, administrative reform, the employment of advanced techniques of psychological warfare—but the first requirement is providing [military] protection." Nixon did not truly understand the war as a struggle for unity, independence, and social change arising out of the soil of Vietnam; he understood it as a subversive strategy of aggression with international origins and global implications. He used the term "revolutionary war," but what he described was something else: a war in which the "foreign" regular army of North Vietnam had invaded the South, where it controlled its guerrilla fifth columnists, the Vietcong. In his view the Vietcong was created to serve as an auxiliary of the North Vietnamese army and would not have existed without its instigation and support. In fact, however, the Vietcong, or NLF, was an indigenous southern dissident movement with revolutionary political and social aims. It was both an outgrowth of the all-Vietnamese Vietminh of the French-Vietminh War and a southern insurgency of the post-Geneva, Diem period. In 1968 it was still a predominantly homegrown southern political organization with a military wing, the People's Liberation Armed Forces (PLAF), although it also received material aid and infusions of manpower from the North and strategic policy direction from the Hanoi Politburo. The Politburo, however, had southern members, just as the Saigon government had northerners.[23] To the Politburo in Hanoi and the frontline fighters in the South, Vietnam was one country; South Vietnam was no more an independent nation than the secessionist American South had been in the eyes of Abraham Lincoln and the Union Army.

NIXON'S VIETNAM

Geneva, Diem, Vietminh, Vietcong, National Liberation Front, North Vietnam, South Vietnam—it was all very complex history, which many Americans did not know or understand. In his career, Nixon had had ample opportunity to learn that history, but he viewed it from the perspective of a dedicated cold war warrior. Vietnam, he asserted, was a testing ground of Mao's "wars of liberation," which served both Chinese and Soviet interests. Hanoi, which he claimed controlled the Vietcong, was not a "puppet," he conceded, but it had to be a "respectful client" of the Soviet Union "in order to keep Soviet aid flowing and to balance the influence of nearby Peking." The war, he maintained, was not "an isolated trial, a war in a vacuum."

> Beneath the struggle among Vietnamese lies the larger, continuing struggle between those nations that want order and those that want disorder; between those that want peace, and those that seek domination. It is this larger conflict which gives the war in Viet Nam its importance far beyond Southeast Asia. . . . We must recognize if we are to restore a realistic perspective on the war . . . the deep and direct involvement of the Soviet Union.[24]

This was the view of one who made and unmade the destinies of small countries, played the great game on a global chessboard, had his own clients, and projected his view of reality onto others. Even had Nixon really understood the indigenous authenticity of the Vietnamese enemy, it would probably not have altered his reaction, for he believed their war *functioned* to serve the global interests of the Soviets, Chinese, and international Communism, as well as other forces of "disorder"—leftism, socialism, and nationalist rebellion:

> While the United States is tied down in Viet Nam, the Soviets are loose in the World—free to challenge us in the Mediterranean, free to move into the vacuum left by retreating colonial powers in the Middle East and along the vast rimland of the Indian Ocean. . . . The war bitterly divides the people of the United States, and separates us from our allies. . . . In their support of Hanoi, the Soviets have encouraged violent disorder rather than peaceful stability.[25]

Big powers as well, the Soviet Union and the PRC did play much the same game of global balance of power as the United States, attempting to shape the affairs of smaller nations in their own interests and against that of other powers. The Vietnamese revolutionaries were clients of these Communist realpolitikers, as Nixon said, in that they received services and material aid, but their motives and aims were their own. They were not always respectful of their suppliers, and they were ready to carry on even if their allies abandoned them. They were self-motivated. Theirs was the view of the angry movers and shakers within small nations—of those who believed their people had been exploited and their nation's resources plundered by the great powers, and who had committed themselves to revolutionary change.

Over the course of a half century, Ho Chi Minh and other revolutionaries had migrated intellectually from liberal and socialist understandings of classic colonialism to a Marxist-Leninist worldview about capitalist first world neoimperialism in the second and third worlds. Ho Chi Minh's encounters with the liberals and socialists of France and America in the early twentieth century had convinced him that they were not seriously committed to removing the yoke of French colonial rule from Vietnam, even though they voiced support for the principles of equality, liberty, justice, self-determination, and the pursuit of happiness. In Lenin's theories of imperialism, however, he discovered an explanation of French rule in Vietnam. In the international Communist movement, he found allies committed to overturning capitalist imperialism. In the Communist Parties of the Soviet Union and China, he recognized an organizational model for achieving Vietnam's independence.[26]

This worldview of the leaders of the VWP, combined with their practical need for diplomatic, military, and economic aid from the Eastern bloc in their wars against the French and the Americans, had led them to participate on the chessboard of global diplomacy. Their experience in the French-Vietminh war, and later with what they regarded as the "American war" in Vietnam, could not help but impress them with the international dimensions of their struggle. In the post–World War II period, they, like the statesmen of the great powers, were also concerned about the problem of balance of power, particularly the balance between the United States, the USSR, and the PRC, for it directly affected their fortunes. They fought, however, not for global goals but for local, Vietnamese goals—for their square on the board.

AVOIDING DEFEAT

Despite his misapprehension of the origins and purposes of the Vietnamese Communists and their allies, Nixon nonetheless understood that they had played a crucial role in producing a frustrating military stalemate. On Friday, March 29, he told his speechwriters, Richard Whalen, Raymond Price, and Patrick Buchanan: "I've come to the conclusion that there's no way to win the war. But we can't say that, of course. In fact, we have to seem to say the opposite, just to keep some degree of bargaining leverage."[27] Nixon had just learned important news: President Johnson's Senior Advisory Group had recommended at a luncheon meeting on Tuesday, March 26, that he begin to disengage from Vietnam.

Johnson had often consulted these "Wise Old Men" of the foreign policy Establishment. A "rich blend of Wall Street and Washington soldiers and diplomats,"[28] many were now retired from government service, but in their heyday they had been among the original architects of America's global hegemony. They still supported the goal of Pax Americana and still accepted the American responsibility for policing the globe. In the past few years they had repeatedly ratified Johnson's policies in Vietnam. Since 1967, however, several had become uneasy about the war and its impact on American society and foreign policy. Their friends, former colleagues, and family members were either becoming dovish or, if remaining hawkish, souring on the endless war. They knew that high-level officials in the State and Defense Departments now had serious doubts about the course of the war and were holding their own private strategy meetings. Robert S. McNamara, whose name had once been synonymous with the waging of the war, had recently left his position as secretary of defense because of his reevaluations of strategy and his differences with the president. Promilitary congressional Democrats, including two key members of the Senate Armed Services Committee, Henry Jackson and John Stennis, believed the war was hopeless.[29] The Wise Men were increasingly cognizant, too, of the dramatic decline in public support for the war and constantly surprised by the strength of vocal antiwar opposition. They worried about growing racial conflict, the president's flagging popularity, the challenges to his presidency from within the party, and the implications of all for the conduct of foreign policy. Most of all they fretted about the military stalemate, which was draining American military power and threatening U.S. commitments elsewhere, especially those in Europe.[30]

At the Tuesday luncheon meeting, General Wheeler, referring to the Tet offensive, told the group that Westmoreland had "turned this around," and therefore "this was the worst time to negotiate." Henry Cabot Lodge, one of the Wise Men, whispered sarcastically in Dean Acheson's ear, "Yes, because we are in worse shape militarily than we have ever been."[31] The enemy's military and political successes during its Tet offensive had caused many in the group to be skeptical of the sanguine briefings from the president's military advisers. Acheson, who had had enough of it, had recently warned Johnson, "Mr. President, you are being led down the garden path."[32] Particularly troubling to several was the apparent contradiction between Westmoreland's upbeat assessment of the Tet battle and Wheeler's request in late February for 205,129 more troops for the Vietnam theater.[33]

The recommendations from the group at this dramatic meeting shocked the president, who remarked: "You have been hearing things that I haven't." The majority believed, the group's reporter McGeorge Bundy told Johnson, that "we must begin to take steps to disengage"; the minority felt "we should not act to weaken our position." On the military's request for troop reinforcements, Bundy continued, "most of us think that there should not be a substantial escalation, nor an extension of the conflict. This would be against our national interest."[34]

Although this was a fateful moment in the history of American foreign policy, in which these formidable elder statesmen were advising retrenchment in Vietnam, they were not calling for retreat or surrender. The most skeptical within the Senior Advisory Group were primarily casting doubt on the possibility of military victory, or, as one member of the group, Arthur Dean, phrased it: "There is no military conclusion in this war—or any military end in the near future."[35] They had simply and finally come to the view that neither more American troops nor more bombing would lead to military victory.

Lodge, who was in the minority and against disengagement, nonetheless recommended the abandonment of big-unit search-and-destroy operations, which were aimed at military victory, and proposed instead a politico-military strategy of counterinsurgency, which would have the effect of reducing American casualties and winning public support in America. Behind this American counterinsurgency shield, the South could reorganize its government and army to be competitive with the North.[36] The majority side believed the war must soon end in the interest of addressing the military, political, and economic crises facing the American nation. Save for recommending negotiations and a "clear and hold" strategy of engaging enemy territorial guerrillas, however, they had no sure solutions of their own, no magic formulas to achieve what they wanted to achieve and what the U.S. government had long sought in Vietnam as its minimal goal: the "avoidance of defeat." W. Averell Harriman, who was not present at the meeting but had been kept informed, was one of the main "doves" within the group and was probably the strongest advocate of negotiations. In this approach, he believed it very important to enlist Soviet cooperation.[37] But the Wise Men, even the most dovish, continued to hope that somehow the North Vietnamese and the Viet Cong would conclude that they could not win and the United States could not be defeated. Perhaps then they would agree to a negotiated settlement acceptable to Washington, one that would preserve the Saigon government, thereby enabling the United States to exit from the war while maintaining its honor.

It was wishful thinking, and it illustrated how trapped these men were in their commitment to credibility. How could the continuance of current military strategies—which is what some in the group supported—succeed when they had failed before and, in any event, could not be sustained politically and economically? How could military disengagement—which is what the majority wanted—bring about negotiations that would lead to the preservation of South Vietnam as a non-Communist, independent state when massive engagement had failed?

Nixon had received a remarkably accurate report on the meeting. He knew that the Senior Advisory Group "had reversed its former stand . . . [and] no longer believed that the war could be brought to a successful end by military means." His own assessment of the conflict resembled that of the defecting Wise Men. When he confided to his speechwriters that "there's no way to win the war," he meant that there was no way to defeat the other side militarily. Yet, like the Wise Men, he continued to hope for a successful political outcome. To this end, he needed "bargaining leverage" to conclude the war "promptly on a basis consistent with the strategic interests of the United States and the free Asian nations."[38]

He, too, believed that American foreign policy was in crisis. But to him, in a world of challenge and change, it was a crisis of will and understanding, of power and credibility, of public order and economic health. The stalemate in Vietnam was both a cause and a symptom. The antiwar opposition, the counterculture movement, and the Black revolt were, he thought, rebellions against legitimate authority, which had produced social disorder and compounded the already difficult task of global leadership. Ominously, the erosion of public and elite support for intervention in Vietnam had undermined the almost two-decade-old consensus supporting the principle of military intervention itself. The nation, he thought, was on the precipice of a "new isolationism," threatening American goals and leadership abroad.[39] In a parallel development, the Soviet Union had improved its ability to project conventional forces beyond its borders, and its achievement of nuclear parity with the United States had neutralized one of the crucial elements of American military credibility. "The thinly stretched forces of the United States," Nixon argued, "no longer are backed by the decisive nuclear superiority which in past crises made our power fully credible."[40] This development, he noted, might also ignite a new arms race, which would pose additional dangers to global stability and national economic health. Meanwhile, spiraling inflation at home and the growing balance-of-payments deficit with America's trading partners alarmed corporate and political leaders, lowered Americans' standard of living, and weakened the nation's ability to support high levels of military spending.[41]

Speechwriter Whalen thought the news coming out of the Senior Advisory Group's meeting with the president had "a calming effect" on Nixon, "as though freeing him from an unwanted burden of choice and decision." Whalen may have misinterpreted Nixon's inner emotions, but he sensed that a burden had been lifted. "Now," Whalen thought, "he could think exclusively in political terms, preparing counters to Johnson's expected moves."[42] Perhaps Nixon was relieved that

Johnson would have to bear the brunt of responsibility for the initial decisions associated with disengagement, decisions that would undoubtedly rankle hawks in the military establishment, in the leadership of both parties, among the voters, and in the Saigon government. It was the backlash of hawks, of all the wartime factions, that both men feared most. As for doves and moderates, Nixon knew that the president was not likely to take the "peace issue" entirely away from him by ending the war before the election in November. Johnson might use the advantages of his office, however, to gain points by suspending the bombing or opening negotiations. These two old political fighters were used to sparring with one another.[43]

Nixon was not surprised when, on March 31, Johnson announced a halt to the bombing of the Democratic Republic of Vietnam (DRV) north of the twentieth parallel of latitude, appealed to Hanoi to begin peace talks, and appointed W. Averell Harriman, an old Soviet hand and one of the Wise Men, to head the American negotiating team.[44] He was, however, critical of the military wisdom of Johnson's decision to stop the bombing. Well into his own presidency, Nixon would regard the bombing halt as a "great mistake, because we could have closed the whole thing down if we'd stayed with it."[45] Nixon was also "privately shaken and uncertain" about Johnson's unexpected withdrawal from the presidential race and its implications for policy and politics: "He wants to play the peacemaker. Can he do it? We don't know what moves have been made off the board. . . . Hanoi may never be in a better bargaining position than now."[46] Nixon had hoped to face a battered and bruised Democratic opponent in November, either Johnson or Kennedy. Now, however, the campaign was even more unpredictable. The race was between Hubert H. Humphrey and Bobby Kennedy, neither of whom, Nixon thought, was as vulnerable as Johnson on Vietnam, but the president was still in the position of making a peace gesture that would help the Democratic nominee, or perhaps he could reenter the race, as if responding to a party draft.[47]

Nixon's public reaction was to continue his "do-nothing strategy"—to say as little as necessary about Vietnam, biding his time. His statesmanlike excuse was that he wished to say nothing that would interfere with Johnson's peace initiative or undermine his own bargaining leverage should he become president; meanwhile, he would assess Hanoi's response to the partial bombing halt. Continuing to pursue a Republican centrist approach, he publicly warned Johnson against "the temptations of a camouflaged surrender,"[48] but he let it be known to the press that "he resented those who continue to label him as a 'classic' military hawk who would escalate the war," and he believed "there is plenty of room for negotiation of a settlement that would not encourage other guerrilla-type wars in the Pacific." As his qualification suggested, Nixon never yielded on key American goals. He rejected "the notion of a settlement that would involve imposing a coalition government on South Vietnam, on grounds that this would not serve the long-range interests of peace in the Pacific."[49] But he did speak less about stopping Communism in Asia and more about the necessity of ending the war, the opportunities for negotiation, and his ability to provide new leadership unburdened by the mistakes of the past.

Through the dreadful, calamitous months of 1968, with its wars, international crises, interventions, assassinations, and civil disorder, Nixon became, in the eyes of many, a peace candidate—an old cold war warrior who now wanted to end the war honorably. Many in the press and the public thought of peace as simply a cessation of violence, a condition that reasonable men should be able to accomplish, or that some better technique of diplomacy could bring about. Relatively little attention was paid to the specific terms of a possible settlement—the shape of the peace—and how these terms, which were what the war had been all about, could be compromised. And what did ending the war *honorably* mean? The novelty of the new Nixon declaring his interest in terminating the war was of more interest during the campaign than other familiar reminders of the old Nixon.

NOVEMBER SURPRISE

Meanwhile, the old Nixon and members of his staff were involved in secret diplomacy with Saigon in an effort to prevent peace from breaking out prematurely, that is, before the election. For well over a year before the voting, even before Johnson's announcement of a bombing halt, Nixon had worried that Johnson would make a politically motivated, timely gesture toward peace in Vietnam. In particular, he feared an "October surprise,"[50] and, in anticipation, he took steps in 1967 and 1968 to influence events. These included making contact with the Thieu regime through intermediaries.

In the spring of 1967, Nixon asked Anna Chennault to be his liaison with Thieu.[51] Nicknamed "Little Flower" by her friends and "Dragon Lady" by Nixon's staff for her involvement in their diplomatic intrigues, Chennault was a major Republican fund-raiser and the grande dame of the "China Lobby." She had business interests in Asia and friends in Saigon and among both political parties in Washington.[52] According to her account, she first met Thieu in the late fall of 1967 to deliver "a message from Nixon requesting that I be recognized as the conduit for any information that might flow between the two." During the next year, she traveled to Saigon frequently and kept "Nixon . . . informed about South Vietnamese attitudes vis-à-vis the peace talks"—mainly through John N. Mitchell, Nixon's law partner and campaign manager. Her "job" in her "many encounters with Thieu," as she put it, was to assure him that Nixon would be a strong supporter of Vietnam, and therefore Thieu should "hold . . . back" from caving in to Johnson.[53]

In July 1968, at Nixon's request, Chennault arranged a meeting with Saigon's ambassador to Washington, Bui Diem, in Nixon's New York hotel suite.[54] Diem had become "increasingly attracted to the Republicans." Like Thieu, he believed that Hanoi favored Humphrey because of Nixon's cold war reputation; by the same token, he and Thieu "thought that Nixon, through his statements, was stronger than Humphrey; Nixon was known to be a very anticommunist politician. . . . This gave us the idea that he knew how to deal with the communists."[55] Nixon, Diem, and Thieu believed that Johnson's peace efforts were a political ploy to help Humphrey. At the meeting Nixon promised "to see that Vietnam gets better treatment from me than under the Democrats." Diem recommended the provision of better training and equipment to the RVNAF in the face of inevitable withdrawals of U.S. troops, while Nixon spoke of the possibility of pressuring Hanoi's allies, the Soviet Union and China. After the meeting, Diem remained in contact with Nixon through Chennault and Mitchell;[56] he also spoke often with prominent pro-Nixon, hawkish Republicans and other members of Nixon's staff, including Richard V. Allen and Senator John Tower.

Thieu appreciated Nixon's backing, for he feared that his opposition to negotiations would invite a Johnson-instigated coup. Moreover, having concluded at a 1967 meeting with Humphrey that the vice president was in favor of tempering the American position on the NLF, he welcomed the opportunity to frustrate Humphrey's ambition to become president. Nixon's election, on the other hand, would buy him more time. A new Republican administration would require a period of adjustment, and, as Thieu explained to a confidant, he would have more "rope to play with," especially if Nixon were in his debt. "With Nixon at least there was a chance" to stay in power.[57] Nixon's encouragement of Thieu in this affair probably emboldened him to resist U.S. pressure to cooperate.[58]

Meanwhile, in early to mid-September 1968, Henry Kissinger informed the Nixon camp through Allen that he was available to assist them with advice and information.[59] Kissinger had been Rockefeller's foreign policy adviser before Rockefeller's withdrawal from the Republican presidential race, but he had also served the Johnson administration in the summer and fall of 1967 as a private channel to representatives of Hanoi. One of many third-party diplomatic efforts during the Democratic years of the war, this episode began when Kissinger's French contacts visited Hanoi in July 1967 and carried back a message that "an unconditional end to the bombing [of the North] would lead promptly to negotiations." But the "Kissinger Project," as it was dubbed by the White House, soon came to naught, primarily, it appeared, because the United States bombed Hanoi while these private contacts were taking place.[60] Kissinger subsequently maintained his contacts with American negotiators, particularly Harriman, although he did not always agree with the administration's position or tactics.[61]

Aware of Kissinger's diplomatic role in 1967 and his contacts with Johnson's negotiators, Nixon's 1968 campaign camp accepted his offer of aid. Several days later, Kissinger met with Harriman, Cyrus Vance, and other members of the American delegation during a personal business trip to Paris. Kissinger's trip was at least one month in the planning, for on August 15 he had written his longtime friend Harriman: "My dear Averell, Your telegram meant a great deal to me. There is a chance that I may be in Paris around September 17 and I would very much like to stop in and see you then. I am through with Republican politics. The party is hopeless and unfit to govern. Warm regards, . . . Henry."[62]

In Paris Kissinger learned that the delegation's talks-about-talks with DRV counterparts were at a delicate stage. Since May the preliminary discussions had been deadlocked. Hanoi had refused to approve Saigon's participation in negotiations until Washington extended its bombing halt to include the area between the DMZ and the twentieth parallel. Johnson hesitated to order a complete cessation of bombing until he could be assured that the Politburo not only would agree to Thieu's participation but also would promise to refrain from large-scale military violations of the DMZ and attacks against South Vietnam's major cities. When an arrangement on these questions was worked out in October, new problems emerged, one over the length of the interval between a bombing halt and the beginning of negotiations, and another over the structure of the talks. The United States wanted talks to begin within twenty-four hours on an "our side, your side" basis, that is, between the four parties organized in two groups. The DRV complained that the "next day" schedule did not allow enough time for the NLF delegation to organize itself; it also objected to the two-sided structure, preferring instead a four-sided arrangement. Then South Vietnam entered the dispute and objected to the NLF's participation.[63]

On his return to the United States in the last week of September, Kissinger warned Mitchell that "something big was afoot" in Paris and that Nixon should "avoid any new ideas or proposals regarding Vietnam."[64] During the next month, Kissinger continued to provide information and advice to Allen and Mitchell, including news about the likelihood of a bombing halt.[65]

Alerted to the possibility of a diplomatic breakthrough in Paris, Nixon played his political cards. To "put the Vietnam monkey on Humphrey's back, *not* Johnson's,"[66] he publicly attacked the vice president on October 1 for a speech the day before in which Humphrey had announced that as president he would, among other diplomatic and military steps, "stop the bombing of North Vietnam as an acceptable risk for peace" on condition of "evidence of communist willingness to restore the . . . [DMZ]." As though rushing to the president's defense, Nixon accused Humphrey of lacking clarity, of squandering the "trump card" of a bombing halt by telegraphing to Hanoi what he would do as president, and of undermining Johnson's efforts in Paris. Thus, he insinuated, Humphrey had put the Paris negotiations at risk and also imperiled American lives. Explaining to the press what his own position was on a cessation of bombing, however, Nixon described a policy that was hardly distinguishable from Humphrey's. It was also hardly distinguishable from the then secret U.S. position in Paris, to which Nixon was probably privy. He therefore avoided a direct public challenge to Johnson. The DRV negotiators knew, of course, what was happening in Paris and pointed out to the press that Humphrey's proposals were "nothing new," for they barely deviated from Johnson's. Humphrey's speech had, however, been something of a turning point in personal and political terms, for he had taken a small step away from

Johnson's *public* intransigence on a bombing halt, declaring in a small way his independence from Johnson's oppressive grip on his campaign. Humphrey had also called for Vietnamization, implied he would get tougher with the South Vietnamese, and talked about a cease-fire.[67]

Growing more nervous with the approach of the election, but also stepping up the pressure, Nixon sent warning signals to Johnson in mid-October. He had his aides urge Republican and Democratic notables in Washington to "nail Lyndon hard to find out what's happening," but also to suggest that he, Nixon, knew "what's going on" and believed the president was trying "to throw the election to Humphrey by pulling something in Paris." Spiro T. Agnew, meanwhile, was to "ask Secretary of State Dean Rusk whether there was anything to 'rumors' we had heard."[68] On October 26, worried that an announcement of a bombing halt was at hand, Nixon spoke out publicly about "reports" that Johnson was engaged in a "cynical, last-minute attempt . . . to salvage the candidacy of Mr. Humphrey."[69] Believing he walked "a fine line between political necessity and personal responsibility," Nixon rationalized his behavior with the thought that "the actions of Johnson and many of those around him were sufficiently political to permit my taking at least some action."[70]

Although sanctimoniously criticizing Humphrey for sabotaging the negotiations, Nixon secretly sent word to Thieu to "hold on." On October 23 Diem cabled Thieu: "Many Republican friends have contacted me and encouraged us to stand firm." On the twenty-seventh he wrote, "I am regularly in touch with the Nixon entourage," that is, Chennault, Mitchell, and Tower.[71]

On that same October day the DRV delegation in Paris informed Harriman and Vance that it had dropped all of its unresolved demands. The delegation proposed a complete bombing halt for October 30, with negotiations between the United States, the RVN, DRV, and NLF to begin on November 3. Secretary of State Rusk told Johnson that the other side had "made the major step. . . . If ten steps separated us, they have taken eight and we have taken 2."[72] The North Vietnamese had most probably been influenced by information from Moscow that Nixon was likely to win the presidential election, suggesting they ought to make their compromise proposal before the American presidential election took place. Working backstage, in prior months Soviet officials had helped to resolve all of the disputes between the quarreling delegations in Paris. Their interest in facilitating talks was no doubt partly the product of their negative views of Nixon and their appreciation of his lead in the presidential race: a bombing halt coupled with the announcement of an agreement on negotiations might assist Humphrey's chances for election; even if Nixon won, the commencement of talks would at least initiate momentum for a negotiated settlement before he was inaugurated. The Soviets favored Humphrey because they were used to dealing with Democrats, on balance associating them with episodes of improved relations and Republicans with periods of heightened cold war. Nixon had a hard-line reputation and was seen as anti-Soviet, anti-Communist, untrustworthy, and unpredictable, and the Soviets doubted that he would continue the Democrats' attempts to achieve détente.[73] For his part, the Republican candidate "suspected that the Soviets might have counseled the North Vietnamese to offer to begin the Paris talks in the hope that the bombing halt would tip the balance to Humphrey in the election," and he resented it.[74]

Although Thieu expressed reservations, he persuaded Ellsworth Bunker, the U.S. ambassador in Saigon, that he would probably come around to accepting the diplomatic arrangements made in Paris. Johnson, after additional consultations with aides, finally announced a bombing halt on October 31, five days before the election. That night Mitchell phoned Chennault to say: "Anna, I'm speaking on behalf of Mr. Nixon. It's very important that our Vietnamese friends understand our Republican position and I hope you have made that clear to them." Chennault assured him as much.[75]

Just hours after Johnson's announcement, Thieu surprised and confounded the American administration by publicly proclaiming in an address before the RVN National Assembly that he opposed both the bombing halt and negotiations with the NLF, and he demanded that Hanoi talk directly with his government. The balloon of voter support for Humphrey that had expanded after Johnson's television appearance deflated as news of Thieu's rejection of the peace initiative spread. Johnson's good news had been tarnished, and the start of negotiations would have to be delayed.

On November 5 Nixon won the election by a narrow margin in the popular vote, 31,770,237 to 31,270,533. No presidential election has ever been a referendum on a single issue, but some issues are more important than others, and the war was a very important issue in 1968. In his memoir William Safire speculated: "Nixon probably would not be President were it not for Thieu. Nixon remembered."[76]

Accused by Nixon of acting to assist Humphrey, Johnson had in fact done little for his vice president and had not kept him fully informed of diplomatic or political developments. His procrastination had actually harmed Humphrey, for there had not been enough time left between Thieu's announcement and the election to overturn the public's mood of cynicism about the president's diplomacy and the prospects for progress toward peace. Johnson might have assured Humphrey's election and advanced his own public image and negotiating efforts by exposing Nixon's contacts with Thieu, which he had learned about through FBI and CIA surveillance of Chennault and Diem.[77] Or he might have followed the advice of his national security adviser, Walt W. Rostow, who on the morning of October 31 recommended that Johnson coerce Nixon into assisting him to force Thieu's cooperation.

> Have in Nixon alone. . . . Tell him flatly that you are confident that he has had nothing whatsoever to do with this; . . . you might remind him of the trouble that President Eisenhower . . . had when Syngman Rhee kicked up his heels towards the end of the Korean War. . . . We simply cannot let these inexperi-

enced men snatch defeat from the jaws of victory. Therefore, you would ask him to join in a private message to Thieu, with the other candidates.[78]

Of course, for Johnson to have told Nixon face-to-face that he "had nothing whatsoever to do with this" would have meant that he believed Nixon had a lot to do with it. Instead of forcefully confronting Nixon, the president, two hours before his October 31 speech, arranged a conference call with all three candidates, Nixon, Humphrey, and George Wallace, ostensibly to inform them of the forthcoming bombing-halt announcement and deny suspicions that it was a political maneuver. He also said, in a not-so-veiled comment to Nixon: "Some old China hands are going around and implying to some of the Embassies and some others that they might get a better deal out of somebody that was not involved in this. Now that's made it difficult and it's held up things a bit." But then he added, perhaps too disarmingly, "I know that none of you candidates are aware of it or responsible for it."[79] He asked only for comments, and they gave him their verbal backing, but no joint message went out to Thieu.

It was too little too late. Pundits later argued that Johnson's mysterious, self-defeating behavior was partly the result of his ambivalence about Humphrey, but also of many other reasons, including his fear that exposing Thieu's intransigence and machinations would weaken public support for the war and strengthen Hanoi's negotiating position.[80] The South Vietnamese tail continued to wag the American dog.

The likely connection between Nixon's secret diplomacy and Thieu's "November surprise," and the latter's probable contribution to Nixon's election, bound the two men together in an alliance of convenience and secrecy. The affair illustrated Nixon's habit of confusing his self-interest with the national interest and Thieu's determination to stay in power. Kissinger's involvement revealed his penchant for self-aggrandizement and devious dealings. Nonetheless, it influenced Nixon after the election to appoint Kissinger as assistant to the president for national security affairs.[81]

As he had hoped, Thieu had bought more time for himself as a result of Nixon's election. Through November he resisted Johnson's calls to participate in the negotiations, and when the Saigon delegation arrived in Paris on December 8, a new controversy developed over the seating of RVN and NLF delegates. The South Vietnamese wanted to seat the DRV and NLF as a single delegation on one side of the table with nameplates and flags signifying Saigon's view of their close relationship. The North Vietnamese insisted on an arrangement in which the DRV and NLF would be seated behind separate nameplates and flags on separate sides of a square table—a placement that would be matched by the U.S. and RVN delegations. The dispute lasted for ten weeks and was resolved once more with Soviet help. The Soviets proposed an adaptation of the U.S. proposal for an oval, or oblong, table, with no nameplates and no flags, but added two small square or rectangular tables, which would be aligned on opposite sides of the main table.

The oblong table, where the negotiators would sit, would have the effect of treating the four delegations as separate but equal, while the two cornered tables, where aides and translators would sit, would suggest a two-sided separation.[82]

After the DRV and American delegations agreed on the compromise at their meeting of January 15, 1969, Bill Rogers, a longtime Nixon friend and incoming secretary of state, authorized outgoing Secretary of State Dean Rusk to tell Thieu that president-elect Nixon urged him to accept the arrangement. Kissinger claimed in his memoirs that he regarded such cooperation as a political blunder, for the preinauguration compromise allowed Johnson to claim a success, and it put the incoming president and his special adviser in the position of having to account for the deadlock in negotiations that followed, thus rekindling "the domestic debate," with new criticism of them both for their subsequent inflexibility.[83] Nixon was silent on the issue in his memoirs, but he had no doubt authorized Rogers to confirm the compromise because he recognized he was trapped by circumstances: if there had not been an agreement on starting the Paris negotiations before he came to power, he would have been saddled with the problem of fashioning one, and he would also have faced the possibility of being accused by the Johnson administration and Hanoi of sabotaging the negotiations.

It was time to pay the piper. Nixon had stated in the campaign that he was in a better position to negotiate with the enemy; now, as president-elect, it was time to begin. Moreover, had the deadlock continued, Thieu would have been seen as the obstacle to negotiations, thus weakening Nixon's own standing with the American people. Furthermore, the criticism directed by opponents of the war against Nixon and Kissinger months later had everything to do with their actual policies and nothing to do with the preinaugural deal on holding meetings in Paris.

Nixon's successful presidential campaign, which had combined private intrigue with a public rhetoric of deception, had led many to believe that he wanted to end the war, thereby achieving peace in Vietnam and America. He did want to end the war, but on his terms. His election victory brought to power two men, himself and Kissinger, who viewed the conflict in Vietnam from a global perspective and were committed to *winning* a "peace"—coercing or coaxing the other side to consent to a settlement that served U.S. global interests. Their challenge would be to square their goals and convictions with political and military realities—to develop a plan or strategy that could achieve the successful outcome that had eluded Johnson.

4

NIXON, KISSINGER, AND THE MADMAN THEORY

Henry bought into the madman theory.
—H. R. Haldeman[1]

NIXINGER

Nixon and Kissinger were an unlikely pair of policy makers, with apparently little in common.[2] Nixon was of pioneer stock with a Quaker mother and a Scots-Irish father, and he believed his rise to great political power from humble, small-business beginnings exemplified the American saga of the self-made man. He tried to project an all-American image of personal moral rectitude, especially in matters of family and sex, and he was also anti-Democratic, antipress, antiliberal, anti-Establishment, anti-intellectual, anti–women's lib, and anti-Semitic.[3] Kissinger was an immigrant Jew whose family had fled Nazi Germany. During his service under Nixon, his personal moral reputation was that of a playboy, which he considered useful because it "reassures" people "that I'm not a museum piece. Anyway, this frivolous reputation amuses me."[4] His rise to prominence in academic and government circles rested on his intellectual brilliance, but also on his ability to cultivate influential patrons, initially in the U.S. Army and later in bastions of the eastern Establishment—Harvard University and the Council on Foreign Relations. His most recent sponsor had been Rockefeller, Nixon's Republican rival, yet he also had liberal friends, acquaintances, and colleagues in academe, government, and the Democratic Party.

Before his appointment as assistant for national security affairs, Kissinger had taken every opportunity to criticize Nixon in private. Theodore H. White remembered being called aside by Kissinger at the Republican National Convention in Miami: "'Teddy,'" he said, "'we have to stop this madman Nixon.' Kissinger went on a prolonged indictment of Nixon, that he was not to be trusted, that he represented everything dark and dangerous."[5] Even after serving under Nixon, in his memoir *White House Years* Kissinger mixed praise of Nixon's courage and boldness with criticisms of his irrationality and indecisiveness, while portraying himself as steady and thoughtful.

There were many other differences between the two men. Uncomfortable with small talk, Nixon possessed a strange and limited sense of humor. His presidential administration, except for Kissinger, who could be charming and witty, would acquire a reputation for humorlessness, which Nixon would attempt to rectify with occasional lectures to his staff about the need for joviality and with feeble jokes of his own. The president-elect was skilled in debate, and, publicly at least, he spoke and wrote forcefully and effectively in concise, simple, direct language, drawing examples from practical experience and popular mythology—even though his political and diplomatic actions and remarks were often deliberate ploys of misdirection. Kissinger spoke with a heavy accent, even though he had lived in the United States for many years and his German was imperfect; his brother Walter sarcastically attributed the persistence of Henry's Germanic pronunciations to his habit of not listening to what others had to say.[6] Reflecting the bent of his mind, Kissinger's writing was suffused with references to paradox, contradiction, nuance, indirectness, and ambiguity. Always the professor—"Doctor" Kissinger, as Nixon and others often referred to him—he filled his books with didactic epigrams and maxims. His turgid, complex, and obscure writing seemed to conform to the stereotype of German scholarly treatises, and in fact much of his thinking was derivative, drawing on classical German and European philosophers and contemporary national security intellectuals.[7] Nixon's ideas about foreign affairs were probably more original, even though he too borrowed from the leaders under whom he served and synthesized the policy choices the bureaucracy had developed.

Each needing the other, their contrasting personalities and backgrounds became ironically complementary. Kissinger, the self-seeking, chameleon-like courtier, needed Nixon, the president, in order to gain access to power. Appealing to Nixon's desire to concentrate foreign policy decision making in the White House, Kissinger, during the transition period, designed a new National Security Council system that made the NSC the principal forum for foreign policy issues requiring interagency decisions. This change in turn had the effect of making Kissinger, as chief of the NSC staff, Nixon's principal adviser on foreign policy, superseding William Rogers, Nixon's secretary of state.[8] Nixon, the combative, conservative southern California outsider, needed Kissinger to appease moderate Republicans and skeptical intellectuals, as well as to solidify his standing with the foreign policy and Wall Street establishment. Nixon despised the press corps and tried to intimidate them, and he failed in winning their affection or sympathy, even though he and his staff, some drawing on their public relations backgrounds, were masterful propagandists. Kissinger was vigilant toward the press, but he was willing to leak information and was able to use self-deprecating humor to win reporters' appreciation and admiration. Kissinger's scholarly credentials conferred intellectual legitimacy on Nixon's action-oriented foreign policy; his tactical diplomatic skills counterbalanced Nixon's renowned militancy and supplemented his broad, strategic conceptions; and his demonstrated ability to carry out secret schemes meshed with Nixon's modus operandi.

Different in so many ways, Nixon and Kissinger nonetheless shared common traits and views and were, in strange ways, kindred spirits. Noting this, one historian referred to them collectively as "Nixinger," especially since the foreign policies of the Nixon administration were jointly made and carried out.[9] Although neither man would acknowledge it, both had been psychologically scarred in their youth: Nixon by his lonely childhood of perceived deprivation; Kissinger by his fearful experiences in Nazi Germany.[10] Neither would open themselves to a candid assessment of their personalities. "I won't tell you what I am." Kissinger said to one interviewer. "I'll never tell anyone."[11] Each was an outsider to old, northeastern power and wealth: Nixon the middle-class Californian, Kissinger the Jewish immigrant. Rootless and ambitious, they were unhampered by traditional loyalties and affiliations. Nixon was the pragmatic conservative, neither firmly right-wing nor indeed firmly moderate, and represented the emerging political power of the American West and South. Kissinger was one of the new class of civilian national security intellectuals who was willing to serve any government in power.

Neither was a hollow man in the sense of lacking convictions about society, politics, economics, or diplomacy, but both were pragmatically flexible in response to circumstances. They also seemed to lack moral compunctions about using unethical means to achieve their ends and were ruthless players in the arena of power and politics. Nixon was a political scrapper who aggressively sought power and asserted the prerogatives of the offices he held. He preferred an authoritarian style of administration but shied away from personally disciplining his subordinates, leaving that dirty job to other subordinates, especially Haldeman.[12] Kissinger was a competitive, bureaucratic infighter who remorselessly expanded and defended his territory. He also preferred a top-down style of administration but, in contrast to Nixon, was abusive toward his aides. Leslie Gelb, one of his former students, decided that his teacher was "the typical product of an authoritarian background—devious with his peers, domineering with his subordinates, obsequious to his superiors."[13]

If Nixon was paranoid, moody, devious, and insecure, Kissinger was suspicious, brooding, devious, and insecure. Both were wary of others, always gauging whether they were friend or foe, and whether they should be recruited or neutralized. Both believed in hard work and merit but nurtured thoughts of exalted self-importance. Each in their careers owed much to sponsors and mentors.

Nixon had been Eisenhower's "prat boy"; Kissinger, according to others' testimony, had been sycophantic toward his benefactors—and continued to be so with Nixon. While contemptuously deriding Nixon behind his back, he shamelessly praised him in face-to-face meetings and personal messages. Kissinger would engage in servile flattery to assuage Nixon's insecurities and gratify his vanities from the inception of the new administration to its expiration. After Nixon's first meeting with the NSC on January 25, 1969, when Kissinger was attempting to secure his place in the inner circle, Haldeman recorded in his notes that "Kissinger was *very* enthusiastic about the way P handled the NSC, K is really impressed with overall performance, and surprised!"[14] Almost four years later, on election day 1972, one of the low points in their relationship, when Kissinger had reason to be concerned about his future with the administration, he wrote to the president:

> It seems appropriate before the votes are counted to tell you what a privilege the last four years have been. I am confident of the outcome today. But it cannot affect the historic achievement—to take a divided nation, mired in war, losing its confidence, marked by intellectuals without conviction and give it a new purpose and overcome its hesitations. . . . It has been an inspiration to see your fortitude in adversity and your willingness to walk alone. For this— as well as for the unfailing human kindness and consideration—I shall always be grateful.[15]

Kissinger's flatteries always emphasized characteristics Nixon cared very much about: his own leadership, fortitude in crisis, and audacity in the use of force. When Nixon ordered the bombing of Hanoi in December 1972, against Kissinger's previous recommendations, Kissinger made "the point that the P's best course is brutal unpredictability."[16]

On one very important matter, foreign policy, Nixon and Kissinger thought similarly. They considered themselves "realists" and assumed that nation-states existed in a world of international anarchy, in which power was the fundamental determinant of relationships. Like many other self-styled realist thinkers, they were critical of what they regarded as the excessive idealism, moralism, legalism, and sentimentality of the American people, ideas they associated with the liberal traditions they rejected. Nixon wrote: "Americans are hopeless idealists. They reject the idea of seeking power as an end in itself or of pursuing an imperial role for the United States. They are turned off by European concepts of the balance of power and diplomacy. . . . They will fight only if convinced that a larger moral cause hangs in the balance. . . . But that is not the way the real world works."[17] Similarly, Kissinger argued that Americans were reluctant to think in terms of power. The American "national psychology," he claimed, "has few doubts that reasonable men can settle all differences by honest compromise."[18] But the reality is that "force has always been the ultimate sanction at a conference table. . . . Diplomacy by itself cannot be effective unless . . . our opponents know what pressures we will be willing to bring to bear."[19] At his core he was philosophically conservative (as his former mentor Fritz Kraemer observed) and a foreign policy hawk (as his protégé Lawrence Eagleburger affirmed). Kissinger wanted the Vietnam War ended, for example, but from his perspective it could be ended satisfactorily only through force.[20]

Nixon and Kissinger constantly maintained that the American tendency had been to substitute the pursuit of unrealistic, abstract goals for achievable, limited ends, which through history had caused U.S. foreign policy to oscillate between the extremes of wrongheaded isolationist withdrawal and impossible missionary crusades. Americans, in their view, naively believed their New World experience was exceptional—immune to history's necessities and limitations, its ironies and compromises. But, as Nixon advised, "a nation can advance a cause, however just, only through the exercise of power, and a statesman can pursue a cause only by constantly balancing the tension between what he wishes to achieve and what he has the power to achieve." Kissinger agreed: statesmanship must be accompanied by the recognition of limits.[21] Included among these limits in the America of the sixties, according to Kissinger and Nixon, were the "slothfulness" of youth, the "detachment" and effeteness of intellectuals, the "civil war" conditions within the body politic, and the "general moral decay" of the American people. In particular, Nixon thought, "homosexuality, dope, and immorality are the basic enemies of a strong society, and that's why the Russians are pushing it here, in order to destroy us."[22]

On many critical matters, including the Vietnam War, neither Nixon nor Kissinger matched deeds with words when it came to restraining the expansiveness of their own causes by acting in accordance with the limited power they commanded. Despite the crisis of means and ends that Nixon and Kissinger faced around the globe and in Vietnam in early 1969, for example, they steadfastly pursued the cause of preserving the Saigon government and a non-Communist South Vietnam. Perhaps they did not recognize the impracticality of their goal, but if they did not, the reason was that their realism was counterbalanced by their deep-seated faith in the possibilities of creative statesmanship and the efficacy of excessive force.

"Great leadership," Nixon asserted, "is a unique form of art, requiring both force and vision to an extraordinary degree." It is not, as many Americans believed, merely the exercise of management skills or the application of superior technique. Great leaders must not only "*know* the right thing"; they must "*do* the right thing."[23] They must be highly disciplined, hardworking, supremely self-confident, driven by a dream, and farsighted. Winston Churchill, who topped Nixon's list of "leaders who changed the world," had been, he thought, a realist who courageously overcame failure, rightly took risks, and successfully met major crises, and also dreamed great visions. These were, of course, qualities Nixon admired and believed he possessed as well.

Like Nixon, Kissinger thought that Americans placed too much faith in technical analysis and management and not enough in intuitive genius. Great statesmen achieved "freedom" from historical "necessity" through "self-transcendence," a creative, heroic process of willpower and bold action. As he explained in his scholarly books, Castlereagh, Metternich, and Bismarck—Kissinger's examples of the genius-statesmen of history—each possessed most of the required qualities of creative leadership: intuition, wisdom, knowledge, farsighted perceptiveness, inspiration, artistry, and charisma.[24]

Like Nixon, Kissinger, too, believed in the value of crises. These were opportune moments for transcendence, when "contingency" ruled and "the elements from which policy is shaped suddenly become fluid," creating "an unusual capacity for creative action" in which great men could "dominate and impose coherence on confused and seemingly random occurrences."[25] Kissinger, who practiced personalized diplomacy under Nixon, believed he too possessed qualities of the creative statesman: "I feel my greatest strength," he confided in one interview, "was in intuition on where the main historical currents were."[26] In another interview, he confessed: "I've always let myself be guided by spontaneous decisions. . . . In a sense, however, I'm a fatalist. I believe in destiny. I'm convinced, of course, that you have to fight to reach a goal. . . . I believe more in human relations than in ideas. I use ideas but I need human relations."[27] He possessed charisma and enjoyed popularity with the public in large part, he thought, because "I've always acted alone. . . . Americans like the cowboy who leads the wagon train by riding ahead alone on his horse, the cowboy who rides all alone into the town, the village, with his horse and nothing else. . . . He acts, that's all, by being in the right place at the right time."[28]

Both men put great stock in the utility of force, but its use required indomitable willpower and courage, the marks of a strong leader. "The willingness to apply force has been the ultimate test of will," Kissinger declared in 1957, "and the ability to use force has been the ultimate test of the strategic concepts of a society."[29] In April 1969, agreeing with remarks Kissinger had recently made to him, Nixon explained to Haldeman that what was needed to "galvanize people into overcoming" America's moral decay and influence the course of events in Vietnam and around the world was "a really strong overt act" of "hard retaliation," which would require "self-assurance" in the face of contrary public opinion.[30]

Although Kissinger was ten years younger than Nixon, his views on the role of force in foreign policy had been formed, like Nixon's, during the cold war crises and seminal strategic debates of the 1950s. In 1957 he gained a certain prominence within elite foreign policy circles with the publication of *Nuclear Weapons and Foreign Policy,* a best-selling book in which he had drawn from the deliberations of a panel of military and foreign policy experts called together by the Council on Foreign Relations. Until Kissinger's book there had not been a coherent intellectual exposition of U.S. nuclear strategy and the "paradoxes" of the nuclear age. Nixon read the book, was impressed by its thesis, and was photographed carrying a copy[31]—even though it questioned the deterrent credibility of the Eisenhower-Dulles-Nixon policy of massive retaliation. Implicit in the threat of massive retaliation was an attack on China or the Soviet Union, with all of its risks of general war. Kissinger maintained that this strategy undermined America's deterrent credibility because it implied a resort to total nuclear war, which made it an unbelievable threat to enemies in areas where U.S. interests were peripherally involved. Like his fellow national security experts, Kissinger thought of deterrence as the discouragement of Soviet, Communist, leftist, or nationalist aggressions, which he understood not only as a Soviet nuclear attack on the United States and Europe but as all other Communist or revolutionary actions on the periphery that threatened Pax Americana. What America needed, Kissinger argued, was a flexible deterrent capability and, to support it, a doctrine of limited nuclear war—considered limited because it could be contained short of total nuclear war.

Kissinger misrepresented the policy of massive retaliation because, as practiced by Eisenhower and Dulles, it had in fact included considerations of the use of "tactical" nuclear weapons in places like China, Korea, and Vietnam, which, had they been employed, would have amounted to a one-sided, limited nuclear war waged by the United States. He was correct in arguing, however, that there existed no formal doctrine of such war, without which there could be no systematized planning and implementation. This was his main point and criticism. But even though he raised doubts about massive retaliation and its apparent all-or-nothing emphasis, his proposals were designed not to replace it but to augment it. He had disparaged the apparent inflexibility of the strategy, not those inherent principles of forceful diplomacy that deterred or coerced the enemy by demonstrating one's willingness to risk destruction while making credible one's own threats of inflicting unacceptable damage.[32] Undergirding Kissinger's critique was a desire to strengthen the credibility of massive retaliation with a doctrine and practice that would demonstrate to aggressors that the United States had the ability to resist all types of aggression and the will, through limited nuclear war, to *risk* escalation toward general nuclear war. Like Eisenhower, Dulles, and Nixon—as well as all those who espoused nuclear deterrence—Kissinger believed in the psychological value of threatening the unthinkable. He simply wanted to make the incredible credible with the doctrine of limited war. "Above all," he wrote, the strategy of limited war "requires strong nerves. . . . Its effectiveness will depend on our willingness to face up to the risks of Armageddon."[33]

An intellectual who advised government on national security matters, spoke with a German accent, seriously discussed the advisability of using nuclear weapons, and calmly supported the strategic value of risking the end of the world, Dr. Kissinger became one of the prime models for the popular-culture character Dr. Strangelove.[34] His ideas were not abnormal for the times, however, for they were consistent with the traditions of atomic strategy and diplomacy, and in that sense he was not strangely enamored of nuclear war. The development of tactical nuclear weapons had preceded *Nuclear Weapons and Foreign Policy* by several years, and policy makers like Nixon and Admiral Radford had previously advocated their use in local conflicts. Kissinger's book could be seen as an example of the attempt of national security intellectuals to catch up with technology and practice. Their strategic rationalizations and debates also reflected the struggles between competing bureaucracies, agencies, military services, and corporations for military dollars, which in the late 1950s were between those who advocated the New Look and those who proposed flexible deterrence, whether nuclear or conventional. Some thinkers were also concerned about the all-or-nothing implications of massive retaliation. Arms control alternatives were popular mainly within the antinuclear peace movement.[35]

It was probably not until the early 1970s that Kissinger came to appreciate the difficulties associated with containing so-called limited nuclear wars short of total nuclear war:[36] How could both sides realistically prevent such a war from progressively escalating to ever-higher levels of nuclear violence? In addition, there was bureaucratic resistance within the Strategic Air Command to relinquishing its control of nuclear targeting to include more flexible strategies and capabilities. These reservations aside, the principles of force Kissinger enunciated in *Nuclear Weapons and Foreign Policy* were ones he continued to espouse during the Vietnam years.[37]

KISSINGER'S VIETNAM

Kissinger had toured Vietnam in November 1965 and July 1966 as a consultant to Henry Cabot Lodge, and once again in October 1966 at the request of Averell Harriman. In *White House Years* he said of Vietnam: "Psychologists or sociologists may explain some day what it is about that distant monochromatic land, of green mountains and fields merging with an azure sea, that for millennia has acted as a magnet for foreigners who sought glory there and found frustration, who believed that in its rice fields and jungles some principle was to be established and entered them only to recede in disillusion."[38]

Like an unfinished silkscreen, his portrait of Vietnam's seductive geography was both incomplete and inaccurate. The earth, air, and water of Vietnam are distinctive but are not monochromatic. Although covered by vibrantly green-toned trees and grasses, Vietnam is a land of many hues: dusty red soil, seasonally golden rice crops, exotic fruits and flowers, painted Buddhist temples, and colorful children's clothing—all merging with the aqua-tinted South China Sea. Kissinger's wistful, retrospective reflection on Vietnam was not intended to be complete, but its omissions and inaccuracies were also the result of his tunnel vision. His was a defense of his own involvement, attributing to mysterious psychological and sociological processes the attraction of foreigners to an alluring land of fiercely resisting people, an intentional criticism of his adopted country's alleged naive idealism. Hidden or erased from the palimpsest on which he wrote his history of the Vietnam War were the documents, manuscripts, conversations, and scenes that historians require for a fuller account. Through history, some individuals may have had high-minded purposes or peculiar personal, psychological reasons for their sojourns in Vietnam—some finding satisfaction, some, frustration, some, disillusion, some, a heart of darkness—but there was no great mystery about the fundamental purposes of their nations' policies. The long record of foreign invasion and Vietnamese resistance revealed that the Chinese, Mongols, Portuguese, French, and Japanese had gone to Vietnam for reasons having to do mostly with the quest for wealth, power, and hegemony. Despite their reputed idealistic delusions, Americans, or at least American leaders, were not exceptions to the rule, as Kissinger, the realist policy maker, should have known.

Vietnam had been a magnet for Kissinger, too, and he, like some of the other foreigners he mentioned, was also to leave in frustration and disillusion. His role in these last Nixon years of military intervention was so important and his commitment so deep, despite the paradoxes and futility of fighting a failing war, that other analysts would argue that Kissinger's psychology—like Nixon's—largely accounted for his involvement. Psychohistorian Dana Ward argued that Kissinger was a "depressive personality" with multiple symptoms, which included "an undervalued sense of self," "compulsive confrontation with risks," a "drive for supremacy," an "inability to empathize with others," and a "heroic vision" of foreign policy.[39] Kissinger would surely have ridiculed this analysis, although he interpreted others' behavior in and about Vietnam in a similar manner, referring to critics of the war in particular as people whose "self-hatred" led them to express "inchoate rage," a demeanor, he said, he had been determined to avoid since the "cruel and degrading years" of his youth in Germany.[40]

Kissinger confessed to an interviewer in 1972 that he had "never been against the war."[41] His own slow education about the conflict, he said, had paralleled America's involvement, which had been "imperceptibly gradual and progressively sobering." According to his account in *White House Years,* he had considered the initial intervention contrary to America's vital interest, writing that U.S. "entry into the war had been the product not of a militarist psychosis but of a naïve idealism." After Diem's assassination, he took "strong exception to a government policy" that "committed us to a course we could not foresee while undermining the political base for it." But through it all he was part of the "silent majority that agreed with the Johnson Administration's commitment of combat forces" in 1965 "to resist Hanoi's now clear direct involvement."[42] By 1968, however, the Johnson-Westmoreland strategy of attrition had been unable to translate "military successes . . . into permanent political advantage."[43]

In contrast to hawks, who interpreted the war as one of aggression by North Vietnam against South Vietnam, Kissinger acknowledged its civil war characteristics. Even so, Kissinger's views were still orthodox and very close to Nixon's: while he conceded the war was a civil war, it was so only in the South, insofar as there were guerrillas fighting the Saigon government, which, he insisted, had to be preserved. The United States must not negotiate away the Saigon government. He did not see the war as a struggle for unification, independence, and reform, but regarded the Viet Cong as the instrument of North Vietnam.[44] Despite all of his concerns, reservations, and criticisms of the war and its management, by 1968 Kissinger had resolved that the "commitment of 500,000 Americans has settled the importance of Vietnam," for this huge investment meant that "the collapse of the American effort" would undermine U.S. credibility and prestige. It "would add the charge of unreliability to the accusation of bad judgment."[45]

Kissinger thought in global terms. Stability rested upon allied confidence in American promises, and the task at hand was to figure out a way to avoid defeat. "However we got into Viet Nam, whatever the judgment of our actions, ending the war honorably is essential for the peace of the world."[46] Kissinger, the realist, was speaking as a philosophical idealist.

Before he came to power, Kissinger's most famous treatise on the question of what was to be done to solve the Vietnam riddle was an article in the January 1969 issue of *Foreign Affairs* entitled "The Viet Nam Negotiations." In a typically complex and didactic exposition, Kissinger discussed the paradoxes of the war, the conceptual confusion of the Johnson administration, the dilemmas of negotiation, the state of international relations, and the perversity of Hanoi. All pointed to his conclusion that negotiations between the parties were likely to be prolonged. Therefore, "a new administration must be given the benefit of the doubt and a chance to move toward a peace which grants the people of Viet Nam what they have so long struggled to achieve: an opportunity to work out their own destiny in their own way." Kissinger implied that prolonged negotiations were not only inevitable by the nature of inherent complexities; they also might prove beneficial, for they would provide time for Saigon to expand its political base, while leaving the enemy "so exhausted as to jeopardize the purpose of decades of struggle." But Kissinger did not propose a plan to accomplish these goals, save for advice on "*the way*" negotiations should be carried out and the listing of proposals that citizens, policy makers, bureaucrats, politicians, and the Wise Men had already begun discussing—an enclave strategy, the gradual withdrawal of American troops, and Vietnamization. It was not Kissinger but Nixon who, before his election, developed the outlines of a strategic plan to win the peace, one that contained ideas others had proposed but that also bore Nixon's distinct stamp.[47]

NIXON'S NOT-SO-SECRET STRATEGY TO WIN THE PEACE

During the spring and summer of the 1968 presidential campaign, Nixon and his aides had denied that he had a secret plan for peace with honor in Vietnam.[48] Nevertheless, on August 1, as the Republican National Convention was about to begin, the outlines of his nonexistent secret plan became public when he formally proposed steps that he thought should be taken to end the war and win the peace, steps he had revealed piecemeal in prior months. He called for a reappraisal of all aspects of the war's prosecution, "arming the American people with the truth," conducting negotiations with the Soviet Union, putting "greater emphasis" on pacification, giving more "urgent attention" to Vietnamization, and gradually "phasing-out" American troops.[49] Regarding the related issue of how U.S. troops were currently raised for service in Vietnam, in October he criticized the inequities of the draft and proposed ending it "once our involvement in the Vietnam war is behind us," substituting an all-volunteer force.[50] Looking toward a future "structure" of peace around the globe, he proposed arms control, regional security alliances, freer trade, and "eventual conversations with China."[51]

New for Nixon was his apparent advocacy of troop withdrawals, which evoked newspaper headlines that applied the adjective "dovish" to him and his "new strategy." It was a proposal long advocated by the antiwar movement, congressional doves, some Democratic policy makers, and even a few Republican Party leaders and one or two of Nixon's aides. Polls had indicated growing public support for the idea. Nixon, however, coupled it with progress in "phasing-in" the training and equipping of the South Vietnamese in order to reverse their "ever-increasing dependency" on the United States.

Vietnamization—in the generic sense of turning the war over to indigenous allies—was an idea as old as the French-Vietminh War. In October 1967 McNamara had revived it as a step toward disengagement and a substitute for American escalation. He had urged Johnson to impose a partial bombing halt, establish a ceiling on American troop levels, stabilize the ground war, and turn more responsibility over to the South Vietnamese.[52] This was both Johnson's and Nixon's policy by the time the fall presidential campaign was under way. Responding to statements made by Democratic presidential nominee Humphrey in September about supporting reductions in American forces if elected, Nixon commented "that the military presence . . . in Vietnam should remain at its present level, because, in order to negotiate a settlement the enemy must be convinced that he isn't going to be able to win something militarily at the time we are talking."[53]

Vietnamization was also linked in Nixon's mind with pacification, or a "new kind of war" that would include "greater emphasis on small-unit action, on routing out the Vietcong infrastructure, on police and patrol activities, on intelligence-gathering, on the strengthening of local forces."[54] This was not a new approach either. Nixon and the Eisenhower administration had advocated elements of counterinsurgency pacification during the French-Vietminh War. It had been practiced by Ngo Dinh Diem with American advice and support in the late 1950s and was continued in various forms after Diem and throughout the Kennedy and Johnson phases of the war. Phoenix, a program that expanded the role of the South Vietnamese government in pacification, was approved in late December 1967, was set back by the Tet offensive, but, like the bird whose name it bore, was reborn—restored in earnest by the Johnson administration in mid-1968.[55]

Nixon's criticism of the draft was a political tactic aimed at defusing an issue that helped fuel active antiwar opposition, especially among the young, while his support for the phasing-out of American troops was a concession to Republican moderates and opponents of the war alike, as well as an acknowledgment of the shifting mood of the general public. If troop withdrawals actually came about, however, they would unilaterally remove Washington's most important military asset—even if Vietnamization improved Saigon's military capabilities. Pacification and Vietnamization were responses to sagging home-front support for the war, but they were not likely to alter the military balance decisively, break the military stalemate, or provide Nixon with the bargaining leverage necessary to convince his tough-minded enemy to negotiate concessions. They could not be relied upon as the means he said were required to wage the war "more effectively." Insofar as they had a strategic purpose—as opposed to a home-front political purpose— pacification and Vietnamization, as Nixon knew, were stopgap measures designed to hold the line as American troops withdrew. They would not enable him to end the war "honorably, consistent with America's limited aims and with the long-term requirements of peace in Asia."[56]

In public speeches and private statements during 1968, Nixon claimed that such leverage could be found in a "dramatic escalation" of American diplomatic efforts directed primarily toward the Soviet Union.[57] He promised that his new diplomatic offensive would be carried out with "careful and deliberate preparation [and] a full orchestration of the political, economic, and diplomatic resources of the United States on a world scale." The peace campaign would place the war in its proper global setting, linking what he considered to be interrelated and wide-ranging problems between the United States and the USSR, namely, Vietnam, China, Europe, the Middle East, Cuba, nuclear arms, and trade.[58]

To involve the Soviet Union diplomatically in the settlement of the second Indochina War—it was not an original idea. Beginning with UN Secretary-General U Thant's initiative in 1964, numerous private and third-country peace efforts from 1965 through 1967 had included contacts with the Soviet government. Prominent elected officials, such as Senator Mike Mansfield, and even low-level officers, such as the military attaché of the U.S. embassy in Moscow, had unofficially asked the Soviets to act as intermediary. The Johnson administration had pursued many of these third-party initiatives and set in motion some of its own. The State Department had authorized indirect "informal contacts" with the Soviet Politburo through experienced emissaries like Averell Harriman. Direct meetings between high-level American and Soviet officials, including Lyndon Johnson, Dean Rusk, Llewellyn Thompson, Alexei Kosygin, Andrei Gromyko, and Anatolii Dobrynin, had been held. Beginning in 1966 the Johnson administration had waged three major peace campaigns that included a role for the Soviets, code-named Marigold, Sunflower, and Pennsylvania. Unfortunately, it seems to have mismanaged all of these failed attempts. There were bureaucratic muddles, miscommunications with third parties, and leaks to the public, which invited criticisms from all sides. Greater discretion and more effective involvement of the Soviets might have helped, but the greatest problem, as historian George Herring noted, was "the irreconcilable bargaining positions of the two major belligerents and the apparent faith of both sides in the efficacy of military means."[59]

Nixon's approach vis-à-vis the Soviet Union would differ from Johnson's primarily in its emphasis on "linkage," which included carrots and sticks. Opportunities for trade with Europe and the United States, arms control, continued progress toward détente—these were the carrots Nixon planned to offer the Soviets, connecting them with Moscow's willingness to persuade Hanoi to make diplomatic concessions. He doubted, however, that these singly or collectively were sufficiently powerful levers, and thus he hinted that he would use the sticks of diplomacy as well. While he affirmed that the process of détente begun under Kennedy and Johnson would continue, he insisted that Moscow must also be dealt with through "a new policy that will awaken the Soviet Union to the perils of the course it has taken in Vietnam . . . through candid, tough-minded, face-to-face diplomacy cast in the language of realism."[60]

Where was Nixon to find the "realistic" leverage he sought to pry open Soviet cooperation? The next president, he explained, would have to convince the Soviets of his sure "grasp of the realities of power" and his understanding of the relationships between "the military and political aspects of warfare." Part of this effort would be to reestablish U.S. "military superiority" over the USSR,"[61] and another would be to play the "China card." Although his ideas about openings to China were in their embryonic stage in 1968, he was beginning to consider the value of exploiting the Sino-Soviet rivalry in order to foster his own goals in foreign policy. He often sent such a signal in his public statements about relations with the Soviet Union, hardly ever failing to mention the Chinese, with whom he promised to hold talks in order to discuss China's "eventual place" in the community of nations.[62]

Nixon provided few details in 1968 about his plan to win the peace in Vietnam, but his general message was clear: as far as Hanoi was concerned, he intended to combine broad diplomatic strategies with "irresistible military pressure."[63] He emphasized that we must "persist in our effort, by both force and diplomacy, to persuade Hanoi itself that the war is not worth the cost."[64] Determined to establish the independence of South Vietnam, a goal the other side was even more determined to thwart, Nixon was not inclined to abandon the military means by which he might attain it. In what, however, did irresistible military pressure consist? What were the military means? It was unlikely that he would be able to regain sufficient nuclear "superiority" over the Soviets to neutralize their deterrent capability and provide him with an opportunity to actually use nuclear weapons against North Vietnam. In South Vietnam the Johnson-Westmoreland military strategy of big-unit ground operations was failing. Nixon not only had disavowed it during the presidential campaign but also had conceded the improbability of winning a military victory over Vietnamese forces and had already voiced support for phasing out American troops. This, in addition to adverse public opinion and the possibility of Chinese intervention, made it unlikely that he could launch large-scale invasions of North Vietnam, Laos, or Cambodia.

THE MADMAN THEORY

Instead, what Nixon primarily had in mind was a psychological warfare strata-gem. His theory of coercion, as Haldeman described it in his 1978 memoir, *The Ends of Power,* was "the principle of a threat of excessive force," that is, force that normal statesmen would consider not only disproportionate to the issues in dispute but also senselessly dangerous, risking a larger conflict that would actu-ally imperil the interests and security of the threatener. The credibility of such a threat depended on convincing Hanoi and Moscow of his policy obsessions or unpredictable irrationality.

As they walked "along a foggy beach after a long day of speech-writing . . . during the campaign," talking about how the war could be ended, "Nixon," Halde-man claimed, "coined a phrase for his theory which I'm sure will bring smiles of delight to Nixon-haters everywhere":

> I'm the one man in this country who can do it. . . . They'll believe any threat of force that Nixon makes because it's Nixon. . . . I call it the Madman Theory, Bob. I want the North Vietnamese to believe I've reached the point where I might do *anything* to stop the war. We'll just slip the word to them that, "for God's sake, you know Nixon is obsessed about Communism. We can't re-strain him when he's angry—and he has his hand on the nuclear button"—and Ho Chi Minh himself will be in Paris in two days begging for peace.[65]

As recounted by Haldeman, Nixon's madman theory contained at least two meanings of the word "mad": deranged, imprudent, irrational, unpredictable; and angry or easily irritated. Moreover, it included the threat of massive military force—even of nuclear weapons.

Richard Whalen reported a similar conversation with Nixon a year earlier, in the fall of 1967, in which the candidate entertained a proposal for ending the war put forward by retired air force General Lauris Norstad: the United States should call a thirty-day bombing halt of North Vietnam, issue an ultimatum, make an all-out effort to bring about negotiations, and, if these steps failed, "apply whatever level of military force, particularly bombing, proved necessary to end the war." When Whalen pointed out that the only persuasive threat would be that of nuclear strikes, Nixon said, "Well, if I were in there, I *would* use nuclear weapons." Para-phrasing Nixon's other remarks, Whalen wrote: "He explained at once that he did *not* mean that he would use them in Vietnam, only that he would be as willing as John Kennedy to threaten their use in appropriate circumstances."[66]

Ignoring Whalen's less well-known account of his analogous conversation with Nixon, a few scholars have treated Haldeman's famous madman story as implausible—as an anecdote lacking sufficient corroborative evidence. Despite Haldeman's close and long service with Nixon, as well as his reputation for meticulous, matter-of-fact note taking, they have treated Haldeman's recounting as the product of a faulty memory during hectic times.[67] Skeptics have described as unthinkable the idea that Nixon would threaten nuclear attacks, and they have judged those who have taken Haldeman's account seriously as gullible or malicious Nixon bashers. Particularly implausible, perhaps, was the very term "madman theory," which seemed more the psychological fantasy of an abstract, war-game theorist working for a think tank than the strategic linchpin of a politician-statesman who claimed to be a pragmatist.

There is no known or available firsthand documentary evidence of Nixon ever having spoken or written the phrase "madman theory," and he denied using the term to at least one historian, Joan Hoff.[68] Haldeman recorded in his notes that Nixon spoke the words "mad bomber" at a White House meeting on January 14, 1973, but at the time the president was speculating about how "the opposition" would characterize his bombing of Hanoi.[69] Only one other secondhand account, besides Haldeman's walk-on-the-foggy-beach story, quoted his use of the word "madman" in reference to his Vietnam policies. In an *Atlantic* article of 1974, Thomas L. Hughes cited columnist Richard Wilson's notes written after a private meeting Nixon held with Kissinger and Admiral Thomas Moorer on the night of December 18, 1972, during which Nixon said: "[He] did not care if the whole world thought he was crazy in resuming the bombing. . . . If it did, so much the better. The Russians and Chinese might think they were dealing with a madman and so had better force North Vietnam into a settlement before the world was consumed in a larger war."[70]

Until the smoking gun of a firsthand document can be found to prove beyond a doubt that the madman theory was a central element in Nixon's strategy to win the peace—or that Nixon himself voiced the words "madman theory"—there will be doubters. There is, however, ample secondhand *and* firsthand evidence that Nixon had spoken about and acted upon the essential ideas constituting the madman theory from the 1950s through his terms as president, and that he continued to talk about these ideas after leaving office.[71] His public and private statements before, during, and after his presidency are replete with references to irrationality, unpredictability, disproportionate force, risk taking, blackmail, toughness, audacity, defiance, and similar qualities and poses. These he made while recommending or taking forceful steps in his capacity as vice president and president, or while expounding in his writings about the principles of coercion and celebrating historical examples of what he took to be foreign policy effectiveness—Teddy Roosevelt's big-stick diplomacy, Churchill's bravado, Syngman Rhee's unpredictability, Eisenhower's brinkmanship, and Kennedy's successful eyeball-to-eyeball confrontation with Khrushchev during the October 1962 missile crisis.

Reporting on her interview of Nixon in the 1970s, the one in which he denied ever using the term "madman theory," Hoff paraphrased the former commander in chief, saying: "Had he discussed the concept or principle of threatening to use excessive force, it would have been . . . in connection with employing Kissinger in the role of the 'good messenger' to play off against his own well-known anti-communist views when negotiating with communist nations."[72] In other words, he denied speaking the *term* "madman theory" but confessed that he had indeed spoken regularly about the ideas that constituted the *concept* behind the theory. These were the threat of excessive force used in tandem with diplomacy and the reinforcing tactic of good messenger–bad messenger—or, more aptly in the case of outlaw movements like Communism, "good cop–bad cop." Kissinger would act as the good cop pleading for cooperation in order that he could protect the criminal from Nixon, the bad cop—the enforcement officer who was capable of acting violently, excessively, angrily, or irrationally.[73]

Others who worked for the administration, besides Haldeman and Whalen, attested to Nixon's faith in irrational unpredictability and excessive force as though it were common knowledge, almost unremarkable. Herbert Klein wrote in his memoir: "One of the assets he coveted was that the international opposition was never quite certain how he would react. They only knew he would not back away from confrontation."[74] William Safire remembered that at least as early as March 1968 "the essence of the Nixon position was to . . . put diplomatic heat on the Soviets and the Chinese . . . [and] to sharply increase the bombing and naval blockading of the North Vietnamese, thereby forcing an early end to the war."[75] Winston Lord affirmed that both Nixon and Kissinger were "quite serious" about the madman theory. Their understanding of it included the ploy of diplomatic irrationality through the threat of massive military force, which in the context of Vietnam meant carpet bombing of villages and cities, the bombing of dikes, the invasion of the DRV, and the like but did not include the use of nuclear weapons—although they were not averse to having the Vietnamese believe that nuclear weapons might be employed.[76] Morton Halperin said: "It became clear to me, in retrospect, that Nixon's plan was to threaten the Russians with the destruction of North Vietnam unless they cooperated. But, at the time, it wasn't clear to me that he had any plan at all."[77]

Because Lord and Halperin were members of Kissinger's NSC staff, some journalists and scholars have suggested that they were biased against Nixon because of their boss's influence. In his diatribes against Nixon before journalists or his staff, Kissinger not infrequently referred to the president as "monomaniacal," "my drunken friend," and a "madman." During meetings with German officials in February 1969, Kissinger told his assistant, Helmut Sonnenfeldt, to prepare Nixon for his speech before the Bundestag: "You better start writing some talking points for this madman, or there's no telling what he'll come up with."[78]

Doubting that Nixon believed in or implemented the madman theory, Hoff attributed the term and the concept to Kissinger, and treated his claims about Nixon's obsession with madman ideas as one element of Kissinger's own pro-Kissinger, anti-Nixon spin on their foreign policies. While she conceded that the two men discussed and employed excessive force between 1969 and 1973—after all, one can find examples in their memoirs and in the record of their actions— Hoff seemed to deny that it was the result of a consistently applied, systematic theory of foreign policy. Hoff also suggested that the collaboration of the two men in the making of foreign policy brought out the worst qualities in each personality, but on balance it was Kissinger who egged Nixon on when it came to the use of brutally unpredictable force.

Journalist Seymour Hersh, who, contrary to Hoff, considered both Nixon and Kissinger to be madman practitioners, suggested two separate but parallel sources for the madman *concept*. Kissinger's madman theory, he proffered, originated in his researching and writing of *Nuclear Weapons and Foreign Policy*, in which he had discussed the "strategy of ambiguity." Nixon's madman theory, however, had its roots in the lessons he learned from Eisenhower's threats against the Chinese and North Koreans at the end of the Korean War. The *term* itself—the madman theory—Hersh hypothesized, could likely be traced to two lectures on the foreign policy uses of blackmail and madness that Daniel Ellsberg, then a member of the Society of Fellows at Harvard, had delivered before Kissinger's Harvard seminar in 1959. A decade later, Hersh said, Kissinger passed the term on to Nixon.[79]

Hersh's etiology is plausible, but it is unlikely and unnecessary. According to Haldeman, his walk on the foggy beach with Nixon took place "during the campaign" in 1968, before Kissinger's postelection meeting in November with Nixon at the Pierre Hotel, which led to his appointment as assistant to the president for national security affairs. Moreover, the story of Ellsberg's lectures is more complex than that told by Hersh. In addition to his presentation at Kissinger's seminar, Ellsberg delivered a series of public lectures in Boston on the topic of "The Art of Coercion," which were subsequently broadcast by Boston's public radio station, WGBH. A larger audience than Kissinger's pupils heard Ellsberg, resulting during the next decade in numerous citations in the literature of bargaining theory and in requests for copies of selected papers. In 1968, in order to cope with a backlog of requests, Ellsberg reprinted the opening lecture, "The Theory and Practice of Blackmail," which he characterized as a dissection of the "anatomy of blackmail." Other lectures included "Presidents as Perfect Detonators," "The Threat of Violence," "The Incentives to Preemptive Attack," and "The Political Uses of Madness," in which he tried to capture the "*sound* of blackmail."[80]

The word "madness" in relation to policy making was, therefore, in the air, so to speak—in circulation among bargaining theorists, national security intellectuals, and policy makers for almost a decade before 1968. The books and movies *Dr. Strangelove* and *Fail-Safe*, depicting characters who conformed to the madman profile, were part of popular nuclear culture by the midsixties.[81] Reinforcing this image of madness, the acronym for the U.S. nuclear doctrine of mutual assured destruction, which Secretary of Defense McNamara enunciated between 1964 and 1968, read MAD. Although unintended by the Kennedy administration, MAD implied that there was a surrealistic insanity associated with nuclear strategy.[82] Perhaps Nixon heard of Ellsberg's papers or read one, but "madman" was and is a common epithet, which need not have originated with a paper in a particular seminar to enter Nixon's vocabulary. "All passions that produce strange and unusual behavior," Thomas Hobbes wrote in the seventeenth century, "are called by the general name of madness."[83] In any case, Ellsberg, who discussed the political uses of madness in his papers, did not himself use the phrase "madman theory."

The main issue concerning origins has to do not with the term but with content—the concepts behind the theory. One of Ellsberg's themes throughout his lectures was the problem of the disproportion between threatening nuclear attack—then mainly thought of as a mutually genocidal exchange between the United States and the USSR—and the "limited" goals both nations sought. How could this problem be solved to the advantage of the United States? Drawing on bargaining theory, then in its infancy, as well as on the history of Hitler's mad threats and actions during the pre–World War II period, Ellsberg argued that a leader who was mad— that is, willing to risk a general war and his own destruction, or one who could pretend to be so willing—might then be able to blackmail other leaders into concessions because they would regard the threats as real and the risks of resisting as too great.

In Ellsberg's view, madness could be of two sorts. One would consist in the threatener convincing the victim of his unpredictable irrationality: the threatener's real or apparent derangement, rage, impulsive nature, erratic tendencies, or lack of a sense of proportion creates the perception of the real possibility that he would carry through with his excessive threats. Another sort of madness would consist in making the victim perceive that the threatener *wanted* to carry out the threats because, for example, he was a lover of violence, a doctrinaire ideologue, or an obsessive monomaniac, thus conveying a message of predictable madness.

Before the 1968 election, Nixon's record of speaking and acting had included ideas supporting both predictable and unpredictable madness. His explanation of the madman theory to Haldeman during their walk on the beach was a summation of these two principles, emerging from a lifetime of thought and practice, and expressed concisely, bluntly, and clearly in the kind of language Nixon normally used. Translated, it described how he would bring a satisfactory end to the Vietnam War by threatening to act with disproportionate force, a threat made credible by his reputation as a doctrinaire cold war warrior who also suffered spells of uncontrollable anger.

Kissinger was undoubtedly aware of the social science literature on diplomatic blackmail. Thomas C. Schelling, whose ideas on bargaining were similar to Ellsberg's, was a colleague of Kissinger's at the Harvard University Center for International Affairs. But Kissinger's record before 1969 suggested that he supported only the strategy of the madness of predictability, which was more typical of conventional national security intellectuals and bureaucrats—Ellsberg was unconventional. In *Nuclear Weapons and Foreign Policy*, Kissinger had made an argument for predictable nuclear deterrence, calling for "presenting the enemy with an unfavorable calculus of risks" by means of "military operations in phases which permit an assessment of the risks and possibilities for settlement at each stage before recourse is had to the next phase of operations."[84] This approach resembled what became known as "graduated deterrence," a rational strategy that Nixon would criticize when it was applied by the Johnson administration to the use of conventional forces in Vietnam. Kissinger's discussion of the "strategy of ambiguity . . . , which combines political, psychological, and military pressures to induce the greatest degree of uncertainty and hesitation in the minds of the opponent," was a strategy he claimed the Soviets used and was also implicit in the Eisenhower-Dulles strategy of massive retaliation. Kissinger was critical of massive retaliation precisely because it was unpredictably mad: "It has been argued that the deliberate ambiguity of our present position, which refuses to define what we understand by limited war or under what circumstances we might fight it, is in itself a deterrent because the enemy can never be certain that military action on his part may not unleash all-out war. . . . However, it may have precisely the contrary effect; it may give rise to the notion that we do not intend to resist at all and thus encourage aggression."[85] His proposals for a doctrine of limited nuclear war were intended to introduce rationality and predictability to nuclear deterrence by developing the capability of fighting nuclear war below the threshold of all-out war, thus making nuclear deterrence credible.

In *The Necessity for Choice,* published in 1961 after Ellsberg's lectures, Kissinger repeated the arguments he had made for the necessity of possessing a doctrine of and capability for limited nuclear war, but contradictorily cast doubt on the feasibility of containing such a war. The only sure way to prevent escalation to general nuclear war was to restrict limited war to conventional forces. Kissinger thus became even more committed to predictable deterrence. While he did not abandon his support for America's long-standing nuclear "first-use" policy—resorting to nuclear weapons in the event of the failure of conventional deterrents—his rationale conformed to the principles of predictable madness: "If the aggressor accepts [our] renunciation of nuclear weapons at face value as indicating a decision to accept defeat by conventional forces, aggression may actually be encouraged."[86] It was mad to use nuclear weapons, he seemed to be saying, but we must make clear and credible our resolve to use them—even if using them is madness—in order to prevent both Communist aggression and the necessity of their use. These were among the paradoxes Kissinger perceived in the nuclear age.

Ellsberg, the bargaining theorist and student of history, had articulated a full-blown madman theory in 1959, consisting of predictable and unpredictable madness. By that time Nixon, Dulles, and Eisenhower had already practiced such a theory; they had not written seminar papers about it, but they had dropped sufficient hints. Although Kissinger was aware of both types of policy madness, he seems to have favored the predictable kind. He did not seem as captivated as Nixon by the bargaining possibilities in unpredictable madness. Kissinger's attraction to the use of force in diplomacy, his emphasis on the necessity of possessing the willpower to run great risks, and his desire to please Nixon in order to consolidate his own position within the administration made him, however, a willing convert. Nixon likely appreciated Kissinger's ready understanding and sympathy. Haldeman told an interviewer many years after his walk on the beach with Nixon: "Henry bought into the madman theory. He was eager to let the Soviets think that the president might at any moment take tough steps."[87] It was an accurate rendering of how Nixinger madman practice came about.

Nixon was not a national security intellectual, theorizer, or rationalizer. He was a practicing policy maker and a somewhat original strategist, at least more original than Kissinger. He had learned the art of forceful coercion from other practitioners: Frank Nixon, Rhee, Dulles, Eisenhower, and other leaders he admired. In his account Haldeman narrowed this lifetime of experience to one event, claiming that Nixon had learned his lesson about threatening excessive force primarily from Eisenhower's handling of the Korean War. It was a simplistic version of a more complex history, even though the event undoubtedly made a strong impression on Nixon and was relevant to the situation in which he found himself in 1968.

Soon after coming to office in 1953, Eisenhower supposedly threatened to use nuclear weapons against China and its ally North Korea unless they came to terms in the deadlocked negotiations at Panmunjom. Within weeks the Chinese and North Koreans made the requisite concessions. Although Nixon lacked Eisenhower's distinguished military reputation, Haldeman explained that Nixon believed his long public record as an obsessive anti-Communist—combined with his well-known impulsive anger—meant that Communist leaders in Moscow and Hanoi feared him more than any other American politician. For this reason his own threats would be just as credible as Eisenhower's had been fifteen years before.[88]

Indeed, for these reasons Hanoi on balance preferred Humphrey to Nixon, as did the Soviets. By 1970, whether aware of the madman theory or not, Vietnamese Politburo documents, resolutions, and press commentaries referred to Nixon's war efforts as *dien cuong,* which translates into related meanings of madness: rabid, frenzied, violently angry, and crazed.[89] He and Kissinger had, at least, succeeded in conveying the message.

Nixon used the Korean War analogy on August 6, 1968, when speaking to southern delegates to the Republican convention in Miami as he assured them that he knew how to end the Vietnam War.

How do you bring a war to a conclusion? I'll tell you how Korea was ended. We got in there and had this messy war on our hands. Eisenhower . . . let the word go out diplomatically to the Chinese and the North [Koreans] that we would not tolerate this continual ground war of attrition. And within a matter of months, they negotiated. Well, as far as negotiation [in Vietnam] is concerned that should be our position. We'll be militarily strong and diplomatically strong. . . . I'll tell you one thing. I played a little poker when I was in the Navy. . . . I learned something. . . . When a guy didn't have the cards, he talked awfully big. But when he had the cards, he just sat there—had that cold look in his eyes. Now we've got the cards. . . . What we've got to do is walk softly and carry a big stick. And that is what we are going to do.[90]

This version of how the Korean War had ended had been part of Republican historical doctrine at least as early as 1955, when Admiral C. Turner Joy, a senior U.S. negotiator at Panmunjom, published *How Communists Negotiate,* in which he claimed that "the threat of atom bombs" had persuaded the Chinese to finally accept an armistice. As he put it, "It was as simple as that."[91] In January 1956 *Life* magazine published a story in which Dulles claimed to have delivered an unmistakable and effective nuclear warning to Beijing on Eisenhower's behalf in 1953.[92] In his memoir, *Mandate for Change,* Eisenhower asserted that "in India and in the Formosa Straits area, and at the truce negotiations at Panmunjom, we dropped the word, discreetly . . . that, in the absence of satisfactory progress [in negotiations], we intended to move decisively without inhibition in our use of weapons."[93]

Nixon's boasts, therefore, rang true in the ears of hawkish, conservative delegates to the Miami convention,[94] even though this interpretation of the history of the Korean cease-fire was probably apocryphal. In reality Dulles's threat had not been clearly delivered. If it was made at all, it appears to have been a subtle hint dropped to a prospective intermediary, Prime Minister Jawaharlal Nehru, in New Delhi on May 21, 1952. Nehru claimed, however, that Dulles had not mentioned a nuclear threat, and, had Dulles done so, he would not have relayed it to the Chinese.[95] Although the U.S. government seriously considered launching nuclear strikes, these would have taken place only under special circumstances, which did not obtain at the time. The diplomatic risks, military impracticalities, and political complications inherent in their use had caused U.S. decision makers to hesitate, leaving them only the option of *threatening* nuclear attack; whether in fact they clearly made such a threat is open to question. Nonetheless, other indirect threats had emanated from the United States, and the Chinese had monitored them. According to one scholar who studied Chinese attitudes, "The most palpable and credible nuclear threats to China came in the form of the highly publicized U.S. nuclear testing program and the equally open publicity and analysis of the nuclear option."[96]

The coming of the armistice was not as simple as Admiral Joy had claimed. Despite the attention paid to them by the Chinese, the American threats and signals probably played at most a very small role in ending the war. The war had exhausted all belligerents by 1953, and there were signs that all parties wanted to end the conflict. Joseph Stalin's death on March 5 removed one obstacle to an armistice and created an opportune moment for the Chinese and North Koreans to offer a concession, which was matched by the United States, itself led by a new administration that had been elected on the pledge to end the war. Nothing on the diplomatic front or on the battlefield, where the Chinese continued to launch attacks and counterattacks up to the signing of the armistice in July 1953, indicated that they were intimidated by nuclear threats or by the U.S. Air Force's massive conventional bombing of the North Korean dam-irrigation system in May. To the contrary, they were determined to avoid even the appearance of having caved in and were therefore committed to resisting nuclear blackmail. The armistice agreement itself, which was a compromise, indicated that both sides had acknowledged the military stalemate. They had at last concluded that conventional military options were too costly or dangerous to be continued indefinitely and not likely in any case to be efficacious.[97] If any major obstacle remained to a cease-fire in the spring and summer of 1953, it was the stubbornness of South Korea's President Rhee, whom Eisenhower, through Nixon, had to prevail upon to cooperate.

Nixon probably believed that subtle nuclear threats had played a role in ending the war, perhaps even a decisive causal role among other contributory causes. When he retold the story in 1985 to a *Time* reporter on the fortieth anniversary of the destruction of Hiroshima and Nagasaki, he said: "The Chinese were probably tired of the war. And the Russians did not want to go to war over Korea. But it was the Bomb that did it. I'll tell you why." Without providing any actual evidence of Chinese–North Korean motives and actions, he explained that all the requirements—the conditions—for Eisenhower's threat to have worked had been in place: the United States had "unquestioned nuclear superiority"; Korea was of "supreme American interest"; a conventional option was not available; and Eisenhower had credibility, which was probably "the biggest factor."[98]

If Nixon ever had doubts about the importance of America's nuclear threats in ending the Korean War, he did not share them with others. The tale had become part of Republican historical mythology about the cold war, elevating Eisenhower, Dulles, and even Nixon to the level of legendary statesmen; it permitted them to claim that they had ended the Korean War sooner, at less cost, and more advantageously than would have been the case otherwise; and it served to defend the administration's general strategy of massive retaliation against its critics. The myth did not consist so much in falsely claiming that nuclear threats had been made, but rather in falsely claiming that they had worked. For Nixon to doubt this claim in 1968 would have opened to question his own foreign policy record. To have cast doubt on the efficacy of the principle of nuclear threat would have lost him bargaining leverage in the war he would have to end in Vietnam if elected president. Nixon understood the role of psychological warfare. He also understood the value of myths, but he could be their captive as well. As he prepared to be president, he retained his faith in excessive threats and continued to entertain nuclear notions.

The Korean War analogy appealed to Nixon not only because it was an accepted historical myth but also because the predicament he found himself in was similar to the one Eisenhower had inherited from Truman: a stalemated civil war involving outside powers; a war-weary American public; stalled negotiations; and a client government unwilling to accept a compromise. Nixon knew, however, that for all the similarities between the situation Eisenhower faced in Korea in 1953 and the one he would face in Vietnam in 1969, at least one factor that American strategists had regarded as necessary to the credibility of both conventional and nuclear deterrence was absent: dominant American nuclear superiority.[99] In addition, he would have to withdraw American troops unilaterally—at a pace yet to be determined—because the public demanded it and he and other American leaders had committed themselves to it.

Contrary to what he told the delegates at Miami, Nixon did not hold a good hand of cards, as did the quiet, poker-faced player in his colorful metaphor. Instead, he would have to talk big and bluff his opponents. Nixon was an expert poker player and knew that in poker a player holding bad cards can still be a winner by means of bluff.[100] He had learned to play in college and had honed his skills in long hours of free time while serving in the South Pacific during World War II. The game suited him well: he could put on a poker face; he was willing to take risks; he was able to bluff well; and he possessed a drive to win—a jugular instinct. In later life he often used poker analogies to characterize diplomatic dealings. "The time to bluff," Nixon explained to Haldeman, Kissinger, and Haig, "is when you have nothing; the time to keep quiet is when you have the cards."[101] To win, or even to avoid losing too much, he would not be quiet: he would threaten the use of disproportionate force, resting its credibility on his reputation and selected conventional military escalations. To bluff the other side into dropping out of the game, he would raise the stakes not only by the Vietnamization of the war in the South and the diplomatic isolation of Hanoi from Moscow and Beijing but also by the expansion of the war in Indochina and the threatened conventional or nuclear destruction of North Vietnam.[102]

Mixing metaphors, as Nixon did in his Miami speech, he would not walk softly and carry a big stick; he would strut and talk loudly, carrying a small stick, but warning that he might go to the woodshed and fetch the big one. He had been dishonest with his hawkish audience in Miami because he wanted to win the election and also because he had known since March that he would have to pretend that he actually had or believed he had the winning cards in order to carry through with the bluff against Hanoi and Moscow. "We have to seem to say the opposite," he told Whalen, "just to keep some degree of bargaining leverage."[103]

On the other hand, it is possible that Nixon regarded the madman threat not as a bluff but as an ace in the hole.[104] The problem, however, was that he would be going up against equally skillful Vietnamese players who held, or believed they held, better cards than he and were more poker-faced than he. If they were not more mad than he, they were more angry about the war. They had more to lose, they believed, if they threw in their cards before playing out their hand; they were even more determined to avoid defeat and more prepared to accept the risks of raising the ante. To meet this contingency, Nixon would have to be willing and able to carry through with his threats. Would the American people, the bureaucracy, his advisers, his party, America's allies, and the Soviets and Chinese allow him to? Would they deal him the cards he needed?

"In diplomacy, unlike poker," Ellsberg noted in his paper on the political uses of madness, "it is never desirable to be caught bluffing."[105] This maxim was even more true of real war. Nixon's use of the poker analogy was indicative of his love of the game and his legendary deviousness— "shrewd Nixonology," as Whalen characterized this way of thinking—but poker was probably not an appropriate analogy for the actual situation he faced in Vietnam. Chess was more apt. It is a game played with the actual pieces on the board, which a player positions to capture his opponent's pieces or, the ultimate goal, to checkmate his opponent's king; there are no bluffs as such, although one might play a gambit—enticing a false move from one's opponent by sacrificing a piece of one's own. No analogy is perfect, but this was more like the game the Vietnamese played.

Despite his promise to withdraw American troops, Nixon believed that his diplomatic-military strategy would provide him with the bargaining leverage he needed to pry a negotiated settlement out of Hanoi and Moscow within his first year in office. Both he and Kissinger believed they knew why Johnson's war had failed, why he had been unable to terminate it, and what was needed to rectify past mistakes. As it had been for Johnson, the problem for Nixon and Kissinger, however, was not simply that of stopping the war, but of stopping it on their own terms in order to win the peace—one that was consistent with American policy makers' goals and principles dating to the Truman administration. Nixon needed to end the war quickly but, as he later recalled, only "as quickly as was honorably possible." Neither man conceived of peace as only the cessation of hostilities. Nor did they think of it as harmony in South Vietnam. "The obverse of [Americans'] reluctance to think in terms of power has been [their] notion of the nature of peace," Kissinger wrote in *Nuclear Weapons and Foreign Policy*. "[They] assume that peace is the 'normal' pattern of relations among states, that it is equivalent to a consciousness of harmony, that it can be aimed at directly as a goal of policy."[106] Of course, he thought Americans were wrong—and naive. Nixon and Kissinger's conception of peace was one of stability, fixed in an American framework, but it was one their Vietnamese opponents found oppressive and unacceptable. Nixon did not have a new policy that revised Johnson's objectives; he had what he thought was a new strategy that promised success in pursuit of the old goals. The details of this new strategy, however, had yet to be drawn.

5

AVOIDING DEFEAT, SEEKING VICTORY: 1968–1969

But any settlement . . . must provide for the territorial and political integrity of South Vietnam.
—Richard Nixon[1]

POLICY GOALS

Despite his apparent disdain for Americans' foreign policy idealism, Nixon publicly spoke and wrote of his goals in Vietnam as if they were generous in spirit and noble in purpose. Thus, he began his term on January 20, 1969, with an inaugural address reminiscent of Woodrow Wilson's, in which he pledged to open an era of negotiation in search of a peace of compassion and understanding, of opportunity for all, and without victory over others.[2] Explaining ten years later in his memoir, *RN,* why he did not take advantage of the moment, blame the war on the Democrats, and then withdraw from Vietnam—a step recommended by at least one friend in Congress and most of the antiwar movement—Nixon associated the well-being of the South Vietnamese people and their right to self-determination with the survival of President Nguyen Van Thieu's government. "A precipitate withdrawal would abandon 17 million South Vietnamese, many of whom had worked for us and supported us, to Communist atrocities and domination. . . . Almost everything involving a Vietnam settlement was negotiable except . . . I would not agree to any terms that required or amounted to our overthrow of President Thieu."[3]

Nixon's commitments to the people of South Vietnam and President Thieu's government were conditional, however, for they had been made and would be kept not because of their sentimental or idealistic content but because of their relationship to Nixon's own reelection and the global interests of the United States—as he and other policy makers perceived them. Although believing that the American people had "to be appealed to on idealistic terms," he was convinced that in reality nations should and did "go into war for pragmatic reasons."[4] Linking his presidency with previous administrations, Nixon faithfully enumerated these long-standing reasons in his postwar history, *No More Vietnams:*

> Truman, Eisenhower, Kennedy, and Johnson . . . were in total agreement on three fundamental points: A Communist victory would be a human tragedy for the people of Vietnam. It would imperil the survival of other free nations in Southeast Asia and would strike a damaging blow to the strategic interests of the United States. It would lead to further Communist aggression, not only in Southeast Asia but in other parts of the free world as well. I strongly agreed with those conclusions.[5]

The new American president's concern about the fate of the Saigon regime and the South Vietnamese people was probably no greater in degree or quality than that of President Johnson's assistant secretary of defense, John T. McNaughton. In an internal policy memorandum in 1965, McNaughton had made it clear that "to help a friend" for its own sake was "NOT" a reason for America to be fighting in Vietnam. He gave top priority to the aim of avoiding "a humiliating U.S. defeat (to our reputation as a guarantor)," weighting its decisive relative importance with the mathematical value of 70 percent. Specifically, what needed protection was the U.S. reputation as a "counter-subversion"—aka counter-revolution—guarantor. Preventing Southeast Asian dominoes from falling into "Chinese hands" was worth 20 percent. The third and final goal of permitting "the people of SVN to enjoy a better, freer way of life" received a negligible valuation of 10 percent.[6]

McNaughton had been part of an NSC working group in 1964 and 1965 that had considered U.S. interests, objectives, and options in Vietnam. The group had determined that the "initial" national objective was to prevent South Vietnam from coming "under Communist control 'in any form,'" for this would constitute a "major blow to . . . U.S. prestige." Yet it realized that the costs and risks of maintaining South Vietnam's independence might be too great, and that South Vietnam "might still come apart." Thus, America's "fallback" goal was "to hold the situation together as long as possible so that we have time to strengthen other areas of Asia."[7]

Nixon had made and expressed similar conclusions at least as early as 1967, and he continued to hold these views through his presidential tenure. In a briefing paper about American aims in Vietnam he circulated to White House staffers, the president argued that the United States could not survive should it abandon "a continent where 60 percent of humanity will live in the year 2000." If the United States pulled back so fast "as to cause an Asian collapse . . . , a great vital arc of free nations . . . would lose their independence"; "the hard-liners in Peking would be encouraged"; Japan would "go neutral"; and Germany, Japan, and India would "go nuclear" to protect themselves. The United States must therefore "withdraw in [a] way Asians can take over their defense, not withdraw in [a] way Asians will collapse. The mistakes this generation makes will be paid for by the next generation."[8]

In 1969 the survival of the Saigon regime was crucial to Nixon mainly in relation to the goal of creating and maintaining a Pax Americana. "I was not personally attached to Thieu," Nixon wrote in *RN*, "but I looked at the situation in practical terms." Thieu was not the most "enlightened or tolerant or democratic" anti-Communist leader in South Vietnam, but he was the strongest. "My determination to honor our commitment to Thieu was a commitment to stability. . . . To abandon South Vietnam to the Communists now would cost us inestimably in our search for a stable, structured, and lasting peace."[9] The re-creation of an American-centered world order, however, was contingent on the reestablishment of American global hegemony: "[The] power of the United States must be used more effectively, at home and abroad, or we go down the drain as a great power," Nixon told Kissinger, Ehrlichman, and Haldeman in July 1969. "[We] have already lost the leadership position we held at [the] end of WWII, but [we] can regain it, if [we move] fast!"[10]

Kissinger, too, spoke and wrote publicly in idealistic terms about the administration's aims: redeeming the sacrifices of those who had struggled before in good causes; maintaining dignity; keeping faith in the future; pursuing the goal of peace. He most probably believed in these and the other responsibilities and high principles to which he often appealed, but, like Nixon, he put them in the service of a fundamentally pragmatic and self-interested goal: an American-led global system, which itself was portrayed as a high-minded, principled objective. Kissinger recalled in *White House Years,* for example, that he could not allow himself "to succumb to the fashionable debunking of 'prestige' or 'honor' or 'credibility.'" To have abandoned South Vietnam to "tyranny" would have been "profoundly immoral and destructive of our efforts to build a new and ultimately more peaceful pattern of international relations."[11] This attitude matched his perception of Nixon's aims: "Nixon was eager," Kissinger wrote in *Diplomacy*, "to negotiate an honorable extrication, which he defined as almost anything except turning over to the North Vietnamese communists the millions of people who had been led by his predecessors to rely on America. He took credibility and honor seriously because they defined America's capacity to shape a peaceful international order."[12]

Neither Nixon nor Kissinger was personally attached to Thieu in a sentimental sense, but because Thieu had helped Nixon win the election, Nixon may have felt compromised, concerned that Thieu would leak the real story of their November surprise. Convinced that he had contributed to Nixon's election, and knowing that Nixon had encouraged him to withhold "support [for] . . . Johnson's peace initiative," the South Vietnamese president believed that the new American president "owed him a political debt."[13] On this Anna Chennault agreed with Thieu. When she learned after the election that Nixon now wanted Thieu to participate in the Paris negotiations, she, like Thieu, felt betrayed, the victim of "politics," but the kind of politics, she told the Nixon camp, she did not play. Her irritation was such that Nixon became concerned she would reveal their preelection "arrangement with Thieu" to the press. One emissary after another visited or telephoned her—Attorney General Mitchell, Director of Communications Klein, Senators Everett Dirksen, John Tower, and George Murphy, and other Nixon lieutenants— all asking her to persuade Thieu to cooperate and also to remain quiet about past intrigues. "The ultimate handshake came months later, at a White House function," she remembered, "when Nixon took me aside and, with intense gratitude, began thanking me for my help in the election. I've certainly paid dearly for it," she told him. "Yes, I appreciate that," Nixon murmured uncomfortably, "I know you are a good soldier."[14]

Nixon's nascent strategy for the Vietnam War did not yet embrace the so-called decent-interval solution, that is, withdrawing from the struggle without having achieved a clear-cut victory but having created conditions in South Vietnam that would avoid or postpone some future downfall of the Saigon regime— in essence, protecting America's credibility as a counterrevolutionary guarantor, an effective repeller of outside aggression, and a trustworthy ally. Kissinger had seemed to advocate this solution in his *Foreign Affairs* article of late 1968, and some pundits have suggested this was *the* Nixinger strategy from the beginning of the administration: "As for the United States," Kissinger wrote, "if it brings about a removal of external forces and pressures, and if it gains a reasonable time for political consolidation, it will have done the maximum possible for an ally— short of permanent occupation."[15] But this policy was hardly different from that of the Johnson administration at the time of Nixon's election. The operative phrases—the "removal of external forces and pressures" and "political consolidation"—suggested that "victory" was the goal. Kissinger's intention was to consolidate Thieu's government while the United States made an honorable exit. It required not only the expulsion or the negotiated withdrawal of the People's Army of Vietnam (PAVN) from South Vietnam but the strengthening of the RVNAF's military power and the crushing of insurgent resistance before and after a ceasefire. The year 1969 was too early in the Nixinger "game plan" to settle for a solution that would merely bring about a mutual North Vietnamese–American withdrawal, only to be followed by a sufficiently long interval to paper over the collapse of the RVN and the ignominy of policy defeat.[16]

Not sentimentally attached to Thieu, Nixon nonetheless felt personally responsible for his survival. He, like Johnson before him, did not want to be the first president to lose a war. In one private, angry moment, Kissinger, who did not want to be the first national security assistant to lose a war, put the issue this way: we "can't preside over [the] destruction of [the] Saigon government."[17] This was their definition of "defeat" in South Vietnam. Like previous stewards of

American foreign policy, Nixon and Kissinger took seriously the necessity of avoiding defeat, with its personal and global humiliations and consequences. If the collapse of the Saigon government meant defeat, the obverse, its continuance, meant victory, which, however, required not only the survival of Thieu's government but also the expansion of its sovereignty over the non-Communist RVN.

STRATEGIC OPTIONS

During the postelection, preinauguration transition period, Kissinger commissioned a RAND Corporation study of National Security Agency views on the current "realities" of the war and the "future prospects" for victory in South Vietnam. Daniel Ellsberg and Fred Ikle, who led the RAND team, met with Kissinger at the Pierre Hotel after Christmas Day to deliver their findings. In their written report, which was framed as an options paper delineating the alternative strategies proposed by agency heads and staff, they defined the conditions of victory as: "The destruction or withdrawal of all NVA units in South Vietnam, the destruction, withdrawal, or dissolution of all (or most) VC forces and apparatus, the permanent cessation of infiltration, and the virtually unchallenged sovereignty of a stable, non-Communist regime . . . , with no significant Communist political role except on an individual, 'reconciled' basis."[18]

Although government agencies agreed on the meaning of victory, Ellsberg and Ikle reported finding a "systematic, . . . distinct cleavage in opinion" between two groups about the current status of the Saigon regime, the military balance on the field of battle, and the prospects for victory. Designated "Group A" and "Group B" in the RAND report, each included subsets of officials who recommended variant military and diplomatic strategies. In Group A these strategies were aimed at "Communist 'fade-away' or negotiated victory"; in Group B they were intended to produce a "compromise settlement" with the other side. Ellsberg and Ikle noted a third strategy, "C," which called for the "unilateral withdrawal of all U.S. forces within one to two years," even without a settlement. Alternative C, whose goal was to extricate the United States from South Vietnam, had, however, "no advocates within the U.S. Government, but might become necessary if some of the other alternatives failed."[19]

Group A comprised officers and officials at highest levels in the JCS, MACV, the State Department, and the American embassy in Saigon, as well as some CIA analysts. They believed that enemy forces were in strategic retreat and the Saigon regime was growing stronger, with more hamlets than ever under its control. The enemy was in Paris to negotiate "from a sense of weakness and failure,"[20] and hence the United States should insist on the withdrawal of all Communist forces from South Vietnam, Laos, and Cambodia. Although the RVN was stronger than before, Group A recommended that the United States maintain a large military presence and avoid putting destabilizing pressures on the Saigon government until victory was assured: sizable American troop withdrawals should not be made for twelve to eighteen months, and U.S. demands upon the RVN to make political reforms should be restrained.

Meanwhile, if U.S. and RVN armed forces resumed military operations at pre-Tet levels, Group A argued, the war could be concluded in twelve to twenty-four months. Escalation beyond pre-Tet levels, however, would ensure a swifter and more complete victory. There were several escalation options: air and ground operations in Cambodia and Laos; unrestricted bombing and mining of North Vietnam; limited invasion of North Vietnam and Laos; full-scale invasion of North Vietnam; or any combination of these. Depending on the option chosen, U.S. force levels would have to be increased and the reserves mobilized; there would be higher casualties and greater dollar expenditures; and the Soviets and Chinese might take countermeasures. But Group A argued that the American public would accept the costs, while there would be a small risk of a strong Soviet or Chinese response. In any event, it was likely that none of the options mentioned would be necessary, because—they claimed in a recommendation that resembled the madman theory— "the credible threat, explicit or tacit, of unrestricted bombing or limited invasion of North Vietnam might well cause the DRV to accept our conditions for victory immediately."[21] To enhance threat credibility, compromises should not be offered in negotiations.

Dissidents in Group A doubted that the old American military methods of big-unit operations and bombing would succeed. They recommended an alternative that went beyond the "one war" strategy of General Creighton Abrams, who had replaced Westmoreland as commander of MACV in July 1968: a radical re-structuring of U.S. and RVN forces into small units deployed in populated areas to carry out counterinsurgency activities. American troops could be withdrawn more rapidly with this strategy, they maintained, but victory would probably not be achieved for a period of four to five years.

Group B, which included the secretary of defense and most of his staff, a minority at high levels in the State Department, and some CIA analysts, believed that a return to pre-Tet operations or a resort to one or more kinds of escalation would lead to military failure and unacceptable risks and costs, while triggering even greater domestic opposition to American policy in Vietnam. Expanded counterinsurgency would also fail. Hanoi would be encouraged to hold out, and the United States would eventually have to withdraw without winning concessions.

Members of Group B disagreed with those in Group A not because they were ready to surrender—or "cop out,"[22] as Nixon and Kissinger would later phrase it—but because they had become convinced Group A's bankrupt strategy would result in crisis or defeat. Although uncertain of Hanoi's motives, they did not believe that Hanoi was in Paris from weakness or desperation. Group B was less sanguine about the length of time required to reach an agreement or terminate U.S. intervention—two to three years, compared with Group A's one to two. Persuaded that victory through military escalation was unlikely or impossible, they recommended instead that the United States seek a formal or tacit diplomatic compromise—namely, "a coalition government . . . [and] mutual withdrawal [of U.S. and North Vietnamese forces] or ceasefire . . . as part of an agreed overall settlement."[23] A formal settlement was preferable to a tacit one, for "there would be a clear expression, politically useful both for the GVN [Government of Vietnam] and the United States, that the main purpose of the U.S. involvement had been accomplished—hence U.S. withdrawal was appropriate."[24] This, of course, was one of the meanings of "honorable exit." Although compromise fell short of victory, it averted defeat and salvaged credibility.

Agreeing on the wisdom of diplomatic compromise, Group B nevertheless gave diverse specific recommendations: the continuation of current military operations and the negotiation of both a mutual withdrawal from and a coalition government for South Vietnam; a tacit or explicit mutual de-escalation and the negotiation of mutual withdrawal only, while the United States encouraged the South Vietnamese to assume a larger burden of the war; a substantial initial withdrawal of American troops combined with the building up of the RVNAF while seeking a compromise settlement; and variants of the last two. Whether in favor of mutual withdrawal only or a more comprehensive settlement that included a political compromise in South Vietnam, Group B's members were more willing than those in Group A to pressure the Saigon regime into making an accommodation with non-Communist political elements in South Vietnam, refraining from obstructing bilateral talks between Hanoi and Washington, and negotiating in good faith with the NLF.

Those in Group B who favored an agreement on the sole issue of the mutual withdrawal of U.S. and DRV armed forces pointed out that a negotiating strategy that concentrated only on that issue freed the United States from the troublesome task of working out a political settlement for South Vietnam. Following the mutual withdrawal of North Vietnamese and American forces, the Saigon regime, they believed, would have a fair chance of gradually overcoming the NLF's insurgency. "Afterwards, it might survive, like South Korea, with an acceptable level of U.S. support." Yet, willing to accept the eventual defeat of the Saigon government and its army by the VC, their position would later be known as the "decent-interval solution": "The United States could accept such a Communist take-over in SVN, since it would have resulted from a primarily indigenous conflict [during the interval after U.S. withdrawal]. The principal U.S. objective of repelling external aggression would have been met." Besides maintaining credibility, this approach had two additional benefits: a settlement on the military issue of mutual withdrawal alone could more likely be concluded in less than three years than one that included a political component, and mutual withdrawal "would be the one objective for which domestic support in the United States is least divided."[25]

The RAND report confirmed the existence of deep divisions within and between government agencies, leading Ellsberg to suggest to Kissinger that he carry out a more comprehensive survey once the new administration took power, but he proposed that the questions be put to each agency separately, so that Kissinger could compare discrepancies between their responses agency by agency. Kissinger liked the idea of a new survey because it would provide him with more information about agency thinking on the war, while at the same time burdening the bureaucracy with paperwork, thus giving him and Nixon more room to maneuver. He told one aide, "I'm tying up the bureaucracy for a year and buying time for the new president."[26] The procedure of requiring separate responses also appealed to him because it prevented agencies from compromising their differences and colluding against the executive branch, which he considered the bureaucratic bane of presidential leadership.

NSSM 1

On January 21, the day after Nixon's inauguration, Kissinger issued a "study directive," ordering key national security agencies and their heads to respond by February 10 to twenty-nine major and over fifty subsidiary questions.[27] Many of the agency heads and staff were holdovers from the previous administration, but some, of course, were new Nixon appointees. Drafted with Ellsberg's assistance, the questions focused on topics Nixon and Kissinger wanted addressed: the negotiating environment, enemy capabilities, RVNAF capabilities, the progress of pacification, political prospects in South Vietnam, and the effectiveness of U.S. military operations.

The responses revealed general agreement on several issues. All believed the RVN had been strengthened in recent months, but not enough to enable its armed forces to fight alone successfully against the Vietnamese Liberation Armed Forces (VNLAF) "in the foreseeable future." Although it had improved "its political position in certain respects," the Saigon government continued to be weakest, and the VC/NLF strongest, in the countryside, and so it was "not clear whether it could survive a peaceful competition with the NLF for political power in South Vietnam." Even though the other side had suffered military and political reverses, it was able to replace its losses in South Vietnam through recruitment and infiltration and with supplies and equipment from the Soviet Union and China. The VNLAF was still capable of launching offensives, and it also controlled the initiative in battle and thus the attrition rate of both sides. It seemed, therefore, that the NLF and the DRV were not in Paris to negotiate from weakness, "but rather from a realization that a military victory is not attainable as long as U.S. forces remain in SVN, yet a victory in the political area is very possible."[28]

Despite this unpromising consensus, there were those who slanted their interpretation of facts toward hopefulness. These optimists argued that the enemy's "lower profile on the battlefield" and participation in negotiations were the products of a shift in political and military momentum favoring the United States and

South Vietnam. The RVNAF was fighting better, pacification had made real advances, and U.S. operations had been effective—and "with less constraints" could be more so. The RVN was "more stable than at any time since Diem," and it was making progress. American negotiators in Paris should be told that "the tides are favorable."[29]

Others were skeptical. Although improvements had been made in the allied position, the war was essentially stalemated, and "short of unacceptable risks of widening the war," the United States and the RVN "cannot now or in the foreseeable future bring the enemy to his knees." Despite their superior size and more abundant equipment, South Vietnamese armed forces had "great problems." In addition, the optimistic claims made for pacification were inflated, while political progress was inadequate. The other side was not in Paris from political or military weakness, and the strength of the U.S. military position was such that "a compromise settlement is the most likely outcome for Vietnam." The American focus should now be on political actions.[30]

As in the RAND study, most of the optimists were concentrated at the top levels of MACV, the JCS, the U.S. embassy in Saigon, and, to a lesser extent than in the RAND study, in the State Department. The skeptics were to be found among the CIA and civilians in the Pentagon. Opinion varied according to the issues and often was divided between the heads of departments and operatives in the field. In MACV, for example, assessments of progress differed from one military zone to another, but Abrams suppressed the most negative analyses.[31] There were paradoxical divergences, too. Although the CIA and the intelligence divisions of the State Department gave Saigon's armed forces their lowest ratings for improvement and effectiveness, they nonetheless believed that the RVNAF could "hold its own and make some progress" against the PLAF if the latter were not supported by the PAVN.[32]

Kissinger acknowledged that the overall responses in National Security Study Memorandum (NSSM) 1 confirmed the "perplexities" that had given rise to the inquiry in the first place. Very troubling were the "disturbingly large disagreements within the intelligence community over such elementary facts as the size and deployment of enemy forces, and the importance of Cambodia . . . as a supply base." He concluded, "There was no consensus as to facts, much less to policy."[33]

Despite differences between optimists and skeptics, one lesson to be drawn was that, before a complete U.S. withdrawal, the Saigon government needed to eliminate corruption and broaden its political appeal, and its army needed to improve its effectiveness. Both political and military reforms required time, but their accomplishment was plagued by inherent contradictions. The RVNAF was unlikely to improve its performance unless the United States turned over to it the burden of fighting, but if the United States withdrew, the RVNAF's morale might collapse. In a similar Catch-22, government leaders most likely would not attempt serious political reforms unless they were pressured by the United States to do so, but such pressure might undermine their current stability—past U.S. efforts, it was

noted, had failed "at directing Vietnamese political life into desired channels."[34]
Even with political reforms and military strengthening, the consensus was that
neither the Saigon government nor its armed forces would be able to "handle" or
"stand up" to Communist forces without American support in the form of monetary aid, logistical assistance, ground troops, and airpower.[35]

Like the participants in the RAND study, NSSM 1 respondents took "victory"
to mean the establishment of Thieu's unchallenged sovereignty throughout South
Vietnam. But in light of the certainty of American withdrawal, no agency fore-
cast victory coming about as the result of military or diplomatic steps.[36] Instead,
they expected hostilities to be ended by a negotiated compromise. The issue for
these policy makers had become one of deciding the rate of U.S. withdrawal, the
degree of U.S. support for the RVN during withdrawal, and whether U.S. support
should be extended past a cease-fire. The JCS and MACV looked "toward continued U.S. support to assure the sovereignty of the GVN." The Department of
Defense and the State Department required "only that the South Vietnamese be
free to choose their political future without external influence."[37]

PLAN OF ACTION

The primary purpose of NSSM 1, however, had not been to elicit agency proposals for alternative national policies or military strategies. Instead, the questions in
Kissinger's directive of January 21 had been worded to draw forth agency assessments of political and military conditions in Vietnam and the prospects for either
a "victory" or a favorable "compromise" based on options already being considered
during the transition period by Nixon and Kissinger. Question 23, for example,
had asked what the prospects were for "attaining—at current, reduced, or increased
levels of U.S. military effort—either 'victory,' or a strong non-Communist political role after a compromise settlement of hostilities."[38]

The phrase "current levels of U.S. military effort" was a reference to the
bombing halt imposed by President Johnson and the "One War, One Strategy" of
General Abrams. Initiated in September 1968, the One War operational strategy
ended the tacit division of roles and missions between American and South Vietnamese forces, wherein the former had concentrated on attrition and the latter on
pacification; now both armies would engage in attrition and pacification—simultaneously searching and destroying, clearing, and providing security.[39] Implicit
in other questions—as well as in steps taken and intentions expressed by the new
administration—was that current levels of *ground* operations were to be stabilized
or gradually reduced; it was also clear that withdrawals of U.S. troops were to be
made, even if slowly.[40] Consequently, it was not likely that "increased levels"
meant that American GIs would be engaged in big-unit operations in South Vietnam on the scale of those before Tet 1968 (except for those already planned for
early 1969) or participate in large-scale invasions of North Vietnam, Laos, and

Cambodia—although these latter operations in scaled-down form were probably not yet ruled out and were considered viable options under certain contingencies. The remaining options were to strengthen the RVNAF, switch American troops at some point to small-unit operations, accelerate pacification, and resume and expand aerial bombing. Only the latter option—bombing—translated into significantly increased levels of U.S. military effort. Indeed, the questions Kissinger asked and the answers provided about U.S. military operations had to do mainly with "B-52 effectiveness," air interdiction in Laos, Cambodia, and North Vietnam, and the effect of an "alternative" bombing campaign on the flow of Soviet and Chinese aid.[41]

NSSM 1 had followed the RAND study by two to three months. Agency responses were received in early to mid-February, but a summary was not prepared and circulated to the NSC Review Group until March 14, and it was revised during the next week in preparation for a March 26 meeting of the NSC.[42] By then, however, Nixon and Kissinger had already begun to implement their strategy to win the war. They had acted before the facts as known and reported by national security agencies in their own comprehensive survey of their own administration had been collated by the NSC staff and discussed by the cabinet. If NSSM 1 served any purpose, it was to provide Nixon and Kissinger by February and March with information about bureaucratic opinion—a map of the bureaucratic terrain, so to speak—and to move the bureaucracy somewhat in the direction of their preexisting covert strategy, or at least to keep them busy while it was being implemented. It may also have been designed, just as Kissinger later said, to buy them time—to postpone criticism from those who were eager to end the war, whether by escalation or de-escalation.

The RAND study, therefore, was probably much more important to the development of their plan than NSSM 1, for it provided Nixon and Kissinger during the transition period with an early and more timely assessment of the difficulties they faced in Vietnam, and also of the range of options available—or at least those options government agencies in the late fall of 1968 believed were available. Like two mechanics collecting used parts to remodel an old car, the president and his assistant had chosen those that best fit their design for winning the peace, although they added Nixon's own ornaments—diplomatic linkage in U.S.-Soviet relations and credible but "mad" threats of escalation. Group A in the RAND options paper had proposed tacit or explicit threats of unrestricted bombing, but the national security agencies had not broached the idea of diplomatic linkage.

Nixon had denied during the presidential campaign that he had in mind what could be called a "plan" for ending the war. He continued these denials after his presidency, asserting he had "never said" he had a "'plan,' much less a 'secret plan' to end the war," for he had recognized "the difficulty of finding a solution" and how "absurd" it would have been at the time of the campaign to reveal a plan even if he had one. "Premature disclosure" would have doomed "even the best-laid plans."[43] He did admit, however, that he had had "strategic ideas" for achieving a peace with honor: "We could use our armed strength more effectively to convince the North Vietnamese that a military victory was not possible, . . . step up our programs for training and equipping the South Vietnamese," and make "adequate use of our vast diplomatic resources" to influence China and the Soviet Union, where "the heart of the problem lay more" than in Vietnam. The actual strategy that eventually did take shape was assembled, he maintained, in "the first months" of his administration. It had five parts: "Vietnamization" of the war; "pacification" of the South Vietnamese countryside; "diplomatic isolation" of North Vietnam; "gradual withdrawal of U.S. troops"; and "peace negotiations." He described the latter as "diplomatic efforts coupled with irresistible military pressure"—an oblique reference to a carrot-and-stick approach, in which the stick was the application of the madman theory. This combined diplomatic-military-political strategy, he explained, was a practical, realistic compromise between the impolitic course of severe military escalation advocated by the military and the naive policy of "peace at any price" advocated by the antiwar opposition. "I was convinced," he wrote, "that unless we backed up our diplomatic efforts with strong military pressure, the North Vietnamese would continue their strategy of talking and fighting until we tired of the struggle."[44] Aerial bombing was to be the central element of that military pressure, for Nixon believed in 1968 and would continue to believe into his presidency that bombing could close "the whole thing down."[45]

This was an accurate retroactive description of the key elements of Nixon's plan but a disingenuous account of the timing of its "taking shape." The strategy—the "secret plan"—that would be followed in 1969 had actually been outlined by Nixon at least as early as August 1968, and its basic elements were set in place by the time of the post-Christmas meetings at the Pierre Hotel between Kissinger, Ellsberg, and Ikle—weeks before NSSM 1. What remained to be completed after the inauguration were the details of implementation and the issuing of orders to commence the implementation: deciding how, when, and where to send verbal and physical signals that credibly threatened the possibility of "mad" escalations; opening a secret, back-channel contact with the Soviets; establishing the U.S. negotiating position vis-à-vis Hanoi; determining the size and timing of U.S. troop withdrawals; attempting approaches to China; and developing alternatives in case of failure. Only in this narrow sense was it true, as he claimed, that the plan "took shape" in the first few months of his administration.[46]

What took shape, therefore, was the "plan of action," as Kissinger described it in conversations with Dobrynin.[47] Because Kissinger was Nixon's implementer of the foreign policy elements of the plan of action, Haldeman, in his notes and diaries, referred to the military and diplomatic aspects of the strategy as "K's plan,"[48] but its essential elements had been designed by Nixon.

Nixon's postwar description of his plan was inaccurate, or at least incomplete, in one other respect: there were aspects of the plan—notably Vietnamization and de-Americanization—that were designed to win victories on the political home front as well. The plan of action, as Kissinger reviewed it later in the year 1969, was three-pronged: "In effect, we are attempting to solve the problem of Vietnam on three highly interrelated fronts: (1) within the U.S., (2) in Vietnam, and (3) through diplomacy."[49] On the home front, Vietnamization and de-Americanization were accompanied by announcements of prospective changes in the draft laws, which served to buy time for the rest of the plan to take hold.[50]

Nixon's and Kissinger's lack of candor about the matter of having or not having a plan before the "first few months" of the administration was in part probably the result of their desire to uphold Nixon's campaign denials, to avoid the charge or appearance of manipulating bureaucratic opinion, to protect their reputations from the taint of misleading the public, and, not least, to put the responsibility for their bombing of Cambodia on the Vietnamese enemy. But intrigue was also their natural modus operandi, becoming part and parcel not only of how they spoke about their plan but of the plan itself. "The only productive negotiations are the private ones," Nixon told his cabinet officers on March 20, and the only "basis for successful negotiating" is "military strength," by which he meant establishing a credible threat of escalation. This was an approach to which "the intellectuals are all opposed," he said, and, which many others in the citizenry, the bureaucracy, and Congress were also opposed. "It's only us nonintellectuals who understand what the game is all about."[51] Although an intellectual, Kissinger was an exception, then, for he understood the strategy: "We had to continue military pressures sufficient to deter Hanoi from turning negotiations into another Panmunjom, but not act so provocatively as to tempt a fight to the finish, [and] our government had to be sufficiently disciplined to speak with the same voice."[52]

National Security Council aide Roger Morris argued in one of his postwar books about Nixinger foreign policy that the president and his assistant did not at any time have anything that could be recognized as a plan for Vietnam. Instead, their approach was one of indecision, equivocation, outward deceit, and inner self-deception—all mixed with personal ambition, power seeking, distrust of the bureaucracy, and an obsession with projecting an image of toughness.[53] However true, the constants of Nixinger strategy toward the Vietnam War remained: big military plays, Vietnamization, pacification, clever negotiating ploys, Soviet linkage, the China card, and counterattacks against domestic opponents. Under pressure from his critics in late 1969, Nixon's public relations line was: "P has a plan, [and] it's working." It was the kind of statement he often made, publicly and privately. "All the rest are in doubt," Nixon commented to Haldeman in 1971, "but we know precisely what we're going to do and where we're going to be on Vietnam."[54] He was exaggerating about their precision, but he and Kissinger had plans for Vietnam.

Frequently heard in the White House, the word "plan" was used to convey at least two different but related meanings: it could refer to a scheme of proceeding toward a goal or to a program of specific steps in that direction. There were White House plans for all sorts of things: for press conferences, for trips to San Clemente or Key Biscayne, for sabotaging political opponents, for dealing with Congress, or for international problems.[55] If military plans were the issue, the JCS, with the involvement of Kissinger and the NSC, drew up the programs of specific action, and the president decided what parts were to be implemented. The overall "Vietnam plan," however, was more in the nature of a scheme, with a commitment to particular broad approaches. Throughout the war Nixon and Kissinger would need to decide on specific steps and time lines. They usually proceeded to construct their plan piecemeal after reviewing studies of this or that issue, testing the waters of public, congressional, or bureaucratic opinion, and gauging likely Vietnamese, Soviet, or Chinese reaction. Theirs was not ever a finished plan in the sense of a blueprint—a complete diagram of specific events and time lines. It was a plan in the making, some parts complete, some in the drafting. But those sections of the design that were drawn up from time to time were based on an overall concept—a strategy of key principles that guided their ever-evolving specific plans of action.

For Nixon, if not for Kissinger, the war was yet another personal challenge arising from the tumult of national and international events. Struggle, will, boldness, and creativity—all encapsulated in the president's plan—would again prevail, they believed, as it had in Nixon's prior career and for Kissinger's geniuses of history. Reflecting on this period, Ellsberg was not far off the mark when he said of their attitude: "What was in the mind of the new administration was: We will do it better—and more savagely. . . . Only Nixon and Kissinger—coming in fresh, and thinking we know how to launch a threat campaign—could convince themselves that this was going to do the job."[56] Through winter and spring and into the summer of 1969, Nixon and Kissinger believed that in this manner the war could be ended favorably before the year was out.

At this stage of Nixon's administration, his and Kissinger's hubris was nurtured by their confidence in the plan but also by the flush of electoral victory and the headiness of assuming the presidency. It was, Kissinger remarked, an "innocence and exhilaration of newly acquired power."[57] Haldeman noted in his diary a short time after the inauguration: "For the P, as well as for all of us, life in the White House was like entering an entire new world. . . . It was . . . a totally different position from that of VP. There were lots of new things to learn every day, and he clearly enjoyed the process. . . . He loves being P!"[58]

OPTIMISM, APPREHENSION, AND TIMETABLES

Haldeman also asserted that "from the start of his Presidency," Nixon "fully expected that an acceptable, if not totally satisfactory, solution would be achieved through negotiation within the first six months."[59] Two months after his inauguration, Nixon was still hopeful, if not optimistic. On March 20, shortly after deciding to bomb Cambodia, he "flatly" told his cabinet that "the war will be over by next year."[60] On April 15, with a little more than nine months left in the year, and even as a new crisis flared up in Korea, he assured his cabinet officers and their wives that he "hoped we would have it over in a few months," because he had "some real faith in K[issinger]'s plan." A decade later, Nixon publicly confirmed that in 1969 he had entered office believing the war could be ended within the year or earlier: "Ideally the war could be over in a matter of months if the North Vietnamese wanted peace. Realistically, however, I was prepared to take most of my first year in office to arrive at a negotiated settlement."[61] For a self-styled realist, his comment uncovered a naive and arrogant assumption: the possibility of ending on his terms in less than one year a war that had been going on for decades, and one that the United States, by the account of most experts, was losing. Such a view of the world's malleability was more presumptuous than realistic.

Kissinger shared Nixon's optimism: "Give us six months, and if we haven't ended the war by then," he told a group of antiwar Quakers in May, "you can come back and tear down the White House fence." He promised his Harvard colleagues, "We'll be out in a matter of months."[62] It was not uncommon for Kissinger to tell others what he assumed they wanted to hear, but Anthony Lake, a member of Kissinger's NSC staff, thought that "Henry was sincere in believing he could negotiate an end to the war, and do it sooner rather than later."[63] In his memoir Kissinger wrote that he had "great hope" and "even thought a tolerable outcome could be achieved within a year."[64]

Although buoyant and optimistic in those early days, Nixon also appreciated the necessity of having to conclude the war in order to deal with the domestic and international crises facing the United States. There was another, more personal necessity as well: "I'm not going to end up like LBJ," he observed in November after his electoral victory, "holed up in the White House afraid to show my face on the street. I'm going to stop that war. Fast."[65] Nixon believed, as did Kissinger, Laird, and other White House advisers, that his honeymoon with public opinion would last only six to nine months. If by then he had not ended the war, it would become, Haldeman noted, "his war."[66] Distinguished outsiders made the same point and used the same timetable. In a thinly veiled warning, Averell Harriman signaled the president that he would find it necessary to oppose him openly if it became "Nixon's War," by which he meant that Nixon would have failed in bringing peace to Vietnam and that antiwar demonstrations would have begun again. Harriman gave the president until October to succeed, or at least show progress.[67] Kissinger felt they were caught between "the hammer of antiwar pressure and the anvil of Hanoi."[68] In response, their strategy was "to walk a fine line . . . between withdrawing too fast to convince Hanoi of our determination and withdrawing too slowly to satisfy the American public."[69] Meanwhile, linkage and threat—made credible by the bombing of Cambodia—would lever the enemy into concessions.

Nixon was determinedly optimistic as he began his administration, but things could go wrong, and the war might have to continue in order to ensure an "honorable" exit. He was the steward of American global policy, convinced that the national interest—as he, most of the bureaucracy, and many others in the body politic defined it—rose or fell on the preservation of the Saigon regime.

6
TALKING WHILE FIGHTING: 1969

The big stick and the carrot, what is it?
Fighting and talking. . . . It is the same.
—Nguyen Co Thach[1]

BUYING TIME

Although projecting an air of confidence during the first six to nine months of his administration, Nixon walked a tightrope between the need to encourage faith in his policies, however secret, and the need to dampen the citizenry's expectations of a quick peace, however much he had contributed to raising them during the campaign. Above all, he needed to "buy time," postponing antiwar criticism of his policies and the collapse of public patience for as long as possible—for at least the nine months of honeymoon he thought he could have.[2] When television news agencies reported after his inauguration that the negotiations in Paris were deadlocked as soon as they had begun, Nixon instructed Kissinger to tell Henry Cabot Lodge, head of the American negotiating delegation, to "knock down the idea that we should expect any kind of progress at this early date. . . . He should aim everything he says toward the United States indicating that the going is hard and that he does not hold out any false optimism, but that he is convinced that the negotiations will succeed, and that he is getting every possible encouragement from RN."[3] In a similar vein, Nixon explained to his cabinet on March 20 that "the next four to five months will be very tough because we have to take [the] public position that [the] outlook is tough, etc., while we negotiate in private," backed up by "military strength."[4]

It was a difficult balancing act, especially since members of his administration did not always walk Nixon's subtle and complex public relations line but instead delivered mixed messages and revealed information that raised or lowered public expectations, encouraged Hanoi, or unnerved Saigon. On April 6, for example, the day after Vietnam veterans against the war marched in Central Park, the *New York Times* ran a front-page story, based on leaks by "informed officials," that reported on Nixon's "new approach to the war." On the positive side, the headline undoubtedly contributed to public confidence in his policies. It read, "Nixon Has Begun Program to End War in Vietnam," and the ensuing story explained that his plan included "the recall of some American troops," along with a "secret program of diplomatic and military measures designed to extricate the United States from Vietnam" while "providing greater security for some of South Vietnam's major population centers."[5] But in spelling out these diplomatic and military measures, the story also revealed that American military operations on the ground would be scaled down, that secret talks were being arranged, and that Washington was ready "to settle for something less than military victory." The purpose of the strategy, according to the story, was to buy time for "negotiations and the evolution of new political processes in South Vietnam before the final American pullout," which implied a prolonged war. Contradictorily, the report also suggested that this ambitious program of buying time would be accomplished, or at least "become evident," by the end of the year, which was less than eight months away.[6]

This and a flood of similar stories since the inauguration dismayed Thieu's government in Saigon and Nixon's supporters in America. Samuel Berger, Ambassador Bunker's deputy and liaison to President Thieu, cabled Secretary Rogers on April 11 to report that recent rumors of rapid and unilateral U.S. troop withdrawals coupled with new peace proposals from Washington to Hanoi had caused a crisis of confidence in Saigon: "There is a reappearance of nervousness in high quarters here, and confusion and apprehension below." AFL-CIO President George Meany and former University of Oklahoma football coach Bud Wilkinson wrote Nixon about their alarm over the apparent "disarray" in the administration's position on Vietnam.

Believing in Eisenhower's uncertainty principle, Nixon thought it "generally helpful" to send mixed messages "so as to keep the enemy guessing as to what we might do in the event the negotiations did not succeed," but he now believed "that criticism has reached a dangerous point where the President seems to have lost control of his team." Arguing that "the 'Open Administration' approach is not defensible when it injures our negotiating position," he sent a memo to Rogers, Laird, Bunker, Lodge, and Kissinger, in which he demanded a "consistent line with no deviation whatever" on at least "two major issues": troop withdrawals and secret talks. In sum, he insisted, the line should be: "We have no plans to withdraw troops unless and until progress is made on one or all of the three fronts I have mentioned" in press conferences; "with regard to secret talks, . . . there will be absolutely no discussion of whether secret talks are taking place or what will be discussed" or any indication that we are dealing with Hanoi "independently" of Saigon.[7]

PLENARY PUBLIC AND SECRET PRIVATE NEGOTIATIONS: OPENING MOVES

Despite his talk about ending the war through negotiations, from the start of his administration Nixon had little faith in the four-party, public talks in Paris arranged by his predecessor. He purposefully scheduled a European trip to begin on February 23, only a month after his inauguration because, as he told Haldeman on January 27, he "must go early before Vietnam problems set in and [the] Paris talks bog down."[8] It was not just that Nixon believed the involvement of the RVN and NLF guaranteed confrontation and public exposure encouraged posturing. What Kissinger said about Nixon in his postwar memoir was also true: "He did not believe that negotiations would amount to anything until the military situation changed fundamentally. He thought Hanoi would accept a compromise only if it had no other choice. On the whole, he favored a policy of maximum pressure."[9] Nixon took this frame of mind into all negotiations with adversaries. During a cabinet meeting on March 20, at which both the Paris negotiations and arms control talks on antiballistic missile systems with the Soviets were being discussed, the "main thrust" of Nixon's remarks, as Haldeman paraphrased them, were: "We have to have real military superiority and defense as a base for negotiations."[10]

Kissinger asserted in his *White House Years* that he had more trust than Nixon in the technique of negotiation. If he did, it was not because he was an inveterate idealist but because he, representing the president, was going to be the person in charge of directing negotiations and, ultimately, the prime negotiator. "Whatever the Administration and regardless of the issue," he wrote, "American negotiators usually like to succeed."[11] Kissinger usually counted himself an American, and he always liked to succeed. On balance more willing than Nixon to give negotiations a chance, Kissinger, however, also believed that American diplomacy needed to be augmented with force. His preferred negotiating strategy would have been to "make the most sweeping and generous proposal of which we were capable, short of overthrowing an allied government but ensuring a free political contest," and then, if it failed, to apply maximum military pressure to bring about a negotiated "compromise."[12]

Kissinger also shared Nixon's lack of confidence in the four-party, semipublic forum of the Paris negotiations at the avenue Kléber location—known as the "plenary" or Kléber, talks. Both men favored direct, private contacts with Hanoi. Others had recommended such an approach during the Johnson years,[13] and private meetings had already been held between the American and DRV delegations in Paris to make arrangements for the public plenary talks.[14] Still, it was an approach that very much suited their shared desire to control the process by removing it from the public eye and reducing the involvement of third parties and government agencies outside the White House.

A month before Nixon's inauguration, Nixon and Kissinger had made their first but abortive attempt to establish a private channel. On December 20, 1968, they sent a message to Hanoi through Kissinger's friend Jean Sainteny, former French colonial delegate-general to Tonkin, in which they communicated a willingness to engage in "serious" talks, based on "self-respect," aiming at "an honorable settlement but for nothing less," and with a willingness to "discuss ultimate objectives first." The message concluded: "If Hanoi wishes to communicate some of their general ideas prior to January 20, they will be examined with a constructive attitude and in strictest confidence."[15] Both Nixon and Kissinger characterized the tone of the message as "conciliatory."[16]

Hanoi's reply was delivered eleven days later by its representative in Paris, Mai Van Bo, who, on handing it to Sainteny,[17] commented: "At the beginning, I believe that the question is to know if the U.S. [that is, the future Nixon White House] wants peace, if it really wishes to withdraw its troops from South Vietnam, or if it only talks of this to make it possible to do nothing." The reply accused Saigon of obstructing the talks (the dispute about the shape of the table was then under way), and it called on the president-elect to communicate his "specific ideas for making more precise points than are already known, for our serious examination."[18]

Kissinger's comment on this exchange years later faulted the other side: "Thus was the Nixon Administration first exposed to the maddening diplomatic style of the North Vietnamese."[19] Nixon claimed that he was "neither surprised nor discouraged," since he "had never expected to end the long war quickly or easily." Although committed to reaching "a peaceful settlement if possible," he was determined, he wrote, to "see through to an honorable conclusion the commitment we had undertaken."[20] Perhaps it was true that he had not been discouraged by the abortive attempt to open a private channel in December, but the rebuff seems to have confirmed his view that negotiations alone would not succeed, whether they were conducted in public or private. During the next two months the administration moved with only deliberate speed toward private negotiations, talking among themselves, weighing pros and cons, and waiting for the rest of their end-the-war strategy to take effect.[21]

There were others who urged them to move more swiftly. The American delegation at the Paris talks, now led by Henry Cabot Lodge, made several requests for permission to arrange talks between Lodge and his DRV counterpart, Xuan Thuy.[22] (Thuy was only the titular leader of the DRV delegation; he was not a member of the Politburo, and he lacked plenipotentiary powers, which, analogously, was true for Harriman and Lodge as well.) Averell Harriman, who had preceded Lodge as delegation head, endorsed the idea at a meeting with Nixon and Kissinger in the Oval Office on February 21.[23] Both Lodge and Harriman had probably been encouraged in this direction by the comments made by Le Duc Tho at a private meeting in Paris between the delegations on January 14. Tho had suggested that "goodwill" and continued private meetings between the United States and the DRV would assist in making the talks productive.[24] Subsequently, Xuan Thuy also communicated a willingness to meet privately.[25] There had also been useful private bilateral meetings between the American and North Vietnamese delegations during tea breaks in the plenary talks. When Nixon spoke with Charles de Gaulle at Versailles on March 1 on the last day of his European trip, the French president recommended direct conversations with Hanoi as "the best way to make progress," and the American president "indicated great interest in attempting this."[26] It was a feeling Nixon probably communicated to Kissinger after the meeting, for on the same day Kissinger sent a memorandum to him recommending preparatory steps: "Before we agree to private talks in Paris we should have a clear understanding of the strategy we would follow in those talks and the substantive positions we would take" on the mutual withdrawal of forces, the DMZ, and prisoners of war. The draft study Kissinger ordered was approved at an NSC meeting on March 28.[27] Meanwhile, on the tenth the Department of State instructed Ambassador Bunker to broach the subject of regular, bilateral, secret talks between Lodge and Thuy with President Thieu.[28]

Lodge and Thuy held the first of several formal private meetings on March 22. About these Lodge publicly reported months later that "Thuy has been as intransigent in private meetings as he has been in public meetings. . . . We got nowhere because [Hanoi] either refused to consider our proposals—or demanded that we take unilateral actions without any parallel action by them. And they even declined to have any serious discussion in which the government of South Vietnam could participate." He also complained that Thuy subsequently "tried to make it appear as if he has all along been ready to meet privately for serious discussion," but that in fact "every private meeting . . . has been at the request of the United States." His charge was disingenuous, for the act of taking the initiative was part of the diplomatic maneuvering that naturally accompanied talks such as those in Paris. While the American government and its negotiators had in fact taken frequent initiatives for private meetings, they tried to put the "onus" of requesting such meetings "reasonably on the other side at frequent intervals," a tactic that was also practiced by the other side, but with more success. The whole process, moreover, was complicated by other factors: Nixon and Kissinger did not put as much stock in Lodge's effort as in Kissinger's; Thieu refused to talk with the NLF; the collective leadership of the DRV was meticulous and deliberate in its approach; and the United States insisted on a two-track, political-military division in the negotiations.[29]

Kissinger's comment about the first meeting in March was that "it produced not a negotiation but North Vietnamese demands."[30] Thuy's "demands" were consistent with his government's long-standing terms for a settlement, which had been put forward in the NLF's Five-Point Statement of March 22, 1965, and the

DRV's Four-Point Position of April 8, 1965. Among these points, two stood out: calls for the unilateral withdrawal of American troops and the reunification of Vietnam, the latter "to be settled by the Vietnamese people . . . in accordance with the program of the South Viet Nam National Liberation Front, without any foreign interference." The key political component in the NLF's program was a proposal for the formation of "a broad and progressive democratic [coalition] regime," which it and the United States expected would consist mostly of parties sympathetic to the NLF. These demands were diametrically opposed to American demands, which Johnson had enunciated in the "Manila communiqué" of October 1966, and which Nixon continued to insist on after the inauguration: the mutual withdrawal of U.S. and DRV forces—with "residual" American troops remaining in South Vietnam until all North Vietnamese were confirmed to have withdrawn—and the preservation of South Vietnam as a separate state. Rarely stated directly, the latter point was usually framed in a formulation that called for free and democratic elections in South Vietnam—but elections in which the Saigon regime, remaining in power, would have the upper hand over a disarmed NLF.[31]

On taking charge of the public, four-party Paris negotiations, which formally began on January 25, President Nixon and Assistant for National Security Affairs Kissinger had carried over another approach from the Johnson administration: the "two-track negotiating strategy," wherein political issues, such as the status of South Vietnam, would be negotiated by the Saigon regime and the NLF, while military issues would be decided by the United States and the DRV. The two-track position served American goals: it insinuated that DRV forces, like U.S. forces, were "foreign" troops in the nation of South Vietnam; and it implied that the Saigon regime was the legitimate government of South Vietnam. There were added benefits: it vastly simplified the American task of negotiating a withdrawal of American troops, and in the event of a settlement calling for the mutual withdrawal of "foreign" forces, the NLF would be left to its own devices against the American-supported RVN.[32] At no time, however, did the other side accept the description of North Vietnamese forces as "foreign."

To many Americans, their government's negotiating strategy appeared reasonable, but to the DRV and NLF, its purpose was transparently hostile. It was, for them, an obstacle to their version of serious negotiations. On February 21, when the DRV and NLF delegations hosted a meeting with Valerian Zorin, Soviet ambassador to France, at their residence in Paris, they pointed out that the proposals made by the American delegation were aimed not at "solving the problem" but "at putting off its decision." In contrast, they said, the DRV and NLF delegations had "put forward proposals which are necessary to discuss in order to come to a political resolution of the problems," but, they said, the United States wants to "have a chance to strengthen the Saigon regime" and "to improve its position in South Vietnam in order to conduct the negotiations from a position of strength."[33]

In these first encounters there was little goodwill. Whether in public or private sessions, both sides at Paris were rigid in holding to their positions and belligerent in their attitudes. The Americans insisted on the two-track formula, criticized the other side for their military attacks in South Vietnam, and refused to talk with the NLF delegation. The DRV and NLF delegations insisted on the unconditional withdrawal of American troops, the achievement of "true independence" for Vietnam, the inclusion of the NLF in U.S.-DRV discussions, and the "exclusion of the Thieu-Ky-Huong regime" from power.[34] (In their Ten-Point Overall Solution of May 8, however, they hinted that they might not be opposed to the participation of Thieu, Ky, and Huong in a coalition government for South Vietnam. But the parties in the plenary talks in Paris failed to reach agreement on these proposals.)[35]

Nixon and Kissinger were remarkably tardy in either putting forward new proposals at the Paris plenary or turning to their preferred negotiating approach, the private and *secret* contact—secret even from the American delegation in Paris. Their sluggishness seems to have been the result of several interrelated causes: their initial confidence in other elements of their plan of coercion—particularly military pressure and linkage; their desire for these elements to become operational and to have an impact on the enemy; their belief that they held the upper hand in their relationship with Hanoi, enabling them to use the prospect of direct talks as an inducement for Hanoi to make concessions; and their view that premature private talks with Hanoi and the NLF would tend to undermine the legitimacy of the Saigon government. Underlying all of these beliefs was their conviction that the DRV would not "compromise" unless forced to but would continue fighting while negotiating. "The North Vietnamese were less interested in stopping the fighting than in winning it," Kissinger wrote.[36] His view mirrored Hanoi's perspective on the American style of negotiation.

NEGOTIATING STYLES

By the time the four-party negotiations had begun in Paris on January 25, the concept of fighting while negotiating was the guiding principle behind the diplomatic policy and military strategy of the Politburo in Hanoi. Vietnamese Workers' Party leaders and frontline soldiers had become discouraged in 1965 after President Johnson had committed American combat troops in large numbers and begun a sustained bombing campaign against the north. All knew that the United States possessed vast economic, technological, and military resources and was far and away the strategically stronger belligerent. Party First Secretary Le Duan and other leaders exhorted the cadres and the rank and file in the field to take encouragement from the inevitable difficulties American forces faced by fighting in an alien and distant land, while they debated strategy and policy in the Politburo, attempting to fashion the correct formula for ultimate victory.

Drawing on Chinese and Vietnamese theories, decision makers in Hanoi were convinced that protracted war was a necessary response to the problem of the weak against the strong.[37] In a 1966 letter to General Nguyen Chi Thanh, Le Duan had written that "the basic problem is to defeat the imperialists on the battlefield," but he warned that victory would not come immediately: "As far as the general strategy is concerned, we are advocating that the revolution in South Vietnam has to pass through several transitional phases prior to advancing toward national reunification and socialism."[38] A small country subjected to invasion by a powerful enemy could not successfully negotiate until the imbalance of power was brought into equilibrium on the field of battle. In a speech to a congress of the Central Office for South Vietnam in April 1966, General Nguyen Van Vinh, chairman of the VWP Reunification Department, reminded his audience that the fighting-and-negotiating phase of the struggle only became practical when the prior phase—the "fighting" phase—evolved to the point at which "both sides are fighting indecisively."[39]

This was the situation in mid-1968, by which time the war had become deadlocked; or, at least, policy makers on both sides had reluctantly acknowledged that a stalemate existed. Neither side was in a position to impose decisive military defeats on the other. Between the beginning of 1965 and the end of 1968, the United States had inflicted enormous casualties on the VNLAF, while severely damaging North Vietnam, pacifying some areas of South Vietnam, and marginally strengthening the Saigon regime. Yet the resistance was far from being defeated, and it retained its former assets: reserves of manpower, especially in the North; widespread, even if diminished, political support in the South; a reduced but continuing capacity to control the rate of casualties for both sides; "rear areas" in Cambodia, Laos, and North Vietnam; and various forms of material, manpower, and diplomatic assistance from the Soviet Union, China, and others in the socialist camp.[40] At the same time, the United States was burdened globally, divided domestically, and unable to solve the dilemma of shoring up an inept, dependent regime in Saigon, which possessed a small political base and commanded an army unable to fight effectively against its opposition.

During the fighting-and-negotiating stage of war, General Vinh argued, "the side which fights more strongly will compel the adversary to accept its conditions." The final stage of the process comprised "negotiations and the signing of agreements."[41] To Secretary Duan, as well as other Party leaders, the battle to be fought was one of both "armed" and "political struggle." Considered to be part of the latter, the "diplomatic struggle" was of "prime importance."[42]

Kissinger characterized the Vietnamese approach to diplomacy as doctrinaire, intransigent, excessively suspicious, and cynical—as well as "devious and baffling." It was, he said, the product of their Marxist-Leninist ideology, their "legacy of Cartesian logic from French colonialism," and their "indirect" style of communicating, which, given their historical experience with invasion, they had developed to manipulate "physically stronger foreigners." The North Vietnamese conviction that they were engaged in a "life-and-death struggle" was, however, "the fundamental problem." In contrast, Kissinger asserted, the American approach to negotiations presumed good-faith, give-and-take discussions between reasonable parties in search of an evenhanded, compromise settlement. Thus, Kissinger wrote: "Our mode of settling conflicts was to seek a solution somewhere between the contending positions. . . . To them the Paris talks were not a device for settlement but an instrument of political warfare."[43] Nixon phrased it differently, but the meaning was the same: "Ho Chi Minh and his battle-hardened colleagues had not fought and sacrificed for twenty-five years in order to negotiate a compromise peace. They were fighting for total victory. But in the hope that I was wrong, I vigorously pursued the negotiating process."[44]

At times Nixon and Kissinger appeared to regret the American style of negotiating. Kissinger wrote: "Negotiability—an elegant phrase meaning what one knows the other side will accept—becomes an end in itself and the outcome is foreordained: The negotiation will see the constant retreat of the party that is committed to it." Compounding the problem of style was the influence of democratic dissent: "Critics demand greater flexibility; soon the proposition is advanced that the United States has an obligation to overcome the stalemate by offering concessions."[45] Nixon believed he had an answer to the problem: "I was convinced that unless we backed up our diplomatic efforts with strong military pressure, the North Vietnamese would continue their strategy of talking and fighting until we tired of the struggle and caved in."[46]

From the Vietnamese perspective, the American characterization of their own style of negotiation was a deceptive pose, for "experience in world affairs has shown," Vo Nguyen Giap argued in September 1967, "that Americans are more impressed by force than by reason"; therefore, "no agreement can be reached as long as we fail to win on the battlefield."[47] The guiding principle of American negotiating strategy appeared to be that of the position of strength. "U.S. views hold," Le Duan claimed in 1966, "that negotiation is to be conducted from a strong position."[48] The United States used negotiations as a ploy, he argued, professing interest in compromise but in practice drawing on its superior power to turn talks into means by which the weaker side could be pressured into concessions. "The U.S. imperialists," Duan continued, "are attempting to widen the war in a move to save them from the sad predicament and quagmire, but, on the other hand, are trying to force us to the negotiation table for some concessions."[49]

During negotiations, whether preliminary exchanges or formal meetings, the United States employed the supporting stratagem of the carrot and stick—proffering incentives and threatening force to induce compliance. In his history of the talks, Luu Van Loi, a senior DRV diplomat, cited the very earliest contacts between the Johnson administration and Hanoi as examples of this technique. On two occasions in June and August 1964, the White House, via the Canadian ambassador, sent messages to Hanoi containing both military threats and, if concessions were forthcoming, offers of economic aid. But, Loi wrote, "'the carrot-and-stick theme' . . . did not shake the determination of Hanoi to defend the country against foreign aggression."[50]

The madman theory was a variant of this American diplomatic style. Nguyen Co Thach, vice minister of foreign affairs and aide to Le Duc Tho in the private negotiations with Kissinger in Paris, once reproached Kissinger about the one-sided tendency of Americans to criticize the Vietnamese style of fighting-and-negotiating: "It is [your] idea that it is a good thing to make a false threat that the enemy believes is a true threat. It is a bad thing if we are threatening an enemy with a true threat and the enemy believes it is a false threat." Of course, Nixon's and Kissinger's threats were not always false. Thach was not only setting the record straight about the American use of threat bargaining but also putting up a brave front by taunting Kissinger about the ineffectiveness of his threats: "False or true, we Vietnamese don't mind. There must be a third category—for those who don't care whether the threat is true or false."[51]

The reality of American-Vietnamese negotiations was that neither side was interested in conflict resolution for its own sake. The participants had not entered the negotiations in order to find a compromise that would satisfy the other's needs and interests. The Soviets, the Europeans, and the American antiwar movement—all outside the decision-making circles in Washington and Hanoi—might call for compromise and reasonableness and express impatience and annoyance with the men who would not and could not end a dangerous and costly war, but the decision-making insiders believed that a true compromise would mean the sacrifice of substantive goals for which they had long fought. The Vietnamese clearly had more riding on the outcome, but American leaders felt they had much at stake as well. It was the military deadlock, not an interest in fairness, that had caused both sides to recognize the political necessity of talking.

Despite this mutual recognition of the impasse, hawks in the Politburo and the White House in 1969 continued to believe that the avoidance of political defeat required military success. By the same token, they were both convinced that their position of strength at the negotiating table could be improved by shifting the battlefield balance of power in their favor. While both sides remained hopeful about military prospects and tenacious concerning political goals, neither was confident of its own prospects following a cease-fire and a political compromise. In different ways, moreover, the leadership on either side continued to be tolerant of the wartime suffering of its own country and especially of the Vietnamese people.[52]

In these circumstances there was little difference between the principle of fighting while negotiating and the carrot-and-stick approach. Although the VWP Politburo and the Republican White House spoke in distinctive styles, both combined armed and political struggle in practice. To the Politburo, political struggle meant many things, including the proselytizing of refugees in urban slums, the distribution of land to the tillers, the mobilizing of students, intellectuals, and peasants, the forming of alliances with non-Communist nationalists, and the holding of diplomatic meetings in Paris. But the relevance of the political element was not lost on Nixon, Kissinger, and other American strategists either. Not without success, they used political rhetoric, news leaks, and the presidential mystique to sway American domestic and world opinion; they deployed pacification tactics and land reform programs to win South Vietnamese hearts and minds; and they synchronized diplomatic offensives with bombing campaigns.

Although the Vietnamese mode of discourse was, as Kissinger described it, sometimes "indirect" and "opaque" in an attempt to keep their options open, the Americans, for their part, were oblique but transparent in making their offers and threats—hinting of a willingness to compromise while suggesting dire consequences if the other side did not agree. The perspectives of the two sides were quite different: the Vietnamese, under attack, aware of their small-power status, and aspiring for independence; the Americans, under pressure to end the war honorably, feeling the burdens of great power, and expecting the Vietnamese to show deference. Even when he was extending polite compliments, Kissinger's arrogance showed through. Careful to praise both the South and North Vietnamese, he nonetheless could not avoid condescension. Writing of the DRV's representatives, he observed: "Their contact with the outside world had been sporadic and shaped by the requirements of their many struggles. But in meeting with the representative of the strongest power on earth, they were subtle, disciplined, and infinitely patient. Except for one occasion—when, carried away by the early success of the spring offensive of 1972, they turned insolent—they were always courteous."[53]

The members of the Politburo had few illusions about American power, Nixon's intent, and the other obstacles they faced. But they were determined to persevere, "battle-hardened" as they were. They also understood and took heart from the "objective contradictions" in Nixon's own difficult situation. They were reasonably confident that the Soviet nuclear arsenal would deter any plans Nixon might have to employ nuclear weapons, while the possibility of Chinese intervention would prevent him from invading the North.[54] Moreover, as a Central Office for South Vietnam (COSVN) resolution of July 1969 pointed out, the withdrawal issue placed Nixon on the horns of a dilemma. If conditions in Vietnam were such that he could not withdraw troops without producing a "sudden collapse" of Thieu's government, the "internal conflicts" between him and the American people and the Saigon regime would increase. But if he did withdraw troops, it would undermine American strategy, "accentuate" the demoralization of U.S. and RVN forces, and lead to the "political isolation, . . . decay, and ineffectiveness" of Thieu's administration. This predicament, centering on the troop withdrawal question, they believed, was "the *greatest weak point* of the Americans."[55]

Reflecting on Nixon's words and actions, Nguyen Co Thach noted: "Nixon on the one hand was threatening bombing and on the other withdrawing troops. That means . . . [his signal] was very vague. The question for us was not [the threat of] bombing or any kind of force. We should have been able to survive, to stay on. But for the Americans, in any case, they must leave. That was their problem."[56]

LINKAGE

In February Nixon and Kissinger had opened a secret diplomatic channel to Moscow through Ambassador Dobrynin. As Moscow's official representative in Washington, Dobrynin had often met with Secretary of State Rusk to discuss Vietnam and other matters of importance to both superpowers. Governor Harriman had "several rows" with Rusk about these because he had "tried to convince . . . [Rusk] that Dobrynin was only a high-class cler[k], and that he was wasting his time talking with him," but Rusk had taken it as a belittlement of the position of secretary of state. When Harriman told Nixon about these quarrels within the previous administration, he advised the new president "to get through to the Politburo leaders" more directly. But this approach to the Kremlin would have meant sending "special representatives" to Moscow,[57] probably someone like Harriman, which would have defeated Nixon's and Kissinger's desire to control diplomacy from the Oval Office, for it would have involved the bureaucracy or other third parties and risked internal debates over policy and leaks to the press and public. They planned instead to bypass the State Department and other policy agencies by holding their own private, unpublicized meetings with the Soviet ambassador. Dobrynin was to be their *back* channel to the Politburo, not their open channel.

Kissinger made his first contact with Dobrynin at an official Soviet embassy reception on February 14; three days later, Dobrynin paid an official visit to the president at the White House. In these first two meetings the tenor and format of subsequent unofficial meetings was agreed upon. Kissinger, "as confidant to Nixon," and Dobrynin, "on behalf of the Politburo," would hold frequent discussions, during which they would "think out loud," speak candidly, and express both their personal views and their governments' official positions. They would "conduct preliminary negotiations on almost all major issues, . . . clarify the basic purposes of our governments," head off crises, and make formal and informal proposals on a "noncommittal" basis. Normally, they met in the Map Room of the White House, with the ambassador discreetly entering from the seldom-used East Wing diplomatic entrance, which was screened by rhododendron bushes. When requested by the Soviets, Kissinger would visit Dobrynin in the embassy. Dobrynin met with Nixon at the White House irregularly and on special occasions.[58]

It was Kissinger who had suggested to Nixon the establishment of this private channel, arguing that informal talks would likely produce more "forthcoming" exchanges than formal talks.[59] The arrangement suited well the personalities, goals, and tactics of both the president and his assistant. It gave Kissinger, who believed "more in human relations than in ideas,"[60] a chance to establish a personal relationship with an important Soviet official, while solidifying his influence over foreign policy, and, as Dobrynin put it in a memo to Gromyko, strengthening "his own personal position with Nixon."[61] It provided Nixon, who believed more in ideas than in human relations, an opportunity to insulate himself from "the give and take of negotiations,"[62] while maintaining White House control over American policy toward the Soviet Union. Wary of leaving negotiations primarily in the hands of cabinet agencies, and believing that the presummit expectations of the press and the public often exceeded summit results, Nixon and Kissinger hoped that back-channel discussions would prepare the ground for formal negotiations between government agencies on both sides and productive meetings between the American president and the Soviet leader.[63] Through this private channel, moreover, they would better be able to pursue their strategy of linkage and employ their tactic of offering carrots while brandishing sticks.

In the February meetings with Nixon and Kissinger, Dobrynin was conciliatory and diplomatic. To both he lamented those "opportunities" for reconciliation that both sides had lost in the past, and to Nixon he presented a seven-page note from Moscow in which his government expressed a willingness to improve relations and solve problems between the two great powers, particularly about strategic arms, Vietnam, the Middle East, Eastern Europe, and Berlin.

The American leaders delivered mixed signals. Kissinger, too, spoke of the need for accommodation. But he blamed historic tensions between the two countries on Soviet behavior, which he claimed was the real cause of friction, not mutual mistakes or lost opportunities, and he insisted on "reciprocity" in behavior and agreements, without which, he said, additional crises would be inevitable.[64] Nixon was amiable, but he introduced the notion of linkage, saying "that progress in one area must logically be linked to progress in other areas." Then he delivered a veiled threat: "I think it is incumbent on us, when we begin strategic arms talks, to do what we can in a parallel way to defuse critical political situations like the Middle East and Vietnam and Berlin, where there is a danger that arms might be put to use."[65]

According to Kissinger's memoirs, Nixon thought his meeting with Dobrynin had been a "tough confrontation." Kissinger reported a different impression, however, writing that the exchange had been "conciliatory," but in the competitive spirit of "the opening in a chess game between experts." In any event, he assumed that Dobrynin's conversations with both of them could only have reinforced the ambassador's apprehensions about the administration's future course—would it be in the direction of conciliation or confrontation? This uncertainty was all to the good, Kissinger thought; moreover, it was what Nixon wanted.

The morning after the Nixon-Dobrynin conversation, Kissinger sent a memo to the president, in which he theorized that the Soviets' interest in negotiations "stems in large measure from their uncertainty about the plans of this Administration"; that is, whether "'adventurous'" forces in Washington will outweigh "'reasonable'" forces. Playing up to Nixon's attraction to the coercive virtues of toughness and uncertainty, Kissinger rejected the advice of the reasonable faction, which believed that "we should not let this moment of Soviet interest pass." He recommended instead that "we should seek to utilize this Soviet interest, stemming as I think it does from anxiety, to induce them to come to grips with the real sources of tension, notably in the Middle East, but also in Vietnam. This approach also would require continued firmness on our part in Berlin."[66]

Dobrynin had indicated the Soviets' willingness to negotiate a number of issues simultaneously, which both Nixon and Kissinger initially took as their acceptance of the concept of linkage. But to the Soviets, simultaneity and linkage were not identical;[67] issues had to be negotiated "on the basis of the merits" of each. What was particularly upsetting to the ambassador was the American linking of political issues, such as Vietnam, with military matters, such as nuclear arms control. Dobrynin informed Harriman of as much two days after meeting with Nixon. In a conversation he undoubtedly expected the former chief negotiator in Paris to report to Nixon, Dobrynin explained that Soviet leaders had debated among themselves for over a year whether they wanted to negotiate an arms control agreement, and a majority had finally decided to proceed. It was not now possible, he said, "to tie political settlements with nuclear questions." The Soviet government "would not be bribed or intimidated . . . and nothing would induce them to give in on some political issue in order to get our agreement on nuclear matters." Dobrynin was "most anxious" to clarify this matter.[68] The Soviets' interest in negotiating was not the result of their anxiety about the new administration's adventurism, as Nixon and Kissinger assumed. On the contrary, as long as the Americans insisted on linkage, they were less likely to negotiate, particularly if they believed Nixon and Kissinger were trying to blackmail them with threats of one kind or another.

Harriman conveyed Dobrynin's clarifications to the president when he called on him with Kissinger on February 21, two days before Nixon was to leave for Brussels. "I argued against linking political and military negotiations," Harriman wrote in a personal memorandum of his conversation. "Henry seems to think this has been satisfactorily explained to Dobrynin. I told him I didn't get that impression."[69] Harriman was correct in his suspicions. As he and Kissinger left Nixon's office, Kissinger confessed: "You will be pleased with our policy with the Russians on Viet-Nam. We want to get hold of them at a top level and come to an agreement with them as to what will happen in Viet-Nam. If we do this, it will be possible to have progress militarily."[70]

These meetings with Dobrynin and Harriman, and the memos about them, revealed how much faith Nixon and Kissinger had put in the madman theory and how little commitment they had made in reaching compromise agreements. Their strategy was not only to link other issues to the settlement of the Vietnam War but to link linkage itself to threats designed to induce anxiety. Vietnam was the linchpin issue, but all others were to be accomplished as well through the tactic of producing uncertainty about their "adventurous" plans.

It was an odd strategy, particularly on the matter of nuclear arms control, and it reflected their peculiar response to the American nuclear predicament. By 1969 the Soviet Union had nearly achieved numerical equality with the United States in land-based ballistic missiles and had begun the construction and deployment of their own nuclear-powered ballistic-missile submarines. Although the United States led the USSR in weapons technology and in the number of long-range bombers and nuclear-powered ballistic-missile submarines, the Soviet land-based nuclear weapons program continued to gather momentum, while the American program was in abatement.[71] Hawks called for a policy of renewed expansion, but the president and his assistant understood that the domestic environment of antimilitarism, compounded by strains in the economy, made this course unlikely. It was also impractical, for the Soviets could match an American buildup—or at least were determined to do so despite the cost.[72] To many experts, the only rational course left to the administration, if it was to halt a Soviet buildup and rein in the arms race, was to enter into an arms control agreement.

At the same time they recognized the folly of an arms race, however, Nixon and Kissinger deeply regretted the Soviet Union's achievement of nuclear parity, because it undermined the credibility of America's willingness to use nuclear weapons "in defense of allies." Trapped on the horns of this self-inflicted dilemma, they thought they had a solution. With or without arms control, they could not reestablish numerical nuclear superiority, but they might nonetheless reestablish nuclear credibility by two other methods: retargeting American nuclear weapons in order to permit their use in "limited applications,"[73] and communicating an irrational, adventurous spirit, which might unnerve the Soviets sufficiently to elicit their cooperation in ending the Vietnam War in exchange for an arms control agreement. As Nixon and Kissinger viewed the situation, much seemed to turn on the Vietnam War: unless it were ended, political and economic constraints would hamper the American nuclear program, thereby encouraging *Soviet* adventurism, but unless the United States could reestablish its nuclear credibility, the Vietnam War could not be ended on acceptable terms. The original solution they investigated seemed designed to enable them to have their cake and eat it too. In their February meetings with Dobrynin, they had established the principle of linkage; but a few weeks earlier, on the day after Nixon's inauguration, he and Kissinger had ordered NSSM 3, a study of the conventional and nuclear balance of forces, which led to a follow-on study in June requesting the Pentagon to examine limited nuclear targeting options. These might provide the United States with a flexible nuclear capability, which could thereby serve as a credible deterrent for local wars, thus frustrating the Soviet Union's achievement of nuclear parity and also enabling the United States to offset the Soviets' putative superiority in conventional forces.[74]

The role Kissinger played in his meetings with Dobrynin was not solely that of the "good messenger" or "good guy," moderating warnings he was carrying from the "bad guy," President Nixon. Each posed as Jekyll and Hyde, or at least Dobrynin thought so after one meeting: "One could feel that he had instructions from Nixon to give us precisely this kind of argument, though Kissinger expressed it as if in his own words."[75]

Although Dobrynin did not like to hear threatening messages from Kissinger, he did find great value in the Kissinger channel, which provided him with insights into White House power relationships and opportunities for conveying Soviet perspectives on issues. Kissinger was, Dobrynin observed, "a smart and erudite person, [who] is at the same time extremely vain, . . . boasting of his influence." Indeed, Dobrynin believed, Kissinger did have "dominant influence" over Nixon because he had "concentrated the collection and presentation to the President of all material on foreign policy" in his office, and he meets with Nixon "significantly more often than any other aide." Therefore, Dobrynin concluded, "it would be expedient over time to more and more actively develop and use the channel with Kissinger in order to influence and through him drive home directly to President Nixon our points of view on various important questions, especially in situations where a certain delicacy is called for or where any sort of publicity is undesirable."[76]

From these personal contacts he understood that "problem No. 1" for the American administration remained that of finding "an exit from the Vietnam War under acceptable conditions, which would guarantee . . . [Nixon's] reelection." Dobrynin predicted that Nixon would continue to try to "'convince' the USSR to help settle the conflict," and that this effort would affect Soviet negotiations "on other international questions, if not directly, then at least as a definite slowing of the tempo of these negotiations or settlement of other problems."[77]

In his postwar account, Kissinger characterized these exchanges with Dobrynin on the issue of Vietnam during the next two years as "inconclusive." Despite his attempts to enlist "Soviet cooperation" to end the war, Dobrynin, he wrote, was "evasive . . . ; he never came up with a concrete proposal to end the war."[78] What he meant, of course, was that the Soviets never came up with a concrete proposal to end the war on American terms.

In exchanges with the American government, the Soviets consistently supported the position of the DRV and NLF, even though they may not have agreed with it. Under dire circumstances they might have accepted a solution that provided for a divided Vietnam, for they were genuinely interested in preventing a confrontation with the United States in Southeast Asia and the globalization of the conflict. They were, on the other hand, trapped in their own logic of credibility: they could not let down their allies, particularly since the Chinese were challenging them for leadership in the developing countries. Moreover, the Soviets had proactive goals in Southeast Asia—namely, to continue their policy of rapprochement with the DRV in order to rid the Vietnamese of "narrow nationalistic errors in the area of foreign policy," and to "utilize" Hanoi's prestige "in our interests." According to Soviet diplomats in Hanoi: "When the DRV has become the leading force in the struggle of the peoples of Indochina, we will possess comparatively more possibilities for establishing our policy in this region. It is not excluded that Indochina may become for us a key to all Southeast Asia. In addition, in this region there is nobody, so far, we can lean on, except the DRV."[79]

Despite these aims, the Soviets had been helpful in the past in bringing about the negotiations in Paris, which even Nixon and Kissinger acknowledged, and they continued to work for a diplomatic solution. On the day Harriman visited Nixon at the White House and told him that "we could find ourselves in parallel positions in Southeast Asia,"[80] Zorin had met with Thuy and Kiem at the Soviet embassy in Paris, urging them to develop a "concrete program" to propose to the American delegation. Zorin argued that specific questions and proposals put to the Americans might help bring about a political settlement. Distrusting U.S. motives and concerned that Washington might consider any proposal a sign of weakness, "the Vietnamese comrades," Zorin reported, were at first skeptical, but at the end of the meeting they "treated this idea with interest." Zorin's insistence on concreteness was probably influential in the NLF's presentation of their Ten-Point Overall Solution to the Paris plenary on May 8.[81]

TRIANGULAR RELATIONSHIPS

The consensus among national security agencies as reported in NSSM 1 had been that "Peking opposes negotiations while Moscow prefers an early negotiated settlement on terms as favorable as possible to Hanoi."[82] Despite this, Nixon and Kissinger chose to follow a course that was more hostile to the Soviet Union than it was to the People's Republic. The "China-card" portion of their triangular policy was designed to signal the USSR that the United States would somehow ally itself with the PRC unless the Soviet government was cooperative on international problems like Vietnam. At the time, it was a strategy that ran counter to conventional wisdom. NSSM 14, an interagency study of America's China policy ordered on February 5 and completed in May, indicated, for example, that U.S. national security agencies, in Kissinger's words, put "excessive emphasis on China's ideology and alleged militancy," treating these concerns "as if they existed in a vacuum," and making "no reference . . . to the global implications of Sino-Soviet tensions and the opportunities for us in the triangular relationship."[83]

In his postwar accounts, Nixon was ambiguous about the motives behind the triangular strategy. "Contrary to the conventional wisdom," he wrote in *In the Arena,* "my primary motive was not to enlist China's aid in ending the war in Vietnam or to play the so-called China card against the Soviet Union."[84] In *No More Vietnams,* however, he ascribed coequal status to the China card: "Though rapprochement with China and detente with the Soviet Union were ends in themselves, I also considered them possible means to hasten the end of the war."[85] Kissinger was uncharacteristically more direct. In *White House Years* he explained his motives in realist terms: "History suggested that it was usually more advantageous to align oneself with the weaker of two antagonistic partners, because this acted as a restraint on the stronger."[86] Of the three schools of thought within the government about relations with China and the Soviet Union—the "Slavophile," the "Sinophile," and the "Realpolitiker"—Kissinger and Nixon counted themselves among the latter.[87]

Whichever motive took priority—intimidating the Soviets or improving relations with China—the actual playing of the China card against the Soviet Union preceded concrete moves to bring about rapprochement with China. Although Nixon had written and spoken about the need for normalizing relations with China since 1967, in early 1969 he continued to be ambivalent about taking steps in that direction, uncertain whether such a course was more advantageous than detrimental to American interests. Rapprochement with China might calm the anti-American rage of an isolated people, contribute to stability in the Pacific Rim, lever the Soviets into greater cooperation, and serve as an additional counterweight to the Soviet Union's global power. On the other hand, rapprochement with a revolutionary power might unsettle Pacific Rim allies, clients, and trading partners, as well as conservatives in the United States. Kissinger put a positive spin on this ambivalence, claiming in *White House Years* that Nixon wanted to keep his options open, prepared either to move immediately or to postpone the opening of China.

Despite Nixon's uncertainty concerning whether, how, and when to approach the Chinese about better relations, once in office he used the discussion of the possibility as a means of influencing Soviet behavior. On February 1, 1969, he wrote in a memorandum to Kissinger: "I think we should give every encouragement to the attitude that this Administration is 'exploring possibilities of raprochement [*sic*] with the Chinese.' This, of course, should be done privately." Kissinger commented, "The maneuver was intended to disquiet the Soviets."[88] Following Nixon's lead, Kissinger recommended in a mid-February 1969 memorandum that the president should use the China card in his first meeting with Dobrynin: "I also included an ambiguous formulation to the effect that if Soviet support failed to materialize 'we do not exclude that others who have an interest would be enlisted to bring about progress. . . .' This was a cryptic reference to the Chinese—though it would not be opaque to the astute Dobrynin."[89]

These schemes were hatched several months before Nixon and Kissinger took concrete steps toward improved relations with China; when they did decide to begin a process of rapprochement, the primary motive seems to have been the China card. In June 1969, reacting to the escalating crisis in relations between the Soviet Union and China, Kissinger wrote the president: "Soviet concern [with their China problem] may have finally reached the point that it can be turned to our advantage, if they are in fact attempting to ensure our neutrality in their Chinese containment policy, if not our active cooperation." Nixon's response was, "This is our goal," by which he meant turning it to the advantage of the United States. "We now redoubled our own efforts," Kissinger later remarked, "to establish contact with Peking."[90]

The timing of approaches toward China was influenced by the deterioration of Soviet-Sino relations and by the Nixon-Kissinger plan to extricate the United States from Vietnam, which was the most important link in the policy of linkage. The triangular relationship between the United States, the USSR, and the PRC, as seen by Nixon and Kissinger, was supposed to assist them in extricating the United States from Vietnam: the China card and the carrots of détente would encourage Moscow to put pressure on Hanoi to negotiate an agreement allowing the United States to withdraw with honor, while rapprochement with Beijing would intimidate not only the Soviets but Hanoi as well.

China's advocacy of radical revolutionary movements around the world and its opposition to negotiations over Vietnam was less important to Nixon and Kissinger than the Soviet Union's challenge to America's global aims and interests and the critical significance of its aid to Hanoi.[91] By 1969 the USSR had replaced China as the DRV's largest supplier. Although it paled in comparison with the amount of aid given by the United States to South Vietnam, in that year Moscow provided Hanoi with 50 percent of the assistance it received from the Communist bloc, almost $.5 billion dollars. About $200 million of this amount was military aid. In addition, nearly 2,000 Soviet military experts maintained equipment and operated radar and antiaircraft installations.[92] The Chinese troop presence before 1969 had been considerably greater. Over 320,000 Chinese engineering and artillery units had performed maintenance, construction, and antiaircraft tasks north of the twenty-first parallel. The peak year had been 1967, when 170,000 Chinese troops were in the DRV. Subsequently, their numbers declined sharply until, by late 1969, only a handful of units remained behind to complete their projects.[93]

The decline in Chinese assistance was the product of multiple, interconnected causes. From the early to the late sixties, Beijing grew annoyed with North Vietnam's rejection of China's historic presumptions about the centrality of its cultural and geopolitical role in Asia. In addition, the DRV's acceptance of increased aid from the USSR became embroiled in the Sino-Soviet conflict, further straining DRV relations with the PRC. Meanwhile, by the end of the decade the debilitating effect of Mao's Cultural Revolution on China's political and economic system made it necessary for Beijing to curtail its overseas commitments. Not the least of the causes of friction between Hanoi and Beijing was Beijing's disapproval of Hanoi's decision to begin negotiations with Washington.[94] As the DRV's foreign minister Nguyen Duy Trinh remarked in February 1967, among its allies there were three views on Hanoi's diplomatic initiatives: China disapproved; the Soviet Union "very much" welcomed them; and North Korea, Cuba, and Romania supported "everything we are doing."[95]

It was the DRV, however, that seemed to enjoy the relative advantage in this tangled web of relationships. No matter how strained the Sino-Vietnamese alliance, Beijing was unwilling to relinquish its influence in Southeast Asia to Moscow or to accept a permanent American presence in South Vietnam. In fact, that was the reason for its disapproval of negotiations to end the war, for it had favored an indecisive, protracted conflict that might thwart the American goal of preserving an outpost in South Vietnam, while simultaneously reducing the possibility of an armed confrontation with the United States and delaying Hanoi's drive to unite Vietnam. Nor did Beijing want to approve negotiations with Washington when the policy of the United States was to isolate and contain China. By the same token, Moscow's own global aims and regional goals prevented it from bullying Hanoi.

The DRV relied on aid and assistance from the USSR and the PRC, and it had to accept the "advice" of its stronger allies. Despite fissures in its alliances and concerns about the impact of American triangular diplomacy, it was able to juggle the competing interests of Moscow and Beijing in Southeast Asia well enough that it continued to receive sufficient aid to wage an effective war against the United States and the Saigon regime while maintaining a significant degree of independence from its allies.[96] Soviet diplomats in Hanoi even complained about their lack of influence over DRV policy. One 1970 political report of the Soviet embassy read: "The Vietnamese comrades have remained in the previous position of incomplete confidence in the USSR"; they do not want to "spoil or aggravate relations with the Soviet Union, but do not draw closer to it with complete confidence." The North Vietnamese treated Soviet citizens in the DRV with suspicion, resisted Soviet ideological influence in their country, did not adequately credit Soviet assistance in their public statements, and often "forgot" to inform Moscow of their diplomatic activities.[97]

Like Kissinger, the Soviets and the Chinese might have thought of this behavior as the ungrateful bad manners of a xenophobic, "morbidly" suspicious, perversely obstinate, and "ferociously" self-righteous people,[98] but the Vietnamese considered it the prudent vigilance of a small country, historically colonized and currently besieged. They remembered, too, their experience in the Geneva negotiations of 1954, when the Soviets and Chinese, concerned about American intervention, persuaded them to accept a compromise that gave them less than they had won.[99]

As NSSM 1 analysts had observed, "Neither Peking nor Moscow have exerted heavy pressure on Hanoi and for various reasons they are unlikely to do so, although their military and economic assistance give them [potentially] important leverage." Two of the reasons were that "Peking and Moscow tend to cancel out each other," while Hanoi "is attempting to chart its own independent course."[100]

Nixon and Kissinger disregarded this assessment. They chose to view Communist interrelationships not as obstacles to their plans but as opportunities to square the triangle, interposing the United States between the Soviet Union, China, and North Vietnam. Determining that Hanoi's reliance on Soviet supplies and global power gave Moscow leverage over Hanoi, they intended to encourage Moscow to use it. As far as China was concerned, if Beijing was irritated with Hanoi, then the gap between the PRC and the DRV might be widened through a policy of rapprochement with the United States, which would also affect Sino-Soviet relations. A more bitter feud between the USSR and the PRC would complicate the DRV's position because most of the military aid from the Soviet Union came by rail through China and required Sino-Soviet cooperation. Kissinger noted a final bonus: the "drama of ending estrangement" with China could have an important impact on domestic politics, countering the despair brought on by the "agony of Vietnam" with the hope engendered by the "possibility of creative policy."[101]

7

TARGET OF OPPORTUNITY: 1969

If in doubt we bomb Cambodia.
—Richard Nixon[1]

CAMBODIA

Kissinger claimed in *White House Years* that before he and Nixon could develop their negotiating strategy or resolve the internal strategic debate uncovered by NSSM 1, "Hanoi preempted our analyses by launching a countrywide offensive in South Vietnam" on February 22. By these actions, he maintained, the enemy had breached the 1968 bombing-halt understanding, wherein they were supposed to scale down their attacks across the DMZ.[2] Nixon treated this "post-Tet" offensive more personally, arguing in *RN* that the enemy's "small-scale but savage offensive into South Vietnam" was a "deliberate test, clearly designed to take the measure of me and my administration at the outset." In another revealing comment, he said, "My immediate instinct was to retaliate." In this he was supported by Kissinger, for they agreed that "if we let the Communists manipulate us at this early stage, we might never be able to negotiate with them from a position of equality, much less one of strength."[3] Their explanation of the origins of their "retaliation," which would take place in Cambodia, was disingenuous.

A common refrain among hawks and military officials inside and outside of government, the proposal to attack Communist bases and supply lines in Cambodia had antedated Nixon's election and represented both the mind-set of those optimists who favored military solutions to the war and the doctrines of those strategists who believed that VNLAF bases should be attacked wherever they might be found. General Lemay had urged such attacks in March 1964; General West-moreland had recommended them in March 1967 and again after Tet 1968; and the JCS had lobbied for them in May, September, and December 1968.[4] In November 1967, when former president Eisenhower had advocated "hot pursuit" of the enemy into Laos and Cambodia, candidate Nixon publicly called it an unsound step, but with the qualification "at this time."[5]

By January 8, 1969, however, the president-elect had come to believe the time was ripe for developing an option that had long appealed to him, and he ordered his assistant to begin the process: "I want a precise report on what the enemy has in Cambodia and what, if anything, we are doing to destroy the buildup there. I think a very definite change of policy toward Cambodia probably should be one of the first orders of business." In reply to Kissinger's ensuing inquiry, the mili-tary provided information about Vietnamese logistics routes from Sihanoukville to base camps along the Cambodian border, pointing out that very little was being done to destroy them and that MACV's many requests for authority to con-duct operations in Cambodia either had been denied or were pending.[6]

Pressed by Nixon, Kissinger began to do something about it. "In the first few weeks of the new administration," according to journalist Seymour Hersh, Kissinger ordered Colonel Ray B. Sitton, known in the Pentagon as "Mr. B-52," to develop a list of bombing options in Cambodia. Sitton told Hersh in a postwar interview that Kissinger "wanted them [the enemy] to know that we were serious about possible escalation" and had charged him with the task of recommending "military steps you might make that would signal North Vietnam that we meant business."[7] Although Haldeman referred to a mysterious "Pentagon planning of-ficer" in a diary entry about Cambodia, a reference to Sitton, Kissinger, intrigu-ingly, did not mention him in his memoirs.[8] Sitton's options study apparently followed a track parallel to, but separate from and more secret than, other inquir-ies and studies on the bombing of Cambodia.

Kissinger's NSSM 1 directive of January 21, for example, included questions about the importance of Laos and Cambodia as channels for enemy supplies to South Vietnam.[9] All agencies agreed in their replies that Laotian routes were vital, but the CIA and State Department dissented from MACV's view that Cam-bodia was a significant conduit as well, with the recommendation that "the act of sealing off the enemy's Cambodian supply lines must be considered as an inte-gral part of any plan to prevent supplies from reaching enemy forces in the Re-public of Vietnam."[10] This meant, Kissinger explained, the bombing of one or more of a dozen Communist bases or "sanctuaries" along the Cambodian–South Viet-nam border.[11]

Meanwhile, two other expressed concerns impinged on the issue of bombing Cambodia: the probability of an enemy offensive and the potentially damaging military consequences of imminent U.S. troop withdrawals. At the first meeting of the NSC on January 25, Wheeler said that everything but the bombing of North

Vietnam was being done to anticipate the contingency of enemy attack.[12] But at a subsequent meeting Kissinger held with Wheeler and Laird on January 30, the secretary of defense pointed out that the public would not support the renewed bombing of the North. As an alternative Wheeler then proposed the bombing of enemy base complexes in Cambodia. Two days later Nixon sent a note to Kissinger that read: "I do not like the suggestions that I see in virtually every news report that 'we anticipate a Communist initiative in South Vietnam.' I believe that if any initiative occurs it should be on our part and not theirs."[13]

Whether in response to this comment or another request, the MACV commander, General Creighton Abrams, cabled General Earl Wheeler on February 9 that "recent information, developed from photo reconnaissance and a rallier gives us hard intelligence on COSVN HQ facilities in Base Area 353." From its dispersed, mobile headquarters under the jungle canopy along the Cambodia–South Vietnam border, the elusive Central Office for South Vietnam directed VNLAF operations in the South. Abrams argued that a large, concentrated B-52 attack on COSVN would ensure its destruction and disrupt future offensives the enemy might be planning.[14] Passed on to Nixon, these recommendations, Kissinger recalled, "fell on fertile" ground."[15] General John P. McConnell, the acting chairman of the JCS in Wheeler's absence, cabled Abrams that "the highest authority" had seen his request, was seriously considering it, and wanted estimates of the number of probable civilian casualties.[16]

Although "the highest authority" told Abrams through McConnell that there was no need for a briefing team to be sent to Washington, Abrams sent one anyway. On February 18 two unnamed colonels from Saigon met with Wheeler, Kissinger, Laird, and the military aides to the presidential assistant and the secretary of defense—Colonels Alexander Haig and Robert Pursley. Abrams's men assured the group that COSVN was headquartered in Base Area 353, but that even if the intelligence were mistaken and COSVN were not present, the base complex held enemy regiments, military hospitals, and large caches of supplies. Because the meeting with Abrams's colonels took place over their morning meal, the operation they were planning against Base Area 353 was given the tasteless code name Breakfast.[17]

Kissinger claimed in *White House Years* that the officers assured him there were no civilians living in the area.[18] In a private memo, he passed this information on to Nixon and urged the attack, commenting that the greatest risks would be military retaliation by Hanoi, Cambodian and Soviet protests, and a public outcry. Supported by advice received at the breakfast meeting, he recommended a delay until the end of March or until there was an enemy provocation: "I advised against an unprovoked bombing of the sanctuaries," he wrote.[19]

These Nixon administration discussions and Kissinger's counsel were reminiscent of the deliberations within Johnson's government in January 1965, which had led to the decision to launch a sustained campaign of bombing against North Vietnam. Its commencement, too, had been postponed until a "provocation" occurred. When the Viet Cong attacked U.S. Army barracks at Pleiku on February 6, the Johnson administration used it as the pretext to order "retaliatory" air strikes against the North. As McGeorge Bundy, Johnson's national security adviser, observed, however, "Pleikus are like streetcars": if you miss one, another will soon come along. In *White House Years* Kissinger wrote that he had advocated a delay in bombing the Cambodian base because he wanted to "give negotiations a chance" and also "seek to maintain public support for our policy." It was a half-truth. It was not true that the Nixon-Kissinger strategy was *either* to bomb *or* to negotiate. To the contrary, their plan was to use "irresistible military pressure" to force the other side into accepting a negotiated settlement favorable to the United States, and they regarded the Cambodian strike as an integral part of that pressure. The postponement was of too short a duration to give the four-party negotiations in Paris a chance to produce a favorable result; in fact, in January and February both Kissinger and Nixon believed the talks would "bog down," taking "several months" to be fruitful.[20] On the other hand, it was true that Nixon and Kissinger wanted to maintain public support for their Vietnam policy, but this wish meant that the bombing, when it came, would be carried out covertly, hidden from the public, or, in case the secret leaked out, under the pretext of retaliation against enemy initiatives.[21]

The operational military plan was being drafted by the time the post-Tet offensive began.[22] As Kissinger confessed in a self-congratulatory yet unintentionally revealing aside, the postponement he recommended was a "classic bureaucratic stalling device," which served the purpose of "easing the pain" of Laird, Rogers, and other advisers who had reservations about this momentous step but were "being overruled."[23] In addition, Nixon was soon to leave on a European trip, visiting heads of state to shore up the NATO alliance and also discuss the prospects for peace in Vietnam. A postponement was prudent. And, of course, public relations strategy called for a provocation.

COSVN'S INTENTIONS

The reality of military initiatives in the waging of this war was that both the Vietnamese and the Americans pursued them as a matter of course. Strategic doctrine on both sides dictated seizing the initiative; strategically, no specific provocations were required. In 1969 the belligerents were convinced that their war aims could be accomplished in negotiations only by shifting the stalemated balance of power in their favor.[24] Nixon reminded his subordinates that American and South Vietnamese military strength and the maintenance of a sufficient level of public support constituted the foundation of successful negotiating.[25] COSVN instructed its cadres that "our actual military and political forces *on the battlefield* will determine the attitude of the enemy at the conference table and the issue of the negotiations."[26] The military offensives of both had the main purpose of strengthening their position by causing attrition among enemy forces and resources, undermining enemy morale, and holding on to territory and populations gained. Obversely, a good offense was the best defense: by seizing the initiative and keeping up the pressure, the other side was put off balance.

One of the strategic advantages COSVN enjoyed and exploited was its ability to influence the rate of casualties through its offensive and defensive initiatives. In its NSSM 1 report the American JCS bemoaned its lack of control over the enemy's casualties: "'The enemy, by the type of action he adopts, has the predominant share in determining . . . [its own] attrition rates.' Three fourths of the battles are at the enemy's choice of time, place, type, and duration."[27] COSVN's predominant control over the strategic and tactical initiative also meant that it influenced the rate of American casualties. Beyond this control, VNLAF forces had increasingly made American soldiers the target of their attacks after 1966, and a major aim of their offensives in 1969 was to inflict casualties on U.S. forces in order to influence home-front opinion in America.[28] Nixon's and Kissinger's worried and angry response to their attacks was in part a reflection of their concern about these casualties, which were reported in front-page news stories about intensified fighting.

The offensive launched by the VNLAF on February 22, which Kissinger self-righteously described as "an act of extraordinary cynicism," but which did not mainly involve North Vietnamese troops or mainly proceed from across the DMZ, followed on the heels of over a dozen American ground operations begun soon after Nixon's inauguration. Many were carried out by battalion- and brigade-sized units, but at least two were division-sized search-and-destroy sweeps. The first, Operation Dewey Canyon, got under way in I Corps on January 22, with the objective of disrupting VNLAF logistics and base areas threatening the city of Hue; the second, Operation Toan Thang 3 ("Total Victory"), began on February 17 in III Corps, as part of a continuing effort since Tet 1968 to maintain pressure on the other side.[29] All of these ground operations were augmented by artillery, helicopter, and aerial attacks, inflicting heavy casualties not only on VNLAF troops but also on civilians. The post-Tet campaign or, as COSVN referred to it, the Phase X spring offensive, was small by comparison. Both MACV and COSVN described it as a "non–all out" campaign.[30] PLAF and PAVN forces attacked 125 targets with sappers and 400 others by shelling, which during March exceeded the artillery barrages of the 1968 Tet offensive. Two attacks were carried out by regiment-sized units, sixteen by battalion-sized units. According to Philip B. Davidson, the chief intelligence officer for General Abrams, all attacks were repulsed, and the offensive had little impact on American operations. Casualties were another matter. Kissinger reported to the president that the enemy had been "able to achieve a relatively high casualty rate among U.S. and South Vietnamese forces while not exposing their own main units"—1,140 American and over 1,500 South Vietnamese soldiers were killed after three weeks of fighting.[31] VNLAF casualties cannot be definitively known, but in this war they were usually greater than U.S. and RVN losses.

COSVN documents indicate that the 1969 Phase X offensive was a prelude to what was to be a larger Phase H summer campaign. Both had the purpose of contributing to "decisive victory," which in the long term was understood as the ultimate goals of "independence, democracy, peace, and neutrality for South Vietnam [leading to] . . . the reunification of the country."[32] Decisive victory in the short term, however, encompassed interim aims: "The Americans must withdraw all troops from South Vietnam; . . . our military and political forces must be stronger than the remaining forces of the puppet army and administration; . . . our . . . forces must be master of the major part of the rural area, the important strategic areas, the areas bordering the cities, and some parts of the cities; . . . and [we must be in a position to] . . . achieve the immediate objectives of the Revolution in the South."[33]

COSVN regarded Phases X and H as continuations of the 1968 Tet or General Offensive and Uprising, which it claimed had achieved a long list of notable successes: inflicting heavy casualties on American forces; frustrating the initial stage of the accelerated pacification program; weakening the Thieu regime and its army; undermining American will and morale on both the war and the home front; cutting short Johnson's presidential career; winning a halt to the bombing of North Vietnam; opening the Paris negotiations; forcing the United States to sit at the table with the NLF; compounding the global economic and strategic crises faced by the United States; and beginning the process of American troop withdrawal.[34] COSVN conceded, however, that the General Offensive of 1968 had fallen short of its most optimistic aims of producing a general uprising in the cities, toppling Thieu's regime, and causing an American withdrawal.[35]

This litany of limited but nonetheless significant gains, while accurate, was intended to bolster the resolve of their own cadres and troops for the struggle ahead, for in addition to exposing deficiencies in command coordination and combat leadership, the fighting in 1968 had undermined the morale and confidence of many cadres and units, who now "overestimate the enemy and underestimate the revolutionary capacities of the masses; therefore, when faced with difficulties, they become skeptical and lack resolution."[36] Victory, COSVN promised, would be "won step by step, bit by bit" by pushing forward on three fronts: political, economic, and military. Specifically, it planned to renew resolve, improve leadership, coordination, and tactics, step up political organizing, counter American propaganda, raise village living conditions, create a Provisional Revolutionary Government (PRG), put forward a peace plan, and press the attack in urban, rural, jungle, and mountain areas.[37] "Flexibility" in meeting "objective" difficulties was to be the guiding principle of the new strategy.[38]

COSVN's pursuit of victory step by step, bit by bit, was a call for protracted war, but the "precept of protractedness" did not mean it intended or wanted to prolong the war. On the contrary, it was to be a flexible, practical response to newly appreciated difficulties and a realistic acknowledgment of the unlikelihood of swift victory. In highlighting past successes, COSVN sought to offer hope for the future, but recognizing obstacles, it needed to lower expectations. Nonetheless, it intended to press the attack as much as possible in order to hasten U.S. troop withdrawals and prevent Nixon from prolonging the war, which would give Vietnamization an opportunity to succeed. "We must" COSVN urged its cadres, *"highly concentrate our efforts to win a decisive victory within a relatively short period of time."*[39]

While many Americans thought of Nixon's strategy as one designed to honorably extricate the United States from South Vietnam as quickly as possible, COSVN viewed it as something quite different. The COSVN's description of American strategy and purpose resembled Nixon's and Kissinger's, except for its reverse perspective, which gave U.S. aims an opposite meaning. Instead of a noble, defensive endeavor to maintain American credibility and global peace, the American war was seen as aggressive and neocolonial, with the aim of preserving America's self-interested global power:

> They will strive to . . . strengthen the puppet army and administration, and . . . maintain . . . U.S. troops at an essential level and for an essential period; . . . go on with their "clear and hold" strategy; . . . strive to hold major strategic positions; . . . accelerate . . . pacification . . . to gain control of the people and territory; seek . . . to weaken our military and political forces; . . . create conditions in which they could gradually withdraw American troops while keeping the puppet troops strong; and on this basis, find a political solution to *end the war while still maintaining neocolonialism in South Vietnam; . . . and in which the U.S. lackeys still keep a strong force and hold advantageous positions to compete with us economically and politically after the war;* to maintain by all means their position in Southeast Asia without affecting the U.S. influence and prestige over the world.[40]

COSVN reminded its cadres and soldiers that if their own offensives were "not sufficiently strong" and "the Americans are able to temporarily overcome part of their difficulties," the war would be prolonged. If their own attacks were strong enough, however, their control of rural and urban areas would be expanded, pacification and Vietnamization would be thwarted, American forces could suffer increasing losses, and the United States "may be *forced to seek an early end to the war* through a political solution which they cannot refuse."[41]

As Nixon suspected, his mettle, the "subjective" factor in these calculations, was indeed a target of COSVN's campaigns. The immediate goal of Phase X was to "force Nixon to reconsider his plan and re-examine the situation." Phase H, coming at the end of Nixon's "honeymoon period," in which he had "freedom to make calculations," would add to his difficulties at a time when he "is under the pressure of various factions."[42] In either eventuality, but "especially in the case of a prolonged de-escalation," COSVN predicted, Nixon "may, in certain circumstances, put pressure on us by threatening to broaden the war through the resumption of bombing in North Vietnam within a definite scope and time limit, or the expansion of the war into Laos and Cambodia."[43]

DECIDING TO BOMB CAMBODIA

The attacks of Phase X began on Saturday, February 22, Washington, D.C., time, the day before Nixon departed for Europe. According to Kissinger, the president was "seething" about the offensive as he read stacks of briefing books in preparation for the journey. "All his instincts were to respond violently." But Nixon was in a quandary. Although wanting to avoid the appearance of passivity—which he felt contradicted his reputation, encouraged the other side, and allowed it to seize the initiative—he hesitated, concerned that bombing Cambodia would provoke antiwar demonstrations in Europe and spoil his goodwill visits with other leaders. For the time being, he settled for a telephone call to Soviet Ambassador Dobrynin, warning of retaliation if the attacks continued.[44]

Still angry during the transatlantic flight on Sunday, Nixon decided while aboard *Air Force One* to order the bombing of Cambodia. Kissinger concurred but advised a forty-eight-hour postponement of the "execute order" because, he argued, a step of this "magnitude" required consultation with "relevant officials" and "a detailed plan for dealing with the consequences."[45] Kissinger wired his military assistant, Alexander Haig, to join him in Belgium and to bring Sitton. Haig was an ardent advocate of bombing; Sitton was the B-52 operations expert who would know how to carry it out secretly.

On Monday morning, February 24, they met with Kissinger and Haldeman on *Air Force One,* parked at the Brussels airport. Kissinger had just returned from a NATO convocation he had attended with Nixon. To avoid attracting attention to the deliberations on the plane, the president had chosen not to be present but instead carried on with his schedule of wreath laying at the Tomb of the Unknown Soldier and lunching with the Belgian king and queen. Later in the day Nixon boarded the plane for the flight to London, near the end of which he came to the briefing room, where the planning session was still in progress, apologized for not having attended, and said that he would discuss the matter with Kissinger. To Sitton this meant that Kissinger's recommendation would carry considerable weight.[46]

With Haldeman looking on during the meeting, Kissinger, Haig, and Sitton developed, as Kissinger put it, "both a military and a diplomatic schedule as well as guidance for briefing the press."[47] In the process, they prepared their scheme of dual reporting, designed to resolve Nixon's and Kissinger's greatest worry: preventing Congress, the press, and the public from learning of the raids and their rationale. This concern had most probably been the true purpose of Sunday's postponement of the execute order.[48]

In their memoirs years later, after the deception was exposed, the president and his assistant maintained that the overriding purpose of secrecy, as Kissinger phrased it, "was to avoid *forcing* the North Vietnamese, Prince Sihanouk of Cambodia, and the Soviets and Chinese into public reactions they might not be eager to make."[49] He meant that Hanoi might be impelled to retaliate militarily and also break off the Paris negotiations; Sihanouk would feel the need to tilt diplomatically toward Hanoi and oppose the bombing, which Nixon and Kissinger claimed would run counter to his private endorsement; and the Soviets and Chinese would also have to oppose the raids, which would complicate America's global diplomacy.[50]

This reasoning did make some sense—but only to minds that followed Byzantine paths and were obsessed with secrecy for the control it appeared to give them over the rest of the government and the course of events, as well as its putative value for their Vietnam plan of action. It did not make sense in other ways. Concerning the Paris negotiations, the bombing was, after all, supposed to influence them favorably: "The state of play in Paris is completely sterile," Nixon told Rogers and Laird. "I am convinced that the only way to move the negotiations off dead center is to do something on the military front. That is something they will understand."[51] Should Hanoi retaliate militarily and cancel the talks, it would mean the bombing had failed.

But if Nixon and Kissinger doubted the efficacy of their own actions, why then order the raids and risk both military and diplomatic failure? Concerning Sihanouk, it was apparently true that he was unhappy about the Vietnamese presence in his country and had indirectly indicated that he would not protest Americans' "hot pursuit" of VNLAF forces or air raids against the bases. But these were the vague hints of a leader forced to sail his ship of state along a hazardous diplomatic course between the rock of Vietnamese bases and the whirlpool of American counteractions. No one has yet deciphered what Sihanouk really thought, but it is not likely that he welcomed large-scale invasions or sustained B-52 raids, which would plunge his country into chaos. The fact remains that he was not officially asked for permission to bomb; nor did he give it. Kissinger would praise the attention Nixon's government gave to legal niceties about whether the enemy offensive violated a prior agreement, but there was little concern for the moral, constitutional, or international legal implications of bombing a neutral country with B-52s.[52] Despite their public explanations, Nixon and Kissinger expected that there would be North Vietnamese and Cambodian protests, and thus they had prepared their cover story of "retaliation" and developed a procedure for diverting the press.[53] Had Hanoi or Phnom Penh complained, the Soviets and Chinese also may have been compelled to object publicly or privately, but that was a risk they were willing to accept.

Their elaborate, implausible account of the need for secrecy was both a reflection of their habits of intrigue and, coming in the postwar, postdisclosure years, their cover story. Nixon's true concern, or at least his primary reason for secrecy, was to prevent the American people, and particularly the antiwar movement in the streets, universities, press, and Congress, from learning of the raids: "My administration was only two months old," Nixon wrote, "and I wanted to provoke as little public outcry as possible at the outset."[54] They were more concerned about awakening "the dormant beast of public protest," as Kissinger phrased it, than about the constitutional requirement to obtain permission from Congress to make war on another country. Had Nixon consulted Congress or the public before acting, there would have been an uproar. Had there been public disclosure after the initial raid, he might have had to call off subsequent bombings, thus undermining his purpose, which was to send a signal to the other side of his irrational willingness and ability to escalate the war—to demonstrate that he would not be and could not be constrained by domestic opposition.

Neither Laird nor Rogers was initially privy to the decision made on board *Air Force One*. Even though Rogers was on the plane, Nixon informed him later in London, giving the secretary of state, Kissinger boasted, only "a cryptic account of his thinking but no details."[55] It was not Nixon or Kissinger but Haig who, on his return to Washington, briefed Laird. The secretary of defense supported the idea of bombing Cambodia but doubted that it could be kept secret, warned that the attempt to do so could backfire, and argued that if the bombing of COSVN was a legitimate target, it probably could be defended publicly.[56] In the least, he advised delay until the provocation would be clearer.

Nixon postponed the raid once more, not, apparently, because of Laird's objections, however, but because of Rogers's concerns about the impact on the Paris talks, concerns that compounded the president's worry that "a leak of plans to bomb Cambodia may have triggered serious antiwar demonstrations abroad."[57] About the cancellation, Haldeman noted in his diary: "It has had to be called off because State will not accept responsibility, and risk otherwise is too great. K very disappointed."[58]

Nixon returned to Washington on March 2, but he continued to be buffeted by conflicting advice. Laird straddled the fence between support for military retaliation and concern about public and congressional reaction. Rogers persevered in advising postponement. The JCS advocated air strikes against both Cambodia and North Vietnam. Kissinger used their proposal for attacking North Vietnam as a foil to encourage Nixon to order the Cambodian operation because he knew Nixon wanted to do "something." The president was frustrated, impatient, and angry; moreover, the bombing of Cambodia was an integral part of his military and diplomatic strategy. It had to get under way soon in order to back up warnings they had already sent through the Soviets and before they held direct, private talks with Hanoi—but also as a psychological warfare counter to troop withdrawals, which were being discussed publicly and would begin in 1969.

At a press conference on March 4, Nixon delivered several public warnings to Hanoi and Moscow as he answered questions about events in Vietnam and relations with the Soviet Union. In response to one, in which the reporter asked whether he considered the bombing of North Vietnam to be an appropriate response, Nixon answered: "I will only say . . . we have several contingency plans that can be put into effect. I am considering all of those plans. . . . We will not tolerate a continuation of this kind of attack without some response that will be appropriate."[59] Although promising at one point that he would explain the option he selected to the American people, he said at another moment that he would not: "I will not indicate [my decision] in advance, and I am not going to indicate [it] publicly."[60] On the same day Nixon ordered an air strike against the Cambodian bases for March 9, only to postpone it again at the last moment because of Rogers's objections and persistent concern about press reaction should the secret leak. Deputy Secretary of Defense David Packard was "very disturbed" about the cancellation, and Kissinger thought it was better to be "clobbered now" by the "establishment press" than to extend the delay.[61]

Press, public, and congressional opinion about the war continued to be poised between those who criticized Nixon for stepping up the war and those who urged escalation. Now, however, there was growing sentiment for retaliation against the enemy offensive, which was causing American casualties and testing the patience of the president of the United States. At another press conference on March 14, reporters pressed the president repeatedly about what he would do in response to the attacks. Nixon now seemed closer to a firm decision: "You may recall that on March 4, when I received a similar question, . . . I issued what was interpreted widely as a warning. It will be my policy as president to issue a warning only once, and I will not repeat it now. Anything in the future that is done will be done. There will be no additional warning."[62] When on the following day the VNLAF fired five rockets into Saigon, Nixon's frustration exceeded its bounds, or he now felt he had a clear provocation, or he thought public opinion was prepared for retaliation. He phoned Kissinger to order the attack: "State is to be notified only after the point of no return. . . . The order is not appealable."[63]

Yet there was to be one more discussion of the Cambodian bombing. After church services on Sunday, March 16, Nixon met with Kissinger, Rogers, Laird, and Wheeler in the Oval Office. Kissinger claimed in his memoirs that he had recommended the meeting to Nixon, arguing that "such a decision should not be taken without giving his senior advisers an opportunity to express their views—if only to protect himself if it led to a public uproar." In any case, it would take at least twenty-four hours for the bombing order to be executed. But Kissinger probably had an additional motive: to expose those who disagreed with the president, alienating Nixon from them. Kissinger had already learned enough about Nixon to know that when he arrived at a firm decision, as he now had about this matter, he nonetheless wanted to pretend that the issue was still open until his advisers voiced their opinion. Such sessions "led to hours of the very discussion that he found so distasteful," Kissinger wrote, "and that reinforced his tendency to exclude the recalcitrants from further deliberations." Kissinger's main target was Rogers, the only one of the group who persisted in objecting to the raid, and who as secretary of state was the main threat to Kissinger's growing influence over foreign policy. Just one week before this Oval

Office meeting, Kissinger had accused Rogers of "self-interest . . . so paramount that he can't adequately serve the P." He had recommended that Rogers be fired and made chief justice of the Supreme Court. Kissinger was already seen within Nixon's inner circle as the czar of foreign policy, but his control was not yet solidified. It was also his nature to be obsessively insecure.[64]

BREAKFAST

As controllers in their radar hootches on the ground in South Vietnam radioed countdowns to the bombardiers at 30,000 feet in the air over Cambodia, sixty B-52s flying in twenty "cell" formations of three bombers each released their strings of bombs into the night upon Base Area 353 in the "Fish Hook" region of Cambodia. In the jungle below, the thirty-ton payloads of each of the black-bellied planes erupted in a "box" pattern one-half mile wide by two miles long.[65] An NLF official who survived a similar raid one year later described his experience:

> We were awakened by the . . . thunder. . . . The concussive *whump-whump-whump* came closer and closer, moving in a direct line toward our positions. Then, as the cataclysm walked in on us, every one hugged the earth—some screaming quietly, others struggling to suppress attacks of violent, involuntary trembling. Around us the ground began to heave spasmodically, and we were engulfed in a monstrous roar. Then, abruptly, it stopped, leaving behind it nearly a hundred dazed Maquis [VNLAF soldiers], shaking their heads in an attempt to clear the pressure from their ears. The last of the bomb craters had opened up less than a kilometer away. . . . Miraculously, no one had been hurt.[66]

At the White House it was 2:00 P.M. on March 17 when the operation "came off"—a "historic day," Haldeman noted in his diary. Nixon and Kissinger were "really excited." Kissinger returned the next day "beaming." B-52 crews had reported secondary explosions, which implied that ammunition and fuel depots had been destroyed—"a lot more than had been expected." The raid was judged "very productive, . . . a great success."[67] Subsequent analysis revealed, however, that the crews were mistaken about the number of secondary explosions. Moreover, COSVN had not been destroyed, and the raid—for all the terrible sound and fury wreaked upon earth and people—had been, as one Green Beret officer put it, the same as poking a beehive the size of a basketball with a stick.[68] A top secret Daniel Boone Special Forces unit sent into the area to mop up was, in the words of one member, "slaughtered" by the VNLAF. Ordered to follow, a second unit mutinied.[69]

Breakfast would be succeeded by Lunch, Snack, Dinner, and Dessert, collectively known as Menu. In a period of fourteen months, from the first raids in March 1969 to May 1970, 3,825 B-52 sorties dropped 103,921 tons of bombs on six of the seventeen border base camps. Even when Menu ended, the bombing of

Cambodia continued, but now farther into the interior. By March 1973, B-52s had delivered 212,678 tons of bombs upon the formerly neutral country, helping turn it into a killing field.[70]

Nixon recorded in *RN* that Operation Breakfast "was the first turning point in my administration's conduct of the Vietnam War."[71] Originally proposed by MACV as the logical next step in military strategy—the destruction of enemy troop concentrations, the interdiction of supply lines, a deterrent against attack, a counterweight to the impending withdrawal of American troops—the bombing of Cambodian sanctuaries had been transformed by Nixon into a demonstration of his will. He had challenged the Hanoi Politburo, overcome the Department of State bureaucracy, and bypassed Congress and the citizenry. Because the renewal of bombing against North Vietnam seemed politically impossible in January and February, Nixon and Kissinger found in Cambodia a target of opportunity, one which at least half of the national security bureaucracy believed contained viable military targets, and one which, having previously been off-limits, they hoped would also serve to lever the Politburo in Hanoi into making diplomatic concessions. As Kissinger explained to his NSC aide for East Asia, Richard L. Sneider, who doubted the military value of bombing the bases and scoffed at the likelihood of destroying COSVN, military usefulness was secondary to the psychological principle of "always keeping the enemy guessing," which was, of course, Nixon's madman theory.[72]

After interviewing contacts in the Pentagon, William Beecher—the *New York Times* correspondent who within weeks of Breakfast broke the story of the bombings—learned that one of the "principal factors" underlying the air strikes was "to signal Hanoi that the Nixon administration, while pressing for peace in Paris, is willing to take some military risks avoided by the previous Administration . . . to demonstrate that the Nixon Administration is different and 'tougher.'"[73] Although there was little press follow-up to[74] and apparently little public interest in Beecher's story, the White House inner circle became even more obsessed with leaks, leading them to wiretap NSC aides. By 1973, after the raids had been uncovered,[75] they and the wiretaps would meld into the scandal publicly known as Watergate.

Nixon and Kissinger's determination to bomb Cambodia did not result primarily from a desire to strike a military blow against COSVN and enemy logistics routes or to stop an enemy offensive in order to save American lives. Breakfast was an offensive, military-diplomatic initiative followed by subsequent Menu raids. Military purposes and diplomatic signals were combined in other escalations through Indochina. B-52s and fighter-bombers no longer permitted to strike North Vietnam after Johnson's October 31 bombing halt were diverted to neighboring Laos, where they augmented preexisting air campaigns against villages and Communist military units in the Plain of Jars and against the complex of logistics highways and jungle paths known as the Ho Chi Minh Trail. During 1969 the number of combat sorties in Laos increased by 60 percent over 1968. Between

January 20, 1969, and May 1, 1970, tactical aircraft dropped 476,571 tons of bombs on Laos; B-52s dropped 244,586 tons. American planes pounded South Vietnam even more heavily than in the past. B-52 sorties increased threefold over the rate in 1967, from 1,000 to 3,000 sorties. Compared with the period 1965 through 1968, the total expenditure of munitions deployed by airpower across all of Indochina from the beginning of 1969 through 1972 increased dramatically, from 3,190,458 to 4,213,073 tons, even though the number of combat sorties declined, from 1,765,000 to 1,687,000. A sharp rise in B-52 sorties accounted for the rise in tonnage dropped: from 36,809 in Johnson's final term as president to 75,539 in Nixon's first term.[76]

Airpower was Nixon's primary war-making weapon—a weapon not only possessing military value to the fighting on the ground but also, because of its expanded use throughout the rest of Indochina, having diplomatic value as a credible offensive threat of dramatic escalation against North Vietnam in the future. Nixon hoped that airpower would constitute the decisive element in his multi-pronged strategy to win the peace. In the language of the RAND study of December 1968, the president, like Group A, wanted a "negotiated victory," not, like Group B, a "compromise settlement." To achieve it, he hoped to combine a patchwork of options proposed by Groups A and B, which ironically also included a modified version of alternative C—the unilateral, albeit gradual, withdrawal of U.S. troops. The ground war in South Vietnam would not be expanded to pre-Tet 1968 levels. It would be continued at its current level for as long as possible, while pacification was intensified, Vietnamization expanded, and the option of limited land campaigns into Cambodia and Laos kept open. The Soviets would be prevailed upon to put pressure on the North Vietnamese to make diplomatic concessions, and the administration would deliver tacit and explicit threats of unrestricted bombing against the North through the Soviets and by means of its bombings in Cambodia and Laos.

DE-AMERICANIZATION/VIETNAMIZATION

On March 13, three days before his final decision to proceed with Breakfast, President Nixon met with Secretary of Defense Laird to receive his recommendations for the withdrawal of American troops from South Vietnam.[77] Laird had just returned with General Wheeler from Saigon, where they had discussed the matter with General Abrams and his MACV staff. Although commanders in South Vietnam for the past year had expected troop withdrawals, they had not received specific guidance from Washington and consequently had not begun to plan for them. They assumed that reductions would take place as part of a negotiated mutual withdrawal of American and North Vietnamese forces. In lieu of an agreement, Abrams argued that American withdrawals would be feasible only if three "indicators" were favorable: progress in pacification, improvements in the RVNAF, and a lessening of the enemy threat.[78] While approving these conditions in principle, Laird put greater priority on the political need to make plans for withdrawals before Nixon's honeymoon period expired—"before the time given to the new Administration runs out," he told Abrams, "be it three, six, or nine months, but probably with[in] the next three or four months."[79]

Laird was not a dove, and he favored stronger military measures than had been employed in the past, but he was an astute observer of home-front political winds, and because of the direction in which they were blowing, he knew that most of the hawkish options floated in Washington and Saigon would not fly. He had therefore come to believe that military victory in South Vietnam was unlikely. At best, Nixon's plan of action would bring about a negotiated mutual withdrawal, while Vietnamization would enable South Vietnamese forces to take the place of the Americans who were leaving. He was dissatisfied, however, with the doctrinal "orientation" of MACV, which had the effect of putting more emphasis on military operations than on preparing the South Vietnamese to fight alone. He was also skeptical of the possibility of rapid progress in the negotiations. With these considerations in mind, he was determined to initiate the process of American troop reductions independently of Kissinger's negotiations and Abrams's conditions.[80] The secretary of defense's policy amounted to a gradual but unilateral withdrawal, an option no one in the government had advocated in 1968.[81]

In his report to Nixon of March 13, Laird recommended withdrawing 50,000 to 70,000 American troops in 1969 and the drafting of a long-range, comprehensive plan as soon as possible. Nixon did not immediately approve the recommendation, but it is unclear whether this meant he was uncertain about the matter or simply biding his time before ordering its execution. When asked at a press conference the next day about rumors of forthcoming withdrawals, the president responded that "in view of the current offensive on the part of the North Vietnamese and the Vietcong, there is no prospect for a reduction of American forces in the foreseeable future."[82] He then cited three conditions that would have to be met before withdrawals took place; these were worded differently than Abrams's conditions, but they were similar: "the ability of the South Vietnamese to defend themselves" where Americans are now defending them; progress in the negotiations; and the level of the enemy threat. He was dissembling, however, for at that moment he was preparing to give the order for withdrawals before any of these conditions had been met.

As with other elements in his plan of action for an honorable exit, Nixon had been pondering the matter of troop reductions for a long time—ever since the campaign and especially during the transition period. He had brought it up for discussion at his first NSC meeting of January 25, during which both he and Laird, according to Kissinger's account, "kept their counsel," an act of discretion that usually meant Nixon was already committed to a particular course of action.[83] Two weeks after receiving Laird's report, the president discussed troop withdrawals at another NSC meeting on March 28, in which the policy seemed a foregone conclusion. It was at this meeting that Abrams assured the group—despite his real doubts—that the RVNAF's performance had improved substantially; it was also the occasion on which Nixon praised Laird's political subterfuge of substituting the title "Vietnamization" for "de-Americanization."[84] On April 10 Kissinger, with Nixon's approval, issued NSSM 36, which ordered Laird to prepare specific alternative timetables for Vietnamization that would result in "the progressive transfer . . . of the fighting effort" from U.S. armed forces to RVN armed forces, leaving only a support and advisory mission in place at the end of the process.[85]

While the withdrawals were to be unilateral, their pace would depend on circumstances. NSSM 36 was a contingency plan. Troop reductions were to begin on July 1, 1969, with options to complete them in December 1970, June 1971, December 1971, or December 1972. Unfavorable contingencies, such as lack of progress in Nixon's and Abrams's three conditions, could prolong the process of withdrawal into the next presidential campaign.[86] As it turned out, they did, but in the beginning the president did not expect they would. He believed he could end the war before the year was over, for despite the initial withdrawals he was confident in the coercive parts of his plan.

That the order to prepare a specific, comprehensive plan was not given before April 10 was probably less the product of Nixon's ambivalence and more the result of his having had to consult relevant officials, persuade reluctant agencies, draft studies and orders, and prepare Thieu, with whom he scheduled a meeting for June. Nixon was as sensitive as Laird to political winds, and the withdrawal of troops was part of the home-front battle to win support for his Vietnam policies.

"ANOTHER PROJECT"

Nixon and Kissinger had apparently believed as early as the first week of March that their plan of action—as they envisioned it at the time—had more or less been set into motion. They had explained the principle of linkage to Dobrynin; they had begun to play the China card; MACV was pushing forward with its ground operations in South Vietnam; Laird was about to make his recommendations for Vietnamization; Lodge was soon to begin direct, private talks with the DRV in Paris; and they had chosen Cambodia as a target of opportunity.

Inevitably and soon, however, things began to go wrong. Secretary of State Rogers met with Dobrynin on March 8 and, according to Kissinger's view of things, "unilaterally abrogated the two-track approach of separating military and political issues."[87] Rogers, Kissinger claimed, had proposed to begin immediate private talks with the DRV on both political and military matters. This, Haldeman noted, put Kissinger "in *great* distress," leading him to telephone the White House the next day and complain that "Rogers had reversed United States policy." Rogers's "stance" implied, Kissinger said, that the United States was not "fully backing the Thieu government." With this "disastrous" diplomatic error, Rogers had created the conditions for the eventual "destruction" of the Saigon regime and also given away the administration's "chance" of taking a "hard line" with the Soviets and North Vietnamese. At the White House on March 10, Kissinger continued to rail against Rogers: "In reversing our policy about private talks with North Vietnam about political matters as well as military, [he] has seriously jeopardized our negotiating ability and our chance to end the war[,] especially . . . because it follows right on their shelling of Saigon, and at a time when [the] Soviets are in trouble with China at the border."

This was also a moment when Rogers was expressing reservations about the prospective bombing of Cambodia—which led to the cancellation of the strike scheduled for that day—and a time when Kissinger believed the secretary of state was challenging his control of foreign policy. Kissinger was so "upset" that he threatened to resign if Roger's policy prevailed, but he indicated to Nixon that he preferred that Rogers be kicked upstairs to the Supreme Court.

Haldeman suggested that Kissinger try to turn the whole thing to their "advantage by a maneuver designed to totally confuse the Soviets." Kissinger, not unexpectedly, replied that it might be possible to do this.[88] What Haldeman specifically recommended is unknown, but the immediate remedy taken by Nixon was to order Kissinger to tell Dobrynin on March 11 that "the Soviet impression of a change in the U.S. position was 'premature.'" Three days later, on the day of Nixon's press conference, Kissinger "explained delicately" to Rogers that U.S. policy was to begin bilateral talks first with Hanoi, but to include Saigon and the NLF only later. Rogers replied that he was "very anxious" to start serious negotiations.[89] Three more days later, Nixon made the decision to go ahead with Breakfast.

Nonetheless, Kissinger wrote in *White House Years* that he "concluded that time was working against us and that we should find some means of bringing matters to a head. I sought to involve the USSR in a complex maneuver and recommended Cyrus Vance as the ideal man for the mission."[90] He began to plan the maneuver at least as early as March 18, the day he met with Vance to discuss it. Agreeing that a move had to be made, Nixon approved it after several discussions of project details between April 5 and 11.[91]

Referring to this development in his diary entry of Monday April 14, Haldeman noted that Kissinger was "about to launch another project." It had "started last Friday" when Nixon decided to proceed with a "program of mining Haiphong to look tough." The "program" was both diplomatic and military. In his meeting that Monday night with Dobrynin, Kissinger was "to say we'll take only one more try at [a] settlement, [and] then [we will] have to move. [We are] putting a two-month deadline on results. . . . K [was] very impressed with P's guts in making this hard decision."[92]

The previous attempts at a settlement to which he referred were probably the other discussions held with Dobrynin. The new effort was to be their first attempt at establishing a secret contact with the DRV—one separate from the Paris negotiations.[93] To arrive at a Vietnam agreement, Vance was to be authorized to undertake a "mission to Moscow," where he would begin talks with the Soviets on the Middle East and strategic arms limitation and, linking these with Vietnam, also meet secretly with a "senior North Vietnamese representative." In these latter discussions he would be empowered to negotiate both political and military issues, which was a radical departure from the previous two-track strategy, but one that Kissinger believed Rogers had compromised. When Kissinger broached the Moscow idea with Vance, he omitted telling him that the administration would force a "military showdown" with Hanoi if the mission failed.[94]

Kissinger claimed in his memoirs that Nixon expressed doubts that the "Vance ploy" would work, but he did not explain which part of the ploy the president questioned—linkage, military escalation against North Vietnam, or sending Vance on a mission. Since Nixon was the originator of the linkage concept and had written to Premier Kosygin on March 26 reiterating the points he had explained to Dobrynin in their conversation on February 17, it is doubtful that his reservations concerned this aspect of Kissinger's new project.[95] It is also unlikely that he was dubious about the value of making military threats against North Vietnam, for this too was a Nixonian concept, and the president had already told Kissinger that he was prepared to take "tough escalatory steps" if the Vance mission failed.[96] Perhaps he thought that the military measures would have to be carried out before Hanoi would cave in. Or perhaps the president doubted the efficacy or wisdom of sending a third person to Moscow—in this case an eastern-Establishment corporate lawyer who had served in diplomatic roles for the Johnson administration. In any event, in a subsequent exchange with Kissinger, Nixon extended the escalation deadline from six weeks to two months and added economic cooperation with the Soviets to the list of Vance's bargaining points.[97]

The Vance ploy seems to have been one of those cases wherein a specific maneuver was invented and decided upon in the context of madman assumptions, the nature of the complex personal relationship between Nixon and Kissinger, and the vicissitudes of war and politics. It was a proactive coercive stratagem, on the one hand, but on the other it was also a reactive remedy for their frustration—and in between, it may have been another bid by Kissinger to ingratiate himself with Nixon.

Senator Barry Goldwater, who spoke with Nixon sometime during this critical period of mid-March to mid-April, provided some evidence of Nixon's sense of feeling entangled in a web of conflicting constraints and goals but holding on to violent escalation as a way to avoid becoming ensnared:

I asked President Nixon how long he intended to continue the bombing halt. . . . Nixon said he intended to give the peace effort at least six months. He didn't think the American public would stand for an all-out military assault on North Vietnam. He said he was in a no-win situation. He told me that Secretary of Defense Laird, who had just returned from Saigon, was hopeful we could soon commence withdrawal of American troops and substitute South Vietnamese replacements. If this didn't work, if no progress were made in Paris, he would then, perhaps, have to order a resumption of bombing [against North Vietnam].[98]

Whatever the true origins of the scheme, Kissinger met with Dobrynin on the night of April 14. To prove he and Nixon were in sync, Kissinger resorted to a technique he often used with Dobrynin: showing him a memo he had previously written to Nixon and on which the president had made marginal notations. Kissinger also presented Dobrynin with a three-point statement addressed to him and initialed by the president. In point one Nixon reiterated "his conviction that a just peace is achievable." In point two Nixon stated his willingness "to explore avenues other than the existing negotiating framework," including direct meetings between U.S. and DRV negotiators to "discuss general principles of a settlement," with the technical details to be worked out in Paris. In closing, he expressed the conviction "that all parties are at a crossroads and that extraordinary measures are called for."[99] Kissinger drove this point home by warning Dobrynin that unless there was a Vietnam settlement, "we might take measures that would create 'a complicated situation.'"[100] He probably did not specify the measures they had in mind: blockading the DRV by mining its ports, halting troop withdrawals, and bombing rail lines from China.[101]

According to Kissinger's account, Dobrynin took serious note of his references to linkage, repeated the Soviet rejection of the principle, and argued that this American policy could only serve Chinese interests. His parting remark was to say that their conversation was "very important." Kissinger further claimed that no official reply "was ever received from Moscow" and that, even after the war, he remained in the dark about whether his message was ever conveyed to Hanoi.[102]

Soviet documents prove that the message was sent to Hanoi, and that Premier Pham Van Dong responded to Moscow on May 5, saying that the issues Kissinger raised could better be settled at the Paris negotiations than in a special mission. There is yet no evidence that the Soviets passed this reply on to Nixon. But their records do establish that Moscow told Washington that its rejection of Hanoi's terms—a coalition government for South Vietnam and the unilateral withdrawal of American troops—precluded Soviet diplomatic assistance.[103] On May 27, in a related communication, Kosygin replied to Nixon's letter of March 26, rejecting linkage and repeating the Soviet position that each problem between the United States and the USSR should be resolved on its own merits.

It seems that Moscow and Hanoi looked at the card Washington played and then sloughed it off. Kissinger's account of their alleged nonresponse may have been an attempt to make them appear intransigent or to cover up the failure of their ploy. Nixon's and Kissinger's manful threats—which were at the core of their gambit—had backfired, for Moscow and Hanoi could afford to appear no less courageous and resolute than Washington. Despite these uncooperative responses, however, Nixon and Kissinger persisted in their strategy of coercion and linkage. Referring to Kosygin's letter, Kissinger wrote: "We decided not to argue the point; we would simply continue our approach in practice."[104]

Meanwhile, in order to lend credibility to their threat of a major showdown with North Vietnam, it appears they intended "to look tough" by mining the harbor of Haiphong before the two-month deadline expired and the other military steps were taken.[105] But no sooner had Nixon and Kissinger decided on the Vance ploy and the Haiphong mining than their plans were overtaken by another event.

At 11:50 P.M. on April 14, the very night Kissinger met with Dobrynin, North Korean MiGs shot down a U.S. Navy EC-121 reconnaissance plane with a thirty-one-man crew aboard. It had been flying a "routine spy mission" forty-eight miles off the coast of North Korea. Both Nixon and Kissinger referred to the incident in their memoirs as the first major crisis of the administration. Both believed that it presented a challenge to the credibility of their will and ability to meet force with force.[106] On the following day, backed up by his staff, particularly Morton Halperin, Kissinger recommended the bombing of the airfield whence the MiGs came. Nixon agreed, thinking "we need to show [a] strong reaction."

The Haiphong operation, however, was "temporarily . . . louse[d] up," Kissinger complained, because if carried out "it would look like [a] reaction to" the North Korean shootdown.[107] The most important plan considered over the next few days was to bomb the North Korean MiG airfield as soon as possible, then "move in four carriers, plus a lot of other strength." It would be dangerous, Nixon and Kissinger thought, but it would "back up K's earlier conversation [with Dobrynin] this week" and be "potentially very productive toward ending the Vietnam War."[108]

At an NSC meeting on April 16, however, Laird, Rogers, and Wheeler opposed the air strike, raising several objections: the fight with North Korea could escalate into another Asian ground war; suitable forces were not ready; there might be adverse domestic and world reaction, which would end Nixon's honeymoon with the public. Kissinger continued to argue not only that the administration was being tested but also that a tough move would serve the purposes of the madman theory, particularly with regard to Vietnam: "If we strike back . . . they will say, 'This guy is becoming irrational—and we'd better settle with him.' "[109] After the NSC meeting Kissinger consulted with Haldeman and Ehrlichman about possible domestic reactions to an air strike against the MiG base. Ehrlichman asked, "What if they knock out something of ours?"

"Then it could escalate." Kissinger replied.

"How far?"

"Well, it could go nuclear."[110]

Nixon's choices came down to three "viable alternatives": bomb the airfield; do not bomb the airfield, but continue the reconnaissance flights with fighter escorts; or "do nothing but protest." The president continued to believe, with Kissinger, that he had "to retaliate in some fairly strong fashion." On Thursday,

April 17, Haldeman's "bet" was that they would go through with the air strike at noon on Monday.

Nixon, however, began to vacillate. As he weighed the risks, he lapsed into a typical Nixonian pattern: rambling "introspective rumination"[111] in the presence of a confidant, in this case Haldeman. The president commented, in agreement with Kissinger's thesis, that a strong presidential act was necessary to "galvanize people into overcoming slothfulness and detachment arising from general moral decay," but he expressed disquiet that all of his advisers except Kissinger were opposed to the air strike. He was also worried about the risk of another war and concerned that the public would not "buy" it. On the other hand, he consoled himself with the thought that because the public reaction to the incident had been mild, it seemed they did not "expect hard retaliation." Haldeman now noted: "K feels this was ideal time and place, P concerned that it's not."[112]

Kissinger was the "principal proponent" of military retaliation, but with the president wavering, he no longer felt comfortable in the role. On Friday he announced that he had changed his mind, telling Nixon that "he's determined to make a big positive move, but *not* convinced this is the best time and place for *us*."[113] He knew that "if we don't retaliate in Korea we'll have to either find another similar incident in three to four weeks, or go with Operation Lunch," the second phase of Menu. On Saturday, April 19, Nixon made his decision, which was to cancel the Korean operation and approve Lunch.

Both Nixon and Kissinger blamed the president's other advisers for causing them to fail the test of decisiveness presented by the shootdown. The president accused Ehrlichman, for example, of having "sold out to the doves too."[114] Nixon's reaction was to withdraw even more into himself, determined to make future decisions alone, or only with Kissinger. Taking advantage of the president's mood, Kissinger strengthened his control over the advisory process by forming a new committee called the Washington Special Action Group (WSAG), consisting of the second-ranking officers from the other national security agencies, which he would chair.

"IF IN DOUBT WE BOMB CAMBODIA"

Three weeks after the decision to proceed with Operation Lunch, Cambodia for a third time became the receptacle of Nixon's and Kissinger's opportunistic fury. On May 11 Nixon, Kissinger, and other aides were on board the top secret Airborne Command Post jet, returning to Washington from Key Biscayne. During the flight they were put through a nuclear test exercise, which Haldeman described as "pretty scary," yet they were fascinated with the command-room display boards and communications equipment. Nixon became "quite interested," asking "a lot of questions about nuclear capability and kill results," leading Haldeman to infer that he worried "about the lightly tossed-about millions of deaths."[115] During another part of the journey, Nixon read a report on nuclear operations plans—possibly NSSM 3, which he and Kissinger had ordered the day following the inauguration and which had been completed on May 8. One of this study's findings was that the Single Integrated Operational [Nuclear War] Plan contained no flexible, limited options in its massive attack scenarios. The authors, however, included an argument in their summary papers supporting the development of nuclear plans and capabilities to target U.S. forces more flexibly and selectively.[116]

A few of the president's scribbled notes on three pages of his ever-present yellow legal tablet have been declassified, but their meaning remains intriguingly obscure: "These plans are a disgrace. They really have no options outside these in last, because if you use the force separately the SIOP becomes impossible. If in doubt we bomb Cambodia."[117]

In the game of chess the phrase is "If in doubt, move a pawn." Had they been looking for contingency plans that would allow them in present or future contingencies to flexibly employ nuclear weapons somewhere, anywhere, in order to impress the Soviets? Had they been considering "limited" nuclear strikes against North Vietnam? Perhaps neither of the above, but about what were they in doubt?

8

NIXON'S WAR: 1969

This does make it his war.
—H. R. Haldeman[1]

"VIETNAM PLANS AREN'T WORKING OUT RIGHT"

Before boarding the Airborne Command Post, Nixon had been "preoccupied" with making arrangements for a "peace plan announcement." Kissinger was "stirred up," Haldeman noted, "because he thinks Hanoi may be folding; [he] has some feelers." What feelers Kissinger had in mind is unknown. Haldeman's notes are silent on the details, and neither Kissinger nor Nixon mentioned them in their memoirs. Perhaps Kissinger was engaging in the usual wishful thinking or boosterism.

The decision to make a public peace proposal was, however, primarily a response to moves by the other side. On April 25 Xuan Thuy had remarked: "If the Nixon Administration has a great peace program, as it makes believe, why doesn't it make that program public?" Kissinger claimed that he then urged the president to publicly "elaborate a clear-cut position of our own." Nixon listened but decided to delay, hoping for a response to the Vance-Dobrynin gambit—only to be disappointed.[2] In the interim, on May 8 the NLF delegation announced its Ten-Point Overall Solution, which was consistent with previous positions articulated by the DRV and NLF but provided more concrete proposals on a number of key issues, including U.S. withdrawal, the formation of a coalition government, and the release of prisoners of war. Kissinger regarded the proposal as "one-sided in content and insolent in tone,"[3] yet it received a great deal of attention in the United States, causing Nixon "to take the initiative once again" by detailing his "first comprehensive peace plan" in a televised appearance on Wednesday, May 14.[4]

The president and his assistant considered the main significance of their eight-point proposal to be its call for the simultaneous withdrawal of U.S. and DRV troops within a twelve-month period, which was, Kissinger claimed, a "quantum advance" beyond Johnson's 1966 Manila formula (the withdrawal of all DRV troops six months before "residual" U.S. troops were out). Nixon also made gestures toward the NLF's ten-point proposal by accepting the right of South Vietnam to be neutral, welcoming the full participation of all political elements of South Vietnam in its political life, opening the door to a coalition government and national unification, renouncing any U.S. intention of maintaining permanent bases or ties in Vietnam, and accepting the unification of the country (but only after a period of five years).[5]

Kissinger was initially encouraged by the response of the DRV/NLF delegations, writing a memo to Nixon saying that the "Communist presentations" at the May 22 plenary session in Paris indicated that they were interested in hearing "further elaborations or modifications" of the U.S. position. Unsurprisingly, he took this apparent interest by the other side to be an opportunity for tactical finessing: "There would appear to be considerable room for the U.S. to tailor a response at the next plenary meeting to the specific points made yesterday by the Communists in an effort to advance the process of movement by the other side."[6]

But the other side was not so easily seduced. Although Xuan Thuy acknowledged "points of agreement," Nixon's proposal still retained the old U.S. demand for the mutual withdrawal of U.S. and DRV forces. In addition, it conditioned the participation of the NLF in South Vietnam's politics on its abandonment of "the use of force," while leaving Thieu's regime in power; and it put the supervision of postwithdrawal elections in the hands of an "international" body, which was inconsistent with the NLF's rejection of "foreign interference."[7] At a private DRV-U.S. meeting between Le Duc Tho and Henry Cabot Lodge and their deputies on May 31, both sides reiterated their customary terms. The United States called for mutual withdrawal of "non-South Vietnamese" forces and the two-track procedure of separating political and military negotiations; the DRV insisted on the ten-point proposal, unconditional withdrawal, and exclusion of the Thieu regime.[8] Kissinger soon became frustrated by the "labored pace" of the Paris negotiations.[9]

Nixon and Kissinger were disappointed as well in home-front reaction to the peace plan announcement. Elated after his speech on Wednesday, May 14, Nixon had become dejected by Sunday after hearing and reading press comments, which he felt were either neutral or negative. If JFK had made the speech, he thought, "they would have been ecstatic."[10] For reassurance he began reading General George S. Patton's *War as I Knew It,* from which he learned that "a successful commander has to have leadership and be a superb mechanic, but most important be ruthless in analyzing his staff."[11] Confident in his own leadership and organizational abilities, Nixon thus complained that his staff had not done a satisfactory job in "building up the P, even though the press had been generally good," and he now thought "we" had to do better at broadcasting the story of how hard he worked, especially on speeches. His inner circle—Kissinger, Haldeman, and Ehrlichman—the only staff members he considered "smart and strong enough" to do it, should work on the problem. He, the president, needed to streamline his schedule and become more like de Gaulle—"aloof, inaccessible, mysterious," and not "too chummy."[12]

Kissinger's postmortem on the day after the speech was more technical: it was "too complex with too many nuances that are totally unintelligible to the ordinary guy." In hindsight he and Haldeman thought Nixon should have presented the full plan as a diplomatic white paper but summarized it on television in a brief, inspirational talk.[13]

As spring was ending and summer beginning, the mood of the administration was turning. Haldeman and Ehrlichman supposed that the president sensed the "end of the easy going and is getting ready to deal with adversities, both internal and external, plus bad press coming up." They had been on a "shakedown cruise" but now must "tighten up" for the storms ahead—"the big stuff."[14] On July 7, after a story appeared in *Newsweek* criticizing him for lack of leadership, Nixon concluded that the White House needed "to reverse the PR trend and get our own line out"; namely, that the record so far, while "not spectacular," was better than *Newsweek* had portrayed it: they had made proposals to Congress and had not yet lost a vote, and soon there was to be a "flood" of administration-initiated domestic legislation.[15]

Having enjoyed a honeymoon from serious public criticism for the first six months after the inauguration, the president and his assistant had nevertheless been vexed during this period by public and elite opinion about the war. In February Nixon had been annoyed with hawks, complaining about their "constant right-wing bitching, with never a positive alternative."[16] They could not be mollified, and by July the Republican Right had become even more unhappy about his failure to cut government domestic spending and his "softening in Vietnam."[17]

On the other side of the spectrum, the antiwar movement had, despite its temporary quiescence, bothered Nixon and his close advisers almost to the point of distraction. In February the president had "wanted to do something about campus disorders," not so much because they presented a real crisis but because he was angry about their corrosive effect on support for his policies.[18] On May 28, for example, Nixon and his inner circle were disappointed in a group of young GOP congressmen who visited the White House after having "been out talking to students at colleges." Kissinger, who was present at the meeting, complained, "These fellows sound just like the French aristocracy two years before the revolution." Haldeman agreed: "They take the radicals at face value, [and] vastly overrate their influence. Only George Bush seemed to understand . . . [the students'] desire for confrontation, not solution."[19]

But Kissinger was critical of the radical, liberal, pacifist, young, middle-aged, and elder doves alike. They could not be satisfied, he complained. Their demands for a negotiated settlement were in constant flux, escalating beyond what Bobby Kennedy, Eugene McCarthy, and George McGovern had proposed in 1968. The antiwar crowd, he asserted, was congenitally critical of the administration.[20] Nixon thought of youthful antiwar activists as draft-dodging "rabble" who had been pampered by their parents and misled by faculty "agitators." Their nationwide activities challenged his authority, constricted his movements, and frustrated his policies, and their shouts near the White House prevented him from sleeping.[21]

Even when free of domestic protesters, Nixon and his men worriedly ruminated about the problem of non-American protesters. While planning Nixon's European tour in February, there had been, Haldeman noted, a "lot of talk about demonstrations on the trip," and their concern had delayed plans to bomb Cambodia. The precautions taken in England, moreover, made members of the president's entourage feel as though they were "in an armed camp,"[22] and throughout the European trip they were wary of demonstrators.

Several weeks later and back in the United States, they became concerned about expected protests during a speech Nixon had scheduled to make at Ohio State University in June, and he and his advisers decided to cancel the event. At first their cover story was to be the announcement of a meeting with President Thieu in California on the day the OSU speech was to have taken place, but then, fearing "riots" in California, they arranged the meeting with Thieu for Midway. Kissinger's conservative sensibilities were piqued: these conditions were "a symptom of the morass into which the Vietnam war plunged our society that a meeting between the president and the leader for whose country over thirty thousand Americans had died had to take place on an uninhabited island in the middle of the Pacific."[23]

President Thieu also sensed dire portents. Although relieved that the Johnson-inspired coup he had feared before the November 1968 election had not come to pass, and thankful that Nixon was president, Thieu had become discouraged before his meeting with Nixon at Midway on June 8. Reluctantly, he had formally agreed to new bilateral talks between Kissinger and Thuy, with the understanding that these would not begin until July,[24] but he was particularly troubled by rumors of an impending official announcement of American troop withdrawals. He knew what the start of withdrawals forebode: "*dau xuoi duoi lot,*" was the Vietnamese saying ("if the head slides through easily, the tail will follow"). Thieu was also concerned about the call for reforms in his government and the danger of appearing to be subservient.

When Nixon officially informed Thieu at Midway about his intention to withdraw 25,000 American troops beginning in July, he pleaded necessity—explaining that he faced domestic pressure from Congress, the press, and the antiwar movement. But the American president attempted to diminish the significance of the withdrawals by characterizing them as a ploy designed to buy time for implementation of his strategy. To soften the blow, he assured Thieu of eight years of continued support—four years of "military Vietnamization" during his first term and four more years of "economic Vietnamization" during his second term. Vowing to accept nothing less than the mutual withdrawal of American and North Vietnamese forces in negotiations, he consoled Thieu by pointing out that by the time most American troops had withdrawn, the North Vietnamese would have pulled out as well.[25] Thieu believed, however, that Nixon had already made a concession in his May 14 proposal, reneging on Johnson's pledges in the Manila formula to keep some U.S. troops in South Vietnam six months past a North Vietnamese withdrawal.

The South Vietnamese president tried to make the best out of the situation, asking Nixon to commit funds and equipment for two new elite, mobile South Vietnamese divisions. He expressed the hope that in the long run a Korea-like solution would come about for Vietnam—that the country would be divided along the DMZ, with two divisions of American troops serving as a deterrent to a North Vietnamese invasion. Nixon, however, was noncommittal, and Thieu could do nothing to alter the course of events. He even accepted Nixon's news about wanting to open secret, direct talks with Hanoi, satisfied that he would be informed of the political issues discussed.[26] American relations with the Saigon regime, for the time being, had proved manageable.

But by this time Kissinger, too, had become concerned about what he perceived as the waning resolve of the other members of the administration.[27] Made soon after his peace plan speech of May 14, Nixon's decision to begin troop withdrawals from South Vietnam was, he thought, one sign of this irresoluteness. Another was the constant pressure put on Thieu by Rogers and the State Department to quicken the pace of political and economic reform in South Vietnam.[28]

Compounding matters, Kissinger—and Haldeman as well—thought that the president had made some "startling" statements in a June 19 press conference, which followed on his return from Midway. Asked about comments by former secretary of defense Clark Clifford concerning his schedule of troop withdrawals, the president said that he would make another withdrawal decision in August and added that he hoped he could beat Clifford's proposed timetable of having all troops out by the end of 1970. Asked whether he was "wedded" to the Thieu regime, Nixon responded: "I would not say that the United States, insofar as any government in the world is concerned, is wedded to it in the sense that we cannot take any course of action that that government does not approve."[29] In the context, it was a measured, responsible statement; in his next sentence he made a point of affirming the commitment of the United States to the Saigon government.

But, as Haldeman noted, "all this shook K pretty badly." He feared that Thieu would "consider it a betrayal, as will all South East Asia, and it will be interpreted as unilateral withdrawal." Haldeman told him that the president had probably wanted to "hit back" at Clifford and had simply overplayed his hand, but Kissinger nonetheless thought it would be extremely difficult to shore up their tough line.

Kissinger had been "pushing" for an approach opposite to that of Laird and Rogers, but now he feared that Nixon, like them, had "decided to pull out." Haldeman's view was that Kissinger was overreacting, yet at the same time he felt he had "good reason" because of his disappointed expectations: in the "last few days" Kissinger had become "deeply discouraged" that their "Vietnam plans aren't working out right." Perhaps, Haldeman conjectured, Nixon knows this too and has reacted accordingly in the press conference, that is, politically.[30] As Nixon prepared to meet with Henry Cabot Lodge on June 24 to discuss the Paris negotiations, Kissinger suggested that the ambassador would recommend greater flexibility in the talks, but Kissinger advised the president to take the position "that we must play a harder line in Paris for the present."[31]

During the next few weeks Kissinger became even more distressed that "his plans for ending [the] war aren't working fast enough," and he carped that "Rogers and Laird are constantly pushing for faster and faster withdrawal." This, he felt, meant a "cop-out" in twelve months. If this was the policy, he argued, the administration might as well cop out now.[32]

"GO FOR BROKE"

Matters came to a head at a "big meeting" on the *Sequoia* on July 7,[33] at which Kissinger, Laird, Rogers, Abrams, Attorney General John Mitchell, and CIA Deputy Director Robert Cushman made recommendations and thrashed out differences while Nixon presided. The results were mixed, for the policies that emerged were an amalgam of both the Laird-Rogers and the Nixon-Kissinger positions.

To appease Laird, Rogers, and the American public, MACV's "mission statement" was changed from that of defeating the enemy and forcing the withdrawal of the PAVN from South Vietnam to one of providing maximum assistance to the Saigon government, strengthening its armed forces, bolstering pacification, and interdicting supplies to the enemy.[34] It may also have been at this meeting that a decision was made to expedite American troop withdrawals.[35] Kissinger had gone into the *Sequoia* conclave, however, determined to "push for some escalation, enough to get us a reasonable bargain for a settlement within six months."[36] It was an approach Nixon viscerally supported. While Laird and Rogers were granted additional troop withdrawals and a change in MACV's mission statement, he and Kissinger came out of the meeting planning to "'go for broke' in the sense," Nixon explained, "that I would attempt to end the war one way or the other—either by negotiated agreement or by an increased use of force."[37]

By way of implementing this plan, Kissinger telephoned Ambassador Dobrynin on Friday, July 11, to request a meeting that evening (Dobrynin was scheduled to leave on Saturday for Moscow). In his report of the rendezvous to Foreign Minister Gromyko, the ambassador described how Nixon's assistant had dangled carrots of conciliation by affirming that the American government was prepared to work with the Soviet government toward the resolution of major problems in U.S.-USSR relations. These included trade, strategic arms control, nuclear proliferation, German nuclear policy, the Middle East, Eastern Europe, and Berlin.

Later in the conversation Kissinger pointed out, however, that compromise on all or most of these issues awaited progress in stopping "the Vietnam conflict as soon as possible," and to that purpose the United States required the cooperation of the Soviet Union "in overcoming the existing dead end in Paris." It was "evident from everything," Dobrynin commented, that "the Vietnam question . . . occupies the main place in the minds of the president and his most important advisors."[38]

Kissinger then brandished sticks of antagonism. His first threat was to suggest indirectly that Nixon might play the China card. He reminded Dobrynin at one point that "there are people who think that the USA and China can somehow come to an understanding in opposition to the USSR," but, demurring from this course, he said it "would not satisfy the interests of the U.S. itself" to do so. Instead, the United States and the USSR, which are the only powers capable of confronting one another in "different parts of the world," need "to conclude concrete agreements" and "follow appropriate parallel courses in the most important and dangerous questions." Besides, Mao Zedong's "actions can't be evaluated using rational logic," whereas "the Soviet Union is governed by realistically thinking politicians who are interested in their people's and their country's well-being." Unless, however, the Soviet Union played "a more active part" in settling the Vietnam War by moving "Hanoi from its own, specific and narrow point of view," it would not be possible for the United States and the USSR to "unite their efforts . . . to prevent dragging the world into major military conflicts."[39]

Kissinger proceeded to defend "Nixon's program to settle the Vietnam conflict." He explained that the American side was willing "to discuss 'any suggestions and to look for compromises,'" but he insisted that, among other things, Hanoi cannot be allowed to "'reject Thieu, because that would represent . . . a political capitulation'" by the United States and South Vietnam. He then made a second threat: if the DRV continued to "obstruct" the negotiations in Paris, the administration would consider "other alternatives."[40] Dobrynin alerted Gromyko to the potential of the threat:

> This sufficiently firm-sounding theme of "other alternatives" in talks with both Nixon and Kissinger cannot but be noted. Although at the current stage these comments carry, evidently, more the character of attempts to blackmail the Vietnamese and in part the USSR with hints that upon expiration of a certain period of time Nixon might renew the bombing of the DRV or take other military measures, it is not possible to entirely exclude the possibility of such actions by the current administration if the situation, in Nixon's opinion, will justify it.[41]

Kissinger, Dobrynin reported, also "threw out a comment" that if the administration turns to these other alternatives, they hoped that "Soviet-American relations do not fall any further than a 'dangerous minimum.'" It was necessary,

Dobrynin therefore suggested to Gromyko, for the Soviet government "to be ready" for developments, "especially if Beijing's provocative course against the USSR will gather strength, and, if in Washington they start to believe that the situation in this sense may be unfavorable for Hanoi."[42]

During his conversation with Kissinger, Dobrynin reaffirmed Soviet policy on the Vietnam War: "There cannot be any other alternatives to peaceful negotiations and a peaceful settlement. . . . Any attempt of the USA to solve the Vietnam question by forceful means unavoidably is destined to fail and that such a course . . . undoubtedly will bring in its train a general increase in international tension, which could not but touch on our relations with the USA." Matching Kissinger's irony with satire, Dobrynin told him that Nixon should not repeat Johnson's mistakes, the consequences of which were made "sufficiently clear by the example of the previous owner of the White House."[43]

A few days later Nixon launched a supporting carrot-and-stick stratagem aimed at Hanoi. At Kissinger's suggestion the president met on July 15 with Jean Sainteny in the Oval Office and asked him to serve as an intermediary between the White House and the Politburo. Sainteny suggested instead that Kissinger meet with Le Duc Tho, but the president and his assistant chose their original course. Sainteny's first task was to be their courier, carrying an undated personal letter from Nixon to Ho Chi Minh that the president had drafted earlier. Because Hanoi refused to grant Sainteny a visa, however, after his return to Paris he delivered the letter to Mai Van Bo.

Nixon opened the letter with words of peace:

I realize that it is difficult to communicate meaningfully across the gulf of four years of war. But precisely because of this gulf, I wanted to take this opportunity to reaffirm in all solemnity my desire to work for a just peace. . . .

There is nothing to be gained by waiting. . . .

The time has come to move forward at the conference table toward an early resolution of this tragic war. You will find us forthcoming and open-minded in a common effort to bring the blessings of peace to the brave people of Vietnam. Let history record that at this critical juncture, both sides turned their face toward peace rather than toward conflict and war.[44]

But he closed with a warning that unless a breakthrough in the negotiations was made by November 1—the anniversary of Johnson's bombing halt—he would be obliged to resort "to measures of great consequence and force."[45] Describing this episode in *RN*, Nixon wrote: "I felt that I had gone as far as I could. . . . My letter put the choice between war and peace in his hands."[46]

Nixon claimed that the first response of the North Vietnamese was to propose a secret meeting between Kissinger and Xuan Thuy. Kissinger's story was different: when Hanoi refused to accept Sainteny as an intermediary, Nixon and Kissinger asked him to arrange a meeting between Kissinger and North Vietnamese negotiators in order "to try for a breakthrough."[47]

DISENGAGEMENT COUPLED WITH THREAT

Meanwhile, on July 23, the president embarked on an around-the-world trip, which, among other purposes, served, Nixon said, to "camouflage" Kissinger's forthcoming clandestine meeting with Xuan Thuy, scheduled for August 4 in Paris. Flying west to Johnston Atoll in the Pacific, the president's entourage, which included Kissinger, flew by helicopter to the aircraft carrier *Hornet* to observe the splashdown of the *Apollo 11* moon-mission spacecraft *Columbia* and greet the returning astronauts. Nixon became exuberant during the event, on one occasion ordering the ship's band to play "Columbia the Gem of the Ocean," and on another remarking that they had witnessed "the greatest week in the history of the world since the Creation."[48] The president was in good spirits not only because he was inspired by the July 20 moon landing and his meeting with the astronauts on July 24 but also because of "Teddy Kennedy's escapade" at Chappaquiddick on the night of July 18 and its harmful impact on Kennedy's prospects for mounting a challenge in the 1972 presidential election.[49]

Nixon's enthusiasm—as well as his desire to continue making news for home consumption—encouraged him to be more talkative and forthcoming than usual.[50] On July 25, although tired after two days of travel through several time zones, the president gave reporters an informal background briefing while chatting with them at the officers' club on Guam. In reply to a question about American support for Asian allies who might find themselves in South Vietnam's predicament, he made a surprise announcement of what the press at first called the "Guam Doctrine."[51] Asian nations, he declared, have primary responsibility for defending themselves from internal and external threat, except when a major power with nuclear weapons was involved.

His remarks appeared to be impromptu, but he had been thinking about this policy for some time. Receiving more attention than he expected and disliking the press's title for his declaration, Nixon told Kissinger to find a more exalted appellation. It was soon dubbed the "Nixon Doctrine."[52]

Kissinger subsequently took partial credit for developing the principles it stood for,[53] but the president did not support his claim. Nixon later told one historian that he had kept his thoughts to himself until giving the Guam backgrounder in order to avoid bureaucratic leaks—as well as additional NSSMs from Kissinger and more NSC meetings.[54] Although both men had previously discussed the question of post-Vietnam American policy in Asia, Nixon's announcement and his particular formulation of the doctrine surprised Kissinger. Eyewitnesses said that the assistant was displeased (most probably because he had been kept in the dark and because the declaration came at a time when he was worried about the drift of the administration's Vietnam policies). To Kissinger's complaints, Nixon condescendingly replied, "You'll learn, relax."[55]

The immediate response from allies and Congress was mixed, with some interpreting Nixon's statements to mean that he intended to withdraw U.S. forces from Asia. Patrick Buchanan, whose job was to cull news stories on selected topics for the president's perusal, reported that there was "widespread confusion on the meaning of the Nixon Doctrine." Charged with investigating the accuracy of this assessment, Kissinger's staff reported in late August that Buchanan had "clearly overstate[d] the case."[56] Nixon had clarified his remarks during the remainder of his global journey and upon his return home, persuading most commentators to praise the new doctrine. Don Oberdorfer, for example, wrote: "Mr. Nixon showed on his recent trip that he has learned many things. . . . The most pertinent seemed to be that security begins at home, and that the first positive steps toward a new Asian era must come from Asia itself." Roscoe and Geoffrey Drummond called the policy a "major turning point in American Foreign Policy."[57]

Giving the policy backhanded praise in his postwar memoir, *White House Years,* Kissinger observed: "There was less to the Nixon Doctrine than met the eye. . . . That we should no longer involve ourselves in civil wars was—in 1969— the conventional wisdom. On the other hand, a formal statement of the American position provided for the first time clear-cut criteria for friend and foe."[58]

In practice these criteria were not clear-cut, no more, in fact, than the Eisenhower administration's New Look and "nation-building" strategies of the 1950s, from which Nixon had borrowed. His newly enunciated doctrine was a response to U.S. foreign policy problems similar to those these older policies had attempted to meet in prior decades, but instead of solving problems such as Vietnam, they had drawn the United States into the quagmire from which Nixon now dearly wanted to extricate himself. As with several other foreign policy initiatives of the Nixon administration, moreover, it would not endure. Indeed, Nixon violated the doctrine in Cambodia and would soon do so in Laos. It is tempting to view Nixon's remarks—developed in virtual solitude and delivered without careful preparation by the NSC—as his attempt to rationalize the policy of Vietnamization and provide a general theory of global retrenchment, while at the same time defend America's global policing role, which was then under attack by influential segments of the American body politic.[59]

From Guam the presidential party flew on to Manilla, Djakarta, Bangkok, and—in a surprise stop on July 30—Saigon, where Nixon broke more discouraging news to Thieu: additional American withdrawals would take place on the basis of a systematic timetable and American initiatives. Kissinger complained: "We were clearly on the way out of Vietnam by negotiation if possible, by unilateral withdrawal if necessary."[60] With the word "negotiation," however, Kissinger meant diplomatic linkage in dealing with the Soviets and the use of irresistible military pressure against the North Vietnamese to force them into concessions.

In contrast to Thieu, Nixon and his aides were elated by the visit. The helicopter landing at the Presidential Palace had been risky but exciting, and their tour of the First Army's base at Xi Nam was uplifting. Nixon gave an "emotional charge" to Haldeman "never to let the hippie college-types in to see him again. He was really taken by the quality and character of the guys he talked to, and by reaction [became] really fed up with the protesters and peaceniks" back home.[61] Nixon had been complaining and continued to complain about the failure of his White House in "not adequately getting the story out" to the American people—that is, the story of his active presidency and particularly of his success on this global tour. He must have been pleased when Kissinger's staff later discovered that his visit to South Vietnam had been generally well reported and well received. "The emphasis was on your ability and willingness to go to the South Vietnamese capital in the heartland of the country," and the visit to American units had lent credence to the administration's claims of having increased "territorial control."[62]

But the personal high point of the trip for Nixon occurred in the two days in early August he spent in Bucharest, visiting President Nicolae Ceauşéscu, touring the city, and receiving a warm welcome from large Romanian crowds, who lined up to see him drive by. At the guest house late at night after the first day, Nixon called Haldeman and Kissinger to his room to share in his marvel at the event's historic significance. In his pajamas and puffing on a cigar, he told them that "history was made" by his visit. The "turnout and emotional reaction" of the people, he said, must have "scared" Communist officials, who were aware they were "sitting on a tinder box." They, Nixon thought, did not have the "guts" of their leader, whose political shrewdness and intellectual brightness impressed him. At the airport the next day, the two leaders bid farewell with arms around one another.[63]

Among the reasons Nixon thought Ceauşéscu gutsy was that he had maintained good relations with China despite Romania's proximity to the Soviet Union. A major purpose of his visit was to "needle our Moscow friends"[64]—not only by appearing on the soil of a country in the USSR's East European sphere of influence but also by dealing the China card. He implemented this latter ploy by asking the Romanian leader to act as a channel of communication to Beijing, a request he knew Ceauşéscu would pass on to Moscow.[65]

Nixon also tried to take advantage of Ceauşéscu's good relations with North Vietnam. In one meeting the American president reinforced his earlier threat to Hanoi: "We cannot indefinitely continue to have two hundred deaths a week in Vietnam and no progress in Paris. On November 1 this year—one year after the halt of the bombing, and after the withdrawal of some of our troops and several reasonable offers for peaceful negotiations—if there is no progress, we must reevaluate our policy."[66] Nixon had dropped similar hints to other leaders on his global trip and with state visitors in Washington, "in the expectation," Kissinger said, "that these warnings would filter back to Hanoi."[67]

As Nixon flew from Romania to England, then on to the United States, Kissinger split off from the presidential party and headed for Paris, where he, his personal assistant Anthony Lake, and the American military attaché in Paris, General Vernon Walters, met secretly with Xuan Thuy, Mai Van Bo, and their assistants on August 4 in Sainteny's apartment on the rue de Rivoli in Paris.

Kissinger opened the conversation by asking Thuy whether there had been an answer from his government to Nixon's letter of July 15. Thuy replied that the letter had not been forwarded to Hanoi because it had not been dated. Kissinger proceeded to enumerate American terms for a settlement, which included the mutual withdrawal of "outside forces" from South Vietnam and the maintenance of "the existing relationship of political forces," and he revealed that Nixon was prepared to "open another [secret] channel of contact" with Hanoi and "appoint a high-level emissary who would be authorized to negotiate a conclusion to the war." If the negotiations proved "serious," Nixon would appoint him (Kissinger) "to conduct the negotiations." To facilitate the effort, Nixon was willing to "adjust military operations" downward. However, "if by November 1, no major progress has been made toward a solution, we will be compelled—with great reluctance—to take measures of the greatest consequence." Kissinger drove home the point by admonishing the North Vietnamese for attempting in their propaganda and in the plenary Paris discussions to make the conflict "Mr. Nixon's War." It was not in their interest to do so, Kissinger warned them, because "if it is Mr. Nixon's War, he cannot afford not to win it. . . . We cannot continue to accept the procedures that have characterized our contacts in the last 15 months after November 1."[68]

Ignoring American threats, Thuy asked Kissinger to speak with greater clarity about whether the pace of American troop withdrawals would be accelerated before November 1, whether the proposed secret talks between Washington and Hanoi would supersede the Paris plenaries, and the meaning of the American call for the "neutralization" of Vietnam. Apparently dissatisfied with Kissinger's vague answers, Thuy spoke for several minutes about the history of Vietnam's struggle for "independence, freedom, and peace . . . against foreign aggression"[69] and then presented a point-by-point critique of American terms, recommending instead the PRG's ten-point proposal as the basis for a solution for the war. When Kissinger ridiculed the ten points as the other side's "Ten Commandments," Thuy defended them as the "logical and realistic" starting point for negotiation.[70]

The second half of the meeting was taken up with an exchange of differences on key issues. Thuy rejected the American call for a separation of political and military issues, a five-year period of reunification for Vietnam, the mutual withdrawal of American and North Vietnamese troops, and elections, to be organized by Thieu, for a new South Vietnamese government. Kissinger rejected the DRV/PRG call for the unilateral withdrawal of American troops and the formation of a provisional, transitional government that would exclude Thieu, Ky, and Huong. At the end of the meeting, Thuy stated that he wished "to meet with Dr. Kissinger again if we can make progress."[71] Although agreeing to future contacts, Kissinger was sufficiently irritated with and disappointed in the meeting that he would not again use this "newly established channel" in 1969.[72]

Soon, however, he availed himself of the services of Professor Joseph R. Starobin, previously a member of the Communist Party USA and foreign editor of the New York *Daily Worker,* who on July 26 had renewed his former acquaintance with Xuan Thuy in Paris. Intrigued by Thuy's remarks and believing he had new information to convey, Starobin reported his conversation to Kissinger at the Western White House in San Clemente on August 12. Kissinger apparently authorized him to recontact Thuy, for they met again in Paris on September 2. Neither Kissinger nor Thuy informed Starobin that direct secret talks had already begun.

Little, if anything, in Starobin's meeting with Thuy indicated that new proposals were exchanged, which led journalist Tad Szulc in 1978 to wonder why Kissinger and Thuy had played this "curious" game. Nonetheless, extant information about the meeting provides insights into both sides' negotiating styles. Starobin, for instance, reported that Thuy had referred to Hanoi's insistence on an American withdrawal as a "principle," which may have been significant, perhaps indicating that the terms and timing of an American pullout were negotiable.[73] The DRV Foreign Ministry's notes of the meeting indicated that Nixon and Kissinger considered the occasion an opportunity to deliver, albeit indirectly, yet another threat of military escalation, for Starobin told them that prolonged negotiations would invite American right-wing hostility, leading to a resumption of bombing or the mining of North Vietnamese ports, which was what the administration was seriously considering at the time. Starobin also relayed Kissinger's sentiment that the "U.S. disliked the present Saigon government, but did not want a complete disruption of it." This oblique admission and qualified endorsement of the Saigon regime, however, probably implied less political flexibility than tactical guile in the tradition of the carrot and stick.[74]

DUCK HOOK

Nixon received Ho Chi Minh's reply to his July 15 letter on August 30. In his letter, dated August 25, Ho acknowledged the need to "allow the United States to get out of the war with honor," and he closed with a possibly conciliatory sentiment: "With good will on both sides we might arrive at common efforts in view of finding a correct solution of the Vietnamese problem." But Nixon chose to characterize it as a "cold rebuff" because Ho, although "deeply touched at the rising toll of death of young Americans," attributed them to the policies of U.S. "governing circles," while Kissinger viewed the response as "peremptory" because Ho called for a negotiated solution based on the PRG's ten points. In his own letter Nixon had expressed a willingness "to discuss any proposal or program that might lead to a negotiated settlement," including the other side's ten points, but he had equated these with the "other proposals" put forward by other groups, while identifying his own eight-point proposal as the fairest to all parties. Ho had reversed this hierarchy of peace programs, and although he had called for goodwill on both sides, he had made it clear that his government would not bend in the face of threats.[75]

Ho's letter exacerbated a long-developing crisis in the White House's Vietnam strategy. The anxieties Nixon had begun to feel earlier in the year about the viability of his plan to end the war were now magnified, and his closest advisers were seriously divided about how best to proceed, with each lobbying for the president's attention. No one was more active than Kissinger. In *White House Years* he wrote about this period as one of strategic "reassessment," explaining that his "preferred course was the one that had been at the heart of the proposed Vance mission": "To make the most sweeping and generous proposal of which we were capable, short of overthrowing an allied government but enduring a free political contest. If it were refused, we would halt troop withdrawals and quarantine North Vietnam by mining its ports and perhaps bombing its rail links to China. The goal would be a rapid negotiated compromise."[76]

The contingency plan Nixon and Kissinger ordered to be developed in support of this scenario came to be known as Duck Hook, "for reasons," Kissinger said, "that totally escape me today."[77] In his 1978 description, which was probably based on orally transmitted information, Tad Szulc mistakenly reported the plan's code name as "Duck Hoop," and he quoted Kissinger as having explained that the plan referred to "all the 'ducks' of American power 'circling in' for the kill; a drawing of a flight of ducks appeared on the cover of all documents pertaining to Duck Hoop."[78]

Just as muddled and improbable as that illustration was Kissinger's disingenuous chronology of the plan's evolution, which has obfuscated this episode ever since. In his memoirs he declared that Nixon's threat of taking strong action unless the other side facilitated progress in the negotiations before November 1 was not backed up by a concrete plan. Kissinger implied that planning for the November attacks by his staff only began "in September and October" and "proceeded in a desultory fashion," which suggested that it was in response to Ho Chi Minh's rejection—an implication Nixon made in his memoir as well.[79] The desultory planning period, however, preceded Ho's letter and may have begun in April, when Nixon had decided to proceed with a "program of mining Haiphong to look tough."[80] When the North Koreans downed the U.S. Navy's EC-121 reconnaissance plane, Nixon, with Kissinger's advice, temporarily shelved the project. But in July, when they decided to "go for broke" and Nixon issued the November deadline ultimatum, it was probably this April program that was revived and expanded, whereupon it was dubbed the "November Option" by military planners. The April program itself may have derived from a previous JCS attack plan that was taken off the shelf.[81]

After the war, informants told Tad Szulc and Seymour Hersh that the hawkish chief of naval operations, Admiral Thomas Moorer, had allowed his staff to carry out "studies" for a November operation without the knowledge of Secretary of Defense Laird. Moorer's unbecoming conduct was likely made possible because the plan they scrutinized was a preexisting one. In any event, their studies were completed on July 20, and it was either at this time—or in early to mid-

September, when Kissinger assembled a special group to assess the operation—that the November Option was renamed Duck Hook.[82]

Haldeman's diary lends credence to a chronology that extends back to a period before the exchanges with Ho, revealing that Kissinger's support for a plan was greater than he admitted in his memoirs. On August 18—two weeks after Kissinger returned from his secret meeting with Thuy in Paris, and two weeks before Nixon received Ho's letter—Kissinger, with John Mitchell already firmly in his corner, tried to consolidate Haldeman's and Ehrlichman's support for his "Vietnam alternatives." His long and bitter battle with Laird and Rogers to influence Nixon on the direction of Vietnam policy was coming to a head. Haldeman recorded that Kissinger "feels strongly that he, E[rhlichman] and I, plus Mitchell, must hang tight and provide the backup." Since domestic politics was a battleground that also engaged Nixon's careful attention, Kissinger recommended that there be "a domestic [PR] plan to go with it [i.e., the military plan], covering actions and reaction here [in the United States]." He needed to enlist Haldeman's, Ehrlichman's, and Mitchell's help in nudging the president; that is, encouraging him "to make [a] total mental commitment and really be prepared for the heat." The latter was a reference to anticipated criticism not only from dissidents in the bureaucracy, such as Laird and Rogers, but also from the public, Congress, and the antiwar movement should Nixon choose the escalation option. On August 28 Nixon reviewed "K's contingency plan for Vietnam," which was most probably the November Option, but he did not make a decision one way or the other.[83]

As he had done before and would do again, Kissinger had accurately divined Nixon's mood. Haldeman's notes reveal that by mid-August Nixon already understood the need for mental resolve and was getting "ready for what lies ahead." The president knew that a go-for-broke military operation would require a go-for-broke public relations campaign, in which he would have to expend most or all of his political capital to survive "the heat." This realization by Nixon, Haldeman noted, was "at least part of the reason for the efforts to build a strong space thing, and certainly the reason behind the push for better PR capability," and also the reason he was then vacationing in San Clemente.[84] The stay at the Western White House, which commenced after the around-the-world trip, lasted four weeks and in part reflected the stress felt by Nixon. By the "space thing" Haldeman meant Nixon's attempt to piggyback onto the public's enthusiasm for the American astronauts' recent voyage to the moon.

Inspired by the astronauts' walk on the moon, the president had begun emphasizing, even more than usual, the need for a new public relations campaign or "Presidential Offensive" to "establish the mystique of the presidency." Borrowing from space program argot, he recommended "GO" as the theme word for the promotional effort; melding the latter with foreign policy, he bonded GO with the traditional colloquialism "go for broke": "[GO] means all systems ready, never be indecisive, get going, take risks, be exciting. Can't fall into dry rot of just managing the chaos better. Must use the great power of the office to *do some-*

thing. Boldness. Now is the time to go. We've organized things, now use them. Go for broke. . . . Power of the United States must be used more effectively at home and abroad or we go down the drain as a great power."[85]

In late August and into September, however, the president was not resolute in preparing to take the political heat, even though the go-for-broke military campaign had been his own inspiration. Indeed, he obsessed about the problem of maintaining or improving his public image, convening frequent meetings of "HEHK"—Haldeman, Ehrlichman, Bryce Harlow, and Kissinger—to plot public relations strategy.

Kissinger feared that Nixon was approaching a perilous state of indecisive nervousness on the Vietnam problem; he therefore took what he later described as "quixotic" steps to appeal to the president's instinct for the jugular and persuade him to approve the November Option. (Roger Morris, one of Kissinger's aides, thought that Kissinger himself was being egged on by Haig.)[86] On September 10, two days before another "big Vietnam meeting" of the NSC in the Cabinet Room, Kissinger sent a long memo to Nixon, in which he expressed his deep concern "about our present course in Vietnam." Their strategy of "attempting to solve the problem of Vietnam on three highly interrelated fronts" was, he argued, failing on the first two (in the United States and in Vietnam), which had the effect of undermining their effort on the third—diplomacy.

Although acknowledging that polls indicated citizen satisfaction with the administration's handling of the war, Kissinger predicted that home-front public pressure to bring the war to a swift conclusion would increase. The "student" antiwar demonstrations planned for October, along with the increasingly strong opposition of "moderate" opinion makers, would "polarize" public opinion, putting the president in the position in which Lyndon Johnson had found himself— that is, "caught between Hawks and Doves." This would "confuse" Hanoi but also would "confirm it in its course of waiting us out."

On the Vietnam front, Kissinger argued that the administration could not "win the war" with current military operations and pacification within the two years some advisers had predicted, although "success or failure in hurting the enemy remains very important." Vietnamization would not likely succeed, because the RVNAF was fundamentally incapable of assuming the full burden of the war, and the withdrawal of American troops would have serious side effects: emboldening the enemy; causing the American public to demand continued disengagement that could lead to de facto unilateral, complete withdrawal; and undermining the morale of soldiers who were among the last to leave. Then he pointed out the obvious: Thieu's regime was politically weak. It was chronically unwilling and inherently incapable of broadening its base, and it lacked the full confidence of even non-Communist elements in the South Vietnamese body politic. Of enemy strategy, Kissinger's estimation was that they were prepared to "wait us out." Characterizing their diplomatic policy as one of "intransigence," he predicted that they were not likely to make "concessions" in Paris.[87]

Little is known of the discussion that took place at the big meeting on Friday, September 12. Haldeman noted that in attendance were "NSC types plus Vietnam Commanders and [the U.S.] Ambassador [to Saigon]," and that the main topic on the agenda was the laying of plans for additional troop reductions. On September 16 Nixon announced an additional troop withdrawal of 35,000 by December 15, which was almost certainly designed to please the American public.[88]

But there are indications that with this announcement Nixon also hoped to impress Hanoi with the seriousness of his desire for a settlement.[89] On September 3, only four days after Nixon received Ho's letter, the legendary Vietnamese leader died, leading the administration to speculate on the implications of unsubstantiated rumors that a power struggle had broken out in the Hanoi Politburo, which might possibly produce enemy concessions. Nixon wrote in *RN* that his September 16 withdrawal announcement "was intended to let the new leaders of North Vietnam know that I was not assuming that they were bound by Ho's reply to my letter." His hopes for a change in North Vietnamese policy were soon dashed, however, when on September 20 Kissinger received a discouraging letter from his friend Jean Sainteny. The former colonial delegate-general had attended Ho's funeral and spoken about Nixon's desire for peace with the new premier, Pham Van Dong, who, according to Nixon, said to Sainteny: "I see that they have convinced you. But we, we are not able to take them at their words; only acts will convince us."[90] Even though Nixon conceded that Dong had been "notably unvituperative," he interpreted his comment to mean that the Politburo had not budged from the position taken by Ho. Believing he had demonstrated his own earnestness through his troop withdrawal actions, Nixon felt the sting of rejection and failure. In reaction he thought of violence, remarking that "once again the choice lay with Hanoi."[91]

Kissinger had emerged from the September 12 NSC meeting frustrated and unhappy. The gathering seems to have been taken up less with strategic boldness and more with the mollification of the American public and peaceful, even if meaningless, gestures to the enemy. Kissinger must have thought he was losing control of both the correct strategy and influence over the president, but he took little part in the discussion. Haldeman's diary confirms what Kissinger in his memoirs claimed was one of the few things he said: "We need a plan to end the war, not only to withdraw troops. This is what is on people's minds."[92] The tough steps he advocated may not, however, have even come up for discussion. The participants had been too busy addressing issues connected to public relations, namely, troop withdrawals and the developing story of Green Berets accused of murdering a South Vietnamese they had believed to be a double agent. On top of that, Kissinger was upset by another of Nixon's attempts to convince the enemy of his sincerity. Haldeman reported that at the meeting there was a "big flap over [a] 36-hour halt of B-52 raids in South Vietnam."[93]

It may have been at this juncture—that is, shortly before or after the NSC meeting—that Kissinger assembled a "trusted group" of his staff "to explore the military side of the coin"—that is, the existing Duck Hook studies. The "September Group," as some members called it, included Anthony Lake, Winston Lord, Laurence Lynn, Roger Morris, Peter Rodman, Helmut Sonnenfeldt, William Watts, Colonel Alexander Haig, Colonel William Lemnitzer, and Captain Rembrandt C. Robinson. In *White House Years* Kissinger wrote that he told them the president was not willing to "capitulate" but had "lost confidence" in their current strategy of walking a fine line "between withdrawing too fast to convince Hanoi of our determination and withdrawing too slowly to satisfy the American public." What was needed, therefore, was a "military plan designed for maximum impact on the enemy's military capability" in order to "force a rapid conclusion" to the war.[94]

Kissinger met individually with each adviser before bringing him into the special group. Roger Morris, who was assigned the task of compiling everyone's research, later reported that Kissinger told him that the negotiations were not going well, but because the bureaucracy was endemically incapable of coming up with fresh initiatives, he, Kissinger, would "have to do it" and take the president, Congress, and the people along with him.[95] To the assembled group, Kissinger declared that he and Nixon had offered "concessions which have been unrequited." Therefore, options were now needed. "I refuse to believe that a little fourth-rate power like North Vietnam does not have a breaking point. . . . It shall be the assignment of this group to examine the option of a savage, decisive blow against North Vietnam. You start without any preconceptions at all."[96]

When one staff member asked about the possible use of nuclear weapons, Kissinger replied that it was "the policy of this administration not to use nuclear *weapons.*" But he did not exclude the use of "*a* nuclear *device*" to block a key railroad pass to China if that should prove the only way of doing it. Morris said he had been shown nuclear targeting plans. Charles Colson, who was not a member of the special group but who asked Haldeman about the affair in 1970, claimed that Haldeman said "Kissinger had lobbied for nuclear options in the spring and fall of 1969."[97]

Testimony on this matter, however, has been inconsistent. Other aides told Seymour Hersh that they did not recall encountering any evidence that Nixon and Kissinger considered using a nuclear device in the Duck Hook operation.[98] Winston Lord expressed incredulity to another interviewer: "I'm absolutely convinced that nuclear weapons were never considered, even hypothetically. There were never any options made; I never heard it discussed. It's beyond my comprehension that they would even think of doing that."

But he added: "There's a difference between their never considering nuclear weapons and it occurring to them that [the] madman [theory] . . . might even make them [the North Vietnamese] think, god, would they ever use nuclear weapons? And of course we wouldn't go out of our way to allay their fears about that. . . . Let them worry about it, even though we know it's not true. Do you see the distinction?"[99]

While Kissinger's staff examined the military, diplomatic, and legal consequences of Duck Hook, drafted a presidential speech announcing the raids, and prepared a "scenario" for the final negotiations, the JCS turned the original Duck Hook studies into a plan of operations. Kissinger described it as a four-day attack that would begin on November 1 and incorporate the mining of DRV ports and harbors and air raids on twenty-nine "targets of military and economic importance."[100] Accounts of the plan by Kissinger's aides revealed that this initial four-day retribution would be followed by a pause to give the other side an opportunity to assess its predicament. If Hanoi failed to make diplomatic concessions, Washington would launch additional four-day attacks—each followed by a reprieve—until the desired result was achieved. These accounts suggest that the Duck Hook studies included contingency planning for an invasion of North Vietnam, the bombing of Red River dikes, and the blockading of Sihanoukville.[101]

Even though Nixon had declared in March that his administration would serve warning on the enemy only once, he continued during this period of planning and assessment to repeat earlier threats of dramatic escalation. When Kissinger received Dobrynin in his office on September 27, he and Nixon played out a prearranged plan of intimidation: Nixon telephoned his assistant while the meeting was in progress, and after their conversation Kissinger turned to Dobrynin to tell him that the president wanted to emphasize that the Vietnam War was the critical issue in the U.S.-USSR relationship, that "the train had left the station and was heading down the track," and that the next step had to be taken by Hanoi. Dobrynin retorted, "I hope it's an airplane rather than a train, because an airplane can still change its course in flight." Kissinger responded, "The President chooses his words very carefully and I am sure he meant what he said."[102] On the same day, Nixon met with nine Republican senators and "planted a story" that he hoped would "attract some attention in Hanoi" and have the effect of turning up "the pressure . . . a notch." He told the senators that he was considering a plan to blockade Haiphong and invade North Vietnam. Within a matter of days, his stratagem had the desired effect: leaked by one or more of the senators, the rumor was repeated by the press.[103] To bolster these threats, according to Seymour Hersh's informants, Nixon ordered a Strategic Air Command B-52 alert "sometime in October," which lasted twenty-nine days.[104]

Learning by early October about Duck Hook and Nixon's November deadline, Laird and Rogers vigorously opposed the strategy and continued to urge an emphasis on Vietnamization.[105] In making his case, Laird drew on the critical assessments of members of Kissinger's own staff. Lynn, Watts, Lake, and Morris had argued in personal and group reports that the air raids and the blockade would produce indecisive military results that would not significantly reduce the North's ability to wage war in the South. There were few industrial targets in North Vietnam, the destruction of viable targets would be incomplete, no blockade could ever be thorough, and the Soviets and Chinese would find a way of resupplying the North Vietnamese. Despite these inconclusive results, the costs on both sides would be great: B-52 losses would be heavier and North Vietnamese civilian casualties would be greater than those estimated by the military. Since there were no serious negotiations under way and 450,000 American troops remained in Vietnam, the timing of the operation was wrong, for it would appear that the administration was attempting to win the war (which was in fact Nixon's and Kissinger's intention). At home the escalation would call forth widespread protests and disorder, resulting in a political catastrophe for the administration.[106]

PR, PROTESTS, AND POWS

Meanwhile, the president and his inner circle were already fretting about domestic politics and public relations on a wide range of issues, but with the Vietnam War occupying a central place. Things "sort of hit the fan," Haldeman noted, when they learned on September 15 that RVN Vice President Nguyen Cao Ky had leaked the troop withdrawal story before Nixon was to make his announcement; Ky had also provided a figure for the number of troops to be withdrawn that was higher than Nixon's. The White House "spent quite a while" trying to work out a public explanation for the numerical discrepancy.[107] On September 18 Nixon was disappointed in the lukewarm reception given by the UN General Assembly to his speech, in which he had urged other governments to persuade Hanoi to negotiate. Later he was cheered by the public relations prospects associated with Laird's plan to cancel draft calls for November and December. But he became "*really* upset" late at night when he discovered that the army intended to proceed with the court-martial of the accused Green Berets. A few days later Kissinger succeeded in persuading the CIA to refuse to allow its agents to testify as witnesses, which brought the matter "under control" and soon led to the cancellation of the trial by Army Secretary Stanley Resor. On September 30 Nixon met most of the day with Kissinger and Ehrlichman, trying to decide how to prevent key administration figures from having to testify before a Senate Foreign Relations Subcommittee hearing on the administration's secret operations in Laos, which had recently been exposed by two *Washington Post* reporters.[108]

Their greatest public relations concerns were two major antiwar actions scheduled for mid-October and mid-November—the Moratorium and the Mobilization Against the War. Nixon was apprehensive because these were the first nationwide, mass demonstrations directed against him. Believing that Hanoi's will to resist was encouraged by division within the United States, he worried that peace rallies and marches would serve to undermine the impact of his and Kissinger's diplomatic-military strategy. Aware that public support for his Vietnam policies was tenuous, he feared that a resurgence of antiwar activity would further erode confidence in his leadership.[109] In April 44 percent of adults polled by Gallup had approved of his handling of the war, with 30 percent suspending judgment; 26 percent disapproved but were split between those who favored an immediate withdrawal or dramatic military escalation. In July Nixon's ratings began to decline, and by September 52 percent indicated dissatisfaction with his handling of the war, with only 35 percent approving. Dissatisfaction with the war itself increased, too. In February 52 percent of those polled had said that it had been a mistake to have originally sent troops to fight in Vietnam; the figure rose to 58 percent in September. No wonder that public support for a sustained schedule of troop withdrawals gained momentum after Nixon's troop withdrawal announcement in June; in September 71 percent of respondents extended approval to his second withdrawal announcement. But the trend in public opinion against the war continued to rise—55 percent counted themselves as doves, 31 as hawks, and 14 as having no opinion in November 1969, compared with 42, 44, and 31 percent thirteen months before.[110]

This public relations crisis called forth the old Nixon—the preemptive striker and scrappy counterpuncher. As early as June, when he visited two conservative campuses, Nixon had begun to speak out against college protesters. On September 26, as the Moratorium and Mobilization approached, he announced that they would not affect his policies. On the same day, in an attempt to throttle press coverage of demonstrations, Vice President Agnew severely criticized the media for its alleged bias in covering antiwar protests. During a political strategy session at the White House on the twenty-seventh—the day Kissinger met with Dobrynin and Nixon leaked his Duck Hook intentions to Republican senators—the president "cranked . . . up" House and Senate leaders, campaign chairs, and White House speechwriters "to get out and hit hard on the offensive." The demonstrators, he told the group, would be "prolonging the war by this attack, because our only hope for negotiation is to convince Hanoi we are ready to stay with it." What was needed in the next thirty to sixty days was public trust in his assurances that "we know what we're doing" and national unity behind his policies. The enemy must not be given additional evidence of national division. They must understand that they will continue to have to deal with Richard Nixon for "three years and three months," and that he is determined not to be the "first President to lose a war."[111] Following a review of the White House's PR activity two days later, Nixon "turned the House hawks loose" by having them demand that the administration "resume bombing, etc., as a counter on the right to all the pressure on the left to cop out." While Nixon became increasingly combative, he also began to act in a manner for which he had criticized LBJ—"using every occasion to plead for support." During a September 30 medal ceremony for marine veterans of Vietnam, for example, he called for national unity behind his wartime leadership.[112]

One component of Nixon's public relations offensive—a project to merge public support for the release of American prisoners of war with support for his policies in waging the war—was to have far-reaching, long-term consequences for diplomacy and domestic politics. The POW campaign had actually begun shortly after his inauguration in January. At the opening plenary session of the Paris talks, Lodge made an unusual request for the "early release of prisoners on both sides," which signified a call for separating the matter of returning prisoners from the main issue of terminating the war.[113] In March the administration studied the question of whether to include the demand for early prisoner releases as one of its terms in private negotiations with Hanoi. The combined PR and diplomatic strategy it decided to adopt, however, seems to have been one of stressing the POW issue in the public plenary talks in Paris, while omitting them—for the time being, as it proved—from the private talks, which began in August. This strategy of going public in order to marshal public opinion behind a call for the prompt release of all American POWs was supported on the home front by a vigorous public relations campaign. State and Defense Department officials, for example, assisted in organizing families of POWs behind the effort, while the White House tapped into an existing right-wing network of anti–peace movement and pro-war individuals and groups. One of these was Texas multimillionaire H. Ross Perot, who formed United We Stand, an organization that lobbied in support of the war, opposed the antiwar movement, and publicized the POW matter in cooperation with Nixon's campaign, thereby helping to make it an "issue." The press and members of Congress quickly joined the bandwagon.

The motives behind the administration's demand for the rapid release of POWs were manifold. They included the diversion of public attention from the Saigon government's mistreatment of political and military prisoners in South Vietnam by drawing attention to enemy cruelties; the establishment of a "public record" of having tried to win the release of the POWs; the creation of a propaganda counterweight to the antiwar message of the American peace movement; and the development of public tolerance for Nixon's insistence in negotiations on the mutual withdrawal of "foreign" forces from South Vietnam.[114] Most Americans thought of the war's purpose as one of "fighting communism," "stopping aggression," "withdrawing with honor," or "achieving peace." Fewer citizens would have supported a sustained war had these terms been clearly and concretely understood as the maintenance of Thieu's regime and the preservation of South Vietnam as a non-Communist state, which were and had been the core policy goals of the U.S. government, and were the main obstacles to the termination of fighting and therefore the release of prisoners on both sides. As a negotiating strategy, it would ultimately backfire because the other side, which came to appreciate the strength of American public concern about prisoner releases, continued to link such releases with the conclusion of a peace agreement and the termination of the war, which, in any case, was the normal protocol in wartime negotiations. By adding a superfluous demand for the release of POWs to his list of negotiating terms, Nixon provided Hanoi with an additional diplomatic lever, thus overturning his own intent and compounding his own diplomatic task.

As a public relations strategy, the POW campaign was ultimately successful, for the demand for a quick release of POWs deflected attention from the real policy purposes of Nixon's strategy while creating "deep emotional support" for the war[115]—thereby winning over the hearts, if not the minds, of many Americans.

They came to see prisoner release as the main reason for continuing the war, an illogical inference that nonetheless elicited greater patience for a gradual, as opposed to a rapid, withdrawal of troops. And because Nixon and his lieutenants also succeeded in associating the demand for an early prisoner release with the loyal sentiments of "supporting our troops" and "supporting the flag," they were better able to cast antiwar protestors in the role of unpatriotic dissidents. By the fall, as the Moratorium drew near, the POW campaign gathered momentum. Several events were scheduled: Paris trips in September and October by families of prisoners to demand meetings with the DRV and PRG; a congressional bill declaring November 9 a National Day of Prayer for POWs; full-page newspaper ads by United We Stand on the same day demanding the release of POWs; House subcommittee hearings in mid-November to denounce Hanoi's cruel treatment of American prisoners; and similar activities into December, including meetings between Nixon, Laird, and POW relatives.[116]

Kissinger later commented that Nixon was ungenerous toward dissidents at a time in history that demanded a leader possessing nobility of spirit. Suspecting a liberal conspiracy against him, and misunderstanding both the protesters and the nature of his conflict with them, Nixon, Kissinger asserted, viewed his differences with critics of the war as a "political battle for survival" when it was really a "foreign policy debate." He reacted with the "methods that had already brought him so far," thereby polarizing American politics and more.

But Kissinger, too, was ill equipped to understand the foreign policy argument offered by those who questioned the policy wisdom, strategic morality, and human and material costs of the war. Whether because of his own political partisanship, his conservative-intellectual's mentality, or both, he simplistically portrayed the antiwar opposition as primarily composed of college youths who suffered from "the metaphysical despair of those who saw before them a life of affluence in a spiritual desert." They and their dovish elders—particularly those in Congress—were, he claimed, "unpacifiable," perversely demanding more of the administration than of the Politburo.[117]

The private record indicates that Kissinger was disturbed by the uncooperativeness of his rivals within the government and the protests of the antiwar movement, both of which evoked for him youthful memories of the last traumatic days of the Weimar Republic.[118] "Very concerned" that the president would reject Duck Hook, Haldeman noted, Kissinger continued to argue that the choice was between the extremes of a "bug out" and an "acceleration" of military pressure on Hanoi.

In the beginning of October, the president began to fear that his special assistant was becoming unhinged: Kissinger, he thought, was "obsessed" about his rivalry with Rogers and Laird and overreacted to their participation in the making of policy. Growing intolerant of Kissinger's peculiar "attitudes and habits," Nixon instructed Haldeman to help make Kissinger "upbeat" and keep him "on an even keel," for he was "extremely valuable and effective and any deterioration would be damaging to the overall operation." By the end of October, however, Nixon's patience was almost exhausted. On October 27 he abruptly walked out on Kissinger's foreign policy briefing when the latter repeatedly mixed criticisms of Rogers and the State Department with information about global issues.[119]

Kissinger's perturbed behavior during this period was the product of a complex mix of several causes: melancholy about the failure of their original scheme to win the war; a fervid attempt to ingratiate himself with the president by continuing to advocate the original tough Vietnam line; and dread that Nixon would cave in to public pressure and accept the compromise approach of his rivals, Laird and Rogers, thereby endangering Kissinger's standing in the pecking order of presidential power.[120] Confounded by his statements, Kissinger's own aides were uncertain about his purpose and motives. Some thought he favored Duck Hook and was its strongest advocate; some thought he opposed the plan and wanted their critical assessment in order to convince Nixon that it should not be adopted.[121] This latter assessment was probably the result of Kissinger's habit of criticizing his "mad" boss in order to maintain the support of those of his aides who had dovish views on the war. Kissinger did in fact support the plan, but he would do so only as long as Nixon, its originator, did, for if the president decided against it, Kissinger would be isolated.

A DEFINING MOMENT

Nixon's resolve eroded rapidly in October. He sensed that he was "lost" if he chose a "cop-out" or a dramatic escalation. Without Duck Hook he believed he could not quickly end the war, but he was also convinced that if he embraced the plan, he could not—as Kissinger phrased it in October—"hold the government and the people together" for the three to six months required for it to work. On October 3, with his threat deadline looming, he began his own final assessment of the plan, telling his staff that he would have to concentrate on Vietnam and foreign affairs for the next six weeks, leaving domestic matters to them.[122] After an NSC meeting and a rambling, unsuccessful television speech on nonwar issues on October 8, he took solace in the thought that his public relations malaise had been inevitable because the "main problem is Vietnam." He told Haldeman that he had "bought nine months" and had "kept the doves at bay," but he could no longer "expect to get any more time." He would have "to take them on," first, by using Vice President Agnew to attack the antiwar movement and the press, which he had already begun to do, then by going on the attack himself. The "problem," he now knew, was that "this does make it his war."[123]

It was a defining moment, not because he accepted responsibility for the continuing war or was giving up on the struggle but because he acknowledged that his original plan had failed and that to salvage it he would have to launch a military operation that would entail grave domestic consequences. He had long before taken on the conflict as his own (as evidenced by the secret bombing of Cambodia and Laos), but he could not now bring himself to accept the domestic risks attendant upon a more drastic—and public—escalation. Although still "pondering the course" of the war through the night and into the next day, he confided to Haldeman over lunch that he "does *not* yet rule out K's plan as a possibility, but [he] *does* now feel [the] Laird-Rogers plan is a possibility, when he did not think so a month ago."[124]

Nixon would review Vietnam alternatives one more time on October 11, but he had crossed the line, and Kissinger knew it.[125] Although rejecting what they considered to be the "cop-out" option of withdrawing precipitously while blaming it on the doves, the president abandoned Duck Hook—at least for the time being.[126] His decision was to ride out the Moratorium and then make a major speech to the American people, in which he would explain his policies and ask for their support. Decided on at least by October 9 but not publicly announced until the thirteenth, the address was scheduled for November 3, after the November 1 deadline and an important November 2 gubernatorial election in New Jersey but well ahead of the November 13 Mobilization. The president and his inner circle hoped the anticipation engendered by the announcement would divert public attention from the protesters' message, keep the antiwar movement at bay, throw fear into the heart of the North Vietnamese enemy, and also allow Nixon to withhold further public comments on the war until the night of the November 3 speech. Nonetheless, there was, Haldeman noted, a "lot of concern about . . . Moratorium Day as it nears and [the] heat builds."[127] On October 14 Pham Van Dong broadcast a message of encouragement over Hanoi Radio to participants in the Moratorium and Mobilization, expressing confidence that the "Vietnamese people and U.S. progressive people" would be victorious in the struggle "against U.S. aggression." Nixon recalled later: "I knew for sure that my ultimatum had failed."[128]

When Moratorium Day came to Washington and other cities and villages across the country on October 15, millions of Americans participated in suspensions of business as usual, teach-ins, memorial services, and a multiplicity of additional nonviolent actions. Well received by many among the nondemonstrating public, the Moratorium did not, however, live up to the dire expectations of the White House, in part because the press, intimidated by Agnew's attacks, reduced its coverage of the event. Nixon's inner circle breathed "a great sigh of relief."[129] Yet they continued to worry about the impact of the antiwar movement and the upcoming Mobilization in particular. Although hopeful that Nixon's November 3 speech "would clearly state the case and . . . under normal circumstances be very effective, . . . probably buy[ing] us another couple of months," they also knew that the circumstances were not normal: "a massive adverse reaction could conceivably be developed the next day, and built up over ten days into the November 13–15 demonstrations with horrible results."[130]

TOWARD A NEW STRATEGY FOR VIETNAM

On the foreign policy scene, meanwhile, Nixon was unable to free himself of old habits. Although having already decided against Duck Hook, he issued yet other threats against Moscow and Hanoi in an October 20 meeting with Dobrynin. They were designed, he said, to make sure that the Soviets did "not mistake as weakness that lack of dramatic action on my part in carrying out the ultimatum." He would demonstrate "continuing resolve to the North Vietnamese" on the battlefield, but the Soviets needed "a special reminder."[131] According to Nixon's account, he and Dobrynin first discussed the Mideast, European security, and Berlin, but then he took control of the meeting to scold the Soviets for having done "nothing to help" with the Vietnam imbroglio except to arrange for an oblong table in Paris, while the United States had made "all the conciliatory moves." Offering a carrot to Dobrynin, he promised that "if the Soviet Union found it possible to do something in Vietnam, and the Vietnam war ended, then we might do something dramatic to improve our relations." But playing the China card, he predicted that if the Soviet Union did "not help us get peace," the chance would be lost to "build a different kind of world"; that is, one based on friendly tripartite relationships between the United States, the USSR, and the PRC rather than one in which the USSR stood in lonely isolation. Reminding Dobrynin that his government could not afford the "humiliation of a defeat," Nixon warned that he would, if necessary, pursue his "own methods for bringing the war to an end." Neither the apparently "unmanageable . . . American domestic situation" nor the heavy costs of the war would deter him. When finished, he rose from his chair and escorted Dobrynin to the door.

Haldeman's take on the meeting was that the president "really blasted him for Soviet intransigence on Vietnam and other matters." Kissinger's characterization in *White House Years* was slightly different, for he claimed that Nixon's threats were empty, and that he had been more eager to solicit Soviet support than willing "to face down his old friend by escalating the menace to the Soviet Union." Moreover, Kissinger claimed, Dobrynin had shrewdly succeeded in applying "reverse linkage" by extending a Soviet carrot that Nixon could not refuse: an offer to move up the opening date for SALT talks to mid-November, coincident with both the Duck Hook and the Mobilization timetable. He had thus taken advantage of the eagerness of "much of our government" to get arms negotiations under way and of Nixon's fears about a negative public reaction should the offer be denied and the story leaked.[132] Concerning the many threats made by the president since July to take drastic military action against North Vietnam by an early November deadline, Kissinger alleged: "As always, Nixon tried to play for all the marbles; and as was not infrequently the case, he began it with a maneuver that appeared portentous though it reflected no definitive plan. In short, he was bluffing."[133]

Because the operation was not carried out, it was true that Duck Hook was not a *definitive* plan, but it was a carefully considered plan, and Nixon had *not* been bluffing in the sense that Kissinger implied; that is, by making false threats, never having intended to follow through. Although the president possessed the military means by which to gravely damage North Vietnam, and although he did seriously consider their use, he and his advisers came to doubt that these means would be militarily and politically decisive, and they proved unwilling to pay the price of risking a try at finding out. In the end Nixon decided against Duck Hook not because he had been bluffing from the outset but because he backed down in the face of opposition from Rogers and Laird, NSC staff criticism of the plan, anxiety about negative public reaction and antiwar demonstrations, Soviet non-cooperation, and Vietnamese defiance. He had judged that the operation would not have fundamentally changed the military and political situation in South Vietnam; that Hanoi and the Viet Cong had not been intimidated; that the Soviets, Chinese, and Europeans would have reacted adversely; that part of his own government was opposed; that world and domestic public opinion remained dangerously volatile; and that the antiwar movement retained its vitality.

Nixon was remarkably candid in his own accounts of the decision to shelve Duck Hook. "I underestimated the willingness of the North Vietnamese to hang on," he wrote in *RN*. Although he had "wanted to orchestrate the maximum possible pressure on Hanoi," he could not "depend on solid support at home" if Hanoi "call[ed] my bluff."[134] "I believed," he commented in *No More Vietnams*, "it would be very hard to hold the country together while pursuing a military solution." Bombing and mining "would have been more than the traffic could bear" in government and bureaucracy; they would have offered only "a temporary respite from enemy actions," which "would not by itself guarantee South Vietnam's survival"; and the chances of détente with the Soviets and Chinese would have been "snuffed out."[135] The Moratorium, in particular, he wrote in *RN*, "had undercut the credibility of the ultimatum,"[136] by which he meant that in early October it implied to him that a dramatic escalation of the war would "risk a major American and worldwide furor and still not address the central problem of whether the South Vietnamese were sufficiently confident and prepared to defend themselves against a renewed Communist offensive at some time in the future."[137]

Nixon's emphasis in his postwar accounts upon the role of public opinion in causing him to postpone drastic military solutions in 1969 was in part an attempt to saddle the press and the antiwar movement with responsibility for losing the war. But the private record indicates that he was personally impressed with and worried about current antiwar activity and its future potential. The impending Mobilization served to bolster the impact on Nixon of the Moratorium, but coming on the heels of Duck Hook attacks, had they taken place, the demonstration carried with it the potential to grow into something much larger.[138]

For the moment Nixon's political pragmatism had defeated his gambling instinct, and by abandoning Duck Hook, he had chosen prudence over boldness— the better part of valor. This choice, however, tormented both Nixon and Kissinger, for it exposed a deficiency of that very willpower both had touted as an essential quality of decisive leadership.

With the hindsight of their postwar disappointment, Nixon and Kissinger expressed regret at having backed down. After the signing of the Paris Agreement in 1973 Kissinger told Safire: "We should have bombed the hell out of them the minute we got into office. . . . The North Vietnamese started an offensive in February 1969. We should have responded strongly. We should have taken on the doves right then—start bombing and mining the harbors. The war would have been over in 1970."[139] In 1978, at the start of his post-Watergate campaign of rehabilitation, Nixon told the Oxford University Union: "We should have begun bombing North Vietnam and mining its harbors at the time of our Cambodian operations in 1970." And in *No More Vietnams,* published in 1985, he wrote: "In retrospect . . . I would have to agree that a good case can be made by those who believe that we should have taken strong action against North Vietnam much earlier than we did."[140]

In October 1969, however, Nixon consoled himself with the thought that U.S. casualties were down, which might indicate enemy de-escalation, and also that Ho Chi Minh's death might still produce "new opportunities for reaching a settlement that deserved a chance to develop."[141] Haldeman thought that in his speech on November 3 Nixon would reveal his heretofore secret diplomatic steps and explain to the American people that he had done everything he possibly could. Then he would cancel the public Paris talks, announce additional and continuing troop withdrawals, and, if the Politburo were willing, send a personal envoy to Hanoi. If the other side continued to de-escalate, the United States would withdraw rapidly; if, instead, they escalated dramatically, Nixon would quickly implement an operation similar to Duck Hook in order to get military victory in three to six months, hoping that his prior explanations and enemy perfidy would have created the conditions for public support.[142] Haldeman was correct about the general drift of Nixon's thinking but mistaken about the details.

In *RN* Nixon indicated that although he had given up on ending the war in 1969, he believed that "victory" could still be achieved within two years by convincing the North Vietnamese that the United States was "there for the duration," building South Vietnamese confidence in American resolve, and continuing current U.S. diplomatic tactics and military strategies.[143] The record suggests, however, that although his hopes of ending the war in 1969 had indeed been dashed, he was optimistic that he could achieve his goals before the end of 1970. He was not as prescient as he implied in *RN* about the length of time it would take or clear in his own mind about the means by which it could be accomplished. He now appreciated that Moscow's leverage on Hanoi was limited, but he did not yet envision the China card as a real possibility. Nor did he—or Kissinger—yet appreciate the strength of antiwar sentiment and the determination of the enemy in Vietnam. Nixon's hopes lay in dampening antiwar sentiment with a new public relations campaign, holding home-front support with troop withdrawals, and building up Saigon through Vietnamization—all this while Kissinger worked the diplomatic angle and he looked for opportunities to make a big military play.[144]

The November speech, which originally had been conceived as the president's public announcement of the commencement of Duck Hook, now became the launching pad of his accelerated PR campaign. It was entitled "The President's Pursuit for Peace." Structured like an elaborate syllogism, Nixon's speech began with the premise that the absence of national unity behind his policies was the major obstacle to progress in ending the war. Attempting to rebuild confidence in his administration, Nixon pointed out that the enemy had caused the war, that he had inherited it from the previous administration, and that his responsibility was to uphold critical preexisting foreign policy obligations. Then he outlined his version of the positive steps he had taken in pursuit of "America's peace." In refusing to cooperate, however, Hanoi had blocked a solution. Warning of "bloodbaths" in Vietnam and a "collapse of confidence" abroad if the United States were to precipitously withdraw from Vietnam, he explained his own plan, which he promised would finally succeed; namely, Vietnamization, de-Americanization, the search for a negotiated settlement, and the determination not to hesitate in taking "strong and effective measures" should the other side increase "its violence." Concluding, he returned to his original premise about the critical need for national unity and the necessity for confidence in his government. To achieve "unity" (or consensus behind his policies), he appealed to the "silent majority" to support the war until an honorable peace through negotiations could be achieved, but he rebuked the "vocal minority," which, with its criticisms of the war, had caused division at home. North Vietnam could not "defeat or humiliate the United States," he proclaimed. "Only Americans can do that."[145]

To most Americans the nation's vital interests did not seem to be in jeopardy, and the purposes of this ugly war were not tangible. Nixon, however, attempted to transform this intangibility into an asset. The antiwar movement had doubted the wisdom of sacrificing American lives and taxpayers' dollars in a war fought by immoral means in defense of dishonorable, globalist goals, while militarism and social injustice persisted at home. Nixon redefined the meaning of such concepts as wisdom, honor, and morality by portraying the struggle as one for personal and national self-respect, patriotic loyalty, the saving of POW lives, the prevention of a Communist bloodbath, and the honoring of America's commitments. The final punctuation of his argument was to attach these symbols not only to support for the war but also to his own policies in waging it.

The televised address, and events before and after it, blunted the impact of the antiwar movement's campaign. A majority of senators and congressmen rallied in support of the president, and polls taken immediately after the speech registered 77 percent approval.[146] Nixon would remember it as his most "significant" and "effective" speech.[147] To ensure its effectiveness the White House developed a post-speech "game plan" of follow-through, which included orchestrated pro-war street demonstrations, patriotic presidential events, supportive speeches by legislators and show business celebrities, full-page newspaper ads, letter-writing campaigns, legal and verbal attacks against the antiwar movement, flag-waving, the declaration of National Unity Week (to begin on November 14), and a long list of other activities and events.[148] Primarily targeted at energizing the Silent Majority, the campaign's major themes were support for the war, the president, the country, veterans, and POWs. The icon of the effort was the American flag, which was waved, raised, reproduced on automobile bumper stickers, and worn as a political button or lapel pin. Associating his Vietnam policies with the flag, America's only universal symbol of patriotism, Nixon identified the opponents of the war as unpatriotic scoundrels, countering those in the antiwar movement who had used it as a symbol of blind, nationalistic loyalty in a militaristic war.[149]

But appealing to its own traditional American symbols, the Mobilization that followed the Moratorium was not without impact. In the cold wind and rain from the night of Wednesday, November 12, through the morning of Friday, November 14, thousands of protesters carrying candles and name placards memorializing the 45,000 Americans who had died in Vietnam silently filed across the Arlington Memorial bridge from Arlington National Cemetery to the Mall, as drummers beat a somber funeral roll. On November 15 the March Against Death was followed by the largest single demonstration against the war. Perhaps as many as 500,000 people gathered near the Washington Monument in song, speech, and silent witness, calling for American withdrawal, peace in Vietnam, and justice at home.[150]

In the White House, huddled by the fireplace on the night of November 14, even Nixon and his inner circle were impressed by the March Against Death. Nixon, Haldeman recorded, entertained "helpful ideas like using helicopters to blow their candles out, etc."[151] About the demonstration on the following day, Haldeman noted, "It was really huge."[152]

Although 77 percent of Americans polled had rallied in support of his November 3 speech and, by a margin of 51 to 36 percent, disagreed with the tactics of the antiwar movement, 81 percent believed the demonstrators were raising important questions, which should be answered, and 50 percent thought the war was a mistake and morally indefensible. By the end of November, public approval of Nixon's management of the war rose 5 percent compared with figures in September but, by a ratio of 55 percent to 33 percent, citizens rejected Nixon's characterization of protesters as "hippie, long haired, and irresponsible young people." In addition, the Congress was deeply divided on the war, and the press was skeptical of Nixon's claims.[153] Nixon, who continued to feel besieged by the movement, adjusted his schedule and travels to avoid demonstrators, but he was not always successful. To his consternation, for instance, antiwar protesters vociferously heckled when he lit the national Christmas tree on December 16.[154] He became more combative not only because of his disdain for opponents of the war, which spurred him to fight back, but also because he knew that support for the war remained fragile, which drove him to struggle harder. And struggle meant fighting back.[155] Ominously, even loyal Republican corporate executives were expressing a longing for peace. On November 26 Cyrus Eaton, chairman of the board of the Chesapeake and Ohio Railroad, wrote the White House to assure Nixon and Kissinger that "from the standpoint of the American businessman, there is no issue between us and the communists that cannot be quickly settled." The matter was urgent, he argued, because the financial markets must be restored to their "normal state." With peace Republicans could hold the presidency for twelve years. "The alternative is the complete disappearance of the Republican Party."[156] Then there were the unexpected turns of the war at home about which one had to worry: in late November Nixon became apprehensive that the 1968 My Lai massacre, which had recently come to light, might do "harm" to public support for the war. He hoped, however, that the damage could be reduced by arguing that My Lai "was contrary to national policy" and by pointing out that it happened as the war was escalating under the previous administration. Now, of course, it was de-escalating.[157]

Nevertheless, Nixon believed he had dodged a bullet during this fall of public discontent. Haldeman noted in mid-December: "Seems that P has pretty thoroughly gotten into the position of calming down the war opposition, killing the mobilizations and assuring the people that he has a plan and that it's working. Can probably keep it that way for a while. Problem will be if Viet Cong mounts a big offensive, or some other turn-around."[158] Nixon's concerns about an untoward turnabout were warranted as the fateful year of 1969 ended and the war entered yet another new phase. As he noted in *RN,* within four months he would "be forced to order an attack on the Communist sanctuaries in Cambodia," and in the next two years the war "would once again bring America to the brink of internal disruption."[159]

9
BITING THE BULLET: 1970

Cold steel, no give, nothing about negotiation. Hanoi can now
choose between peace and war.
—Richard Nixon[1]

PASSIVE-ACTIVE MOODS

The elation Nixon had felt after his television appearance on November 3 was short-lived, and during the next several months he lapsed into one of his sporadic postsuccess letdowns. Nixon watchers—close aides and psychobiographers alike—have commented on this recurrent phenomenon in his behavior, considering it to have been out of the ordinary. Haldeman recorded some of the incidences of letdown in his *Diaries,* describing them as states of boredom and psychological depression that followed peaks of triumph during periods of "activism." Nixon was well aware of his own mood swings, anticipating letdowns either by trying to prepare mentally for their onset or by avoiding activism in favor of "passivity." Defending his occasionally passive postures during one of his introspective soliloquies in the Oval Office, Nixon told Haldeman that his self-styled "low-key presidency" was necessary in order to bring about "a cooling of the country" in an era of turmoil. Yet periods of passivity caused him to worry about the "need" for activism, and, as well, to emphasize the importance of maintaining the "momentum" of success through follow-up procedures and combativeness toward opponents.[2]

The intermittent doldrums Nixon experienced had significant policy implications: a period of depressive inactivity spurred him to turn problems into crises or to overreact to real crises. A crisis, Nixon had written in *Six Crises,* "is bigger than the man himself [and] takes his mind off his own problems. . . . The natural symptoms of stress in a period of crisis . . . become positive forces for creative action."[3] In turn, the higher he rode "on the crisis wave," as Haldeman put it, the more likely and severe would be the subsequent letdown.[4] Determination turned to irresoluteness; a desire for public or bureaucratic approval alternated with denial and self-deception; constructive achievement was matched by destructive counterattack; and back and forth. Fearful of appearing weakly passive but concerned about becoming overly aggressive, Nixon would remind himself to avoid extremes. During the difficult period of preparing his November 3 speech, he scribbled a note on his draft: "Don't get rattled—don't waver—don't react."[5] Attempting to put a positive spin on the process, he rationalized his behavior in terms of a functional strategy: "It's good to have a fight to stir people up, sprint, then lie low." When angered, however, he often vented his wrath in unrealistic, hyperbolic threats, some of which he intended to carry out and some of which he did not. Agitated by a postal workers strike in several major cities in March 1970, he fumed to Haldeman that he would "bring all [the] troops home from Vietnam if he must [to] keep [the] mail moving."[6] When resisting contrary bureaucratic advice and "ruthlessly and courageously" making a controversial decision, as Kissinger put it, he retreated more deeply into "his all-enveloping solitude."[7]

One remedy Nixon frequently pursued in attempting to strike a balance between passivity and aggressiveness was to prioritize his workload and goals. On February 28, following an important NSC meeting on Laos the previous evening, and after telling Haldeman that they should have more stag dinners during the following week when Pat Nixon would be out of town, he decided to "get really hard-nosed about [foreign- and domestic-policy] priorities." Paraphrasing Nixon, Haldeman noted that the president wanted to "do better on the high priorities[,] so [he] will cold-bloodedly eliminate the secondary. [He] will send revolutionary memos to K and E, i.e., wants K to cut out everything about Africa, Latin America, etc. Only cover Russia, China, Vietnam, Middle East, the ones that matter. Eliminate all he can't do anything about."[8] The memos went out two days later.[9]

There was a fine line between the extent to which Nixon's mood shaped events and circumstances and, on the other hand, the extent to which they shaped his mood. In January 1970 Nixon predicted that the coming year would be the worst of his presidency, for he anticipated monetary inflation, economic recession, "no turn on crime" or other domestic problems, and the usual off-year election criticism. The White House public relations operation must therefore accumulate "equity" in public perceptions of his leadership and character, enabling him during the coming months to stay above the fray or to "ride it through." But he reassured himself that the situation "will improve in '71 and build up to '72. [We] must be prepared." Voicing another of his many political axioms, Nixon told Haldeman: "No leader survives simply by doing well. He only survives if the people have confidence in him when he's *not* doing well."[10] As events demonstrated, his pessimistic predictions were not without foundation. Writing in mid-April about the four months following Nixon's November speech, Haldeman observed that Nixon seemed "to have lost a lot of the basic 'feel' of the job," allowing himself to be distracted by nonessentials. It was "partly a result," Haldeman inferred, "of multiple unsolvable problems bearing in, and partly a function of less newness in the job. He really needs crises to deal with, and is not at his best with a period of general erosion such as this"; he is "not good on self-initiated momentum." Among the external causes of erosion in Nixon's mood during the first few months of 1970 were defeats and disappointments in public relations and public opinion polls, increasingly bitter infighting between Kissinger and Rogers, and sundry domestic and international conundrums. Having observed Nixon's bouts with ennui, procrastination, and depression on previous occasions, however, Haldeman considered the president's state of mind as "perfectly natural," representing a "normal doldrums period through which we'll pass."[11] Haldeman jotted these notes as Nixon was preparing to invade Cambodia.

REAPPRAISING VIETNAM STRATEGY

The president's passive-aggressive interaction with external challenges was reflected in his approach to the Vietnam War, the greatest of those "unsolvable problems bearing in." In late 1969 and early 1970, as he had during previous periods of doldrums, he embarked upon a reappraisal of strategy. On December 9, 1969, he told a group of visiting congressmen that he would "have a new review of Vietnam policy" soon after he announced the next increment of troop withdrawals on the fifteenth. The president was preparing to undertake a systematic reassessment, one that now included a careful review of NSC staff reports and expert outside advice.

Nixon had begun to question the efficacy of his original plan for Vietnam sometime in late September or early October—during the period in which he was backpedaling on Duck Hook and rewriting the November speech. Seeking alternatives, he had invited British counterinsurgency expert Sir Robert Thompson to the White House to discuss his "plan for ending Vietnam." They met on October 17. Already familiar with Thompson's previously successful record of battling the post–World War II Communist insurgency in Malaya, as well as with his subsequent books on counterguerrilla warfare, the president now heard him deliver an upbeat assessment of the prospects for Vietnamization, which, Sir Robert argued, could succeed within two years. "I began to think more in terms of stepping up Vietnamization," Nixon recalled in *RN,* "while continuing the fighting at its present level." This would prepare Saigon "to continue the war" after the Americans left. Thus encouraged, Nixon hired Thompson as a consultant and then sent him off to Vietnam in order to confirm his evaluation firsthand. After Thompson returned to Washington in November, he reported that the Saigon government held the "winning position" and would continue to do so unless the United States withdrew its troops and aid too rapidly.[12]

In support of his own report, Thompson arranged a meeting between Nixon, Kissinger, and John Paul Vann, an unconventional but veteran American adviser in Vietnam, who over the years had met with, befriended, or gained the respect of other advisers and influential journalists, including Daniel Ellsberg, Kissinger, and Neil Sheehan, a correspondent for United Press International and the *New York Times*. Vann had previously served as a uniformed military adviser but was now the senior civilian official for the Civil Operations and Revolutionary Development Support program in the Mekong River delta. He had escorted Thompson on his tour of the region in early November. Both shared an experience with and attraction to counterguerrilla, pacification tactics, an optimism about prospects for victory, and a dislike of the antiwar movement. When he met with the president in the White House on December 22, Nixon, at Kissinger's suggestion, asked Vann to explain why he thought the situation in the delta was improving, to comment on the capabilities of the RVNAF, to assess the intentions of the NVA, and to give his opinion on improving the American effort. Vann not only assured Nixon that pacification would continue to succeed but also argued that the South Vietnamese could be trained to fight as well as Americans—on the condition, however, that they were provided with heavy weapons, artillery, and air support. Thus aided, he predicted, they would even be able to contain a PAVN offensive from the North after the departure of American troops.[13]

Meanwhile, Kissinger's Vietnam Special Studies Group (VSSG), an interagency committee he had formed in the fall of 1969, had been discussing the status of pacification.[14] Among the studies considered was one produced by an NSC Working Group headed by Laurence Lynn and Robert Sansom of Kissinger's staff. The statistics they gathered indicated that since the Tet offensive of 1968 the United States and the RVN had made substantial gains in controlling the countryside at the expense of the NLF. But some on the committee doubted these trends could be maintained as American troops pulled out, and they questioned whether the Saigon government had the ability to establish itself permanently in the rural heartland. In any case, they could not be sure whether recent favorable trends were the result of the VNLAF having been forced to retrench in the face of American and South Vietnamese programs or of a decision by Hanoi to curtail operations for its own strategic reasons. The VSSG was skeptical of upbeat assessments as well, but it nonetheless endorsed Robert Thompson's report after Kissinger distributed it to the various departments. Several members of the VSSG, including Under Secretary of State Elliot Richardson, believed there was too much pressure from the top to produce encouraging reports.[15]

"The top" included Nixon, Laird, and Rogers, but not Kissinger. Rogers, according to Kissinger, was sensitive to public and congressional opinion and thus favored the largest reductions possible within the shortest period of time. In discussions of Vietnamization, he and the State Department did not give great consideration to the military impact of troop withdrawals and their impact on negotiations but instead emphasized the achievement of reforms within Saigon's military and political structure. Like Rogers, Laird believed Vietnamization was necessary in order to maintain domestic support for the president's goals, but he also believed Vietnamization was militarily sound, or at least that it should be given a chance to succeed. Concerned about the impact of the war on the Defense Department's budget and global military posture, Laird favored rapid reductions. Although he endorsed the policy of keeping a large "residual force" in place after an agreement on mutual withdrawal, he advocated the subsequent reduction of this force according to a timetable that Kissinger considered rapid.[16] Kissinger felt he had to concur with the president's growing interest in turning the war over to the Vietnamese and accelerating the pace of American withdrawals, but he voiced doubts about optimistic reports and urged a go-slow approach in de-Americanization. His concerns were fueled in part by his continuing personal rivalry with Laird and Rogers, but also by his previous experience with excessively optimistic bureaucratic studies and his intuition about the enemy's commitment to their cause.[17]

As 1969 ended and 1970 began, Kissinger interpreted a series of speeches by General Vo Nguyen Giap as an indication of his and the Politburo's faith in the efficacy of "protracted struggle" against America's "superior technology."[18] Kissinger's analysis of Giap's meaning was closer to the mark than those of some other American observers. Douglas Pike, for example, suggested at the time that the enemy's new strategy, which he dubbed "neo-revolutionary," marked a break with their earlier revolutionary war concept of a gradual progression from small-scale guerrilla tactics to regular, main-force warfare. However, he maintained, the new approach could not tip the balance against the United States.[19]

Giap had obliquely acknowledged in his speeches that North Vietnam was sorely besieged by American airpower and that the VNLAF had lost ground in the South, but he was nevertheless defiant and determined. The new strategy he advocated was one of technologically modernizing the PAVN and strengthening the air defenses and the economy of the North, while in the South the VNLAF should improve its political and military techniques of revolutionary war, rebuild its political infrastructure, and militarily wear down their American and South Vietnamese enemies. As in the past, Giap spoke of combining military and political means of struggle and of maintaining an indomitable will to persist. The ultimate goal was still that of passing from guerrilla war to regular war at some point in the future in order to liberate territory, but what was different about his summons to endure was a new emphasis on advanced weaponry and flexibility in moving from one stage of warfare to another.[20]

Supporting Giap's argument, General Van Tien Dung explained in January 1970 that the new circumstances of Nixon's war required them to "be constantly creative" in adapting to changing circumstances and to avoid "mechanically," or dogmatically, adhering to past theories about progressively moving from one distinct phase of war to another. The Politburo's review of the situation in January was that the war would be "long and complicated," but it predicted that the decisive phase would come in late 1970 to early 1971.[21] The Politburo continued to believe that the status of the military balance on the battlefield and the political conditions in South Vietnam would influence negotiations in their favor, but the time was not yet ripe, and therefore, they needed to prepare positions of strength.

Summarizing Giap's message in a report to the president on January 7, 1970, Kissinger called attention to the enemy's determination, observing that "the North Vietnamese cannot have fought for 25 years only to call it quits without another major effort," and he cast doubt on recent optimism in Washington about improvements in the fighting capacity of the RVNAF.[22] The president saw Kissinger's report but probably did not read Giap's speeches, and Kissinger probably did not quote Giap's remark—which was undoubtedly intended to bolster the morale of his own troops—that Nixon's strategy of bombing the North while withdrawing American soldiers from the South was a "passive" approach compared with the "aggressive" approach of the Politburo's liberation strategy.[23]

Kissinger recommended that the president dispatch another team of analysts to conduct another study of the military and political situation in South Vietnam. Headed by Alexander Haig, Kissinger's hawkish military assistant, the team surveyed several key provinces between January 19 and 29 and concluded: "There is no sign that the enemy has given up. . . . The pressures on the GVN resulting from U.S. troop withdrawals may lead to . . . a deterioration of territorial security force performance and a loss of popular support for the GVN."[24]

To reinforce the team's findings, Kissinger sent Nixon a CIA report that identified a fatal psychological flaw in Vietnamization and its corollary de-Americanization: the agency had discovered that South Vietnamese leaders were becoming increasingly pessimistic about their future prospects as a result of their fear of a rapid American withdrawal. Nixon responded with an observation about the obverse, perhaps based in part on his acceptance of a capitalist ethic: "K— the psychology is enormously important. They must take responsibility if they are *ever* to gain confidence. We have to take risks on that score."[25]

Nixon was not so foolish to think that Vietnamization alone could win the war, but because of the domestic political pressures upon him to withdraw American troops, he needed Vietnamization to succeed, and because he did, he wanted to believe it could. At the turn of the year, as his new strategy for Vietnam evolved, Vietnamization and de-Americanization received new emphasis. On December 15, 1969, the president declared that another 50,000 Americans would be pulled out of Vietnam by April 15, 1970, bringing the total withdrawal figure to 115,500.[26] He had considered announcing a larger number but, as Haldeman noted, "decided against [a] really big chunk now in order to save some for the spring," when he was planning to make a dramatic public relations announcement of 150,000 reductions in several stages between the fall of 1970 and the spring of 1971.[27] It was a difficult balancing act: pleasing the public with significant withdrawals, but not so significant that they would undermine Vietnamization or deny the administration leverage in negotiations with Hanoi. Kissinger acknowledged this problem in *White House Years* as having been part of their "basic dilemma": "An enemy determined on protracted struggle could only be brought to compromise by being confronted by insuperable obstacles on the ground." As American troop withdrawals proceeded apace, he worried that "they were evaporating Hanoi's need to bargain about our disengagement."[28] He became "disturbed" in mid-January 1970 when Rogers stated publicly that the administration's troop withdrawal plan was "irrevocable," and he complained to Haldeman that the secretary of state had breached the president's announced policy of making withdrawals contingent on progress in negotiations and enemy reactions in the field.[29]

Nixon's withdrawal timetable was indeed contingent on events and circumstances, and both he and Kissinger wanted to retain control over the pace of withdrawals so as not to undermine their negotiating position. When Nixon made a dramatic announcement on April 20 that 150,000 troops would be pulled out by the spring of 1971, the plan—urged by Kissinger—was to withdraw only one-third of this total by October 15, 1970, with most leaving after August. But Rogers's assessment was nonetheless correct: continuing withdrawals were inevitable. Their timing was at issue, but the process could not be reversed without incurring heavy political costs. At the beginning of 1970, it was not yet a major problem for the administration because 434,000 troops would remain in Vietnam in April 1970, despite the previous withdrawals approved in December 1969. By December 1970, 344,000 would remain. At the beginning of 1970, Nixon and Kissinger still expected to arrive at an acceptable settlement of the war before they would have too few troops left on the ground with which to bargain, and Nixon was not to feel the weight of that problem until April and May of 1971, when troop strength was down to 284,000 and more reductions were scheduled to take place at a more rapid pace.[30]

In the first year of his tenure, President Nixon had "passively" accepted or caved in to pressure for de-Americanization. But optimistic reports of progress in Vietnamization encouraged him to believe that he could sufficiently shore up the Saigon regime to keep it in power when an "honorable peace" would have been achieved, after which ample time would remain to "redeem the interim difficulties" on the home front and wage a successful presidential campaign in 1972. Thieu could then be sustained through the post-cease-fire future with continuing American aid.

"As 1970 began," he recalled in *RN*, "I felt that we had to think about initiatives we could undertake to show the enemy that we were still serious about our commitment in Vietnam." Although he had postponed a decision to proceed with a Duck Hook–like military action in the face of international and domestic opposition, he "aggressively" continued to bomb Indochina, while seeking opportunities to carry out a dramatic air or ground operation.[31] In 1970, as he told Laird, "we must play a tough game."[32] Nixon had determined "to continue the war despite the serious strains . . . on the home front" and the "ineffectiveness" of his attempts to persuade Moscow to put pressure on Hanoi. He "envisioned" a new military-diplomatic strategy, one that included diminished fighting by Americans on the ground in the coming year and a continuation of Kissinger's secret diplomatic ventures. While frustrated by Moscow's inability or unwillingness to pressure Hanoi into making concessions, Nixon believed he had made it clear to the Soviets that his administration would not tolerate "any major increase in aid or belligerent encouragement" to the North Vietnamese. The China card, he wrote, "would not be a major factor until the middle of 1971," which implied that it was not a major factor in his thinking in 1970—except as it had been previously, a rhetorical device to lever the Soviets. Nixon and Kissinger knew, because Dobrynin had told them, that the prospect of better relations between Washington and Beijing was a "neuralgic point" with Moscow.[33] It would not be until October 1970 that the limited direct contacts and indirect signals between Washington and Beijing appeared ready to develop into an opening for rapprochement.[34]

For his part, Kissinger—who increasingly dominated the machinery of foreign policy on behalf of and at the bidding of the president—had resigned himself to Vietnamization, but he, too, adhered to the madman theory. Blaming the enemy for basing diplomatic success on military success, Kissinger commented in *White House Years:* "There was no purely diplomatic alternative. Unless military and political efforts were kept in tandem, both would prove sterile. . . . It was precisely for this reason that I urged a military strategy that would persuade Hanoi to compromise and negotiate," and this he conceived in terms of "air operations."[35]

Military pressure was necessary because the political "compromise" Nixon and Kissinger sought was one that kept South Vietnam a non-Communist state by preserving Thieu's regime, which in turn served the larger purposes of protecting Nixon's presidency and American global credibility. Paradoxically, these goals were to be accomplished even while withdrawing American troops and achieving the release of American POWs. Nixon and Kissinger would continue the war for diplomatic victory in South Vietnam, but now more than before, Nixon needed to buy even more time for his extended timetable in order to persuade enemies and allies alike of American resolve, while at the same time fashioning, or at least maintaining, political support for his own presidency.

The new Nixinger timetable—which was not, however, firmly fixed—anticipated a turnaround in the war in late 1970 or by early 1971.[36] What they thought would bring about the turnaround is not clear, yet the old strategic recipe, consisting of the same ingredients but in different proportions, continued to be used. Some combination of Vietnamization, diplomatic linkage, madman threats, and dramatic military actions would, he and Kissinger hoped, succeed. As a component in this strategy, their hope of playing the China card against Moscow and Hanoi was just that, a hope; until it became a real possibility, which depended on Chinese intentions, Nixon and Kissinger could not develop a precise triangular plan. Before the card could be played, the Chinese had to be sitting at the poker table with the Americans and Soviets.

The Politburo's timetable, which now relied on a more "creatively" fought protracted war, coincidentally paralleled that of the White House. Reacting to the political and military realities of the struggle as they interpreted them, both sides had settled down to waging a more extended war than they had thought necessary the year before. They were retrenching in order to reorganize their assets, strengthen their base, and position themselves for the forthcoming negotiations, but meanwhile they intended to carry out decisive military actions in the future, if necessary. Both acknowledged the need to be militarily flexible in anticipation of untoward developments in the field, but both still fought on to decide the future status of South Vietnam.

DIPLOMATIC MANEUVERING

Affirming his long-standing belief that "the optimum moment for negotiations is when things appear to be going well," Kissinger asserted in *White House Years* that in November 1969 the administration had been in the "strongest" position to negotiate since coming to power, and he had therefore recommended another try at secret talks. It was an odd and questionable claim, because the administration had recently acknowledged the failure of its original plan to end the war. Kissinger contended in his memoir, however, that their pluck in the face of adversity and their resilience in recovering from strategic reversals had augured well for diplomatic success. They had withstood a VNLAF offensive as well as the Moratorium, and by going to the people with his televised speech Nixon had regenerated substantial public support for his policies. In addition, he claimed that Hanoi's leadership had been discombobulated by the president's response to Lodge's resignation as ambassador to the Paris talks.[37]

Lodge had asked to be relieved as senior negotiator in June 1969 but at Kissinger's request had remained in his post until officially resigning in late November. Although Lodge had told Nixon and Kissinger that he was not "dissatisfied" but was resigning in order to spend more time with his family, he was frustrated by his lack of influence in the negotiations. Proposed in January 1969, his idea for coupling a cease-fire proposal with military demands—such as mutual withdrawal, POW releases, respect for the DMZ, and international supervision—had been adopted, but his recommendation to establish a regular schedule of private negotiations with the DRV and PRG had been rejected. He also lacked plenipotentiary powers to negotiate, and he thought that madman threats against Hanoi would undermine relations with the Soviet Union and cause the Paris negotiations to collapse.[38]

Nixon refused to appoint a successor because, Kissinger claimed, the president wanted to demonstrate his "displeasure" with the lack of progress in the Paris talks. As a result, he said, Hanoi suspected that Nixon would soon resume the bombing of North Vietnam, and it therefore "clamored" for the appointment of another senior American negotiator. But it does not appear that the other side was intimidated. Instead, they responded with reciprocal measures. Lodge's counterpart, Xuan Thuy, did not attend the plenary Paris meetings that took place after Lodge's departure.[39] When in late November Kissinger requested a secret meeting with Thuy, he was rebuffed, apparently because Hanoi was "not ready." In mid-December, having deliberated Kissinger's proposal, the North Vietnamese formally rejected renewed secret talks between Kissinger and Thuy, citing Nixon's "warlike" speech of November 3, his failure to appoint Lodge's replacement, and the absence of a new proposal from the United States. Weeks later, Mme Nguyen Thi Binh, the chief delegate of the PRG, refused to meet directly with Philip Habib, the second-ranking member of the American delegation to the Paris talks and Lodge's de facto successor.[40] In a written response to letters from Lodge and Habib on POW issues, she referred to Habib as "Mr.," not as "Ambassador," while using her own title of "Foreign Minister" of the PRG, not "Chief Delegate" of the PRG to the Paris talks.[41]

The likely reason for Kissinger's recommendation to Nixon in November that he authorize secret talks was not that the times were propitious. As he confessed in *White House Years*, "I fell into the trap of . . . becoming an advocate of my own negotiation."[42] Nixon was then, had been earlier, and would remain more skeptical than Kissinger of achieving an acceptable termination of the war through diplomatic tactics; that is, without Hanoi having been forced to concede as a result of military setback. Kissinger's explanation of the president's attitude was that Nixon was wary of pursuing negotiations for fear of being rebuffed. To save the secret talks—or, as he phrased it, "to keep the channel alive"—Kissinger was often overly sanguine in his reportage of negotiating prospects. Nixon confirmed Kissinger's admission: "I was rather less optimistic."[43]

According to Kissinger's account, only with great difficulty did he succeed in persuading Nixon in mid-January to approve one more effort to reopen secret talks. Even so, the president expressed continued skepticism: "I don't know what these clowns want to talk about, but the line we take is either they talk or we are going to sit it out. I don't feel this is any time for concession."[44] On the other hand, Nixon claimed in *RN* that he believed the North Vietnamese by this time may have been diplomatically weakened by his rise in the polls, Soviet proposals to begin talks on Berlin, and Chinese offers to hold ambassadorial talks in Warsaw. Kissinger's most persuasive argument, however, was that even if talks failed, they should "build a record by which we would be able to demonstrate that Hanoi was the obstacle to negotiations." If Nixon's "aggressive" side opposed talks, his "passive" or "pacific" side inclined him to explore acceptable diplomatic means of ending the war, especially if the enemy could be blamed should these fail.[45]

After considering Kissinger's second proposal for several weeks, the North Vietnamese informed the Americans that they would be willing to meet on February 21. Within twelve hours the administration accepted—a decision Kissinger later regretted, not because it made any difference in the end but because he felt it had communicated excessive eagerness.[46] Both he and Nixon had taken it as a promising omen that Le Duc Tho, who was attending a French Communist Party congress in Paris, had told the French government that he might stay past the February 8 date of the end of the meeting, "depending on developments in the talks."[47] According to Haldeman, at the time Kissinger was "all cranked up," believing, or at least telling Nixon, that the other side's willingness to talk "may mean something."[48] Kissinger also reveled in the "intrigue" surrounding arrangements for the clandestine meetings—a sentiment that Nixon shared.[49]

Roger Morris, a Kissinger aide, thought his boss appeared nervous before leaving Washington for his first meeting with Le Duc Tho, for he paced back and forth, rehearsing his opening remarks. Kissinger knew that Tho, a Politburo member, had more power to reach an agreement than Thuy, but also that he was a formidable negotiator. "Luckily for my sanity," he wrote in *White House Years*, "the full implications of what I was up against did not hit me at that first meeting in the dingy living room in [the North Vietnamese residence in Choisy-le-Roi, Paris, at number 11] rue Darthé, or I might have forgone the exercise." The face of the Vietnamese enemy that Kissinger saw in his mind's eye was a portrait in stereotype. For Tho's demonstrated strength of character and dignified demeanor, Kissinger came to have considerable respect, but for his revolutionary cause and disrespectful impertinence toward representatives of the United States, only contempt. To others he condescendingly referred to his adversary as "Ducky" and recorded in his memoirs that Tho and his compatriots were "insolent."[50]

There were to be three secret meetings on February 21, March 16, and April 4 before the talks were overtaken by events in Cambodia. At the first, Kissinger opened with arguments designed to gain a psychological advantage. He claimed that public support for Nixon's policies was greater than before, that Hanoi's military position had not improved, and that its international situation was weaker as a result of the Sino-Soviet dispute. Thuy and Tho countered, pointing out that opinion polls indicated more Americans favored immediate withdrawal than before and that key legislators and leaders were calling for flexibility in the negotiations. More important than public opinion in measuring relative strength, Tho maintained, was the actual military situation in Vietnam, which had not yet been determined in favor of one side or the other. Yet he reminded Kissinger that Nixon's assessment of the military prospects for Vietnamization was in error, for how could the United States expect to succeed through reliance on "puppet troops" when it could not win previously, before Nixon had begun to withdraw American troops?[51]

When they came to the discussion of concrete issues, Tho repeated the key military and political positions of the DRV and the PRG, insisting on a complete and unconditional U.S. withdrawal from Vietnam and the formation of a tripartite coalition government that excluded key members of Thieu's regime, with elections to follow. If the DRV and PRG had ever considered including Thieu, Ky, and Khiem, they had changed their minds by the end of 1969 because of

Thieu's repeated declarations of opposition to such a government.[52] Refusing to discuss the matter of a coalition, but rejecting it nonetheless, Kissinger focused on military matters. As before, he insisted on a mutual withdrawal of U.S. and DRV military forces, but he introduced a nuanced revision, informing Tho that the Nixon administration would no longer require that North Vietnamese troops be placed on the same "legal basis" as American troops. "Because . . . you do not acknowledge their presence in South Vietnam and you cannot admit that they are 'foreign,'" he told the DRV delegates, "we would take full account of your special view of this question."[53] Kissinger's solution was that the United States would make a de jure commitment in a peace agreement to withdraw all of its troops, if in return Hanoi carried out a de facto withdrawal of its troops. Tho rejected this more subtle but meaningless version of reciprocity,[54] which Kissinger may have proffered to fulfill Hanoi's prior requirement that these talks would take place only if Washington presented something new.

When Kissinger returned to Washington on February 23, he reported that he was "pretty pleased, feels [the talks] made a start toward some real progress," and he had been "pretty tough." Even though Nixon agreed with Kissinger that Tho's suggestion for a second meeting indicated that they were worried about the course of the war and therefore prepared to negotiate "seriously," he—as well as Haldeman—doubted Kissinger's toughness, and they were never confident about the accuracy of his assessments of the talks.[55] After reading Kissinger's memo suggesting tactics for the next meeting, Nixon wrote back with his own recommendations: "Don't haggle so much over 'what did they mean by this or that.' . . . They thrive on this kind of discussion. Come directly to the hard decisions on the two major issues and say 'we will leave details to subordinates'—otherwise you will spend two days on details and make no progress on substance. We need a breakthrough on principle—and substance. Tell them we want to go immediately to the core of the problem."[56]

The two core goals of Nixon and Kissinger were the mutual withdrawal of military forces and a political settlement favoring Thieu.[57] But because the American negotiating strategy was to separate the military and political discussions—with the United States talking to the DRV about the former, and the RVN talking to the PRG about the latter—the two major issues Nixon wanted discussed in Kissinger's meetings with Tho that began in February 1970 were mutual withdrawal and POWs (both defined as "military" issues). If, however, Tho would have offered a political proposal to the Americans that Thieu should remain as president of the RVN, Kissinger would not have objected.

The POW matter had not been a major agenda item in Kissinger's previous private meeting with the North Vietnamese delegation but had been one in the four-party plenary Paris talks. Lodge's delegation had often raised the POW question in the plenaries, calling for an early release.[58] The DRV and PRG had usually rebutted by demanding the release of all of their nationals held by the United States and the RVN, both military and civilian, while pointing out that prisoners on both sides could be freed only upon the resolution of "other questions" and the conclusion of a peace agreement.[59] However, Nixon was now elevating the POW matter to the status of a major issue in the private talks as well.

In the plenary talks, Habib, Lodge's de facto successor, was instructed to confine "himself virtually exclusively to the issue of prisoners of war." Kissinger may have questioned this tactic, however. In March he advised Nixon that Habib should be authorized "from now on to begin speaking on other issues, while continuing to focus on the subject of prisoners of war." On Kissinger's memorandum, however, Nixon scribbled in response, "I'm not sure this suggestion fits with the big picture."[60]

What was the "big picture" in February and March 1970? The American side had first raised the POW issue in the plenary talks in early 1969, mainly to build public support for Nixon's policies. By the end of the year, Nixon and Kissinger continued to pursue it to establish a record of negotiation in order to defend the extension of their timetable for ending the war and to justify dramatic military steps in the future. By that time, Kissinger, if not Nixon, had additionally come to see it as a clever negotiating device to bring about the mutual withdrawal of forces: if the other side acknowledged that there were North Vietnamese prisoners in South Vietnam, then it followed that they had tacitly admitted there were North Vietnamese troops there. This "nuance," as Kissinger suggested in December 1969, against the advice of the State Department, "could give us a handle for pressing the point further, thereby helping to establish one of the basic points in the Administration's policies on Vietnam." But by March 1970, if not before, there was another aim: if the administration could convince Hanoi in the private talks to withdraw its troops *and* release American POWs without a political settlement, then Nixon could declare to the American people that he had brought the troops home, ended the war, and achieved a victory in the process. By means of such an agreement, Thieu, already strengthened through Vietnamization, could be sustained through postwar aid.[61]

The scheme was too cunning. They did not outwit the DRV or PRG, but deceived themselves into believing they could convince the other side by way of Kissinger's shrewd negotiating tactics or Nixon's dire military threats to yield the points for which the enemy had fought the war. But Nixon and Kissinger were unavoidably attracted to ingeniously complex intrigues, which they regarded as skillful strategies of realpolitik. Haldeman noted that Kissinger "is fascinated by [the] complexity of P's mind and approach. K loves this kind of maneuver as does P, and K is amazed by P's ability at it."[62]

The self-deception accompanying their complex cleverness was compounded by secrecy and the compartmentalization of knowledge and decision making, which excluded the public, Congress, and key members of the executive branch, isolating Nixon and Kissinger from productive discourse with significant others about realities and prospects. Even Kissinger admitted that compartmentalization was the "bane of the Nixon Administration." But he myopically saw the fatal injury as that of having exacerbated the bureaucracy's "self-will" and "lack of discipline," which led it in its exclusion from decision making and information to resist the will of Nixon and Kissinger.[63] Kissinger's biographer, Walter Isaacson, conjectured that they would have done themselves a favor by making their own negotiating terms and actions public: "It would have made it more difficult for critics of the war to allege that Washington was the only stubborn party."[64] Perhaps, but it also would have made more apparent the stubbornness of Nixon and Kissinger, exposing to greater scrutiny their negotiating tactics, their military strategy, their extended timetable, their commitment to President Thieu's regime, and their manipulation of the POW issue.

Nixon's and Kissinger's secret methods were not simply the product of their habits of mind or their love of wielding exclusive power but also of their policy and strategy commitments, which they knew were difficult to defend, especially if Thieu became the center of public attention even more than he was already. The goal of preserving Thieu's regime was defensible to many Americans in maintaining the credibility of America's willingness and ability to intervene militarily in trouble spots like Vietnam. But the sacrifices asked of Americans in order to keep Thieu in power caused many others to question the worth of preserving both Thieu specifically and credibility generally. The national consensus in support of unlimited military intervention had already eroded severely, and some believed there were other paths to or forms of credibility. Nixon and Kissinger did not want to encourage the public analysis of these matters or of the administration's management of the war. That was the rub.[65] The other side was indeed stubborn in its adherence to key goals, but it had also given Nixon a way out: a coalition government in South Vietnam, an internationally supervised withdrawal of American troops by a certain date, and a process by which Vietnam would be reunited. From Hanoi's point of view, these terms constituted a compromise that resembled but also improved upon the 1954 Geneva Accords, which had been sabotaged afterward by an aggressive anti-Communist regime supported by the United States.

When Kissinger departed Washington for his second meeting with Tho, he was openly hopeful about a deal, telling Nixon and Haldeman: "If the North Vietnamese have anything positive this time, we'll be on the way to a settlement this year. A real coup if it works out."[66] In Paris on March 16, Kissinger tried what he described as "another approach." He called for a "mutual de-escalation of military operations throughout Indochina" while negotiations were taking place, and he proposed a monthly schedule of American troop withdrawals over a sixteen-month period, a program of prisoner releases during the withdrawal process, and a mixed electoral commission to oversee South Vietnamese elections after an agreement. Unfortunately for Kissinger, he had made a tactical error: the sixteen-month schedule conflicted with the twelve-month schedule Nixon had proposed previously in his public speeches of May and November 1969—a contradiction Tho was quick to point out. In any case it did not matter, for it fell far short of the PRG's call for a six-month withdrawal period, which Tho continued to support.

Tho also rejected Kissinger's proposals for the mutual de-escalation of military operations and the mixed-electoral commission as just more attempts to separate the discussion of fundamental military and political issues and thus preserve Thieu in power. For good measure Tho criticized the U.S. "expansion" of the war into Laos and Cambodia.[67]

In his written report to Nixon from Paris, Kissinger made a point of describing the "warmth" with which the North Vietnamese had greeted him. They had been "more friendly than at the last meeting."[68] When he returned to Washington the evening of March 16, he was in "good spirits," telling Haldeman after briefing Nixon that he was "still very optimistic, because North Vietnam was at least willing to discuss mutual withdrawal, which is [the] first admission they even have troops in [South Vietnam]." Paraphrasing the sense of Kissinger's comments, Haldeman noted that Kissinger was "playing [a] tough, uneager role," but even so the North Vietnamese wanted to "keep going for the next step." Kissinger had wanted to wait another month before the next meeting, but they insisted on a two-week interval, and he therefore thought "maybe there's hope."[69] His optimism, which may only have been intended for Nixon's ears, proved groundless at the next meeting on April 4, when Tho summarized his government's objections to the American position: it did not accept the principle of mutual withdrawal; American troops must depart within six months after an agreement; and Thieu must not remain in power.

Kissinger's account in *White House Years* obfuscated the differences separating the two sides: "Tho's view" was that "our schedule was defective," he wrote, "because it would start to run only after the agreement was completed, while Hanoi wanted us to withdraw unconditionally on a schedule unrelated to any other issue."[70] His implication was that Tho had unreasonably demanded that he accede to the unilateral withdrawal of American troops before a formal agreement and without having settled other issues; namely, those concerning political power in Saigon. That is, Tho was imposing prior conditions on the negotiations. But in reality "the agreement" Kissinger wanted and to which he referred in his memoirs—and one to which Tho objected—was the American proposal for a signed convention that called for the scheduled mutual withdrawal of U.S. and DRV forces from South Vietnam, but which, avoiding the key political issue, left Thieu in power. During the subsequent negotiating and withdrawal period, both sides would observe a partial cease-fire, de-escalate their military operations, and release POWs, while the PRG and RVN negotiated political questions.

Even though Nixon and Kissinger sought an agreement with Hanoi that stuck to military questions, such a settlement, by legitimating Thieu's rule by default, would in principle and practice be political as well, leaving the political status quo unchanged—*the* central issue of the war. This was obvious to insiders but obscure to outsiders, including the American public and even many in the antiwar movement. Thieu would have the upper hand in negotiations with the PRG for the creation of an electoral commission, whose task would be to organize the holding of elections after the mutual withdrawal had been effected. Tho's other, but even more important, objection was that U.S. forces would stay in Indochina for an extended period to bolster Thieu, the bombing of Laos and Cambodia would continue, and the threat of American air strikes against North Vietnam would remain. Because of the PAVN's withdrawal and the partial cease-fire, the military and political cadres of the NLF would be left to stand more or less alone facing Thieu's army and police supported by American aid and advice. The situation would be similar to that which obtained during Diem's regime before his assassination in 1963.

The Politburo did indeed demand a unilateral American withdrawal, as Kissinger said, but it would be a withdrawal commencing with a political-military agreement—one that removed U.S. forces from Vietnam, left PAVN in the South, and established a coalition government that excluded Thieu. POWs would be released upon the signing of the agreement. Hanoi and the PRG might, however, have accepted a coalition government with Thieu's participation had Washington formally agreed to withdraw unilaterally within a shortened time frame, and many Americans may have considered such a settlement honorable. But as long as the United States held to its own position and Thieu opposed a coalition, the DRV and PRG continued to insist on Thieu's exclusion. With or without Thieu's inclusion, a coalition government would have been led by the PRG and allied groups.

There was enormous irony in the Nixinger position. In January 1973—three years and thousands of deaths later—they would have to accept an agreement that provided for unilateral American withdrawal from Indochina, PRG participation in a tripartite commission of "concord and reconciliation," and restricted postwar aid to Thieu. In February, March, and April 1970, Nixon and Kissinger were in a stronger bargaining position than they would be in 1972–1973 because of the presence of over 400,000 U.S. troops in South Vietnam. No one can say with certainty, but they might have been able to secure a similar or better agreement in 1970 (or 1969, for that matter) had they formally committed to a schedule of unilateral American withdrawal with deliberate speed on a certain date, for this was the most significant concern of the other side.[71]

Whether or not such an agreement would have been possible before 1973, the 1970 Nixinger proposals were patently unrealistic in the context of existing conditions. The same could not be said of the Politburo's terms. After interviewing Premier Pham Van Dong in Hanoi in late 1969, Richard Barnet, a former Kennedy official and now a critic of the Vietnam War, commented that North Vietnamese leaders were not "enticed by the prospect that 'something interesting might develop' in the course of such negotiations." They were stubborn in holding to their demands for an American withdrawal and a major role for the PRG in the government of South Vietnam—an obstinacy that would cost their people many lives. But it was the Americans, after all, who wanted out of Vietnam, and even without a formal agreement, American troops were in fact slowly leaving. Allowing Thieu to remain in power in these circumstances would be, Barnet commented, a "ratification of a defeat on the battlefield, an event which had not happened and seems most unlikely to happen."[72]

Kissinger, an advocate of his own negotiations, could not see these realities clearly. Haldeman noted on April 5: "Hard to tell how well K evaluates these sessions. He tends to be all one way, optimistic or pessimistic, and colors everything based on his basic reaction." In moments of irritation with his assistant, Nixon accused Kissinger of failing to negotiate effectively. On April 13, after reading Kissinger's assistant's report on the talks, the president commented: "It's obvious he can't negotiate, he makes debating points instead."[73] Despite his criticism of Kissinger's abilities and style, Nixon, a practitioner of realpolitik, had nonetheless hoped that military steps taken in Laos, as well as those that they may have already planned for Cambodia, would have levered Hanoi into concessions. Kissinger shared this hope. Both were still seeking an elusive battlefield victory.

THE PLAIN OF JARS

At an afternoon meeting with Kissinger, Moorer, Richardson, and CIA Director Richard Helms on Monday, February 16, Nixon authorized B-52 raids on targets in the Plain of Jars in northern Laos. The raids were launched on Tuesday. The United States had previously bombed Laos north of the panhandle, but these were the first strikes in the region by B-52s. Intended to be hidden from the American public, the bombing was, however, reported in the *New York Times* on Thursday. At 11:30 P.M. Kissinger briefed the president on Indochina affairs, and Nixon gave his assistant final instructions before his Friday morning departure to Paris, where he was to meet with Le Duc Tho for their first private talks on the twenty-first.[74]

The bombings triggered a long-running commotion within and without the administration. Major newspapers editorialized against the operation. Democratic and Republican senators chastised Nixon and Kissinger for their secret methods, for raising the level of violence in Laos, for violating the 1962 Geneva Agreements, and for using CIA operatives in support of the Laotian government. Senator Stuart Symington urged Rogers to recall the U.S. ambassador to Laos in order to testify before his subcommittee, and he wanted to make public previous secret testimony on the war in Laos. Opposing the B-52 bombing, Rogers recommended cooperation, largely because he wanted to "force the issue," but Nixon, with Kissinger's support, rejected his advice. The feuding continued, however. On March 20, after his second meeting with Tho, Kissinger, Haldeman noted, made "an issue out of [the] State [Department's] reluctance to bomb Laos. . . . P told me to tell K to go ahead and bomb; don't make announcement or notify State; just do it and skip the argument."[75]

The administration's initial explanation of the Laotian operation was that it had been undertaken in defense of Premier Souvanna Phouma's neutralist government against a major North Vietnamese offensive, launched on February 12. In a lengthy public statement on March 6, prepared by Kissinger's office but with Nixon's collaboration, there was an additional defense: the expanded bombing of Laos would assist the process of Vietnamization and save American and allied lives by interdicting the flow of enemy supplies along the Ho Chi Minh Trail. The March 6 presidential statement failed to mention the B-52 strikes, referring simply to the use of "air power" and "air interdiction."[76]

In his memoirs Kissinger maintained that the enemy offensive had threatened to overturn the delicate "equilibrium" in Laos between Souvanna's Royal Laotian Army, supported by the United States, and the Pathet Lao, supported by Hanoi. It was designed, he wrote, to "overrun" Laos, which would force Souvanna to succumb to Hanoi's influence and abandon his "acquiescence" in the U.S. effort to interdict the Ho Chi Minh Trail. If the offensive reached the Mekong River, Thailand might deny the United States the use of air bases. As for secrecy about the B-52 operation, it was necessary in order to "limit" the war in Laos.[77]

What made the administration's explanations suspect was the fact that limited enemy and allied offensives had regularly begun at this time each year—the start of the dry season in northern Indochina—and had themselves been a dynamic part of the uneasy equilibrium. Both had sought to maintain the balance of power and position in their favor, which for Hanoi meant protecting Pathet Lao positions in the north and the Ho Chi Minh Trail farther south. It was unlikely that Hanoi intended to conquer Laos, which would have required a larger effort, diverting troops and resources needed for the struggle in South Vietnam. The attack was probably an attempt to preempt a CIA-backed government offensive, as well as a response to Washington's previous escalation of the ground and air war: on coming to power the Nixon administration had initiated operations that expelled Communist forces from the Plain of Jars, and it had additionally increased the number of fighter-bomber missions against villages and other targets in Pathet Lao areas.[78]

Seymour Hersh averred that the B-52 campaign was really designed as a warning shot to convince Hanoi not to prolong the war.[79] Kissinger and Nixon were indeed cognizant of the strategic "symbolism of a B-52 strike,"[80] but at the same time the symbolic value of B-52 raids was related in their minds to their military effectiveness against enemy movements. The North Vietnamese offensive, they argued, "threatened" to alter the existing balance of power in the Plain of Jars, and it therefore needed to be defeated. In a memorandum sent to the president before the NSC meeting on February 27 (an edited version of which he quoted in his memoirs), Kissinger wrote: "Should North Vietnam overrun Laos [that is, the Plain of Jars], our whole bargaining with respect to the Vietnam conflict would be undermined."[81] Although fighter-bomber attacks against enemy concentrations would have been adequate to meet an offensive, Kissinger was told by General Wheeler that B-52s were preferable because the smaller planes "could not compare in effectiveness."[82] This was advice he and Nixon welcomed, for it served larger strategic-diplomatic purposes as well.

Kissinger admitted in his memoirs that he and Nixon believed at the time that the Politburo's willingness to make concessions at the table would depend on the balance of power in Indochina and America's continuing ability to deploy efficacious military force. Airpower was the one instrument of force at their disposal that appeared potentially decisive at the negotiating table, if not on the battlefield, and at the same time seemed acceptable to the American public.[83] "No one cares about B-52 strikes in Laos," Nixon told Kissinger after an NSC meeting on February 27, "but people worry about our boys there."[84]

They had chosen the occasion of a North Vietnamese dry-season offensive as an excuse to use B-52s in order to accomplish at least two interconnected aims: to prevent the other side from reestablishing the equilibrium in Laos; and to send a warning signal that would influence negotiations. Their stratagem was a mixture of careful calculation and groundless optimism, mixed with exaggerated anxiety and disingenuous claims. On March 24, when domestic matters occupied Nixon's agenda, Haldeman quipped: "Poor K, no one will pay any attention to his wars, and it looks like Laos is falling."[85] Yet only several days later the North Vietnamese halted their offensive. On April 8 Nixon commented: "We've saved Laos for four weeks at least, and maybe we can hold a few weeks more."[86]

Because they believed that the outcome of the negotiations was contingent on the strength of the public's approval of Nixon's leadership, Nixon and Kissinger were doubly troubled that their Laotian policy had provoked a public outcry on the home front. Haldeman noted in his diary that Kissinger's optimism about progress in his private talks with Tho was related to the maintenance of "balance in [the United States], and this is getting tougher as Senate critics fire up again, especially about Laos. Also we have a Gallup [poll] that shows P down 11 points on handling Vietnam."[87] The quasi honeymoon Nixon had enjoyed with critics of his policies following his November 1969 speech had come to an end. Since critics opposed the war, and Nixon continued to wage it, this development was perhaps inevitable. He and the White House inner circle believed, however, the reason was personal and partisan, and that the honeymoon had actually ended weeks earlier, when national magazines and dovish senators had raised questions about his policies. Echoing Nixon, Haldeman had recorded after a staff meeting about PR questions on February 4 that it was "obvious" that the "Establishment" wanted to reopen the Vietnam debate. "They gave us 90 days after the November 3 speech and are now back at it. Also lot of effort to revive the Moratorium activities."[88]

Kissinger unwittingly contributed to the president's PR problems when he placed false information in the March 6 statement on Laos. Attempting to demonstrate that no Americans had participated or were participating in Laotian ground combat, Kissinger had written: "No American stationed in Laos has ever been killed in ground combat operations."[89] Nixon was publicly embarrassed when the Defense Department and the press subsequently pointed out that Americans had indeed been killed and wounded in Laos during the past decade. Kissinger blamed the error on ambiguous information supplied by the Defense Department, but

Nixon was nonetheless furious with his special adviser's blunder, and he refused to meet with him for almost a week.[90] When he was finally readmitted to the inner sanctum, Haldeman commented, Kissinger was "in pretty bad shape, feels he goofed and thus let P down and was taken in . . . by both Defense and State, and has lost P's confidence." On March 11 Nixon tried to "get him back in gear," reproving Kissinger for "beating a dead horse" and urging him to "move on the more constructive efforts."[91] "The Laos flap," Haldeman complained, "took an enormous amount of P's time."[92]

Nixon's disquietude was compounded by the struggle between Kissinger, Laird, and Rogers, and he was perplexed about what to do about it—"it's impossible because of the characters, especially K," Haldeman noted after hearing Nixon explain his dilemma.[93] Kissinger's ranting against Rogers, especially with regard to the secretary of state's opposition to the Laotian bombing and his initiatives to bring about a compromise in the long-running Israeli-Egyptian imbroglio,[94] led Nixon on March 18 to grumble about Kissinger's "psychopathic obsession with the idea that Rogers is out to get him."[95] After meeting with Rogers a couple of weeks later, Nixon decided that Kissinger had not given him accurate descriptions of Rogers's and Laird's views on foreign and military policy. Yet he also felt that Rogers "clearly maneuvers to clobber Henry,"[96] and he knew that Laird often pursued his own course.

Toward the end of March, Nixon and Haldeman believed Kissinger needed "time off and rest." They "had him stashed away at Paradise Island [in the Bahamas] for a week's vacation." But Kissinger was "all stirred up . . . , afraid to be away if [a] crisis breaks, and Cambodia is brewing one." Haldeman managed to persuade Kissinger to stay a little longer, however, "much to P's relief."[97] Nixon was then feeling the heavy weight of the presidency. "If anything breaks" on the "postal [strike], Cambodia, etc.," Haldeman worried on March 31, Nixon would be "overloaded."[98] His mood may have influenced a "big retaliation move" he ordered the next day against surface-to-air antiaircraft missile sites in North Vietnam, after surface-to-air missiles (SAMs) had downed an American photo-reconnaissance plane. Haig—who did not oppose such steps in principle—thought the moment was unpropitious: an attack would "screw up K[issinger]'s secret talks in Paris," where he was scheduled to meet with Tho on April 4. Filling in for Kissinger in his absence, Haig was gaining the president's confidence, and the attack was postponed for a few days—until Kissinger was ready to return home. The first "protective reaction strikes"—a title that obscured the resumption of bombing in North Vietnam—had begun in February, and they were to escalate in number during the next three years.[99] Nixon misleadingly justified such strikes by referring to an alleged understanding that President Johnson had made with the North Vietnamese during negotiations over the bombing halt in 1968.[100]

"March and April," Kissinger confessed in *White House Years,* "were months of great tension."[101] The causes of his own stress included the Laotian struggle, his "maddeningly ambiguous" negotiations with Le Duc Tho, the Mideast crisis, new and fateful developments in Cambodia, and the president's testiness toward him. All but the last bothered Nixon as well. In the gloom of his other frustrations, Nixon's "nervous energy," as Kissinger put it, was additionally sapped in April by an internal squabble over troop withdrawals, congressional demands that he negotiate limits on multiple-warhead, strategic missiles, the Senate's defeat of his Supreme Court nominee, Harrold G. Carswell, and the plight of *Apollo 13,* as it spun out of control toward Earth on its return voyage from the moon.[102] Personal frustration merged with political frustration when Nixon canceled his attendance at his daughter Julie's graduation from Smith and his son-in-law David's from Amherst on the advice of the Secret Service, whose agents were worried about the possibility of antiwar protests. Pat and Julie were very disappointed. Vice President Agnew undoubtedly roused Nixon's anger with the remark: "Don't let them intimidate you, Mr. President. You may be President, but you're her father, and a father should be able to attend his daughter's graduation."[103]

By mid-April Nixon had once again become greatly concerned about being and appearing decisive. Soliloquizing before Haldeman in the Oval Office about how well he compared with other presidents, Nixon convinced himself that he possessed to a greater degree than Kennedy, Johnson, or Eisenhower the "ability to command a group," which was "his main strength." Although the equal of Teddy Roosevelt, Woodrow Wilson, and Charles de Gaulle, he believed he got "no credit for it." Unlike these great leaders, who had aides who "got [them] enormous coverage of the[ir] mystique," his own staff had failed to build up the public's perception of his ability and "make it even more effective" in relation to his own mystique. Then, as they talked about the astronauts, he told Haldeman about his own funeral plans.[104]

"Historians rarely do justice to the psychological stress on a policymaker," Kissinger complained in *White House Years.* "What no document can reveal is the accumulated impact of accident, intangibles, fears, and hesitation."[105] Haldeman's notes and diaries, however, do offer a glimpse into Nixon's and Kissinger's emotions during this period, indicating that Nixon's doldrums and Kissinger's distress influenced the manner in which they responded to unfolding events in Cambodia. But these and other documents, as well as their memoirs, also reveal their policy goals. Psychological proclivities and foreign policy purpose—it was an explosive combination.

THE DECISION

On March 18 General Lon Nol (the minister of defense and prime minister of Cambodia), Prince Sirik Matak (cousin to Prince Sihanouk and leader of the Cambodian business community), and their coconspirators in the legislature and army deposed Sihanouk and seized governmental power in the capital, Phnom Penh. Sihanouk was in Moscow at the time, preparing to fly to Beijing. The coup d'état had been preceded by ten days of discord between pro- and anti-Sihanouk factions and several anti-DRV/PRG demonstrations, which Lon Nol and his clique had organized in the capital and in villages along the border with South Vietnam, particularly in areas bombed by B-52s. On March 12 Lon Nol and Sirik Matak canceled Sihanouk's trade agreement with the DRV and PRG that had permitted them to purchase supplies in Cambodia and to use the port of Sihanoukville on the coast of the Gulf of Siam, and they ordered Vietnamese Communist troops to leave the country. Vacationing in Paris during the pre-coup period, Sihanouk had immediately denounced his opponents, but instead of rushing back to Phnom Penh, he left Paris on March 13 for previously scheduled talks in Moscow. On March 15, as North Vietnamese negotiators met with Cambodian officials to discuss the troop evacuation ultimatum, Lon Nol requested South Vietnamese military assistance in attacking VNLAF base areas.

After the coup of March 18, Sihanouk, now in Beijing conferring with North Vietnamese and Chinese diplomats, grudgingly accepted the leadership of the Cambodian Communist Khmer Rouge insurgents, whom he had previously hunted down, jailed, and killed when he ruled Cambodia. On March 23 he issued a public call to arms against Lon Nol's de facto regime. The DRV, PRG, and the Pathet Lao extended their support, although Hanoi left a skeletal diplomatic staff in Phnom Penh, and the PRC tried to negotiate a compromise with Lon Nol's government on the status of the sanctuaries. Meanwhile, Lon Nol sought to mobilize the support of the Khmer population with denunciations of Sihanouk's corruption and his excessive tolerance of Communist troops in Cambodia, but also by arousing Khmer nationalism against Vietnamese-Cambodians. In Phnom Penh the middle class, the educated elite, and the army, hoping for a new era of economic prosperity and the receipt of bounteous American aid, welcomed Sihanouk's ouster and ignored his call to arms, but in the countryside, where Sihanouk's rule had been less resented and his removal regarded as a desecration, peasants rioted in several villages against Lon Nol's officials. Government arrests, more violence, and atrocities by both sides ensued. Long dormant below the surface of Khmer society, "savage . . . forces were aroused," William Shawcross observed in his important book on the Cambodian calamity, "and for years to come they simmered and shifted as war spread."[106]

At his meeting with Henry Kissinger on March 16, Le Duc Tho accused the United States of having organized the anti-Sihanouk riots; on April 4 he charged American intelligence agencies with instigating Sihanouk's ouster.[107] The assessment of VNLAF security units in Cambodia was that the coup "was under the direct leadership of the Americans . . . [and] had the complete cooperation of the French."[108] On the American home front, many of Nixon's antiwar critics had similar thoughts and suspected the administration of wanting to widen the war. But Nixon and Kissinger blamed the war's widening on Hanoi and denied charges of Washington's plotting,[109] although in 1977 Kissinger qualified his denial of U.S. involvement with the remark: "at least not at the top level."[110] No direct evidence has yet surfaced identifying the White House, the CIA, or the French in a formal conspiracy. Yet, as Shawcross pointed out: "It was clear . . . that American officials in Vietnam were aware of its planning and were indirectly in touch with the plotters. In some circumstances there is only a fine line to be drawn between foreknowledge and complicity."[111] In his 1983 book on Kissinger, Seymour Hersh developed indirect evidence that American operatives in the Green Berets and in military intelligence had encouraged Sihanouk's overthrow since 1969.[112]

Although obscured by disinformation, the absence of full documentary disclosure, and political controversy, it is clear that the origin of the coup, which set in motion the baneful actions and reactions of all sides, had been the result of a chain of complex causes rooted in the events of the previous several years. Generally these had to do not only with the underlying tensions in Cambodian society and politics but also with the spreading of the Vietnam War into Cambodia. The B-52 bombings of Operation Menu had been decisive in triggering the profound military, social, and political perturbations in eastern Cambodia. They had led the VNLAF to expand their sanctuaries during the previous year, which in turn had conjured additional frictions between the Vietnamese and Khmer and between factions of the Cambodian elite who held different views about the appropriate policy to follow regarding Hanoi and Washington.[113] For personal and policy reasons, Lon Nol and his Cambodian coconspirators had tired of Sihanouk's reign. The policy reasons had to do with their objections to Sihanouk's lenient, albeit practical, posture toward the VNLAF sanctuaries, and their belief in the putative advantages of throwing in their lot with that of Washington and Saigon—a belief encouraged by the U.S. government and its agents.

Lon Nol had expected American support,[114] and he was soon rewarded by a White House that welcomed the coup: it "was all right with us," Haldeman noted at the time.[115] The United States extended diplomatic recognition to Lon Nol, Nixon ordered arms and money to be channeled to his government, and the American command in Saigon authorized South Vietnamese military operations against the sanctuaries.[116] Preceded by B-52 raids, the RVNAF launched the first of what Kissinger called "shallow" cross-border operations against VNLAF positions on March 27.[117] These continued through the third week of April. Some attacks penetrated as far as ten miles into Cambodia, and some were carried out in cooperation with the Cambodian army. Defending these steps publicly, Kissinger asserted that they were provoked by the aggressive actions of the North Vietnamese before and after the coup. He accused them of rejecting an all-Indochina cease-fire, inciting Sihanouk's anti-American belligerence, initiating widespread attacks against Lon Nol's government, sponsoring the Khmer Rouge, and pursuing "total victory" in Cambodia.[118]

Although DRV/NLF actions undoubtedly contributed to the descent of Cambodia into total war, all the signs suggest that the Politburo had not welcomed the coup or the problems it created. Hanoi's diplomatic posture was initially ambivalent. It did not immediately embrace Sihanouk after the coup and continued for a time to press for a diplomatic compromise with Lon Nol, hoping that he would adopt the neutral stance of his predecessor and accept the existence of the sanctuaries in Cambodian territory.[119] Based on his own contemporaneous meetings in Paris with Le Duc Tho, Kissinger privately commented that Hanoi had been surprised, "thrown . . . completely off balance," and "confused" by the coup—an appraisal Nixon accepted. On his return to Washington from Paris on April 5, Kissinger reported to Nixon that Tho "didn't close things off." It was Kissinger, Haldeman noted, who told Tho he "wouldn't meet again unless they had something positive to offer."[120] Their understanding of Hanoi's position encouraged Secretary of Defense Laird and several of Kissinger's aides to recommend that Lon Nol should be encouraged to negotiate a return to the pre-coup status quo.[121]

Although it may have been diplomatically confused, Hanoi had not been militarily surprised. Since the latter part of 1969 its intelligence sources in Phnom Penh had reported increasing American pressure on Sihanouk to alter his policy toward the bombing of the sanctuaries, and in the first part of 1970 Soviet and Chinese intelligence warned of the possibility of a coup. Still, the other side's overt military steps in March and April contradicted Kissinger's public claims about its intentions. By March COSVN had begun to prepare evacuation routes out of the border area and had moved additional military units in to protect them. From the Mimot plantation in the Fish Hook, or Base Area 353, as it was designated by the United States, the COSVN command staff trekked north across the Mekong River to Kratie province around early March, and the PRG and NLF retreated north from their positions on the east flank of the Parrot's Beak as the South Vietnamese and Cambodian attacks began at the end of March. Their new locations on the west bank of the Mekong in east-central Cambodia put them in position to retreat toward Laos if necessary. VNLAF attacks on Cambodian government troops and positions did not begin until April 3, after RVN and Cambodian attacks had been under way for at least a week. But according to participants' accounts and captured documents, these had developed out of attempts to cover evacuations from border areas and protect their old and new bases, their communications lines, and the "50,000 tons of weapons, ammunition, military equipment, and supplies and medicine stored in the depots" at the port of Sihanoukville against the military movements of the Cambodians from the west and the South Vietnamese from the east.[122]

The post-coup declarations of the DRV/PRG in support of the Khmer Rouge–Royalist alliance against Lon Nol may have represented an attempt to "exploit" the situation, as Kissinger and others asserted, but at least as late as the latter part of April, they were uncertain about the possibilities and uneasy in their association with the Khmer Rouge.[123] Their support of the "Revolution" in Cambodia had as its primary purpose the protection of VNLAF communications and rear-base areas and the countering of what they took to be Nixon's strategic aims in Indochina: "The Americans had wanted to overthrow S[ihanouk] in order to strike VN and implement the Vietnamization plan," COSVN argued. "They wanted to cut our transportation routes, destroy our storage facilities, and base areas in order to cause difficulties to us, weaken our forces, force us to make concessions at the peace talks." Worrisome, too, were the frictions between Cambodians and VNLAF troops, which had been aggravated by the new fighting: "The population is still trying to evaluate our behavior and actions while cooperating with us to attack the enemy," a field security unit cautioned. "In many places, some cadre and soldiers are still violating discipline, which is adversely influencing the morale and thinking of the people and harming the good nature of the revolutionary army."[124]

Reacting combatively to the turmoil in Cambodia from the beginning, Nixon had authorized planning for a major U.S.-RVN offensive against the sanctuaries either before or soon after the coup—"several weeks" before a "big . . . meeting of the NSC types" on April 26.[125] It was an idea that had long been on his mind and on the military's agenda. As Kissinger outlined the strategic options in *White House Years,* the choices were "doing nothing (the preferred course of the State and Defense departments); attacking the sanctuaries with South Vietnamese forces only (my recommendation); and using whatever forces were necessary to neutralize all of the base areas, including American combat forces, recommended by Bunker, Abrams, and the Joint Chiefs of Staff."[126] Helms was another top adviser who approved option three. To Laird and Rogers, option one, "doing nothing," meant no major ground invasion, but they also favored the use of diplomatic means to defuse the crisis. According to Kissinger, Rogers even opposed "substantial" cross-border attacks by the RVN but accepted the necessity of "unrestricted" American air raids. Laird strongly supported "shallow" cross-border South Vietnamese operations but opposed a major, joint U.S.-RVN offensive into the sanctuaries. By at least April 18 Nixon and Kissinger had rejected option one and were seriously considering options two and three—that is, a two-stage, combined U.S.-RVN operation.[127] (It would later be referred to publicly as an "incursion." Privately, the word "invasion" was sometimes used.)[128] Option two, the RVNAF attack into the Parrot's Beak, a salient of Cambodian territory jutting toward Saigon, was referred to in the White House inner circle as "Phase I." Option three, or "Phase II," was a joint U.S.-RVNAF thrust into the Fish Hook region of Cambodia, a shallow salient that bordered South Vietnam's Tay Ninh and Binh Long provinces and the VNLAF's Iron Triangle stronghold. It would involve mostly American troops. Both the Parrot's Beak and Fish Hook attacks were configured as pincer movements, designed to envelop enemy forces and base areas within each salient.[129]

In the post-event controversy about the Cambodian invasion, the main issues argued have concerned the timing and motives of Nixon's decision to proceed and Kissinger's role in it. A briefing Nixon received from Admiral John McCain at a breakfast meeting with officers from Commander in Chief Pacific headquarters (CINCPAC) on April 19 in Honolulu, where he had gone to present the Medal of Honor to the crew of *Apollo 13,* gave "focus to his inchoate anxieties about Cambodia"—as Kissinger phrased it.[130] McCain—whose presentations were known for their

emotionally pugnacious flair, and whose son was a POW in North Vietnam—
argued that in light of Nixon's decision to withdraw 150,000 troops during the course
of the year, which he was scheduled to announce on television the next day, South
Vietnam's western flank needed to be protected, which meant that Cambodia had
to be saved if Vietnamization were to succeed. In the least, the sanctuaries had to be
attacked. Nixon was so impressed that he arranged for McCain to go to San Clemente
in order for Kissinger to hear the same briefing.[131]

Awake early on April 20, Nixon spent the morning polishing his withdrawal
speech, which he had worked on during the flight to California. In midafternoon
he met with McCain and Kissinger. At 6:30 P.M., one hour after he had gone on
the air, Nixon and his entourage took off for Washington, D.C.[132] During the flight
Nixon presided over long discussions about "revving" up the "team" and the
"troops" in support of his withdrawal plans. By taking "the offensive," they could
preempt opponents. The vice president and the cabinet were to be encouraged to
line up behind him; his speechwriters were to prepare the follow-up public relations spin; supporters in the Congress and press were to be mobilized. Meanwhile,
he was to "cut [the] crap" in his own schedule in half in order to have more time
to think and write, while in his public demeanor he should "be more aloof."
Anticipating that Secretary of Defense Laird would take advantage of the withdrawal decision by accelerating the schedule, Nixon contrived to bypass him and
other cabinet members by setting up a back channel directly from the White House
to the military. He "was not," he insisted, "going to let Laird kill this by pulling
out too fast."[133]

Shifting the topic to Cambodia, Nixon, Haldeman noted, began "really pushing on strong moves in Laos and Cambodia—hit all the sanctuaries." The matter
would be on his agenda the next day. He would "take over the war in Cambodia
and take resp[onsibility]." On this matter, they "need to pull all together." His
decision would be made "w/o Rogers, etc." Haldeman was to confront Rogers and
Laird and tell them that the "P said [he] can't bug out." His speechwriters would
prepare to meet opposition from other quarters by hitting hard on these points:
"Do you want [the] U.S. to lose? do you want us to bug out? what more do you
want in way of negotiation?" The withdrawal decision was a "boy'[s] job." Cambodia was "a man's job," and it "really needs to work."[134]

After little sleep during the night, Nixon was awake at 6:00 A.M. Washington time, April 21, "cranking in full gear." At 9:30 A.M., after two other meetings, he met with Kissinger and Helms to discuss Cambodia. Helms reported on
VNLAF attacks and the fragility of the new Cambodian government. According to Kissinger, Nixon was "beside himself" on hearing the news of bureaucratic
"foot-dragging" in delivering the money, arms, and communications equipment
to Lon Nol and the CIA that he had ordered previously. He demanded immediate
action on the matter and also called for an NSC meeting the next day to decide on
his government's "overall strategy" for Cambodia. Only NSC principals were to
be in attendance; there were to be no undersecretaries; no one was to take notes;

and Kissinger was to sit at the table. During the rest of the day Nixon was simul-taneously angry with cabinet aides who were disgruntled about sundry ancillary issues, relieved that his economic advisers had predicted there would be no reces-sion in 1970, and excited about dealing with the crisis in Cambodia. Haldeman thought he was "really rolling in spite of no sleep as he enjoys taking command of foreign policy, with a little good news domestically."[135]

Nixon was awake at 5:00 A.M. on April 22, dictating a memorandum to Haldeman for Kissinger. "In high gear" and roaring on "in his new energy" when he arrived at his office, he had ordered Haldeman to cancel everything on his schedule so that he could concentrate on Cambodia. In the memo he told his national security adviser that "we need a bold move . . . to show that we stand with Lon Nol." Claiming that "we have really dropped the ball on this one" for fear of provoking the North Vietnamese, he argued that it was now time to "do something symbolic to help him survive," because the Communists, never need-ing any provocation, were already "romping" in Cambodia, and Lon Nol's gov-ernment would likely fall. The bold move should be coupled with diplomatic efforts: Kissinger should take steps to inform "the lily-livered Ambassadors from our so-called friends in the world," and a special emissary should be sent to Phnom Penh to reassure Lon Nol of support. "We are going to find out who our friends are now, because if we decide to stand up here some of the rest of them had better come along fast." In three other memos to Kissinger that day, Nixon accused Sihanouk of parroting the Communist line, spoke of calling on the Japanese, French, British, and other allies to back up the United States, and asked Kissinger to summon the Soviet chargé to tell him that the president had arrived at a "com-mand decision." Kissinger did not, however, carry out Nixon's instructions re-garding America's allies or the Soviets because the "pace of events," he claimed, preoccupied his time.[136]

Although his schedule of meetings on Cambodia was full, Nixon "simmered down," Haldeman thought, as the day wore on. In several sessions with Kissinger throughout the morning and early afternoon preceding the NSC conclave at 3:00 P.M., he decided to go ahead with the Phase I attack and ordered South Vietnamese troops moved to the border.[137] Nixon and Kissinger viewed the NSC gathering as simply "advisory," or, more to the point, as a perfunctory forum to allow dissi-dents to air their views. After Nixon informed the group of his decision, there followed a discussion on the level of American participation in support of the South Vietnamese. Eventually, Vice President Agnew, whom Kissinger had briefed the previous day in order to prepare him "to work on the hawks,"[138] spoke up, blurt-ing out his view that the discussion was irrelevant. He favored attacking all of the sanctuaries, not just those covered by Phase I—the South Vietnamese Fish Hook offensive. Anything short of invading both the Fish Hook and the Parrot's Beak, Agnew insisted, was "pussyfooting."[139]

Nixon's reaction to Agnew's outburst—as claimed by Kissinger in *White House Years,* the only source for what was said at the meeting—was to weigh in on the side of tactical air support for Phase I "on the basis of demonstrated necessity," which was a position in between that of the vice president and dissident cabinet members. There was nothing that Nixon hated more, Kissinger wrote, than to be "shown up in a group as being less tough than his advisers." After the NSC meeting Nixon scolded Kissinger for having failed to forewarn him of Agnew's position.[140]

In his account of this period of decision making about Cambodia, Kissinger suggested that Nixon's manic state of mind and the "idiosyncracies" of his personality "propelled" him toward more violent steps in Cambodia. The president was "overwrought," "irritable," and "defiant." With flashes of romantic grandiosity, he thought of himself as "a beleaguered military commander in the tradition of Patton." He was sometimes intoxicated, which slurred his speech and lubricated his belligerence; he was frustrated by his foot-dragging bureaucracy, which threw him into "monumental" rages; and he was egged on by select hawkish advisers. The emotional response Agnew's "outburst" provoked in Nixon—to take one example—had the long-term effect, Kissinger argued, of "accelerating" his ultimate decision to go ahead with Phase II.[141]

Haldeman's notes and diary entries reinforce this portrait of Nixon's aggressive mania. He appears hyperactive, more talkative than usual, and irritable. Despite directing his energies toward the goal of invading Cambodia, he was easily distracted by other, less relevant matters (another sign of mania): seating arrangements for state dinners, his distant funeral, and finding a room into which his new pool table would fit. He went without much sleep and committed himself to a strategic course that was personally exciting, but certain to have painful consequences. Nixon repeatedly screened the recently released motion picture *Patton* and frequently quoted passages from the flamboyant World War II general's autobiography. George S. Patton's life and words appealed to Nixon's grandiose self-image. As Nixon explained it to Haldeman, the general had been an inspiring leader, superb administrator, tireless worker, aggressive fighter, courageous defier of the Establishment, overcomer of crises, and conquering hero.[142]

In spite of his own exquisitely detailed description of Nixon's odd behavior and his own stress and strain, however, Kissinger denied that the decision to invade Cambodia with American troops was "a maniacal eruption of irrationality as the uproar afterward sought to imply." By the time the decision was made, there had been considerable hesitation, deliberation, and consultation on Nixon's part. It was a rational, noble, lonely, courageous step "by a man who had to discipline his nerves almost daily to face his associates and to overcome the partially subconscious, partially deliberate procrastination of his executive departments." Kissinger implied that throughout the crisis he was a levelheaded and circumspect adviser to the president, serving to channel Nixon's bouts of rage into reasonable and constructive action toward a necessary solution to a difficult problem. The "objective" conditions in Cambodia, where North Vietnamese attacks threatened to topple Lon Nol's regime and bring Cambodia under Hanoi's hegemonic control, demanded that tough military steps be taken. Behind the sound and fury, "the merits of the case were overwhelming."[143]

Overall, Kissinger's account in *White House Years* was muddled, contradictory, and self-serving. His own mental state, for example, was not as rational as he portrayed it. He, too, was deeply moved by his emotions, psychological proclivities, and personal ambitions. He enjoyed the excitement of the Cambodian crisis, the satisfaction of acting forcefully in Indochina, and the opportunity for outmaneuvering his rivals in the intricate infighting of the executive branch. Both he and Nixon became temporarily buoyant—now and then elevated above their regular condition of joyless stress and despondency. As Nixon followed Kissinger into the NSC meeting on April 22, he turned to Haldeman "with a big smile and said [that] K's really having fun today; he's playing Bismarck." Haldeman noted after the NSC meeting and several more sessions between Kissinger and Nixon: "Funny, just when K is getting really low and discouraged a new break comes along and cranks him back up."[144]

While at times Kissinger may have moderated Nixon's rage, he also encouraged his foreign policy belligerence, and, without Kissinger's support, Nixon may not have taken the steps he did. Although determined on a course of boldness and possessing the support of Abrams, Agnew, Bunker, Helms, Moorer, and the Joint Chiefs, Nixon was faced with the unpleasant and significant opposition of Rogers, Laird, and their departments. As much as he may have enjoyed going against the bureaucracy in general, he disliked and shunned personal confrontations with top aides. Nixon required Kissinger's loyalty and assistance, which Kissinger readily gave, partly out of conviction but partly to solidify his place in the administration. Another national security adviser might have failed him in this role.[145] Deliberately obscured by Nixon and Kissinger, their complex, interwoven motives and moods were impossible to unravel and were not fully understood even by those who were close to the decision-making process.[146]

Nixon's mood swings were probably as much an effect of the tense circumstances in which he found himself as they were a cause of his own assertive actions. They were the product of the obstructions of his opponents and his bitter encounter with the dilemmas of Vietnam; they were also symptoms of his having to work himself into an irritable, belligerent state in order to accept the inevitable consequences of the escalatory decisions he wanted to make regarding Cambodia. Haldeman noted on April 23: "He's very much absorbed in Cambodia, and realizes he's treading on the brink of major [political] problems as he escalates the war there. Will have to do a masterful job of explanation to keep the people with him. And there'll be a monumental squawk from the Hill." Before leaving the office that night, Nixon stood looking out the window and said in angry frustration: "Damn Johnson, if he'd just done the right thing we wouldn't be in this mess now."[147]

However much the decision to invade Cambodia with American troops was driven by the subconscious moods of these men, it is clear that it was also made in the conscious pursuit of their firmly held, long-standing strategic aims and policy goals. Implementing Phase II not only would send a symbolic, threatening message to Hanoi but also could achieve decisive military results: Lon Nol would be saved; the port of Sihanoukville would be closed; the sanctuaries and the VNLAF troops in them would be destroyed; COSVN headquarters would be captured; and Vietnamization would be protected.[148] On April 23, after listening to more of Nixon's ruminations, Haldeman noted: "He still feels he can get it wound up this year, if we keep enough pressure on, and don't crumble at home. K agrees." They believed Phase I would cause few domestic political difficulties, "but it only cripples North Vietnam, [and] doesn't really knock out their sanctuaries. That comes with Phase II, which . . . could be a [political] problem."[149] It was true that both men feared strategic setbacks in Cambodia, and in that sense the decision was "defensive." But it was also "offensive," for they had rushed to take advantage of the crisis, viewing it as an opportunity to end the war on their own terms.

Although Nixon and Kissinger claimed to have come only gradually to a final decision on the American phase of the offensive—that is, not before April 26 or April 28[150]—there are indications in Haldeman's notes and Kissinger's memoirs that Nixon had actually decided on a combined South Vietnamese Phase I–American Phase II invasion before these dates, and that Kissinger had concurred.[151] Nixon, already drawn to Phases I and II, was considering their implementation by the time he was briefed by McCain on April 19. Intellectually and viscerally inspired by McCain, Nixon had worked himself up to greater enthusiasm for the combined operation during the flights back to California and Washington, D.C., on April 19 and 20. Kissinger, who claimed he had originally supported only Phase I, admitted in *White House Years* that he had been won over to Phase II "at least a week earlier" than April 28, when the "final," formal decision was made.[152] If in fact they had decided in favor of Phase II on April 20 or 21, one or two days before the first NSC meeting on the matter, then what happened in the next week was an elaborate charade whose purpose, Kissinger indirectly admitted, was to give "all parties an opportunity to express themselves," "reduce the inevitable confrontation with Rogers and Laird to a minimum," and "figure out a way to bring along . . . [the] Cabinet."[153] Nixon also needed time to steel himself for an inevitable adverse congressional and antiwar reaction to an American invasion of Cambodia.[154]

Agnew's outburst on April 22, although piquing Nixon's manful pride, was less important as a cause of accelerating his decision for Phase II than Kissinger made it out to be. Obversely, Rogers's and Laird's objections and Nixon's worried anticipation of criticism from Congress and the citizenry delayed the start of the operation. Nixon and Kissinger saw Agnew as a counterweight to internal and external criticism, and they encouraged his belligerence more than he encouraged theirs.[155]

On April 23, following the perfunctory NSC meeting of the previous day, Nixon and Kissinger set out to surmount the bureaucracy, implement Phase I, and plan for Phase II. The president, Haldeman noted in his diary, had little interest "in domestic affairs as the whole focus is on the war. He finds it much more absorbing at any time, and especially when things are tight and he has to make major decisions, going against the bureaucracy."[156] The immediate bureaucratic impediment was Laird's "foot-dragging" on the provision of American tactical air support for the South Vietnamese. He was insisting on Washington's approval for every air strike and objecting to the stationing of American air controllers in Cambodia. In two meetings with WSAG—which Kissinger held in between three sessions with Nixon—Kissinger succeeded in persuading the agency assistants who constituted the group to bypass Laird by authorizing air controllers to accompany the RVNAF and granting General Abrams authority to order tactical air strikes without approval from Washington.[157]

By evening Nixon was in a "monumental rage." He had discovered that his weeks-old order to provide signal equipment to the CIA had still not been carried out and also that the *New York Times* had published a story revealing a highly classified decision to provide rifles to Lon Nol. Nixon phoned Kissinger ten times that night, with three calls going to Senator Fulbright's house, where Kissinger was meeting "informally" with members of the Senate Foreign Relations Committee. He wanted certain midlevel personnel fired, the communications equipment delivered, and Phase II to go forward. He called a meeting for early the next morning with Helms, Moorer, and General Robert Cushman (of the CIA)—men who strongly supported Phase II and would finalize plans for it.[158]

Kissinger spoke with Haldeman that night, "very worried" that the president was "moving too rashly without really thinking through the consequences"—a reference to the threatened firings and the Helms-Moorer meeting, which would be held without Laird's knowledge. In his memoirs he referred to the situation as "bizarre," because the Defense and State Departments were dragging their feet on Phase I, while Nixon was preparing to launch Phase II without their knowledge.[159] Although he speculated that Nixon would finally "scratch" Phase II— perhaps thinking the president would cool down or be deterred by fear of domestic consequences—Kissinger affirmed his own belief on the day of the meeting that it was "a good move," assessing "55-45" odds that Phase I and II combined would "force a decision one way or the other," resulting "in our either winning or losing this year, depending on what Hanoi decides to do."[160]

On Friday, April 24, with Nixon "still really driving about Cambodia," Kissinger in tow, and Rogers and Laird out of the loop, Nixon told Helms, Moorer, and Cushman to schedule Phase I for Sunday, April 26, and Phase II, for Wednesday, April 29.[161] This schedule could not be met, however, because of delays in moving up South Vietnamese troops, Laird's foot-dragging on the mobilizing of tactical air support, and the political need to thrash out internal disagreements about the wisdom of Phase II. Nixon therefore scheduled a meeting for Sunday with his principal national security advisers—Kissinger, Laird, Rogers, Wheeler, and Helms.[162] After sundry other meetings with aides, including Kissinger, during the rest of the day on Friday, Nixon helicoptered to Camp David with his crony Bebe Rebozo.

Meanwhile, Kissinger briefed Senator Stennis, met once more with Helms and Moorer to review planning,[163] and then spent an hour with his own rebellious aides—Lynn, Lake, Lord, Morris, and Watts. Lynn complained that the plans were imprecise and the civilian costs would be devastating. Lake objected to the invasion of a sovereign nation, warning that Cambodia would be engulfed in war and the United States would be bogged down in a wider conflict; he recommended the negotiation of the pre-coup status quo concerning sanctuaries. Lord warned that the operation would erode home-front support for Vietnamization. Morris repeated this prediction and also maintained that the invasion would be politically and militarily indecisive. Watts pointed out that the invasion would lead to other escalations, such as the bombing of Hanoi and Haiphong. Their arguments only solidified Kissinger's conviction that the invasion was the right thing to do, for how else would they win the war or sustain Vietnamization if Cambodia fell to the Communists?[164] (Watts would resign on April 26, Morris and Lake, on April 29, and Lynn during the fall of the year. Lord stayed on—the only one of Kissinger's "bleeding hearts" to do so. If Lord was "dovish," at the other end of the axis was Haig—deeply conservative, ambitious, and willing to indulge the president.)[165]

Matters became more bizarre on the night of April 24. As Nixon and Rebozo drank martinis and watched *The Cincinnati Kid,* a movie about an over-the-hill poker champion, Nixon called Kissinger at the White House. Slurring his words and using obscenities, he talked about the decision to send American troops into Cambodia. Suddenly he put Rebozo on the phone: "The president wants you to know, Henry, that if this doesn't work, it's your ass."[166]

The next morning, Nixon called Kissinger to Camp David to review planning for Phase II of the invasion.[167] While he swam in the pool and Kissinger walked along its edge, Nixon entertained thoughts of "going for broke" by invading Cambodia *and* bombing and mining North Vietnam. Kissinger objected, pointing out that this would be unwise, considering divisions in the national security team and the likelihood of massive domestic protest.

In the afternoon Nixon, Rebozo, and Kissinger flew back to Washington to cruise down the Potomac on the *Sequoia* with Attorney General Mitchell. Uplifted by military planning and liquid refreshments, the president insisted that they stand at attention while the ship's loudspeaker played "The Star-Spangled Banner" as they passed Washington's tomb at Mount Vernon. At 6:00 P.M. the president invited everyone to another viewing of *Patton,* but Kissinger, having seen it before, left midway through the screening to prepare for the NSC meeting on Sunday.[168]

Nixon treated the Sunday evening gathering as an advisory meeting, whose purpose was to discuss contingencies. Neither Laird nor Rogers knew that he had already decided on Phase II.[169] According to Kissinger, the two secretaries did not raise objections, which Nixon chose to interpret as acquiescence, and that night he signed a directive to proceed.[170]

The next day, April 27, Nixon began work early on preparations for an address to the nation on the Cambodian offensive, stopping only briefly on his way to his Executive Office Building office to admire the crab apple blossoms in the White House garden, while Kissinger chaired a meeting of WSAG to discuss implementation of the directive. Rogers and Laird, however, telephoned Kissinger to inform him that they had reservations about the go-ahead directive. Kissinger told them to call the president, who then arranged another conference with his three advisers later in the morning. Just before the meeting began, Nixon told Kissinger that he would "carry the ball"—he would "play Rogers and Laird as if they're with us." Nixon was set on the operation. It was a "tough decision," but he had "stepped up to it." In the past they had been "praised for all the wrong things"—the Nixon Doctrine, SALT, U.S.-Japanese agreements on Okinawa, germ warfare negotiations—but now they were "finally doing the right thing."[171]

During the one-hour discussion, the two cabinet secretaries expressed support for the South Vietnamese Phase I attack against the Parrot's Beak but objected to Phase II, which mainly involved American troops attacking into the Fish Hook. Rogers's points were telling: the decision had been made without full consultation; COSVN, whose destruction was the ostensible purpose of the invasion, was an elusive target; the operation would not deliver a crippling blow; and there would be little gain for the casualties suffered. Laird objected to WSAG's control over the operation, predicted heavy casualties, voiced opposition to the use of American combat troops in Cambodia, and argued that Abrams and Wheeler thought the combined U.S.-RVNAF operations were infeasible.[172] Nixon pointed out that he had no alternative. Almost a year later he described the scene to Nelson Rockefeller:

> I sat right here with two cabinet officers and my national security adviser, and I asked what we needed to do. The recommendation of the Department of Defense was the most pusillanimous little nit-picker I ever saw. "Just bite off the Parrot's Beak." I said you are going to have a hell of an uproar at home if you bite off the Beak. If you are going to take the heat, go for all the marbles. . . . I have made some bad decisions, but a good one was this: When you bite the bullet, bite it hard—go for the big play.[173]

After Laird and Rogers left, Kissinger argued that their objections presented a serious challenge to the president's authority, and he urged implementation. But Nixon thought it prudent to delay the operation for twenty-four hours, while they checked with Abrams and Bunker about their views regarding Phase II—it would demonstrate, Nixon said, that at least he was "willing to listen." Nixon's interpretation of his aides' motives was that Rogers was mostly worried about his appearance before the Senate Foreign Relations Committee that afternoon, which might question him about American involvement in Cambodia; that Laird was trying to fathom the president's position and protect his prerogatives; and that Kissinger was "pushing too hard to hold control."[174]

In the evening, with replies received from Abrams and Bunker affirming their support for a combined Phase I–Phase II operation, Nixon reviewed pros and cons once again with Kissinger and Mitchell until nearly midnight. The president decided to proceed with the operation and instructed Kissinger to issue a new directive with only minor changes in wording to address Laird's objections to WSAG's role. Alone later, Nixon sat in his darkened Executive Office Building office and, with yellow pad in hand, once again listed the pluses and minuses of the plan. At "loose ends" the next morning, he met with Kissinger and Mitchell at 9:30 to review the operation yet one more time. He and Kissinger compared notes, for Kissinger, too, had engaged in the same lonely reassessment. At 10:20, Kissinger left by a side door, and Nixon, with Mitchell taking notes, informed Rogers and Laird of his decision to launch the operation.[175] After several other meetings during the day, Nixon, "really mad," phoned Haldeman to reprimand him "worse than he ever has" for giving permission to CBS to limit its television segment on "Tricia's White House Tour" to thirty minutes during the *Sixty Minutes* show. Haldeman thought the outburst was "basically a release of tensions on the big [Cambodian invasion] decision, but potentially damaging if he starts flailing in other directions." Haldeman concluded, however, "this one is under control."[176]

THE INCURSION

On the morning of April 29, Saigon time, twelve infantry and armored battalions of the RVNAF totaling 8,700 men attacked the flanks of the Parrot's Beak in Operation Toan Thang 42, Phase I of the Cambodian incursion. Toan Thang 43, or Phase II, began on May 1 at 7:30 A.M. Saigon time, with armored and heliborne American units plunging into the Fish Hook from the south and east and a smaller number of South Vietnamese striking from the north. The assaulting forces, totaling 15,000, were preceded by heavy artillery preparation and B-52 and fighter-bomber sorties. Although there was sharp fighting during the first two days, military engagements subsequently tapered off as VNLAF units moved north and west. Within a week after the offensive began, there were 31,000 American and 19,000 South Vietnamese troops in Cambodia. Ultimately comprising thirteen separate multibattalion, search-and-destroy operations through the months of May and June, Toan Thang spread across the border region, encompassing an area that extended from Sihanoukville (now called Kompong Som) in the south to Phnom Penh in the west and Snuol in the north, but which also included territory astride east-west Highway 19 in northeast Cambodia.[177] American naval vessels and patrol aircraft took up stations outside Kompong Som, and U.S. aircraft bombed supply depots north of the DMZ. And the bombing continued in Cambodia.[178] Nixon wanted to "pour a lot of stuff into Cambodia." It was the "big game."[179]

When night had fallen in Vietnam on April 29 and Washington awakened to the news of the RVN's move into the Parrot's Beak, there was swift and adverse criticism from the Senate, led by Republicans John Sherman Cooper and George Aiken, and Democrats Frank Church and Mike Mansfield. Surprised by this strong reaction to Phase I, Nixon and key advisers speculated on the causes. Not untypically, Kissinger theorized that Rogers and Laird had tipped off the senators in the hope that their criticisms would dissuade the president from proceeding with Phase II. After discussing what to do about it, Nixon "sat back and relaxed" with Kissinger and Haldeman for another "of those mystic sessions." Paraphrasing the gist of Nixon's thoughts, Haldeman noted: "[He] reviewed DDE's Lebanon decision and JFK's Cuban missile crisis. Decided this was tougher than either of those, especially since it didn't have to be made. But P is convinced it had to be this now, or get out now, no chance to go along the same path." During the afternoon and into the evening, Nixon secluded himself in the Executive Office Building to work on his forthcoming address to the nation.[180] After another night without much sleep, he was awake at 5:30 A.M. on April 30 and spent the day completing the speech and reviewing follow-up public relations plans. In midafternoon he previewed his address to Kissinger and Haldeman, who thought it "very strong" and "felt it will work"—although in his memoirs Kissinger characterized parts of it as "self-pitying" and "vainglorious."[181]

At 9:00 P.M., one and a half hours after the American Fish Hook attacks had begun, President Nixon went on television to deliver his "Address to the Nation on the Situation in Southeast Asia." It was a syllogistically structured but repetitive speech, during which the president appeared intensely defiant, rose from his desk to point to places on a map of Indochina, and temporarily lost his place in the script. The situation in Indochina necessitated action, he argued: the United States had offered compromises at the negotiating table and was withdrawing its troops, but North Vietnam had responded with diplomatic intransigence and a massive military offensive against the neutral state of Cambodia that could overrun the entire country, cost the lives of Americans in South Vietnam, force a cessation of American troop withdrawals, and slow the progress of Vietnamization. If North Vietnam were allowed to succeed, "the credibility of the United States would be destroyed in every area of the world where only the power of the United States deters aggression." The alternatives to the action he had taken—doing nothing or sending massive aid to the Cambodian government—were either unacceptable or inadequate in meeting the threat. The operation he had launched would strike at the "heart of the trouble," for it would "clean out" the sanctuaries and destroy COSVN. It "puts the leaders of North Vietnam on notice that . . . we will not be humiliated. We will not be defeated." Even so, this was "not an invasion," because the purpose was not to occupy Cambodia. In the end, it would save American lives, facilitate the negotiations, and bring the war in Indochina to a swifter end and a just peace.

The speech was disingenuous and artful. Although making reference to the defenseless, neutral government in Phnom Penh, Nixon failed to mention the coup against Sihanouk, the American role in it, or the steps Lon Nol had taken in over-turning Sihanouk's policies. Claiming that the United States had previously re-spected the neutrality of Cambodia, whereas the enemy had not, he did not discuss the secret B-52 campaign or South Vietnamese–American cross-border operations. Announcing that he would transcend the deep divisions between Americans about how the war should be conducted, he associated antiwar dissent with anarchy and subversion abroad, destructive, "mindless" attacks at home, and the counsels of "doubt and defeat" from segments of the opinion-making elite. Rejecting personal concerns about the political risks to his administration, he nonetheless appealed, even though indirectly, for votes in the upcoming elections. Maintaining that the operation was defensive, he stressed the offensive-minded diplomatic, strategic, and psychological motives that had led to the decision: all policy issues were on the table except the maintenance of the Saigon government, which the other side found unacceptable; the fall of Cambodia would undermine Vietnamization, which was related to his diplomatic strategy; the incursion was a warning shot to Hanoi, promising bolder actions in the future if the North Vietnamese did not agree to his terms; South Vietnam needed to be saved because American global credibil-ity was on the line; the character of the United States and its president were being tested in the crucible of crisis. "If, when the chips are down, the world's most powerful nation . . . acts like a pitiful, helpless giant, the forces of totalitarianism and anarchy will threaten free nations and free institutions throughout the world." Claiming to depart from the customary practice of concluding such presidential speeches with an appeal to the nation to rally behind the president of the United States, he nonetheless identified his decision with the safety of American troops and called on the citizenry to support America's "brave men fighting tonight half-way around the world" for peace, freedom, and justice.[182]

In the White House, the days following the speech were to be a time of "follow-up": keeping track of military developments in Cambodia; holding the line vis-à-vis Hanoi; and seeing through the implementation of the public rela-tions plan of speeches, news spinning, and lobbying of Congress. Toward both his strong and weak supporters, Nixon's theme was one of firmness on the "need to keep an absolutely strong posture, show no sign of weakness or give, keep people rolling, . . . keeping them from backing down. . . . Mainly stay strong, whole em-phasis on 'back the boys,' sell courage of P." Toward the Vietnamese enemy, it was "cold steel, no give, nothing about negotiations. Hanoi can now choose be-tween peace and war." Nixon knew he needed to turn his attention to domestic matters, which he had neglected during the past month, but he could not help but keep "coming back to things related to 'The Decision'"—as the incursion was referred to in Nixon's inner circle. Even though their own instant public opinion poll on the speech "came out darn good," this was not a moment to relax, "when we've got things rolling," Haldeman said to Nixon's pleasure. "[We] will let them up later."[183]

"Psychologists or sociologists may explain some day what it is about that distant monochromatic land, of green mountains and fields merging with an azure sea, that for millennia has acted as a magnet for foreigners who sought glory there and found frustration."
—Henry Kissinger (Photo by Jeffrey Kimball)

(Left, top) Richard and the Dragon, acrylic painting, 1997, by Leslye Sherman.
(Left) Kissinger reporting to Nixon on his previous day's meeting with Le Duc Tho,
September 16, 1972. (National Archives) *(Above)* Nixon's favorite position for thinking and
writing, October 7, 1970. (National Archives)

Charles de Gaulle's farewell speech on Nixon's departure from France, March 1, 1969. Left to right: Haldeman, Ehrlichman, Kissinger, Nixon, Rogers, de Gaulle. (National Archives)

Discussing plans for Lam Son 719. Left to right: Helms, Kissinger, Rogers, Nixon, Laird, Moorer, January 18, 1971. (National Archives)

Thieu and Nixon, Midway, June 8, 1969. (National Archives)

Nixon with GIs in Vietnam, July 30, 1969. (National Archives)

Peace demonstration on the Mall, November 15, 1969. (Swarthmore College Peace Collection, courtesy of Theodore B. Hetzel)

Nixon delivering his address to the nation on the incursion into Cambodia, April 30, 1970. (National Archives)

HOCHIMINH ROAD NETWORK

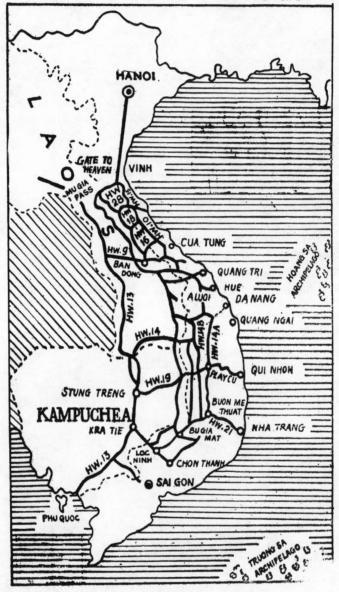

From *The Ho Chi Minh Trail.* (Hanoi: Foreign Languages Publishing House, 1985)

North Vietnamese transports on the Ho Chi Minh Trail during Lam Son 719 (U.S. Army Center of Military History)

Camouflaged B-52s over Hanoi, December 1972. (Department of Defense)

Bach Mai Hospital after B-52 bombings, December 22, 1972. (Vietnamese Revolution Museum, Hanoi)

Kham Thien residential area after B-52 bombings, December 26, 1972. (Vietnamese Revolution Museum, Hanoi)

(Top) *Diamond Lil,* a B-52 that saw service during the Linebacker II operations, now a monument at the U.S. Air Force Academy. A plaque near the plane reads: "The extensive B-52 raids against targets in North Vietnam in December 1972 known as 'Linebacker II' brought the North Vietnamese to meaningful discussions in Paris that led to the release of the American POWs in February 1973." (Photo by Jeffrey Kimball) *(Bottom)* Remains of a B-52 shot down on December 27, 1972, with monument in background, Ngoc Ha suburb of Hanoi. (Photo by Jeffrey Kimball)

MiG-21 atop debris from downed B-52s, a monument at the rear of the National Military Museum, Hanoi. An antiaircraft gun sits in front of the museum. (Photo by Jeffrey Kimball)

I REPLIED BLUNTLY THAT WE NOW HAD SERIOUS QUESTIONS
ABOUT NORTH VIETNAMESE SINCERITY, AND I DESCRIBED THEIR TACTICS
THIS WEEK, SAYING I WOULD NEVER AGAIN COME TO PARIS FOR MORE
THAN TWO DAYS. THE CRUCIAL ELEMENT OF CONFIDENCE WAS FAST
BEING JEOPARIZED, AND WE BOTH NOW HAD IMPORTANT DECISIONS TO
MAKE BETWEEN PEACE AND PROLONGED CONFLICT WITH AN UNCERTAIN
OUTCOME. I AGAIN REMINDED HIM THAT THIS WOULD BE THE LAST TIME
WE WOULD TRY TO NEGOTIATE A COMPREHENSIVE AGREEMENT. I CLOSED
BY SAYING THAT WE HAD CHOSED PEACE AND WOULD SEE IN THE NEXT WEEKS
WHETHER THE PROCESS COULD BE COMPLETED. THO'S DEPARTURE MAINTAINED
HIS RECENT CORDIALITY, WHICH HAD BEEN UNDERLINED AT THE OUTSET OF
MEETING BY GIFTS TO ME FROM THE MINISTER AND HIM.
5 O PS E C R E T SENSITIVE EXCLUSIVELY EYES ONLY
    5. WHERE THEN DOES THIS LEAVE US? I EXPLAINED OUR BASIC
DILEMMA YESTERDAY. HANOI IS ALMOST DISDAINFUL OF US BECAUSE WE
HAVE NO EFFECTIVE LEVERAGE LEFT, WHILE SAIGON IN ITS SHORT-
SIGHTED DEVICES TO SABOTAGE THE AGREEMENT KNOCKS OUT FROM UNDER
US OUR FEW REMAINING PROPS. THIEU'S CEASEFIRE OFFER COULD
FURTHER COMPLICATE THE SITUATION, BECAUSE IF HANOI ACCEPTS IT
WE WILL HAVE STOPPED BOMBING NORTH OF THE 20TH PARALLEL IN
PURSUIT OF OUR PEACE EFFORT WHILE THIEU WOULD HAVE FORCED US TOSTOP
EVERYWHERE ELSE TO SABOTAGE IT. WE WILL SOON HAVE NO MEANS OF
LEVERAGE AT ALL WHILE PRESSURES WILL BUILD UP DOMESTICALLY IF
WE FAIL TO REACH AN AGREEMENT OR GET OUR PRISONERS BACK. WE
WILL NEITER GET AN AGREEMENT NOR BE ABLE TO PRESERVE SAIGON.
    6. WE NOW HAVE TWO ESSENTIAL STRATEGIC CHOICES. THE FIRST
ONE IS TO TURN HARD ON HANOI AND INCREASE PRESSURE ENORMOUSLY
THROUGH BOMBING AND OTHER MEANS. THIS WOULD INCLUDE MEASURES
LIKE RESEEDING THE MINES, MASSIVE TWO-DAY STRIKES AGAINST THE
POWER PLANTS OVER THIS WEEKEND, AND A COUPLE OF B-52 EFFORTS.
THIS WOULD MAKE CLEAR THAT THEY PAID SOMETHING FOR THESE
PAST TEN DAYS. CONCURRENTLY WE WOULD TRY TO LINE UP SAIGON
AND AT LEAST PREVENT THIEU FROM MAKING FURTHER UNILATERAL PRO-
POSALS. PRESSURES ON SAIGON WOULD BE ESSENTIAL SO THAT THIEU
DOES NOT THINK HE HAS FACED US DOWN, AND WE CAN DEMONSTRATE THAT
T O P S E C R E T SENSITIVE EXCLUSIVELY EYES ONLY
WE WILL NOT PUT UP WITH OUR ALLY'S INTRANSIGENCE ANY MORE THAN
WE WILL DO SO WITH OUR ENEMY.
    THE SECOND COURSE IS TO MAINTAIN PRESENT APPEARANCES
BY SCHDULING ANOTHER MEETING WITH LE DUC THO IN EARLY JANUARY.
THIS WOULD TEST THE EXTREMELY UNLIKELY HYPOTHESIS THAT THO MIGHT
GET NEW INSTRUCTIONS. IF WE WERE ONCE AGAIN STONEWALLED, WE
WOULD THEN TURN HARD ON HANOI. WE WOULD GIVE UP THE CURRENT EFFORT,
BLAMING BOTH VIETNAMESE PARTIES BUT PLACING THE MAJOR ONUS ON
HANOI. WE WOULD OFFER A BILATERAL DEAL OF WITHDRAWAL AND AN
END OF BOMBING FOR PRISONERS. UNDER THIS COURSE AS WELL WE WOULD HAVE
TO MOVE ON SAIGON, TO BRING THIEU ABOARD IN THE EVENT OF AN
AGREEMENT IN JANUARY OR IN THE LIKELY EVENT OF FAILURE, TO LAY THE
BASIS FOR GOING THE BILATERAL ROUTE.

Excerpt from a cable to Nixon from Kissinger. When the Paris talks recessed on December 13, 1972, Kissinger recommended two courses of action. The first—"to turn hard on Hanoi"—reflected Nixon's preference and led to Linebacker II.

At the initialing of the Paris Agreement, January 23, 1973. Right to left: Henry Kissinger, Le Duc Tho, Nguyen Dinh Phuong (interpreter), Xuan Thuy, Nguyen Co Thach. (National Archives)

American helicopter deactivating mines in Halong Bay, north of Haiphong, 1973. (Department of Defense)

Nguyen Co Thach and the author, Institute of the History of Vietnam, Hanoi, September 24, 1994.

10

TRANSITIONS, CONTINUITIES: 1970–1971

He still feels he's got to make a major move in early '71.
—H. R. Haldeman[1]

THE CONDITION OF THE COUNTRY

Nixon's attention was riveted on follow-up to the Cambodian invasion decision not only because he believed in the value of assertive foreign policies and proactive public relations campaigns but also because there were adverse domestic repercussions to the incursion, which he had only dimly foreseen, and which now demanded and received his attention. The most visible and dramatic were the street and campus demonstrations, which greatly influenced his decision to withdraw U.S. troops from Cambodia by June 30; the most significant in the long run in their impact on the prosecution of the war were the related reactions in Congress and among the general public.

The organized, national antiwar coalition had declined since the Chicago convention of 1968 and had only temporarily revived during the fall 1969 Moratorium and Mobilization. Riven by internal divisions and suffering from burnout, national organizations and leaders were also stymied by external developments. They were unable to sustain mass antiwar enthusiasm in a war-weary citizenry. They were assailed by a public and press backlash against street demonstrations. They were harassed by federal and local surveillance and arrests. They were outflanked by Nixon's public relations campaign, which had combined Agnew's and others' rhetorical attacks against the movement, nationalistic appeals to support the flag

213

and the troops, and Nixon's promise of terminating the war through troop withdrawals. The left wing of the movement was disorganized and leaderless, with militant minorities engaging in what even the left-liberal, but ever acerbic *Nation* magazine called "mean and mindless" words and actions. Although successful in organizing scores of town meetings around the issue of the war's constitutionality during the winter and spring, the efforts of liberal national organizations were, as one historian characterized them, "diffused."[2]

At the grassroots level the heterogeneous, unstructured movement was reeling, too, but it remained vital on scores of campuses and in hundreds if not thousands of local community organizations across the country. Local coalitions had been responsible for peaceful, nonviolent Moratorium rallies at universities and in small and large cities on the fifteenth of every month since October 1969. During the months preceding the invasion of Cambodia, there had been turbulent protests against the war on private and state-university campuses from Yale to Ohio State to Stanford, with some resulting in clashes with police.[3] There was unrest even at staid, middle-class universities in the small-town hinterland, such as Miami University in Oxford, Ohio, where the April 1970 Moratorium rally had spun off a spontaneous, nonviolent sit-in protest by 300 students at the ROTC building, unleashing official retribution, followed by additional protests.

Haldeman thought that Nixon found it difficult to understand why the young protestors could not see that he was really sincere in trying to end the war. The president thus settled on the theory that the "radicalization" of students was caused by young men's fear of being drafted or was the consequence of a "nihilistic" few or of Communist agents having led a narcissistic and directionless generation astray. It was directionless because of "permissiveness," which "denies the child the opportunity to look in a mirror and finally realize that the problem is me—not my teachers, not the war, not the environment, but me." Their middle-class parents should not be blamed, however, because their children had been given so much by society. What youth needed was a challenge, something to struggle for. Challenge and struggle also built character, like the character of his mother, who had cared for his sick brothers. Struggle was what made nations great, and the United States needed to be great to "maintain the peace, to do good, rather than to do evil, to help rather than to harm others." In 1971, again musing about permissiveness, he told Haldeman that among the major accomplishments of his administration would be the termination of the war and the reduction of student unrest and permissiveness.[4]

Nixon did not credit other explanations for the participation of youths in protest: that antiwar protest, for example, was also the result of a widespread, genuine moral or constitutional opposition to his and others' policies; to impatience with a very long war; to frustration with the violent intransigence of decision makers; to the struggle of dealing with the death of friends and relatives called to battle; and to the challenge of their country's complicity in the destruction and death wrought in Vietnam. Despite his misconstruing of motives, the president worried a great deal about the impact of protest on the "condition of the country" and on his ability to wage the war effectively. He was, in addition, personally vexed by campus unrest: not only did he cancel his plans to attend Julie's and David's graduations for fear of protests, but on April 29 he called them "away from campus problems" to be home with him, the family, and Bebe Rebozo. (Later, in mid-October, he became angrily "cranked up" because students at Macalester College had given his daughter Tricia "a bad time with obscene signs.")[5] Annoyed and distracted by presidential and personal concerns, he sought ways of quelling dissent. Expecting trouble at Yale University in response to the forthcoming Cambodian incursion, for instance, he and his close advisers debated whether to station troops in New Haven on a "standby basis."[6]

Although Nixon had anticipated street and campus protests in response to his April 30 speech, he had thought these would not be very serious; he believed that the broad antiwar citizenry was mainly concerned about casualties, which were down, and students about draft calls, which he had reduced. He had hoped his speech would have served the purpose of explaining his goals and rallying supporters. Rogers had a different take on the likely import of the speech. On reading it and its concluding appeal for national unity just moments before the president went on the air, the secretary of state exclaimed: "Unite the country! This will make the students puke."[7]

Students and other citizens around the nation did indeed find Nixon's announcement of April 30 unpalatable. Spontaneous protests broke out in scores of communities and campuses. Most were peaceful, but some were not. In Cincinnati, Nashville, and Chicago, for instance, students and other dissidents peacefully protested at government centers; but ROTC buildings were set afire on the campuses of Maryland, Yale, Michigan State, Wisconsin, and Washington; and students fought police at Ohio University and Stanford. While visiting the Pentagon on May 1, Nixon referred to those who were "blowing up the campuses" as "these bums," which many took as a reference to all student protesters. Although he and his staff felt his statement had been quoted out of context by the newspapers—thereby implying that he had directed his remarks at all student protesters and not just the few troublemakers—they privately acknowledged that it had not been helpful in calming the nation.[8]

At Kent State University in Ohio, students peacefully protested the Cambodian invasion on the campus Commons on May 1, but a confused series of actions and reactions in the downtown area during the night, involving students, townspeople, and outsiders, produced a riot, property damage, and arrests. Without consulting university officials, the mayor of Kent declared a state of emergency and requested the help of the National Guard. During the night of May 2 the ROTC building was torched by Weathermen, police provocateurs, or anonymous others (accusations have been made regarding all three possible perpetrators, but no solid evidence has surfaced). Troop G of the Guard, which had been trained to put down strikes and riots but not to prevent, manage, or resolve conflict, then occupied the campus. At a press conference on May 3 Governor James Rhodes promised to "eradicate" the "Communist element," but, mixing historical epithets, he referred to radicals as "brownshirts." Later, Guardsmen with their bayonets fixed charged a group of students who were engaged in a sit-in at a downtown intersection, stabbing several and arresting many others. As the confrontation continued into May 4, the exhausted, tense, and angry Guardsmen aimed their rifles and fired off sixty-one rounds for a period of thirteen seconds at an excited crowd of students, some of whom had been protesting the Guard's presence and behavior on campus, some of whom had been bystanders or on their way to other campus locations. When the shooting stopped, four students were dead and nine were wounded.[9]

Over 4,350,000 students nationwide participated in demonstrations against the Kent State killings and the invasion of Cambodia at over 1,300 universities and colleges during the month of May. As historians DeBenedetti and Chatfield remarked in their account of the anti–Vietnam War movement, "it was easily the most massive and shattering protest in the history of American higher education." Authorities responded by closing down one-fifth of America's colleges for periods ranging from one day to the remainder of the spring semester. Most protests had been peaceful, but significant violence was reported at 73 schools. Students bore the brunt of personal violence. On May 6 police shot and wounded several SUNY-Buffalo students going to their classes; others fired tear gas into dormitories. On May 14 police and National Guardsmen attacked a dormitory at Jackson State University in Mississippi, killing two.[10]

Once the postinvasion protests had begun, Kissinger became "uptight," mainly because he was worried about Nixon's reaction, thinking that "he will toss babies to the wolves instead of hanging tight." When Haldeman informed the president about the shootings at Kent State, Nixon was "disturbed," "troubled," and "distressed." He was "afraid," Haldeman cryptically noted, that "his decision set it off, and that [it] is the ostensible cause of the demonstrations there." However much his discomposure was the result of sympathy for the dead and wounded students, it was also the result of anxiety that he would be blamed, that the incident would set off more turmoil, and that few Americans would really understand the personal trial he "was going through"; namely, that he must bear the calumny of critics and the second-guessing of cabinet members and bureaucrats for having made a necessary but difficult presidential decision. He wrote personal letters of condolence to the parents of the dead students, but in his public statement on May 5 he implied that the protesters were to blame for the killings: "This should remind us all once again that when dissent turns to violence, it invites tragedy."[11]

His reaction to this new crisis was, typically, to try to turn it to his advantage—to use it as "an opportunity"—though for now it was unclear how that could be done. In the meantime, he told his aides to "maintain calm," while continuing to lobby Congress and the cabinet "to keep a firm position, but not inflammatory." To do otherwise would be to fall into the "trap" of the "Left," whose goal it was "to panic us." Kissinger recommended that they "just let the students go for [a] couple of weeks then move in and clobber them" with news of "Cambodian success," while taking care "that we not appear to give in any way." Haldeman thought that doing nothing, or the military success itself, would only give protesters "a new excuse." Ehrlichman suggested that better communication would be helpful. Their compromise "plan," as Haldeman summarized it in his diary, was to "ride-out the crises with a show of cool strength and no inflammation, but no waffling[,] . . . then to make one or two good firm moves to maintain leadership." But the "real test is how the Cambodia venture turns out. If it can be proclaimed as success and we can get out in six weeks; it will set him up pretty well for a while. If not, we're in for a bundle of trouble."[12]

Nixon aides were troubled—or at least bothered—by developments. As troops occupied federal buildings to protect them from potential protest, Colson, Ehrlichman, Haldeman, Moynihan, and Ziegler felt the nation was embroiled in the equivalent of a civil war, with the White House under siege. Although previously predicting there would be domestic reaction to the invasion, Lord was shocked by its depth and scope. Leonard Garment thought things were coming "unhinged." Disturbed by the defection of members of his staff and concerned about the impact of domestic protest on policy, Kissinger was disconsolate, although he continued to support the decision. He was also exhausted. With his apartment ringed by protesters, he had to move to the White House basement to get some sleep. Wanting to be understood by his critics, he met privately with antiwar leaders, congressmen, the press, and Harvard colleagues in the weeks and days after the invasion had begun, attempting to convince them that the invasion decision was a strategic issue, not a moral one—as though it had to be one or the other. He charmed many and persuaded few, but his encounter with academic colleagues had the effect, he recalled, of confirming him in his own opinions. As he put it, "the meeting completed my transition from the academic world to the world of affairs." He had concluded that academics did not understand international realities and did not have alternatives to administration strategy that satisfied his and the president's requirements for a settlement in Vietnam.[13]

For days after the Kent State killings, Nixon, too, was exhausted from stress and lack of sleep. Haldeman described him as "pooped and . . . not up to his usual performance." The president's closest advisers were worried about his "condition," believing that his "judgment, temper, and mood suffer[ed] badly." Nixon felt "helpless" in his inability to deal with the campus revolt. His woes were intensified by the "omnipresent media problem": an "establishment" press that always made things "look as bad as possible" and "crying doom" about domestic tension. Although Haldeman consoled himself that, despite it all, the president "has come through extremely well," he was concerned that "there's a long way to go and he's in no condition to weather it. He's still riding on the crisis wave, but the letdown is near at hand and will be huge."[14]

After a press conference in the early evening of May 8, Nixon briefly experienced "great relief and almost exhilaration." He had approached the event with tense anticipation, knowing there was "an awful lot at stake," but he and Haldeman concluded that his performance had been masterfully presidential. He had skillfully steered a course between excessive belligerence toward dissenters (which would have suggested "non-understanding") and excessive forgiveness (which would have implied lack of "strength" and "leadership"). He had even gotten a laugh or two from the audience.[15] The most important news item to emerge from the questioning was Nixon's announcement that all American units would be withdrawn from Cambodia "by the end of June."[16] He defended this step on the basis of the operation's success, but campus demonstrations and other protests had clearly influenced his decision.

Asked whether he planned to talk to protesters who were then gathering in Washington, Nixon was noncommittal, although he expressed openness. Leaders of the New Mobilization Committee to End the War in Vietnam, which had organized the Mobilization demonstrations in November 1969, had called for demonstrations on Saturday, May 9, immediately upon hearing news of the Cambodian invasion. Hastily organized rallies came together in several cities, with 100,000 protesters, mostly young, collecting on the Mall near the Lincoln Memorial in the nation's capital.[17]

"Agitated and uneasy as the events of the last few weeks raced through [his] mind," Nixon confessed, he slept only a few hours during the night of May 8. Awake before 4:00 A.M., he went to the Lincoln Sitting Room, put on a recording of Rachmaninov's rhapsodically nostalgic Piano Concerto no. 2, and, looking out the window, noticed small groups of students on the Ellipse. When his valet, Manolo Sanchez, came in to offer him coffee, Nixon suggested they go to see "the most beautiful sight in Washington"—the Lincoln Memorial at night. Exiting his limousine at the memorial around 4:40 A.M., the president of the United States, with Sanchez at his side, approached a small group of students and tried to engage them in conversation. Either too stunned or too sleepy to carry on a dialogue, the youths mainly listened as Nixon rambled on about sports, the environment, global travel, racial tension, and his own college days—a time when, as a young man, he had mistakenly welcomed Neville Chamberlain's appeasement of Hitler, just as they, he implied, were now mistakenly advocating peace at any price in Vietnam. For the most part, however, Nixon said little about Cambodia, the war in general, or the repressive measures he was preparing to take against dissent. By his own account he was primarily trying to communicate with the young—trying to gain their understanding of his personal sincerity and diplomatic wisdom, while identifying with what he considered to be their deepest, inner concern, as he projected onto them his own past and present quest for meaning: "I knew that young people today were searching, as I was searching forty years ago, for . . . the great mystery of life. . . . I didn't have the answer. . . . I just wanted to be sure that all of them realized that ending the war, and cleaning up the streets and the air and the water, was not going to solve spiritual hunger which all of us have."[18]

By about 6:15 the president and his valet had made their way to the Capitol, where they were joined by Haldeman, Chapin, and Ziegler. After a breakfast at the Mayflower Hotel, Haldeman persuaded Nixon to visit soldiers guarding the Executive Office Building. The president was "very impressed by them." In a sentimental mood, he even felt "very kindly toward the students, who were apparently all hippie types." Haldeman's own reaction to Nixon's quixotic wanderings was that they had made this "the weirdest day so far."[19]

Student and newspaper accounts over the weekend drew attention to the president's odd verbal meanderings. Ehrlichman was critical too, telling the president directly that he had been too tired to be effective and had evaded the war issues for which the protesters had come to Washington. Feeling defensive and wanting to set the record straight, Nixon dictated his own version of the Lincoln Memorial encounter to Haldeman on May 13, an edited version of which later filled over six pages of *RN*.[20]

Nixon's spirit temporarily improved, however, when polls surprisingly revealed rebounding support for his presidency and disapproval of antiwar demonstrations and campus protests. His approval rating rose in the next few weeks, standing at 59 percent on June 2. On May 18, at the beginning of the turnaround period, as he and the inner circle flew back to Washington from Key Biscayne, he awarded the "Blue Heart"—a heart cut out of blue cloth—to Kissinger, Haldeman, and Ehrlichman, who had taken "the brunt of the heat these past weeks." Meant as a symbolic substitute for the Purple Heart, the decoration had been made by Jane Lucke, Bebe Rebozo's friend.[21]

Amazed that the polls were good despite Cambodia, student protests, bad press, a downturn in the economy, and an expected deficit, the president could now marvel at "how easily everyone crumbles." Even after weeks had passed, Nixon found it "remarkable" that they had "survived," which led him to observe, or to console himself, that their exaggerated fears were fundamentally caused by their own Beltway myopia: "We are in the teapot (of DC) and see only the tempest; [the] country isn't stirred up the way we are." The public, he thought, was "simmering down" after the Cambodian announcement and the Kent State shootings. He could console himself that the operation had been helpful at home, in Indochina, and around the world. Paraphrasing his musings on May 27, Haldeman noted: "If we had *not* gone into Cambodia[,] it would have fallen, our casualties would be way up, we'd be under enormous pull-out pressure from within, and P would have badly deteriorated in world position." Nixon was "pretty optimistic on overall outlook." He had decided that this after all had been a good time "to take our lumps." By the fall elections "all could be in damn good shape": the economy now seemed to be improving a little; the stock market would probably gain; the Cambodian operation was "a success and completed"; there was "a good chance" that the Paris negotiations would get "back on track"; and the likelihood of holding a summit meeting and closing a SALT deal with the Soviets was high. "We would have a lot going," Nixon thought.[22]

Guardedly optimistic by early June, Nixon attempted to shift into a more passive mode, Haldeman noted, not "driving hard," but trying to "coast along for a bit, then . . . be ready for the next crisis."[23] Kissinger described Nixon's state of mind similarly, but less positively, characterizing it as one of fatigue and a search for reprieve. He recalled that in the aftermath of the "trauma of Cambodia," the administration suffered from "psychological exhaustion; the fear of another round of demonstrations permeated all the thinking about Vietnam in the Executive Branch that summer—even that of Nixon, who pretended to be impervious. So weariness provided the respite that a consensus could not finish."[24] In reality, both Nixon's and Kissinger's moods swung back and forth from worry to hope, from a desire to coast to a determination to take the offensive.

While encouraging, the polls carried warning signs. Nixon had enjoyed momentary blips of increased support for his presidency and the war since January 1969, but the long-term trends pointed steadily toward greater disapproval of both the war and the president's handling of it among all major political, age, and education groups.[25] The downward cline had been and would remain a slippery slope, impelling Nixon to accelerate unilateral troop withdrawals, while causing Kissinger to worry that it would "sink his chances in Paris."[26] Declining public support for himself and the war aggravated Nixon's congenital concern about his public image, which resulted in greater psychological stress, affected his ability to govern, and led him to pursue parlous countermeasures against the antiwar movement and Democratic opponents. Haldeman wished "he would quit worrying about it and just be president."[27]

The polls had mixed messages for the antiwar movement as well. On top of other difficulties facing activist opponents of the war, the majority of the public was now more than ever turned off by street demonstrations and campus protests, which since at least 1965 had been two critical methods of calling attention to the evils of the war. Moreover, nonactivist opponents of the war among the "lower" or "working" classes felt antipathy toward activist, better-educated, "privileged" students and intellectuals, who in their protests often transgressed traditional methods of political discourse and patriotic symbolism.[28]

Demonstrations, rallies, and marches continued to take place as long as the war went on, however, serving as before to energize antiwar activists and keep the war issue before the "mainstream" public. Although more unpopular with the majority than before and muted by diminished press coverage, they contributed to a general perception of national malaise and crisis that made ending the war even more urgent. And they were not the only form of protest, as those opposed to the fighting and bombing persisted in their letter writing, lobbying, civil disobedience, boycotts, strikes, draft resistance, and desertion from and resistance within the military. Antiwar protests may have been even more widespread and numerous in the last year of the American war, 1972.[29] Regarded by its harshest critics as an alien contingent outside the pale—or as subversives within—the dispárate antiwar movement was itself just the most visible and articulate grassroots expression of a broader national unease about the war.

Like Johnson before him, Nixon was unmovably committed to the goals for which the U.S. government had long struggled in Vietnam, and he was impervious to the peace movement's arguments about the war's immorality and folly. He was attentive, however, to the political costs that dissent exacted: the erosion of support for him and the war; the division within his own bureaucracy; the constriction of his military options in Vietnam; and the growing challenge from an emboldened Congress to his control of foreign policy. Dovish congressmen and senators, for example, had proposed war-limiting legislation since at least the fall of 1969, with different bipartisan proposals variously calling for U.S. withdrawal by a specified date, or threatening the cutoff of funds for the American intervention, or terminating U.S. backing for Thieu's regime unless it reformed. The White House had to expend energy, time, and political capital mobilizing its supporters in Congress in order to defeat or amend these measures. A few days after the Cambodian incursion got under way, Senators John Sherman Cooper and Frank Church proposed a bill to cut off funds for the operation by June 30, and Mark Hatfield and George McGovern drafted an amendment to a military authorization bill that would terminate all funding for U.S. operations in Indochina by December 31, 1970.[30] On June 24 the Senate repealed the Tonkin Gulf resolution; it did so once again on July 10 when Thai troops entered Cambodia. On June 30, the day U.S. troops exited Cambodia, a revised version of the Cooper-Church amendment, which prohibited money for U.S. ground operations in Cambodia and Laos without congressional authorization, passed the Senate, but it was rejected in the House on July 9. The McGovern-Hatfield amendment failed on September 1 by a vote of 55 to 39, but new war-limiting legislation would be proposed in 1971 and garner more support.[31] Nixon ignored the constitutional import of these votes, insisting on his right as commander in chief to act as the "sole organ of foreign affairs" and to protect American forces from potential danger.[32] Still, the administration was concerned about the trend. "The pattern was clear," Kissinger wrote in his memoirs. "Senate opponents of the war would introduce one amendment after another, forcing the Administration into unending rearguard actions to preserve a minimum of flexibility for negotiations. Hanoi could only be encouraged to stall, waiting to harvest the results of our domestic dissent."[33]

Hanoi and the NLF probably *were* encouraged by dissent against the war in Congress, among former decision makers, and in grassroots America—as well as in Europe. After the war, Politburo members commented, for example, that the antiwar movement was "one of the important elements that led to the end of the American War in Vietnam," and for this the "Vietnamese people will always be grateful."[34] In its morale-boosting exhortations to cadres and rank-and-file fighters during the war, COSVN was able to claim with some justification that "the world peoples' movement . . . has created an increasingly stronger pressure on Nixon and promoted the support of our people's struggles."[35]

In suggesting the movement had advanced their cause, COSVN had three things in mind: the very growth of the world peace movement was evidence that Nixon had failed to convince large numbers of citizens in the West to support his "false peace policy"; he was being "thrown into a state of [international political] isolation"; and he was under pressure to withdraw American troops. These developments were auspicious, but COSVN did not believe or claim that the peace movement's growth determined the DRV/PRG posture at the negotiating table, as Kissinger and Nixon asserted. The cause-and-effect relationship was just the opposite: the DRV/PRG's negotiating stance served to call the world's attention to the "falseness" of Nixon's peace policy. This stance was an expression of their long-standing national and revolutionary goals. World opinion could help the DRV/PRG achieve these goals if it hampered Nixon's plans, but success in achieving their goals fundamentally depended on three other factors: their military power; the health of the North Vietnamese economy; and the support they received from the South Vietnamese people. Nixon's and Thieu's military-political programs— Vietnamization, pacification, bombing, and diplomatic linkage—would be defeated not through the American or world peace movement but by the VNLAF's military capabilities, its political proselytizing, and its social reform program in South Vietnam; by the efforts of the North Vietnamese leadership and people; and with the assistance of allies. "The rich experiences gained during our revolutionary struggle tell us," the Central Committee declared at its Nineteenth Plenary Session in February 1970, "that the aggressors will agree to end the war only when they cannot continue to fight and when their hope of victory has definitely been checked. The balance of forces on the battlefield determines the way the war develops."[36]

Then and later, Nixon and Kissinger exaggerated the antiwar movement's influence on the DRV and NLF and its responsibility for the failures of their own military-diplomatic strategies. As Kissinger phrased it in *White House Years:* "The ideal bargaining position would have existed if our public had trusted our goals and our enemy had been uncertain about our tactics. Our domestic discord produced exactly the opposite state of affairs."[37] It was an obscure and circular argument, which has confused the debate ever since. Like their Vietnamese enemies, they believed that the war would turn on the military and diplomatic balance of forces. From the beginning, however, Nixon and Kissinger had not themselves been willing to incur the political, social, military, and international risks and costs that a greater military effort would have exacted. Similar risks and costs had brought down Lyndon Johnson's government and turned much of the foreign policy establishment against an ever-enlarging war. Besides, the efficacy of such a military effort was uncertain, given the nature of the war itself. Thus they had adopted their "tactics of uncertainty"—namely, the madman theory and diplomatic linkage—in order to finesse their way past these dilemmas. But this was the rub, as Kissinger commented about Senate and general antiwar opposition: "It dealt a serious blow to the psychological basis for a coherent strategy."[38]

In any case, the Nixinger "tactics of uncertainty" were transparent to Hanoi not because of American domestic discord in 1970 but because as long as Nixon and Kissinger continued to pursue their goal of an independent South Vietnam while withdrawing American troops, they had no other recourse but the strategy of the madman theory or diplomatic linkage in relation to the Soviet Union and China. Contrary to Kissinger's argument, Hanoi expected that at some point down the road Nixon would unleash his big bombers on the North—despite the antiwar movement.[39] If there was uncertainty in the minds of Politburo strategists, it was not about the "psychological basis" of Nixinger strategy but about material realities; namely, whether Vietnamization would progress sufficiently that, with American support, Thieu would be able to prolong the struggle interminably.[40] Thus it was that Nixon and Kissinger, and not the DRV and NLF, were most affected by dissent from inside and outside the American government. It served, for example, as a major influence on Nixon's decisions to withdraw American troops from Cambodia and to place increased reliance on the uncertainties of Vietnamization, bombing, and global, linkage diplomacy.

RESULTS

When U.S. troops vacated Cambodia on June 30, allied casualties totaled 638 South Vietnamese and 338 Americans killed, and 3,009 South Vietnamese and 1,525 Americans wounded. American figures for VNLAF casualties were 11,349 killed and 2,328 captured, although these estimates were most probably too high. There were no official figures on civilian casualties. The "majority" of South Vietnamese forces were withdrawn as well, but RVNAF units continued to hold border areas and conduct operations deep into Cambodian territory until the end of the war.[41] American air operations continued too. Although the secret Menu bombings ended on May 26, an increasing number of B-52 sorties struck an enlarged target area in what Kissinger called "open operations" until mid-1973, when Congress forced their termination, and tactical air missions, many carried out secretly, were flown against targets throughout eastern Cambodia.[42]

In his report to the nation on June 30, Nixon claimed substantial success: the incursion would have the effect of saving American and South Vietnamese lives; ensuring that U.S. troop withdrawals proceeded on schedule; safeguarding Vietnamization and boosting pacification; and enhancing "the prospects for a just peace." In sum, it had demonstrated the "futility of expanded aggression." All of these gains came or would come from having separated the enemy's main force units from the guerrillas; destroyed enemy base areas; interdicted the flow of supplies from the sea; demonstrated America's will to punish Hanoi's intransigence at the negotiating table; killed or captured considerable numbers of enemy troops;

and, mostly, destroyed or seized large quantities of VNLAF weapons, ammunition rounds, mines, explosives, food, supplies, vehicles, bunkers, and structures.

Despite the impressive statistics cited by Nixon in his report,[43] the operation had been in many ways a failure; if successful in other ways, it had not been militarily decisive, which had been the hope of Nixon, Kissinger, and military planners at the outset. COSVN had not been found and destroyed, and the base areas had not been completely "cleaned out." A CIA study concluded that VNLAF supplies could be replenished within two or three months.[44] Nor had the other side been intimidated by the invasion's symbolic, "madman" intent. Instead of forcing them to make concessions at the bargaining table, the Cambodian coup and incursion had led the DRV/PRG to cancel a scheduled May 6 meeting of the public, plenary talks and to suspend the secret, private talks between Kissinger and Tho after their April 4 rendezvous.[45]

Lon Nol's army had been supplied with additional arms, but neither his regime nor Cambodia would be saved. Kissinger claimed in *White House Years* that without the invasion, Cambodia would have fallen to the Khmer Rouge several years earlier than 1975. But his assertion begged the question of whether it would have fallen at all had Cambodia not been plunged into full-scale civil war by operation Menu, Lon Nol's coup, and the American–South Vietnamese invasion, which had led Hanoi and the Khmer Rouge to put aside their differences for the time being and cooperate in ousting Lon Nol.[46] Meanwhile, frictions had developed between Lon Nol's Cambodian army and Thieu's South Vietnamese army. RVNAF commanders were angry with the Cambodians for imprisoning large numbers of Vietnamese-Cambodian citizens and resentful that the Cambodians "refused to fight."[47]

Although American casualties declined in the months and years after the incursion—not counting those incurred in Cambodia—the drop was due more to the withdrawal of U.S. combat units from South Vietnam than to the destruction of enemy capabilities during the Cambodian operation. Meanwhile, in the next three years the RVNAF suffered higher casualties than in any year except 1968. Military Region 3, which bordered the old sanctuaries, continued to be the scene of heavy fighting and undiminished casualties.[48]

Nixon asserted in *RN* that the operation "had demonstrated Vietnamization was working," and in his June 30 report he had claimed that it had assisted the progress of pacification. Yet at the time Abrams and Laird worried that South Vietnamese units would be badly bruised by their North Vietnamese opponents in Cambodia and felt that the pacification program in South Vietnam was being hurt by having the RVNAF "wandering all over Cambodia." Subsequent American reports on the status of Vietnamization questioned the quality of South Vietnamese command leadership and logistics capabilities.[49]

At home the incursion had given rise to what even Nixon described in his June 30 report as "broad disagreement and dissent within the society." He conceded that "there remains disagreement about . . . [the operation's] long-term significance, [and] about the cost to our society of having taken this action."[50] There could be no disagreement about three long-term results, however. He would not be able to send American troops into Laos or again into Cambodia. More than before he would feel the need to carry out large-scale troop withdrawals from South Vietnam. And if the Cambodian incursion had damaged the VNLAF and forced a postponement of a spring offensive, as Nixon and Kissinger claimed, the obverse had been true as well. Because it had been militarily indecisive, they would be unable to bring the war to a favorable conclusion by the end of 1970 or the beginning of 1971, as they had hoped when launching the operation.

OTHER CRISES

Although the Vietnam War continued to be Nixon's major concern, posing exasperating challenges at home and abroad, it was not the only foreign policy crisis with which he had to deal or the only matter on his programmatic agenda. During the year 1970, American-Soviet negotiations on strategic arms limitation turned new corners, Washington and Moscow discussed the possibility of a summit meeting, Sino-American relations edged fitfully toward rapprochement, the Biafran crisis continued, and new crises in Cuba, Chile, and the Middle East evoked American responses. There would be other emergencies in the years ahead: a Polish uprising (1971); the Indo-Pakistani War (1971); an international monetary crisis (1971); the Yom Kippur War (1973); and the OPEC oil embargo (1973).

To be sure, the other crises Nixon and Kissinger encountered around the globe had roots in endemic historic processes that were independent of Vietnam, and some of these—the U.S. balance of payments deficit, the U.S.-USSR rivalry, relations with China, and the intractable Mideast conflicts, for example—were more fundamentally important to their long-term goals than was Vietnam. But the war in Vietnam was the crucible of testing and change.[51] They believed they needed to end it in order to confront these challenges fully; if it were not ended soon, what was left of the interventionist, globalist consensus at home would be shattered. But if it were ended unfavorably, the consequences would be detrimental to America's global standing and their own goals. "I am utterly convinced that how we end this war will determine the future of the U.S. in the world," Nixon told advisers at a breakfast meeting on July 22, 1970, with Kissinger, Bunker, and David Bruce, Lodge's replacement at the Paris plenaries. "We can maintain the American position in Europe and Asia if we come out well."[52]

The Vietnam War heightened Nixon's sense of world crisis, contributed to his emotional tension, compounded his personality disorders, and influenced his stratagems and tactics for dealing with home-front and foreign issues. It also influenced his grand strategy. The Nixon Doctrine—later applied to other second world and third world trouble spots, such as Iran—had originally been conceived in reaction to the dilemmas Nixon encountered in Southeast Asia. Vietnam influenced relations with China and the Soviet Union. In his comprehensive survey history of détente, Raymond L. Garthoff observed: "While President Nixon would probably have pursued an opening to China even if his principal foreign policy preoccupation from 1969 through 1972 had not been ending the war in Vietnam, that circumstance certainly contributed to the priority he assigned the task." As well, détente with the USSR, which related to issues as diverse as trade and arms control, was tightly linked by Nixon—and Kissinger—to Soviet cooperation in settling the war.[53] Even as they were negotiating a strategic nuclear arms treaty, the difficulty they encountered in applying credible and decisive diplomatic leverage against Hanoi encouraged them to maintain America's nuclear edge over the Soviet Union.

Indochina was also the testing ground of the madman theory, a stratagem Nixon on occasion applied elsewhere, and if the war was not the cause of its use elsewhere, it may have been the catalyst. When informed by Kissinger from Washington on September 17, 1970, that a civil war had erupted in Jordan between King Hussein and the Palestine Liberation Organization's *fedayeen,* for example, Nixon, then in Chicago on a speaking tour, decided to send a warning signal to the Soviet Union, whose role in this crisis both he and Kissinger exaggerated. At the time Kissinger's mood matched Nixon's, for he felt "we are pissing away all we've gained in 18 months, both with Russia and North Vietnam. . . . The real stake is Nixon['s] credibility with [the] Soviets."[54]

The contingency plan for military deployments that Nixon now approved had been drafted at a WSAG meeting chaired by Kissinger the previous day as the Jordanian crisis was building. During their telephone conversation at 8:00 A.M., Nixon told Kissinger: "The main thing is there's nothing better than a little confrontation now and then, a little excitement."

During a previously scheduled briefing of Chicago newspaper editors during the midmorning, he warned that the United States "is prepared to intervene directly in the Jordanian war should Syria and Iraq enter the conflict and tip the military balance against Government forces loyal to Hussein." He added that the United States would make the Soviets pay dearly for their involvement in the concurrent Israeli-Egyptian conflict: "We will intervene if the situation is such that our intervention will make a difference." Questioned about his threats, he answered that it might be generally beneficial for American interests if the Soviets thought he was capable of "irrational or unpredictable action. . . . The real possibility of irrational American action is essential to the U.S.-Soviet relationship."

Nixon had been deliberately enigmatic about the specific actions he was prepared to take. The editors of one of the newspapers, the *Chicago Sun-Times,* nevertheless believed his threat to be newsworthy and reported his "strictly off-the-record" remarks in a separate story written by Peter Lisagor for the paper's afternoon edition on September 17. On the basis of this account, the Voice of America broadcast Nixon's message to the world. On September 18 TASS, the Soviet news agency, took note of the story, as well as of U.S. naval movements in the Mediterranean, and warned that intervention by "outside nations" could widen the Mideast conflict. Meanwhile, Nixon's entourage learned of the *Sun-Times* story while flying back to Washington on the evening of the seventeenth and persuaded the newspaper's management to withdraw it from the evening edition. Later, however, the president phoned Lisagor to congratulate him on his skilled handling of the story, and Nixon's press spokesmen did not deny its import, leading the press to conclude that "the White House was not unhappy that its tough tone was being communicated to other countries."[55]

POLITICS AND VIETNAM

Even as the public furor over the Cambodian incursion had seemed to subside by late May or early June, Nixon and Kissinger came to feel they were walking a "tightrope" between the steadfastness of their Vietnamese enemies and the end-the-war tendencies within Congress, the bureaucracy, and the citizenry. Describing one aspect of their predicament, Kissinger wrote: "We were caught between an enemy unwilling to compromise and an antiwar movement in the Congress refusing either to admit that Hanoi might be implacable or to countenance military action that might have induced Hanoi to alter its terms."[56] Compelled by domestic political and economic pressures to withdraw American troops from Vietnam, their military leverage on the ground in South Vietnam was slowly but steadily fading, despite the intended compensatory effect of Vietnamization. Kissinger knew that "a strategy relying on Vietnamization would not be compatible indefinitely with a strategy of negotiations," and although he reminded Nixon as much, he was helpless to prevent the relentless momentum of American troop disengagement. Pleading budgetary constraints imposed by Congress and political pressures to reduce draft calls, Secretary Laird was by early July once again pressing for accelerated troop withdrawals as well as decreases in strategic and tactical bombing sorties. In these proposals he garnered the support, however grudgingly, of CINCPAC, the JCS, and the State Department. Kissinger fought to retain current schedules of withdrawals and bombing, and Nixon pledged to back him in the bureaucratic struggle. But Laird proceeded on his own fiscal schedule, Nixon wavered, and in October Kissinger "threw in the towel."[57]

The president sometimes wavered, but he also often declared his resolve to stay the course of prosecuting the war despite bureaucratic, grassroots, congressional, or liberal opposition. In July he told advisers: "The American people are evenly divided. The establishment is against me, but I'll see it through if I'm the only person in the country to do it. We'll see the end of our participation one way or another. . . . I came into office without the support of all the people who oppose me today and I can get reelected without their support."[58]

Although feeling pressure from the antiwar movement in and out of Congress, the encouragement Nixon took from polls that revealed his strength among particular segments of voters led him to follow his instinct for counterattack. He took steps and entertained schemes to isolate or destroy opponents of the war and his presidency while building support for himself and his party. The offensive had covert and overt prongs. The covert prong included wiretaps of Kissinger's aides, expanded counterintelligence operations against the antiwar movement, and dirty tricks against his liberal political challengers. The overt prong included a pro-war, antiliberal, antiradical public relations campaign. With polls indicating the unpopularity of demonstrators and radical students among a majority of voters, Nixon had decided by late May to make his opposition to student radicals and their alleged liberal allies a centerpiece of his public relations and political campaigns, one of whose aims was to build support for his war policies and another to forge a new conservative political coalition. This "real majority," as Nixon and his speechwriters dubbed it, embraced Republicans, conservative Democrats, "Poles, Italians, Elks and Rotarians, . . . Catholics," hard hats, and southern whites but excluded "Jews, blacks, youths," and, of course, radicals and liberals, who, lumped together, were designated "radiclibs." For the most part, Vice President Agnew continued to be the public relations point man on war-related issues, contrasting pestiferous student radicalism and liberal journalism with the wholesome Silent Majority, while a team of speechwriters, led by Buchanan and Safire, spun out fresh phrases for him and Nixon. Republican candidates, Nixon ordered, were to be encouraged to "tie their opponents into hippies, kids, Demos." Sometimes trying to appear above the fray, Nixon expropriated central national symbols, declaring July 4 to be Honor America day, for example, and deciding on July 10 to wear an American flag pin on his lapel.[59]

As fall approached, Nixon mused about long-range political plans, such as replacing all key people in the administration by mid-1973, creating a Conservative Party to supersede the Republican Party, and "building *our* establishment in [the] press, business, education, etc." Meanwhile, there were more pressing, immediate concerns: We "should gear everything to '72 reelection and winning Congress." By mid-October Nixon was "really geared up to hit the [campaign] trail," hoping to make big gains for the Republicans in the November congressional elections. "I just hope we've taken the right course," Haldeman noted, "because he's really committed now. If the general view that voters are really confused and seeking direction this year proves to be right, our tour may make the difference."[60]

While campaigning, Nixon emphasized partisan themes: his liberal congressional opponents were undermining his peace efforts and slandering the nation's patriotic values; he was for law and order, but liberal "permissiveness" contributed to violence and crime; and student radicalism was a threat to order. On October 16 Nixon and his staff were greatly excited by the news that the Kent State grand jury had indicted twenty-five students, but no Guardsmen, a step that served Nixon's intention to "counterbalance" the findings of the FBI and the William Scranton Commission, which had investigated the incident during the summer and faulted the National Guard.[61] At San Jose State University on October 27, Nixon "wanted some confrontation," Haldeman matter-of-factly admitted, but "there were no hecklers in the hall, so we stalled departure a little so they could zero in outside, and they sure did. Before getting in [his] car, P stood up and gave the V signs, which made them mad. They threw rocks, flags, candles, etc. . . . Made a huge incident and we worked hard to crank it up."[62]

When in the November election the Republicans lost eleven state houses and nine seats in the U.S. House, gaining only two seats in the Senate, Nixon was disappointed and "brooded" over it for several days afterward. With Washington, D.C., papers portraying the results as a defeat for his presidency, he was eager to launch a concerted public relations attack to spin the story the other way, showing it "as a failure of [the] Party." In White House political strategy sessions he tried to "put the whole thing in perspective," and part of this perspective was to deny that public dissatisfaction with his handling of the Vietnam War had been a factor in the poor Republican showing in the election.[63]

To assuage Nixon and develop a basis for spinning the story for the press, Charles Colson worked up an analysis on the congressional campaign, in which he maintained that "the war issue became neutralized in the campaign." But that meant good news and bad. On the one hand, "people are generally very satisfied with your handling of the war, . . . and the issue would have been an enormous plus had you been the candidate." On the other, "because it . . . has become something of a non-issue, they weren't motivated to vote *against* those who have opposed you on the war. In short, . . . it didn't significantly benefit our supporters or hurt our opponents."[64]

Nixon's instinct once again was to raise himself above thorny, ambivalent issues such as Vietnam by having his public relations people call attention to his personal mystique. Although congratulating himself on his management of the presidency and his "major accomplishments" in foreign policy (the Cambodian incursion, his Mideast diplomacy, and his speech of November 3, 1969), he repeated his old argument to Haldeman and others that his staff had not gotten across the "kind of man he is"—his "warmth," "courage," "independence," and "boldness." His speechwriters would do well to use more anecdotes and "human interest" stories, and even to bring in "poetry, excitement, and spiritual quality." Former Texas governor John Connally, who now served as a consultant to Nixon on political matters and, in 1971, would become secretary of the treasury, agreed with Nixon that "we don't really get out the points that we should be getting." But Connally made one other argument that resonated with the president: that Nixon, in the manner of Lincoln, Churchill, and de Gaulle, should not emphasize his conduct of war but instead the "comeback from defeat . . . story."[65]

Despite talk of having neutralized the Vietnam issue, Nixon was becoming concerned about the long-term impact of the war on the solidity of his political base as he looked forward to the 1972 presidential election. Kissinger claimed that the president believed the war "was sapping his domestic support and therefore had to be ended before 1972." If it were not, he might lose in his bid for re-election, and, considering his likely Democratic opponents, this would have the effect of undermining "America's world position."[66] Nixon's political base included those who had been willing to trust his promises that de-Americanization, Vietnamization, and negotiation would bring about a timely peace with honor, but it also included those hawks who believed that the application of greater military force, particularly more bombing, could achieve the desired end. When in August several hawkish Senators urged Nixon to end the war quickly, Nixon complained: "We've got the Left where we want it now. . . . All they've got left to argue for is a bug-out, and that's their problem. But when the Right starts wanting to get out, for whatever reason, that's *our* problem."[67]

PRIVATE AND PUBLIC DIPLOMACY

As early as May, Kissinger had directed his staff to prepare a special study of the administration's diplomatic options regarding the Vietnam War. These were discussed in interagency meetings and the NSC during June and July.[68] On July 5 he instructed Vernon Walters in Paris to request the reopening of secret talks. To his delight, Hanoi replied in the affirmative on August 18, proposing a meeting date of August 29. Not wanting to appear as eager to talk as he had in February, but also concerned about an imminent vote on the McGovern-Hatfield amendment in Congress and its impact on talks, Kissinger delayed his government's response, then proposed a date of September 7, one week after the amendment had been defeated.[69]

Kissinger intended to go to Paris as he had before—secretly. But Nixon had doubts. The president felt that he could not "go on having Henry conduct operations independently of Rogers without Rogers' knowledge." His concern applied not only to the Paris negotiations but also to Kissinger's secret channel through Dobrynin and other clandestine foreign policy steps. Moreover, Nixon was exasperated with Kissinger's behavior, tired of his complaining about Rogers and of turning every issue with the secretary into a crisis; and he was beginning to doubt the accuracy of Kissinger's descriptions of State Department positions. In mid-August the president told Haldeman that Kissinger "may have reached the end of his usefulness." But Nixon needed Kissinger, and, as Haldeman reminded him, should live with his "weakness" toward Rogers in order to profit from his "enormous assets." At the same time and on the other hand, Rogers and the Department of State were a hindrance to Nixon's foreign policies, and Nixon thought that Rogers frequently made public statements that undercut presidential credibility. (By November, the president was seriously thinking of having Rogers resign as secretary of state in his next term and replacing him with Nelson Rockefeller.)[70]

Kissinger claimed in his memoirs that before leaving for his September 7 meeting in Paris he told Nixon he did not expect progress because he would be talking not with Le Duc Tho but with Xuan Thuy, who lacked plenipotentiary powers. Anticipating vituperative complaints from Thuy about the Cambodian invasion, Kissinger was, however, pleased to find him in a diplomatically cordial mood, willing to hear him out on the American proposal. Nonetheless, Kissinger opened the meeting with a madman threat that was not very subtly masked in a call for fruitful negotiations: "We are nearing the time when the chances for a negotiated settlement will pass. After a certain point you will have in effect committed yourselves to a test of arms. I do not want to predict how this test against a strengthened South Vietnam, supported by us, will end nor how long it will last. But you must recognize that it will make any settlement with the United States increasingly difficult."[71]

He then put forward his proposal: a twelve-month schedule of mutual withdrawals; a promise to leave no residual American forces or bases in South Vietnam "after the war"; and a mixed electoral commission of Communists, Saigon-regime, and neutral representatives to supervise free elections, with "international observers" to provide "additional guarantees." According to Kissinger's account in *White House Years,* his renouncement of the residual forces demand was intended as a concession, while the twelve-month timetable was a superficial change that brought their private and public proposals into line, correcting the faux pas he had made at the April 4 meeting, when he had proposed a sixteen-month schedule.[72] (He could afford to be more generous on this matter because five months had passed since April.) In a postmeeting report to Nixon, Kissinger informed the president that he also told Thuy that this was the administration's "final proposal," and that his government "would not set a date [for withdrawal] until we know that the POWs will be released in exchange, making this a key element in the package."[73]

Kissinger sarcastically wrote in his memoirs that Thuy had defiantly spurned his implied threat "by the perennial claim to epic stature": "We are not afraid of threats. Prolongation of fighting doesn't frighten us. Prolongation of negotiations doesn't frighten us. We are afraid of nothing." Thuy showed little interest in the twelve-month timetable, Kissinger asserted, but, in his "opaqueness," Thuy seemed at the time to be indicating more flexibility regarding the extension of the DRV/PRG's six-month timetable. Above all, Thuy wanted to comment on the political issues, holding to his government's position, which insisted on excluding the Thieu regime from any political settlement.[74]

The DRV Foreign Ministry's notes of the meeting indicate that Hanoi considered the twelve-month timetable for troop withdrawals and the willingness of the Americans to "include political issues" in the discussions as the most interesting of Kissinger's proposals. The North Vietnamese may have seen the new withdrawal timetable as a step, however small, toward the setting of a reasonable date for an American pullout, and the inclusion of political questions as a change, however subtle, in the long-standing American insistence on separating military and political issues. The notes also reveal that the American political proposals were "based on [the] three principles [enunciated] by Nixon in his April 20 speech."[75]

In this speech, the same one in which he had announced the 150,000–man troop withdrawal, Nixon had called for a "just political settlement" that expressed the "will of the South Vietnamese people . . . without outside interference"; that reflected "the existing relationship of political forces"; and for which the United States would "not agree to the arrogant demand that the elected leaders of the Government of Vietnam be overthrown before real negotiations begin."[76]

Kissinger and Thuy scheduled another meeting for September 27, but before it took place, Mme Binh, the PRG foreign minister and head of the PRG delegation in Paris, presented an "Eight-Point Clarification of the Ten-Point Overall Solution" at the eighty-fourth plenary session of the Paris conference on September 17. The PRG continued to insist on several of its long-standing principles: the unconditional and unilateral withdrawal of U.S. forces; free elections supervised by an interim coalition government; the gradual reunification of North and South by the Vietnamese themselves without American interference; and a diplomatic policy of neutrality after reunification. But Binh's proposal included "clarifications" on several points—details that had been absent from previous PRG proposals, and that now brought their position more or less into line with that of the DRV at the private talks: a general cease-fire that would take effect only after a settlement that included an American commitment to withdraw and an agreement on a tripartite, provisional, or interim government that included representatives of the PRG, parties committed to peace, independence, and neutrality, and the Saigon regime, excluding Thieu, Ky, and Khiem; a specific withdrawal date for American forces, June 30, 1971; a guarantee that the VNLAF would refrain from attacks against American troops as they withdrew; and a commitment to begin discussions immediately on the release of POWs.[77]

In *White House Years* Kissinger described the coalition government proposal as one that was "stacked" in favor of the Communists, and the June 30 withdrawal date as a deceptive concession, which on the one hand extended the DRV's six-month schedule to nine months but actually amounted to a "retrogression" in their position because it would take effect before, not after, a settlement. In a private memorandum to Nixon on September 17, however, Kissinger acknowledged at least "two new elements" in Binh's proposal that implied "flexibility": "The suggestion that they will talk to us about POWs. (. . . This included pilots downed in North Vietnam.) The lengthening of the schedule for our withdrawal to nine months, . . . and to a completion date frequently proposed in this country." He remarked that while these elements were "probably intended to generate maximum impact in the U.S.," they should be explored "to see how much flexibility is behind their schedule and the degree to which we can separate their hard demands for our unilateral withdrawal from our desire to pursue other subjects." By "other subjects" Kissinger probably meant the coalition commission and POW releases.[78]

In a follow-up analysis of the full text of Binh's proposal on September 22, Kissinger seemed even more hopeful, for he characterized it as "less assertive than the earlier ten points regarding the United States." Specifically, it implied that "we can quickly and painlessly extricate ourselves from Vietnam if we will only . . . set a withdrawal date"; the POW matter could be settled after an American withdrawal announcement, not in the "aftermath of the war," as the other side had previously stated; there was no demand for reparations or for the international supervision of U.S. withdrawals; and there was no "assertion . . . that we must 'renounce' Thieu-Ky-Khiem, as the Communists have frequently demanded (although unilateral withdrawal would amount to the same thing)."[79]

Kissinger's subsequent talks with Thuy in Paris on September 27, however, were "unproductive," as Kissinger characterized them in his report to Nixon, and they concluded their discussions without setting a date for another meeting.[80] In *White House Years* Kissinger claimed that Thuy had been inflexible, for he had adhered to the June 30 withdrawal date and continued to insist on the "removal" of Thieu, Ky, and Khiem. Kissinger's account was cryptic and censorious, but it implied that he had hoped to win political concessions favorable to Thieu's government in exchange for the setting of an American withdrawal date; that is, the United States was still insisting on Nixon's three political principles of April 20 as a precondition for withdrawal.

There had been a hint in Kissinger's memo of September 22 that he and Nixon were considering the possibility of a decent-interval solution of the political questions, for he had commented that the Binh proposal conveyed "the impression that we could get out easily if we were not concerned about what happened later."[81] On October 3 Kissinger told Safire: "The big question is, does the other side want to settle for anything less than total victory? Their demands are absurd: they want us to withdraw and on the way out to overthrow the Saigon Government. If we ever decide to withdraw, it'll be up to them to overthrow the Saigon Government— not us."[82] And in a chapter of *White House Years* in which he described the American negotiating position in late 1970, Kissinger claimed that the administration was searching for a political solution that gave Thieu "a reasonable chance to survive."[83] But the record of negotiating positions taken by the United States in September and early October indicates that if he and Nixon were entertaining the possibility of such a decent-interval solution, they had not yet embraced it.

In their memoirs, neither Nixon nor Kissinger discussed the POW question as one of their negotiating points. But it seems to have loomed large in the talks. American negotiators had previously emphasized the issue in both public and private statements, and Kissinger had raised it again on September 7. The Vietnamese appeared to have made a significant gesture in the direction of American concerns in the PRG proposal of September 17, a point Kissinger had acknowledged privately. Now apparently realizing that he would have to make concessions in return, Nixon balked. In a marginal notation on a September 23 memo from Kissinger, in which he had outlined for Nixon the approach he intended to take at the September 27 meeting, the president wrote: "Plus prisoners issue—to be considered separately, as indication of their desire for peaceful settlement." Kissinger's staff therefore rewrote their boss's opening statement for the meeting, "trying to underline our interest in this matter without letting it get entangled in the political and military bargaining." When he met with Thuy, Kissinger emphasized the American concern about POWs but did not press the matter, explaining that "we consider it a humanitarian issue, not one where our men can be used as hostages."[84] For Nixon and Kissinger, then, the POW issue was important in scoring political points at home but not negotiable in Paris if it meant the United States would have to trade Thieu, Ky, and Khiem for American POWs.

In a televised address to the nation on October 7, just two weeks after Kissinger's last meeting with Thuy, the day after Nixon returned from a European tour, and the day before he was to take to the campaign trail, Nixon announced what he referred to as "a major new initiative for peace": a cease-fire throughout all of Indochina. Although stating that his offer was "without preconditions," he coupled the proposal with two other provisions: supervision of the cease-fire by international observers, and the convening of a multinational "Indochina Peace Conference." Avoiding mention of Kissinger's secret talks, Nixon disingenuously stated that the plenary sessions in Paris would remain the "primary forum" for negotiations until the "international conference produces serious negotiations." He declared his readiness to negotiate a timetable for withdrawals, but only after agreement was reached on a political settlement that incorporated the three principles he had enunciated on April 20. As a separate item, he proposed the "immediate and unconditional release of all prisoners of war held by both sides." Concluding, he called attention to the welcome he had received from crowds in Europe: "They were not cheering for me as an individual. They were cheering for the country I was proud to represent—the United States of America." Having identified his person with the nation, he ended the speech with a reaffirmation of his goal to build a "structure of peace in the world."[85]

Nixon had delayed his presentation of the proposal in order to "further defuse the war issue"[86] and to achieve political effect in the midst of a campaign, but it was also designed to assuage internal bureaucratic sentiment. Not only were former U.S. negotiators, bipartisan doves, and grassroots antiwar groups advocating a cease-fire, but senior officials and advisers in the Defense and State Departments supported this approach as a means of trimming the budget by de-escalating the war or of appeasing public and congressional opinion. Kissinger explained in *White House Years* that interagency opinion on the administration's diplomatic options, which had been discussed through June and July, had "crystallized" in August around the Indochina-wide cease-fire, and Thieu had reluctantly accepted it. Nixon had approved it "during August" with a target date of announcing it in mid-September, following which Kissinger was to have presented it in person to the Paris plenary conference. A few days later, Nixon would have commenced his European trip. These plans had been changed after Hanoi accepted

Kissinger's invitation for another round of private talks.[87] The White House inner circle now felt that the speech "puts us on the initiative and [the] ball is now in Hanoi's court."[88]

The "standstill ceasefire," or "ceasefire-in-place," as it was dubbed, was but the public unveiling of the armistice proposal previously presented by Kissinger in private negotiations. Once Hanoi abandoned its demand for the "removal" of Thieu from power, as Kissinger phrased it, the cease-fire would take effect, followed by the mutual withdrawal of U.S. and North Vietnamese forces. The other side had rejected it on grounds having to do with principle and practicality, but as Kissinger acknowledged, "its [public] appeal as a 'compromise' proposal was that both sides would thereby be renouncing military victory."[89] But this was all appearance, for a political-paramilitary struggle between the Thieu regime, supported by the United States, and the NLF, supported by the DRV, would inevitably have followed such an agreement.[90]

Drafted by the NSC, Nixon's speech had been put in final form by William Safire after Nixon's October 4 meeting with Kissinger, Rogers, Bruce, and Habib at the Dromoland Castle hotel in Ireland, the last stop on his European tour.[91] By this time Kissinger had become pessimistic about the likelihood of Hanoi accepting a cease-fire, or so he claimed in his memoirs. But thinking the proposal "would give us some temporary relief from public pressures," he kept his doubts to himself during the meeting. Bruce was optimistic on diplomatic grounds, believing that the DRV/PRG "would take the bait." The others were upbeat as well, favoring "anything," Kissinger claimed, "that might get the negotiations off dead center and our critics off the front pages."[92] Safire, who was also at the hotel, later wrote that "the proposal was what Nixon would call 'grandstanding' or 'showboating,' presented primarily for its political impact in the States, buying Nixon some more time, with little chance of its acceptance by the North Vietnamese, but with every chance of its embrace by editorial writers who wanted a dramatic offer which they thought would break the logjam in negotiations."[93]

The standstill cease-fire appeared new and promising to the press and citizenry, and initially it was well received. That Nixon had not directly called for mutual withdrawal in the speech suggested to some that he had abandoned the demand, and thus the cease-fire proposal represented a key change in the American position.[94] In press briefings Kissinger reinforced this impression, intimating that the cease-fire amounted to a substitute for mutual withdrawal.[95] In his memoirs Kissinger explained that even though Nixon had "put" his call for total withdrawal "in the context of mutual withdrawal," he had done so "in a language so deliberately fuzzy as to invite exploration" by the other side.[96]

But to those who paid attention, Nixon had contradicted this interpretation in a remark he made to the press less than twenty-four hours after the speech. Denying that he had delivered the address to win political points, he said: "We made this proposal because we wanted to cover every base that we could. . . . That is why we offered a total withdrawal of all of our forces, something we have never offered before, if we had mutual withdrawal on the other side."[97] His reference to "total withdrawal" was an allusion to the American renunciation of residual American forces in South Vietnam after the war, a "concession" offer Kissinger had made in his proposal of September 7 in Paris. Nixon had obscurely referred to this particular point when he used the term "complete withdrawals" in his October 7 speech.[98] Despite their fuzzy allusions, Nixon and Kissinger were still calling for mutual withdrawal, coupled with a political settlement that kept Thieu in power.

If Nixon, Kissinger, and the NSC had indeed intended to invite the exploration of their ideas by the DRV/PRG—in addition to building political support at home—it was that in July and August they had planned to put forward a series of proposals in private and public with the intention of drawing the other side to the "bait." They hoped to entice the DRV/PRG to accept a cease-fire in return for the offer of no residual American forces, the twelve-month withdrawal schedule, and an American willingness to discuss political questions—namely, a tripartite electoral commission that included Thieu. But the administration had not given up on its basic military and political goals. The cease-fire was seen as a device for precluding a North Vietnamese offensive in 1971 or 1972, and as a way of safeguarding the process of Vietnamization. As Kissinger explained in his memoirs, it was "provisional": if accepted by Hanoi, it must be followed by an international conference on settling the war, at which the United States would demand the withdrawal of North Vietnamese forces. Then, if Hanoi rejected the demand, the administration might be in a better political position at home to insist on keeping "residual forces" in Vietnam, which would have included advisers, aircraft, and perhaps combat troops.[99]

From Paris on October 9, Binh and Thuy shot down Nixon's October surprise, criticizing it as "a maneuver to deceive world opinion" and pointing out that the United States was still insisting on mutual withdrawal. The cease-fire would have the effect of "prolonging the U.S. war of aggression" while keeping Thieu in power. Binh reiterated points in her side's proposals that provided a process for American withdrawal, a cease-fire, a political settlement, and immediate discussions of the prisoner issue. Although denouncing Nixon's speech, the DRV and PRG delegations did not "reject" it, instead describing their reaction as "preliminary." The Vietnamese were undoubtedly also unenthusiastic about Nixon's call for an international conference on Vietnam, since it was possible, as had been the case in the Geneva Conference in 1954, that the cards could be stacked against them in such a body. When diplomatic speculation turned to the likelihood of private talks between Bruce's Paris delegation, the RVN, and the DRV/PRG on Binh's eight points and Nixon's October 7 proposals, a North Vietnamese spokesman, Nguyen Than Le, only denied that such talks had already taken place.[100] On November 17, however, Bruce proposed secret quadripartite meetings.[101]

RAID ON SON TAY

Three days later, fifty-six American Special Forces and Ranger volunteers led by Colonel "Bo" Gritz carried out a helicopter assault on the Son Tay prison compound twenty-three miles west of Hanoi, with the objective of rescuing an estimated ninety to one hundred American POWs, most of whom were bomber pilots shot down over North Vietnam. But they found the camp empty. Because of flooding, the Vietnamese had relocated their prisoners on July 14.

JCS planning for the operation had begun early in the summer, and Laird presented the plan to Nixon "late" in the summer. In September, when traveling in Europe, the president was informed that the operation was ready to be executed. Planners gave Kissinger a full-scale briefing on October 8, recommending an attack date of October 21, but Nixon postponed a decision, fearing that failure during the congressional campaign would have adverse political repercussions. On November 18 the president met with Kissinger, Rogers, Laird, and Moorer to review the operation. No longer worried about the elections, he was, however, concerned about protests similar to those that followed the invasion of Cambodia. He told the gathering: "This time they will probably knock down the gates and I'll have a thousand incoherent hippies urinating on the Oval Office rug." Despite this worry, and despite recent intelligence assessments that there was a very good chance American prisoners were no longer at Son Tay, Nixon approved the raid for November 21, Washington time. Soon afterward, D day was moved forward to November 20.[102]

Nixon had been anxious before the Son Tay operation. He had told Kissinger hours before it was launched, "Don't do any planning for success, it's bad luck." Haldeman noted that on the day of the raid "all were on pins and needles awaiting outcome. Too bad it didn't work. Turned out no prisoners were there. Still went ahead with big bombing, etc."[103] The "big bombing" was carried out by two hundred fighter-bombers over a period of two days against targets in the Hanoi and Haiphong areas and against supply depots, bridges, and mountain passes along the Ho Chi Minh Trail.[104]

The administration's public explanation of the purpose of the Son Tay mission was that it was humanitarian and diplomatic—American POWs were likely being mistreated in North Vietnam, and this raid would free some of them and give the administration leverage in negotiations for others' release. Nixon asserted in his memoirs that his prior meetings with the families of men held prisoner and those listed as missing in action (MIA) had the effect of personalizing the issue, and "obtaining their release became a burning cause."[105] (Some Americans, including the families, assumed that many of the MIAs were being held prisoner by the enemy.) But there were political reasons for the operation as well. The successful rescue of American POWs in a daring behind-the-lines raid by U.S. commandos would have boosted Nixon's approval rating and the public's support for the war. At Nixon's direction the public relations campaign emphasized the explanation that "it was his idea and initiative. [It] all started by his instructions to use some imagination about POWs." Five days after the rescue attempt, Nixon held an awards ceremony at the White House with congressmen in attendance. Earlier he had met with "Bo" Gritz and "was really impressed . . . about how great these guys were." "Cranked up," he told his press secretary, Ron Ziegler, "to treat any skeptics with utter contempt."[106]

There was a political connection, too, between the Son Tay raid and the two days of bombings. While the air attacks were intended, as Kissinger wrote, "to divert Hanoi's defenses from Son Tay," it was also true, as Haldeman noted, that a public relations "push . . . about the effort to spring POWs . . . was a good counter-story to the bombings even though it [the rescue operation] failed." The air attacks did indeed produce a swell of criticism, but the Son Tay mission momentarily diverted public attention from them, while the White House tried to deflect blame for the bombings from Nixon by a prearranged plan to "leave all explanations to Defense."[107]

At the time the bombings were explained as "protective reaction" strikes, which had been launched against North Vietnamese radar and missile sites in reaction to their antiaircraft fire against unarmed American reconnaissance planes.[108] In his memoirs, however, Kissinger revealed the broader diplomatic and strategic reasons behind the November 1970 air raids. Besides diverting North Vietnamese defenses from Son Tay, they were designed "to retaliate for the abrupt rejection of our peace proposal; and to slow down the North Vietnamese dry-season supply effort in to the South."[109]

Thus, besides its humanitarian and political purposes, the combined operation of rescue and bombing had military and "psychological" purposes—an adjective Nixon used in his memoirs. He commented that "it revealed their vulnerability to a kind of attack they had not experienced before." The rescue mission, as Nguyen Co Thach explained to Seymour Hersh, demonstrated that the United States could get past North Vietnamese air defenses and "operate in our rear." It "was a true [rescue] activity but designed to show that their false [madman] threat is [also] true."[110] This result could hardly have escaped American military planners or Nixon and Kissinger at the time of the decision. The bombings sent a related signal: that the administration could and would use the bombing of North Vietnam and Laos as a lever in negotiations and a military tactic to retard Hanoi's offensive military capability in South Vietnam.[111] Nixon drove this point home at a press conference on December 10. Defending the air strikes, he expanded the definition of "protective reaction" to include the protection of American troops in Vietnam and the policy of Vietnamization: "If, as a result of my conclusion that the North Vietnamese, by their infiltration, threaten our remaining forces, if they thereby increase the level of fighting in South Vietnam, then I will order the bombing of military sites in North Vietnam, the passes that lead from North Vietnam into South Vietnam, the military complexes, the military supply lines. . . . Let there be no misunderstanding."[112]

SETTING THE STRATEGY

Restless the night before the Son Tay operation was to take place, Nixon "worked out a new plan for Vietnam at 2:00 this morning," Haldeman noted in his diary. "[The president] wants to blast talks, give last chance, then pull out. Mine Haiphong (or blockade), take offensive, and announce stepped-up withdrawals at same time. Put real heat on North Vietnam."[113] It was not, however, a new plan but a revived plan, one that Nixon had floated earlier in August. Encircled by the political pincer of hawkish and dovish demands to end the war sooner rather than later, Nixon had begun at least by August to consider a plan that incorporated hawkish and dovish elements: he would massively bomb, mine, and blockade North Vietnam while simultaneously withdrawing all remaining U.S. ground forces except those considered "residual." Kissinger had objected, however, arguing at that time that public and congressional protests against the Cambodian incursion had demonstrated that domestic opinion would not support such an escalation without "overwhelming provocation" from the other side. Obversely, de-escalation on the ground through an immediate and complete withdrawal of American troops would send a contradictory signal to Hanoi and trigger the collapse of Thieu's government.

Nixon dropped the matter—until he brought it up once again on November 20. Still driving his plan were concerns about politics, centering on citizen impatience with the war and the problem of winning reelection in 1972. These had to be balanced against the goal of avoiding defeat, or at least the appearance of defeat, in Vietnam.[114]

Kissinger continued to take exception. His objections were not about the political necessity of troop withdrawals or the strategic efficacy of massive bombing, mining, and blockade. They were about their timing. For the moment, the main issue was the pace of troop withdrawal and its relationship to Nixon's electoral concerns. Haldeman paraphrased the argument Kissinger made during November and December in his diary:

> Henry argues against a commitment that early to withdraw all combat troops because he feels that if we pull them out by the end of '71, trouble can start mounting in '72 that we won't be able to deal with and which we'll have to answer for at the elections. He prefers, instead, a commitment to have them all out by the end of '72 so that we won't have to deliver finally until after the elections and therefore can keep our flanks protected. . . . If any bad results follow they will be too late to affect the election.[115]

A complete withdrawal of combat troops made too soon—that is, in 1971—would, Kissinger explained in his memoirs, "wreck the South Vietnamese government and the prospects for Vietnamization." It would send such a signal of American "impatience" to Hanoi that the resumption of massive bombing, mining, and blockade "would serve little purpose." The other side "would simply buckle down and endure, counting on the domestic uproar here to stop our military pressure." The result would be "a collapse in Vietnam in 1972."[116]

Haldeman recorded that on December 21 Nixon came to accept this argument: "This would certainly seem to make more sense, and the P seemed to agree in general. He still feels he's got to make a major move in early '71, and he could make the commitment at that time that there would be no further use of draftees in Vietnam and also make the long-range troop-withdrawal commitment."[117]

There remained the details of pacing troop withdrawals. Kissinger argued against multiple periodic announcements, advocating the one-fell-swoop approach that Nixon had taken in April 1970 with his announcement of a 150,000-man reduction extending over a twelve-month period. In January 1971, when Thieu would urge them to keep American levels above 200,000 until after his own reelection in October 1971, Nixon's plan was to visit Vietnam in April, thereby bolstering Thieu politically by showing confidence in him, then announce approximately 100,000 reductions over six months between June and December. This would take American troop strength down from approximately 280,000 in April to 225,000 in August and 185,000 in December 1971. There would be periodic reductions after that, and then Nixon would announce the end of American participation in combat operations on the ground. At the negotiations, Kissinger would offer more rapid reductions in return for a cease-fire agreement.[118] "The outcome of the war," Kissinger wrote, "would then depend on whether the South Vietnamese, aided only by American air power, would be able to blunt the assault. Peace would thus come either at the end of 1971 or at the end of 1972—either by negotiation or by a South Vietnamese collapse."[119]

Implicit in Nixon's and Kissinger's calculations was their acceptance, at last, of the decent-interval solution, for with the departure of American combat troops near the end of 1972, there could be no guarantees that Thieu's government would survive permanently. They now seemed prepared to countenance his demise, as long as it would take place after an appropriately extended period following American withdrawal, thereby salvaging American credibility and Nixon's honor.

They had not, however, abandoned the hope that Thieu could survive into the indefinite future, and in any case, the administration would try to provide enough of a margin of safety so that his collapse, if it came, would not be sudden. American troops would stay two years more to assist the process of Vietnamization; Nixon and Kissinger were planning a major military offensive for early 1971; airpower would continue to be applied; a climactic Duck Hook type of operation would be held in reserve; and linkage diplomacy vis-à-vis the Soviet Union and China held out the possibility of levering political and military concessions from the DRV/PRG.

Anticipating extreme measures, such as the massive bombing of all of the DRV, and additional military pressure on other fronts to drive them to the brink of defeat and make concessions in negotiations, the other side steeled itself for the coming struggle. As 1970 came to an end, the North Vietnamese let Soviet embassy officials in Hanoi know that despite their great losses, they had preserved their power and determination and would continue the fight on every front—military, political, and diplomatic.[120]

LAM SON 719

Perceptions of opportunity and necessity had propelled Nixon and Kissinger in 1970 to consider making a major military move in Indochina in early 1971. The primary operation Nixon authorized at the turn of the new year was code-named Lam Son 719, whose military objective when it began on January 30 was the disruption of vital North Vietnamese logistics bases on the Ho Chi Minh Trail in southern Laos. It was scheduled to last ninety days, but it endured scarcely sixty before the PAVN drove the RVNAF back into South Vietnam at the end of March.[121]

As with many other things about the war, the provenance of Lam Son 719 remains obscure and assessments of its denouement are mixed, but of what is known, the processes of decision making and of battle conformed to previous patterns. In *White House Years* Kissinger vaguely asserted that in the "last few months" of 1970 he called on his staff and other government experts to submit estimates of the military and diplomatic prospects for the next two years.[122] These "last months" constituted the period of Nixon's growing unease about the ominous relationship between the costs of the war in Vietnam and the politics of the forthcoming American presidential campaign. Thus, Kissinger's request for staff studies most probably arose out of discussions he had with the president in the second half of 1970 concerning their need to find diplomatic leverage, pace the withdrawal of American troops, and provide for the military defense of South Vietnam—all timed in relation to the forthcoming American presidential election in 1972.

As Kissinger described their military goals for this period and beyond, they were to win "another test of strength" in 1972 and, following American withdrawal, enable the RVNAF to resist an anticipated North Vietnamese "main-force" invasion of South Vietnam in 1973.[123] (The president and his adviser were also concerned about an enemy drive into Cambodia or Laos in 1971.)[124] One solution would have been to redeploy "surplus" South Vietnamese battalions from Military Regions 3 and 4 in southern South Vietnam, where the military balance favored the RVNAF over the VNLAF, to Military Regions 1 and 2 in northern and central South Vietnam, where there was an RVNAF battalion "deficit" in relation to actual and potential VNLAF strength. But this option was not available because RVNAF battalions were tied by considerations of morale to the locales from which the troops were recruited and by reasons of South Vietnamese politics to the generals who commanded the army divisions in affected military regions. An obvious remedy to the problem, Kissinger said, would have been to keep at least one American combat division in South Vietnam through 1972 to serve as a "shield" for accelerated pacification in central and northern South Vietnam, which would have freed up South Vietnamese divisions to battle the North Vietnamese. The "domestic situation" in the United States, however, prevented the administration from choosing this option, and the year 1971 would be the last year in which American combat troops could be used with effect. Puzzled by these dilemmas but determined to resolve them, American planners concluded that the best defense would be a good offense—namely, an RVN-U.S. offensive midway through the October to May, 1970–1971, dry season, which "would disrupt the Communist logistics effort, reduce the battalion deficit expected for 1972, and enhance Hanoi's incentive to negotiate."[125]

Kissinger wrote that he strongly urged such an offensive in the face of interagency "indifference," initially favoring another incursion into Cambodia. Nixon agreed with this recommendation, but when Haig returned in December from a trip to South Vietnam, where he had consulted with Abrams, Bunker, and Thieu about a dry-season offensive, he reported that they had proposed an even bolder strike into Laos (although there is reason to wonder whether Thieu was enthusiastic). Thus was born Lam Son 719. As characterized by Kissinger, Abrams's reasoning was that an attack on primary arteries of the Ho Chi Minh Trail would significantly curtail, if not eliminate, Hanoi's ability to carry out major offensive operations in South Vietnam and Cambodia into "the indefinite future."[126] Although Kissinger would later fault Abrams for designing a faulty plan and Thieu for undermining its implementation, he was an earnest advocate, telling Haldeman—even after the plan's flaws were becoming apparent in late January 1971—that "it . . . would in effect end the war, because it would totally demolish the enemy's capability."[127]

Approved by the JCS by December 1970, Abrams's plan called for a three-phase operation. In Phase I, 9,000 U.S. troops would take up positions along Route 9 south of the DMZ in order to reactivate Khe Sanh as a base of operations and clear the area leading to the Vietnam-Laos border. American forces would not enter Laos but would provide helicopter, fighter-bomber, and artillery support for the South Vietnamese incursion. In Phase II, one South Vietnamese division would strike along Route 9 toward the crossroads village of Tchepone in southern Laos, establishing fire bases along the way. Midway through this advance an airborne division would seize and hold Tchepone until the troops coming overland could link up. Phase II was projected to require only four or five days. In Phase III, which was planned to last almost three months, the 17,000 troops of the RVNAF would raze Base 604—the American command's designation for the PAVN logistics complex around Tchepone—and interdict supply trails in the area. Then, in its withdrawal back to South Vietnam, the RVNAF would demolish Base 611, which bordered South Vietnam south of Route 9. In an ancillary move farther south, one RVNAF division would strike across the border from Military Region 3 in South Vietnam toward the town of Snuol in Cambodia to destroy a new base the VNLAF was believed to be setting up nearby.[128] Nixon's contribution to the planning was to urge a maximum bombing effort to divert PAVN's attention from the main thrust into Laos, but also to isolate the battlefield. Haldeman noted: "He pushed the military to go further than they themselves had intended to go."[129]

Nixon and Kissinger discussed the plan in the White House on December 18, 1970.[130] Determined on the operation but equally resolved, as Kissinger put it, "not to stand naked in front of his critics" as he had with the Cambodian decision in 1970, Nixon intended to involve Laird and Rogers in the decision-making process. But he would draw them in individually, hoping to use Laird, with whom he would meet first, to help persuade Rogers, who might then convince others in the State Department. Of all the top advisers, Rogers was the most important and likely recalcitrant.[131] Haig briefed Nixon on his Vietnam trip in Kissinger's presence on December 22,[132] then Laird on the next day, with Moorer, who had already been consulted, in attendance. Laird approved the concept of cutting the Ho Chi Minh Trail, agreeing that doing so could demonstrate the success of Vietnamization and gain another year's time for American policy to work its course. Relieved by Laird's support, Nixon approved the operation "in principle," subject to review after Laird's return from a trip to Vietnam. Another meeting was held on January 18, with Rogers and Helms now added to the group. Following Laird's positive briefing on the operation and a discussion of the timing of troop withdrawals from South Vietnam, however, Rogers joined the Laotian bandwagon, and Nixon gave his authorization for detailed interagency planning to begin. Kissinger initiated a series of WSAG meetings beginning on the following day.[133]

Influenced by Under Secretary M. Alexis Johnson, Rogers, however, soon began to question the plan, which led Kissinger to make his usual complaints in the Oval Office about the secretary and, with Nixon's approval, bureaucratically outmaneuver him through WSAG. Apparently because of State Department objections, it began to dawn on the White House that by launching an allied strike against a vital hub of enemy communications the PAVN would be determined to fight and able to mass its troops effectively. The administration had just learned, moreover, that enemy intelligence had acquired the plan and were redeploying their troops to meet the attack.

In addition to these concerns, Nixon and Kissinger began to worry about congressional and public reaction. News of the Cambodian buildup had led Senator Cooper and others in Congress to complain. Despite his reservations, Rogers helped the White House calm Cooper's fears, arguing that the operations were necessary to interdict supplies and would not involve American troops or advisers. On January 21, however, sixty-four members of the House proposed to ban air and sea support for operations in Cambodia. Six days later, Senators McGovern and Hatfield reintroduced their revised Disengagement Act, which would require the withdrawal of all American troops by the end of the year.[134]

State Department reservations about Lam Son 719 gave rise to another high-level meeting in the Oval Office on January 27. Before it took place Kissinger met with Moorer on January 25 and then with Moorer, Haig, and the president the following day to review possible military defects in the plan, along with three other complicating factors: congressional ferment, possible adverse public responses, and potential Soviet reactions. Dobrynin had just conveyed to Kissinger Moscow's acceptance of a midyear date for a Nixon-Brezhnev meeting, with a SALT agreement in the offing. The group wondered whether the Laotian invasion would derail the sought-after summit, but for the moment they were more concerned about military and political matters. On the military front, Moorer provided assurances that the operation could still be "decisive," a judgment Nixon and Kissinger accepted, and one that Kissinger approvingly repeated to Haldeman: "By going ahead with our planning and letting them go ahead with their counterplanning, we can draw them into a monumental trap and then move in and bomb them, maybe with the same effect as going ahead with the plan." Concerning congressional and public opinion, they concluded that the bombing option "would be a much more salable alternative domestically." With a nuanced turn of logic, Kissinger additionally maintained that the Cambodian invasion in 1970 had served to clear the air, leaving them with fewer concerns in 1971 about a repetition of explosive protests against their major military moves, "but [we] could have them in '72." It therefore followed that "this new action in Laos now would set us up so we wouldn't have to worry about problems in '72, and that of course is most important." The argument was not yet convincing, however.[135]

At the meeting on January 27 with Rogers, Kissinger, Packard, Haig, and Moorer, the secretary of state delivered, even by Kissinger's account, a telling critique of Lam Son 719: How could the operation be successful now when previously, at the peak of American strength, decision makers had thought allied forces were not strong enough to carry it off? All of what the Nixon administration had gained in the past year would be risked in Laos, Rogers warned, and Thieu's position could be shaken. But Nixon was not to be dissuaded, and he ordered that the Cambodian offensive and Phase I of the Laotian operation begin.[136]

Kissinger remembered that he considered the president's partial decision to mean that Nixon, once committed to Phase I, would go forward with Phase II. But, given his reluctance to confront close advisers, Nixon had chosen this piecemeal decision-making approach to avoid having to face down Rogers. Yet, there was to be another period of indecision and reconsideration after network television news leaked hints of Lam Son 719 on February 1, two days after Phase I was under way; these leaks were followed in the next few days by editorials in major national newspapers that raised doubts about the prospects for the operation. Kissinger immediately briefed Agnew, Connally, and Mitchell on February 1 about the pros and cons of Phase II. Nixon held more meetings on February 2 with Rogers, Laird, Helms, Moorer, and Haig, and his cabinet. They talked of polls and of the spirit and intent of the Cooper-Church amendment and the McGovern-Hatfield act, but according to Kissinger's and Haldeman's accounts, no one was opposed to going ahead.[137]

In a long meeting with Nixon that evening, however, Kissinger advised the president—according to Haldeman's notes—that they should "cancel the plans and hold up on the Phase II operation." Nixon was wavering, too, but he deferred a decision until the next day. In the morning the president met with Kissinger, Connally, Mitchell, and Haldeman to thrash out the issue. By the time of the meeting, Nixon and Kissinger had "pretty much changed their minds and swung back to feeling that we should go ahead with the operation." In outlining his case, Nixon pointed out that this would be "our last chance for any major positive action, since we won't be able to do anything after the dry season ends, and next year we won't have enough troops in place to be able to do anything." But both he and Kissinger emphasized another reason for proceeding: "If the P[resident] now allowed himself to be talked out of it, in effect by the press reports which had been leaked from State and Defense, . . . [then] he would lose any hope of controlling the bureaucracy," which they believed was already "completely out of control." Haldeman, Mitchell, and Connally did not disagree with Nixon's concern about the threat to his bureaucratic leadership, but they stressed other reasons for going ahead: the move was necessary in order to safeguard troop withdrawals, and it was unlikely that congressional, campus, press, or public protests would be as strong as Nixon and Kissinger were now assuming they would be. The meeting concluded after two hours without a decision. During a late-afternoon review of the arguments with Haldeman and Kissinger, however, the president— wearing only his shorts as his chiropractor adjusted his vertebrae—told Kissinger to give the execute order.[138]

The RVNAF crossed the Laotian border on February 7, but five days into the invasion and meeting light resistance, the advance stalled. Kissinger later claimed that on February 12 Thieu, who feared that some of his best units were at risk, ordered his commanders to proceed cautiously and to cancel the operation once 3,000 casualties had been incurred. (Hung and Schecter, who interviewed Thieu, said that he denied setting a casualty limit, although he was deeply concerned about walking into a trap.)[139]

When the 17,000 soldiers of the South Vietnamese army had entered Laos, they had been met by 22,000 North Vietnamese troops, mostly lightly armed logistical units. By mid-February more powerful PAVN units supported by tanks and heavy artillery appeared on the western, northern, and southern flanks of the RVNAF. As the fighting escalated, they overran several South Vietnamese fire bases, attacked convoys on Route 9, stepped up their artillery barrages, and with intense antiaircraft fire took a costly toll of allied helicopters. Heavy fighting continued for the next several weeks. On February 28, in the midst of the battle, Thieu replaced the original plan of operation, which had called for a ninety-day period of occupation and destruction of PAVN bases, with one that would nominally achieve the original objective of capturing Tchepone: one heliborne division would seize Tchepone, hold it briefly, and then, with the rest of the invasion force, withdraw from Laos. He told his commander, General Hoang Xuan Lam,

"You go in there just long enough to take a piss and then leave quickly." Abrams, who by now was frustrated with Thieu's actions and the RVNAF's dearth of initiative, had little choice but to accept the new plan.

There had been consternation in the White House, too, about the slow, fitful pace of the RVNAF incursion against the gathering strength of PAVN.[140] When a reporter asked the president at his news conference on March 4 whether the "difficulties" encountered by the RVNAF in Laos would cause him to reduce the rate of American troop withdrawals from Vietnam, Nixon dissembled, insisting that the South Vietnamese "had come of age" and had already accomplished enough in Laos to ensure the continuation of his plan for withdrawal.[141]

On March 7 the South Vietnamese occupied the deserted village of Tchepone, and on March 8 they abandoned it. By now it was clear, as a concerned Kissinger told Nixon on March 11, that the South Vietnamese "have decided to pull out as quickly as they can, because they're afraid that the North Vietnamese are massing for a big attack and that their guys are going to get trapped and slaughtered." They were "most anxious" that the RVNAF "hang in" longer, however, in order that more damage could be inflicted on PAVN and its logistics network and thus "buy so much more time for us down the road." Nixon and Kissinger realized that the danger was that "if it's a real disaster, it'll hurt Thieu politically, and we can't afford to let that happen." Haig was to be sent to South Vietnam to examine the situation and see if the RVNAF could stay in Laos for another month, timing their withdrawal to coincide with Nixon's troop withdrawal announcement and "make it all into one big 'ending the war' type deal."[142]

Lam Son 719 was already passing into its withdrawal phase. The RVNAF hung in the fighting only long enough to get out of Laos. By the time the last of the demoralized RVNAF soldiers crossed back into South Vietnam around March 25, they were pursued by a well-equipped conventional PAVN force of approximately 40,000 troops.[143] Both the South and North Vietnamese had suffered large losses of men, artillery, tanks, trucks, ammunition, and equipment in the Laotian battle, although claims from both sides are unreliable. U.S./RVN after-action reports inflated PAVN casualties to 26,000 and understated RVNAF casualties at 7,683, which nonetheless amounted to almost half of the South Vietnamese who entered Laos. Whatever the true numbers of PAVN casualties, most were the result of American B-52 and fighter-bomber strikes. American losses were more accurately recorded and far lower than those of the South and North Vietnamese, but they were comparable to those incurred in the 1970 Cambodian incursion: 270 killed and 1,580 wounded, with 108 helicopters destroyed and 600 damaged.[144]

As he announced a new round of American troop withdrawals in a speech to the nation on April 7, Nixon proclaimed that the South Vietnamese had demonstrated in Laos that "without American advisers they could fight effectively against the very best troops North Vietnam could put in the field. . . . Consequently, I can report tonight that Vietnamization has succeeded." Although the RVNAF had borne heavy casualties, Nixon argued that the enemy had suffered more and their supply lines had been severely disrupted.[145] Privately, however, Nixon and Kissinger thought Lam Son 719 "was clearly not a success." They faulted Abrams for having misled them on what could have been accomplished, and regretted not taking Westmoreland's advice to avoid a frontal assault on Tchepone. Believing forces assigned to Lam Son 719 to be inadequate in quality and number, Westmoreland had instead recommended hit-and-run raids against key points along the Ho Chi Minh Trail south of the village. Nixon acknowledged that Laos had been a military and diplomatic "mess," which had also "broken the thin thread" supporting the public's faith in the administration's promise to wind down the war. Rationalizing their decision, however, Nixon and Kissinger concluded it was "still a worthwhile operation," and Nixon agreed with Kissinger that "if he knew before it started that it was going to come out exactly the way it did, he would still have gone ahead with it."[146]

In their postwar memoirs, Nixon and Kissinger conceded that their original objectives had not been achieved. Nevertheless, they claimed a strategic, long-term success, arguing that PAVN losses in men and supplies prevented Hanoi from launching an offensive in 1971 and delayed the start of their offensive in 1972. Because American cameras had recorded panicky South Vietnamese soldiers clinging to the skids of evacuation helicopters, Nixon accused the press of turning a "military success" into a "public relations disaster" and therefore a "psychological defeat."[147] Although pointing out the putative positive results of the operation, Kissinger admitted, however, that the South Vietnamese performance had exposed lingering deficiencies in Vietnamization.[148]

Military analysts, such as General Philip Davidson in his postwar history of the war, not only agreed there were deficiencies but also viewed them as incurable. RVNAF military leadership was politicized; Thieu was wanting in judgment and nerve; several commanders were inept; many officers, without American advisory support, lacked the professional skills necessary to coordinate ground, tank, artillery, and air operations; the RVNAF lacked offensive initiative and mobile fighting capability; and, like the Americans, the South Vietnamese relied too much on maneuver by helicopter when walking would have been swifter. American blunders—hasty planning, poor judgment, inadequate coordination with the RVNAF, and interservice rivalry—had compounded RVNAF shortcomings.[149] Thieu criticized the insufficiency of American air support and suppressive fire and the reluctance of American helicopter crews to assist the evacuation. South Vietnamese Major General Nguyen Duy Hinh disputed several American criticisms, but he acknowledged that enormous quantities of valuable matériel were lost and officer and soldier morale was shaken. "Almost without exception," the troops who participated in the operation "did not believe they were victorious." Despite official celebrations of victory, the families of soldiers felt that losses had been inordinate, and they were deeply disturbed that many of the dead and wounded had been left behind.[150]

Haig, who had gone to South Vietnam on March 15 to assess the battle, later recalled that "Lam Son destroyed the cream of the South Vietnam army and was far more serious and detrimental than was believed at the time. Our handling of that was very bad." He blamed "bureaucratic mischief in the Pentagon."[151] Kissinger maintained in his postwar account that the consensus-building process Nixon followed in making his decision had worked all too well, for it detracted from a more careful analysis of the demerits of the plan. This was no doubt true, but Nixon chose this approach because of indifference or opposition within the bureaucracy to the operation, which was the embodiment of the "major move" both he and Kissinger thought necessary to accomplish their aims in Vietnam. The main problem was not the process but the intentions of the men who devised it, causing them to be willfully optimistic rather than judiciously wise. Kissinger also implied that the operation's failures were partly the result of congressional action: the 1970 Cooper-Church resolution had precluded the deployment of American troops and advisers in Laos to assist the South Vietnamese. But Cooper-Church, passed by the Senate, had been rejected by the House. The reality seems to have been that Nixon had been reluctant to challenge the spirit of congressional war-limiting measures and deeply concerned about the potential of public and antiwar movement protests against the sending of American troops into Laos and Cambodia.

Hanoi claimed a great victory in throwing back the invasion and proving PAVN's superiority over the RVNAF. "Washington had wanted to make this operation a test for the policy of 'Vietnamization' of the war. But . . . the new strategy had proved a flop."[152] PAVN losses in Lam Son 719 were indeed heavy, but they were not debilitating. In his 1976 account of the last stages of the war, General Van Tien Dung asserted that its defeat of the invasion had presented PAVN with an opportunity to advance toward Khe Sanh, but it was unprepared to extend its logistic capabilities forward so soon after a major battle. (American bombing no doubt added to PAVN's difficulties.) Personal accounts, even those by disaffected former officers and officials, matter-of-factly described the results in positive terms.[153]

Claims by Nixon and Kissinger that the operation had prevented a VNLAF offensive planned for 1971 and delayed the Spring Offensive of 1972 were exaggerated, false, or at least unproven. There is little or no evidence to indicate that Hanoi was planning a major 1971 offensive, and if Lam Son delayed their 1972 offensive by a month, as Kissinger suggested, the delay worked to Hanoi's advantage, since American intelligence at the start of 1972 expected it to begin in February. When it came at the end of March, American commanders were surprised by its timing and scope.[154] Nguyen Co Thach told Seymour Hersh in 1979 that the years from 1969 through 1971 were a period of strategic retrenchment—of husbanding PAVN and PLAF forces in preparation for a peace agreement. After the 1970 Cambodian invasion, the PAVN and PLAF began to position their supplies and arms in preparation for a possible offensive in 1972. "In America you are more sophisticated; you can prepare very quickly. In my country, we must prepare two or three years for a big offensive." Seen as "a big defeat" for Vietnamization, Lam Son 719 encouraged the Politburo to persist.[155] Both sides were girding for a military showdown, but before it would take place, there were major developments on the diplomatic front.

11
Setting the Stage: 1971

It was doomed always just to trickle out the way it is, and that's now become clear.
—Richard Nixon[1]

We should be patient.
—Le Duc Tho[2]

IMPERVIOUS PROBLEMS

The Laotian debacle was only one of the several problems Nixon faced in the first half of 1971, which he recalled in his memoirs were "so overwhelming and so apparently impervious to anything we could do to change them that it seemed possible that I might not even be nominated for re-election in 1972." His list of woes included an ailing economy, rising unemployment, a growing budget deficit, and the declining value of the dollar on foreign exchange markets. The international monetary crisis was in no small part related to expenditures on the Vietnam War, which was also the source of the other problems he listed. In April and May demonstrators mounted impressive rallies against the war in Washington and across the nation; in June the *New York Times* published portions of the *Pentagon Papers*; and the growing strength of antiwar dissenters in Congress caused the White House to take seriously the possibility of a cutoff of funding for the war or legislation calling for its termination "at almost any time."[3]

Nixon neglected to list at least one other Vietnam-related event that greatly concerned him at the time of the Laotian withdrawal: on March 29 Lieutenant William Calley was found guilty for the murder of at least twenty-two Vietnamese civilians at My Lai and was sentenced to dismissal from the army and life imprisonment at hard labor. An overwhelming but divided majority of the public opposed the verdict. One segment, which mostly included Nixon's constituency—citizens in the South and West, as well as hawks—protested on the grounds that the government was punishing a soldier for doing his "duty" in a war it was prosecuting. Another segment, which included combat veterans, doves, and antiwar activists, argued that the government had made a scapegoat of Calley and had failed to follow the trail of guilt through the military chain of command to the presidency, where the strategy of search-and-destroy, the methodology of "body counts," and the war itself had been devised. There were those, too, such as Lieutenant General William R. Peers, who viewed the affair with despair and sorrow: "To think that out of all those men, only one, Lt. William Calley, was brought to justice. And now, he's practically a hero. It's a tragedy."[4]

Nixon's personal reaction was similar to that of fellow hawks and conservatives. It is an "obsolete idea that war is a game with rules," he commented, "we don't condone this, but when men serve their country you cannot, during this crisis of war, follow this line [of prosecuting for war crimes] unless there's a direct breach of orders. . . . War is bad, so we've got to avoid more bad wars." Calley, as well as Captain Ernest L. Medina and the others implicated in the My Lai massacre, "should not be treated like [Charles] Manson." Had pro-Calley sentiment from the public and Congress not manifested itself as strongly and swiftly as it did, however, Nixon might have let the decision stand. Now he pondered "what he should or should not do in reaction." His staff was divided, and the issue was debated for most of the day on April 1. Connally and others wanted immediate action to free Calley or lighten his sentence. Ehrlichman and others were opposed to a radical reversal, especially so soon after the verdict. Kissinger's advice, as usual, was more complex, but it was also based on his decipherment of Nixon's own complex thoughts. He suggested that the president wait "a couple of weeks" before "suspending the sentence while affirming the conviction" in order to give the appearance of "deliberate action" and confuse the doves politically. White House Counsel John Dean's legal recommendation was "nonintervention," unless "political necessity" dictated action, in which case the president should review only the overall problem of military combat conduct.

Although he knew that he should support an "orderly" legal process, Nixon rejected his lawyer's advice because there was "no political gain for us . . . ; we've got to act on the basis of what does us the most good." He was not willing to defend the military's verdict because "there's not enough in it for us to fight for the military," and he felt in any case that the military was not so much concerned about the "honor of the military service" as it was interested in proving to the "liberals that they move expeditiously with the system of which they're a part." He told his advisers that he wanted to act from a "personal, human viewpoint," show compassion, and "be on the side of the people for a change, instead of always doing what's cautious, proper, and efficient." Besides, there was a "bigger cause, which is the question of how can we hold enough support for a year and a half to maintain our conduct of the war. . . . If we don't move, the support we have for withdrawal from Vietnam, etc., [that is, Vietnamization] will evaporate or become discouraged." He agreed with Haldeman that he could not ignore "the general public reaction," which "has been stupendous." After discussing the matter once more with his close advisers on April 2, the president decided to free Calley from the stockade and place him under house arrest while he began the process of reviewing the verdict.[5]

The Laotian invasion, the decision to review Calley's conviction, and the president's national address on April 7 announcing additional troop withdrawals and a continuing commitment to the policy of Vietnamization formed the backdrop to the spring season of peace demonstrations. There had been many and varied antiwar actions across the country in the first months of the year, but three in particular during April and May got the attention of the administration. During the third week of April, the Vietnam Veterans Against the War (VVAW) began a series of poignant protests in Washington, D.C., which, as two historians of the movement characterized them, "carried the weight of tested patriotism, seeming to arise from the Vietnam conflict itself."[6] On April 19 veterans laid wreaths at Arlington Cemetery, and on subsequent days they conducted candlelight marches, staged mock search-and-destroy missions, attempted to turn themselves in as war criminals to Defense Department officials, and picketed the Supreme Court to demand that it rule on the war's constitutionality. Some, including Navy Lieutenant John Kerry, testified before the televised hearings of the Senate Committee on Foreign Relations. On April 23, 700 VVAW members marched from their encampment on the Mall to the Capitol, where each in turn announced his name, then threw his war medal over a makeshift fence to the other side—back to the government that had sent them to war.[7]

Of all the demonstrations in the spring of 1971, this one unnerved Nixon the most. It was well covered by the news media, and Nixon sensed that the veterans' antiwar message was getting across to the public. This point was driven home on April 23, when the administration's own quick poll showed a three-point drop in Nixon's approval rating, which to them was inexplicable but for the VVAW's demonstrations. Nixon's consternation was compounded by his inability to do anything about it. Initially, the Justice Department had obtained a federal district court order to remove the veterans from their illegal encampment. But Nixon—perhaps remembering President Herbert Hoover's politically disastrous eviction of the World War I veterans' Bonus Army in 1932—was reluctant to carry it out, and decided he would just "negotiate the issue to death." Now, however, Chief Justice Warren Berger pressured the White House to seek a rescission of the order, lest the court be embarrassed by the veterans' defiance. The district court judge, however, was furious at having to cooperate, pointing out that the reversal embarrassed the administration as well as his court, while sanctioning the veterans' violation of the law. All the administration could think of doing next to counter the VVAW's public relations success was to have the pro-war Veterans of Foreign Wars ask the television media for equal time, get turned down, and then use the rejection as a public relations "arguing point" against the press and the anti-war movement.[8]

Two other demonstrations followed that of the VVAW: a mass rally and lobbying effort organized by liberal antiwar organizations and trade unions; and a massive nonviolent direct action organized by the more militant May Day Collective, whose plan was to block key bridges and street intersections in Washington in order to stop traffic and bring a temporary halt to government business as usual. In the first, a crowd variously estimated at 200,000 to 500,000 gathered in Washington, and another 125,000 demonstrators gathered in San Francisco on April 24. The marches and speeches in Washington were followed by lobbying efforts on the Hill and nonviolent civil disobedience at government agencies. The throng that assembled at the Capitol was orderly and peaceful, and there was a sense among the organizers that the rally had reestablished the viability of the movement. On the other hand, the demonstrators were pessimistic, for they expected the war to go on despite their efforts. Nixon had left Washington for Camp David, but he phoned the White House several times to receive reports from Haldeman, who had stayed behind to monitor developments. Haldeman's take on the event was that the demonstrators were "basically a pretty non-stirred-up group. . . ، No problems from our viewpoint." Nonetheless, the president's "principal interest" in his calls the following day was "the whole PR question": deciding how best to "counterattack" against the demonstrators while avoiding "over-exposure" on Vietnam.[9]

Anticipating the "May Day" actions, Nixon flew to San Clemente on April 30. Although Haldeman and Ehrlichman dissuaded him from voicing his combative sentiment at his Saturday, May 1, press conference—where he wanted to announce that "the party's over and it's time to draw the line"—the president was determined "to go hard" on the demonstrators.[10] On May 2, two days before the protest was scheduled to begin, federal authorities launched a preemptive raid, dispersing a crowd at the Jefferson Memorial and arresting several hundred from among them. On May 3 and 4, city police, federal officials, marines, and army troops swept the streets, disrupted marches, broke up attempts to block traffic, and arrested 7,000 persons, incarcerating them in the Washington Coliseum and RFK Stadium. The arbitrary arrests ordered by Nixon provoked protests from "the Left and civil liberties types," as the White House characterized them, but he enjoyed the support of a slim majority of the public.[11]

Despite domestic protests, Nixon consoled himself and his staff with the argument that the war had been "neutralized." What really mattered in their preparations for the forthcoming campaign, the president repeatedly told his aides, would be their success in building a favorable image of "the man"—the mystique of his forceful persona and skillful leadership. Considering de Gaulle's death in November 1970, he thought, they could build Nixon up "as *the* world leader." In addition, as Connally urged, they should emphasize that he "can operate effectively, . . . is highly disciplined mentally and physically, knows his people . . .

and his adversaries and their strengths and weaknesses, . . . [and is] ruthless enough to be a great" president. The voters, Nixon thought, should be made to realize that his problems as president were more substantial than those of any president since Abraham Lincoln, and, as Connally pointed out, repeating Nixon's own view, the "big thing" about him was his ability to "comeback [*sic*] from defeat," like Churchill and de Gaulle, the two great figures of the twentieth century.[12] Nixon's strategy of mystique building would continue in the future to undergird his public relations campaign and would soon receive a boost with his announcement in July of a historic presidential trip to China in 1972.

Meanwhile, his respite from the domestic vexations of the Vietnam War in the spring of 1971 was short-lived. On Sunday, June 13, the *New York Times* began publishing installments of the *Pentagon Papers*, which Daniel Ellsberg had given to reporter Neil Sheehan. The heretofore top secret study, officially known as "The History of U.S. Decision-making in Vietnam, 1945–1968," had been commissioned by Secretary of Defense Robert McNamara in 1967 to learn the "lessons" of the Vietnam intervention. When completed in 1968 it comprised forty-three volumes and 7,000 pages of selected government documents accompanied by the analyses of over two dozen professionals from government agencies and think tanks, including Ellsberg, who in 1969 was the only researcher authorized to possess and analyze the entire study. Revealing the policy-making rationales and deceptions of all presidential administrations since World War II, but primarily those of the Kennedy and Johnson administrations, the *Pentagon Papers* contradicted the belief of many Americans that the United States had been reluctantly drawn into a war of someone else's making.[13]

When the first installment of the study appeared in the *Times*, Haldeman recorded that the White House immediately understood that "it really blasts McNamara and Kennedy and Johnson." Although Haig believed it hurt the Nixon administration's "war effort," he advised that they "keep completely clear of it, because it doesn't hurt us."[14] But this course was not followed. The administration soon obtained indictments against Ellsberg, and it asked the Supreme Court to block continued publication of the *Pentagon Papers*. Nixon even considered arguing the case himself in order "to indicate the importance of it."[15] The White House campaign expanded in ways that endangered the administration and its war effort much more than the publication of the papers. The president ordered his operatives to break into the Brookings Institution, where he thought other Vietnam papers were stored; he talked of stealing documents from the National Archives that he believed liberal former policy makers had deposited for safekeeping; and in early July he formed a secret investigating unit, the "Plumbers," who later broke into the office of Ellsberg's psychoanalyst in order to steal possibly incriminating records, and who engaged in other illegal activities that would lead to the Watergate scandal and Nixon's resignation from the presidency.[16]

Haldeman, Ehrlichman, Colson, and other defenders of Nixon later argued that the president had not initially been disturbed by the publication of the *Penta-*

gon Papers, but that it was Kissinger, in his rage toward Ellsberg, who persuaded and even goaded the president to pursue an excessively aggressive course. Subsequent histories of the affair maintained that Kissinger's motives were a mixture of fear that the Pentagon study indirectly indicted him, because of his previous role as a diplomatic consultant to the Johnson administration, and that his past associations with Ellsberg and other former aides and RAND employees who had turned against the war now undermined his standing with Nixon. His tirades against Ellsberg in the Oval Office and his acquiescence in illegal countermeasures were attempts to distance himself from liberals, leakers, and the study itself. It was also a time in which Kissinger was overextended and under considerable stress. He was deeply engaged in negotiations on Berlin, a SALT agreement, a China trip, and the Vietnam War, and his differences with Secretary of State Rogers on these and other issues concerning the making and conduct of foreign policy exacerbated his anxieties about his position in the administration.[17] On several occasions during 1971, he threatened to resign.[18]

Nixon confessed to Haldeman that the continuing feud between his two top foreign policy aides was a great "emotional drain." It also confounded him. Although he often felt that Kissinger was obsessively paranoid about Rogers, and although he distrusted Kissinger's staff and former associates, the president was on balance more dissatisfied with Rogers and the State Department, whose interference in foreign policy he did not want and whom he believed deliberately obstructed his and Kissinger's policies. Nixon—as well as Haldeman—thought Kissinger more valuable, if not essential, and even more loyal and less vain than Rogers. "If we ever got to the state where somebody had to fall on a sword in order to save the P[resident]", Nixon told Haldeman, "Henry would do it, but Rogers wouldn't." Haldeman agreed, but he quipped that Kissinger "would do it with loud kicking and screaming and make sure the blood spurted all over the place so he got full credit for it, whereas Rogers would find a way to avoid it and get someone else stuck." Nixon knew that he would have to get rid of Rogers, but, loathe to confront his secretary directly, he hesitated; in any case, he felt he had to move carefully, lest Kissinger's ego become "overblown" by Rogers's ouster.[19] Kissinger knew he was the more valuable servant, but he was never completely secure in his position and knew that Nixon's favor was dependent on the president's perception of his loyalty and doctrinal compatibility.

As with other Vietnam policy questions, the hard line Kissinger put forward regarding Ellsberg and the *Pentagon Papers* no doubt encouraged and reinforced Nixon's truculence, but on this issue, as with others, Nixon was inner-directed, believing from the start that swift and sure measures had to be taken. Kissinger most probably felt that he had best match or exceed the president's belligerence or he would lose the president's favor.

When the story broke on Sunday, June 13, Kissinger was out of town. Nixon was at the Executive Office Building with Rebozo and in touch with Haldeman and Haig. The president's view, with which Haldeman and probably Rebozo agreed, was that "it's criminally traitorous that the documents got to the *New York Times*, and even more so that the *Times* is printing them." Before Kissinger returned the next day, Nixon told Haldeman that he did not agree with his staff that "we ought to lay low," for the publication of the *Pentagon Papers* harmed his Vietnam policy and raised questions about "leakage" by some of Kissinger's present and former aides. Moreover, there was the problem of Kissinger having talked with researchers at the Brookings Institution, who were also thought to hold the *Pentagon Papers* as well as other documents on the Nixon administration. While the papers did "make the war look bad," he remarked, "there's nothing that we can do about that." But there was something he could do about his critics. Nixon believed in the need and wanted to seize this opportunity to move against the press, the antiwar movement, and those liberal, Establishment intellectuals who had opposed his Vietnam policies. At the start and later, his primary motive seemed to be that of taking revenge on the press. Nailing Ellsberg "hard" would make the case against the press in general and the *Times* in particular that they had done something "bad." Paraphrasing his boss in his diary, Haldeman noted: "Nothing else that we do in the rest of this Administration will give him more pleasure than to carry out the [temporary restraining] directive now with regard to the *New York Times*."[20]

Nixon realized that his administration was "out of its mind to oppose release of the papers, since they involve previous Democratic papers and how they got the United States into Vietnam," and that the steps he was taking would serve to associate his administration with "the same kind of deception that was practiced" by Kennedy and Johnson. But the risk could be countered by a vigorous public relations offensive that clearly established that the administration's concerns were about "the violation of top secret classifications," the betrayal of the "national interest," the endangerment of national security, the compromising of sources, and the harm done to relations with foreign governments. The presidency, and its need to maintain the "privacy of communications" in order to receive "true advice" and be able to "conduct diplomacy" successfully, must be protected. The culprits should be portrayed as disloyal lawbreakers. In San Clemente on June 20, however, Nixon worried that their public relations campaign lacked direction and focus. Since Ehrlichman was too busy with legal matters, he wanted Haldeman to be in charge, with Buchanan carrying out the practical details. Nixon felt that a parallel effort should be mounted to keep the government in line. Because Haig was on vacation, Kissinger should "get off of China and his other problems for a while" and be the one to "ride herd" on the bureaucracy.[21]

If the press was the main target of prosecutorial and propaganda offensives, Nixon soon widened his aim to include not only dissident national security intellectuals but Democrats as well. He considered declassifying documents on World War II and the Korean War to drive home the point that "Democratic presidents got us into them. . . . All the wars are theirs. . . . Getting out those other papers . . . will clearly paint them as the war party." And then Nixon remembered the Bay of

Pigs invasion, the Cuban missile crisis, and Diem's assassination, whose secret stories would indict his former nemesis, Kennedy. Besides, raking up the past would help take the public's mind off Vietnam. He ordered Haldeman to tell Haig to have Tom Huston, the White House Special Operations director, "to set up a small team under E[hrlichman] to start rifling through secret documents. . . . Get some pros to handle it." A few days earlier, he had wanted Kissinger to obtain Henry Cabot Lodge's files on "the murder of Diem," which he had long argued was the major turning point in the war and had not been fully treated in the *Pentagon Papers*. Now, however, Kissinger was to be kept out of the operation in order to "shake" him up, or perhaps shake him down, since, Haldeman noted, the president "knows that Henry is concerned with covering up some of this stuff, because he was involved in the early part of it."[22]

In September, after new frustrations had accumulated concerning the war and Democratic opposition to it, Nixon returned to the *Pentagon Papers* case as a way to "tear the Democrats up." His opponents wanted to "crawl" off the issue of their responsibility in the war, he complained, but we have to "keep it grinding." The challenge was how to do it. If he demanded congressional hearings, he could not control the investigation; if he went to the courts, the process would extend past the elections. Thus, the administration itself must "play up" the papers. Heretofore, they had emphasized the issue of theft; now they must emphasize "content." And the only way to do that would be "to get into the assassination of Diem." Since the Defense Department study contained only part of the story of Kennedy's culpability, additional files would have to be uncovered. Kissinger had not been cooperative on this matter, Nixon thought, because of his connections with former "students and associates" and his concern "that his [own] name is in the files; also he feels that discussion of the war now is not helpful."[23]

E. Howard Hunt was eventually given the task of acquiring or inventing files on Kennedy's role in Diem's assassination. He chose the latter course. The documents found in Hunt's White House safe after the Watergate arrests in 1972 and then turned over to the FBI included forged State Department cables linking Kennedy with the assassination. L. Patrick Gray, director of the FBI, later destroyed the files. In the end, Congress's indictment of Nixon did not cite the forged Diem papers, but, ironically, in his own mind Nixon associated the forgeries with other illegal actions loosely included under the rubric of "Watergate": illegal intelligence gathering about political opponents; the use of sensitive information to punish critics; the withholding of information from Congress; the falsification of documents; and criminal cover-up.[24]

From the beginning of the *Pentagon Papers* affair, Nixon's state of mind was ensnared in past obsessions, not only with Kennedy but also with the Alger Hiss case, in which he had played such a prominent role in the late forties. He was acting forcefully, he thought, just as he had then, when everyone else was "jittery." The cases were similar, although no one else realized it. In the Ellsberg case, as in the Hiss case, he told his staff in June, "the papers themselves didn't make any difference. They were old and outdated and unimportant [to national security]; the key thing was that we got across the point that Hiss was a spy, a liar and a Communist. That was the issue. The question on this one is basically the same thing. These papers are not what are important in themselves; what is important is that someone stole them and that the *Times* printed them."[25]

During what Haldeman called an "out-in-front-smash-them-over-the-head" session with his cabinet on June 29,[26] Nixon linked the "pip-squeak" Ellsberg not only with Hiss but also with the Rosenbergs. He, like they, had claimed to make a decision for the good of the country, but they did not have the right, the "responsibility." Their actions ruined orderly government. "We're going to go forward on Ellsberg and prosecute him." Nixon told the group that his staff had given him a lot of public relations advice on the importance of wearing his "nice-guy hat," but he wanted "to make it clear that's not my nature."[27]

Beyond vengeance, Nixon's motive in taking the offensive against opponents included at least one substantive concern that affected his Vietnam policies: he thought the Defense Department study might embolden senators and representatives to question presidential control of foreign policy, demand information on what he was doing, and attempt to limit his war powers,[28] which was precisely what Ellsberg had hoped. The long-developing congressional campaign to legislate an end to the war had already picked up momentum in 1971. In the first six months of the year there had been almost two dozen proposals to either restrict Nixon's authority to prosecute the war or to end the war by a fixed date, usually within nine months or by the end of 1971. The latter were attempts to separate the issue of Thieu's survival from that of obtaining the release of the POWs. In June Senators McGovern and Hatfield reintroduced their measure to withdraw American troops by December 31, but on June 16, even as the *Pentagon Papers* flap was underway, the Senate defeated it by a vote of 55 to 42. On June 22, however, Majority Leader Mike Mansfield's resolution to withdraw American troops within nine months of the enactment of the bill, subject to the release of POWs, passed the Senate 57–42.[29]

Mansfield met with Nixon in the White House the next day to discuss the turning over of the *Pentagon Papers* to Congress. Toward the end of the meeting, the president steered the conversation to the Senate's vote on the majority leader's withdrawal resolution. He told Mansfield that the Senate may have "ruined" the negotiations in which the administration was now engaged with Hanoi. If this proved to be the case, he warned, he would go to the people to explain that the Senate was responsible and that he, Mansfield, would have to take the blame.[30] The majority leader was not intimidated, and in the months ahead he would tell his fellow Democrats that the lines were drawn in the legislative-executive struggle, that the question of ending the war was a major political issue for 1972, and that it had better be ended by a Democratic Congress and not a Republican president.[31] Mansfield's resolution, meanwhile, lost in the House after a major countereffort by the administration; when it emerged from a conference committee a month later, the withdrawal deadline had been dropped.

The publication of the *Pentagon Papers* had added force to the legislative campaign to stop the war, but the effort had nonetheless failed in 1971. Into the next year the grassroots and congressional antiwar movements would increasingly emphasize electoral politics as a means of ending the fighting, as their leaders looked ahead to the 1972 elections.[32] Opinion surveys indicated that voter support for Nixon and his presidency was soft and that the continuance of the war was a factor. Polling evaluations of his strength and decisiveness, the two basic characteristics he considered most important to his mystique, were high but declining. At the end of March his approval rating had sunk to 50 percent in the Gallup survey and 41 percent in Harris's; his credibility score was down; and the public's assessment of his handling of the war was at its lowest level since the beginning of his presidency.[33] The citizenry was also becoming more dovish or, if not that, exhausted by the war. By the fall, solid majorities indicated that the public believed the struggle was "morally wrong" and opposed keeping a residual American force in Vietnam, bombing on behalf of a postwar South Vietnam, and continuing massive monetary aid to the Saigon regime.[34]

TRIANGULAR DIPLOMACY AND TOTAL BOMBING

The seemingly impervious problems of the first half of the year did not, however, plunge Nixon into a trough of despair—as similar difficulties had previously. The president's "general attitude," as well as that of his inner circle, according to Haldeman, was "upbeat, positive, and optimistic."[35] Their generalized optimism was a contradictory mixture of sober assessment, wishful thinking, and earnest striving. After two years in office, Nixon, Kissinger, the White House staff, and cabinet officers were more confident in their jobs, better accustomed to perpetual crises, and less prone to panic. They realistically understood that events on the international and domestic fronts could turn either way: "There are all sorts of unforeseen possibilities on the bright side, as well as many on the dark side, that could come up," Haldeman noted, reporting his discussion with Nixon and Kissinger.[36] But they were just as often the victims of self-delusion, especially about the Indochina war. On March 30, for example, and right on the heels of the failure of Lam Son 719, Kissinger predicted that there was "a 50-50 chance at least of getting a Vietnam settlement this summer and ending the war completely." The president, Haldeman noted, "now agrees with Henry's long-held view that there is a remote possibility of a settlement on Vietnam with Hanoi, probably partly as a result of Laos. The P clearly has sort of a mystic feeling about the Laotian thing, and says so. He's not sure what it is or why, but he has the feeling that there may be more involved here than has so far met the eye."[37]

Yet in late March there was little in the objective military situation in Indochina or in the status of the diplomatic talks with Hanoi that warranted Kissinger's superficially cautious, fifty-fifty prognosis of "ending the war completely." Reports from the American embassy and CIA station in Saigon during the first half of 1971 did claim improvements in the internal security position of the Thieu regime, and captured enemy documents did indicate that COSVN acknowledged U.S./RVN achievements in Vietnamization, pacification, and the defense of strategic hamlets and difficulties caused by American–South Vietnamese military operations against their supply efforts, rear areas, and staging areas. On the other hand, these same documents claimed COSVN successes in both the political and military arenas.[38] The reality was that the fighting in South Vietnam was still stalemated, the invasion of Laos had not succeeded in accomplishing its original objective, and there had been no meaningful talks with the other side for five months.[39]

Despite Nixon's brave front, the combined effect of demonstrations, congressional resolutions, and polls was to remind the president that he must end the war sooner rather than later. Because he had not given up on his aim of saving the Saigon regime, he needed to play for time. Thus, he walked a tightrope between having to strengthen Thieu's position and having to withdraw American troops from South Vietnam before the 1972 elections. Beneath the veneer of outward optimism lay a deeper layer of inner concern and frustration, which often bubbled to the surface, revealing Nixon's traditional instincts for either combative striving for victory or tactical withdrawal from failure, instincts that helped to shape his strategy toward the war on both the home front and the international arena. In late April, as he worried about the antiwar demonstrations in Washington and complained about the impatience of the American people, he lectured himself and others about the need for patient persistence—a quality he thought he had exhibited in the Hiss affair of a quarter century before. But his patience had bounds. Deciding in early May that the "battle lines are drawn" on the issue of Vietnam, he spoke of the tactical advantages in isolating "the people that are against us, . . . youth, [the] press, [the] business elite, intellectuals, volunteers, etc.," and of not wasting time playing up to their issues. And his persistence wavered in the face of domestic protests. He and Kissinger were apprehensive that Hanoi may have "misinterpreted" the demonstrations and taken encouragement from them, with the result that the administration's "position" vis-à-vis the enemy had been weakened. Nixon attempted to suppress this concern with the thought that there was no point in worrying, since there was nothing they could do about it, and in any case, in "a couple more months, we won't have anything left to negotiate anyway, except the residual force and the bombing vs. the release of POWs." He suggested that the best course would be to "play the propaganda role more skillfully," by which he meant using the negotiations in such a way that he could at least mollify public opinion. Abandoning the persistence he valued, they would take "one more stab at negotiations," and "if it doesn't work, we'll just go ahead and set the time certain [for withdrawal], and that's it."[40]

As usual, however, Nixon alternated between passivity and activity. He was not one to put his trust entirely in mystic intuition and good fortune or to resign himself to a less than satisfactory outcome. He would strive to outmaneuver his domestic opponents and overcome the dogged resistance of his Vietnamese enemies. He would play the cards dealt him. In the first half of 1971, as portentous developments unfolded on the domestic and international fronts, the plan of action he and Kissinger had begun discussing in late 1970 following the Son Tay operation took on more definite form.

The goal, as previously, was to save Thieu, but Nixon and Kissinger now accepted the alternative of a decent interval after an American withdrawal. The South Vietnamese would then have to "protect themselves." It was therefore imperative, Nixon told close advisers on March 26, that they be given "all they need in the way of helicopters, planes, artillery, and supplies" before "U.S. force levels will have been drastically reduced" and in consideration of the likelihood that Congress would not support "additional equipment for South Vietnam . . . once we have withdrawn." He still hoped for "a break on the negotiating front"—that is, "a prisoner exchange and mutual withdrawal by July 1 of 1972." To force these terms, they would continue with Vietnamization and "a high level of air sorties at least through the U.S. elections." If they failed to obtain the desired agreement, they would trade the cessation of bombing and the retraction of their commitment to U.S. residual forces in a post-cease-fire South Vietnam for the release of POWs.[41]

Without an agreement on mutual withdrawal, however, there remained the problem of prolonging Thieu's survival in the face of PAVN's continued presence in the South, and even if the negotiations succeeded in bringing about PAVN's withdrawal, there was the possibility of a future invasion from the North. Nixon had long felt that if the negotiations failed to deal with these contingencies he could play his ace in the hole: the massive, climactic bombing and mining of North Vietnam, including Hanoi and Haiphong. Applying the madman theory, he and Kissinger had repeatedly threatened to take such a step as they tried to lever concessions in talks with Hanoi and Moscow. The ongoing aerial campaigns in Vietnam, Laos, and Cambodia had in part been designed to achieve concrete military goals, but they had also been designed to lend credibility to their threats of mad bombing. In the fall of 1970 Nixon had talked of unleashing his bombers in 1971, only to be persuaded by Kissinger for tactical political reasons to wait, but bombing remained his "hole card."[42]

What might obviate the need for playing this card, he thought, was one other critical element in his optimistic calculations of leverage. Now, in the spring of 1971, there were dramatic breakthroughs in détente with the Soviet Union and rapprochement with China. Whether Nixon in his pursuit of better relations with these two Communist powers was primarily motivated by a statesman-like vision of global stability (as he claimed), or by Machiavellian calculations of balance of power (as others have argued), or by something in between, three things are clear in the record: the Vietnam connection was critical in the framing of his policy; domestic political considerations influenced the timing of his moves; and détente with the Soviet Union was linked to rapprochement with China.

Nixon had originally offered détente as a reward to be given in return for Soviet cooperation on Vietnam, but he had soon been disappointed. By the end of 1969, he realized there were limits to how far Moscow could and would go to pressure Hanoi.[43] As he began to think ahead to the congressional campaign of 1970, Nixon came to appreciate the political benefits of détente—a dramatic announcement in that direction would be "another good maneuver before [the] elections." To that end he had planned to make public on October 29, 1970, the recent U.S.-Soviet agreement to hold a Moscow summit meeting in the late summer of 1971. But the Soviets rejected Nixon's schedule, arguing that they needed more time to prepare. Although Nixon was the supplicant and viewed the Soviet refusal as an unwillingness to "help us in the elections," he was "not very disturbed," Haldeman observed. It was as if he expected Moscow's recalcitrance, and while previously eager, he now decided to "hold off" on the summit "until [it] serves our purpose."[44] Whether Nixon's calculations were the result of wounded pride, practical resignation, or ingenious planning is uncertain.

Moscow, following the lead of Washington, was also playing the diplomatic game of linkage. In January 1971 Ambassador Dobrynin indicated Soviet readiness to move forward on a summit meeting if the administration was willing to discuss the issue of Berlin as well as SALT. Previously, Kissinger had suggested the reverse, linking progress on Berlin to progress on SALT. Meanwhile, in December 1970 Moscow had put forward a revised proposal on SALT. After much diplomatic jockeying in the weeks ahead, a procedural compromise was reached in May 1971, when both sides agreed to split the difference between Washington's insistence on coupling offensive- and defensive-missile talks and Moscow's insistence on decoupling them.[45] At the end of March 1971, in the midst of these arms control developments, Nixon was encouraged to expect that there would indeed be a high-level meeting between him and First Secretary Brezhnev in the fall of 1971, when they would finalize an arms control treaty and deal with other outstanding issues. This expectation in turn helped encourage White House optimism about achieving a Vietnam settlement within the year.[46]

Fortuitous diplomatic developments on the China front, meanwhile, had a profound effect on Nixon's negotiations with the Soviets and his hopes for a Vietnam settlement. The president had long used the threat of improved relations with China to lever the Soviets, but, uncertain about the strategy to follow vis-à-vis the PRC, he had moved hesitantly toward rapprochement as the means with which to play the China card. Although both the United States and China had sent subtle signals of cordiality to one another in 1970, progress was delayed because of policy divisions within China and the administration's tactic of secret diplomacy, which led Beijing to be suspicious of Nixonian deviousness. Then, too, the Vietnam War had intervened, when the Cambodian invasion in May interrupted their diplomatic minuet for the remainder of the spring. It was not until August that Nixon and Kissinger began to believe that "something big is stirring . . . about Soviet-China probabilities."[47]

Despite this appreciation, they failed to perceive the significance of meetings Mao Zedong and Prime Minister Zhou Enlai held with the American journalist Edgar Snow in October and November. Assuming that the White House would understand the signal, Mao told Snow that he had received several inquiries from Nixon regarding a presidential visit and quipped that he would be happy to receive him "either as a tourist or as president." The administration appears to have dismissed Snow's meeting with Mao because Snow was a leftist, but in January 1971, after receiving an invitation to visit Beijing from Zhou via the Romanian channel, Nixon and Kissinger, for reasons yet unexplained, again failed to seize the moment. The Laotian invasion in February temporarily halted Chinese steps toward rapprochement until it became clear to Beijing that Washington was not prepared to commit American troops to an expanded war.[48] Then, on April 28, after additional signals from both sides, including goodwill Chinese-American Ping-Pong games initiated by Beijing, the White House received a handwritten message from Zhou indicating Chinese willingness to receive a special envoy of the president.[49] On May 9 the administration responded by proposing secret meetings between Kissinger and Zhou on Chinese soil to be followed by the announcement of a visit by President Nixon to Beijing.[50]

Unexpected by Nixon and Kissinger, Chinese Ping-Pong diplomacy in early April had the effect of encouraging them to believe that a major development in Chinese-American relations was about to take place, which in turn led them to consider its broader ramifications. In a meeting with Nixon and Rogers on April 12, Kissinger pointed out that "the current moves on China will help to shake the Soviets up," which Nixon of course understood as well. These moves would have the added benefit of confusing liberal, leftist, and press critics at home, who would be surprised that he, the cold war warrior, was engaged in rapprochement with China. The president then raised the question of "the timing on these" propitious developments. Three days later, Nixon calculated that while a summit meeting and a SALT agreement would boost his standing in the polls, the history of the impact of summitry on presidential popularity indicated that the benefits were short-lived; he thus began to consider postponing the summit until 1972.[51]

The Soviets, yet unaware of Nixon's China moves, were not, however, oblivious to Nixon's political strategy. In his report of April 19 to Party Secretary Dimitri Ustinov, KBG chief Yuri Andropov noted that "Kissinger in a private talk said that from a political point of view it may be more beneficial for Nixon if the agreement with the USSR were to be achieved closer to the presidential elections." Therefore, he argued, the administration's public comments about its sincere desire to achieve a SALT agreement before the end of 1971, lest the 1972 campaign complicate the negotiations, was a ploy "to influence the position of the USSR during the negotiations."[52]

By early May Nixon's optimism about a China breakthrough, a SALT agreement, and a summit reinforced his desire to stay the course in Vietnam, even though he expressed doubt that Kissinger could budge the North Vietnamese in forthcoming negotiations and was "concerned," according to Haldeman, about the public's eagerness to end the war and Congress's efforts to set a date for withdrawal. "Dramatic involvement of the P[resident] for the China matter" would help him on the home front; on the international front, he believed that "the Chinese might put . . . some pressure" on Hanoi, enabling him to continue with his own protracted withdrawal schedule. U.S.-USSR steps toward détente would similarly undermine Hanoi's position and strengthen his standing at home. From much contact and many conversations with the president, Haldeman was confident that Nixon was therefore "as hard line as he's ever been on running out the war on the proper basis as we see it. And I'm very certain in my own mind that's the case. . . . I don't think there's any danger of his softening at this point, at least not until all these other things," he said prophetically, "fall through."[53]

If things did fall through, Nixon had his alternatives. On June 2, when momentarily unsure about the possibilities for a SALT agreement, a summit meeting, and a negotiated end to the war by the end of the summer, he told Haldeman that despite Kissinger's objections he would have to "go for a trip to China this fall." But if this, as well as all of his other initiatives failed, "he will not go out of Vietnam whimpering; . . . he'll play his hole card in November." Never mind that his critics accused him of waging an immoral war. Was Allied bombing in World War II immoral? The same point applied to Vietnam, he thought. While the bombing of North Vietnam was a "tragedy, . . . it's even more immoral to send Americans abroad and not back them up with air power."[54]

Nixon's end-the-war strategies consistently reflected his ideology of world power and his experience in the arena of foreign affairs, but his decisions were also influenced by his angry frustrations with events and developments. Retelling the story of his June 23 conversation with Mansfield to the inner circle, for instance, Nixon, as described by Haldeman, said: "If we do get to the point where we have to withdraw because the negotiations failed, he will do it with a total bombing of the North to eliminate their capability of attacking; so in order to get out, we escalate to accelerate our withdrawal."[55] The plan, such as it was, contained enormous uncertainties, but it gave him confidence. "Of all the major issues, the only one that is a sure thing for us is Vietnam. . . . All the rest are in doubt, but we know precisely what we're going to do and where we're going to be on Vietnam."[56] More accurately, they knew where they wanted to go, what they could do in order to get there, and, depending on other circumstances, more or less when they would try to do it.

BACK TO THE TABLE

On May 13 the North Vietnamese responded affirmatively to an April 14 American proposal for another secret meeting in Paris. Hanoi recommended a rendezvous date of May 30; Washington countered with May 31, which the other side accepted.[57] Each side seems to have viewed the new round of talks as a last-chance effort at a negotiated settlement before turning to a last-resort round of military escalation.[58]

Kissinger, Haldeman noted, was "ecstatic" that the other side had agreed to talk.[59] In his memoirs, Kissinger claimed that he more than Nixon had faith in the negotiating process,[60] even though he, like Nixon, favored "strong military reaction[s]." He explained that the "nuance" of difference between him and Nixon regarding the strategy for ending the war was that he wanted to "weave a complex web" of options that would give them more flexibility, whereas Nixon, "wary of negotiations," was less concerned about maximizing options than he was worried about the political fallout from failure in the negotiations. Consequently, Kissinger wrote, he always advocated combining a military move with a diplomatic one, as well as establishing a record of negotiation, which, if necessary, could be made public in order to counter Hanoi's public propaganda. Indeed, he confessed that he always conducted the talks with the public impact in mind.[61]

Put another way, it was probably the case that the issue between them over the matter of military versus diplomatic means was not as much their comparative skepticism about the intrinsic value of negotiations as it was one of differences over the timing of forceful measures in connection with negotiations. On balance, Nixon, nervous about electoral factors, wanted to put Vietnam behind him as soon as possible; prone to outbursts of fury, he often considered scuttling the talks and deploying massive, climactic violence at the end of the process of unilateral American troop withdrawals. Kissinger, as the prime negotiator, wanted great-power triangulation to work its course and give negotiations with Hanoi a chance to succeed, even if it took them into 1972, and, although not unopposed to the use of massive force, he was more inclined to postpone it. Almost as much as Nixon, Kissinger believed that the war could not be settled in negotiations until the military balance on the field of battle in Vietnam had been altered in their favor—or, as he put it in referring to the president's position, "until there had been a military showdown."[62]

For their part, the Politburo in Hanoi also believed that a shift of the military balance in their direction would serve to influence the negotiations favorably. If Washington did not agree to withdraw its forces by the end of 1971, their military alternative would be a main-force invasion of the South during the spring dry season of 1972 and before the fall American presidential election.

Even without the withdrawal of PAVN from South Vietnam, both Nixon and Kissinger thought that a combination of accelerated Vietnamization and continued Indochina-wide bombing would give them a military edge. If this approach failed, they would then resort to a culminating air and sea offensive against North Vietnam. Kissinger explained in *White House Years* that they believed the Laotian invasion had sufficiently disrupted North Vietnam's logistical system to force the postponement until March 1972 of any major offensive Hanoi might have been contemplating against South Vietnam. In this case, Nixon and Kissinger assumed that the Politburo was in the difficult position of having to choose between "serious negotiation" in 1971 or "gamble on the outcome of an offensive in 1972." This assumption implied that they believed they might be able to strike a bargain that would solidify Thieu's position, gain the release of POWs, and sanction their extended timetable for troop withdrawal. If the agreement contained provisions for a cease-fire, it would also prevent a VNLAF offensive in 1972. Hanoi was indeed ready to bargain, but not at the cost of conceding political legitimacy to Thieu's government, pulling the rug from under the NLF, and postponing their goal of reunifying Vietnam. The critical issues for them were the timing of an American withdrawal and American aid to the RVNAF, both of which were the main props of the Saigon regime, as well as the main cause of the war's prolongation.[63] Both sides understood that the time frame in which a bargain might be struck was defined by two forthcoming events: the spring season of military campaigning in Vietnam and the fall season of political campaigning in the United States. Washington wished to prevent a North Vietnamese offensive, secure Thieu, and score political points before the presidential election. Hanoi wanted Thieu and the Americans out before the spring; if they could not accomplish that in the negotiations of 1971, they would attack, hoping to weaken Thieu politically and militarily, encourage Congress to accelerate American withdrawals, and thereby strengthen their position in the preelection period of talks in 1972.[64]

At his May 31 meeting with Xuan Thuy in what Kissinger frequently described as the "dingy" Paris apartment of the North Vietnamese on rue Darthé, the American delegation tabled a seven-point proposal that Kissinger characterized in his memoirs as "the most sweeping plan we had yet offered."[65] Although claiming in *White House Years* that it had been "worked out" by him and two members of his staff, Winston Lord and Richard Smyser, it was, as he noted in his secret memorandum to the president, "our package proposal"—the product of previous discussions he had had with Nixon, which had then been "marked up" by Kissinger on May 24, submitted to the president on May 28, and revised according to Nixon's marginal comments on May 29 by Kissinger on the plane to Paris.[66] Kissinger considered it a sweeping proposal primarily because the U.S. government had for the first time offered to set a terminal date for the withdrawal of its and allied troops without specifically demanding the mutual withdrawal of North Vietnamese forces. This provision was, however, tied to six others: the withdrawal of "outside forces," to be decided by the Vietnamese and other Indochinese peoples; a cease-fire, to commence when U.S. troops began to withdraw; no further infiltration of "outside forces into the countries of Indochina"; international supervision of the agreement; respect for the Geneva Accords of 1954 and 1962, to be formalized at an international conference; and the release of all prisoners and "innocent" civilians, if not immediately, then to be completed two months before American troop withdrawals.[67]

Reviewing their objectives two days before his meeting with Thuy, Kissinger reminded the president that the offer to set a fixed date for withdrawals would "clearly establish" whether the other side had "any interest at all in negotiations" or whether they would "continue to insist upon the overthrow of the Saigon government." If the latter were the case, the administration would at least have "improved" its "negotiating record," which could be made public at a propitious time in order to "strengthen our position both here at home and around the world"—a public relations goal in which Nixon, anticipating a breakdown in the talks, was increasingly interested. On the other hand, if the other side accepted all or most of the package, Kissinger continued, an agreement would hold "many attractions for us": a cease-fire, international supervision, and no infiltration, leaving the GVN "in a good position," while at the same time American POWs would be returned. Nixon's last-minute contribution to the plan was to instruct Kissinger to "negotiate" the proviso banning North Vietnamese infiltration into South Vietnam,[68] by which he probably meant that Kissinger should use the no-infiltration proviso as a bargaining chip in order to gain the other side's acceptance of a residual American force after a general withdrawal—or vice versa.[69]

In their postmeeting assessment of the American proposal, Hanoi took careful note of Washington's abandonment of its long-standing mutual withdrawal demand, but the Politburo was also aware of the inherent pitfalls and ambiguities of the package proposal. The references to "outside forces" implied that the United States had not yet accepted the *right* of PAVN to be in the South, and Washington might later have insisted that international supervisors put pressure on Hanoi to withdraw its troops. The American demand for "no infiltration of outside forces" during a cease-fire meant, moreover, that PAVN units could not be reinforced, while the withdrawal timetable for American troops, which extended the process well into 1972, and Vietnamization, which would continue, worked to the advantage of Saigon.[70] Most important, the Americans had not put forward a concession or compromise on the political status of Thieu, whose regime would be assisted by a cease-fire that muzzled the offensive and defensive activities of the VNLAF. The DRV therefore interpreted the purpose of the American plan to be that of "keeping Thieu" while "obtaining a POW release." The North Vietnamese decided that their focus would be that of calling for a swifter American withdrawal, the exclusion of Thieu from the Saigon government, a cessation of attacks on the North, and war reparations,[71] which Hanoi viewed not only as compensation for war damages and money for reconstruction but also as "an opening for future [non-neocolonial] American involvement in Vietnam."[72]

Despite their differences, both sides agreed to continue the talks, setting a date of June 26 for the next meeting. The administration soon learned that Le Duc Tho had departed Hanoi for Paris, with stops in Beijing and Moscow. It was a sign, Nixon and Kissinger thought, that the North Vietnamese were intent on serious negotiations. The White House was also encouraged by an interview Xuan Thuy granted to journalist Chalmers M. Roberts on June 8 and published in the *Washington Post* the next day. As Kissinger pointed out to the president, Thuy had indicated that Hanoi "was prepared to separate military and political issues and to link only military issues to the release of POWs." The catch, Kissinger noted in his memorandum, was that they probably expected to "be able to shape the military issues in a way which would have telling political effect"; that is, Hanoi would demand an end to military and economic assistance to the GVN as part of the package, which would "obviously . . . have major political effects in South Vietnam, far beyond those which might result from a withdrawal deadline in itself."[73]

Kissinger's analysis illustrated the complex mix of cross-purposes and misunderstandings that divided the two sides. On balance, the most important issue to the U.S. government was the survival of the Thieu regime for an extended period following an American withdrawal; the most important issue for the DRV and PRG was a rapid and total withdrawal of American combat units as well as military, technical, and economic assistance personnel (the "residual" force Washington wanted to leave in South Vietnam). With reasonable clarity Hanoi was signaling Washington that it was offering a cease-fire and the release of POWs in exchange for the total pullout of U.S. troops, and that it was extending the withdrawal period past their and the PRG's previous deadline of June 30, 1971. Significantly, Thuy did not directly demand Thieu's removal from power; by emphasizing instead Hanoi's long-standing call for the cutoff of military and economic aid to Saigon, he seemed to imply a new definition of what was meant by Thieu's "exclusion"—the cessation of U.S. support for him. Without such a cutoff of aid, Thuy explained to Roberts, American involvement would continue, and the United States would one day have to reintroduce troops and air forces to salvage an unstable, repressive regime. "It is what we call neo-colonialism." Hanoi appeared to be floating a trial balloon, hinting that it was open to a formula for Thieu's exclusion that partially met Nixon's requirements for an "honorable" exit. Kissinger either misunderstood the importance of Thuy's signals or chose to ignore them, concentrating instead on the implications of the proposal for Thieu's survival, to which the administration was fundamentally committed.[74]

When the American delegation entered the North Vietnamese apartment in Paris on June 26, they found it set with a green, cloth-covered conference table in the manner of formal negotiation venues, in contrast to the previously informal arrangement of easy chairs. Kissinger and his aides viewed the new decor as another sign of the other side's serious purpose.[75] Extant fragments of Kissinger's report to the president emphasized North Vietnamese cordiality and their "pointed questions" about the May 31 American proposal. During the opening exchanges Thuy called on Kissinger to clarify an ambiguity: "The last time Mr. Special Adviser said the U.S. would fix a date for troop withdrawal when it knew about the release of POW's, but would not fix a date if it is not clear about prisoners. But from the answer today I understand that even if the U.S. gets the prisoners you would still not fix a date because a date still depends on your other points." After a circuitous response, Kissinger summarized the American position as one that identified the "essential principles" of an agreement, including "the withdrawal date, the ceasefire, neutrality [for South Vietnam], and the return of POWs." Thuy pressed the point: "So, will you fix the date for your troop withdrawal if you know about the release of POWs?" Kissinger answered: "The Seven Points are a package. . . . If you agree that there shall be agreement on ceasefire, release of POWs, and a general agreement on neutrality, which you have already agreed to, we shall fix a date for withdrawal."[76]

At the customary tea break, Thuy went upstairs to finalize his delegation's response, while for the first time Tho joined Kissinger for a sociable chat in the apartment's small garden. When they returned to the table, Thuy presented Hanoi's new nine-point plan,[77] which appeared to be an effort to meet Kissinger's stipulations. The Vietnamese proposed that if American and allied forces set a withdrawal date of December 31, 1971, then they would agree to provisions for which the United States had expressed support: the parallel release of military and civilian POWs; a cease-fire; respect for the Geneva Accords of 1954 and 1962; international supervision of the provisions; international guarantees of the rights of Indochinese countries and the neutrality of South Vietnam, Laos, and Cambodia; and the resolution of Indochinese problems by the Indochinese countries themselves, without outside interference.[78]

The proposal included two other points, two more than the American proposal, which, Thuy joked, "proves our desire is more earnest than yours to end the war."[79] One of these called for American reparations payments. The other required the United States to stop its support of Thieu, Ky, and Khiem in order that a new Saigon administration standing for peace, independence, neutrality, and democracy could be set up, with which the PRG would engage in negotiations about the future of South Vietnam. This was a new formulation of the old demand for a change in Saigon's government and the establishment of a coalition government, but without an outright demand for Thieu's ouster.[80]

"After two years of Communist stonewalling and domestic flagellation," Kissinger and his staff were "elated" by the meeting. He reported to Nixon that for the first time the other side had made a "concrete rejoinder" to the U.S. proposal, presenting their plan as a "negotiating document" and offering to talk "on the basis of both our proposals and theirs." To his every objection, he said, the DRV delegation had stressed that their provisos were "subject to bargaining." Among the other "positive elements" of the North Vietnamese plan, Kissinger listed their explicit agreement to release prisoners concurrently with withdrawals, their acceptance of international supervision, and their offer to enter a cease-fire upon the signing of an agreement—a schedule that went beyond the American proposal of May 31, which had called for a cease-fire to commence only as American withdrawals began. But Kissinger found negative elements in the DRV's plan as well: their demand for reparations, which he claimed he "rejected out of hand," and their enjoinder to cease supporting Thieu, Ky, and Khiem, which at best he regarded as "ambiguous," for it "could mean anything from withdrawing our forces, to ending all economic and military aid, or even conniving in their overthrow."[81]

Kissinger seemed wary and confused, torn as he was between an inveterate mistrust of the other side and his own desire to continue talking. Then, too, he had to sail a course past the shoals of Nixon's visceral skepticism about talking instead of fighting. The result was a hairsplitting analysis suggesting that the North Vietnamese were either "masking" their unyielding demand for Thieu's ouster in order to "gain time" in their quest for military victory or that they were moving toward the American negotiating position of settling the military issues, but first going through the "exercise of fighting for their political demands and showing that we were unyielding."[82] Kissinger could not bring himself to entertain a third possibility: that Hanoi may have been seeking common ground on military and political issues in order to offer Nixon a way to withdraw from Indochina and abandon Thieu with honor, however defined, before it was too late—before the negotiating string ran out and Vietnam descended more deeply into the inferno of battle.

The two delegations had agreed at the June 26 meeting to resume their talks on July 12, when Kissinger was scheduled to stop in Paris on his way back from Asia. Nixon had authorized the preparation of an American counterproposal for the July 12 meeting, but before it could be presented, Nixon passed through yet another period of "ambivalence," as Kissinger described his mood. Haig cabled Kissinger in Beijing on July 10 to warn him about the "atmosphere" in the White House: "You should be aware that he is seriously considering the alternative plan which he has mentioned previously of moving out precipitously and concurrently undertaking [a] major air effort against [the] North."[83] Kissinger claimed that on the morning of the July 12 meeting with Tho, Nixon telephoned him on an open line, which he assumed Nixon knew would be tapped by the French, who would then pass on what they heard to the Vietnamese. If the phone was tapped, what the French heard was Nixon giving Kissinger "graphic and bloodcurdling instructions even while repeating his approval of the counterproposal I was about to submit."[84]

Kissinger explained Nixon's ambivalence as having been caused by his usual skepticism about the negotiations, compounded by his "outrage" at the "duplicitous stunts" of Mme Binh and Le Duc Tho and the consequent criticisms of his Vietnam policies by domestic opponents. On July 1, at the 119th plenary session of the Paris talks, Mme Binh had announced the PRG's seven-point program for a settlement. On July 7 the New York Times published Anthony Lewis's July 6 interview of Le Duc Tho, with a headline reading, "Hanoi Aide Says P.O.W. Agreement Can Be Separate." According to Kissinger, Binh's seven-point plan was inconsistent with the DRV's nine-point plan, while Tho deceived Lewis, claiming that the DRV was prepared to exchange American withdrawals for prisoners, whereas in the private negotiations the DRV had tied such a settlement to other provisions. It was, Kissinger argued, another attempt by Hanoi to whipsaw the administration: in the secret talks they were intransigent, but in public interviews and speeches they appeared flexible, encouraging Nixon's domestic opponents to put political pressure on him to give in.[85]

Binh's plan, however, was not inconsistent with the DRV's private positions in the secret talks. It did not, for example, renege on the cease-fire provision of the DRV's nine-point proposal, as Kissinger claimed in his memoirs. Moreover, both Binh and Tho offered clarifications to other provisions in private proposals. Binh's plan called on the United States to "cease backing" Thieu in order that a new Saigon administration could be organized to negotiate with the PRG on forming a tripartite, interim government, which would govern until general elections were held in South Vietnam.[86] Tho offered a two-step plan to end the war. The first stage, which was highlighted in Lewis's interview, offered to exchange prisoner releases for a total withdrawal of the forces of the United States and its non-Vietnamese allies. As he explained to Lewis, total withdrawal meant the withdrawal of all combat troops and advisory personnel, the removal of military equipment, the dismantlement of bases, and the cessation of aerial bombing and naval shelling. Such an agreement, Tho maintained, would open the way for a comprehensive settlement, resolving the question of political power in South Vietnam and Vietnam's future relationship with the United States. In this second phase, Tho explained that the Thieu administration would have to be changed, and he suggested a way it could be done: "The forthcoming election in South Vietnam is an opportunity for Mr. Nixon to change Thieu. . . . It is the U.S. that will decide who will win. . . . It is also a yardstick to show whether Mr. Nixon desires a peaceful settlement on the war or not."[87]

Although Tho, as Kissinger claimed, had linked the military agreement to a political change in Saigon, he had not called for a coup d'état as the precondition of a settlement, although undoubtedly he would not have objected had Nixon and Kissinger decided to carry one out. Nor had he demanded the formation of a coalition government. Instead, Tho had proposed that the United States either assume a neutral posture in the election, or withdraw its support from Thieu, or throw its weight behind a candidate other than Thieu; more likely he meant all three; that is, what might be called "proactive neutrality." In any event, both Binh and Tho had emphasized privately and publicly that their various provisos were subject to bargaining. Hanoi regarded American proactive neutrality in the presidential election as a sign of good faith, and probably offered it as a device by which Nixon could have withdrawn under conditions in which the people of South Vietnam would have democratically chosen a new leader who was willing to negotiate with the PRG. The U.S. government might have tested the DRV's and PRG's sincerity regarding a separate military settlement, if that were the issue, by agreeing in July to carry out a total withdrawal of its forces by or soon after December 31, 1971, with an accompanying cutoff of military assistance to the Thieu regime. This it did not do, not because it would have been impossible to trade fixed withdrawals for prisoners without having to remove Thieu directly but because a total withdrawal and an aid cutoff by the end of the year in themselves would have seriously weakened Thieu's position. Kissinger had and would secretly remind Nixon of this consequence in his reports.[88]

There were other reasons for Nixon's ambivalent mood during the period before the July 12 meeting. At least as late as the end of May, he had seriously expected an acceptable settlement by the end of the summer,[89] but that prospect was now fading. Frustrated, he was also in a rage about war-limiting resolutions in Congress and the publication of the *Pentagon Papers*, which ironically had encouraged Congress to challenge his Vietnam policies but had made him more determined to stick with Thieu, lest Thieu's removal in 1971 be compared to Diem's in 1963.[90] More important, Nixon, as well as Kissinger, had been emboldened by the China opening. On the night of June 2 the White House had received a message from Beijing accepting the May 9 American proposal for a presidential visit to be preceded by preparatory talks between Kissinger and Zhou Enlai on July 9. When Kissinger joined the president the following morning in the Lincoln Room to discuss the news, he was trembling with excitement. As they raised their brandies in a toast, Kissinger argued, and Nixon no doubt concurred, that it "will put a lot of pressure on North Vietnam to settle with him when he meets with them secretly at the end of June." He was "extremely optimistic that we may get all of the settlements that we're working toward on all of our initiatives, and if we do that we'll really be in great shape."[91] Nixon put off the public announcement of his trip until July 15, after Kissinger returned from his first reconnaissance in China and his meeting with Tho. It was a time, Kissinger reported, of "extraordinary hope" because of movement on several diplomatic fronts, but also one in which they were "shell-shocked" by the battles on the home front and in Vietnam.[92]

When he met with Tho on July 12, flush from his Asian sojourn, Kissinger believed "the negotiating framework would never be the same again; it had been fundamentally changed by my trip." The North Vietnamese knew that Kissinger had been in Saigon, but they did not know that he had also been in Beijing, and so the advantage at the moment was in Kissinger's mind. He began the meeting "testily," accusing them of bad faith in publishing Binh's seven points.[93] Eventually he turned to the main agenda: Washington's reply to Hanoi's nine points. Kissinger expressed his government's desire for an early solution, and although he did not have a formal counterproposal, he made two gestures: accepting the other side's proviso to initiate a cease-fire upon the signing of an agreement, which was preferable to one beginning with American withdrawals, and redefining reparations as economic assistance. Kissinger remarked that the administration would not pay compensation as an act of penance but would of its own accord generously contribute economic aid after the war to Indochina, including North Vietnam, as Johnson and Nixon had said publicly. After four and a half hours the talks adjourned with an agreement to meet again on July 26.[94]

Kissinger reported to Nixon that the issues had narrowed to one: political power in Saigon. "We cannot do their political work for them," he wrote.

For all his faults, Thieu has been a loyal ally. Moreover, the recent publication of the Pentagon papers with their revelations about American complicity in the coup against Diem would make our involvement in Thieu's removal even more unpalatable. . . . I am not even sure we could remove Thieu if we wanted to, unless we were prepared to engage in a major confrontation whose only certain result would be the destruction of South Vietnam's political fabric and everybody's self-respect.[95]

Apparently encouraged by the meeting and perhaps desirous of preserving Nixon's and Kissinger's self-respect, Tho and Thuy proposed an eleven-point revision of their nine-point plan to the Politburo on July 19. It included three clarifications: changing the term "war reparations" into "U.S. contributions to heal the destruction of war"; stating more clearly that POW releases would meet the same deadline as U.S. troop withdrawals; and specifying that only Thieu need be excluded from a new government in Saigon. The latter revision was a retreat from their earlier demand for the exclusion of Thieu and his "clique" and seemed to formalize their public suggestion for proactive U.S. neutrality in the forthcoming elections, leading to Thieu's defeat.[96]

Kissinger's account of the July 26 meeting in *White House Years* described the North Vietnamese as representatives of "an underdeveloped country," who were "sinuous," "wily," "disciplined," and "overbearing," with a courage that was heroically "out of scale" and a superb skill in the "nuances of formulation"—a trait he was sure to notice. He had offered, he wrote, a total withdrawal of American forces, the closing of U.S. bases, and a guarantee of South Vietnamese neutrality, but they had wanted more: a cutoff of all military aid to Saigon and the replacement of Thieu. Kissinger claimed that, in an aside, Tho told him that if the United States "did not know how to replace Thieu by means of the presidential election, assassination would do admirably."[97] Tho's aide, Thach, denied the story, however, saying, "It went something like this: he told Henry Kissinger that they have replaced their stooges many times in many places in the world, so they have enough imagination to do it again. Le Duc Tho said nothing about this assassination of Thieu."[98]

Kissinger's secret report of the meeting to Nixon described a more complex negotiation, and one that was not as black and white as Kissinger publicly portrayed it. Although a "breakthrough" had not been achieved, he wrote on July 26, there had been gains for the administration: a "superb public record of genuine willingness to compromise" more than what "our domestic opposition" had demanded; the DRV's clarification of the POW release timetable; and a narrowing of the other issues, except for one, "the replacement by us of Thieu."[99] Kissinger had come to the meeting with several proposals. He specified dollar amounts of postwar grants and loans to Indochinese countries, and he told the other side that the administration was "prepared" to set a withdrawal date of nine months "after an agreement is made." In addition, the United States would take the following steps: "indicate that South Vietnam would be neutral"; "pledge to accept restrictions on our future military aid to South Vietnam"; and "declare our total neutrality in all political processes."[100]

The pledge of diplomatic neutrality for South Vietnam was directed at the fifth point of the PRG plan. The promise of military aid restrictions, however, only partially met DRV and PRG demands for a complete cutoff, which meant that the United States, while reducing its military assistance, would remain unneutrally committed to an anti-Communist, antiunification government. The assurance of neutrality in all political processes apparently included noninterference in the current South Vietnamese presidential campaign, thus acknowledging Tho's suggestion, but Kissinger rejected proactive neutrality, or, as Thuy put it, he refused to "give up" or "change" the present Saigon administration. He also refused to even discuss "the question" of administration in South Vietnam. And since the administration in the United States wanted to continue sending military aid to South Vietnam, it was clear that Nixon and Kissinger expected Thieu to win the election and remain in power, while a residual force would be left behind to provide military and technical advice. Even assuming an agreement were signed in August 1971, the "nine months" Kissinger proposed for American troop withdrawals exceeded by four or five months the DRV/PRG deadline of December 31, 1971, taking it to April or May of 1972, past the dry season of that year. In reality, however, Nixon and Kissinger were actually thinking of a nine-month period of withdrawals that began after November 1 and ended on August 1, 1972, making it a twelve-month timetable from the date of the current Paris negotiating session. And although he had specified a withdrawal period that the United States was "prepared" to meet, Kissinger was not willing to actually fix the final deadline until an overall settlement was reached that incorporated other issues, including the release of POWs—not only those in Vietnam but throughout Indochina.[101]

The Vietnamese told Kissinger that their own withdrawal deadline of December 31, 1971, was "flexible"; they argued that if he would only fix or set the withdrawal deadline during the talks and discuss the question of government in Saigon, they could move rapidly to settle the military and political issues. At one point in the conversation Thuy said: "The question of prisoners is not difficult at all. But you want to use the question to overshadow the other questions and therefore the negotiations are protracted." After more conversation, Kissinger replied: "This proposition that we give you a deadline no matter what happens [regarding Thieu] may impress . . . [your] friends at the *New York Times*. . . . If we are going to retreat regardless of what happens, you must get used to the idea that we will do so at our own pace and one convenient for us. . . . And we will not settle the war just for prisoners. This is another point you should have no illusions about."[102]

The war was, as it had always been, about political power in Saigon and what that meant for the future of South Vietnam. But the impasse in the negotiations was not primarily about the overt ouster of Thieu by the United States but instead about U.S. withdrawal and military aid, because Thieu's position in Saigon rested fundamentally on American military power and assistance. The DRV/PRG refused to agree to a withdrawal schedule that extended into mid-1972 or beyond, particularly if Thieu remained in office and continued to receive American military assistance and advice. If he were no longer in power, however, they probably would have accepted a withdrawal-for-prisoners deal that extended the deadline past 1971. Or, if the United States had agreed to their withdrawal deadline and a termination of aid, they may have shown flexibility, as they appeared to be doing already, regarding how Thieu would be eased out of office and by whom he would be replaced. The United States refused to set a deadline for withdrawal or to agree to an aid cutoff, since that would likely cause the demise of Thieu's government, and except for a vague promise of neutrality in the South Vietnamese presidential race, it refused to fix a withdrawal deadline or talk about the issue of political power in Saigon, unless the other side would first agree to Thieu's remaining in power.[103]

Kissinger returned home on the evening of July 26, Washington time, and reported to Nixon in person the next morning. He also "filled in" Haldeman, who understood from Kissinger's remarks that there had been a good negotiating session, with concurrence on all points except Hanoi's insistence that "we agree to overthrow the Thieu government." Kissinger said that when he told Tho that there was therefore no further need to meet, Tho replied that there was, "that they would come back . . . with a new proposal for a political solution."[104] The North Vietnamese interpretation of Tho's exchange with Kissinger had a somewhat different emphasis: they understood that Kissinger had expressed American willingness to discuss military and political issues toward the goal of arriving at a "final solution."[105] Despite these different slants, both sides wished to talk at the next meeting about military and political issues, each returning with clarifications of their position.[106]

When the two delegations came together three weeks later on August 16, Tho was still in Hanoi. Kissinger interpreted his absence from and Thuy's remarks during the session as a "holding action," believing that "they have not yet made their decision about accepting our political formula."[107] That formula, which Kissinger now presented as part of an eight-point counterproposal, declared that the political future of South Vietnam should be decided by the people of South Vietnam without external interference. The United States would stay neutral in the fall elections, respect the voting results, and be ready to establish economic and military relations with any government that came to power. The plan included three other key revisions or written clarifications of the American position: it adjusted the previous demand that prisoner releases be completed two months before the completion of troop withdrawals to agree with the other side's idea for releases to run parallel with withdrawals; it repeated the American demand for an Indochina-wide cease-fire, as opposed to one for Vietnam only; and it fixed a date for American withdrawals at August 1, 1972, provided that a final agreement was signed by November 1, 1971.[108]

Thuy praised Kissinger for presenting his points in writing and for his rephrasing of the withdrawal pledge. Although he complained about the American withdrawal timetable, which was "too long" in Hanoi's view, he indicated that it was subject to discussion. He also stated that the desire of the DRV and the NLF was for a neutral South Vietnam that was neither Communist nor allied with the United States. He dropped their previous reservations about the release of American POWs throughout all of Indochina and consented in principle to the presentation of POW lists on the day an agreement was signed. But he took a firm stand on residual personnel, requesting the total withdrawal of U.S. forces, by which he meant that "all U.S. forces, ground forces, naval forces, air forces, marine forces, military advisers, military personnel, technical personnel, war material, [and] military bases . . . should be withdrawn, without any exceptions and without any reservations." It was a matter of "principle."[109] On the main political question, Thuy told Kissinger that Thieu's withdrawal from the presidential race would present a "favorable opportunity" for a settlement,[110] implying that the United States should discourage him from running. The American pledge of neutrality was meaningless, for it "would have no effect." Despite Nixon's recent public statement of neutrality, for example, Thieu continued to use "all his machinery to win." Nonetheless, Thuy assured Kissinger that while "the political problem is still unsettled and . . . our withdrawal deadlines are far apart, . . . the other issues, including the ceasefire [which the United States insisted should apply to all Indochina] can be resolved."[111]

Kissinger summed up the American position, saying that he did not consider their remaining differences on the major issues of withdrawals and POWs to be matters of principle. Washington, for example, could "slightly" adjust the date of its pullout.[112] Withdrawals and prisoner releases were matters "that could be resolved once we had reached a political understanding." The United States, he said, did not quarrel with Hanoi's desire for a neutral government in Saigon but "differed on how to bring it about. We could not interfere in the South Vietnamese political process."[113]

The August session failed not only because of deep divisions on the withdrawal timetable, residual forces, and military assistance to Saigon but also because Washington, despite its pledge of neutrality in the South Vietnamese election, was unneutral, demonstrating, as Thach put it, that "the biggest goal of Nixon and Kissinger was the maintenance of the Saigon government, and not the sharing of power with the PRG. We see that they would like to have all the cake."[114]

In private and public comments during this year's round of negotiations, the DRV and PRG had offered the United States a face-saving compromise on the key political question of political power in South Vietnam. If Thieu were to be "excluded" from the government, the United States could then withdraw, POWs would be released, and a cease-fire would go into effect, all with international supervision. Over time, the other side had recommended several methods for Thieu's exclusion: through a coalition or new-government arrangement that excluded Thieu but included other members of the RVN; by deposing him or cutting off aid; by withdrawing support for him in the 1971 presidential campaign; or by persuading him not to run at all. To many Americans and perhaps even to Hanoi and the PRG, it seemed possible that without American interference, Vice President Ky, who was a candidate in the three-person race, might draw enough votes from Thieu to allow General Duong Van "Big" Minh, the national hero of the coup against Diem in 1963, to win. Minh's most important political support came from retired RVNAF officers, peace groups, and influential Buddhist organizations. Minh favored the temporary division of Vietnam and opposed negotiations with the PRG unless the latter abandoned its demand for a coalition government,[115] a demand that the PRG had seemed to meet in Mme Binh's seven-point proposal of July 1.

Although the American embassy in Saigon officially instructed its employees to be neutral in word and deed, Ambassador Bunker and the CIA tolerated, encouraged, and cooperated with Thieu in sabotaging the chances for an open and free election. In a move to exclude his competition, Thieu, probably assisted with funds from the CIA, overrode the South Vietnamese Senate's objections and bribed the lower house of the National Assembly to win passage of a bill requiring that prospective candidates would have to receive the endorsement of either forty members of the assembly or one hundred province chiefs in order to qualify for the election. He then proceeded to coerce or buy signatures from local councils and a majority of the assembly in order to reduce Ky's potential pool of endorsers. Nonetheless, Ky gathered 102 signatures, only to have the Supreme Court of South Vietnam disqualify 40 on August 6, which happened to be ten days before Kissinger's meeting with Thuy in Paris. Minh, rejecting a tax-free, $3 million American bribe proffered by Ambassador Bunker to stay in the rigged race and provide it with a veneer of legitimacy, withdrew as a candidate on August 20.[116]

Three weeks later Nixon remarked in a press conference: "You cannot expect that American-style democracy, meeting our standards, will . . . come in a country like South Vietnam, which has no tradition whatever. . . . But we have made progress."[117] In the uncontested election of October 3, Thieu won 94.3 percent of the votes cast. The South Vietnamese secret police had threatened citizens with arrest if they opposed Thieu; his government had not distributed voting cards in areas where Thieu was unpopular; and province chiefs had been instructed to do whatever was necessary to bring about his victory, such as intimidating voters and defrauding the vote count.[118]

Kissinger acknowledged in his memoirs that Thieu had acted heavy-handedly in "discouraging" rivals. But while rejecting the charge of American complicity, he defended his and Nixon's decision not "to toss Thieu to the wolves,"[119] thus conceding what Thuy had argued, that American neutrality, as practiced in the campaign, had "no effect." It was meaningless if it were not backed by persuasion or the cutting off of aid. Thieu's reelection was key to American policy, even though, as Kissinger told Nixon shortly after his return from Paris, the campaign "screw up" had meant that the North Vietnamese, foreseeing the outcome of the presidential campaign, had not "come through with a settlement" on August 16.[120]

The August session was a critical juncture in the negotiations. Disappointed by the talks, Hanoi was now turning its thoughts to final preparations for a spring 1972 offensive. Tho commented to Thuy on September 7: "The strategy for diplomatic struggle has to be attached to the military strategy; therefore, in the immediate future, nothing can be solved. We should be patient."[121] Nixon, after listening to Kissinger's analysis of the election screwup, was frustrated and impatient with diplomatic developments, insisting "that we have to settle Vietnam one way or the other before Congress returns in January."[122] He was once again threatening to break off the talks and resort to his "alternative plan,"[123] which was to expose the secret Paris channel, report the administration's record on negotiations to the American people—thus making Hanoi "deal with us publicly" —and attack Senate opponents, "saying they forced us to abandon our secret negotiations."[124]

The president may have been blowing off steam and expressing his ambivalence. Even so, his declamations concerned Kissinger, who tried to counter Nixon's predilections with empathy for his "heartbreak" about the "whole war situation" and by offering an upbeat argument for patience: since we really won the war, we just need one more dry season of fighting to break the backs of opponents in Vietnam and at home, and of course more time for talking while fighting. Haldeman, probably reflecting Nixon's view, was sarcastically skeptical: "This is, of course, the same line he's used for the last two years, over and over, and I guess what all of Johnson's advisors used with him, to keep the thing escalating. . . . It sounds like a broken record."[125]

In the week before the next Paris meeting on September 13, Kissinger, either desperate to avoid Nixon's abandonment of secret negotiations or supremely confident in personal diplomacy, had proposed that he be sent to Hanoi to settle the war. Nixon, however, thought he suffered "delusions of grandeur as a peacemaker." "Henry" did not understand that it was "no use" meeting with Communist leaders in Hanoi. Their "method of working is to keep talking and to screw you behind your back while you're doing it. To them, talking is a tactic to win, not to work out an agreement." In any case, the risk was too great. "It would be disaster to do it and fail," and the failure could not be kept secret.[126]

Kissinger did not go to Hanoi, but he did meet once more with Thuy in Paris. The short, two-hour session only confirmed the impasse reached in August: Tho was not in attendance; Kissinger reiterated the administration's eight-point proposal; Thuy concluded that the United States had not "come to grips with solving the political problem in South Vietnam";[127] and Kissinger decided that Thuy had nothing new to say.[128]

The Paris talks were near collapse, and Thieu's transparent electoral machinations had given dissidents at home another issue with which to criticize White House policy. In Congress, Senator Henry Jackson, formerly a firm supporter of the war, had urged the administration to ensure a fair election or face a cutoff of aid to Saigon; and a revised Mansfield amendment calling for a troop pullout within six months was on its way to passage. In this "atmosphere," Kissinger's main concern was with Nixon's reaction.[129] Angry with opponents on the domestic battlefront, the president told his staff that it was time once more to form another "attack group," have Agnew "unlimbered," and launch an "all-out assault" on the Democrats, accusing them of partisanship and isolationism in foreign policy. Against his infuriating Vietnamese opponents, Nixon was inclined to vent his rage by stepping up military pressure. Complaining on September 17 about the DRV/ PRG position in the talks concerning Thieu, he repeated his anti-Kennedy, anti-Democrat refrain "that the way we got into Vietnam was the overthrow of Diem, and the way to get out is not by throwing out Thieu." To make the point to the North Vietnamese, it was time for another dose of madman-theory medicine. "It was important," he told Kissinger, "to give them a hard shot now to create in them the fear that the P may do more." The president ordered his special assistant "to get a bombing attack going over the weekend" but to play it "low-key" in public relations, explaining the raid to the American public as a "protective reaction" to Hanoi's violation of the DMZ.[130]

The differences between the president and his special assistant on how and when to conclude the war had reached another crossroad. Nixon's patience was wearing thin, but with the stakes both personal and global, Kissinger persisted in his advocacy of their current policy of talking while fighting instead of walking away and turning up the bombing. On September 14, the day he returned from Paris, he again proposed a special diplomatic mission for himself, this time a trip to Moscow to meet with Pham Van Dong to work out an agreement.[131] As doubtful as he had been about the Hanoi proposal, the president, however, did not immediately reject the Moscow gambit. On September 18, the day after Nixon had ordered the air strike against the DMZ, and in the light of other "recent events," Kissinger submitted a long memorandum in which he tried to make his case through what he characterized as a "dispassionate" analysis of the situation in Vietnam, the prospects for the future, the policy options remaining, and the relationship of the war to larger issues.[132]

Given Nixon's state of mind, it was a well-crafted, timely, and quite passionate appeal. In the introduction to his analysis of options in Vietnam, Kissinger reminded the president that "the underlying assumption remains what it has been from the outset of your Administration: the manner in which we end the war, or at least our participation, is crucial both for America's global position and for the fabric of our society." Elaborating, he argued that a solution with "dignity" in the form of an act of government was far preferable to a "precipitate American withdrawal . . . in response to pressures and in the form of a collapse [of Thieu's government] . . . or ignominious rout [of Thieu's forces]." Either result would spell the loss of credibility abroad, deepen the "crisis of authority," call into question "the heavy sacrifices" made, and fuel "impulses for recrimination." The wrong choice of options in Vietnam, Kissinger argued, would damage "your effort to shape a new foreign-policy role for this country," and the likely impact would be "to swing us from post World War II predominance to post Vietnam abdication, instead of striking the balanced posture of the Nixon Doctrine."[133]

In recent months the president had spoken often about the importance of maintaining the United States as the "number one" global power, for through its predominance America had been able to hold together the "free world alliance," keep the peace, and "help the world." But now U.S. leadership was threatened by its waning ability to compete economically with other capitalist states, which crippled its capacity to remain militarily strong in the face of the rising political and military challenge of "the Communists," who, he maintained, were waiting in the wings to take over as world leaders. The "real problem" underlying America's decline, he argued, was not only the excessive demands of American labor or the immorality, decadence, and purposelessness of youth, hippies, homosexuals, and others who had "fallen away" but also the ministers, professors, teachers, and "business leadership class" who have "become soft." Nixon agreed with Billy Graham that the American people needed to be made strong by a president who challenged them to "sacrifice and work" and to recognize the "spiritual side of things." Government must not continue to give them "everything." When Nixon felt obstructed by his Vietnam critics in the Democratic Party, which was often, he also agreed with those aides, such as John Scali, who argued that "our problems at home are accurately the legacy of another Administration, who spent the money in Vietnam, billions of dollars, not realizing what it would do to the domestic economy." But whether the problem was moral or structural, Nixon believed that in order to restore "prosperity without war and without inflation" and to keep America "the biggest leader in the world," he must do more than simply issue a challenge. He must revamp government, adopt bold, effective policies, and inspire consensus and cooperation by strengthening his image as a doer, a man of character and compassion, and a great international leader.[134] The China opening would go a long way toward ending the Vietnam War, splitting the Communist bloc, rebuilding a favorable world order, curing his "approval problem" at home, building up his leadership, and restoring presidential "authority." It was the greatest "watershed" in history since World War II. And as he retrospectively and self-flatteringly reconstructed his words and writings on China since his *Foreign Affairs* article of 1967, he credited his own farsighted vision and creative initiatives for the achievement. It remained to see it through and to have the American people acknowledge his role. America's future and Nixon's future were bound together.[135]

Option 1 of Kissinger's September 18 analysis, "Fixed Withdrawals for Prisoners," was his take on where the negotiations stood at the moment. "We could probably negotiate such a deal and thus get our prisoners back soon and our forces out safely" under the cover of a cease-fire. But "the heart of the problem," as Nixon noted in the margin of Kissinger's analysis, was that there would be an unacceptable "asking price," as Kissinger characterized the likely bargain. The time frame for withdrawal would be "impossibly brief," and Hanoi would probably demand a cessation of air support throughout Indochina, the removal of some American equipment, and restrictions on further aid to South Vietnam. They would also likely insist on Thieu's removal. "Whatever package we put together would probably weaken the GVN fatally." South Vietnam could begin to unravel immediately as the result of the settlement itself, or it might topple within months from military pressure, perhaps even while American troops were in the process of withdrawing. Unhindered, North Vietnamese troops and supplies would stream down the Ho Chi Minh Trail; without American air support, Laos and Cambodia would also probably fall.

Option 2, "Play Out Vietnamization," was probably the choice Nixon was then considering. The administration would carry out its current unilateral troop reductions, then stop on August 1, 1972, leaving a "residual force" of 40,000, which, along with American air forces, would be used as bargaining chips for POWs. "Necessary economic and military assistance to the GVN" and "heavy bombing in the Panhandle [of North Vietnam]" would continue, at least through the spring dry season of 1972. Meanwhile, the American people would be told about the administration's "extensive negotiating record," which would be portrayed "as our only realistic alternative," given Hanoi's unreasonable intransigence. The advantage of this approach, Kissinger argued, was that by providing maximum possible support to the regimes in South Vietnam, Laos, and Cambodia, it prevented their destabilization and enabled them to fight on, while it retained "what is left of our fading assets for negotiations." The "fatal flaw," however, was the "domestic front," for pressure could build for swifter troop withdrawals, Thieu would be singled out as the obstacle to a settlement, and POWs could become "stakes in a bigger game." (Of course, Thieu was already seen by antiwar critics as the obstacle, and POWs had long ago become stakes in a bigger game.)

Option 3 has been deleted by censors from the otherwise declassified document, but considering statements and actions by the administration before and after Kissinger's memorandum, it may have combined elements of one or more of the other options, plus an all-out bombing campaign against North Vietnam north of the Panhandle at a propitious moment during the withdrawal period.

Option 4, "Another Major Negotiating Effort," which Kissinger favored, was to be accomplished by a secret, personal trip by him to Moscow in late November to work out an agreement in principle with DRV Prime Minister Pham Van Dong by mid-December based on new American proposals. These were a seven-month withdrawal period beginning in January 1972, leaving a residual force of 10,000; concurrent prisoner exchanges; an accompanying cease-fire with no further infiltration of outside forces; a process for the formation of an international electoral supervisory body as well as an Electoral Commission, which would include the NLF; and South Vietnamese elections in September, a month before which Thieu would resign, leaving a caretaker government. One of the "understandings" associated with the agreement-in-principle was a pledge that Nixon would seek congressional authorization for a five-year, $5.5 billion program of economic assistance to Indochina in the form of grants and low-interest loans, $2 billion of which would go to the DRV. Should this negotiating effort fail, Kissinger averred, "we would be in a much better position to go with option 2 in January," and the residual force of 40,000 along with aerial bombing would remain "until we get our prisoners."[136]

Nixon was discouraged by the choices Kissinger had laid out. He was "sorry that we hadn't been able to actually end the war directly, but . . . there really was no way to end it. It was doomed always just to trickle out the way it is, and that's now become clear."[137] Perhaps fearing failure, or concerned that Kissinger might receive most of the credit for a settlement should one be reached, or worried that Rogers would complain if Kissinger and not he went to the Soviet capital,[138] Nixon did not approve Kissinger's Moscow trip, but he did endorse the other provisions of option 4 with at least one adjustment: the U.S. troop withdrawal date with an accompanying parallel prisoner exchange was moved up one month.[139] If the plan failed to win Hanoi's acceptance, which was likely, they could turn to options 2 or 3.

Haig acquired Thieu's acceptance of the plan on September 23 in Saigon, after affirming Nixon's "determination to carry on U.S. support in this terminal phase of our involvement" and explaining "the corollary need for an impressive negotiating record to hold domestic opposition and restrictive legislation in check, especially in view of the recent political developments in South Vietnam." Thieu made a theatrical offer to remove himself as a candidate from the special 1972 presidential election proposed in the new American negotiating plan, but the administration rejected it. The gesture earned Nixon's praise, however: "This indicates character and great stability," he wrote in the margin of Kissinger's report.[140] On October 11, a week after Thieu's reelection in this year's one-man presidential race, General Walters presented the proposal in writing to the North Vietnamese delegate-general, Vo Van Sung, in Paris and read a message from the White House describing the offer as "one last attempt" to reach an agreement in 1971. Hanoi replied on October 25, proposing a meeting between Tho, Thuy, and Kissinger on November 20, a date Washington accepted on November 3.[141] On November 17 Hanoi informed Washington that Le Duc Tho was ill and would not be able to meet, but that Thuy was "still agreeable." On the nineteenth Walters told Sung that if Tho could not be in attendance, "no point would be served by a meeting."[142]

In his memoirs Kissinger described Hanoi's claim of Tho's illness as a bogus excuse to cover the Politburo's insolent unwillingness to compromise as they bent "their energies toward one last test of strength."[143] In a postwar interview with Hersh, Thach said that Tho was truly ill, but that this was only one cause of the Politburo's posture regarding further talks: "We saw in the context of the time that it was not propitious after the election of Thieu. The Nixon government was going ahead with its plan, and so it was useless of us to meet at this time." Concerning the substance of the U.S. proposal, he remarked that Thieu's resignation one month before the proposed election in 1972 was "meaningless," since one month was not a sufficient interval "when they are working all the time to decide the election outcome."[144] Moreover, other elements of the proposal, including the long troop withdrawal period, indicated no change in the American position. According to Foreign Ministry records, the Politburo decided on November 11 that Tho would not go to Paris because Nixon had not yet announced a change in his Vietnam policies and assumed that the administration was still committed to the "preservation of Thieu and [its] continuation of [the] war." Thuy would meet with Kissinger, if he agreed, in order to "maintain contact."[145]

In response to questions at his press conference on October 12, a month before the Politburo's decision to keep Tho in Hanoi and a day after Walters handed the new American proposal to Sung, Nixon had deferred public discussion of his Vietnam policies until November. When he made his announcement on the twelfth, it was mainly to reveal another increment of troop reductions—45,000 to be removed by the end of January 1972. His other statements on Vietnam made it clear, however, that his goals and strategies remained unchanged: military aid would continue in support of Saigon; airpower would be used to "defend" American troops but also to assist the South Vietnamese after a settlement; residual forces would stay behind; and in the negotiations the "humanitarian" issue of prisoner releases should be separated from other questions and a cease-fire should apply to all of Indochina.[146] Haldeman thought he did a "superb job." The "content was excellent, as was his attitude and style." TV network coverage "came out very well," proving to the president "that [good] technique is worthwhile."[147]

Hanoi obviously distrusted the American pledge of neutrality in a 1972 election, and it regarded the timetable for U.S. withdrawals as too long. American troops and airpower would have remained during the period leading up to the election, and Vietnamization would have continued, while an Indochina-wide cease-fire would have removed the DRV's option for an offensive in the dry season of 1972. There were still serious ambiguities in the American proposal. While Washington made no direct demand for PAVN withdrawals, there was a vague reference to postelection military assistance to the South Vietnamese government and a call for no "outside interference" in the process by which the people of South Vietnam would decide their future, which seemed to imply that the United States still considered North Vietnam a nation separate from the South and therefore an outside or foreign power. The same implication of mutual withdrawal was contained in another clause: "Among the problems that will be settled [by the Indochinese countries] is the implementation of the principle that all armed forces of the countries of Indochina must remain within their national frontiers."[148] Vietnamese leaders believed that Washington had, once again, passed up a chance to end the war. Had the United States stopped supporting Thieu in the 1971 election and agreed to withdraw all its troops, there would have been an agreement.[149]

THE DIE IS CAST

President Nixon had also informed the nation at his October 12 press conference that he would meet with Soviet leaders in Moscow in the latter part of May, hinting that this summit, as well as the one in Beijing, would take up the subject of Vietnam. The actual agreement for a Moscow summit had been reached by both sides in mid-August, shortly before Kissinger's critical meeting with Thuy in Paris on August 16, but they had decided to postpone the public announcement until a joint communiqué could be drafted and after Nixon held a scheduled meeting with Gromyko at the White House on September 29.[150] On October 16 Kissinger departed Washington for his second visit to Beijing, where, among other things, he and Zhou Enlai agreed on February 21 as the starting date for Nixon's visit.[151] That the Beijing trip would precede the Moscow trip was purposeful, intended mainly to reward the Chinese and pressure the Soviets. Both meetings were also strategically timed in relation to the 1972 American presidential campaign and Nixon's plans regarding Vietnam. Coming during the dry season period of military campaigning in Indochina, the two summits might encourage Beijing and Moscow to discourage Hanoi from launching an offensive and embarrassing its allies.

"This then," Kissinger rhapsodized in his memoirs, "was the manner in which we maintained our momentum" in a year begun in "stagnation." The door was opening to China; a time had been set for the Moscow summit following understandings on Berlin, the Middle East, and nuclear arms; and the Vietnam War, which "still dominated the passions of many, . . . was now less a national obsession than a painful legacy on the way to resolution." The reason, Kissinger surmised, was that "Hanoi could not help but be affected by the knowledge that its two great Communist allies were each improving their relationship with Washington despite the war in Indochina. This was bound to improve our negotiating position." Moreover, with the summit agreements, he and Nixon had prevented Vietnam from sapping the "spirit and confidence" of the American people and had made it possible for the creation of a new international order. "We were using an era of negotiation to achieve *our* purposes of securing peace and defending freedom."[152]

This was, at least, what he and Nixon hoped at the time would be the case and what then and later they wanted posterity to believe. But the war was far from being resolved and was in fact soon to escalate toward a higher level of violence. Even though the secret history of decision making in Hanoi and Washington is shrouded in mystery and controversy, the visible record of diplomatic-military events is well known: the negotiations did not enter their final stage until after Hanoi's Spring Offensive of 1972, which was launched between the times of Nixon's trips to Beijing and Moscow, while the final diplomatic settlement was preceded by a stepped-up campaign of American bombing in North Vietnam. The progress they had made thus far in triangular diplomacy had encouraged Nixon and Kissinger to hold the line in Vietnam, passing up the opportunity, however slim, for a settlement in 1971.

Although U.S. diplomatic moves vis-à-vis the PRC and the USSR were undoubtedly important additional factors in the DRV's calculus of negotiation and war, it remains unclear to what extent these momentous developments between the world's three great military powers influenced its decisions. Hanoi was of course displeased with and disappointed by the actions of its most important allies. Between May and August 1971, the Soviet embassy in Hanoi cautioned its Vietnamese comrades that an offensive would "risk too much"; it explained that while there was a necessity to defend themselves, they should "constantly keep the diplomatic initiative in hand."[153] At his first meeting with Zhou in Beijing in July, Kissinger had obtained a measure of Chinese support for American policies in Vietnam in return for American concessions on Taiwan. On July 18, just days after Kissinger left Beijing, China transmitted the American plan for a diplomatic settlement to Hanoi. The terms were already known to the Politburo, but China's intermediation seemed to signal an erosion of its support of Vietnam. During his second visit to Beijing in October, and after the United States acquiesced in a UN vote to expel Taiwan from the international body, Kissinger won a firmer commitment from China to urge the North Vietnamese to compromise diplomatically without another test of military power. When Premier Pham Van Dong, who had rejected an invitation to visit Beijing following Kissinger's first visit, accepted a second invitation in November, his meeting with Mao was tense. The Chinese leader suggested that Vietnam should allow Thieu to stay in power in South Vietnam just as China must allow Chiang Kai-shek to stay in Taiwan. Dong sarcastically replied that in contrast to China, Vietnam's strength was sufficient to "sweep all of these dogs out of Vietnam."[154]

The Vietnamese knew that Mao was making a case for Nixon, and they asked him, as they asked the Soviets, not to meet with the American president. Both China and Russia refused. Perhaps it was then, sometime in November or December, that the Politburo decided finally on the spring offensive. Although Hanoi had begun to position supplies in early 1970 in anticipation of a possible offensive in 1972, preparations had not begun in earnest until May 1971 and were stepped up in October.[155] The collapse of the Paris negotiations with the United States between the time of the August 16 session and Thieu's reelection in October was a turning point in the Politburo's decision making, although Thach, in an interview with the author, denied that the final decision to go ahead with a spring offensive was made at this time or earlier, as Kissinger asserted. He affirmed, however, that Hanoi was "preparing for the worst."[156] The uncompromising American proposal of October 11, combined with Kissinger's trip to Beijing, Nixon's Moscow summit announcement, and Beijing's gesture toward the American position in November, were additional factors in turning the Politburo from negotiations to battle.

These were the negative incentives. An additional but positive incentive perhaps was Nixon's November announcement of more troop withdrawals. Although insufficient to justify the signing of a peace agreement, they did mean that American troop strength would be down to approximately 140,000 by January 31, 1972, with only a small percentage consisting of combat infantry.[157] Even though the RVNAF exceeded 1 million men while PAVN had less than 200,000 in the South at the end of 1971, the northern army was confident. And despite their steps toward better relations with the United States, both the Soviets and the Chinese had signed agreements with North Vietnam in 1971 for supplemental aid, over and above their existing commitments.[158] CIA estimates of seaborne imports in 1971 to North Vietnam, which constituted 90 percent of total imports, put them at a record level, nearly 20 percent over the 1970 figure, and the pattern continued through May 1972. Eighty-eight percent of total seaborne shipments came from the Soviet Union and the PRC. Those from the former were "at an all-time high," and those from the latter were "the largest in three years." Additional supplies also came in by coastal shipping, roads, and railroads from China, with oil pipelines under construction. There were other eastern bloc suppliers. In January, the DRV signed an agreement with Poland for military and economic assistance, technical and scientific cooperation, and commodities exchanges for the year 1972.[159]

What diplomatic compromises each side had made in 1971 had failed to bring a settlement. Nixon, eager to withdraw but loathe to lose, was banking on triangular diplomacy and the hole card of airpower to retrieve victory from the jaws of defeat. The DRV and PRG, appreciating American determination and power but suspicious of allied irresoluteness, were preparing to use forceful means in order to improve their political-military situation in South Vietnam and, in turn, their diplomatic prospects in Paris and for the period after a settlement. The stage was set for a showdown.[160]

12

Fighting, Then Talking: 1972

Le Duc Tho: *"Do you really want to bring this to an end now?"*
Kissinger: *"Yes."*[1]

TO BUG OUT OR NOT TO BUG OUT

On New Year's Day Kissinger telephoned Haldeman in a panic, anxious to share his concern "that the P's looking for a way to bug out." In recent conversations, the president had complained to him about the "terrible pressure" he was under regarding Vietnam,[2] and, as he had many times before, Nixon had probably talked about the need to cut his political losses on the home front by turning to his alternative plan for ending the war. Although he would continue to "play out Vietnamization" by providing assistance to the RVNAF and standing firm on maintaining Thieu in power, at least for a decently long period, he would shore up domestic support for his policies by publicly exposing the secret Paris channel, recounting the administration's version of the negotiating record, battling Hanoi on the propaganda front, and rapidly withdrawing American troops. Residual forces, triangular diplomacy, domestic public support, and stepped-up bombing would provide leverage against Hanoi, and in the end his hole card would be the massive bombing and mining of northern North Vietnam.[3] A bug-out by Nixon, therefore, was not the same as a bug-out by Congress. When the White House inner circle accused Congress and other antiwar doves of wanting to bug out, they were referring to congressional resolutions and movement proposals for a swift unilateral withdrawal in exchange for the repatriation of American prison-

286

ers, but without guarantees for Thieu's government and without bombing. None-theless, Kissinger believed that if Nixon replaced fighting-while-negotiating with bombing-while-running, he would be bugging out on the kind of negotiated settle-ment they had long sought, and which he, Kissinger, was trying to negotiate.

Nixon was already determined to make another troop withdrawal announce-ment and go public about the secret talks, and there was nothing Kissinger could do to change that. The immediate issue was timing and tactics. The president was thinking about giving "an all out speech" before Congress reconvened on Janu-ary 18, in which he would combine his announcement of withdrawals with the revelation of secret talks. But Kissinger was recommending that he separate the two, delaying the latter as long as possible. Not to do so would "focus" the atten-tion of the president's opponents on Vietnam, giving them another "rallying point" from which to criticize their "peace plan." Better to let them "wallow around for awhile undirected." The president should simply ignore the upcoming war-limiting resolutions from Congress and proceed on his own timetable. Regarding negotia-tions with the North Vietnamese, Kissinger's "instinct" was that Hanoi was "ready to give," and therefore it "would be a disaster" to "show any nervousness" too soon.[4]

Nixon felt other pressures besides congressional resolutions. Although *Time* magazine had finally chosen him "Man of the Year" and opinion surveys during the past few months had registered his approval rating above 50 percent, he was steadily losing ground in the polls. As the new year began, the Democratic front-runner for the presidential nomination, Senator Edmund Muskie, had drawn even with him in preelection canvasses. He attributed his decline to varied causes: the general "depression" of the public, the erosion of "presidential authority," a di-vided government, the economy, Vietnam, and the China issue—his base con-stituency in the West and South and the right wing of his party were uneasy about Taiwan's expulsion from the UN, even though the majority of the country sup-ported his opening to Beijing. The voters simply did not understand him or know how to "judge him," Nixon thought; and they were not "mesmerized" by him as they had been by John F. Kennedy. Nixon worried also about the impact of un-foreseen developments on his chances for reelection: the economy might worsen, something might go wrong with his Sino-Soviet summitry, or there could be an unexpected turn for the worse in Vietnam. As if to remind him, the war had made headlines again during the latter part of December as a result of public protests and editorial criticisms of his expanded "protective-reaction" air raids. With some success, John Connally reassured the president on January 2 that, while he should not be overly optimistic, the attitude of the people about the state of the nation was generally good, there had been progress on the international front, the stock market was bullish, and the controversy over the recent bombing of North Viet-nam was blowing over.[5]

Kissinger had his own personal worries, fueled in part by his psychic insecu-rities but also by his and Nixon's mistakes. In their most important and recent foreign policy blunder, they had badly mishandled the India-Pakistan conflict by "tilting" policy toward Pakistan. The result was that the administration had contributed to the outbreak of war between the two South Asian countries in early December, alienated India, risked a confrontation with the Soviet Union and the cancellation of the summit, and drawn criticism from the rest of the government, the press, and the public. The administration was perceived as having erred diplomatically and behaved immorally in supporting a country that had brutally tried to suppress a democratic independence movement in Bangladesh and launched a war against India. The tilt had been the joint policy of both men, motivated by petty and misguided assumptions. They personally disliked India's leader, Indira Gandhi, and had also supposed that India's predominance over Pakistan would benefit the geopolitical interests of the Soviet Union. But their most important motives had to do with their China policy. Pakistan's president, Yahya Kahn, had served as their prime intermediary during secret diplomatic approaches to China and should, they thought, now be shown appreciation. In addition, they assumed that Beijing favored Pakistan over India and might even enter the conflict on the side of the former. Rather than endanger rapprochement, they tilted toward Pakistan, although it was not necessary, since Beijing preferred to contain rather than escalate war on the subcontinent. Kissinger had prodded the president and voiced opinions to the press that had embarrassed the administration and opened a new credibility gap with the public, and Nixon thought that Kissinger, as his agent, was most responsible for the misadventure.[6]

Among critics of their policy toward Pakistan and India was the State Department, which had previously taken issue with the Nixinger tilt toward China and away from Taiwan. Kissinger whined incessantly about Rogers's interference and launched tirades against the obstructionism of the bureaucracy. Arguing that the situation was intolerable, Kissinger threatened to resign, as he had before—although, not wanting, as he said, to "leave the P[resident] alone to go to China," he wavered in his determination to carry it out. Nixon agreed with Kissinger about the "State Department problem." Expounding another "Nixonism," he declared that "the bureaucracy has a vested interest in the chaos with which it lives." Still, Nixon believed "there was something wrong with Henry," something "personal" that went beyond the substance of the "Pakistan problem," which he knew deeply bothered his national security assistant, because Kissinger's insecurities made it difficult for him to deal with failure. The president and the rest of the inner circle were familiar with Kissinger's resignation threats, which by now were an outworn ploy. But Nixon, unwilling as ever to confront subordinates, was at a loss to deal with the issue, except to "take a hard line" and not "back down." Thus, he formed a "Henry handling committee," consisting of Haldeman, Ehrlichman, and Haig, to assist him. Haig argued that Kissinger was tired and bored as well as unstable, an analysis with which the president mostly agreed, since he, too, thought Kissinger had "mental problems" and was exhausted. Nixon decided that Haldeman or Ehrlichman should tell Kissinger to seek psychiatric help to deal with his "persecution complex"—to tell him that "the president knows about such things. . . . He has some experience in these matters." No one gave Kissinger this advice, but Nixon soon considered firing him, especially because he began to worry that Kissinger might betray him after the China trip and during the heat of the upcoming presidential campaign, just as he had betrayed the Democrats in 1968.[7]

On the heels of Indo-Pakistani flap came another crisis: the White House learned in mid-December that a member of Kissinger's staff and the liaison between the NSC and the Joint Chiefs, navy yeoman Charles Radford, had been handing secret NSC documents to the JCS. Nixon decided to cover up the spy scandal not only because it would embarrass the military and his administration if discussed in the press but mainly because he believed it had compromised the JCS chief, Admiral Moorer, and would make him more pliant. Instead of drawing him closer to Kissinger, however, the affair caused Nixon to assign fault to Kissinger's duplicitous and fractious management of the NSC, as well as for not keeping him fully apprised of the facts of the case.[8]

In the dark about Nixon's thoughts of dismissing him, Kissinger nevertheless feared he had lost favor. There were signs. He had been slighted, he believed, when the president allowed Rogers to speak at a dinner for Prime Minister Pierre Trudeau of Canada and had called on Rogers again during a television appearance in the Executive Office Building. At the end of the year Nixon canceled their regular morning meetings and did not return Kissinger's phone calls. Nixon had also decided to write the negotiations speech himself, without Kissinger's help.[9]

Thus Kissinger's panicky phone call to Haldeman on New Year's Day about the president's forthcoming Vietnam announcements may have been motivated as much by anxieties about his place in the administration as by his substantive thoughts about tactics and timing. Knowing that the president had "lost confidence" in him and would not tolerate his ranting much longer, he had admitted to Haldeman and Ehrlichman that he was indeed "egotistical and nervous." But he insisted nonetheless that he was of great value to the president—"essential," in fact, to the forthcoming China trip. He was right.[10] Nixon needed him. Kissinger's personal crisis passed. He did not resign, he was not fired, and the president decided to take his advice about Vietnam.[11] But the affair illustrated that public policies were intertwined with personal idiosyncracies, and despite their elation about summitry in Beijing and Moscow, all was not well among the White House inner circle.

The president made a short troop withdrawal speech on January 13. Another 70,000 would be out by May 1, he proclaimed, leaving the total of those still in South Vietnam at 69,000.[12] He promised more withdrawals, and when these were announced on April 26, June 28, and August 28, successive reductions of 49,000, 39,000, and 27,000 brought the number of American uniformed personnel in South Vietnam on December 1 to 12,000.[13] In 1972, prior to the cease-fire agreement of January 1973, Nixon therefore followed a ten-month, unilateral withdrawal schedule, leaving a residual force of several thousand noncombat troops by the end of the year. It was not a precipitous withdrawal in the sense that Kissinger had feared, and in fact it extended the withdrawal schedules the administration had offered to Hanoi during the 1971 round of negotiations. But it did match the withdrawal plan outlined by Kissinger in option 2 of his September 18, 1971, memorandum to the president, which he had entitled, "Play Out Vietnamization." On September 1, 1972, just weeks before a breakthrough in the negotiations, 39,000 American troops—along with accompanying bases, equipment, logistical infrastructure, combat air support, and civilian intelligence and diplomatic personnel—would remain in Southeast Asia.[14]

On January 25 Nixon delivered his second speech on Vietnam in two weeks, lifting the veil of secrecy from the private talks in Paris in order, he said, to "lay out the record" of negotiations and "break the deadlock." The other side had misled the American people by publicly berating his administration for failing to respond to their proposals. But, he argued, on his behalf "Dr. Kissinger" had indeed put forward good-faith counterproposals, recently offering in particular to set a terminal date for withdrawals in exchange for a cease-fire and the return of POWs. It was the North Vietnamese who had refused to negotiate, for they were not interested in reasonable give-and-take but wanted him to abandon an ally by overthrowing the Saigon government. Consequently, Vietnamization would proceed, "as the South Vietnamese develop the capability to defend themselves," while American forces were withdrawn and he presented his peace plan at the Paris plenaries. But in an indirect reference to bombing, he promised to protect American troops if the enemy should increase its military attacks.[15]

If Nixon was sincere in his stated goal of breaking the deadlock in negotiations, he had not attempted to accomplish it by putting forward new proposals. The plan he made public was the same one he had presented on October 11, with an added emphasis on the old dual-track approach, in which he called on the United States and the DRV to settle the military issues, while the Vietnamese settled the political ones. The tactic he had chosen was not diplomatic but political—designed to shore up domestic support for his policies by placing in the best light the efforts he had heretofore made. He had not chosen to win public support by emphasizing the progress made thus far in the negotiations. The record he revealed was incomplete. Except for his own plan, no documents of the negotiating record were presented for scrutiny by the public or Congress; and none of the other side's secret proposals or compromises were detailed. His speech was hardline and belligerent. He did not offer the American people hope, but, stressing the intransigence of Hanoi, he appealed for public backing of his own determination to persist, intending thereby to lever the enemy to relent.[16]

North Vietnam responded to Nixon's speech on January 31 by publicizing its nine-point proposal of June 26, 1971, and arguing it was the United States that had canceled the private meeting scheduled for November 20, not the DRV as Nixon had asserted. On February 2 the PRG issued two "clarifications" to its seven-point proposal of July 1, 1971, concerning issues Nixon had highlighted. These called on the United States to propose a precise date for the total withdrawal of its forces, which would also be the date for the final release of all military and civilian prisoners, and demanded that Thieu resign, which would then lead to negotiations for the formation of a three-segment government of national concord.[17]

Reaction to the address in the United States and South Vietnam was mixed. Learning that Nixon had engaged in secret talks, some who had criticized him in the past and many in the larger public came to believe, for a time at least, that he had striven to end the war with honor. In one poll taken after his speech, Nixon leaped 4 percentage points ahead of Muskie. Opponents of the war, however, soon renewed their criticisms. Some concentrated on the moral implications of Nixon's continuance of the war. During a Medal of Freedom award dinner at the White House four days after the speech, for example, a young woman pulled a "Stop the Killing" sign from inside her dress and with a coconspirator read a statement about ending the war. The audience was shocked, Pat Nixon was disturbed, and the incident made news the following morning. Many prominent doves called attention to what they considered flaws in Nixon's peace plan. Clark Clifford maintained that the kind of cease-fire demanded by the president erected a roadblock to a settlement. Ted Kennedy argued that the president's plan should have only one point, the return of the POWs, not eight—that the setting of conditions for free elections and cease-fires, and "any other such trappings" would take the United States up a blind alley, just as they had in the past. The *Washington Post* editorialized that Nixon's plan amounted to "the same old shell game." Muskie rebuked the administration for its support of Thieu, which appeared to many from Nixon's speech to be the main sticking point in the negotiations, and he recommended a cutoff of aid to Saigon. Despite Nixon's avowals of support, even President Thieu was annoyed with the speech because the American president had revealed in public what had previously been secret—that the administration had dropped its demand for mutual withdrawal—and he believed this revelation would demoralize his supporters in South Vietnam.[18]

In his postwar memoirs Kissinger placed a positive slant on the events of January 1972. Nixon's speech, he wrote, had been one of his most "dramatic and impressive"; the base of support for the antiwar opposition had been narrowed; and the DRV and PRG had been thrown "off stride." Judged by "normal standards," their Vietnam policy had been a "considerable success," for though the public was weary of war, it was still unwilling to assist the enemy by overthrowing Thieu, and the administration was "in a solid position to take strong action in South Vietnam's defense." Having avoided collapse in Vietnam, he further argued, they had impressed the Soviets and Chinese with America's ability and determination to stand by its allies, thereby making possible the scheduling of summits in Beijing and Moscow, which had put the administration in a position to construct a "new international order."[19]

These were lofty claims. A more realistic assessment would have been that their success had been to buy a little time on the domestic front as they prepared to embark on their voyages to China and Russia, where they intended to isolate the DRV from its powerful allies, and by which Nixon hoped to build a mystique of statesmanlike leadership in order to expand his electoral base at home. The DRV had not been thrown off stride, and the Politburo and the PRG had become more convinced than ever that Nixon remained committed to maintaining Thieu in power and keeping Vietnam divided. It was not the administration's steadfastness in Vietnam that had persuaded Moscow's and Beijing's leaders to meet with Nixon, as Kissinger claimed. The interest of the PRC and the USSR in détente and rapprochement was driven by their own internal politics, national needs, and international goals. If anything, Washington's commitment to Thieu since 1969 had postponed détente with the Soviet Union, insofar as Nixon had alternately dangled the carrot of better relations and brandished the stick of escalation in order to enlist Soviet help in bringing Hanoi to terms. Concerning rapprochement, Nixon's and Kissinger's resoluteness in standing by Thieu had delayed its development by exacerbating the political struggle within China over the issue of cordial relations with the United States, since purist Chinese ideologists viewed rapprochement with imperialist America as a betrayal of their revolutionary solidarity with Vietnam and of their own government's raison d'être. Ironically, it was Washington's irresoluteness that had served as an incentive for the Mao-Zhou faction in Beijing to improve relations with the United States. Nixon's initial steps toward diplomatic and military disengagement from Taiwan and his continuing unilateral withdrawal of troops from Vietnam demonstrated that, in relation to the past, American power in Asia was declining, while that of the Soviet Union was rising. Beijing's leaders calculated that they could counter Moscow's moves by playing their American card. Nixon's and Kissinger's commitment to credibility in Vietnam had, however, served as one of *their* major incentives for rapprochement. As the likelihood of levering the Soviets had diminished after 1969, their interest in playing the China card had concomitantly increased.[20]

On January 3, ten days before the withdrawal announcement and three weeks before the peace plan address, Nixon and his aides had expected that the two speeches together would work as a one-two punch against his opponents. The first speech would "suck all the peaceniks out, and the second move will chop them all off." The second speech would be a public relations "blockbuster," because with it he would make public the secret negotiations and present his plan for a settlement, pulling the rug from under the antiwar movement. By the time he delivered this speech, White House expectations for its political impact had been lowered. It was now mainly "to try to get . . . across somehow . . . that the P has done exactly what he said he would." After the criticisms came, Nixon had to turn to a defensive counterattack. He reminded aides that opponents will "hit the point of Nixon trying to keep Thieu in power, and we don't want to get the argument out on this basis. We can't let them make Thieu the issue, and we need to figure out how we get off of that." The best way to divert attention from Thieu as the issue was to "attack our opponents," to make the case that the Democrats and other

opponents of the administration, posing as advocates of peace, are in fact "prolonging the war, and hurting the peace. . . . We have to make the issue of their
sabotage of the peace plan, and not let the issue be the preservation of Thieu."[21]

PROTECTIVE REACTIONS AND DIPLOMATIC MANEUVERS

The administration's original justification for resuming the bombing of North Vietnam in February 1970 had been that the raids were "protective reactions" to antiaircraft attacks upon unarmed American photoreconnaissance planes, which had
continued to fly their missions even after Johnson halted the bombing of North
Vietnam in 1968. In December 1970 Nixon had expanded the definition of protective reaction to include the protection of American troops in Vietnam and the policy
of Vietnamization, which made the bombing campaign potentially open-ended.

The overall pattern of individual air missions over North Vietnam was superficially deceptive. The number of sorties declined sharply after 1968, from
172,000 in that year to 37,000 in 1969 and 1970, with another drop to 24,000 in
1971. Despite the 1971 decline, however, the attack sorties, as opposed to the
nonattack sorties, rose in late 1971 and into 1972 as planes were shifted from
missions in Laos, where, as in Cambodia, bombing sorties had increased dramatically after 1968 and 1969. There were 60 "protective reaction" raids against targets in North Vietnam during 1970 and 108 during 1971, with the pace of attacks
accelerating in the fall and especially after Christmas, when Nixon authorized
Operation Proud Deep, a five-day campaign in which 1,025 sorties were flown
against airfields, missile sites, petroleum storage areas, supply depots, and truck
parks south of the twentieth parallel of latitude. On February 17, 1972, there were
two days of air strikes against North Vietnamese artillery, which had been firing
on RVNAF positions across the DMZ. Altogether, during the first three months
of 1972, 90 raids were launched, nearly equaling the total flown in the previous
year. Through 1972 the number of attack and nonattack sorties rose sharply to
106,000.[22]

To be sure, there was a reciprocal relationship between Washington's actions
and Hanoi's. In late 1971 the North Vietnamese began to shift their air defenses
south into the Panhandle in response to American air strikes and in order to protect their logistics system as they prepared for the Spring Offensive.[23] SAM sites
and antiaircraft guns fired on American planes attacking in Laos and along the
DMZ, and MiGs flying out of new bases in the Panhandle sporadically struck
American ground radar installations in northern South Vietnam. In turn, the United
States sent out more reconnaissance planes and more fighter-bombers, with the
number of the former deliberately increased to justify the use of the latter in "protective reaction" strikes. However much the raids had been intended as defensively
protective of reconnaissance planes, troops, or Vietnamization, their primary
purposes had been proactive—to destroy military targets, weaken the VNLAF's

capacity to wage war, and signal Hanoi that Nixon was prepared to resume and escalate the bombing of North Vietnam. These purposes became more important as the administration suspended the Paris negotiations, made and planned more troop withdrawals, prepared for an expected dry-season enemy offensive, and implemented Nixon's triangular diplomatic strategy in late 1971 and into the first months of 1972. In a letter to Brezhnev on January 25, in which Nixon gave the Soviet first secretary advance word of his address to the nation on the secret negotiations, he also delivered another madman warning, which he no doubt thought had been given credibility by the "protective reaction" strikes against North Vietnam: "The Soviet Union should understand that the United States would have no choice but to react strongly to actions by the North Vietnamese which are designed to humiliate us." Although a similar message was sent to Beijing, to Moscow he made an additional and not so subtle stick-versus-carrot allusion, warning that hostile actions by Hanoi "would be to no one's benefit and would serve to complicate the international situation."[24] Hanoi, meanwhile, made ready. Old bunkers were renovated, new ones were built, and evacuation plans were refurbished.[25]

In a manner reminiscent of President Johnson before him, President Nixon became more personally active in ordering raids and selecting targets, whether in South or North Vietnam. In September 1971, for example, he directed Kissinger to give the enemy a "hard shot" in the area of the DMZ. In the Proud Deep operation in late December 1971, he approved the JCS's target list and agreed to their request to extend the period of bombing from three to five days. On February 5, as Haldeman noted: "He told Henry that he wants some non-routine approaches rather than the usual military thinking. For example, a 48 hour stand down all over Vietnam, and then a 48 hour total force attack against one area. For instance, hit everything there is in the B3 area [in the central highlands of South Vietnam]."[26] Nixon must have thought that the maneuver somehow implemented, even if a little, his strategy of unpredictability, and that it would discombobulate the enemy.

The JCS, which favored expanded bombing and understood the spirit of "protective reaction," responded to Nixon's criticisms of unimaginative military rigidity. In December 1971 the chiefs prodded air commanders to be more flexible in their interpretation of complex rules of engagement, which restricted the bombing of some military targets. One officer, General John D. Lavelle, commander of the Seventh Air Force in South Vietnam, decided to make liberal interpretations. In late 1971 and early 1972 he authorized at least twenty-eight missions in which air crews were ordered to attack targets that were potentially threatening but had not fired on American aircraft, as well as targets that were only "associated" with sites that had fired at American planes, such as airfields, radar installations, and SAM transport trucks. When Lonnie D. Franks, a young air force sergeant stationed at Udorn air base in Thailand wrote a letter in early March to his senator, Harold Hughes, revealing that Lavelle had ordered the falsification of reports by air and ground crews to make the raids appear to be responses to enemy fire, the scandal led to Lavelle's demotion and retirement. Nixon, who had done so much to create an environment of falsification, approved these disciplinary steps because Lavelle had become a public relations liability.[27]

The expanded air campaign was progressively undergirded by a massive buildup of air and sea attack capability. Between December 29, 1971, and May 20, 1972, Nixon sent an additional 207 air force F-4 fighter-bombers to South Vietnam and Thailand, raising the total to 374. Between February 5 and May 23, he also dispatched 161 B-52s to Anderson Air Force Base in Guam and Utapao Royal Air Force Base in Thailand, bringing the total to 210, more than half the fleet of the Strategic Air Command. Into April he reinforced the two aircraft carriers in the Gulf of Tonkin with four more, increasing the navy's total of attack planes to more than 300. Additional cruisers and destroyers were also sent to stations off the Vietnamese coast.[28] Kissinger noted in his memoirs: "We found ourselves in the anomalous position of augmenting with forces that did not count against the troop ceiling . . . , while continuing the promised withdrawals."[29] But it was not at all anomalous; it was part of a plan to compensate for troop withdrawals with airpower, while preparing for a military showdown. Much of the air buildup was in response to the North Vietnamese Spring Offensive, which began on March 30, but much of it had been initiated before the offensive and in anticipation of it, as well as of the presidential election and the final withdrawal of U.S. troops.

The administration had long expected a North Vietnamese dry-season offensive, but on January 4 General Abrams formally warned the White House of an impending invasion, which he believed could come as early as the first part of February, preceding Nixon's February 17 departure for China. Arguing that this might well be the decisive battle of the war, with the survival of Vietnamization hanging in the balance, he requested authority for "maximum flexibility" to disrupt enemy preparations north of the DMZ with airpower. Even though Kissinger accepted "the probability" that "while the P's in China, . . . [North Vietnam] might well move to cut [South] Vietnam in half and create a super crisis that we would have trouble dealing with,"[30] he inexplicably delayed convening a meeting of the Senior Review Group until January 24.[31]

Perhaps the reason was that the White House deemed it unnecessary to take emergency measures, since the bombing of North Vietnam had already been stepped up. Or Nixon may have already made up his mind about what he would and would not do, and therefore consultative meetings may have been held, like other such meetings in the past, only to soothe bureaucratic feathers by allowing advisers to express their opinions formally in a collective setting. While Abrams and the JCS wanted maximum flexibility, Rogers and the State Department believed that more bombing would interfere with negotiations, Laird and the Defense Department were concerned about the additional budgetary burden, and the White House, including Kissinger, thought it would have an adverse impact on the China trip. Proposed by Laird, but agreed to by Nixon and Kissinger, the compromise that emerged from the Senior Review Group meeting in late January was to increase air attacks in the area of the Central Highlands of the South, where the group believed the North Vietnamese blow would fall, and to place electronic sensors in the DMZ to monitor enemy movements in that threatened area. Nixon and Kissinger favored the compromise for two reasons: a dramatic expansion of attacks on the North preceding Nixon's trip to China would be "provocative";[32] and, because they would have to be sustained over a period of time to be effective, the escalated bombing would be difficult to defend before the public unless it were seen as having been provoked by an actual invasion. Although supporting the compromise, Kissinger advocated using the period before the invasion to beef up American air forces—keeping as many helicopters as possible in South Vietnam in spite of troop withdrawals, and sending more B-52s, fighter-bombers, and aircraft carriers to the area.

On February 2 Nixon presided over a meeting of the NSC to consider the implementation of the Senior Review Group recommendations. The president presented the "talking points" Kissinger had drafted: if failure should occur in the upcoming battle, he did not want it attributed to lack of preparation, leadership, or decisiveness; the South Vietnamese must be given the means and will to meet the enemy challenge; and the United States must make an "all out effort" to convince the enemy that he could not succeed through military means; he must be made to engage "seriously" in negotiations. After the meeting concluded, Nixon authorized the sending of "another carrier, more B-52s, and additional all-weather planes." In essence, the decision was to increase bombing in South Vietnam and instruct the military to keep the White House informed of enemy movements, but to delay a more massive response against North Vietnam than was currently under way until the dry-season offensive commenced.[33]

The offensive did not come before Nixon's China trip. Instead, there seemed to be good news on the diplomatic front. On February 14 General Vernon Walters in Paris informed the White House that the North Vietnamese had invited Kissinger to a luncheon meeting on March 17. Kissinger, as Haldeman described him, was "ecstatic" because, as Kissinger had characterized the invitation, the North Vietnamese had been "pleasant" and invited him to lunch. This was "significant." They had never before asked him to share a meal, even though many previous sessions had gone through the morning, past the lunch hour, and into the late afternoon. The invitation seemed to ensure that there would be no major offensive as they had feared, and it could lead to a diplomatic breakthrough. With no offensive in the offing and serious negotiations likely, this development was nothing short of "spectacular." After questioning Kissinger "strongly" on his reasons for thinking the invitation was "significant" and not just another "ploy," Nixon joined him in gratitude that they would get some "relief from the offensive" and in self-congratulation about the steps they had taken that had brought about this very "positive" situation. The "progress" they had made with Hanoi was the result of having attacked antiwar critics at home, demonstrating, he averred, that he was not to be "kicked around." It was also the product of their imminent China trip, the current heavy bombing of South Vietnam, and the deployment of three carriers "into position and that sort of thing." These things "must have had an effect."[34]

On February 16 the White House responded to the North Vietnamese invitation by proposing a meeting date of March 20, warning that "the attempt to place one side under military duress by escalating the level of military activity is inconsistent with the purpose of these meetings."[35] It was a veiled reference to the other side's preparations for an offensive, of course, but it was also rather sanctimonious, since Nixon and Kissinger had applied and were applying as much military—and diplomatic—pressure on their opponents as they could muster.

To the DRV and other small nations in the Communist camp, Nixon's visit was at worst indicative of a shift in Chinese policy away from their support of revolutionary movements and, regarding the struggle in Vietnam, of acquiescence in the U.S. policy of preserving Thieu's government and delaying or preventing the reunification of the country.[36] In the least, Nixon's meetings with Mao and Zhou and his walk on the Great Wall were signs to the Vietnamese, who hardly had to be reminded, that China's foreign policy was motivated less by Communist solidarity than by Chinese perceptions of national interest, which did not necessarily include a united, strong Vietnam.

Nixon's appraisal is unclear. Although in a "positive, radiant mood" at the time of his return to Washington, he said little to the public or to those in the administration who were outside the inner circle about the impact of the trip on the Indochina War, but he stressed instead its broader positive import for long-term U.S.-PRC relations. "The most important thing out of the China trip," he told his cabinet, "was that there's a profound new relationship between the PRC and the United States." They had both agreed not to resort to force or the threat of force with one another or with others. Apparently he was not even thinking of Vietnam when he said that.[37] No doubt he thought the trip would help him in dealing with the Soviets, and he also thought that by boosting his public image, he would have a stronger domestic base in support of his Vietnam policies—a strategy he had decided on beforehand. During the flight to China, Nixon and his staff discussed again the form of the public image they should project about this historic trip to an alien and enemy culture. Their conclusion, as in previous discussions, was that it should stress his leadership in achieving long-range goals, which led Nixon to observe about both foreign and domestic matters: "We need to create an aura of confidence and mystique that we believe in the leader, and not that we're self-examining and critiquing. . . . We should go on our strong points, take the offensive."[38]

Kissinger's assessment in *White House Years* was more direct. He wrote that the Chinese summit amounted to a successful first step in Washington's diplomatic strategy of isolating Hanoi.[39] There was little to justify this claim, however, in the joint U.S.-PRC Shanghai Communiqué that was released on February 27, the day before Nixon's departure from China. The United States affirmed its support for the Saigon regime and repeated its espousal of a diplomatic solution based on its eight-point proposal of January. The People's Republic affirmed its support for the peoples of Vietnam, Cambodia, and Laos and repeated its approval of a diplomatic settlement based on the PRG's seven-point proposal and its two clarifications of February.[40] Nixon claimed nothing about Vietnam when he spoke to his cabinet but said instead that the heart of the communiqué was the Chinese-American agreement "that no nation should dominate Asia."[41]

There was also little in Nixon's or Kissinger's reported conversations with Mao or Zhou that might clearly be interpreted as a Chinese promise of cooperation with America's triangular policy toward Vietnam. In a meeting with Zhou Enlai, Nixon had warned that "we would react violently if Hanoi launched another major offensive."[42] He made this remark while attempting to link the maintenance of American credibility to rapprochement between China and the United States, saying that if he submitted to Hanoi's demands "we would cease to be a nation worth having as a friend, and which the people of the world could depend upon as an ally." Both Nixon and Kissinger reported in their memoirs that Zhou expressed sympathy and support for the Vietnamese, predicted that a protracted withdrawal would create more difficulties for the United States, and urged Nixon to settle quickly lest the quagmire of war prevent his country from adequately performing its regional and global roles. If the views expressed in his memoirs reflected his views at the time, however, Kissinger, and presumably Nixon, chose to interpret Zhou's remarks as "a masterpiece of indirection." Zhou, he wrote, criticized the American negotiating position only "perfunctorily" and never "really" championed Hanoi's demand for a coalition government or Thieu's ouster. Because Zhou did not say that China shared a community of interest with Vietnam but supported Hanoi and the PRG in recompense for imperial China's past treatment of Vietnam, and because he said that Chinese and American difficulties would be settled peacefully, Kissinger said he and Nixon construed Zhou's words to mean that China would not intervene militarily in Vietnam.[43] Perhaps Mao or Zhou provided private assurances that neither Nixon nor Kissinger reported publicly.[44] More likely, Nixon and Kissinger may have been so taken by the historic symbolism of the trip, the gracious hospitality of their hosts, the thrill of meeting with Mao and Zhou, the expectation that it would influence the Soviets, and the boost it gave to Nixon's sense of personal achievement and his standing in the polls that they could not but regard Zhou's comments in a positive light.[45] Other, more sober statesmen could have interpreted Zhou's remarks as the Chinese version of linkage: get out of Vietnam as soon as possible or we may find our new relationship developing more slowly than desirable. Or they could simply have considered it good-mannered ambivalence, reflecting China's interest in better relations with the United States, but not at the cost of losing credibility with *its* allies.

Insofar as the Soviet Union was concerned, Nixon and Kissinger did of course see the China trip as a way of putting pressure on Moscow. But the Chinese perspective on triangulation was that its rapprochement with the United States would frustrate the presumed Soviet aim of fomenting tension between China and America, while the withdrawal of the United States from Taiwan and Vietnam meant that its aggressive power was weakened in Asia.[46] Hanoi was hardly being "isolated," although Beijing might have been advising it to settle the war as soon as feasible.

In any case, Nixon's trip did not immediately turn the war's diplomacy in his favor. On February 29, just as the president and his entourage returned from China, Hanoi informed Washington of its acceptance of their March 20 date for a Kissinger-Tho meeting. But on March 6 it told Washington that it wanted to postpone the meeting until April 15, citing, according to Kissinger's account, air attacks made before and after Nixon's China visit.[47] In his memoirs Kissinger claimed this was a questionable pretext, since some of the attacks had occurred almost two weeks before Hanoi had accepted the March 20 date, that is, on February 17 and 18. And he denied that the attacks Hanoi alleged to have taken place after Nixon's return from China had in fact occurred: "They would have been totally inconsistent with our strategy. We were staying well clear of the North precisely to avoid this sort of accusation."[48] It was not, however, a categorical denial.

The DRV's expressions of willingness to negotiate were part of the same elaborate game being played by the United States: combining military preparations with diplomatic maneuvers, one intended to assist the other, while also satisfying political requirements. Among other purposes, the North Vietnamese may have intended to establish a record of having tried to reach a negotiated settlement, thereby mollifying Beijing and Moscow, just as Washington, by making known its record, hoped to appease the American public. The reason Hanoi gave for postponing the March 20 meeting may indeed have been a pretext, but its real motives can only be speculated upon. Perhaps the Politburo felt that a gesture of protest and of determination had to be made against the continuing air raids, recent American air and sea deployments, and Nixon's threat while in Beijing to take strong military measures should the DRV invade South Vietnam. Hanoi's postponement of the prospective meeting was also likely related to the impending offensive. By holding out the prospect of negotiations, or by actually engaging in negotiations, the North Vietnamese might confuse Washington about the timing of an attack and curb American efforts to impede it. If this was the purpose, it worked, especially because Nixon and Kissinger were predisposed to delay an all-out response until after the attack in order to put themselves "into the best political and psychological position to overcome the approaching onslaught and to sustain our retaliation publicly." Kissinger bitterly reflected in his memoirs that the White House should have realized that Hanoi's invitation to negotiate was a ploy, because Hanoi had really intended to hold talks at a time of "maximum pressure and discomfiture for us" as they prepared to attack.[49]

On March 8 General Abrams made the case to his superiors that North Vietnamese preparations were by now so advanced that the offensive might as well be considered under way. Citing NSC 149, which had called for air attacks against targets in North Vietnam between the DMZ and the nineteenth parallel once the offensive had begun, he asked for permission to launch strikes against several nettlesome antiaircraft sites in the Panhandle. On the basis of Abrams's assessment of the military situation, Haig warned Kissinger on March 10 that the North Vietnamese offensive would be stronger and broader than originally thought. The projection now was that attacks would fall not only on Military Region 2 in the Central Highlands, but also on Military Region 1 from Cambodia and across the DMZ, with supporting thrusts in Tay Ninh province (Military Region 3) and in the Mekong delta (Military Region 4). These latter actions, he surmised, were designed to prevent South Vietnamese reserves in Military Regions 3 and 4 from being redeployed northward, as well as to wreak havoc in heavily populated towns and cities. Nixon nonetheless refused Abrams's request, preferring to delay his response until the offensive was actually launched, when public opinion would probably allow him a freer hand.[50] He did, however, advocate what he called his "Churchillian strategy," which he had suggested previously in relation to the bombing of South Vietnam; that is, to break with military routine by grounding all aircraft in Indochina for several days, then on another day send them all out in a single massive blow. Kissinger and Laird agreed to the maneuver. For two days American planes stood down, and on the third day they attacked.[51]

Meanwhile, diplomatic exchanges between the United States and the DRV continued through March. On the thirteenth Washington protested Hanoi's postponement of a secret meeting, denied Hanoi's allegations, declined their proposed date of April 15, and suggested April 24. On March 23, with Hanoi not yet having responded to this suggestion, William Porter, the current American ambassador to the plenary Paris talks, called off the scheduled general session at avenue Kléber. He had acted without Washington's authority but assumed his step was consistent with Nixon's tough posture and disdain for the public negotiations. At a press conference the next day, Nixon took responsibility for the postponement, accusing the other side of using this Paris forum for purposes of filibuster and propaganda.[52] On March 27 Hanoi accepted the April 24 date for a private meeting, but only on the condition that the semipublic plenary were held before then. Kissinger wrote that he persuaded Nixon to agree, and on April 1 Washington proposed a plenary-meeting date of April 13. The Spring Offensive had already begun, although Kissinger claimed afterward that its full scope had not become evident until April 2. By this date, military events overcame the grim diplomatic dance.[53]

Until the last minute, Kissinger and his aides had been deliberating what stance the administration should take in the forthcoming negotiations. Should the DRV be asked to make a gesture on POW releases? Should the DRV be asked about the negotiability of the PRG's two-point elaborations of their seven-point plan? Should the United States press again for the separation of military and political issues?

They were also considering a unilateral and complete troop withdrawal—except for a residual force—by November 1.[54]

Nixon was insistent regarding this matter. On March 11 he had written Kissinger that in "looking ahead on Vietnam we must take several political factors" into account, especially as the July Democratic National Convention drew nearer. Even though Vietnam was not in his judgment a major political issue at the moment, he thought it would be made one by the Democrats at their convention. They would point out that the administration had not been able to end the war after more than three years in office. Because the majority of delegates would be from the "anti-war crowd," there would be a plank against the war in their platform. The nominee would probably give an acceptance speech that would hit the administration hard on the issue "unless we have defused [it] substantially by that time." The best way to defuse it would be to announce more troop withdrawals in April and again before the Democratic National Convention, even though these would undermine Kissinger's leverage in the negotiations. He told Kissinger, however, that while they must continue to "play the negotiating string out, . . . we must not let that string hang us in the fall by failing to do what we can to present the very best possible case for our position on the assumption that no negotiated settlement will have been reached. . . . As you know, I have very little confidence in what . . . [the April] meeting may accomplish, and I do not believe that they are going to negotiate until after the election." Without a withdrawal announcement in June, he concluded, "we will be in very serious trouble."[55]

Nixon had reiterated his "bug-out" strategy. After the Moscow trip, and regardless of events on the battlefield, he would announce in April or June that all troops would be out by the election except for a residual force, which would be kept in South Vietnam until the POWs were returned. The negotiations would be pursued at least through June,[56] with only residual forces, airpower, and triangular diplomacy left as leverage. The war was being continued in order to save Thieu, but if all failed, in the end Nixon would settle for a decent interval and the return of POWs.

He was determined on his course, which was, like other policies and strategies in the past, a blend of pragmatic political calculation and dogged adherence to hegemonic international goals, of his "passive" acceptance of the inevitability of withdrawal and his "aggressive" predilections toward ruthless counterpunches. Airpower, his remaining military tool, served defensive and offensive purposes. General Abrams explained its defensive role to reporters on March 17: enemy arms could not prevail as long as American planes dominated the battlefield, but if these were withdrawn too rapidly, "the psychological effect on South Vietnamese commanders in the field could be 'catastrophic.'"[57] Nixon agreed, of course, but viewed aerial bombardment primarily as an offensive weapon that should be employed against the North with devastating force in order to teach Hanoi a stern lesson and drive it to a settlement. Coming after the enemy offensive began, such bombing could be publicly portrayed as a response to North Vietnamese aggression and would likely be tolerated or even welcomed by many of the voters.[58]

THE SPRING OFFENSIVE

The long-anticipated dry-season Communist offensive began on March 30. Following a massive, preparatory artillery barrage, an estimated 15,000 North Vietnamese troops with armored vehicles, artillery, and mobile antiaircraft guns attacked across the DMZ from the north and northwest into Quang Tri province in Military Region 1. The broad scope and main outlines of the offensive began to unfold during the next several days. From the hills in western Thue Thien province, a reinforced PAVN division thrust toward Hue. In Military Region 2 several PAVN divisions advanced from Laos and Cambodia toward Dak To and Kontum in the Central Highlands, while along the coast to the east one PAVN division supported by PLAF regiments attacked in Binh Dinh province. Far to the south in Military Region 3, a single PAVN regiment attacked north of Tay Ninh, while three PLAF divisions, reinforced with North Vietnamese personnel, advanced from their Cambodian base areas toward Loc Ninh and An Loc. In Military Region 4, even farther south, one PAVN division supported by PLAF regional forces attacked from Cambodia into the northwestern section of the Mekong delta.

Within a week half of Quang Tri province was in VNLAF control, and Quang Tri City was in danger of falling. Loc Ninh fell within days, and by mid-April South Vietnamese defensive positions west of Hue were under heavy pressure. The performance of South Vietnamese officers and troops was mixed. Whole units surrendered, others were defeated, large numbers fought poorly or joined refugees fleeing the advance, but many also held their ground.

The timing and breadth of Communist attacks surprised most intelligence analysts and American and South Vietnamese leaders. They had originally expected the offensive to come in February. When it did not, they noted signs pointing to its commencement in March, but they were still taken aback when it came on March 30. Despite evidence and warnings to the contrary, they were doubly surprised by the dramatic shift in VNLAF strategy from guerrilla to conventional war. The major thrust had been expected in the Central Highlands of Military Region 2, but there the fighting developed more slowly than in the north, where the heaviest blows had been delivered first upon Quang Tri and Thue Thien provinces. In Military Region 3 they had expected a major offensive in Tay Ninh province, but the VNLAF had directed its main attacks farther north against Loc Ninh and An Loc.[59]

Even though he had not fully appreciated the strength of the developing offensive during its first few days, Nixon's initial reaction had been to step up the massing of sea and air power that he had earlier set in motion, and on April 4 he authorized fighter-bomber strikes up to the eighteenth parallel.[60] He was ready, too, Haldeman noted, to "move in hard . . . using B-52s for the first time to bomb North Vietnam," while intending to defend his decision to the American public on the basis of the enemy's "violation of the DMZ." But bad weather delayed attacks on North Vietnam. Nixon, who believed the military was using the weather as an excuse, criticized Admiral Moorer on April 4 for the "Air Force's inability to get moving."[61] At an afternoon meeting the next day, he told Haldeman and Mitchell that "the bastards have never been bombed like they're going to be bombed this time." But the problem was that "the Air Force isn't worth a—I mean, they won't fly." The weather "isn't bad," he insisted.[62] Nixon was angry, now insisting that everyone refer to the North Vietnamese as "the enemy," "Communist," and "invaders," not as "the other side."[63]

Ron Ziegler remarked during this period that the president was emotionally "high again."[64] Kissinger approvingly told Haldeman that the president was acting "quite strongly" and "taking control."[65] On April 5 Rogers phoned the White House to say that "everybody's steadfast on the Vietnam move," but he added that he was troubled by the poor performance of the South Vietnamese and concerned that American planes would be shot down, creating more POWs. Haldeman, who took the call, privately noted that Rogers's POW caveat was "a fairly obvious negative that hardly seems necessary for him to enumerate."[66]

On April 6 Laird forwarded a JCS contingency plan to mine Haiphong Harbor and bomb and shell targets near Hanoi on a onetime basis. But, reflecting Abrams's views as well, he thought the plan militarily imprudent. Laird argued that it would divert air resources from South Vietnam, where they were sorely needed to assist the RVNAF. Moreover, attacks against Hanoi and Haiphong would only produce a limited, long-term military impact, since the DRV's bases of supply were in untouchable rear areas in the Soviet Union and China, while the DRV itself possessed a diverse and flexible system of distributing supplies to the South. The threat to North Vietnam's small but rebuilt industrial base was considerable but would be short-lived once the bombing destroyed it. Meanwhile, the political impact at home and abroad of such bombing would be adverse, providing the antiwar movement with an issue around which to rally. Although Laird understood that Nixon wanted the mining and bombing campaign to have a "political" impact on the Soviets, influencing them to reduce their support for North Vietnam, he expressed doubt in a cover memo he attached to the JCS plan that the operation called for would actually achieve this goal.

In passing Laird's memo to Kissinger, Haig reminded him that if Laird were correct in his judgment that the diplomatic and military benefits of the JCS plan were not worth the negative domestic and international price incurred, then the president had in mind a much bigger plan, one that would prove cost-effective.[67] Following Kissinger's instructions, which had undoubtedly originated with the president, Haig had just completed preparing a planning paper calling for the mining of all North Vietnamese ports and the bombing of all military targets in North Vietnam, save for those in a buffer zone along the Chinese border.[68]

On this day, too, Nixon, Kissinger, and Haldeman happened to be meeting with air force General John Vogt, who had been slated for promotion and assignment to NATO but had now been reassigned to Vietnam to replace the outgoing General Lavelle. At a briefing a day or two earlier, Vogt had told Kissinger that he was distressed with the military's failure to carry out the president's bombing orders and to develop innovative ideas of their own, and that he would gladly give up his promotion to go to Vietnam and get "the thing straightened out." Impressed, Kissinger told Nixon the story, and Nixon decided to send Vogt to Vietnam, while allowing him to keep his promotion. Upset with the military's handling of bombing operations in Vietnam, Nixon wanted Vogt to step in and take charge. At the "dramatic" White House meeting on April 6, Nixon told the general that it would be "tragic" if the air force missed what might be its last historic opportunity to wage this kind of air battle. Promising to back him up, he ordered Vogt to bypass Abrams in order to get the job done.[69]

What needed to be straightened out was the complex and divided command structure for ordering and controlling air operations in Vietnam. Despite his assurances to Vogt, Nixon did not change the command-and-control system, fearing the reform would cause too much internal dissension at this time of crisis.[70] As Kissinger related it in his memoirs, however, the larger and more important issue had to do with the differing assumptions governing bureaucratic and White House thoughts about the bombing strategy to be followed in Vietnam. Abrams, Laird, and Kissinger's staff, with the exception of Haig, saw the Spring Offensive mainly as a critical trial of South Vietnamese armed forces; airpower should therefore be used primarily to assist the RVNAF fighting in the South, thus preserving the integrity of Vietnamization. Convinced that bombing should be directed against the North as well, Nixon and Kissinger, however, thought these advisers too cautious, unimaginative, and strategically narrow-minded.[71] Since they believed the expected enemy offensive was "a desperation move," it presented them with an opportunity to hit North Vietnam hard with massive airpower, thus creating "a good chance" of successful negotiations, which Nixon felt they had not "really . . . had up to now." There was, too, a larger context: airpower employed against North Vietnam could lever the Soviets and Chinese into putting pressure on Hanoi.[72]

Yet for all of Nixon's anger, resolve, and opportunism, he also suffered doubts and anxieties. Should he deliver a speech or hold a press conference in which he would discuss the North Vietnamese offensive and explain that he was responding not with American troops but with American airpower? On April 10 Kissinger convinced him that such a speech would tend to "soften" the "tough line" they were taking with the Soviets and North Vietnamese. But their evaluation of the merits of a public statement led to a long philosophical discussion, in which they considered the possibility of a Saigon collapse. Nixon felt he was dealing with a "very major crisis." It was "do-or-die" in Vietnam: Hanoi and Saigon had committed all of their resources; and the United States had committed all of its assets short of putting in more troops, "which we won't do." The United States might break the back of the North Vietnamese, but on the other hand, South Vietnam may not hold. In this event, Nixon complained that it would prove to others the superiority of Soviet methods in the third world; it would destroy the foreign policy of the United States; it would mean the loss of the free world; and he would be ruined politically. He mused about the relative merits of capitalist versus Communist culture, wondering whether America's emphasis on materialist values and economic abundance softened up its allies in the battle with revolutionary movements, which stressed a spirit of sacrifice and whose members lived Spartan lives.[73]

For the time being, Nixon followed a middle course in his Vietnam strategy. He postponed a decision on the mining operation but ordered the air and sea attacks on targets around Hanoi to be carried out on April 16 and 17, Vietnam time. On the tenth, meanwhile, B-52s bombed supply depots near Vinh, just below the nineteenth parallel. It was the first time during Nixon's tenure that the big bombers had struck North Vietnam.[74] Abrams chose the moment to cable a request on April 14 for a delay in the far-north attacks, arguing that major battles were shaping up in South Vietnam near Quang Tri and An Loc. The sortie requirements were so great that air operations in North Vietnam would impair his ability to provide the air support so essential to the defense of critical areas in the South. The northern bombings would also require additional maintenance of aircraft and the movement of aircraft carriers from south to north and back again, forcing delays and risking the consequences of more bad weather should it develop.[75] Kissinger thought Abrams's warning put them in a public relations bind: if "anything went wrong," as Haldeman paraphrased his remarks, Abrams could say he had advised against the far-north bombings. The president, however, rejected the general's request.[76] The attacks against Hanoi went ahead, while Nixon encouraged Kissinger to develop even "stronger action" against the North. On the fifteenth Haldeman recorded that the president was seriously "considering putting on a blockade later this week."[77]

Although Nixon and Kissinger agreed on the necessity of the all-out bombing of the North, they continued to differ over their approach to the Soviet Union and China in relation to North Vietnam. Nixon wanted to lump them together, confronting Hanoi with sticks and withholding carrots from Moscow and Beijing, but especially Moscow, unless they committed themselves to "help end the war" by reducing support for Hanoi. Kissinger concurred about the sticks-and-carrots strategy vis-à-vis Moscow but opposed setting rigid preconditions, preferring to use "negotiation as a weapon" by distinguishing between the interests of the three Communist powers in order to isolate Hanoi from its suppliers. In practice, as Nixon explained Kissinger's approach, it was to make "flexibility the cornerstone of successful negotiation," during which he would "feel out the situation."[78] Although not entirely confident about this tactic, Nixon allowed Kissinger to try it, in large part because his scheduled May summit in Moscow was at risk should he take a hard line with the Soviets. Kissinger's personal stake was the cancellation of his own pre-summit trip to Moscow at the end of April.[79]

Deciding on this course during the first days of the Spring Offensive, they moved quickly to implement it. But in protesting both China's and the Soviet Union's support of the invasion, their means differed from one to the other. They complained to Beijing through private channels, but to Moscow both through public statements made by Nixon and other U.S. officials and in private meetings Kissinger held with Dobrynin. To Beijing, they emphasized the American stake in Vietnam and the importance of the new Sino-American relationship. But to Moscow they warned of canceling or slowing down progress on specific measures the Soviets wanted: U.S. encouragement of West German ratification of treaties concerning Eastern Europe; U.S. grain sales and U.S.-USSR commercial talks; or the holding of the summit itself. To the Soviets they also delivered threats of decisive military blows against North Vietnam.[80]

Meanwhile, in the midst of great-power posturing and the fighting in Vietnam, Washington and Hanoi continued to exchange messages on when and whether to hold plenary and private talks. Neither wanted the onus of canceling the scheduled secret meeting, but at the same time neither wanted to appear overly eager, and both wanted talks for political and strategic purposes. On April 4 Washington withdrew its proposal to resume the plenaries on April 13 but left standing the April 24 date for a private meeting. On April 15 Hanoi rejected the April 24 date unless Washington agreed to resume the general session. The White House countered on April 16 with a proposal for a plenary on the twenty-seventh if there was a secret meeting on the twenty-fourth; on April 19, the North Vietnamese proposed April 25 for the plenary and May 2 for a Kissinger-Tho meeting; on the twenty-third, when Kissinger was in Moscow, the Americans agreed.[81]

In Kissinger's account, his meetings with Dobrynin and the fighting in Vietnam formed the backdrop to this diplomatic game. He suggested that Moscow and Hanoi were made nervous by his and Nixon's diplomacy of linkage, the tide of battle in South Vietnam, and the bombing of the North, particularly the mid-April raids around Hanoi. Although driven back in places, the South Vietnamese were generally holding ground, as American airpower pounded North Vietnamese formations and threatened greater devastation in the North. "Our bargaining position was stronger; our threats were more plausible," Kissinger claimed. In diplomatic exchanges, the Soviets were "falling all over us" and passing messages to and from Hanoi, while Hanoi was anxiously "thrashing around."[82]

No doubt Hanoi was concerned about the massive U.S. buildup of force and the possibility of mining, blockade, and bigger air raids in the far north, and the Soviets worried that the summit might fall victim to the renewed fighting. But there was nervousness on all sides. Nixon and Kissinger worried about the fate of South Vietnam, the status of the Paris negotiating process, the prospects for the summit, and the relationships between all three. Moreover, Hanoi's interest in resuming the talks was probably less that of caving in to pressure than of preventing or delaying the American bombing and mining in the far north of the DRV.[83]

On April 12 Dobrynin suggested that Vietnam could be put on the agenda of Kissinger's still tentative pre-summit visit to Moscow, in addition to discussions on preparations for the summit. This marked the first time Moscow had offered to carry out direct, high-level conversations on Vietnam. Kissinger was in favor of his going to Moscow, partly out of "vanity," he confessed, but also because it would "disquiet" Hanoi. Nixon decided to authorize Kissinger's Moscow trip for April 20, with instructions to discuss Vietnam and the summit.[84]

Three days later, Kissinger learned that Hanoi wanted to postpone the secret April 24 meeting, which Dobrynin had previously hinted would be an important one. Kissinger shot off a complaint to the Soviet ambassador, but the news produced another crisis of decision making in the White House. In several conversations that day, the president and his national security adviser debated what should be done. Nixon at first thought Kissinger should not make his pre-summit trip after all, since the postponement implied Moscow's unwillingness or inability to influence Hanoi. What game were the Soviets playing? Nixon was concerned that he would be unable to throw in his hole card of blockading the North and bombing Hanoi while Kissinger met with Brezhnev, or else the Soviets would cancel the May summit. Perhaps he should cancel the summit first and go ahead with the bombing and blockade. Thinking about the dismal political impact of these steps, he talked of finding a presidential successor. Kissinger pleaded that he should not allow the North Vietnamese to destroy another president. He conceded that Moscow might have been "playing the same game" as Washington—using the summit as a means of restraining the violence of the other—but he argued that during his own pre-summit trip, air and sea attacks against the North could continue, except for the bombing of targets around Hanoi and the mining of harbors. The hole card would only be delayed for the few days of his trip to Moscow. Because the Soviets wanted a summit too, they would just as likely go ahead with it despite bombing and mining. The summit, he further maintained, was itself a political hole card, which would serve to muffle domestic and Soviet criticism of the far-north bombing and mining. Nixon later relented when Kissinger phoned him after dinner to say that Dobrynin was still eager to have him appear in the Soviet capital, had promised to give priority to Vietnam in the talks, and held out the prospect of a Kissinger-Tho meeting in Moscow. Nixon authorized the trip. The negotiating string, he said, should indeed be played out.[85]

It was on this same Saturday that Nixon overrode Abrams's objections to the air raids on Hanoi, which were scheduled to begin that night, Washington time. After church services on Sunday, Nixon told Haldeman that reports he had received on the B-52 strikes indicated they had been "exceptionally effective, the best ever in the war. . . . The Pentagon was jumping up and down. We really left a good calling card."[86] During the attacks, however, four Soviet ships were struck, with loss of life, and Moscow made a formal protest. But the White House thought it restrained under the circumstances and significant that the Kremlin's invitation to Kissinger had not been withdrawn.[87] Still "cranked up" on Monday, Nixon instructed Press Secretary Ziegler to counterattack the press for raising questions about the impact of bombing on the prospects for a Moscow summit and to explain that the president would take whatever steps were necessary to drive back the invasion, regardless of the risk to his political future.[88]

KISSINGER'S SECRET MOSCOW TRIP

When Kissinger left Washington for Moscow at 1:00 A.M. on April 20, he believed he understood Nixon's thinking about the purpose of his trip: to prepare the ground for an international breakthrough on world order at the scheduled Nixon-Brezhnev summit, but primarily to persuade the Soviets to use their influence with the North Vietnamese to de-escalate their fighting. Pointing out that the president was prepared to do what was militarily necessary to turn back the Spring Offensive, even if these steps endangered improved relations with the USSR, he should wave the stick of escalated bombing and insist on talking about Vietnam before turning to the summit-related issues of SALT, East-West trade, the Mideast, and European security. There must be an understanding on Vietnam prior to the summit, but he should also extend the carrot by continuing preparations for the summit and maintaining the prospect of improved U.S.-USSR relations.[89]

En route to Moscow on April 20, however, Kissinger received new instructions. "After reflection" on Kissinger's Moscow briefing book, Nixon had decided that he wanted him to omit his "philosophical" introductory statement and other background material. He should "cut to the quick" and get to "brass tacks" with Brezhnev on Vietnam. The Soviet leader should not be allowed to "filibuster." Brezhnev should be told bluntly and brutally that the president will not stop the bombing until the invading forces withdraw to the North; the president demands that Moscow desist from strong rhetoric in support of Vietnam; and he insists that progress cannot be made on summit-related issues unless progress is made on the issue of Vietnam. In the evening, Nixon traveled to Camp David—his "cover story" in explaining to Rogers why Kissinger had made a secret trip to Moscow. While at Camp David to consult with Kissinger, as the story went, they had received an urgent request from Brezhnev for a meeting with Kissinger.[90]

Kissinger reported to Nixon after a five-hour conversation with Brezhnev on April 21. He informed the president that Hanoi had "in insolent terms" rejected Tho's appearance in Moscow; that he had been "brutal" in telling Brezhnev the United States could settle for nothing less in Vietnam than a guaranteed de-escalation for a year; and that he and the Soviet leader had spent almost all of their time talking about Vietnam.[91] On the twenty-second Kissinger met twice with the Soviet leader, using the "stick of bombing and [the] carrot of being forthcoming on summit-related matters in order to get mutual de-escalation in Vietnam." He had, he wrote in his report to Nixon, "gone to the brink with repeated declarations that we will continue military operations." He had presented demands through the Soviets to Hanoi: they must withdraw the divisions that had entered South Vietnam since March and restore respect for the DMZ; only then would the bombing stop; in the forthcoming Paris talks, the United States would demand the immediate release of POWs, even before a settlement was concluded. Devoting most of his attention to Vietnam, Kissinger made, however, what he called in his memoirs a "crucial" decision: having made his point about the war, he decided to put Vietnam aside and move on with summit preparations. He also informed Nixon that Brezhnev had asked him to stay in Moscow for an additional day.[92]

During the next two days more cables were exchanged between Nixon and Kissinger and between Kissinger and Haig, who, with Haldeman, worked with Nixon at Camp David on presidential business, although Nixon gave most of his time to Bebe Rebozo. Despite his polite references to Kissinger's negotiating skills and tough talk, Nixon's messages to him indicated displeasure and agitation. The USSR was getting what it wanted—discussions on the summit and a Kissinger visit that was longer than what he had with the Chinese. But the United States was not getting what it wanted—effective Soviet action on Vietnam. Only a few foreign policy "sophisticates" would understand the subtleties of what Kissinger would accomplish toward long-term U.S.-Soviet relations. Without a public report confirming Soviet cooperation on Vietnam, the Left would be "contemptuous" and the Right would be "frustrated." Nixon was determined to go ahead with bombing north of the twentieth parallel, which had been suspended during Kissinger's trip.[93]

Kissinger pleaded with Haig to keep everyone "calm" until he returned. To Nixon he reported his earnestness and success regarding Soviet cooperation on Vietnam, such as it was, concluding, "To kick them in the teeth would be an absurdity." Brezhnev had said that the Kremlin was doing all it could to help Nixon politically. In any case, the Soviets would not cancel the summit; the White House, Kissinger told him, would have to do that.[94]

Kissinger thought Nixon's cables were mainly the product of too many hours and drinks with his feisty pal Rebozo, and his fear that the Soviets would cancel the summit before he could.[95] These suspicions were not without foundation, but Nixon's contradictory emotions were more complex. His aggressive mood had been reinforced by several pieces of information, including intelligence reports from an informant in Hanoi that the Politburo was deeply concerned about the bombings;[96] Haig's report on the night of Kissinger's departure for Moscow of the beneficial effects of the mid-April, far-north bombings on South Vietnamese morale;[97] and a recent poll showing that public support for the president had gone up 11 points since the escalation of fighting.[98] Nixon suspected that the Soviets and the North Vietnamese were holding out the prospect of more talks in order to delay expanded bombing. Kissinger's arguments about the beneficial impact of his Moscow negotiations upon the enemy in Hanoi and dovish critics at home, he thought, were just more of his "gobbledygook." He also resented Kissinger's "unbelievable ego," which Kissinger had exhibited by ascribing so much importance in his cables to the attention he was receiving from the Soviets. He worried, too, about the likelihood of Kissinger taking public credit for diplomatic progress on his return. The Moscow trip and its long-term prospects would play with the intellectual elite but not with conservative hawks and down-home constituents, who favored simple, short-term, forceful measures on Vietnam. They would think that Kissinger's meetings and Nixon's upcoming summit with Brezhnev amounted to a surrender, since the Soviets had supported and supplied the North Vietnamese invasion. He felt the Soviets had trapped him into going through with the summit. Despite polls, which indicated that he need not worry as much about the criticism of doves, as Kissinger said he should, as about the defection of his hawkish supporters, he felt he was nonetheless caught in a bind between liberals and conservatives— damned if he did and damned if he didn't meet the Soviets at the summit. Nixon expected that the North Vietnamese would yield nothing during Kissinger's May 2 meeting with Tho in Paris; this would both justify and make necessary the bombing and mining of·Hanoi and Haiphong. Moscow, however, might as a result cancel the summit, and he would be hurt politically, since it would appear that he had chosen an expanded war in Vietnam over better relations with the USSR. On the other hand, if he canceled the summit first, he would be harmed politically as well.

In an "eerie session" before the fireplace at Camp David during a violent thunderstorm on a cold, dark evening, Nixon vented his frustrations to Haldeman and Haig. Although sympathetic, Haig observed that there was nothing that could be done, and that most of these problems would have existed even without Kissinger's trip. Nixon knew this was true. He had even reminded Kissinger in one of his cables of what both of them had long known, that there was little more that the Soviets or Chinese could really do regarding Vietnam.[99] Still, he was frustrated. It bothered him that the madman theory was not working and that Moscow had not done more.

In the end, it was much ado about nothing of substance. Although Kissinger had been insubordinate—in the sense that he had not terminated the talks and had instead moved on to discuss summit matters once the Soviets had listened to his blunt remarks and pleaded limited influence with Hanoi—he had been more or less true to the instructions Nixon had originally given him before his departure for Moscow. For his part, Nixon had nagged Kissinger to be tougher with the Soviets on Vietnam, but he had not given him direct orders to cut short his visit or cancel the summit if nothing more was achieved regarding Vietnam. Although Nixon was "primed," as Haldeman noted, "to really whack Henry" on his return to Washington, while Kissinger was "distressed that he had been sabotaged and undercut," their reunion, thanks to Haig's mediation and Nixon's change of heart, was good-spirited.[100] Nixon did not scold Kissinger, for he not only disliked confronting subordinates face-to-face but also fundamentally agreed with Kissinger's assessment of the manifold value of his conversations: Kremlin leaders had received him despite the bombing of Hanoi and Haiphong in mid-April; the Soviets agreed to transmit severe American proposals to the North Vietnamese and to urge private talks despite continued bombing, which they thought was likely to disconcert them; progress had been made on arms control and other issues; the joint Soviet-American communiqué included indirect language indicating that Vietnam had been discussed, which should please the doves and appease the hawks.[101] Kissinger appeared to have saved the day with the Soviets concerning the summit, holding the line while Nixon passed through another period of passive-aggressive anxiety. Nonetheless, insofar as the war was concerned, little had been accomplished and little had been lost, save that the bombing north of the twentieth parallel had been temporarily suspended.

On April 25 the White House made public Kissinger's Moscow trip and announced the resumption of plenary talks in Paris. On the twenty-sixth Nixon delivered an address to the nation, accusing Hanoi of "naked and unprovoked aggression across an *international* border." After reviewing the history of his negotiations and troop withdrawals, and announcing the withdrawal of another 20,000 by July 1, Nixon warned in his conclusion that North Vietnam could not be treated as a sanctuary. The bombing would continue as long as the invasion continued.[102] It was a threat he intended to be "damn frightening" to the North Vietnamese.[103] Displaying similar grit in his briefing of the White House staff shortly before Nixon's speech, Kissinger declared that it was not a time for "flinching." Both sides had put all their "chips into the pot." We have come this far by convincing "our opponents" that we "mean business" and are not "backing off," and now we have a better "possibility" of getting serious talks started "than at any time in the Administration." The president has made the North Vietnamese "believe they might lose everything," and if they do not win with their offensive, "they will lose everything."[104]

Still pumped up during his evening flight to Key Biscayne, Nixon ordered Kissinger to "hit" Hanoi over the weekend and to "orchestrate" air strikes in Military Region 1, where the North Vietnamese had launched new attacks. All B-52s in the Indochina theater should be launched. Kissinger delayed the attacks because, as he told Haldeman, he could "not possibly" put all B-52s in the air—or because, as Nixon thought, Kissinger did not want to bomb Hanoi before he went to Paris.[105] Even though Nixon himself would soon vacillate about the bombing and mining of North Vietnam, for political reasons he desperately wanted it to take place sooner rather than later. If the operation was launched too close to the summit, the summit might be canceled. But because it could not be carried out during the summit when he was in Moscow, the period remaining afterward was too close to the Democratic National Convention; and the more it was delayed, the more likely it was that Congress would tie his hands.[106]

LINEBACKER

With limited logistics capability to sustain mobile, armored warfare, especially in the face of all-weather American air strikes, the North Vietnamese offensive had been marked by alternating periods of attack and pause, while units regrouped, reinforced, and resupplied. Now, as April turned to May, the North Vietnamese, after several pauses, renewed their attacks. In Quang Tri province, panicky South Vietnamese troops abandoned their defensive positions guarding the provincial capital and joined the thousands of civilian refugees fleeing south. Farther south, the fate of Hue and Kontum hung in the balance.

At 6:00 P.M. on May 1, soon before he was to depart Washington for Paris, Kissinger informed Nixon of the fall of Quang Tri City. Abrams's report suggested that the South Vietnamese may very well have "lost the will to fight." Although he admitted it was a serious blow to South Vietnamese morale, Kissinger commented that Quang Tri City was not as important as Hue, for which the decisive battle was now beginning. Nixon was taken aback, but after an inconclusive discussion about the causes of South Vietnamese defeats, he repeated the instructions he had given to Kissinger on April 30 for his talks with Le Duc Tho.[107] The North Vietnamese must be told that they have to negotiate seriously. "The President has had enough and now you have only one message to give them—Settle or else!"[108] "Our Soviet friends" must also be informed that the summit is at risk, for he would not go to Moscow if "we're in a bad position on Vietnam at the time."[109]

Nixon's emphasis on far-north bombing was a mixture of anger, fear, and calculation. He was angry that the North Vietnamese and Soviets were, he thought, getting the better of him. He was fearful of losing his conservative constituents and of losing South Vietnam, in which case he would have no alternative but to blockade North Vietnam and demand the return of POWs. Bombing and related measures, such as mining and blockade, were therefore a means of lashing out at Hanoi, of signaling the North Vietnamese and the Soviets that he meant business, a way of mollifying his constituents, and a device by which he might now possibly "tip the balance in favor of the South Vietnamese for battles to come when we no longer will be able to help them with major air strikes."[110] At this high tide of the Spring Offensive, Nixon expected Tho would be intransigent when he met with Kissinger the following day. But even at this moment of military foreboding, he searched for hopeful auguries about the longer-term diplomatic future. Despite his visceral mistrust of the Paris negotiations, he thought on May 1 that it was "quite possible" Kissinger could eventually negotiate a cease-fire, because it was "probable that the North Vietnamese are hurting even worse than the South Vietnamese, and that both sides may be ready to fold."[111]

At the May 2 meeting in Paris, neither side was prepared to negotiate. In between mutual recriminations, Kissinger presented the new American demands: stop the current offensive; return to the status quo ante March 29; separate political and military issues; present a political solution that did not include the installation of a government dominated by Communists; respect the DMZ; and offer counterproposals to the standing eight-point plan presented by the United States in 1971. Although he told Tho and Thuy that "our political proposal was not inflexible," he did not accept the concept of anything resembling a coalition government, and, contrary to subsequent conventional wisdom, he did not advocate a cease-fire-in-place, but instead called for a cease-fire and the withdrawal of invading North Vietnamese forces. However legitimate he may have regarded these demands, his was not a serious negotiating proposal, but at the same time he insisted that the North Vietnamese "negotiate seriously."

Tho and Thuy responded that they stood by their previous proposals and were not prepared to stop the offensive, which by this time had made significant gains, with the prospects of more. They complained to Kissinger that he continued to avoid setting a fixed date for withdrawal, and they challenged him to demonstrate the "flexibility" on this and other issues that American officials had touted publicly. In their other remarks, however, they seemed, as they had before, to be setting up Thieu as the main issue, in order that, if necessary, they might at a later date relent on the question of his retention in power, as though he were a chess piece to be sacrificed in a gambit to win checkmate—U.S. troop and aerial withdrawal and a cessation or diminution of aid to the Saigon regime. For them to ultimately concede on the question of Thieu remaining in power was, in poker parlance, their ace in the hole, something for which the Americans would throw down their remaining cards.

Kissinger broke off the meeting and instructed Ambassador Porter to suspend the plenary sessions when he met the North Vietnamese delegation on May 4. Three days after Porter's announcement, the Politburo decided to cancel Tho's next scheduled meeting with Kissinger on May 21. In his report to Nixon on May 2, Kissinger concluded that the "major utility of this session was to reconfirm their intractability on negotiations, both for our own calculations and, when necessary, the public record."[112]

Kissinger's phrase "our own calculations" was a reference to the expansion of attacks against the North, for which Hanoi's predicted "intractability" in the negotiations would serve as a justification. At a meeting on the presidential yacht *Sequoia* in the evening of May 2, soon upon Kissinger's return from Paris, Nixon, Kissinger, and Haig discussed all of the military options, including an invasion of the North, the bombing of Red River dikes, and the use of nuclear weapons. Nixon rejected these choices, favoring the blockading of DRV ports and the expansion of bombing north of the twentieth parallel. Kissinger agreed but also recommended calling off the summit.[113] He made several interrelated arguments: to meet with the Soviets in Moscow while their tanks, driven by North Vietnamese, were rumbling into Hue, would make the president of the United States appear weak. The administration's hand would not be strong enough to negotiate with the Soviets. The bombing was, therefore, necessary to send both Moscow and Hanoi a psychologically important message. But such a step would likely cause the Soviets to scrub the summit, which would make it appear to the public as though the president had chosen the bombing of North Vietnam over world peace. Hence, by this odd logic, the administration should itself cancel the summit and go ahead with bombing and blockading. Although inclined to preempt the Soviets and cancel first, Nixon was not now sure it was the right move. The result of quick polls indicated strong support for a summit despite the offensive. He decided to postpone a decision for several days and told Haldeman to make a strong case to Kissinger against cancellation. Haldeman's position was that they should try to have the "best of both worlds": go ahead with the summit, but, taking the chance that the Soviets would not cancel it, proceed with bombing and blockading.[114]

May 4 proved a turning point, when Nixon invited outgoing Secretary of the Treasury Connally to meet with Kissinger and Haldeman and render an opinion. Upon hearing Kissinger enumerate the options—do not bomb, cancel summit and bomb, bomb and see what happens—Connally immediately chose the last, arguing, even before Haldeman could speak, that the American people wanted the summit, and if it was to be canceled, the Soviets should be the ones to do it. The first priority, he asserted, was to do whatever was necessary to stop the offensive and to make it clear to Moscow that the president will not accept defeat. The president was in good shape politically and had to have the "guts" to meet the crisis. When Nixon learned of Connally's remarks, he began to reminisce about two previous turning points in his administration when he should have followed his "instincts" and massively bombed—during the EC-121 crisis with North Korea and at the time of his November 3, 1969, speech on Vietnam. He decided that "we can't lose the war, that we're going to hit hard, that we're going to move in."[115]

Told later by Nixon that he had made up his mind and wanted no more discussion, Kissinger responded that he had already changed his own opinion about the issue and now had some suggestions for a bigger and better operation: they should initiate a blockade before the bombing, since a blockade was unexpected, and "it's better to do the unexpected" (a point sure to appeal to Nixon); it should be carried out on a continuous basis; the blockade also provided more time for bombers to remain in the South, where Abrams needed them; and when the bombing campaign took place, it should be a sustained operation, not just a "one-shot" attack over a few days. Nixon liked these tougher-sounding, more flexible ideas and ordered Moorer to prepare a plan.

At the end of the day, however, when Kissinger met with Nixon to review planning in his Executive Office Building hideaway, he recommended a mining operation in preference to a blockade, which was less likely to force a direct confrontation with Soviet ships. Pacing and gesticulating while puffing on a pipe in a manner reminiscent of Douglas MacArthur, Nixon approved the change. They also decided on the quid pro quo they would demand from Hanoi in exchange for a bombing halt: it must agree to an internationally supervised cease-fire and the return of POWs, in return for which there would be a complete U.S. troop withdrawal within four months of the cease-fire and the POW release.[116] In contrast with what Kissinger had told Tho in Paris, Nixon would not demand the withdrawal of North Vietnamese troops introduced into South Vietnam since March. But to insist on the return of POWs before a complete U.S. pullout would amount to a step backward from previous understandings, while the four-month withdrawal period would clearly be unacceptable to the other side.

The next step was to prepare a presidential address announcing the operation and the terms of a settlement to the nation. But there was to be another delay. Doubting that far-north bombing and mining would have any immediate effect on the outcome of the critical battles for Hue and Kontum, Abrams wanted a postponement in order to provide maximum aerial assistance to the South Vietnamese. It was imprudent to send B-52s "away hunting rabbits while the backyard was filled with lions."

Kissinger cabled Bunker on May 4 that Nixon was "nearing the end of his patience with the general," who should understand that "we are playing the most complex game with the Soviets involving matters which extend far beyond the battle in Vietnam as crucial as it is." Nixon granted a several-day postponement, but, frustrated by the general, decided he would bump Abrams up to chief of staff of the army and replace him at MACV with General Frederick Weyand at a bureaucratically and politically opportune moment. Meanwhile, for good measure, Kissinger cabled Bunker on May 6 with another message for Abrams: the administration "was not interested in half-measures; . . . we really mean business and we want to strike in a fashion that maximizes their difficulties. . . . There should be no question in either your or General Abrams' mind that we want to devote the necessary assets to this action." If more airpower was necessary, he said, then it should be requested and it would be sent.[117]

At 2:00 P.M. on May 8, after a meeting with the NSC, Nixon gave the execute order for the operation,[118] which in honor of Nixon's love of football, the military code-named Linebacker. It "HAS to work," he remarked later at a cabinet meeting. "We've crossed the Rubicon."[119] That night, he informed the nation and outlined the peace plan he and Kissinger had decided on May 4 they would present to Hanoi.[120]

Having "gone through agony" for so long on making the decision and taking the political risks, Nixon was now in a plucky mood. Unhappy with what he considered the military's unimaginative "milk runs" planned for Linebacker, he told Kissinger on May 9 that he wanted to "go for broke." Like the enemy, we must "go to the brink" and "destroy" the enemy's "war-making capacity." Johnson had lacked the will to do so; I "have the *will* in spades." The NSC staff must recommend "action . . . which is very *strong, threatening,* and *effective.*"[121] Inspired during the several days before his departure for Moscow by thoughts about the bold brilliance of Churchill, MacArthur, and Patton, Nixon gave Kissinger orders for other audacious operations: the CIA should initiate a campaign of disinformation, putting out the word that North Vietnamese morale was collapsing; the South Vietnamese should launch a massed tank counterattack; B-52 attacks against Hanoi and Haiphong should be stepped up while he was in Moscow (he said he did not want to make the same mistake he made when in Beijing by "letting up" on the bombing). In his memoir account, Kissinger implied that he ignored some of these orders, viewing them as just more examples of Nixon's habit of rhetorical exaggeration at times when he needed to release his "nervous tension."[122]

Nixon also wanted to make sure that hawks, unhappy with his trip to Moscow, would have no cause to think he had temporized in attacking North Vietnam.[123] In general, any concerns he had about the impact of dovish or hawkish faultfinding were calmed by subsequent opinion polls. Although press and congressional criticism was immediate, and there would be a spate of antiwar demonstrations in the days ahead, many newspapers came to Nixon's defense, and polls indicated that public approval of his speech and support for the bombing were strong, between 59 and 76 percent, depending on the pollster.[124] The immediate political price of bombing had been cheap.

The decision had been inevitable, despite the sound, fury, and vacillation that had attended the process of making it. It was an essential part of Nixon's "bug-out" strategy. He had long considered making a culminating demonstration of his madman theory, which, given his irritable mood and his few remaining military assets, he regarded as necessary if he were to exit Vietnam with what he understood as honor.[125] The Spring Offensive had provided him with an opportunity. Linebacker was aimed less at stopping the invasion and more at pleasing his constituents, frightening the North Vietnamese and Soviets, influencing the negotiations, and diminishing Hanoi's future war-fighting capability in the struggle that lay ahead for the South Vietnamese.

THE SUMMIT AND VIETNAM

Andrei M. Alexandrov-Argentov, foreign policy assistant to Brezhnev, recalled in his memoirs that Moscow's leaders were "shocked and indignant at the provocative character of Washington's actions" concerning Linebacker, but they were divided about how to respond. President Nikolai Podgornyi, Ukrainian party leader Pyotr Shelest, and Central Committee secretary Dmitri Polyanski advocated cancellation of the summit, and there was a "real possibility" that they might carry the majority of the Central Committee. But Brezhnev "saw *only* that the Soviet-American meeting, the preparation of which had taken so much effort and energy, was threatened." Supported by three other influential leaders, Kosygin, Gromyko, and Mikhail Suslov, and benefited by recent news that the Bundestag of the Federal Republic of Germany had ratified the Soviet–West German Treaty of 1970, Brezhnev was able to win the approval of the Central Committee for proceeding with the summit.[126] Soviet and Chinese diplomatic protests immediately after Linebacker had begun were largely confined to the bombing of their ships, while other signals were sent indicating that American attacks would not derail other issues associated with détente or rapprochement.

The White House learned on May 11 that the Soviets would indeed go ahead with the summit; Nixon and his entourage departed for Moscow on May 20.[127] Amid all the other issues to be discussed, it was the Soviets and not the Americans who raised the subject of Vietnam at the first plenary meeting of delegations on the twenty-fourth. Nixon, however, sidestepped Brezhnev's remarks. At a smaller dinner gathering in the evening at a dacha on the outskirts of Moscow, Nixon was bluntly confronted by Brezhnev, Kosygin, and Podgornyi, who took turns censuring his Vietnam policy. It was unlawful, aggressive, cruel, and murderous, Podgornyi said. "There is the blood of old people, women, and children on your hands. When will you finally end this senseless war?" Kosygin recommended that the United States remove Thieu from power. Brezhnev argued that the North Vietnamese plan for a political solution was reasonable, and he warned: "You overestimate the possibility in the present situation of resolving problems in Vietnam from a position of strength. There may come a critical moment for the North Vietnamese when they will not refuse to let in forces of other countries."[128]

Nixon later described his own remarks and demeanor as calm and firm, although he had made a minor concession during the "bullying" session—hinting to Brezhnev that he might agree to modify the previous proposal of late 1971 and early 1972 concerning Thieu's resignation before an election from one to two months.[129] Kissinger told Nixon the next morning that he had been "very tough," "magnificent," and "cold."[130] In his memoirs he recalled that it struck him during the exchanges that the Soviet leaders were players in a "charade." Although their tone was "bellicose" and their manner "rough," they had not threatened any immediate specific countermeasures. The rhetorical attack was for the record, made to please Hanoi,[131] and when the charade was over, they sat down to dinner and a pleasant conversation, returning to the main business of the summit on the following day. Nixon made no claims about the success of the summit in terms of progress on Vietnam, listing instead agreements on SALT, pollution, and medicine, the establishment of commissions on commerce and science, and the signing of a code of Soviet-American conduct.[132] Kissinger was less reserved, asserting that Hanoi had been "faced down" and "isolated," becoming, as a result, more compromising in its approach to negotiations.[133]

But if "charade" was the right term, both parties had played the game. Nixon and Kissinger, who had made so much for so long of using linkage diplomacy to force the Soviets into pressuring the Vietnamese, seemed to have abandoned the strategy, settling for Soviet tolerance of Linebacker and the global and political benefits of détente, barely complaining of Soviet aid to North Vietnam. Although the Soviets had not broken off the summit, neither had the Americans. If summitry had, as Kissinger claimed, given the Soviet Union and the People's Republic a larger stake in settling the Vietnam War through compromise, the same was true for the United States. The DRV had been isolated in the sense that the Soviets and Chinese had not taken proactive diplomatic or military steps to resist the bombing and mining offensive, but they nevertheless continued to criticize American policy and provide matériel to Hanoi.[134] Moreover, Nixon and Kissinger had assured Soviet leaders that they would not destroy North Vietnam.[135] The real success of the Soviet and Chinese summits for Nixon and Kissinger in regard to Vietnam was that they won them popular acclaim at home, which served to diminish the strength and significance of antiwar sentiment before the election.[136]

NEGOTIATIONS RESUME

Nixon took satisfaction in an offer made by Brezhnev during the summit on May 29 to send a high Soviet official to convey Washington's negotiating position to Hanoi "in the interest of peace."[137] Explaining this position to Gromyko the night before, Kissinger had said that the United States would not stand in the way if a Communist government eventually came to power in Saigon. Although he emphasized that the United States could not now "by its own hands" remove Thieu from power, he recommended the formation of a tripartite electoral commission, consisting of PRG, neutralist, and Saigon parties. The United States had previously proposed such a commission, but now for the first time Kissinger pointed out that it could serve as a transition to a coalition government that the United States would tolerate, serving meanwhile as a face-saving compromise on the main political issue:

> Already in the creation of the Electoral Commission, there will be laid down the principle of coalition. In fact the Commission itself will be, in a sense, a transitional form, similar to a coalition government. It would also be possible to consider how, in a flexible though somewhat camouflaged form, to establish the idea of a coalition government early in the coordination of these issues, though as a whole this problem must be a subject for negotiations between the sides themselves.[138]

When Gromyko, obviously surprised, asked if he had correctly understood the meaning of the proposal, Kissinger assured Gromyko that he had and acknowledged that he was deviating from Washington's public position.[139]

Kissinger did not mention this proposal in his memoir account of his meeting with Gromyko. But he obliquely discussed it later in the book in the context of reporting his tactics for his next meeting with Tho, referring to it as an "anodyne," intended to assuage Hanoi's pain upon Washington's rejection of its demand for a provisional but formal coalition government. If Hanoi "played along" with this stratagem, then perhaps the final settlement would resemble what Washington had always wanted: a two-track agreement, in which the United States and DRV had resolved the military issues, leaving the political questions to be settled by the Vietnamese parties.[140] That was his hope, but at the same time it was a concession, for it implied legal recognition by the United States of the legitimacy of the PRG, and Kissinger, of course, knew this to be the case. He also knew that Thieu would not have been pleased had he known.

President Podgornyi traveled to North Vietnam on the Soviet mission of peace in mid-June.[141] Kissinger reported in *White House Years* that in a letter to Nixon on June 22, Brezhnev's characterization of North Vietnamese words and demeanor in their meetings with Podgornyi indicated a softening of tone: they had listened attentively to Podgornyi and were willing to engage in businesslike talks about both their and American proposals. Kissinger, however, was reading tea leaves.

A cable from Deputy Prime Minister Nguyen Duy Trinh in Hanoi to Le Duc Tho in Paris indicates that Hanoi's leaders expressed their unhappiness with the Soviet Union's participation in the summit and its tepid response to the bombing and mining of their country.[142] It was probably also the case that, as in the past, the North Vietnamese wanted to hear American proposals directly from the Americans in the Paris talks. They had no doubt been diplomatically polite toward the Soviet president and had taken careful note of Kissinger's new formulation for a political settlement, incorporating it into their own plans and tactics for the negotiations everyone expected would eventually take place. But already indignant about Chinese diplomatic prodding, their substantive response to Podgornyi's entreaty for peace was probably similar to that given the leader of the German Democratic Republic (GDR), Erich Honecker, during an official conversation with the North Vietnamese ambassador, Nguyen Song Tung, in East Berlin on July 18, one month after Podgornyi's visit and a day before Tho was to meet with Kissinger in Paris. Honecker assured Tung of the solidarity of the people of the GDR with the people of Vietnam, and he promised "great help," conditioned, however, by the cooperation of the PRC. But he advised him that the GDR was in full agreement with the views of the USSR, as transmitted to Hanoi during Podgornyi's recent visit—namely, that in "our opinion" neither the United States nor the DRV could defeat the other militarily, despite the successes of the Spring Offensive, and therefore the DRV—without totally neglecting the military side—should pursue all possibilities in their "political and diplomatic struggle" by "sounding out the American position in Paris." Tung replied that he had been informed of an "unofficial decision" by Hanoi's Central Committee that it would stop the war only if two conditions were met, conditions that Nixon had not yet been ready to accept in the Paris negotiations: the United States must cease all military activities and withdraw all of its forces; and it must agree to the formation of a provisional coalition government.[143]

For all of Kissinger's claims about Hanoi having "blinked" in their long eyeball-to-eyeball confrontation with Washington, it was Nixon and Kissinger who made the first direct offer to resume negotiations.[144] Upon Kissinger's recommendation and with Nixon's authorization, Colonel Georges Guay, who had replaced General Walters as military attaché in Paris, on June 11 proposed a Kissinger-Tho meeting to Sung, the Vietnamese representative. Sung replied on June 20, counterproposing a meeting on July 15 but insisting that the plenaries be resumed as well. On June 26 Washington agreed but proposed July 13 for the general session and July 19 for the private session.[145]

With Kissinger and Tho sounding out one another, their six-and-a-half-hour meeting in the Vietnamese apartment at 11 rue Darthé was the longest ever.[146] Kissinger warned Tho that the talks would not continue if Hanoi used them to "manipulate" the American election, but in general both sides were diplomatically cordial. The main points discussed had to do with the old issues of cease-fire and political settlements, with Kissinger returning to Washington's pre-1971 dual-track approach of separating military and political issues, and Tho continuing to insist on comprehensive, or one-track, political-military discussions. Businesslike, Tho expressed interest in hearing Kissinger's "new views," but Kissinger, determined to exhibit steadfastness, pointed to his thick black briefing book and said it contained "old views." He stood by Washington's previous proposals, which included the terms laid out in Nixon's May 8 speech, his own presentation at the May 2 private meeting in Paris, and Nixon's January 25 speech, which in turn had slightly revised the provisions Walters had presented to Sung on October 11, 1971. Since this hodgepodge needed clarification, Kissinger explained that he was proposing two "modifications": a cease-fire-in-place, which amounted to a retraction of his May 2 demand for the withdrawal of those North Vietnamese troops introduced into South Vietnam by the Spring Offensive; and an American troop withdrawal four months after a cease-fire, but parallel with prisoner repatriation, which was a retraction of Nixon's May 8 demand that the withdrawal would take place only after POWs were released.

Tho replied that Kissinger's remarks lacked specificity, since they were even vaguer than the American eight points of 1971, which had been tabled at the August private meeting. The so-called cease-fire and POW modifications, moreover, simply reiterated American offers of the past. He insisted there should be a parallel agreement on military and political questions, then a cease-fire, which could then lead to a permanent end to the war. Otherwise, a premature cease-fire might lead to renewed hostilities. "There is no positive point" in your comments, Tho remarked. Yours is not a "serious negotiation." He said that he had expected Kissinger to have spoken more constructively in private. Kissinger was not being frank, he added, because he had avoided the discussion of political issues, such as Thieu's resignation, which marked a regression in progress made during 1971.[147] Repeating his side's demand for a tripartite coalition government, Tho allowed that after Thieu's resignation, the rest of his government could stay in power and even receive U.S. aid, pending final negotiations.[148] At the close of the meeting they agreed to meet again on August 1.

To Nixon, Kissinger characterized the talks in terms of Machiavellian tactics. The other side was as "positive" as they could have been, he said, given that we "must have thrown them off-stride by withholding the total package discussed in the USSR" (which was a reference to the proposals for an electoral commission and Thieu's resignation *two* months before an election). If the North Vietnamese "move," he speculated, it could be to accept a cease-fire coupled with American political proposals for Thieu's resignation just before an election; or they might try to use the talks to make Thieu "the obstacle to a comprehensive settlement."[149] Tho's assessment for the Foreign Ministry was similar but more succinct: "In general, the U.S. showed that it wanted a solution, but it still explored our cards and gave nothing new."[150]

The August 1 meeting lasted even longer—eight hours. Kissinger reported to Nixon that it was "the most interesting session we have ever had."[151] Even though he tabled a twelve-point plan, he boasted in *White House Years* that he had offered "nothing new"; the plan had only "cosmetic modifications." It was the North Vietnamese, he wrote, who retreated from prior positions and made new proposals: they dropped their demand for a withdrawal deadline; abandoned their "ancient" insistence on replacing Thieu with a provisional coalition government that would negotiate with the PRG to bring about a permanent government; and recommended talks between Saigon and the PRG on political issues, thus conceding the U.S. demand on a two-track approach by separating political and military questions. They even added fruit, cookies, and thicker spring rolls to the menu, auguries to Kissinger and his aides that the Vietnamese were buttering them up.[152]

The documentary record, though incomplete, suggests, however, that Kissinger exaggerated Vietnamese concessions. Both sides held fast to most of their principles but retreated somewhat from some recent positions, and each, probing the other, proposed cosmetic but potentially significant modifications, some of which were compromises, others bargaining chips. Kissinger continued to insist on an Indochina-wide cease-fire, but he agreed to discuss military and political issues.[153] He proposed a presidential election within six months of a final agreement on a political solution but not later than three months from an agreement on a cease-fire, prisoners, and withdrawals, and he may have brought up his proposal for an electoral commission and talked about Thieu's resignation two months before an election. Although restating that prisoner releases would run concurrent with a four-month withdrawal period, he concurred with the North Vietnamese position that repatriation should begin after the cessation of American bombing and mining, rather than before—although he insisted that prisoners in Laos and Cambodia must also be released.[154]

The North Vietnamese continued to insist on a one-track negotiation linking political and military discussions,[155] repeated demands that the United States accept responsibility for reparations in the formal document of settlement, called on the United States to terminate military aid to Saigon upon the signing of an agreement, and held that the cease-fire be confined to Vietnam. But they indicated a willingness to discuss the modalities of cease-fire, troop withdrawals, and POW releases and to negotiate all issues one by one. Regarding prisoners, the North Vietnamese for the first time formally agreed to exchange lists at the time of signing, although they had agreed to this in principle a year before, and while indicating that the matter of prisoners in Cambodia and Laos could easily be solved after an agreement, they confined their prisoner provisions to Vietnam.[156] They also dropped their demand that the United States set an unconditional, definite deadline for withdrawal, which, by this stage in the negotiations and in light of continuing American withdrawals, was perhaps a moot point. Besides, Tho told Kissinger that his four-month withdrawal schedule was too long, suggesting one month instead, and he continued to insist that all personnel, including civilian advisers, be withdrawn.[157] Although no longer requiring Thieu's resignation prior to the formation of a coalition, Tho, contrary to Kissinger's memoir account, continued to call for and refer to the prospective coalition government as "provisional."[158] Moreover, if the Soviets had passed on to the North Vietnamese the Nixon-Kissinger position on an electoral commission and Thieu's resignation two months before an election, which they must have done, or if Kissinger raised these points informally at the meeting,[159] Tho may have been attempting to whet Kissinger's appetite by meeting the United States halfway, dropping the old demand for Thieu's resignation before the formation of a coalition government. Tho's assessment of the meeting was that "the U.S. point on political issues [the electoral commission and Thieu's resignation two months prior to the election?] seemed to be more flexible, but still opposite to ours."[160]

At the August 14 meeting, each side, now ready to engage in serious negotiations, presented legal papers to the other. Kissinger's packet comprised a general statement of American principles, a procedural document on the method of negotiating particular issues in the private and plenary meetings, and the American ten-point plan, in which he answered each of the North Vietnamese proposals except the political one. Tho gave Kissinger a document acknowledging U.S. principles and procedures, but he offered the DRV's own principles and procedural "clarifications," the most important point of which was the rejection of the U.S. principle of discussing military issues in the private forum and political issues in the plenary forum. The two sides, the document stated, must settle both the military questions and the "main contents" of the political issues in the private forum. They should discuss the total withdrawal of U.S. forces and those of its allies; the cessation of military aid to Saigon; respect for the national rights of the South Vietnamese people; the total release of all prisoners; and "the reality in South Vietnam of the existence of two governments, two armed forces, and three political forces," along with the necessity of forming "a national reconciliation, provisional, tripartite government." The plenary forum of four parties should sign the agreements arrived at in the private meetings, concretely decide how to implement the agreement, and discuss U.S. responsibility for "healing the war wounds in Vietnam." Regarding the cease-fire, Tho emphasized that it should come only after an overall settlement, but he indicated that such an agreement would positively contribute to an Indochina-wide cessation of hostilities as well as the release of POWs in Laos and Cambodia.[161]

Progress had been glacial, if that is the right word for summertime diplomacy between tropical Hanoi and humid Washington, but there had been enough movement in the last three meetings to give Kissinger hope and a sense of "expectancy."[162] From Paris he flew to South Vietnam, but only after a stopover in Switzerland to be with his parents on their fiftieth wedding anniversary, where he enjoyed a brief respite from the "fanatics from Hanoi" and gathered emotional strength for his scheduled meeting with the "desperate men in Saigon." He felt caught, he wrote later, between the two Vietnamese parties, each wanting "victory," "pressed" by an American public weary of the war, and "harassed" by domestic antiwar opponents of the administration. At his meetings in Saigon on August 17 and 18, he would submit Washington's negotiating objectives for Thieu's consideration, but the meeting would also serve the purpose of providing him with an excuse to delay Washington's response to Hanoi's August proposals. Such "procrastination" would force Hanoi's hand, for, he claimed, the North Vietnamese felt the "compulsion of time." They were reeling from the failure of their Spring Offensive, isolated by triangular diplomacy, and anxious to settle before the American presidential election.[163] They were caught in a "dilemma," he would tell Thieu, because, "if there is no ceasefire, their military situation deteriorates, and if they don't give back the prisoners, we keep bombing them."[164] Much of this argument was designed for Thieu, to bolster his confidence and win his support for Kissinger's September meeting with Tho; it was also intended for posterity, for those who would read Kissinger's version of history and be persuaded to think well of his steadfastness of purpose and the wisdom of his and Nixon's four-year war. But Kissinger—and Nixon too—felt the compulsion of the electoral timetable, the pressures of their home front, and the dilemmas of military stalemate, which had not been resolved by the Spring Offensive or the Linebacker bombings.

THE SPRING OFFENSIVE, LINEBACKER, AND THE NEGOTIATIONS

The battles of the Spring Offensive had abated by the end of June but continued through the summer, with neither Hue, Kontum, nor An Loc falling. On September 15, South Vietnamese forces recaptured Quang Tri City, by then barely recognizable from the destruction, although the VNLAF held on to most of Quang Tri province, much of Military Region 1, and smaller sections of Military Regions 2, 3, and 4. The offensive had been stopped, or, depending on one's perspective, by the fall and by the time Kissinger would meet again in September with Tho, it had ground to a halt as the combined result of several causes: North Vietnamese mistakes; South Vietnamese fighting ability; the inherent difficulties of conducting an armored campaign on external lines of supply in harsh terrain; and the critical role played by American commanders, advisers, marines, and, most of all, airpower.

Nixon, Kissinger, and other American analysts asserted then and after that Hanoi's invasion had been defeated by the South Vietnamese, who had been assisted by Linebacker operations. Government analyses that concluded the offensive had achieved significant progress—thus contradicting the official line—were labeled "unbalanced," withheld from public scrutiny, and, if leaked, countered by "balanced" analyses.[165] The "balanced" assessments, which favored White House and air force views, were, however, colored by rosy hopes and Western assumptions about Hanoi's strategic motives.

If it is assumed that these motives were, in the style of Western military strategy, to rout the RVNAF, force the collapse of Thieu's government, or cut South Vietnam in two by seizing most of the cities and provinces in northern and central South Vietnam, then the conclusion can be made that it failed. The Vietnamese revolutionaries, however, conceived of military activity in terms of strategic flexibility and political purpose. While they hoped for a decisive victory, they were prepared to accept less—the enlargement of territory held, especially in Military Regions 1 and 2 and along the Cambodian border in Military Region 3, and the weakening of the RVNAF, both in anticipation of future offensives. Simultaneously, they aimed to reconstitute the NLF in selected areas of South Vietnam, especially in the Mekong delta—where its strength had been seriously eroded by depopulation from American bombing and pacification campaigns carried out by the United States and the RVN—thereby positioning the PRG and the NLF for the political-military struggle with Thieu after an American withdrawal. There were political-diplomatic motives as well: to demonstrate the failure of Vietnamization; reinforce congressional impatience with the endless war in Vietnam; speed the withdrawal of American forces; and strengthen Hanoi's hand in the Paris negotiations before Nixon's reelection. In these more limited or flexible goals, the Spring Offensive made significant gains.[166]

Linebacker operations against North Vietnam were carried out from May 10 through October 22, with a total of 9,315 sorties flown in 141 air missions that delivered 2,346 strikes, in which 17,876 bombs were dropped[167] totaling approximately 150,000 tons. This amounted to as much as one-fourth of the tonnage of all of Johnson's three-year Rolling Thunder campaign. Bad weather hampered flights until September, when four times as many planes flew compared with the previous monthly peak. In mid-October, when the Kissinger-Tho negotiations reached a fruitful stage, Nixon slightly restricted the scope of B-52 operations and reduced the number of sorties sent against the North. In the third week of October, as an agreement seemed near, he limited bombing to points south of the twentieth parallel. By then these far-north raids had inflicted severe damage to the DRV's rail and road network, truck and power facilities, and petroleum-oil-lubricant (POL) system, while the mining operation had effectively closed its major ports to oceanic shipping.[168]

Protagonists for Linebacker, who included Nixon and Kissinger, as well as national security analysts, air force spokesmen, and historians, have in their subsequent assessments muddied the distinction between the northern Linebacker operations and the air operations carried out over the South in support of the

RVNAF. Their general claim has been that the bombing of the South *and* North stopped the Spring Offensive, damaged the morale of soldiers and citizens of the DRV, and, along with pressure from the Soviets and Chinese, convinced the Politburo to compromise at the negotiating table.[169]

There is little doubt that American air strikes against the attacking ground troops of the VNLAF in the South inflicted heavy casualties on its units and imposed burdensome restrictions on its mobility. Although many South Vietnamese soldiers and officers fought well, there is almost unanimous consensus among American commanders and journalists on the scene that without the support of this massive airpower, the RVNAF would have either suffered a decisive defeat or lost significantly more men, equipment, and territory than it did.[170] The impact of the far-north Linebacker bombings on the progress of the Spring Offensive was, however, indirect and delayed, particularly since they were targeted against communications and industry in the North's heartland and not against military formations participating in the southern fighting.

Reliable assessments of Linebacker's impact on Hanoi's ability to wage war into the future were and are hampered by nebulous data. Although mining and bombing statistics were impressive, some intelligence analyses doubted these had a decisive impact. The CIA concluded in August that the amount of interdiction achieved "will not materially diminish the capabilities of enemy main force combat units, at least in northern South Vietnam. . . . The bombing and mining program probably will not, of itself, pose unmanageable difficulties to the North Vietnamese regime—either now or through early 1973." Hanoi had stockpiled supplies throughout Vietnam; it possessed a complex and flexible logistics network; and it, along with Moscow and Beijing, had taken countermeasures to compensate for the mining of major ports and the bombing of rail and road systems—including the transshipment of oil and goods from the Soviet Union through Chinese ports to the border with North Vietnam, the building of additional oil pipelines from the border to Hanoi and South Vietnam, and the increased use of minor roads and coastal shipping.[171]

Defending Linebacker before Congress in January 1973, Admiral Moorer testified that resupply from the Chinese and Soviets was significant, as was the enlargement of storage areas, the stepping up of infiltration, and the redeployment to the South of tanks, artillery, and antiaircraft guns. By December 18, when Linebacker II was launched, North Vietnam's major lines of communication were again serviceable, especially the railroads from China and coastal shipping north of twenty degrees latitude. Even after their losses in the Spring Offensive and the damage brought about by Linebacker I and II, he could only say that, measured against North Vietnam's offensive strength in March 1972, its war-making capacity had been set back one year from January 1973.[172]

Lacking documentation on Politburo deliberations, it is impossible to say with certainty what influence the Spring Offensive had on Hanoi's diplomatic strategy. Their divisions had suffered heavy losses in manpower and equipment, but so, too, had Saigon forces, and on balance, Hanoi and the NLF had improved their military and political position in South Vietnam. They could also expect continued resupply from the Soviets and Chinese at an adequate level. Nixon's anticipated reelection in November was a factor in their planning, but it was not the main determinant. The record of negotiations indicates that they were not panicking; they were calculating realistically. Better to settle with Nixon now if the right deal could be struck than risk having him change his mind, drag out the negotiations, and prolong the bombing. The election might work against Nixon too, desirous as he was of concluding the war before the voting or at least before his next term—and before Congress might end it for him. Nixon's troop withdrawals meant that American combat troops would soon be out of Vietnam by 1973 anyway, except for a residual force of advisers. A settlement could formally assure the total withdrawal of American personnel and the termination of aid to Saigon, while also establishing the legal legitimacy of the PRG and the NLF and the principle of one Vietnam.

In postwar interviews, Nguyen Co Thach, a foreign ministry official who served under Tho in the Paris talks, explained that the Politburo's diplomatic strategy contained three "options," each contingent on flexible military outcomes. The first, which had been pursued through 1971 and into 1972, as the Spring Offensive began, was to bring about Thieu's removal and his replacement by a coalition government dominated by the PRG. But as the offensive stalled—failing to accomplish its maximum objectives—they shifted to the second option, which was a coalition government at the top that included Thieu, the PRG, and third parties, with two governments, the Saigon administration and the PRG, recognized at the lower level—that is, in the territories each controlled. This was the goal sought by Tho when he met with Kissinger during July and August. Resisted by Kissinger in September, Tho would turn to the third option—a looser form of coalition government at the top called the Government of National Concord—but continue to insist on the two local, de facto, de jure governments in the rival territories. In the end, Kissinger, pressured by Nixon and Thieu, would reduce the governmental elements of the coalition and secure an agreement that defined it as an electoral commission. This third option, even with Kissinger's revision, was Hanoi's minimum goal, but it shared a common thread with the other two: the Saigon administration would *not* be "uniquely lawful." There would be two legal governments, the RVN and the PRG, operating in the different territories. This was the most important political goal, but the most important overall goal was an agreed-upon but unilateral American disengagement. After the Americans left, the struggle would continue in the South, with North Vietnamese forces assisting the NLF/ PRG. The Spring Offensive had not been decisive, but it had hastened a settlement and improved the PRG's territorial and political position. The final agreement, Thach said, conformed to "the reality of the time."[173]

Nixinger strategy had possessed its options too. Its maximum goal had been to preserve the Thieu regime as the only legal government in the South and to bring about the withdrawal of PAVN to the North. Vietnamization would strengthen Thieu to resist a future northern invasion, while enabling him to crush the NLF/PRG. Although striving for this goal from 1969 through 1971 and part of 1972 by means of triangular diplomacy and the Cambodian, Laotian, and Linebacker operations, Nixon and Kissinger had realized by 1971 that their second option was more feasible: Thieu's regime as the only government, but PAVN remaining in the South, with the future struggle to be influenced by the effectiveness of Vietnamization (which would be assisted by a cease-fire), continuing American aid, and Sino-Soviet pressure on the North. If Thieu survived, or if he held on for a decently long interval, their midlevel goals would have been satisfied. The purpose of Linebacker was partly to break the back of the offensive, but mostly to weaken the North for the struggle ahead and to lever compromise by the implied threat of more bombing. Now, in the fall of 1972, they were turning to their third option: cease-fire, recognition of the PRG, continuing aid to Saigon, and total U.S. withdrawal. This would bring an end to direct American participation, as well as the return of POWs, which would satisfy most of the public and Congress, while Thieu's continuance in power, especially if it were for a decent interval and even if power were shared with the PRG in a divided South Vietnam, would, with the rest of the package, give the appearance of a peace with honor. POW releases, which Nixon had initially emphasized for domestic propaganda purposes, had over time become a necessary goal of any negotiated agreement, but one that, ipso facto, was also a bargaining chip for Hanoi.[174]

By the fall of 1972, both sides were practicing the diplomacy of military and political stalemate. Neither side judged the military situation as favorable for the immediate future; each understood the realities of the political balance in the South; both considered their overall prospects with a cease-fire to be comparatively better than without one; and the heavy, manifold costs of the war, as well as the psychological exhaustion of the Indochinese and American peoples, now persuaded both groups of leaders to settle. In sum, neither the United States nor the DRV/PRG governments had relinquished their goals, but both had shifted to practical, minimum solutions. On balance, however, Hanoi and the NLF/PRG possessed more military and political flexibility; as a result, they had more influence on the timing of the breakthrough in negotiations.[175]

There had been an inexorability in the long process of war and diplomacy that had brought both sides to this moment of recognition. Yet the depth of recognition felt and acknowledged varied from leader to leader. Little is known of Politburo deliberations and whether or to what extent there was division or unanimity among its members. Much more is known about conversations, memos, and moods in the White House. Kissinger, more than Nixon, wanted to grasp the opportunity to settle. His policy goals in Vietnam were the same as Nixon's, and he was willing to continue indirect American intervention in support of Thieu after a settlement, but he was more accepting of current necessities and realities, which, he believed, required a formal end to direct U.S. involvement before rather than after the American presidential election. Perhaps he was biased in favor of a settlement because he would be the one to negotiate it. Still, he thought the historical moment should be seized.[176]

Nixon understood the necessities and realities of the war and knew that he must soon formally disengage from Vietnam, but he was ambivalent about whether he should agree to a settlement before or after his reelection. His ambivalence, as usual, was the by-product of his psychological makeup, his assessment of political conditions, and his concern for personal and international credibility. Wary and mistrustful of negotiations with Communists, he worried that Kissinger, prone to optimism in this matter, would err in his haste. After the August 1 meeting in Paris, Nixon had written to Kissinger that he had done a "splendid job on what must be a very tedious exercise."[177] But after the August 14 meeting, when he thought there had been no progress and that none could be expected before the election, he told Haig that "Henry must be discouraged" from exuding hopefulness, lest public expectations would be raised, leading to disillusionment, which would be "harmful politically."[178] Better to prepare a public relations campaign to explain the stopping of talks or, if they continued, to define what progress meant. Nixon did not want to fail if he pursued an agreement before the election, but at the same time he did not want an agreement that failed to include his minimum requirements, especially on the matter of Thieu's retention, which would make it appear a "sellout" to his conservative supporters—and also damage international perceptions of American credibility.[179]

Nor did he feel in August and September as much as he had months earlier that he needed to settle before the election. If the antiwar movement and Congress had pressured him to get out of Vietnam, polls now encouraged Nixon to hold on and await developments until after the election. The majority of pollees supported bombing and mining and what they understood to be Nixon's policies, and they opposed a coalition government arrangement. Thus Nixon told Haig in September that "the American people are no longer interested in a solution based on compromise," and he resisted Haig's (and Kissinger's) argument that public support for tough measures was contingent on continued efforts to seek a compromise diplomatic solution. His spirits were buoyed by his reelection prospects. In the race for the presidency, Nixon was polling far ahead of Senator McGovern,[180] who had been nominated at the Democratic National Convention in mid-July and was viewed as a radical antiwar dove by old-guard Democrats, mainline labor, conservatives, and centrist fence-sitters. McGovern was woefully lacking in campaign funds, especially in comparison to Nixon's immense campaign chest, and he had made it appear that he was indecisive, disloyal, and unsympathetic when soon after the convention he dumped his choice for the vice presidency, Senator Thomas Eagleton, whose mental fitness for the job had been publicly questioned.

In a belligerent mood toward critics of the war and McGovern's allies, and relatively confident of his broad support, Nixon was not inclined and saw no need to accept the advice of some of his advisers to move toward the center of the political spectrum. After Linebacker had begun, he had thought it sufficient to have the White House let the "Vietnam story ride," leaving it to the Joint Chiefs to "handle" press coverage of the fighting and bombing, while he talked about being ready to negotiate a peace with honor and basked in the glow of summitry.[181] McGovern's calls for peace in Vietnam would be countered by press leaks that Hanoi and Washington were making progress toward a settlement.[182] The peace-with-honor line would be coupled with rhetorical attacks against the antiwar movement and dirty tricks against political rivals, creating the environment that gave rise to the mid-June break-in at the Watergate headquarters of the Democratic Party by employees of the Committee to Reelect the President.

Although confident, Nixon worried that something could go wrong with the economy, the Watergate flap, or international matters, particularly Vietnam, which, if not costing him the election, might erode his anticipated landslide victory and his chance for a strong second-term mandate. His ambivalence would be compounded in October when polls registered a slight decline in his lead over McGovern.[183] Nixon believed that press coverage of the unfolding Watergate affair was one cause of his drop. It bothered him enough that he was pleased when progress toward a settlement in Vietnam in late October supplanted Watergate in the headlines. Although his presidency was not yet weakened by Watergate, it nonetheless served as another incentive for a settlement.[184]

The something-going-wrong over Vietnam could include an agreement viewed by Thieu and hawks as a "sellout"; or, even if it were seen by the majority of voters as a realistic compromise, it might still be perceived as a politically cynical October surprise. On the other hand, if significant progress were made in the talks before the election, Nixon could be harmed politically if he resisted an agreement and the North Vietnamese publicly revealed the terms to which both sides had agreed.[185] In any case, a settlement before the election was desirable, since the diplomatic opportunity might pass after his electoral victory if the North Vietnamese changed their minds, and he did not want to go too far into his second term with the Vietnam albatross around his neck. Yet, after the election, he could have a somewhat freer hand to escalate the bombing and extend the war in order to benefit Vietnamization, although, counterbalancing this strategy, Congress might not allow him sufficient leeway. All things considered, he was not sure whether it was politically better to settle before or after the election, but he wanted to keep his options open.[186]

THIEU

As Kissinger prepared to meet Thieu in Saigon on August 17 and 18, he hoped to convince him of the value of exploring "whether there is any chance of a serious settlement between now and November." Knowing Thieu would resist, he would argue that the moment was propitious, "in light of the new military pressures we have brought to bear on the DRV," but also point out that he and Nixon wanted "to bolster our negotiating record," which was "essential in our domestic political context" in order to marshal "the broadest possible support for continued assistance to the GVN." Concerning the specific terms of a prospective agreement, Kissinger would tell Thieu that in his negotiations with the North Vietnamese he wanted to be as "forthcoming as possible on the non-essential issues while varying our political position enough to give them a face-saving negotiating exit but without sacrificing any of the principles of an internal political settlement to which both you and we are committed." In other words, he would propose a tripartite committee of reconciliation that would serve not as a government, as proposed by Hanoi and the PRG, but as an electoral commission.[187]

Kissinger opened the first meeting arguing that the enemy wanted to settle all of the issues before agreeing to a cease-fire because they would be disadvantaged by one. He assured Thieu that the United States would not cooperate with the enemy in agreeing to the destruction of a government for which so many Americans and South Vietnamese had died.[188]

Thieu, heretofore relatively tolerant and cooperative regarding the negotiations, was now recalcitrant. On the one hand, he believed that his military situation was sound; on the other, he was worried that the United States was ready to withdraw its forces, stop its bombing, and compromise his political position in the negotiations. He was being egged on in his skepticism about the solidity of Washington's commitment by his nephew and press assistant, Hoang Duc Nha, and his national security adviser, Nguyen Phu Duc, both of whom mistrusted Kissinger and the Americans. Unconvinced by Kissinger's argument, Thieu tested his commitment by posing a hypothetical question: Would you sign an agreement if the other side offered a cease-fire and the return of POWs? Kissinger did not think the North Vietnamese would make such an offer without a comprehensive settlement, but he confessed that if they did, it could not be turned down, since Nixon had publicly stated he would accept these terms. But Thieu took this as evidence of Washington's wavering support for his government—that the United States would choose a cease-fire and POWs over political and military guarantees. Although Thieu also doubted that Hanoi would agree to a cease-fire without a comprehensive settlement, he understood that Washington wanted to get out of the war as soon as possible and was willing to make political and military compromises in order to do so. Kissinger in fact had told him: "At the next meeting I would like to accept their proposal that there be no ceasefire until all is done." This meant, of course, that he would make compromises on the political question and agree to a unilateral withdrawal. Kissinger for the most part evaded the political issue as much as he could, neglecting to note, for example, that Nixon had also publicly promised he would not abandon an ally. Thieu must have also realized that the promise of American aid after withdrawal was only a promise.[189]

Thieu complained that Kissinger had dropped his demand for the mutual withdrawal of North Vietnamese forces, without which he was even more adamantly opposed to political compromise. Although not a government, the electoral commission would, Thieu maintained, nonetheless enshrine the principle of a tripartite administrative arrangement, extend implicit legal recognition to the PRG, and have an adverse psychological impact on his supporters.

Kissinger reminded Thieu that the other side would never accept mutual withdrawal. He tried to reassure him that the modalities of a withdrawal and ceasefire would have to be discussed by the four parties and that the electoral commission was not a significant threat to his power because it possessed no governmental functions, and, in the election to come, the Communists would win few seats. The commission was actually a good idea because it would provide the administration with a "defensible position" at home, putting "to rest" talk of a coalition government.

In reality, Kissinger knew that Thieu's observations were telling, but he also knew that Thieu and his regime were "not satisfied with survival [into the near future]; they wanted a guarantee that they would prevail." At the same time, he and Nixon were being forced into this compromise by their "own imperatives": there was no "convincing military strategy" for victory, only the prospect of prolonged military stalemate, but there were now budgetary constraints on continued fighting and bombing, and, moreover, the public and Congress would not tolerate perpetual war.[190]

Stymied by Thieu's resistance, Kissinger on the next day turned to his and Nixon's fallback option in cajoling cooperation from the South and prying concessions from the North.

I prefer that they don't return the prisoners of war and that there is no ceasefire before the election. . . . It is easier if we keep up the bombing through the elections. . . . Our strategy is that we are prepared to step up the military pressure on the DRV immediately, drastically and brutally one or two weeks after our election. We want to be in a position that they have rejected our reasonable proposals. After that we will put everything on the prisoner of war question. They think they can use the prisoners of war to overthrow you. If we can move quickly after the elections, we can destroy so much that they will not be in a position to come back and harm you for a long time to come. . . . It is out of the question that we will make any additional concessions after the election.[191]

Kissinger's statement of intent was partially disingenuous. Although he and Nixon believed in the advantages of bombing through and beyond the election, especially if it helped to win Thieu's cooperation, mollify hawks at home, weaken the DRV, and secure a decent interval, Kissinger nonetheless thought it wiser, in light of diplomatic, military, budgetary, and political factors, to settle before the election. Nixon favored waiting until after his reelection, then bringing matters to a head through bombing. But although he was so inclined, he was decidedly undecided, choosing to follow Kissinger's diplomatic strategy but hedging his approval, contingent on political circumstances. A third option, continuing the war at its current level, as Thieu proposed, was seen as unrealistic by both Nixon and Kissinger.[192]

Somewhat reassured, the South Vietnamese, however, pressed the issue of cease-fire: What would the United States do if the other side offered a cease-fire without a prisoner return? Kissinger doubted the North Vietnamese would make such an offer, but told him that if they did, the United States would stop the bombing, but not the mining, which Thieu understood to mean that Washington would then trade mining for POWs. Kissinger replied that at some point, probably in the second half of 1973, Washington might have to stop the bombing and end the mining in return for a cease-fire and POW releases, but this would be only after the other side had been weakened. Even after withdrawing, the United States intended to continue sending military and economic aid to South Vietnam, while at the same time it would try to influence Hanoi's "allies not to arm them in such a way that they are capable of repeating military activities on the scale of the past few months." Driving the point home, Kissinger explained: "We have to get to a point where you can continue to fight with a minimum of direct U.S. involvement."[193] Thieu was not convinced, and Kissinger's promise of brutal bombing, rather than persuade Thieu to cooperate, probably encouraged him to resist, because it seemed that after the election, the United States was willing to take a harder line in the negotiations and escalate the bombing.

Thieu refused to meet for consultations with Bunker before the ambassador joined Nixon and Kissinger in Hawaii on August 31 to discuss the Vietnam situation. According to Kissinger, however, Bunker assured Nixon that his and Kissinger's negotiating policy was on the right course. On that basis Nixon signed a letter written by Kissinger that Bunker was to deliver to Thieu, in which he reaffirmed his earlier promises not to desert "a brave ally." Using Kissinger's logic, the letter argued that the proposals to be presented by Kissinger to Tho, including the electoral commission, "would safeguard Saigon's interests if accepted by the enemy and if rejected would strengthen support in the United States for our joint course." Thieu could not have been comforted by wording in the letter that described his government as a "negotiating partner" with the PRG and communicated a veiled threat that Americans would consider him the "obstacle" to an agreement if he did not cooperate. Thieu believed, moreover, that Hanoi's strategy was to allow Washington to withdraw without losing face, while a coalition arrangement would ensure that the United States would not renew its war against the North. In exchanges with Bunker, Thieu reopened several issues, including the wording of the prisoner release clause and procedural matters. On September 13, just two days before Kissinger's Paris meeting, Thieu rejected the American proposal for the Committee of National Reconciliation, "not because the Committee bothered him," Kissinger averred, "but because he was not ready for a ceasefire."[194]

In his memoirs Kissinger described both Thieu's and Tho's behavior as characteristic of the alleged culturally rooted Vietnamese habit of insolently tormenting their physically stronger opponents: both, he said, rejected compromise and wanted victory. Both did want victory—as had the United States until Nixon and Kissinger grudgingly came to accept unilateral withdrawal and the decent-interval solution—but their behavior was less that of being Vietnamese than of fighting for survival and nationalist aspirations. Thieu understood the dire implications of the American solution and was playing for time and to American hawks. Hanoi was seeking a compromise with the United States but understood, as Dobrynin had reported to Kissinger on August 22, that, in Kissinger's paraphrase, the American "formulations had one overriding purpose: to end the military phase of the war while defining the political outcome in general principles whose implementation Hanoi would then have to negotiate with the South Vietnamese, 'a process which might take forever.'" This was, as Kissinger knew, an accurate assessment of his intent.[195]

BUSINESSLIKE PROGRESS

With Nixon's approval, Kissinger ignored Thieu's objection and included the proposal for a Committee of National Reconciliation in the overall plan he presented to Tho on September 15. He called attention to his willingness to settle both political and military issues before a cease-fire, and to speed up the election process. Following Nixon's instructions to be tough, Kissinger chastised the North Vietnamese for recently agreeing to release three POWs to antiwar activists and allowing the PRG to publicly reiterate its seven-point plan on September 11, which demanded, among other things, that the United States stop supporting Thieu. He also warned that the time remaining to settle was short, since the president would receive a new mandate within two months.[196]

Tho tabled a new ten-point proposal, which included a compromise extension of the timetable for troop withdrawals and prisoner releases from thirty to forty-five days, called for the release of all "militarymen and civilians captured during the Vietnam War"—which differed from the U.S.-RVN proposal of releasing military prisoners and "innocent" civilians[197]—and put forward a revised proposal for a "Government of National Concord." This provisional body would supervise compliance with the agreement and the conduct of foreign policy, while Committees of National Concord would govern in the respective areas controlled by either side.[198]

Kissinger rejected Tho's political proposal but recommended that at the next meeting they try to nail down the language on agreed-upon points and principles. Tho suggested, as Kissinger phrased it, that "progress on the political question would facilitate the solution of military issues; it was no longer a precondition."[199] Kissinger thought this an unprecedented concession, which it may have been, but it may also have been an inducement to settle and withdraw. Toward the end of the meeting, Tho asked: "Do you really want to bring this to an end now?" Kissinger replied, "Yes." "Okay," Tho said, "should we do it by October 15?" After Kissinger said, "That'd be fine," Le Duc Tho came to Kissinger's side of the table, shook hands, and said, "We have finally agreed on one thing, we will end the war on October 15."[200]

Kissinger reported to Nixon that "the North Vietnamese displayed extreme eagerness to settle quickly through their most conciliatory tone to date."[201] Although he admitted that "they continue to pose unacceptable demands," he argued that they were "deeply concerned about your reelection," and know that they will have to make political concessions in order to settle before November.[202] No doubt Kissinger believed the North Vietnamese were keen on settling before the U.S. presidential election, but at the same time his upbeat assessments of North Vietnamese eagerness were intended to persuade Nixon to press on with the talks. The effect was that Kissinger and, to a lesser extent, Nixon were also operating within the electoral timetable.[203]

When Kissinger, Tho, and their delegations met again on September 26 and 27, it was at a new location, 108 avenue de Général Leclerc in Giv-sur-Yvette, fifteen miles outside of Paris in the tranquil French countryside. Because the apartment at 11 rue Darthé had become too well-known to the press, the North Vietnamese had found a lovely white-stucco villa with green shutters and an orange-tiled roof. It had once belonged to Fernand Léger, a leftist painter who had bequeathed it to the French Communist Party. The large, quiet room with green baize table where the talks took place was decorated with Léger's "tubist" paintings of the brave new world he had once envisioned, evoking an optimistic spirit with harmonies of primary colors. Kissinger did not think it dingy, and he noted as well that the foods and drinks served by his hosts had increased in quantity and improved in quality.[204]

Kissinger presented a "repackaged ten point plan" with compromise language on general principles, prisoner exchanges, cease-fire technicalities, and international controls and guarantees. Tho tabled a draft agreement and protocol, which Luu Van Loi had recently brought from the Politburo in Hanoi. In their business-like, point-by-point discussions, Tho complained that the Americans were moving too slowly. Kissinger noted, or at least told Nixon in his report, that Tho had demonstrated a "sense of urgency for an early end to the war . . . and continued eagerness for a rapid settlement," although he too had indicated to Tho that the United States desired "rapid progress." Characterizing the sessions as having "both narrowed our differences in some areas, and demonstrated how far we have to go in others," he concluded that the new North Vietnamese plan, "while still unacceptable, contains certain political provisions that might signal a possible opening."[205]

Their main differences centered on the structure of the tripartite political body to be formed, the wording of the clauses on prisoner releases, the length of the U.S.-allied troop withdrawal period, and reparations. Tho requested concrete language from the Americans on their political proposals but meanwhile presented revised proposals on the functions of the Provisional Government of National

Concord: it would still exclude Thieu, who would also have to resign after an agreement, but its role would not include foreign affairs; and it would operate on the basis on the unanimity of the parties, which was what Kissinger had wanted, since it gave Saigon a veto and would only advise and mediate between the two existing governments in the respective territories. Although the proposal was still unacceptable, Kissinger told Nixon that it was not "inconsistent" with what they wanted: an "irrelevant committee" that would provide a "face-saving cover" to a cease-fire and de facto divided government in the territories.[206] It was also not inconsistent with what the other side wanted: de jure recognition of the de facto governments.

Tho insisted that the American troop withdrawal period of three months was unnecessarily and unacceptably long, but Kissinger hinted that the problem could probably be resolved if other issues could be settled. Tho also continued to insist on prisoner-release wording that included civilian political prisoners held by Saigon—that is, members of the NLF—and that the wording additionally avoid specific reference to Indochina-wide releases, since this was a matter requiring the consent of the Cambodian and Laotian parties. But he indicated flexibility on these matters pending agreement on the South Vietnamese political question and reparations. Tho suggested that they should try to reach an agreement within a month, and he invited Kissinger to Hanoi to work out loose ends. Before departing, they agreed to meet in Giv-sur-Yvette for three days beginning on October 7 in order to work out differences and sign an agreement.[207]

Kissinger reported to Nixon that the other side was still not willing to accept a minority position in a future South Vietnamese government, which was what Thieu wanted, and that they were apparently using the prisoner issue to lever the political one.[208] To calm Thieu's fears, he instructed Bunker to inform him that no significant progress and no agreements of any kind were reached: "Disabuse Thieu once and for all of any notion that we are working toward a Vietnam ceasefire or bombing halt in return for our POWs."[209] This was not entirely true, since both sides were moving toward an agreement. Kissinger was in fact optimistic, believing that all military principles had been settled except those having to do with Cambodia, and that the North Vietnamese might make additional compromises on the political question.[210] This expectation, Kissinger wrote in *White House Years,* was reinforced by the receipt of a note from Hanoi dated September 30, in which the North Vietnamese said that they considered the forthcoming three-day meeting to be of "vital importance," that they would negotiate constructively, and that they hoped to reach an agreement according to the schedule discussed by Kissinger and Tho. There was in the message, however, an observation, which Nixon and Kissinger took as a not-so-veiled warning: if no agreement were reached, the war would be prolonged and the United States would have to accept responsibility.[211]

Nixon's thinking at this time about the timing of a settlement was almost entirely conditioned by political calculations, which included assessments of a long list of interconnected possibilities and necessities: the adverse impact of a settlement on perceptions of American global credibility; the possibility that Hanoi might publicly reveal the prospective terms of an agreement if he refused to meet the timetable; the necessity of concluding an agreement far enough in advance of the election so that it did not appear to be a political ploy, but if an agreement were not reached, to take the negotiations as close to the date of the election as possible in order not to appear to be the obstacle to a settlement; the necessity of avoiding the appearance of selling out; and the possibility that Thieu might publicly announce his opposition to American terms.[212] On September 26 Thieu had warned Bunker that he would defend his views publicly if Kissinger went beyond Saigon's terms.[213]

Hanoi's message on September 30 had been sent in response to a September 28 message from Kissinger,[214] which Kissinger did not mention in his memoirs. That was the day he had won Nixon over to his approach. Kissinger successfully argued that the administration's position was not a sellout of South Vietnam to the Communists and that a "break[through]" in the negotiations was more likely before than after the election. Without an agreement, the war would drag on, but "we couldn't maintain our current course forever." Nixon decided to seek a settlement and to send Haig to Saigon to persuade Thieu. He and Kissinger believed there was only an even chance that Thieu would cooperate; if he did not, they could go to "plan II," which would involve modifying their negotiating proposals for South Vietnamese elections and the functions of the Committee of National Reconciliation in favor of Thieu. The North Vietnamese would not likely accept these proposals, but the delay caused by having to make a counteroffer would take the talks into late October, when there would be a hiatus. Thus, it could all work out politically,[215] although it now appeared that the tail, Saigon, was wagging the dog, Washington.

When Haig met Thieu on October 2 and 4 (Thieu refused to see Haig on the third), Thieu would have none of it. On the fourth, Thieu tearfully confronted Haig and, backed by his National Security Council, defiantly rejected the American proposals. In a memo for Nixon given to Haig, he named North Vietnam as the aggressor, insisted that a divided Vietnam be put in the same category as the two Koreas and Germanys, advised a longer timetable for negotiations, and proposed that the United States and the DRV discuss military issues only; the NLF and RVN, political questions concerning South Vietnam; and the DRV and RVN, matters that concerned them.[216]

Nixon's initial reaction on the night of October 3, Washington time, was to worry that Thieu's opposition would make it appear that the prospective agreement he and Kissinger were seeking amounted to the sellout of an ally. Thieu's recalcitrance also made him pessimistic about the possibility of reaching an agreement with Hanoi, even though just hours earlier he had delivered a bold warning to Gromyko, who had come to Washington to sign the SALT Treaty. Nixon told the Soviet foreign minister that he would resort to "other methods" if Hanoi rejected the offer Kissinger would make at the forthcoming talks in Paris.[217] Kissinger tried to counter Nixon's pessimism, adamantly insisting that there was a fifty-fifty chance of reaching an agreement when he would meet with Tho over the weekend. (Haldeman thought, however, that Kissinger could afford to be optimistic because he had nothing to lose, for he would come out ahead personally whether the negotiations succeeded or blew up in Nixon's face.)[218]

By the morning of October 4, Nixon had again come around in support of the October timetable for negotiating an end to the war. He was now angry with Thieu, ordering that Bunker should have a "cold turkey" talk with him.[219] On October 6 Bunker delivered a personal letter from Nixon, in which he expressed sympathy and solidarity but nonetheless informed Thieu that Kissinger "will explore what security guarantees the other side is willing to give us as the basis for further discussions on the political point." Then he warned Thieu of the possibility of a coup, or, as he phrased it: "I would urge you to take every measure to avoid the development of an atmosphere which could lead to events similar to those which we abhorred in 1963 and which I personally opposed so vehemently in 1968." Promising to consult with Thieu, Nixon cautioned him to avoid taking his own unilateral "precautionary measures against developments arising from these talks"; with an additional warning, he pointed out that the North Vietnamese might publicly reveal the record of negotiations "for propaganda or other reasons," which implied that such revelations might reflect badly on Thieu.[220]

For Nixon, the Vietnam War had come full circle since he had criticized the coup against Diem in 1963 and cooperated with Thieu in sabotaging President Johnson's negotiating efforts in November 1968. But Nixon was trapped in the imperatives of maintaining global credibility and in South Vietnamese political realities that he had helped to create. As one White House memo phrased it, Thieu, regardless of his "popularity or lack thereof . . . , and regardless of his dictatorial tendencies," was the "symbol as well as the central point of real power in the present government." If he were ousted, his successor would be seen as a "stooge" of the United States by the South Vietnamese, while the Americans, in turn, would be perceived as wanting only "to bring the war to a quick end so they can get out and get their handful of prisoners back."[221]

13

Bangs and Whimpers: 1972–1973

He . . . made the point that he will not go out of Vietnam whimpering.
—H. R. Haldeman[1]

BREAKTHROUGH AND BREAKDOWN

On the eve of his October 8 meeting with Le Duc Tho at Giv-sur-Yvette, Kissinger was cautiously optimistic about prospects for a breakthrough.[2] He was nonetheless unprepared for what would happen. Following pleasant banter at midmorning, Tho invited Kissinger to present his case. Kissinger had little to offer that was new, but he proceeded to explain his detailed technical proposals on the modalities of the military issues, which included the cease-fire and the release of prisoners, and to propose what he called "a slight cosmetic change" in the functions of the Committee of National Reconciliation.[3] When he finished shortly after noon, Tho proposed a recess, food was served, and Tho returned to chat with Kissinger, after which he recommended another break until 4:00 P.M. in order to allow him to consult with his delegation. Kissinger and his staff took the opportunity on this clear autumn day to drive into the French countryside toward the town of Rambouillet, near which they stopped at a small lake. He and Haig, full of anxiety for the wait, talked as they briskly walked along the shore, which was lined with trees and picnickers. When they returned to the villa, Tho, with two big green folders in hand, cut to the quick, saying that if they continued to discuss technicalities and exchange counterproposals the negotiations would take many weeks. Therefore, he would present a new, simple, and realistic plan. It was, Kissinger later wrote, the most dramatic moment in his diplomatic career, for here, in a French villa bathed in the dappled light of the setting autumn sun, and amid Léger's striking abstract paintings, Tho had tabled concrete proposals that he could accept.[4]

From Kissinger's perspective the key concession made in the North Vietnamese draft was that it substituted the word "administration" for "government" in what was now proposed as an Administration of National Concord, whose functions would be to implement the signed agreements, achieve national concord, and organize general and local elections, while the two governments and their armies would remain in their respective territories. Another was an agreement in principle that war matériel could be replaced. Kissinger claimed in *White House Years* that these concessions amounted to the other side's acceptance of Nixon's essential demands. The North Vietnamese had abandoned their political formula for a coalition government and had agreed to the principle of separating military from political questions. The latter would be decided by the Vietnamese parties.[5] It was hardly so clear-cut. Except for the "cosmetic" change of wording, the DRV had previously backed away from the demand for a coalition government but had held to the principle of the legitimacy of the PRG in the territories it controlled; in addition, the United States had agreed to other provisions the DRV and NLF had wanted. The draft that Tho presented, however, allowed Kissinger to accept what was a compromise, reflecting military and political realities in the ongoing stalemate.

Wanting time to read the draft and consider its ramifications, Kissinger did not immediately agree to Tho's plan. That night, after walking the old streets of Paris on the Left and Right Banks of the Seine near Notre Dame cathedral, he decided to accept it in principle, but he would attempt "to improve it further." As his staff prepared revised wording, Kissinger informed Nixon that progress had been made but that the talks were at a sensitive state; he urged Thieu to be flexible on the political question, while at the same time advising him to seize additional territory before an agreement was signed. Kissinger, Tho, and their delegations spent the next few days in marathon sessions, debating and reworking the various points of the agreement.

To Kissinger, the most important modification agreed upon during these talks had to do with the tripartite political body, now no longer described as an "administration," which had implied governmental functions, but as an "administrative structure of reconciliation and concord," which presumably did not. It would operate on the basis of unanimity, giving Saigon a veto over its decisions. Other key provisions included a cease-fire and a bombing-mining halt twenty-four hours after the signing; the withdrawal of American and allied forces within two months; the release of prisoners within the same period; and American economic contributions to "healing of the wounds of war" in North Vietnam and throughout Indochina.

There remained, however, outstanding issues, which would trouble the process henceforth: whether civilian prisoners (NLF cadres and "criminals") would be included among those released by Saigon; and prisoner releases, cease-fires, and North Vietnamese troop withdrawals in Laos and Cambodia. Nor had there been time to discuss clauses recognizing the right of the South Vietnamese people to self-determination. Nonetheless, at the close of discussions in the very early morning of October 12, Kissinger and Tho parted with words of goodwill, in a mood Kissinger described as one "approaching euphoria."[6]

The North Vietnamese delegation reported to Hanoi that "the requirements of the politburo are basically met, but remaining are three difficult issues: weapons' replacement, political prisoners, and the International Commission [of Control and Supervision] (ICCS)."[7] Kissinger returned to Washington on October 12 to deliver his progress report.[8] He congratulated Nixon that he now had "three for three": China, the Soviet Union, and Vietnam. The Vietnam deal, he argued, was better than expected: a cease-fire, an ineffective Council of National Concord and Reconciliation, and the return of POWs. At first incredulous, Nixon queried Kissinger, who tried to "plow through his folder" and explain the agreement. But Nixon interrupted him repeatedly, philosophizing on broader issues: the collapse of the "Communist principle" of refusing economic aid; the effectiveness of the China card; the efficacy of the Linebacker bombings; and, as Haldeman put it, "his usual litany." By way of needling Kissinger, Nixon asked Haig, who had previously been skeptical about the talks, whether he was satisfied with the agreement. Haig said it was "OK" but wondered whether Thieu could be convinced. On this matter, the plan decided upon was for Kissinger to go back to Paris to "finish up" the political provisions, then fly to Saigon and convince Thieu, who would not be informed that "the whole schedule is set" for Nixon to make a public announcement on October 26 about an October 30 cease-fire. "Cranked up," Nixon told Manolo, his valet, to bring out his bottle of 1957 Lafite-Rothschild. In the past, Nixon had served only California wine to his staff.[9]

In the "cold gray light of dawn" the next day, both Nixon and Kissinger appreciated that their plans could fall apart, because the Politburo might not accept what Tho had negotiated, but especially because Thieu might not go along with what Kissinger had negotiated. Kissinger, however, was optimistic on both counts. Haldeman, who was present at the breakfast meeting, also thought Thieu would cooperate "because the settlement . . . is the best Thieu is ever going to get, and, unlike '68, when Thieu screwed Johnson, he had Nixon as an alternative. Now he has McGovern."[10] A few hours earlier, Kissinger's aide John Negroponte had informed Thuy in Paris: "The President has reviewed the agreement. He is pleased with it"—except for technical issues that needed changing.[11]

During the next two weeks, the pace of events was frenetic, the negotiations complex, the pressures intense. Rogers weighed in, complaining about not being kept fully informed and opposing any settlement that appeared to abandon Thieu, while Laird, Bunker, and Abrams advocated an agreement. Haldeman, Haig, Colson, and some of Kissinger's lower-level staffers raised questions about the hurried pace of the talks and Kissinger's approach in dealing with Thieu (which, however, was also Nixon's approach). Press leaks in Washington, Saigon, Paris, and Hanoi raised expectations and gave rise to speculation. The election timetable, which had determined the schedule for reaching a settlement, and once considered by Nixon and Kissinger as a means of levering concessions from the other side, now caught them, too, in the dilemmas of political and diplomatic advantage or disadvantage. As Kissinger put it, they walked a "tightrope." If they failed to meet the agreed schedule, Hanoi's reaction might be to publicly release the terms of the agreement, generating political pressures to sign for less satisfactory terms. Or the DRV might reverse its position and call off the talks, posing a myriad of diplomatic, strategic, and political problems in the months ahead, including congressional steps to reduce or cut off funding, a result that would likely be assured if Thieu opposed the settlement. Indeed, as the schedule began to slip, Hanoi threatened on October 20 to cancel discussions and go public. Meanwhile, members of Kissinger's staff, along with officials borrowed from the State Department, carried on talks with North Vietnamese counterparts or assisted Kissinger in his own travels and negotiations. On October 17 Kissinger met with Xuan Thuy in Paris, then flew to Saigon to confer with Thieu. Cables were drafted, encoded, and transmitted back and forth through channels from Saigon, Paris, Washington, and Hanoi, crisscrossing in transmission and confused by time-zone differences.[12]

By October 22, as Kissinger was meeting with Thieu, the United States and the DRV reached an agreement. In the previous few days, the North Vietnamese had assented to American language on the replacement of weapons and war matériel and relented on the issue of civilian prisoner releases by Saigon. Both sides had reached a compromise by which Thieu would be able to sign an agreement that did not acknowledge the government of the PRG but would, at the same time, recognize the PRG as a government. There would be two preambles and two signing ceremonies: one omitting reference to the PRG and signed by the United States, RVN, DRV, and PRG; the other preamble naming the PRG and signed by the United States and DRV on behalf of themselves and the RVN and PRG.[13] The settlement was considered complete by both parties, except for the wording of "unilateral statements" on cease-fires and prisoner releases in Laos and Cambodia. The United States wanted stronger language on the role that the DRV would play in achieving these ends, but this was not seen as an insurmountable difficulty, and Nixon had indicated as much to Hanoi on the twentieth and twenty-second.[14] Key points included the following:

- A declaration of U.S. respect for the independence, sovereignty, unity, and territorial integrity of Vietnam as recognized by the Geneva Agreements of 1954.
- A cease-fire throughout South Vietnam and an end to all American bombing, mining, and military activities in North Vietnam within twenty-four hours of the signing.
- The total withdrawal of American and allied foreign troops and military personnel within sixty days, and the discontinuance of U.S. involvement and

intervention in the internal affairs of South Vietnam; the return of captured and detained personnel of the parties, simultaneous with troop withdrawals.
- Replacement by the two South Vietnamese parties of worn-out munitions, weapons, and war matériel on a piece-by-piece basis.
- The affirmation of the right of the South Vietnamese people to self-determination, as defined by principles and steps that included the formation of an administrative structure (the National Council of National Reconciliation and Concord [NCRC]), to implement the agreements and organize general elections; internationally supervised elections; U.S. noninterference; and consultation between the two South Vietnamese parties (the RVN and PRG) to form councils at lower levels, to reduce troops and arms, and to sign an agreement on internal matters concerning South Vietnam without foreign interference within three months of a cease-fire.
- A commitment to the peaceful reunification of Vietnam.
- The formation of an international four-party military commission and a Vietnamese two-party joint military commission (JMC).
- The establishment of an international commission of control and supervision, and the convening of an international conference on Vietnam to guarantee the agreement.
- The establishment of a mutually beneficial relationship between the DRV and the United States, and U.S. agreement to make contributions to healing the wounds of war and achieving postwar reconstruction.
- Provisions regarding cease-fires and troop withdrawals in Laos and Cambodia, and noninterference among the three countries of Indochina in the affairs of one another.[15]

Both sides had made concessions, but President Thieu's view was that the United States had conceded the most by granting legal status to the PRG/NLF, agreeing to allow PAVN to remain in the South, failing to secure ironclad wording on simultaneous cease-fires in Laos and Cambodia, and accepting references to Vietnam as one nation, which vitiated America's former and his own continuing claim that the DMZ amounted to a national border between the North and South. Thieu made these points in meetings with Kissinger and his entourage in Saigon between October 18 and 23. Playing cat and mouse with Kissinger, he initially withheld his strongest objections until the climactic, angry meeting in the late afternoon of the twenty-second, when Thieu informed Kissinger that he would not sign on. On the twenty-fourth, the day after Kissinger left Saigon, Thieu announced his objections to the agreement to the South Vietnamese National Assembly.[16]

In public comments and memoirs since, Thieu and his supporters argued that the agreement was "Kissinger's agreement," rushed through by a man whose opinions about the Vietnamese were condescending, whose words were disingenuous, whose personal ambitions were grand, and who sought only a decent interval—all despite the reservations of the American president in whose name he spoke. They accused him of betraying Saigon, of accepting terms, such as unilateral troop withdrawal, which they had opposed, and of failing to keep Thieu informed. The NCRC, they claimed, was in reality a transitional coalition government, a point demonstrated by the Vietnamese-language version of the agreement, in which the phrase used to describe the council carried the implication of "governmental structure" more than of "administrative structure." This was confirmed, Thieu and his supporters said, by an interview given by Prime Minister Pham Van Dong to *Newsweek* correspondent Arnaud de Borchgrave, the text of which the journalist brought to Saigon on October 20, and in which Dong had referred to a "coalition of transition."[17]

Kissinger was indeed condescending toward Vietnamese, his words often lacking in candor, and his ambitions extending beyond Vietnam, but Nixon fully supported the terms of the agreement Kissinger presented to Thieu during these fateful few days in Saigon, as well as the decent-interval strategy. Nixon was condescending as well, advising Kissinger, for example, to play "poker" with Thieu by withholding discussions on the political question until the last—a stratagem made pointless by Thieu and Nha, who brought up the matter themselves; he had also armed his emissary with letters for Thieu urging him to cooperate, and expressing his support of Kissinger's mission and the settlement he had negotiated.[18] Nixon and Kissinger agreed that this deal was the best the United States could make.

The quarrel that emerged during this period between Nixon and Kissinger did not have to do with the terms of the agreement or with their views of or commitment to Thieu, but instead with the question of the timing of a signing. This issue, in turn, was rooted in the differing emphasis each gave to complex diplomatic and political calculations, and in the resurfacing of the personal mistrust that permeated their relationship. As the election drew near, Nixon, although pleased by the prospects of a settlement, came to feel that he did not need an agreement to win in a landslide; on the other hand, Thieu's public opposition to the settlement might cause him to lose the votes of some conservatives, eroding his majority while also calling his and America's credibility into question. Although concerned about the criticisms he reputedly received from hawks within his administration, such as Haldeman, Haig, Colson, and Moorer, he was not led by these to question the terms of the agreement itself. The October agreement was "RN's settlement," he wrote in the margin of a news summary prepared for him by his staff concerning public speculation that Kissinger was mainly responsible for the breakthrough. Besides, Haldeman and Haig, who were among the most influential insiders, regarded the agreement as the best one possible under the circumstances, even though they may not have been completely satisfied with it. Their objections seemed to center on Kissinger's accelerated timetable and his handling of Thieu, but not on the agreement itself. Nixon stood by the agreement, but he wanted to "knock down" the "code word" of "coalition government" that Thieu and others were using publicly to refer to the NCRC.[19] His concern was with the broader political impact of such characterizations and of Thieu's opposition, which he tried to gauge through quick polls of public opinion about the agreement.[20] Nixon's own visceral hawkish preference for delaying an agreement in order to use military force to lever more concessions was at this time a secondary motivation.

As Nixon had begun to vacillate in his support of the October agreement during the period of Kissinger's meetings with Thieu, Kissinger wondered whether he would be made the scapegoat for failure. Meanwhile, Nixon and Haldeman wondered whether Kissinger would either steal the public limelight by his having negotiated the settlement or put the onus of failure on Nixon should it fall through—especially as Kissinger began copying the negotiating documents for his own files. But Kissinger, too, by the time he reached Saigon, had begun to question the wisdom of proceeding according to the schedule agreed upon with Hanoi. Concerned about getting a proper agreement, and worried about Thieu's opposition, he vacillated between pushing on according to schedule or turning to a second option, their "plan II" of September—that is, "stalling" the talks with new demands in order to postpone a settlement until after the election. The dilemma he perceived was that Washington should not be seen as forcing an agreement on Saigon. But if he went to Hanoi without Saigon's blessing and then was unsuccessful there in achieving the settlement he wanted, Nixon's government would be embarrassed by having received rebuffs from both Vietnamese parties. Aware of Nixon's doubts, offended by Thieu's treatment of him, and pondering the variables, Kissinger had, by the early afternoon of October 22, decided to try for a settlement. If, however, Thieu continued to resist him, he thought it prudent to pursue the second option: postpone the scheduled meetings with Tho, extend the timetable of talks, and, if Hanoi consented, meet Tho in Paris instead of Hanoi, seeking improved terms in the agreement or even a bilateral agreement between the United States and the DRV on a cease-fire and prisoner release. On the twenty-second Nixon accepted this two-option plan, agreeing to seek a settlement on schedule but ready to postpone the talks with Hanoi and the signing of an agreement if Thieu resisted. In this case, the White House would project a public "aura of progress" up to and past the election, while it stepped up military transfers to Saigon.[21]

Thieu had been informed of the main elements of the American negotiating position over the past several months of talks—perhaps not every detail of every term, or even of the White House's preferred schedule, but he would have had to have been a fool to have remained ignorant in light of what he knew from American briefings, press leaks, and his own informants. His observations about the weaknesses of the agreement were astute, and his criticisms of the American perspective were correct; namely, that for the Nixon administration a compromise agreement was only a setback, but for his government it was a matter of life and death. His claim that the NCRC was a disguised coalition government was, however, an exaggeration, despite real or apparent discrepancies between Vietnamese- and English-language texts.

Because his remarks played into Thieu's hands and provided Nixon and Kissinger with an excuse for delaying the signing, Dong had perhaps erred in publicly commenting on the agreement, especially to a journalist who opposed it. But his words did not offer proof that the DRV and PRG viewed or wanted to tout the NCRC as a transitional "government," although it perhaps had that potential. Indeed, Dong had told de Borchgrave that his side would not attempt to transform the NCRC into a coalition regime. That would be "impossible," he said. It would imperil national concord and trigger a resumption of hostilities. Dong's real point in the interview was that Thieu would be on his own within this transitional coalition structure, while there would be two administrations, or governments, in their own zones—a fact that concerned Thieu greatly. Dong conceded to his own supporters, however, that the Thieu regime would remain in power: "It is an undeniable fact. Everyone must respect this state of affairs."[22]

While harboring resentment at his and his regime's psychological and material dependency on the United States, and encouraged in his mood by his advisers, Duc and Nha, Thieu was also panicky, not wanting, as Kissinger accurately observed, to have the "umbilical" cord of America's direct involvement cut. He was, as Kissinger commented, nearly "hysterical," fearing a coup and assassination, and demanding such "insane" terms as North Vietnamese troop withdrawals and the definition of the DMZ as a national border. He was, as all of the Americans suspected, attempting a reprise of his October surprise in 1968, this time ironically against Nixon—not to bring about his electoral defeat but to marshal political pressures that would cause Nixon to delay an agreement and win better terms.[23]

Kissinger, now fully appreciating Thieu's opposition to a settlement, had cabled Hanoi via the Paris channel in the evening of October 22, Vietnam time, to notify the North Vietnamese with Nixon's approval and in his name that the United States was canceling, or postponing, the remaining meetings previously scheduled, and that he was returning to Washington for consultations with the president. He gave several reasons: obstacles encountered in Saigon; Hanoi's impractical schedule; Dong's breach of faith in talking to de Borchgrave; unresolved technical matters; and issues associated with PAVN's presence in the South. Hanoi cabled a reply, complaining about Washington's own breach of faith and lack of seriousness. Kissinger cabled back, proposing a meeting on October 30 for the purpose of bringing about a final settlement, and he promised a complete cessation of bombing in the event an agreement were reached, even without Saigon's approval.[24]

On October 25, Vietnam time, the Politburo responded to these developments in Saigon and Washington by broadcasting over Radio Hanoi the key points of the agreement, the history of negotiations, and the agreed-upon timetable. The statement accused Nixon of negotiating in bad faith in order to "drag out the talks," deceive the public, and carry out its "scheme" to preserve Thieu's regime.[25] Anticipated by the White House, the administration viewed Hanoi's move as an attempt to generate political pressure on Nixon and Thieu.[26] Several hours later, on the twenty-sixth, Washington time, Kissinger declared at a press conference that "peace was at hand," as he tried to explain in a long-winded statement why an agreement already negotiated could not be signed. Essentially, his message was that after careful scrutiny the Nixon administration had determined that nuances, technicalities, and ambiguities had to be clarified, particularly with regard to the modalities of the cease-fire provisions. North Vietnamese insistence on an "accelerated timetable," he argued, had made their resolution impossible.[27] In consultations beforehand, Nixon had approved the substance of Kissinger's peace-at-hand statement, although he had been unaware of the precise words Kissinger would use. Stumping later in the day in Huntington, West Virginia, and Ashland, Kentucky, Nixon made similar, albeit briefer, remarks. "There has been a break-through in the negotiations," he proclaimed.[28]

Press analysis in the hours and days that followed Kissinger's conference on October 26 focused on the political implications of an agreement reached just before the presidential election and Kissinger's claim that, despite the breakdown of talks, peace was at hand. Had the agreement and Kissinger's statement been designed to manipulate the election? Would McGovern's argument that such an agreement could have been negotiated four years earlier sway more voters to support his bid for the presidency and erode Nixon's majority? The consensus was that Nixon's prospects had been enhanced.[29] These speculations were not misplaced. Nixinger negotiating strategy during the previous two years had been highly conditioned by electoral concerns.

In his memoirs, however, Nixon tried to distance himself from Kissinger's comments. He acknowledged that the promise of imminent peace appeared to give credence to McGovern's charges that the October agreement was a political ploy, but he emphasized the diplomatic issues, alleging that the peace-at-hand phrase eroded his bargaining leverage with Hanoi and Saigon.[30] Kissinger's remark no doubt encouraged Thieu's recalcitrance, but it is unlikely that it had any influence on Hanoi one way or the other. In any case, Nixon's concern at the time was not with the diplomatic bargaining leverage allegedly lost but with the political leverage he would lose at home by continuing the bombing or halting it, and he ordered a quick poll to help him decide which course he should take in the future.[31] In recommending the postponement-of-talks option to Nixon in mid-October, Kissinger had proposed a complete cessation of the bombing of the North in order to demonstrate Washington's good faith, but Nixon, with his complex memories and opinions of Johnson's 1968 bombing halt, had refused, preferring to continue the limited bombing halt, which had begun with Kissinger's arrival in Saigon and applied only to the territory north of the twentieth parallel.[32]

Perhaps, as Nixon claimed in RN, he really believed Kissinger had "gone further than I would have,"[33] but his real quarrel with Kissinger's press conference was that it had captured the headlines and was "getting the play." Hanoi, by going public with the agreement, and Kissinger, by being the one to respond first, had taken him, the president, "out of it." Moreover, Kissinger had not made the "anti-McGovern points" he had wanted him to; namely, that his approach was peace with honor, whereas McGovern's was "peace by surrender." Haldeman, however, consoled Nixon with the thought that, on balance, all was to the good, for the coverage of Kissinger and Vietnam had taken Watergate off the front pages.[34]

If Washington suspected nefarious propaganda motives behind Hanoi's public announcement of the October agreement, Hanoi at the same time suspected that Washington's postponement of talks was calculated. It was designed, they believed, to make it possible for Nixon and Kissinger to speak of progress in negotiations before the election, while delaying the signing until after the election; they could use the delay as an excuse to continue bombing as a means of levering new concessions, while prolonging the war in order to strengthen Saigon with additional shipments of weapons and matériel.[35]

Hanoi almost had it right. Inherent in the second option that Kissinger had outlined on October 22, and which Nixon had accepted, was their intention to use a postponement to win additional concessions in renewed negotiations while stepping up arms transfers to Saigon. Operation Enhance, designed to furnish Saigon with ground and air equipment sufficient to meet expected levels of enemy activity in November and December, had been under way since late August. By mid-September, however, it had become clear to the White House and CINCPAC that the force levels provided would not be adequate. After October 26, Enhance was supplanted by Enhance Plus. It aimed at providing in the period before a cease-fire agreement was signed (whenever that might be) all of the tanks, artillery, helicopters, and fighter aircraft projected for delivery in the 1973 military aid program.[36] Meanwhile, Linebacker bombing would continue, albeit below the twentieth parallel,[37] as CINCPAC, "under directives from higher authority," developed a strategy to conduct a "total air warfare campaign" in Southeast Asia. Its goals would be to "isolate the North Vietnamese heartland" with all-weather attacks in the Hanoi and Haiphong areas, interdict supplies moving south through the DRV, and support the battlefields in South Vietnam, Laos, and Cambodia.[38]

Washington's decision in late October to postpone an agreement, however, had not been caused by a deliberate plan to agree to a settlement before the presidential election, then postpone signing, then escalate the bombing. During the latest round of negotiations, Nixon and Kissinger had preferred the first option: a settlement that would be signed prior to the election. Regarding bombing, Kissinger had recommended closing down Linebacker altogether. Although Nixon had refused, preferring the continuance of the scaled-down operation, he was more or less satisfied that the months-long bombing campaign had already demonstrated his true grit, and he was not then committed to a dramatic escalation. It was Thieu's opposition to the agreement and the domestic and global political ramifications accompanying it that had led Nixon and Kissinger to turn to the second option: the postponement of negotiations and an agreement. However, since 1969 a climactic, madman bombing operation resembling the Duck Hook plan had been one of Nixon's favorite options in his long-term strategy to end the war. Now it became a real possibility as CINCPAC planned a total air campaign, and Nixon and Kissinger pondered how they could solve their political dilemmas, cut their losses, and maximize their gains.

DILEMMAS

After his landslide victory on November 7, Nixon was eager to put Vietnam behind him.[39] There were other global problems to solve, domestic programs to push forward, and scores to settle with his domestic opponents. But he faced nagging dilemmas. If the war dragged on, there would be continued domestic turmoil and a budgetary crisis. Both Democrats and Republicans in Congress understood that Thieu was all that stood in the way of consummating the settlement reached in October, and Nixon knew that he could expect open rebellion from both sides of the aisle unless he could persuade the recalcitrant South Vietnamese president to cooperate. But if Thieu resisted and Nixon proceeded without his compliance, there would be the appearance of having betrayed a friend, which would displease hawks within the policy-making establishment and among his constituents in the body politic; moreover, allies and clients of the United States might question the credibility of America's commitments under a Nixon administration. The strategy chosen was to seek revisions in the October agreement that would appease Thieu and American hawks and also enable him to justify to the American people his last-minute rejection of a settlement he had already negotiated. The carrot of promising Thieu revised terms would be combined with the stick of threatening to sever American support of his regime. The alternate strategy, which Nixon seriously entertained but in the end never followed, was to negotiate a bilateral agreement with the DRV for a cease-fire, followed by an American troop withdrawal and a concurrent exchange of prisoners within sixty days. It was similar to the plan McGovern had advocated, except that the administration would try to convince Congress to continue military aid to Saigon.[40] American credibility might perhaps be damaged, but Congress could be blamed if aid was denied or the Saigon regime disintegrated.

With the South Vietnamese president's political leverage somewhat diminished by the American president's impressive reelection, and reports from Bunker that Thieu seemed in a more cooperative mood,[41] Nixon immediately set out to bring him on board. General Haig, who was seen as more likely to influence General Thieu than Doctor Kissinger, arrived in Saigon on November 10, bearing a letter from President Nixon, dated November 8.

Nixon's letter combined bluntness with tact, determination with conciliation. He reminded Thieu of the benefits of Enhance Plus and his promise of retaliating against the North if it violated the agreement, and he offered to meet with Thieu after an agreement was signed to symbolize their continuing alliance. But he also told Thieu that he was disappointed in the emerging split in their relationship and disturbed by Thieu's "self-defeating" public "distortions" of the agreement, which, he insisted, was "sound" and "excellent," containing, as it did, significant concessions by the other side. In an attempt to address Thieu's objections to the agreement, however, he promised to seek revisions during the forthcoming negotiations with Hanoi. On the political issues, he would substitute the words "Indochinese states" in favor of the existing reference to "three Indochinese countries," and he would propose changing the Vietnamese words used by the DRV for the NCRC—*co quan hanh chanh*, or "administrative organ," in place of *co cau chinh-quyen*, or "administrative or governmental structure." He would also strive to weaken the functions of the NCRC. On military issues, he would call for the unilateral withdrawal of some North Vietnamese divisions, as well as mutual demobilizations of RVNAF and PLAF troops, returning the latter to their homes, which would more adversely affect the PLAF than the RVNAF. He would seek language requiring "respect" for the DMZ—a military and political issue. And he would seek as many as possible of the other "technical" changes Thieu wanted. But he advised Thieu that he should be under no "illusion" that the United States would go beyond these revisions. He was resolved to settle, and he warned that Thieu's current and "dangerous" course would only bring about "disaster" in the U.S.-RVN alliance. Thieu should declare that he had achieved military victory and then work with the United States for political victory in the postagreement environment.[42] Haig pointed out during the meeting that although Nixon had won a landslide victory, the elections had also produced a more dovish Congress, which meant that Nixon could not hold its support if Thieu did not cooperate. Unless Thieu relented, Nixon would be forced to "take brutal action" against Saigon.[43]

Taken aback but still defiant, Thieu drafted his own letter to Nixon, which he gave to Haig on the following day. In it he demanded that North Vietnamese forces be made to withdraw completely from South Vietnam, and he opposed elections until they left. He wanted the words *co quan hanh-chanh dac-trach bau cu* ("administrative organ in charge of elections") used for the NCRC, and he also listed other requirements: Communist nations should be excluded from serving on the ICCS; and the postagreement international conference should be delayed until after a cease-fire came about in Laos and Cambodia.[44]

Nixon responded on November 14, rejecting most of Thieu's additional changes, especially those regarding NVA troops and the ICCS, but gave Thieu his "absolute assurance" that he would "take swift and severe retaliatory action" if the other side did not abide by the terms of the agreement. Thieu reiterated his position on the eighteenth, and Nixon responded on the same date, pointing out that he was "not prepared to scuttle the agreement or to go along with an accumulation of proposals." Nor did he think it necessary to meet in Washington with a personal emissary from Thieu.[45]

The U.S.-DRV negotiations, postponed in late October, were about to begin. The usual diplomatic sparring had followed Kissinger's October 25 cable to Hanoi, in which he had proposed another meeting on the thirtieth. In several exchanges of notes, each side put forward alternate dates, until on November 9 Washington accepted Hanoi's proposal for November 20.[46] There would be three more rounds of talks at different locations in Paris, the first from November 20 to 25, the second, December 4 to 13, and the third and final, from January 1 to 8, 1973. In between the first and second rounds, Nixon would edge ever closer to a decision to launch Linebacker II, and when the operation was concluded, both sides would return to the table to conclude the Paris Agreement on Ending the War and Restoring Peace in Vietnam.

At the first meeting on November 20, Kissinger, in order to satisfy Thieu, presented a list of what he characterized in his memoirs as Thieu's sixty-nine "preposterous" changes in the October agreement.[47] Among the significant revisions, Kissinger demanded references to the DMZ that would have implied that PAVN's presence in the South was illegal and would have restricted movement of personnel from North to South. He called for a partial withdrawal of PAVN troops and tied the release of civilian NLF detainees to these withdrawals. He proposed changes in the functions and naming of the NCRC that would have vitiated its status and role, including the elimination of the third segment, which would have reduced it to a two-party, PRG-RVN negotiating body. He demanded that all specific mention of the PRG be eliminated from the document and insisted that the provision for the establishment of administrative councils at lower levels be eliminated. He proposed changes in the postagreement elections, canceling those for the Constituent Assembly, and insisted that cease-fires in Laos and Cambodia more nearly coincide with the cease-fire in Vietnam. Perhaps to sweeten this bitter pill, he offered to discuss the details of reconstruction aid for North Vietnam.[48]

Tho commented that the talks would go on for another four years if all of the changes were being presented as ultimatums. He affirmed four principles of the DRV position that Kissinger had challenged with his proposals: acknowledgment of the PRG as the other South Vietnamese government; the clear definition of areas controlled by each side; the right of the Vietnamese to national self-determination; and no NVA withdrawals from the South. After questioning Kissinger on the manner in which he planned to accomplish certain provisions, such as the cease-fires in Vietnam, Laos, and Cambodia, the return of prisoners, and the organization of the control commissions, he requested another meeting the next day.[49] Later, Haig, William Porter, and William Sullivan met with South Vietnamese officials, who were now to be kept informed of the negotiating sessions, and explained the steps Kissinger had taken to "meet GVN requirements." In this and subsequent meetings with the South Vietnamese, Haig emphasized that both he and Kissinger spoke for the president.[50]

Kissinger admitted in his memoirs that the presentation of Thieu's list was a "major tactical mistake." Tho returned on November 21 labeling the changes as substantive: they were aimed, he said, at violating the fundamental national rights of the Vietnamese people, denying the existence in South Vietnam of two administrations, two armies, and three political forces, and dividing Vietnam forever. He accepted some revisions regarding the timing of elections, respect for the sovereignty of Indochinese countries and of occupied territories, and other more minor issues. He also agreed to a revised provision on respect for the DMZ, although he insisted that the DMZ be defined as provisional, as it had been in the Geneva Agreement of 1954. But he rejected the majority of Kissinger's substantive proposals and presented his own counterrevisions. He withdrew his previous concession on prisoners, in which NLF civilian detainees were to be released separately from American POWs; he added a demand for the withdrawal of civilian American advisers; and he insisted on the North Vietnamese translation of "administrative structure" (*co cau chinh-quyen*) to describe the NCRC. Having reported to Nixon on the previous day that the negotiations were unmanageable, Kissinger now reported that the DRV delegation was getting tougher on substance.[51]

No doubt Kissinger had thought most of Thieu's revisions to be preposterous, for he returned on November 22 and dropped many of them. But he continued to insist on "improvements"; that is, the list of essential changes that Nixon had detailed in his letter to Thieu on November 8 concerning the use of the South Vietnamese phrase for describing the NCRC, the dropping of references to "three Indochinese countries," and the withdrawal of some North Vietnamese troops. He also repeated demands for an earlier cease-fire in Laos and Cambodia (even though he knew that the DRV did not fully control the fighting in those countries), the convening of the ICCS at the time of cease-fire, and the replacement of "destroyed" and "used up" weapons—in addition to the replacement of "worn out" weapons. But he postponed a renewal of the American demand for a strengthened DMZ.[52] Nixon claimed in *RN* that Kissinger had made it clear that all of the issues were negotiable.[53] Perhaps he had, but "negotiable" still meant that the American side expected some concessions. The DRV side, however, had clearly adopted the same tactic of presenting "negotiable" demands. Tho agreed to broaden the categories of weapons that could be replaced, but he stood by his positions on political language, PAVN withdrawals, civilian prisoner releases, and U.S. civilian technician withdrawals.[54]

After receiving Kissinger's report, Nixon cabled him to say that he was disappointed in the progress of negotiations and with the tone of the North Vietnamese. He instructed him to discontinue the talks unless the other side showed reasonableness. Kissinger should allude to the earlier Linebacker bombings and warn that the president would again take "strong" military steps if necessary— "whatever action . . . necessary to protect the United States's interest."[55]

Kissinger read Nixon's cable to the DRV delegation at the next meeting on November 23[56] and then proceeded to negotiate. At lunch, in between their six-hour discussions, the North Vietnamese served a "lavish" meal of roast beef and chicken in honor of the American Thanksgiving Day.[57] Kissinger reported to Nixon, however, that the talks that day were "difficult." Although the DRV delegation had shown flexibility on the DMZ question, conceded minor political changes, and agreed to nonwritten commitments on a Laotian-Cambodian cease-fire and the relocation of some of their forces in Military Region 1, they were, he wrote, adhering to their positions on American civilian advisers and NLF prisoners. They would make an "appropriate response" on troop relocation only if the United States met their demands on prisoners and political issues.[58]

Kissinger then described "two basic options" and a third subsidiary option. Option one was to break off the talks and resume bombing north of the twentieth parallel (which was what Nixon had suggested in his cable of November 22). Option two was to return to the October provisions on NLF prisoners, negotiate minor changes in the political provisions, and insist on the mutual demobilization of RVN and PLAF forces. Option three, which neither Kissinger nor Nixon mentioned in their memoirs, was to exchange the release of NLF political prisoners for the withdrawal of "substantial" numbers of North Vietnamese troops.[59]

Nixon claimed in *RN* that Kissinger favored option one. Although Kissinger denied this,[60] his reports suggest a belligerent tone. He used the adjective "intransigent" to describe the North Vietnamese stance, when it appears from the documents and his own memoir account that they had shown flexibility. True, the North Vietnamese had not been willing to concede basic military and political issues that they, and Thieu, considered substantive, but they seem to have tried to help Nixon partially solve his problem with Thieu by accepting some revisions.[61] Kissinger could have made or suggested trade-offs to Nixon that both men would later make in the final round of negotiations; for example, dropping demands for North Vietnamese troop withdrawals, moderating their demands concerning the DMZ, and acknowledging the legitimacy of the PRG. Indeed, the final January 1973 settlement would resemble the understandings reached on Thanksgiving Day 1972. But Kissinger's tough-sounding report may have been influenced by personal calculations. He had recently received in Paris a cable from his president in Washington ordering him to take a tough stance. Kissinger also knew that Nixon was irritated with him for currying press favor and was engaged in the reshuffling of his cabinet, with the matter of Kissinger's versus Rogers's fate yet undecided. On another occasion, Kissinger might have reported progress in the negotiations; instead, he described a condition of stalemate and recommended a tough stance.

Nixon's behavior was also odd. After receiving Kissinger's November 23 cable, he reversed himself, dashing off one of his own to Kissinger shortly before 2:00 A.M. on November 24, in which he acknowledged that the October agreement "would have been in our interest." Although it should be improved to take account of Thieu's conditions, there was no choice but to accept the October principles. Thieu, he advised, should be informed that if an agreement was not reached, he could not hold congressional support, and all military and economic aid would be cut off. The resumption of bombing against the North (Kissinger's "option one"), Nixon wrote, was "not a viable option." Haldeman and Richard T. Kennedy, Kissinger's aide, were alarmed that he would want to proceed regardless of what

Saigon thought.[62] At 6:14 A.M. Nixon sent another cable, reversing himself again and instructing Kissinger to call off the talks on the pretext of having to consult with his president if the only alternative was an agreement worse than that of October 8. He would then order a "massive bombing strike" against North Vietnam. It was a "high-risk option," he said, but he would take his political "lumps" and end the war with "honor." Even though public opinion could not be mobilized in support of such a step, the election was past and no longer a factor in his decisions. The action would be "right," repaying the sacrifices "so many" have made.[63]

In *RN* Nixon explained his alternating instructions as swift-thinking responses to Kissinger's reports and rational reassessments of his own hurried commands. But there seems to have been something else influencing his actions, something deeply emotional and psychological. It resembled his fabled passive-aggressive moodiness—in this case, passive in confronting Thieu, aggressive in dealing with the North Vietnamese at long distance. He was "ambivalent"—recognizing home-front political realities on the one hand but refusing to accept them on the other. His erratic instructions, each of which seemed contrary to what Kissinger had recommended, may also have been influenced by his annoyance with his emissary, whom he resented, but on whom he so depended. During discussions in the White House in the last ten days of November, Nixon complained that Kissinger had allegedly appointed to positions persons who had supported McGovern; that he was resisting cost-cutting reductions in staff; that the cabinet thought him difficult to deal with; that he was conveying the wrong public image by smiling in press photographs of him and Tho; that he was too open with the press; that he might be chosen as *Time*'s "Man of the Year" and must be brought "back to earth" and prevented from giving an interview to *Time*.

Nixon was still stewing about Kissinger's egotistical interview with journalist Oriana Fallaci in early November. In it Kissinger had been more critical of Thieu than of Tho and had boasted that the reason for his public popularity was that he acted alone, in the manner of a cowboy, thus leaving the impression that Nixon had little to do with his own administration's foreign policy successes. Moreover, with his and Haldeman's long-standing assessment of Kissinger's temperament reinforced by Haig, Nixon, ironically, felt that it was Kissinger who was "paranoid," who was always on an "up-and-down cycle." He had been "down" in Paris in October and was down again now. He had "screwed up," committing the administration in October to an accelerated schedule of negotiations, which had caused the difficulties they were now having with the North and South Vietnamese. He needed a "long vacation," and "we should take him out" of office by mid-1973. In the meantime, he needed to be brought "under control" and shown "who's boss."[64]

In *White House Years* Kissinger described his behavior in the negotiations as an attempt to steer a middle course between Nixon's strange mood, his contradictory orders, and their three options. Thus, on the one hand, he ignored Nixon's instruction to break off the talks and met with Tho on November 24 to discuss where they stood on the issues.[65] On the other hand, at this meeting he read Nixon's November 22 military warning "in detail," which, in a likely effort to appease Nixon, Kissinger reported, had "sobered him [Tho] considerably."[66] He also tabled protocols on the ICCS, the DMZ, and the definition of the areas occupied by the two Vietnamese parties that would have the effect of strengthening the ICCS, weakening PAVN, and reducing the territory recognized as controlled by the PRG,[67] and he tied the release of NLF prisoners and the solution of political issues to PAVN troop withdrawals and simultaneous cease-fires throughout Indochina.[68] Kissinger reported to Nixon that Tho pointed out that his side had, over the course of the negotiations, "emasculated their political demands, agreed to leave Thieu in office, met our demands with respect to the ceasefire in Laos, and had now even agreed to the de facto removal of some troops from" Military Region 1. The North Vietnamese had been flexible, whereas, by Kissinger's own account, the Americans had not. Kissinger concluded: "We have obtained a good deal more" over the October agreement, and "the agreement is already sound."[69] Nevertheless, during an "electric" meeting with Tho on November 25, Kissinger seized the "initiative" against the North Vietnamese by accusing them of leaking a "slanted" story about the talks to the *Washington Post*. Then, declaring that this round of negotiations had reached an impasse on the issues and threatening "a resumption of military activity," he demanded a week's recess, which Tho "grudgingly" granted. Kissinger took this step even though Nixon had earlier reversed himself once more and urged him to "continue talking if there is any chance for movement."[70]

Why did he break off the negotiations? Why not compromise on the remaining issues, then sign an agreement? There were two reasons, Kissinger told Nixon: "First, the still intransigent position of . . . Thieu and his closest advisors; and second, the rigidity of the North Vietnamese on the remaining issue—their demand that South Vietnamese civilian prisoners be released." As a result, he continued, "we need a few more changes primarily for our dealings with Saigon." The DRV delegation had held firm on the substance of the political issues and the presence of PAVN in the South, using their demands for American civilian-adviser withdrawals and the freeing of NLF civilians, which they tied to American POW releases, as leverage against U.S.-RVN demands for further revisions of political and military questions. Kissinger noted, however, that we "have regained the tactical initiative" and given ourselves "negotiating potential." The recess "disarms Thieu who probably expected" that the talks would be finished in this round, and it "shows Hanoi we cannot be stampeded."[71] Had Nixon and Kissinger been willing to break with Thieu, it would have been possible, as Kissinger remarked almost a month later, to have reached an agreement in November.[72]

Nixon's problem, which Kissinger was trying to solve, was not so much with the North Vietnamese as with his friends. The problem was rooted in at least three specific political facts, all of which were related to broader issues of domestic politics and global policy. The first was congressional opposition. On November 24 Nixon had informed "leading" Democratic and Republican supporters in the Senate, including Goldwater, Ford, and Stennis, about the status of the negotiations in order to gauge their views on the war. They were "unanimous" and "vehement," as he phrased it in a message for Kissinger that day, "in stating . . . that if Saigon is the only roadblock for reaching agreement on this basis, they will personally lead the fight when the new Congress reconvenes on January 3 to cut off all military and economic assistance to Saigon." Kissinger should tell the South Vietnamese that it was "time to fish or cut bait." Nixon complained that the door to continuing the war had been "slammed shut hard and fast by the longtime supporters of the hardline in Vietnam," and Congress was prepared to pull the "purse strings."[73] A second difficult political fact was that pockets of the high military command, including members of the JCS and former MACV commander Westmoreland, were not convinced of the necessity of accepting the current diplomatic solution.[74] A third but most important fact was Saigon's continuing recalcitrance. Kissinger had read Nixon's memo about congressional sentiment to Thieu's special assistant, Nguyen Phu Duc, and his entourage, after meeting with Tho on the twenty-fourth, but the South Vietnamese had been unmoved. Kissinger had not followed Nixon's instruction to issue an ultimatum to the South Vietnamese, and he had defended his refusal with the argument that it would cause a "total public blowup" with Saigon.[75] He was passing the buck. Duc was now to travel to Washington at Thieu's insistence to meet with Nixon on November 29.[76] Nixon would have to face him down.

In the Oval Office meeting with Duc, Nixon defended the October settlement and its November revisions, reminded him of congressional sentiment, promised military retaliation against Hanoi if it broke an agreement, and offered to meet with Thieu. But he warned that Saigon's opposition to a negotiated solution would endanger the U.S.-RVN alliance and could lead to a Communist takeover, for which Saigon would have to share responsibility.[77] Nixon, however, was not as "brutal" as he had intended to be. Haldeman thought, in fact, that he "had softened a little bit" during the discussion, with the effect that the South Vietnamese later informed the White House they would fight on alone and that Washington should make its own settlement with Hanoi. Nixon decided Saigon was playing "chicken."[78] Indeed, in the next few weeks, Thieu would bombard Bunker, the White House, and the American and the South Vietnamese public with complaints about the October agreement. When Kissinger resumed talks with Tho in early December, Thieu would successfully bluff Washington by putting forward a proposal that excluded the United States: a Saigon-Hanoi cease-fire, Vietnamese prisoner releases, and talks between the Vietnamese parties.[79]

Nixon was more successful at his meeting with Laird and the Joint Chiefs the next day. Although Saigon was unhappy with the agreement, he argued, it met all of the conditions he had announced in May. In any case, words on paper were meaningless. It was the reality of power that mattered, and on this score, the agreement was supported by "interlocking" understandings with other powers and by his own determination to resort to military force in the future, if necessary. Westmoreland's insistence on the withdrawal of all North Vietnamese troops and on satisfying all of Thieu's political demands could not be achieved, he pointed out. "The main problem facing the United States is the provision of necessary funds" for both domestic and foreign affairs. He had barely been able to stay "one step ahead of the sheriff, just missing fund cutoffs" for Vietnam. Besides, the October agreement is sound, and it has been improved. "If the American people knew all the details of what has been offered, they would never continue to support a prolongation of the war." The military should express pride in its achievement, or else it would have to face criticism that the war had been useless.[80]

Nixon had rallied his troops, or at least some of the most important of them—the JCS. But before advancing toward his goal of "peace with honor" in Vietnam, he had to cover his flanks, Hanoi and Saigon, and he must also gauge the status of his rear, public opinion. Meanwhile, his relationship with his diplomatic "general," Kissinger, was fraught with resentment and mistrust.

As Nixon saw them, there were two main options—basically the same ones he had had before him since at least August. He could accept the agreement, trading American withdrawals and the termination of Linebacker for a cease-fire, the return of American POWs, and a supervised election for a coalition government (which he contrasted to the "imposition" of a coalition government). But Thieu was adamant in opposing any settlement that did not include the delegitimization of the PRG and the withdrawal of northern forces from the South, which meant that Nixon would have to defy Thieu, either by persuading him to accept the settlement he negotiated or by settling bilaterally with Hanoi. Or he could continue military operations until PAVN left South Vietnam. This course, however, was unacceptable to Congress—unless he could rally public opinion behind it. To discover what the public would accept, on December 2 he ordered a broad-based poll regarding his alternative choices, but his instincts told him that neither the public nor the Congress could be mobilized in support of an extension of the war. Nor was he up to the effort it would require.[81]

Between November 24 and 29, Nixon had expressed his intention to flout Thieu and settle bilaterally, if necessary, preferably by early December. Kissinger had advised against breaking with Thieu. He preferred negotiating Thieu's concurrence, taking a firm, or "brutal," tact but also offering the inducement of additional revisions in the draft agreement. Although Kissinger may actually have favored a settlement with Hanoi that resembled the November 23 understandings, he may have had to recommend the negotiation of additional concessions by Hanoi in order to persuade Nixon to accept his diplomatic strategy. To obtain these necessary revisions, Kissinger argued, Hanoi should be given an ultimatum, which of course meant threatening escalated bombing. Thus armed, Washington could "undertake the necessary massive effort" to turn Saigon around.[82]

This was the strategy Nixon decided upon on December 1,[83] in part because Kissinger had proposed it. Even though their relationship was uneasy, Nixon was, for the time being, stuck with Kissinger as his negotiator.[84] Moreover, Kissinger was popular with the public and the press, and he could harm Nixon politically if there were a serious falling out. In any case, Nixon was constitutionally disinclined to confront either his close aides, such as Kissinger, or his Saigon allies face-to-face, although he was considering putting indirect pressure on Thieu by way of withholding additional economic aid.[85] There were also hard strategic realities behind the acceptance of Kissinger's approach. A bilateral agreement was problematic, for Nixon still might have to resort to escalated bombing to achieve it, and a break with Thieu could harm America's and his own credibility, weakening his leverage with domestic and foreign opponents during the second term.

Kissinger's motives were equally complex—a mixture of psychological processes, bureaucratic tactics, political calculation, and global strategic principles. Although a proponent of the diplomacy of threat, he also advocated the deployment of firmness and force against Hanoi because it served to ingratiate him with Nixon. It had always been safer to be tough than soft, but especially now when his position in the administration was more precarious than at anytime before, with Haig waiting in the wings to take his place. But Kissinger's raison d'être was as Nixon's negotiator, and although he favored the combination of military threat and skillful negotiation, he leaned toward a solution that would be achieved in diplomacy. Like Nixon, he had strategic motives, which were tied up with his role and responsibilities, as he saw them, as chief diplomat for the most powerful nation in the world, whose credibility as a counterrevolutionary power had to be maintained. Thus, he advised against a break with Thieu.

The intricate, strange relationship between the two men had reached a dangerous crossroads. Kissinger's approach might take more time than allowed, time Nixon did not feel he possessed. He calculated that the agreement would have to be signed by December 8 in order to settle everything before Congress reconvened. Ever the salesman, Kissinger told Nixon there was a seventy-thirty chance he could conclude the negotiations on December 5, one day after the talks resumed. But Kissinger was in reality less optimistic, believing his position as a negotiator was "less than brilliant," considering his poor relationship with Nixon[86] and his instructions on how and what he should negotiate. The instructions were that he should insist on the revisions Hanoi had rejected in the previous round of talks. If the DRV conceded these, he should proceed without delay to a signing, regardless of Saigon. If the DRV delegation was "intransigent," the negotiations should be suspended, which meant that Nixon would turn to his military option.[87]

Kissinger had, or at least believed he had, little room in which to maneuver. If he had to insist on substantive revisions, Hanoi's negotiators might not be cooperative, and Saigon would have all the more reason to stand fast. Kissinger felt caught between "two implacable Vietnamese sides who specialized in tormenting each other."[88] He knew that if the Paris talks broke down the press would question his abilities as a negotiator. He probably also felt that Nixon held a gun to his back, for if the negotiations failed, Nixon might then blame him for having complicated the already serious dilemma he believed he faced. Haldeman paraphrased Nixon's description of his own dilemma: "He will have to convince the North Vietnamese that if we don't get an agreement we're going to stay in, and he has to convince the South Vietnamese that if we don't get an agreement we're going to get out."[89] If Kissinger did not succeed in Paris, he, Nixon, would have to get tough with Thieu, risking a break with him after all, but by this time it would appear that he had caved in to North Vietnamese diplomats. To solve the credibility problem this caused, and to gain the release of the POWs in time to satisfy the public and POW families, he would have to escalate the bombing. Yet, while he had often expressed his determination to embark on this course—indeed, he had often forcefully indicated his preference for it—he would still have to face up to the decision.

IMPASSE

The DRV delegation entered the negotiations that resumed in Paris on December 4 with the goal of protecting substantive principles in the October agreement against American demands for revisions that went beyond the November 23 amendments. Their negotiating strategy was to begin by insisting on the October draft, offering to withdraw their subsequent amendments if the American side would do the same. If this opening gambit was unsuccessful, they would, by way of levering the United States back to the November understandings, progressively cancel minor concessions they had made in November, then reopen issues that had been settled in October. The strategy effectively countered the "tactical initiative" and "negotiating potential" Kissinger thought he had gained in November, but in frustrating Kissinger's expectations, it would contribute to the impasse that developed.[90]

On December 4 and 6, Kissinger stuck by American demands, whereupon Tho began to withdraw several minor concessions made in November.[91] On the seventh, Tho offered to advance the timing of cease-fires in Laos and Cambodia and dropped his side's request that South Vietnamese civilian prisoners be released as part of an agreement. But he rejected four other points Kissinger wanted: the deletion of the phrase "administrative stucture" in references to the NCRC; the inclusion of references to "South" and "North" Vietnam; a three-month target date for the demobilization of forces; the withdrawal of North Vietnamese troops; and language that would strengthen the status of the DMZ. He also insisted on including mention of the PRG in the document.[92]

Even though Kissinger remarked in his memoirs that December 7 marked the beginning of a "real deadlock,"[93] hard bargaining followed in subsequent meetings from the eighth through the thirteenth. At the meeting on December 9, the Americans agreed to restore mention of the PRG in the preamble of the agreement; to restore Article 1, which pledged United States respect for the independence, sovereignty, unity, and territorial integrity of Vietnam; and to restore Article 4, which pledged United States nonintervention in the affairs of South Vietnam. In return, the North Vietnamese agreed to what Kissinger reported to Nixon were the essential requirements of the United States: deletion of the phrase "administrative structure" in describing the NCRC; the inclusion of a sentence obligating North and South Vietnam to respect the DMZ; "greatly strengthened provisions on Laos and Cambodia"; the deletion of references to *three* Indochinese countries; an accelerated timetable for a cease-fire in Laos; and concessions on military weapons and equipment replacement provisions. Kissinger, however, was unhappy that Tho had not agreed to his proposed restrictions to movement across the DMZ. The sixty-one-year-old Tho, suffering from high blood pressure and fatigue, had pleaded that some of his colleagues in Hanoi were opposed to additional concessions regarding the DMZ.

On December 12, having at last received new instructions from Hanoi, Tho offered a compromise, accepting the American wording Kissinger had proposed several days before calling for negotiations on the modalities of movement across the DMZ. Kissinger now rejected the wording, standing pat on his more recent proposal that the negotiations include the issue of civilian movement across the line. In return for a concession toward American preferences on wording and placement of the clause in the final document, Tho asked for an American concession whereby the PRG would be mentioned in the text, and requested that there be a four-party signing. Although the details of several protocols concerning the implementation of the overall agreement were still unfinished, by December 13 the only serious issue remaining to be settled between the two sides was the status of the DMZ versus the mention of the PRG in the text or a four-party signing. The DMZ issue "was not," as Kissinger, Nixon, and Haig told one another, "a substantive matter of concern, but rather a problem intimately related to our ability to bring Thieu aboard." When the final meeting on December 13 failed to resolve the matter, the talks recessed.[94]

The negotiations had clearly reached an impasse, but several questions have bedeviled American and Western analyses of the causes of the deadlock and of Nixon's next move—Operation Linebacker II. Did Tho break off the talks? Had the North Vietnamese been, as Kissinger claimed, "intransigent"—intent on stalling the negotiations in order to exploit divisions between Washington and Saigon, aiming for a better deal than the October/November agreements? Was Washington therefore justified in launching Linebacker II in order to force them back to the table and win Hanoi's concurrence on what Nixon and Kissinger asserted were their reasonable revisions in the draft agreement? Did Linebacker II succeed in these aims?

The record does not sustain the Nixinger argument that the other side discontinued the talks. On the contrary, since December 4, Nixon and Kissinger had been debating whether, when, and how to "break off" the negotiations but make it appear that the other side was responsible.[95] On December 12 Tho had informed Kissinger that he would have to return to Hanoi to consult with his government, citing disagreement within the Politburo concerning the changes demanded by the United States. On the thirteenth Kissinger recommended a recess until after Christmas. In his farewell to Kissinger, Tho suggested further exchanges between Hanoi and Washington and expressed confidence that "peace was near" but that it would be two weeks before he could return.[96] If the Politburo had more nefarious motives than consultations with its delegation, they cannot be verified. The DRV was no doubt aware of friction in the Washington-Saigon alliance, as well as of congressional impatience with Thieu and the war. But these realities were more specters in the nightmares of Nixon and Kissinger than visions in the dreams of the Politburo, which had to worry about its Soviet and Chinese allies and its own constituencies in the Central Committee, in the villages of North Vietnam, and at the battlefront throughout Indochina. What can be verified is that the Politburo was unwilling to concede substantive principles for which it had fought for two decades, which had not been lost on the battlefield, and which had been agreed to by Washington in October. Nixon and Kissinger had appreciated this fact since at least August and had said as much to one another and to Thieu in private conversations. There had been a harder edge to the tone used by the DRV delegation during the December round, but this was true for the U.S. delegation as well, and the DRV mood can be accounted for in part or whole by its desire to resist American threats of escalated bombing and counter Thieu's public denunciations of the draft agreement.

We cannot know with certainty what the Politburo's strategy or motives were, and we have only spotty evidence of what specific proposals their delegation presented in Paris. We have a much better record of what Washington said, but, as for motives, historians are left with the unhappy task of pychoanalyzing two men, Nixon and Kissinger, who were pychoanalyzing one another and the Vietnamese as the talks were taking place.

From the outset Kissinger had described to Nixon the DRV's strategy as one of "playing chicken," referred to Tho and his entourage as intransigent, and in the next several days escalated his characterizations of them to "insolent," "ludicrous," and "tawdry, filthy shits."[97] Immediately after his first meeting on December 4, he had presented Nixon with two stark options: accept the terms of the October agreement without changes, or risk breaking off the talks. The first was unacceptable, he said, but in recommending the second, he identified two tactics: settle on the basis of the November understandings, which, he ventured, neither Hanoi nor Saigon was likely to accept; or stay with the current plan and push for substantive revisions that Thieu would find acceptable. This would involve boiling down "our remaining requests to two: the correct Vietnamese translation for 'administrative structure' and one of our three formulations designed to establish the principle that North Vietnamese troops do not have the legal right to intervene indefinitely in South Vietnam." All other revisions would be dropped in exchange for the North Vietnamese dropping their changes regarding the release of civilian prisoners and the withdrawal of U.S. civilian personnel. This second tactic within option two was the one he favored. If the DRV delegation refused to cooperate in this approach, then Washington could break off the talks and step up military measures in order to obtain a strictly military, bilateral settlement with Hanoi—a U.S. withdrawal and bombing cessation in exchange for POWs, but without a cease-fire in South Vietnam. This could be achieved within six months. In this case, however, Kissinger argued that Nixon should go public to explain the breakdown of negotiations and rally the American people in support of bombing and a bilateral agreement. Meanwhile, having failed to achieve an agreement by the deadline promised, December 5, he offered to resign.[98]

From this point on the president considered Kissinger his "weak link." Nixon thought he "overdramatized" the importance of North Vietnamese moods in relation to the realities of negotiation. Kissinger's all-or-nothing choices pointed in the direction of escalating the air war, which Nixon did not initially want to do unless the negotiating string had been fully played out. Paraphrasing Nixon's remarks, Haldeman recorded: "K always prefers the big action play, against all odds and winning it. The P says, I do, too, if you win it. . . . K wants, subconsciously, . . . to flee . . . from the complex" dilemmas of the negotiations. Things were never as dark as they seemed, Nixon commented, but Kissinger had a "suicidal complex," and an analysis of his psychology should be placed in the presidential files. Kissinger was tired and "emotional," and his mood affected his judgment. He must be made to realize that the North Vietnamese were observing his behavior, that they believed he possessed more "authority" than he actually did, and that they thought he was boxed in because he had promised the American people that peace was at hand. His offer to resign was foolish and "out of order," Nixon remarked, the product of a mood that was caused by his perception of failed negotiations, his worries about his rivalry with Rogers, and the embarrassment he felt from the Fallaci interview. Because Nixon believed Kissinger was fearful that the press would criticize him for a breakdown in talks, he thought Kissinger was blaming North Vietnam for the impasse, while trying to get him to take the "heat" by rallying the people.[99]

For his part, Kissinger thought the instructions he received from Nixon from December 5 to 12 were erratic and contradictory: "The President wanted me to stay as long as there was any hope of a settlement; to return for consultations if I judged the deadlock to be unbreakable; to recess but not to adjourn the talks; and to brief the press if he decided to resume bombing."[100]

On December 4 Nixon instructed Kissinger to continue negotiating along the lines of option two, but he expressed a willingness to order the immediate B-52 bombing of the Hanoi-Haiphong complex if Kissinger deemed it necessary before his next meeting with Tho. He was also prepared to break off the talks if the North Vietnamese were unmoved by America's stepped-up military actions. Rejecting Kissinger's recommendation that he should address the American people about a resort to bombing, he accepted Kissinger's suggestion that the North Vietnamese should be portrayed as devious and intransigent and therefore responsible for a breakdown in the negotiations. On December 5 Nixon told Kissinger to try to bluff the North Vietnamese by arguing that, because of their intransigence, the president will be able to get funds from Congress to continue American military activity and to support Saigon (although he in fact believed congressional cooperation was unlikely). On December 6, however, he advised Kissinger that "we should not paint ourselves into a corner" in the talks but always leave "a crack of the door open for further discussion." Although prepared to turn to "massively increased bombing . . . for the limited purpose of getting our prisoners back," he doubted that it was "worth the cost in terms of what it will do to our relations with the Congress, to our support in the country, domestically, and to our relations with the Chinese and the Russians." By December 10, although pleased by Kissinger's success in winning concessions, he told Kissinger to "hold tough on the DMZ issue," stalling until December 12, while they waited to see if Moscow would help to soften Hanoi's stance. The delay also created time for Haig and Agnew to travel to Saigon to work on Thieu. When he met with Tho on the twelfth, Kissinger should assume a "tough posture," but if the DRV delegation resisted, then Kissinger should compromise and even "cave [in] completely," with hopes that Thieu could still be brought around. "With or without the additional concessions on the DMZ we must settle." On December 12, however, he reversed himself: Tho should be told that "the United States can not nor will it make more concessions."[101]

Kissinger attributed Nixon's erratic instructions to his moodiness, his political concerns, the conflicting advice of aides, and his attempt to shift responsibility. Although perhaps less perturbed than Kissinger, Nixon, if not moody, was indeed ill at ease. To begin with, he was, as Haldeman phrased it, "going into quite a lot of psychological reaction to K," and he was also quite concerned about political factors. Neither Kissinger's six-month bombing option nor his recommendation for a presidential speech, Nixon thought, was "rational." A national address would associate him with failure, and although polls indicated that the citizenry, other than the press and the "Left," would support a pause in the talks and tolerate escalated bombing, he suspected that they "don't want to hear" about a "breakdown" in the negotiations and a prolonged war during the Christmas season. Moreover, families expecting an imminent release of American POWs would have to be asked to endure; Congress would not support the bombing for long; and, meanwhile, Thieu's government might collapse. The choice he must make, he realized, was one of pressuring either Hanoi or Saigon. The first was preferable, but how could he accomplish it without appearing responsible for breaking off the talks? Yet if he rejected the hard military option and Kissinger succeeded in reaching a compromise with Tho, Kissinger might return home to criticize him for not being tough enough.

Besides engaging in his own agonizing appraisals, Nixon was receiving conflicting advice from aides. Secretary Laird, his deputy, Kenneth Rush, and Admiral Moorer argued that he had only "one viable, realistic choice": sign the agreement now, avoid military action, press for the return of POWs and the accounting of MIAs, put the onus on North Vietnam, and react with force only if there were violations of the agreement. Haig favored taking the military approach now, even if it prolonged the war. Ehrlichman disagreed and recommended diplomatic compromise, if for no other reason than the burdensome monetary cost. Richard Kennedy argued against a break with Thieu, warning that it would mean the "waste" of a decade of making war, destroy "our relations in the world," and have a detrimental impact on the "American psyche." Connally suggested that Nixon should blame Kissinger for the breakdown in talks.[102]

After meeting with the North Vietnamese on December 13, Kissinger reported that they had been "insolent" and "ludicrous" in having introduced half a dozen modifications on technical issues. He told Nixon that he had accused them of insincerity and delaying tactics. The negotiations were therefore deadlocked, leaving him and Nixon with their old dilemma: "Hanoi is almost disdainful of us because we have no effective leverage left, while Saigon in its shortsighted devices to sabotage the agreement knocks out from under us our few remaining props." Kissinger outlined two options. The first was to "turn hard on Hanoi and increase pressure enormously through bombing and other means . . . [and] concurrently, . . . try to line up Saigon." The second was to hold back on bombing and resume talks in January, which, however, would still require an effort to persuade Saigon. If the North Vietnamese "once again stonewalled in January," Washington would place primary blame on them but would also fault Saigon for the collapse of negotiations. Bombing would be expanded against the North as the United States sought a bilateral agreement with Hanoi on the military issues.[103]

Nixon quickly decided on the first option. What remained to be resolved was the nature of the air campaign, final planning for which had begun as early as December 4. Kissinger had first recommended an escalation of bombing below the twentieth parallel, but Nixon, supported by Haig, believed that "if we want to step it up, we've got to make a major move and go all out." He considered Kissinger's suggestion another sign of "insubordination." Very soon, Kissinger came around, supporting the reseeding of mines and "massive" B-52 strikes in the Hanoi-Haiphong area in Operation Linebacker II.[104]

This cataclysmic but brief campaign was the sword that would cut Nixon's Gordian knot—his dilemmas of politics, credibility, and timing, all compounded by his strange relationship with Kissinger and their mutual frustrations with the North and South Vietnamese. It was the product of the "intransigence" of Hanoi only insofar as the Politburo had requested a recess in the talks and, although making concessions, had resisted substantive revisions in the October and November drafts that Nixon and Kissinger had demanded in order to avoid a break with Thieu. The recess was now seen by the White House as a way of avoiding the appearance of a collapse in talks with North Vietnam and giving the Nixon administration time to prepare the bombing campaign in the far north—while simultaneously making a major effort to win Thieu's acceptance of an agreement.[105]

On December 17, the day Linebacker II began, Haig met with Thieu bearing another letter from Nixon, whose relevant passage read: "Haig's mission now represents my final effort to point out to you the necessity for joint action and to convey my irrevocable intention to proceed, preferably with your cooperation but, if necessary, alone."[106] In its purpose, Linebacker II was aimed less at punishing Hanoi into making concessions and more at providing Saigon with incentives to cooperate. By hurting North Vietnam's war-making ability in a relatively brief but massive campaign, it would give Thieu a lease on life; in its boldness, it would signal Saigon—and Hanoi—that Washington might intervene with airpower in the civil war that lay ahead. But Linebacker II was also motivated by psychological processes and political considerations: as a forceful, symbolic closure to the American war, it would fulfil the promise Nixon had made to himself that he would not go out of Vietnam whimpering; and it had the potential of convincing hawks that he had been tough, compelling the enemy to accept an agreement that was in reality an ambiguous compromise, but which he touted as a clear-cut victory for his skillful management of war and diplomacy.

LINEBACKER II

On Thursday, December 14, Nixon issued the order for Linebacker II to begin with the reseeding of mines on Sunday and the bombing of Hanoi and Haiphong on Monday.[107] There was a four-day delay in the bombing because he wanted to avoid starting it on Saturday, when Tho would be in Beijing, and on Sunday, when he, Nixon, would be attending church services. Pleased with himself for deciding to bomb now rather than in January, he was, however, concerned about holding up Kissinger's "dauber." Yet Kissinger was "happy . . . , because we're in control of things again, instead of being in the position of the rabbit," trapped between "two [Vietnamese] snakes." He agreed with Nixon that his best course was "brutal unpredictability."[108] At dinner on the night of December 18, as the bombs were falling, Nixon scolded Admiral Moorer: "I don't want any more of this crap about the fact that we couldn't hit this target or that one. This is your chance to use military power to win this war, and if you don't, I'll consider you responsible."[109] He explained that "the Russians and Chinese might think they were dealing with a madman and so had better force North Vietnam into a settlement before the world was consumed by a larger war."[110]

For twelve days from December 18 to 29, with a stand-down on Christmas Day, the U.S. Air Force, Navy, and Marine Corps flew 3,420 bombing and support sorties into the heart of the DRV. They attacked railroad yards, supply and petroleum depots, radio-communications installations, electrical power and broadcast stations, bridges, port facilities, transshipment points, airfields, and SAM sites. B-52s dropped 75 percent of the total bomb tonnage, and their sorties in northern Vietnam during this brief period amounted to almost half as many as in the previous six months of Linebacker I. According to the air force, the objectives of the two operations differed substantially. Linebacker I was carried out mainly as an interdiction campaign directed at the DRV's supply system; Linebacker II aimed at applying "maximum pressure through destruction of major target complexes in the vicinity of Hanoi and Haiphong" in order to inflict severe damage to the DRV's "logistic and war supporting capability" and make a "psychological impact" on North Vietnamese "morale." Only 12 percent of the sorties were against strictly military targets—airfields and SAMs.[111]

This "December blitz" or "Christmas bombing," as the press dubbed it, produced heavy "collateral" damage, even though civilians and nonmilitary targets were not deliberately carpet bombed. In Hanoi, for example, the An Duong, Bach Mai, Ben Chuang Duong, Ben Pha Den, and Kham Thien residential districts were heavily damaged; the Bach Mai hospital was destroyed; eight foreign embassies were damaged; and 2,196 civilians were killed and 1,577 wounded. Casualties would have been higher had there been more people in the city, but half of Hanoi's population had been evacuated in April after the start of Linebacker I. Although an indeterminate number of evacuees had returned in late October after Kissinger's peace-at-hand statement, nonessential persons had been relocated again beginning on December 3, when the last round of talks began in Paris. As the Nixon administration hoped, there was terror on the ground from the sheer intensity of bombing, from uncertainty about where the bombers would strike from one day to the next, and with many believing that Nixon was mad to be killing civilians. The F-111s were the most frightening, for in contrast to the B-52s, there was no advanced warning of their arrival. Yet the inconveniences of evacuation, the loss of friends and loved ones, and the destruction of property roused many to anger, engendering a defiant spirit of resistance.[112] The air force bombing survey of April 1973 concluded that while the population "suffered a decline in morale . . . , there was no evidence indicating that the North Vietnamese leadership could not maintain control of the situation."[113]

On the other side of the ledger, during what the Vietnamese called the "twelve days of Dienbienphu in the air," SAMs, MiG interceptors, antiaircraft guns, and operational accidents took a heavy toll of American pilots and their planes. By U.S. counts, 121 crewmen were killed or became POWs or MIAs; thirteen tactical aircraft and fifteen B-52s were shot down, with reports of some crew members refusing to fly. B-52 losses amounted to 12 percent of the 129 big bombers deployed in the raids, exceeding the predictions of the air force.[114]

Press reaction to Linebacker II was strongly critical. At a time of profound public war-weariness, Nixon was engaged in the most intensive bombing of the long, tragic conflict. It was being carried out mostly by techno-sky-warriors flying the very planes that most symbolized indiscriminate, capital-intensive warfare—all-weather, high-flying, instrument-guided, electronic-countermeasure-protected B-52 Stratofortresses. James Reston referred to it as "war by tantrum." Anthony Lewis accused Nixon of acting like a "maddened tyrant." Joseph Kraft called the operation an act of "senseless terror." Other prominent press commentators, including David Brinkley, Harry Reasoner, Tom Wicker, Hugh Sidey, James Wechsler, and Eric Sevareid, as well as hinterland editorialists, characterized Nixon as a bully who saw all life as a battle. They complained of his ruthlessness, deception, insecurity, paranoia, insensitivity, brutality, truculence, cynicism, unscrupulousness, and willful use of arbitrary power. Reasoner accused him of breaking Kissinger's promise of peace; Brinkley thought the bombing unnecessary and called on Nixon to simply get out of Vietnam; the *Los Angeles Times* believed the means were disproportionate to the ends sought; the *St. Louis Post-Dispatch* argued that the "shameful," "monstrous deed" of bombing was "Thieu's final price."[115] Their message to the public was that Linebacker II was an unnecessary, irrational act of fury representing the belligerence Nixon felt toward all of his real and perceived enemies, foreign and domestic. If it had any rational purpose, it was to bribe Thieu into accepting the treaty.

To be seen by the North Vietnamese as the "mad bomber" was exactly what Nixon wanted, but it was not the image he wanted to project to American voters.[116] Confirming his concern, his public approval rating dropped 11 percentage points.[117]

Besides journalists and editorialists, doubters and critics included members of Congress, European allies, neutral governments, the Soviet Union, and China. North Vietnam's allies publicly condemned the bombings, but behind the scenes they advised Hanoi to settle. China apparently reinforced this advice by threatening to "obstruct" the delivery of additional, future supplies to the DRV, but the Soviets assured Hanoi that it would pressure the United States to cease bombing and return to the table as soon as possible. To both allies, the North Vietnamese affirmed their intention to resist America's ultimatums and military pressures, but to continue the negotiations and seek an agreement when the bombing stopped. They must show tenacity, they insisted, otherwise Nixon would be encouraged in his "illusions."[118]

THE PARIS AGREEMENT

Nixon and Kissinger were similarly determined to exhibit tenacity, although Nixon suffered periods of doubt and dread as Thieu continued to resist his entreaties and B-52 losses mounted.[119] Extending carrots with sticks, on December 18, the day the bombing began, the administration had informed the Politburo that it was prepared to settle the substantive issues on the basis of the November understandings, with one reservation and one concession: the phrase "administrative structure" in reference to the NCRC should be dropped, but the signing procedure could follow the proposal made by the DRV in October and December.[120] With neither side wanting to break off the negotiations, but Hanoi insisting on the cessation of bombing, and Washington insisting on the resumption of talks by January 3, there followed the usual diplomatic sparring about when to return to the table. On December 26 the Politburo agreed to resume technical talks on the protocols on January 2, and Washington agreed to stop the bombing north of the twentieth parallel on December 29.[121] The Kissinger-Tho meetings began on January 8, achieving a breakthrough on the major questions the next day, Nixon's birthday. Kissinger phoned the White House with the good news and extended his birthday wishes. It was "the best birthday present," he had had " in sixty years," Nixon commented. Later, Kissinger cabled his report on the talks and suggested that the breakthrough had been made possible by Nixon's "fierce posture."[122]

The talks concluded on January 13 with a settlement that retained the principles of the October agreement, included several of the November understandings, and reflected December and January compromises. As the DRV had always insisted, PAVN remained in the South, and the DMZ was designated as a provisional demarcation line, but with the word "civilian" added to the document concerning future negotiations between the Vietnamese parties on the modalities of movement across the line. (In practice, however, PAVN continued to control the DMZ.) The NCRC retained its functions, but the term "administrative structure" was omitted in references to it. Among minor changes, the size of the ICCS was increased in line with U.S. wishes but below levels previously demanded by the United States. The two-party Vietnamese JMC retained its original power to determine who controlled areas of South Vietnam, but how this was to be done would be negotiated within the JMC. Mention of the PRG in the document was eliminated, and one of the references to the RVN was dropped; the phrase "South Vietnamese parties" was used to refer to the PRG and RVN in the text. But the PRG was specifically recognized in the preamble and in the signing procedure, which followed Hanoi's plan. The DRV dropped its demand for the simultaneous release of Vietnamese civilian detainees and accepted the October formulation, by which these releases were to be "resolved" by the RVN and PRG. But the definition of "civilian detainees" followed the DRV's wishes; that is, it would include persons detained for political activities. The United States dropped its demand for more or less simultaneous cease-fires in Laos and Cambodia, but the DRV agreed to a shortened timetable and to the phrase "Indochinese countries" in place of "*three* Indochinese countries." (In a separate, secret proposal one month later, the United States offered postwar reconstruction aid to North Vietnam.)[123]

Although Nixon pressed Thieu to sign the treaty, Thieu continued to resist through the period of negotiations. Encouraged by the bombing, Thieu at first persisted in demanding PAVN withdrawals and other significant changes in the agreement. Nixon wrote more letters, considered using the "dragon lady," Mme Chennault, to lobby Thieu, and sent Haig to Saigon for another meeting with Thieu on January 16. By this time, Kissinger and Tho had reached a settlement, and Thieu had begun to relent, but he continued to object to specific minor provisions in the agreement until the last moment. He finally submitted on January 21, the day after Nixon's inauguration, and two days before Kissinger and Tho initialed the agreement in Paris.[124] On January 27, 1973, eight years after the massive American combat buildup in South Vietnam had begun and twenty-eight years after America had become involved in the Indochina struggle, the United States, DRV, RVN, and PRG signed the Paris Agreement on Ending the War and Restoring Peace in Vietnam.[125]

NIXON'S VIETNAM MYTHS

In January 1973 the mystical sense of history and drama Nixon had sought since the beginning of his presidency crystallized into his myth of the Vietnam War. Irritated by press criticism of his mad bombings and charges that he had "pulled Kissinger back from peace," Nixon had begun as early as December 19 to urge Haldeman to organize an aggressive, public relations counteroffensive.[126] The group Haldeman assembled on Nixon's instructions to "peddle" his Vietnam "line" and "build up" the president[127] was divided between "hardliners," such as Buchanan and Colson, and "moderates," such as Harlow, Klein, Safire, and Scali. Buchanan and Colson wanted "to drive the critics to their knees, to humiliate them publicly." Led by Safire, the moderates felt the time was right for reconciliation "if we approached our opponents with more olive branches and fewer hammers." But the cards were stacked against the moderates because Nixon favored the attack strategy.[128] The historical moment must be seized, he and the hardliners believed, in order to assure for Nixon "for all time the coveted title[s] of Peacemaker" and "peace bringer." Unless the administration acted to "mark the moment as its own," the liberal press and antiwar intellectuals would attempt to "speak for the American conscience," downplaying Nixon's peacemaking role and treating the agreement as the "long overdue end of a morally repugnant war." In order to rightfully "ascend the paths of glory" after having "stayed the course for so long," the administration would have to establish the interpretive context.[129]

The strategy that emerged was to build on the emerging "revisionist school" of history, which defended the morality and purpose of the war, "take advantage of the current crest" of public emotion about the return of the POWs, and launch an "all out effort" to "get a lot of people out selling our line" with a few "key points to emphasize."[130] There were four key points. First, with the support of the Silent Majority and his friends in Congress, the president had the courage, toughness, and wisdom to make hard decisions and see them through—despite unprecedented attacks from critics in Congress and the media. Second, no quarter must be given to his opponents, especially those on the Hill. By their criticisms and their resolutions against the war, it was they who had prolonged it. Their plan for peace, which would have simply withdrawn American troops from Vietnam in exchange for POWs, was nothing more than a plan for "cutting and running," the equivalent of abject, dishonorable defeat and surrender. It also would have led to a bloodbath of continued war, in which the 50 million long-suffering people of Indochina would have had to fight on without the United States. The critics were wrong, therefore, and Nixon was right. Third, "our" peace with a cease-fire was not a "bug out" but a peace with honor that achieved the major goals of the war; that is, it not only got our POWs back but also won "peace with independence for South Vietnam and peace for the people of Southeast Asia." It assured the right of the South Vietnamese to determine their own future without the Communists imposing a government on them. Furthermore, despite the unpopularity of the war and the mistakes made by previous administrations in fighting it, the president's handling of it preserved the credibility of the U.S. commitment, "which is essential not only to our national self-respect but to our continuing role as a force for peace in the world." Fourth, certain misconceptions must be shot down. It was not possible to settle on a peace in December; the peace agreement signed in January could not have been had earlier; the January agreement was an improvement over the October peace agreement; the NCRC is *not* a "coalition" government; the Thieu government has not been abandoned; there was never any division between the president and Kissinger. And with respect to the December 1972 bombing:

> The President never engaged in "terror bombing" or "carpet bombing" of Hanoi-Haiphong; the United States struck only targets of military value; and what the December bombing accomplished was to break the deadlock in negotiations, to bring about final agreement on the DMZ, the return of U.S. prisoners, the sovereignty of the people of South Vietnam. Despite the howling, the bombing broke the impasse and brought the peace that had eluded us for four years. . . . Only by the strong action that we took in December were we able to convince the enemy that the enemy [*sic*] should settle and not take the risk of waiting for the Congress to give them even more than they were willing to settle for with us.[131]

Enveloping the Paris Agreement in his mystique of personal achievement, Nixon obscured its factual content and left many Americans unprepared for Thieu's defeat in April 1975. The agreement was in reality a compromise settlement—a compromise, however, that left North Vietnamese troops in South Vietnam and acknowledged the de facto and de jure legitimacy of the Provisional Revolutionary Government, with both sides fully aware that a civil war in new guise would ensue for the future of Vietnam. Nixon and Kissinger knew, as Kissinger's national security staff had concluded in October 1972, that, after an agreement, the two Vietnamese parties would be left "to slug it out between themselves in a context of reduced main force vigilance but continued political struggle of intensive brutality." Although the South Vietnamese army had become more effective,

North Vietnamese and Viet Cong forces had recouped many of their base areas in the South, "from which it would be more difficult to dislodge them than in the 1969–1970 period; and they are patient." American troop withdrawals would have the effect of undermining Saigon's psychological confidence and resolve. Even before the withdrawal of American forces, Kissinger's staff observed in October that "there are hardly any of us around anymore to prod the ARVN and GVN to high levels of performance."[132] What Nixon had won in his four years of war was a decent interval. It was not a decent interval for Thieu, whose government would be driven from power within two years, but it was a long enough interval to permit Nixon and Kissinger to claim that they had provided Thieu with a chance to survive—if, however, Congress would continue supporting him, if only the American people possessed the will to continue bombing.

In their postwar statements and books, Nixon and Kissinger expanded on the points Nixon's public relations staff had developed in January 1973. They maintained that their Vietnam policies had been guided by their grand global strategy, the outlines of which they had conceived before the inauguration of their administration, but which they conceded was not fully formulated in 1969 or even 1970. Its descriptors were "détente," "triangular diplomacy," "linkage," and the "Nixon Doctrine," and its product was ultimately a "structure of peace." Each claimed more or less credit for the strategic plan or the intricate tactics of achieving it.

The record suggests that Nixon was more the strategist and Kissinger more the tactician. It also shows that the Soviets were major players in the process of détente and the Chinese in rapprochement and triangulation, not only imposing obstacles to Nixon's and Kissinger's global intent but also taking creative initiatives of their own. The record also suggests that the Nixinger grand design was not well conceived in the beginning, was not fully realized in the end, and was as much, if not more, a product of reaction, improvisation, bureaucratic infighting, and political and economic realities as it was of proactive, farsighted planning and wise, coolheaded statesmanship. The crises with which Nixon and Kissinger dealt in Vietnam or the world were often partly of their own making or fostered additional crises. The détente they sought with the Soviet Union also may have been postponed or even subverted by the strategy they chose—linking military agreements to political concessions, seeking to maintain America's nuclear advantage, playing the China card, and continuing to enlarge American global influence while attempting to confine Soviet influence to Eastern Europe. The interlocking guarantees that Nixon told the Joint Chiefs he had worked out regarding Vietnam did not hold, and the Soviets and Chinese continued to supply North Vietnam after the Paris Agreement, enabling them to achieve final victory in South Vietnam in April 1975.

In any case, at the core of Nixon's strategy for dealing with the Vietnam problem was not triangular diplomacy but the madman theory—the reflection of Nixon's "black id" and the strategic lessons he had imbibed during his prior experiences in the cold war. Kissinger, although a proponent of negotiation, had provided the indispensable support Nixon needed within the government for carrying out his madman strategy. Nonetheless, the Cambodian bombing and invasion, the bombing of Laos and North Vietnam, the numerous threats to the Soviets and North Vietnamese, and Linebacker I and II—all of which were attempts to terrorize the other side into compliance—failed to lever the substantive concessions from Hanoi and the PRG that Nixon and Kissinger had sought. Typically, they blamed Laird, Rogers, Congress, public opinion, the press, intellectuals, and the antiwar movement for influencing them to moderate their actions. Yet it was Nixon and Kissinger who had decided to temporize the strategy of brutal unpredictability. They had not shown the "courage" necessary to defy the will of others. Only in retrospect could they make their hypothetical claims: that *if* they had resorted to massive bombing earlier than they did, the Paris Agreement could have been negotiated before 1973; that *if* the Watergate scandal had not hobbled Nixon, he could have resumed bombing in 1973 or 1974 and forced Hanoi's acquiescence in Thieu's survival; that *if* Congress had provided sufficient postagreement aid to Saigon and also allowed President Gerald Ford to unleash American airpower, Thieu could have turned back the North Vietnamese Spring Offensive of 1975 and survived as president of an independent South Vietnam. But before the Christmastime bombings, and before the Watergate investigation had gained its full momentum, Nixon had concluded that direct American involvement in the war must end, because of Congress, because of public opinion, and because he was weary of it. Because of his faith in mad strategies and triangular diplomacy, however, he had unnecessarily prolonged the war, with all of the baneful consequences of death, destruction, and division for Vietnam and America that this brought about. Ironically, in prosecuting the war for as long as he did, Nixon contributed to the erosion of that domestic consensus which had previously supported military intervention abroad. Practicing the politics of division, he brought down his own government in the Watergate scandal. Blaming others for America's failure in Vietnam, he contributed to the bitterness that haunted American politics and the confusion of purpose and meaning that plagued American foreign policy in the years ahead.

Notes

ABBREVIATIONS IN NOTES

AFHRA: Air Force Historical Research Agency, Maxwell Air Force Base, Alabama

CWIHP Bulletin: Cold War International History Project Bulletin

DSM-IV: Diagnostic and Statistical Manual of Mental Disorders (Fourth Edition), DSM-IV

FRUS: Foreign Relations of the United States

GPO: U.S. Government Printing Office

HRHD: The Haldeman Diaries: Inside the Nixon White House, the Complete Multimedia Edition

MDLC: Manuscript Division, Library of Congress

MHS: Massachusetts Historical Society, Boston, Massachusetts

NPM: Nixon Presidential Materials, National Archives and Records Administration, College Park, Maryland

ANF: Alpha Name Files

CF: Central Files

[CF]: Confidential Files

CO: Countries

FO: Foreign Affairs

HAKASF: Henry A. Kissinger Administrative and Staff Files

HAKOF: Henry A. Kissinger Office Files

HAKTF: Henry A. Kissinger trip files

HAKTO: Kissinger to

HRH: H. R. Haldeman

NSC: National Security Council Files

POF: President's Office File

PPF: President's Personal File

PT/M: Paris Talks/Meetings

SF: Subject Files

SF—LCF: Staff Files—Lake Chron Files

SMOF: Staff Member and Office Files

TOHAK: To Kissinger

WHCF: White House Central Files

WH/NSC: POW/MIA: White House National Security Council Files: POWs and MIAs

WHSF: White House Special Files

NSSM: National Security Study Memorandum

NYT: New York Times

VDRN: Vietnam Documents and Research Notes

WHY: White House Years

1. DRAGONS OF MYTH AND MIND

1. *The Haldeman Diaries: Inside the Nixon White House, the Complete Multimedia Edition* [compact disc] (Santa Monica, Calif.: Sony Electronic Publishing, 1994), January 17, 1972. Haldeman often quoted Nixon, but most often he paraphrased him. Quotation marks in my text around citations from *The Haldeman Diaries* indicate either a direct quote or a paraphrase. This is true of Haldeman's references to statements by other figures, such as Kissinger. The CD-ROM version of Haldeman's "diaries" contains the complete text. The book version (New York: Putnam, 1994) does not. Haldeman drew on his handwritten notes of White House meetings to prepare the published editions of his diary (WHSF: SMOF, HRH, NPM). In many cases, the daily entries in the published diary correspond to those in the handwritten notes, but in other cases entries in one do not appear in the other.

2. King Lear, in William Shakespeare, *The Tragedy of King Lear: The Folio Text*, 1.1.121.

3. *HRHD*, February 2 and July 1, 1970. Along with "mystique," the words "myth" and "mystery" were also common in Nixon's lexicon. For the history of Anglo-American ideas regarding executive mystique, see Forrest McDonald, *The American Presidency: An Intellectual History* (Lawrence: University Press of Kansas, 1994).

4. Richard Nixon, *Leaders* (New York: Simon and Schuster, 1982), 330–331. See also Nixon's comments on myth in *HRHD*, April 14, July 10, and September 15, 1971.

5. *HRHD*, July 21, 1969. See also May 18, August 25, 28, 29, September 5 and 8, 1969, and January 7, 1973.

6. Ibid., December 31, 1969. For Nixon's views on his relationship with the press, see, e.g., Memo, Nixon to Haldeman, January 6, 1970, WHSF: PPF, NPM.

7. Memo, January 19, 1973, folder: Action Memos, box 112, WHSF: ANF, HRH, NPM; Key Points to Be Made with Respect to Vietnam Agreement, n.d. [ca. January 1973], folder: Vietnam Peace Reaction, box 178, ibid.; Marginal revisions by Nixon in memo from Haldeman to Kissinger [originally from Nixon to Haldeman], January 25, 1973, folder: Vietnam 2, ibid.; Thoughts Regarding the Peace Announcement, n.d. [ca. January 1973], ibid.; HRHD, January 23 and 27, 1973, 572–573. See also, Herbert Klein, Making It Perfectly Clear (New York: Doubleday, 1980), 387–390.

8. The tale of Nixon's planned post-Watergate comeback is summarized by Michael R. Beschloss in "How Nixon Came in from the Cold," Vanity Fair, June 1992, 114–119, 148–152; and by Marvin Kalb in The Nixon Memo: Political Respectability, Russia, and the Peace (Chicago: University of Chicago Press, 1994), chap. 2. See also, Richard Nixon, In the Arena: A Memoir of Victory, Defeat, and Renewal (New York: Simon and Schuster, 1990), 44–48; and Jonathan Aitken, Nixon: A Life (Washington, D.C.: Regnery Publishing, 1993), 542–543. Nixon had long felt more confident talking about foreign policy than about domestic policy and had long before established a reputation for possessing expertise in foreign affairs. David Frost, "I Gave Them a Sword": Behind the Scenes of the Nixon Interviews (New York: William Morrow, 1978), 172–174, made several fine observations about Nixon's appeal to foreigners, especially foreign leaders.

9. Nixon summarized this argument in In the Arena, chap. 37.

10. RN: The Memoirs of Richard Nixon (1978; New York: Simon and Schuster, 1990), 1084.

11. Alan Brinkley, "Means of Descent," New Republic, October 1, 1990, 28.

12. As late as mid-1996, over 70 percent of the Nixon Presidential Materials staff was tied up in matters having to do with court litigation and the processing of Watergate tapes, which delayed the processing and declassification of documents on other subjects. Karl Weissenbach (acting director of NPM), "Beyond Elvis and the Tapes: Research at the Nixon Presidential Materials Project," The Record: News from the National Archives and Records Administration 2 (May 1996): 11. See also Joan Hoff, "Researchers' Nightmare: Study-- ing the Nixon Presidency," Presidential Studies Quarterly 26 (Winter 1996): 250–266.

13. Nixon repeated his version of history in speeches and interviews. Monica Crowley, who served as a foreign policy assistant to Nixon in his retirement from 1990 to 1994, and who admired the former president, quotes and paraphrases conversations she had with him in Nixon Off the Record (New York: Random House, 1996). Scattered throughout the book are Nixon's views on leaders and leadership, politics and foreign policy, and the crises and battles of his career.

14. In the Arena, 48.

15. Richard Nixon, No More Vietnams (New York: Arbor House, 1985), 21.

16. Richard J. Whalen, Catch the Falling Flag: A Republican's Challenge to His Party (Boston: Houghton Mifflin, 1972), 69–70.

17. Nixon, Leaders, 327.

18. Richard Nixon, Six Crises (New York: Simon and Schuster, 1962), 422; see also his comments to Crowley in Nixon Off the Record, 30.

19. There are many biographies of Nixon, some of which are cited in these notes. One of the standards is the multivolume study by Stephen E. Ambrose, which begins with Nixon, vol. 1: The Education of a Politician, 1913–1962 (New York: Simon and Schuster, 1987).

Brief portraits include: Jonathan Aitken, "The Nixon Character," *Presidential Studies Quarterly* 26 (Winter 1996): 239–247; and Tom Wicker, "Richard M. Nixon, 1969–1974," *Presidential Studies Quarterly* 249–257.

20. After briefing Vice President Nixon on the power of nuclear weapons at the time of the Dienbienphu crisis, J. Robert Oppenheimer said that Nixon was "the most dangerous man I have ever met." Quoted in Fawn M. Brodie, *Richard Nixon: The Shaping of His Character* (New York: Norton, 1981), 322. On the old and new Nixon and Nixon's shallow convictions, see Whalen, *Catch the Falling Flag*, 25, 52, 98.

21. Whalen, *Catch the Falling Flag*, 62, 79. It was Haldeman's idea to control these appearances; Haldeman had been an executive for the advertising firm of J. Walter Thompson. Nixon's own account of his television strategy in *RN*, 303–304, is disingenuous: he referred to these controlled sessions as "spontaneous" because they contained questions and answers.

22. Whalen, *Catch the Falling Flag*, 63, 80.

23. Richard Bergholz and James Wrightson, quoted in *Nixon: An Oral History of His Presidency*, ed. Gerald S. Strober and Deborah H. Strober (New York: HarperCollins, 1994), 25. Strober confused the campaigns; the San Jose State incident was in 1970; see *HRHD*, October 29, 1970.

24. Nixon, *Six Crises*, xii.

25. He listed many of these in ibid., xv–xvi, but in *Leaders* he expanded the list; see, e.g., chap. 9. Whether or not Nixon possessed any of these qualities, he did believe in them and frequently talked about them to his staff. Examples are strewn throughout the *Haldeman Diaries*. Nixon told Crowley that the 1960 campaign was "legendary"; *Nixon Off the Record*, 31.

26. Nixon, *Six Crises*, xii–xvi. Nixon seemed to thrive on what he considered challenges and crises. In *RN*, e.g., he wrote: "In 1968 I had a different and completely unexpected experience: the fatigue and letdown of victory. But then there was the challenge of setting up a new administration" (232). A reading of his public speeches during 1968—not to mention his many books and Haldeman's notes—reveals that he frequently talked about taking hold, gaining mastery, meeting and overcoming crises, and being a leader. See, e.g., *Nixon Speaks Out: Major Speeches and Statements by Richard Nixon in the Presidential Campaign of 1968* (New York: Nixon-Agnew Campaign Committee, October 25, 1968).

27. Quoted by Nixon in *In the Arena*, 8, and *RN*, 1076. Nixon used these words in his resignation speech and had often cited them in campaign speeches. See also Frost, *"I Gave Them a Sword,"* 193.

28. *In the Arena*, chap. 37.

29. The use of cultural motifs by successful political figures in their public comments and behavior is common, if not universal. Nixon's own accounts of his life can best be placed, I think, in the dramatic Western tropes of romance and tragedy, rather than irony and comedy. His stories also drew on American popular myths, grand European legends, and, as I will point out in a later chapter, the game of poker. These motifs or metaphors not only served to legitimate Nixon's behavior, but also probably informed or guided his actions; i.e., Nixon turned to particular "texts," "canons," or "scripts" in order to make sense out of his own behavior.

30. Encapsulating its theme is the motto on the Nixon family coat of arms, which is displayed in Nixon's renovated childhood home on the grounds of the library: *Toujours*

Prêt (always prepared). The Nixon Library in Yorba Linda is not a library in the usual sense of the term, but is more a museum.

31. Roger Morris, *Richard Milhous Nixon: The Rise of an American Politician* (New York: Henry Holt, 1990), 41.

32. Nixon, *In the Arena*, 34. The European literary theme of the fallen king, or wounded fisher king, whose ill health brought ruin to the realm, was famously identified in Jessie L. Weston's classic, *From Ritual to Romance* (Cambridge: Cambridge University Press, 1920).

33. I discussed the universal theme of back stabbing in "The Stab-in-the-Back Legend and the Vietnam War," *Armed Forces and Society* 14 (Spring 1988): 433–458.

34. Nixon, *In the Arena*, pp. 26–27, 45, quoting Arnold Toynbee and Isaiah Berlin. See also Nixon, *Leaders,* 1990 edition, xii; and Whalen, *Catch the Falling Flag,* 77.

35. See, e.g., *RN,* 1072; and Frost, *"I Gave Them a Sword,"* 173.

36. Quoted in Frost, *"I Gave Them a Sword,"* 272, 183.

37. Quoted in ibid., 269.

38. Whalen, *Catch the Falling Flag,* 59.

39. Nixon's marginal note, Annotated News Summaries, October 27, 1972, WHSF: POF, NPM.

40. Whalen, *Catch the Falling Flag,* 12.

41. Hugh Sidey, "The Man and Foreign Policy," in *The Nixon Presidency: Twenty-Two Intimate Perspectives of Richard M. Nixon,* vol. 6 of *Portraits of American Presidents,* ed. Kenneth W. Thompson (New York: University Press of America, 1987), 312.

42. *HRHD,* January 17, 1972, 398.

43. "Is it better to be loved than feared? It is desirable to be both, but because it is difficult to join them together, it is much safer for a prince to be feared than loved"; Niccolo Machiavelli, *Il Principe,* chap. 8.

44. John F. Stacks, "Oh, They Say, This Is the Watergate Man," *Time,* May 2, 1994, 28–29.

45. *NYT,* April 28, 1994.

46. Ibid.; see also March 25, 1996. On April 22, 1996, the Nixon Library and Birthplace awarded Kissinger the annual Architect of Peace award. In 1996 he was also serving as the chair of the Advisory Council of the Nixon Center for Peace and Freedom, which is a division of the Richard Nixon Library and Birthplace Foundation.

47. Other media productions perpetuated the "but-for-Watergate" and "foreign policy success" themes; e.g., a 1995 Arts and Entertainment Television Network biography of Nixon and "This Week with David Brinkley" (ABC network television) on December 24, 1995. In one important variation of the foreign policy theme—developed first by Henry Kissinger—Kissinger appears as the heroic, rational adviser who strives to control the erratic, irrational president. In the end and despite their strange relationship, however, they achieve foreign policy victories together. See, e.g., the 1995 Turner Network Television movie entitled *Kissinger and Nixon.*

48. Andrew Kopkind, "Many Nixons," *The Nation,* May 16, 1994, 652.

49. Quoted by Sidey in "The Man and Foreign Policy," 311–312.

50. Quoted in *RN,* 1072.

51. For example, in 1995 prospective Republican candidates for the presidential race of 1996 still sought Nixon's posthumous blessing; see *NYT,* May 14, 1995, and March 25, 1996.

52. Kopkind maintained that "the habit of removing Nixon from history and placing him in a purely psychological dimension has led commentators to the most outrageous estimations of his genius"; "Many Nixons," *The Nation,* May 16, 1994, 652. In *Richard Nixon and His America* (Boston: Little, Brown, 1990), Herbert Parmet, another scholar, placed Nixon so firmly in the context of larger social and historical forces, however, that, according to Alan Brinkley in "Means of Descent," 30, "Nixon himself at times disappears from view."

53. William Ewald, Jr., *Eisenhower the President: Crucial Days, 1951–1960* (Englewood Cliffs, N.J.: Prentice Hall, 1981), 178. A former Harvard English professor, then a speechwriter for Eisenhower, Ewald was bothered by the imagery in Nixon's speeches, which, he thought, gave one a glimpse into "a dark pit of mind." There have been exceptions to this polarized, for-or-against, psychological historiography. Historian Joan Hoff, for example, took what may be considered a middle position in *Nixon Reconsidered* (New York: BasicBooks, 1994). She analyzed Nixon "without Watergate," an approach she believed necessary to recognize and appreciate his achievements, which she argued were mainly in the domestic arena. But she also identified his failures, which she thought were mainly on the international stage. She thus turned historiography topsy-turvy, challenging some of Nixon's claims about foreign policy but calling upon critics to acknowledge his domestic policy successes without wallowing in the scandal of Watergate. Somewhat more than many others, she examined his policies as well as his personality.

54. Nixon, *In the Arena,* 79.

55. Nixon's response also fit the pattern noted by Paul Fussell in *Class: A Guide Through the American Status System* (New York: Summit Books, 1983), 16: "You reveal a great deal about your social class by the amount of annoyance or fury you feel when the subject is brought up. A tendency to get very anxious suggests that you are middle-class and nervous about slipping down a rung or two."

56. Nixon often told stories about these events and his mother's caregiving; see, e.g., *HRHD,* April 22, 1971.

57. James David Barber, *The Presidential Character* (Englewood Cliffs, N.J.: Prentice Hall, 1972).

58. Quoted in the *Washington Post,* March 23, 1975; and *NYT,* March 23, 1975.

59. Klein, *Making It Perfectly Clear,* 132. See also Tom Wicker's concluding comment in *One of Us: Richard Nixon and the American Dream* (New York: Random House, 1991), 686.

60. Quoted by Sidey in "The Man and Foreign Policy," 301.

61. Nixon, *In the Arena,* 86–87; Aitken, "The Nixon Character," 240.

62. See, e.g., the strange joke Nixon told his staff in 1971 and paraphrased in *HRHD,* November 5, 1971.

63. Leonard Garment, *Crazy Rhythm* (New York: Random House, 1997), 299.

64. David Abrahamsen, *Nixon vs. Nixon: An Emotional Tragedy* (New York: Farrar, Straus and Giroux, 1977), 221.

65. *Diagnostic and Statistical Manual of Mental Disorders,* 4th ed. (Washington, D.C.: American Psychiatric Association, 1994), 673. Examples include passive-aggressive personalities. See also pp. 734–735. Some symptoms in *DSM-IV* match Abrahamsen's, but the match is not exact, and Abrahamsen lists symptoms found in other disorders as well. Moreover, the APA now lists the passive-aggressive personality disorder under the category of those needing further study before their inclusion in *DSM.*

66. See ibid., 629–673, 735. There is abundant evidence for these traits in documents, memoirs, biographies, and the *Haldeman Diaries.*

67. See my discussion in chapter 9 and also *HRHD*, November 5, 1969, April 15, and May 9, 1970, July 26, 1971, and February 6, 1973; Handwritten Note, April 8, 1970, WHSF: SMOF, HRH, NPM; Garment, *Crazy Rhythm*, 298–299. When coming out of his "doldrums," Nixon exhibited most of the criteria, e.g., "inflated self-esteem or grandiosity"; "decreased need for sleep"; "more talkative than usual"; "flight of ideas or subjective experience that thoughts are racing"; "increase in goal-directed activity"; *DSM-IV*, 328–332, 335–338.

68. Henry A. Kissinger, *White House Years* (Boston: Little, Brown, 1979), 247. Like Nixon, however, Kissinger believed that "he [Nixon] had good foreign policy reasons as well for not letting Hanoi believe that he was paralyzed."

69. Quoted in Frost, *"I Gave Them a Sword,"* 183.

70. Charles W. Colson, *Born Again* (1976; London: Hodder and Stoughton, 1980), 48. Anyone reading Haldeman's notes and diaries and listening to or reading White House tapes should come away with a clear sense of Nixon's penchant for revenge and savage counterattack against foreign and domestic enemies. Haldeman and Kissinger became so used to his tirades that they often disregarded Nixon's incessant orders to retaliate against his foes, believing that he needed to blow off steam and would eventually calm down. See, e.g., *HRHD*, January 29, March 18, June 3 and 4, 1969, June 29, 1971, and *Abuse of Power: The New Nixon Tapes*, ed. Stanley I. Kutler (New York: Free Press, 1997).

71. *HRHD*, January 17, 1972; see also June 9, 1971.

72. William Safire, *Before the Fall: An Inside View of the Pre-Watergate White House* (New York: Doubleday, 1975), 385.

73. At a cabinet meeting in 1971, Nixon spoke of Bedell Smith, Eisenhower's long-time aide, as having complained: "All my life I've just been Ike's prat boy, doing his dirty work." *HRHD*, June 29, 1971. Nixon was angry about the leak of the *Pentagon Papers,* and he compared Daniel Ellsberg to Alger Hiss and the Rosenbergs, but he was also angry about the lack of "discipline" among cabinet members, who expressed their own views and did not follow the White House line. Haldeman was charged with imposing discipline. He would be the president's "lord high executioner," telling people what to do. He was "my prat boy"; this was "the worst job that anybody can have in the White House." Nixon repeated the Bedell Smith story in *RN,* 198, where it is clear in context that he thought Eisenhower had used him similarly. For a survey of other resentments, see Wicker, *One of Us,* chap. 5.

74. See, e.g., *RN,* 376–380.

75. *HRHD*, March 28, 1969.

76. Ibid., March 11, 1969. And like ordinary human beings, Nixon wasted his time on trivial pursuits, e.g., examining hardware catalogs for shower heads when he should have been reading the briefing books for his trip to Europe. Ibid., February 22, 1969. Many of Nixon's behavioral traits are summarized by Stanley Allen Renshon in his review of several early Nixon psychohistories, "Psychological Analysis and Presidential Personality: The Case of Richard Nixon," *History of Childhood Quarterly: The Journal of Psychohistory* 2 (Winter 1975): 415–450.

77. Haldeman is quoted in Betty Glad and Michael W. Link, "President Nixon's Inner Circle of Advisers," *Presidential Studies Quarterly* 26 (Winter 1996): 20; Ehrlichman and Price are quoted in Wicker, *One of Us,* 393. Wicker's discussion of the issue on pp. 390–393

is a balanced analysis, for which he cites most of the relevant sources. See also Garment, *Crazy Rhythm*, 144; Seymour Hersh, *The Price of Power: Kissinger in the Nixon White House* (New York: Summit Books, 1983), 108–110; Roger Morris, *Uncertain Greatness: Henry Kissinger and American Foreign Policy* (New York: Harper and Row, 1977), 95, 147–148; and Nixon's own oblique admission in *In the Arena*, 128.

78. Thomas J. McCormick's synthesis of U.S. foreign policy in the post–World War II era is a good example of the kind of historical analysis that emphasizes structural over personal elements in decision-making: *America's Half-Century: United States Foreign Policy in the Cold War and After*, 2d ed. (Baltimore: Johns Hopkins University Press, 1995). Regarding the "chaotic" personal element, "chaos theory" offers useful metaphors. It has been argued in the physical and medical sciences that small differences (the "butterfly factor" or "initial conditions") at the beginning of a natural function ultimately transform an orderly process into "chaos"—i.e., non-linear unpredictability. Nixon's presidency introduced importantly different factors in the rules and structure of the Vietnam War as it stood in 1968–1969. For a popular overview of general chaos theory, see James Gleick, *Chaos: Making a New Science* (New York: Penguin Books, 1987); for a historian's view, H. W. Brands, "Fractal History, or Clio and the Chaotics," *Diplomatic History* 16 (Fall 1992): 495–510.

2. THE WORLDVIEW OF AN IMPROBABLE PEACEMAKER: 1953–1967

1. Quoted in *NYT*, September 13, 1967.

2. Quoted in ibid., July 7, 1971.

3. *Foreign Relations of the United States 1952–1954*, vol. 13, 85–86; *NYT*, March 17, 1954. See also Général Paul Ely, *Mémoires: L'Indochine Dans La Tourmente* (Paris: Librairie Plon, 1964), chap. 3; George C. Herring and Richard H. Immerman, "Eisenhower, Dulles, and Dienbienphu: 'The Day We Didn't Go to War' Revisited," *Journal of American History* 71 (September 1984): 343–363; and Laurent Césari and Jacques de Folin, "Military Necessity, Political Impossibility: The French Viewpoint on Operation *Vautour*," trans. Mark R. Rubin, chap. 5 in *Dien Bien Phu and the Crisis of Franco-American Relations, 1954–1955*, ed. Lawrence S. Kaplan, Denise Artaud, and Mark R. Rubin (Wilmington, Del.: Scholarly Resources, 1990).

4. *FRUS, 1952–1954*, vol. 13, 947–956, 85–86; and Herring and Immerman, "Eisenhower, Dulles, and Dienbienphu," 346.

5. Quoted in Herring and Immerman, "Eisenhower, Dulles, and Dienbienphu," 346.

6. Eisenhower paraphrased by Nixon in *RN*, 153. The concept of "credibility" was the linchpin of American foreign policy in the cold war and Vietnam eras. In *The Time of Illusion* (New York: Knopf, 1975), Jonathan Schell linked it to the doctrine of nuclear deterrence. In "Credibility and World Power: Exploring the Psychological Dimension in Postwar American Diplomacy," *Diplomatic History* 15 (Fall 1991): 455–472, Robert J. McMahon emphasized its connections with psychological or ideational processes. Credibility was indeed intimately connected with atomic diplomacy, and, being a symbolic concept, it was a manifestation of American "ways of thinking." But I would argue that (1) its roots ran deeper than nuclear deterrence; and (2) it was more than just an idea. If the United States was to police the world in order to maintain a global system compatible

with and beneficial to its own—which is what American policy makers sought to do—then it had to be able to isolate the Soviet Union and, at the same time, prevent nationalist and leftist revolutions against capitalism. Since it could not militarily intervene everywhere, it needed to establish the credibility, the believability, of its will and ability to do so—in order that it would not have to intervene elsewhere. All great powers with hegemonic ambitions have sought to establish the credibility of their power of retribution. Defeat anywhere, e.g., defeat in Vietnam, had the potential of undermining this credibility. In this sense, it was a "realistic" approach. It was "unrealistic" in that the costs and risks of maintaining such a system more often than not exceeded the benefits.

7. *Public Papers of the Presidents of the United States, Dwight D. Eisenhower: 1954* (Washington, D.C.: GPO, 1960), 382–383. At an NSC meeting the day before, Eisenhower had deployed similar metaphors, using the words "chain reaction" and "dominoes"; *FRUS, 1952–1954*, vol. 13, 1257, 1261. On January 8 he had warned of flooding: "The President said what you've got here is a leaky dike, and with leaky dikes it's sometimes better to put a finger in than to let the whole structure be washed away"; ibid., 952. William Safire claimed that Joseph Alsop invented the phrase "falling dominoes"; *Safire's Political Dictionary* (New York: Random House, 1978), 179. Even so, the concept is older than the phrase. On April 22, 1947, Senator Arthur Vandenberg talked about a "chain reaction" of aggression unless Congress voted for aid to Greece and Turkey. When Vandenberg added that American leaders "cannot escape a primary interest that America shall not be stranded in a totalitarian world," he voiced the views of a generation of cold war policy makers; *Congressional Record*, 80th Cong., 1st sess., vol. 93, pt. 3 (Washington, D.C.: GPO, 1947), 3772–3773. In the same year over the same issue, Dean Acheson said: "Like apples in a barrel infected by one rotten one, the corruption of Greece would infect Iran and all to the east [and parts south and west]"; Dean Acheson, *Present at the Creation: My Years in the State Department* (New York: Norton, 1969), 219.

8. Nixon, "Meeting the People of Asia," *Department of State Bulletin*, 30 (January 4, 1954): 10, 12. Nixon made similar public remarks on April 16, 1954: "The main target of the Communists in Korea and in Indo-China is Japan. Conquest of areas so vital to Japan's economy would reduce Japan to an economic satellite of the Soviet Union. . . . A Communist victory in Southeast Asia would be a threat to the security of the United States." Quoted in *NYT*, April 17 and 20, 1954; see also, April 18, 1954.

9. See, e.g., Eisenhower, "Address at the Gettysburg College Convocation," April 4, 1959, *Public Papers of the Presidents, Eisenhower: 1959* (Washington, D.C.: GPO, 1960), 310–313. References to "neocolonialism" are strewn throughout Vietnamese writings; see also, *Vietnam Documents and Research Notes Series: Translation and Analysis of Significant Viet Cong/North Vietnamese Documents* (Bethesda, Md.: University Publications of America, 1991), microfilm.

10. *FRUS, 1952–1954*, vol. 13, 952.

11. See, e.g., *The Pentagon Papers: The Defense Department History of United States Decision-making on Vietnam*, The Senator Gravel Edition, vol. 1 (Boston: Beacon Press, 1971), 92–93; and *FRUS, 1952–1954*, vol. 13, 1269–1270 regarding the strategic diversion of military capabilities, Indochina as a nondecisive theater, and the danger of general war.

12. Quoted in Herring and Immerman, "Eisenhower, Dulles, and Dienbienphu," 349.

13. On the March 22 meeting between Eisenhower, Radford, and Ely, see Ely, *Mémoires*, 64; and Césari and de Folin, "Military Necessity, Political Impossibility," 108–109. Césari and de Folin's source for the post–March 23 meeting between Ely,

Radford, and Nixon is an interview with General Raymond Brohon. Ely had previously met with high American officials, including Nixon, at Radford's home on March 20; *FRUS, 1952–1954*, vol. 13, 1137–1141. Also see ibid., 1141–1144, passim. Ely had first raised the issue of American air intervention as a response to possible Chinese air intervention, but such talk rapidly moved on to discussions about American raids to relieve the siege. See also Ronald H. Spector, *United States Army in Vietnam: Advice and Support: The Early Years, 1941–1960* (Washington, D.C.: Center of Military History, 1983), 192–194. On nuclear weapons, see *RN,* 150; John Prados, *The Sky Would Fall: Operation Vulture, The Secret U.S. Bombing Mission to Vietnam, 1954* (New York: Dial Press, 1983), 145–156. See also, *Pentagon Papers,* Gravel edition, 1:92, 97.

14. Even though Eisenhower discussed the possibility of lending France "new weapons" on April 30, Herring and Immerman, in "Eisenhower, Dulles, and Dienbienphu," 357, questioned whether Dulles made such an offer to Bidault, since, they say, Bidault, who despised Dulles, was the lone source for the alleged proposal. In "Military Necessity, Political Impossibility," 113–114, Césari and de Folin point out, however, that Ely and Jean Chauvel mentioned the offer in their memoirs and diaries.

15. *RN,* 154.

16. Radford's position is paraphrased by Douglas MacArthur II in *FRUS, 1952–1954,* vol. 13, 1271.

17. Quoted in Stephen E. Ambrose, *Eisenhower,* vol. 2, *The President* (New York: Simon and Schuster, 1983), 184.

18. *RN,* 155. It was during this period that J. Robert Oppenheimer, after briefing the vice president on the power of nuclear weapons, remarked that Nixon was "the most dangerous man I have ever met"; quoted in Brodie, *Richard Nixon,* 322.

19. Evidence for this can be found in other quotes from Eisenhower scattered throughout Ambrose's discussion of Eisenhower's strategy of massive retaliation in *Eisenhower,* vol. 2, *The President.*

20. See the following articles from a special issue on "Truman, Eisenhower, and the Uses of Atomic Superiority" in *International Security* 13 (Winter 1988/89): Marc Trachtenberg, "A 'Wasting Asset': American Strategy and the Shifting Nuclear Balance, 1949–1954," 5–49; Roger Dingman, "Atomic Diplomacy During the Korean War," 51–91; and Rosemary J. Foot, "Nuclear Coercion and the Ending of the Korean Conflict," 92–112. Also see Edward Keefer, "President Dwight D. Eisenhower and the End of the Korean War," *Diplomatic History* 10 (Summer 1986): 267–289; and Richard Rhodes, *Dark Sun: The Making of the Hydrogen Bomb* (New York: Simon and Schuster, 1995), chap. 7.

21. Interview, quoted in *Time,* July 29, 1985, 49–50.

22. See note 20 for examples of nuclear intentions and threats during the 1950s. Daniel Ellsberg's "Call to Mutiny," *Monthly Review* 33, no. 4 (September 1981): 1–26, was probably the first documented account identifying the pattern of American nuclear bombing plans and threats from 1945 to the 1980s. For recent scholarship on the bombing of Hiroshima and Nagasaki, see the special issue of *Diplomatic History* 19 (Spring 1995), and Barton Bernstein, "The Atomic Bombings Reconsidered," *Foreign Affairs* 74, (January/February 1995): 135–152. In 1968, when asked by the press to compare his intentions regarding Vietnam with Eisenhower's policies toward Vietnam and Korea in the mid-1950s, Nixon acknowledged American policy makers' appreciation of the reality of U.S. nuclear superiority during the earlier period: "At that time we had unequaled nuclear superiority"; *NYT,* March 11, 1968.

23. *NYT,* January 12, 1954. The first American thermonuclear test had taken place in 1952; the first Soviet test, in 1953. The 1954 U.S. tests were the first with operational bombs. Baldwin's story was ostensibly about U.S.-Soviet conversations regarding "the primary problem of our time—atomic energy." It was undoubtedly no coincidence that Dulles chose this time to announce the administration's New Look, "massive retaliation" policy. Thus, for public consumption, talk of arms control; for Soviet consumption, threats of massive retaliation.

24. *FRUS, 1952–1954,* vol. 2, 577–596. For nuclear references see pp. 583, 591, 595. The key phrases used in NSC 162/2 are "adequate offensive retaliatory strength and defensive strength" and "massive atomic capability." Maintaining the "free world" coalition was, of course, the goal, but it was also necessary in order to provide military bases for massive retaliation; ibid., 591. For public statements see the following: *NYT,* January 13 and March 14, 1954; John Foster Dulles, "The Evolution of Foreign Policy," *Department of State Bulletin* 30 (January 1954): 107–110. Dulles publicly articulated the strategy of massive retaliation in "Policy for Security and Peace," *Foreign Affairs* 32 (April 1954): 353–364.

25. In Baldwin's second story on "the atomic problem" in *NYT,* January 13, 1954, a story obviously influenced by administration thinking, he said: "All Russian atomic energy negotiations have been prefaced with the demand for outright prohibition of the use of atomic arms in war. The United States has been, and still is, quite right in rejecting this demand as a condition to negotiations." First-use, or any *use,* was nonnegotiable, since it was an essential element in American policy. "Massive preemption" is from Trachtenberg, "A 'Wasting Asset,'" 34. Trachtenberg concluded: "It is now often taken for granted that even in the 1950s nuclear war was simply 'unthinkable' as an instrument of policy; and that the threat of 'massive retaliation' was at bottom just pure bluff, because the United States would never be the first to launch a nuclear strike. . . . But one cannot immerse oneself in the sources for this period without coming to the conclusion that something very basic has been forgotten. The historical documents themselves give a very different picture" (49). See also Rhodes, *Dark Sun,* chap. 7.

26. *FRUS, 1952–1954,* vol. 2, 584. The wording of NSC 162 is unclear about whether Indochina was seen as of "vital strategic importance" or of "such strategic importance" or whether there's a difference. American leaders themselves seemed to be unsure; i.e., the domino theory made this area, which was on the periphery and for which there was no treaty obligation, vital.

27. *NYT,* January 13, 1954.

28. Quoted in Anthony Eden, *Full Circle: Memoirs of Anthony Eden* (Boston: Cassell, 1960), 102–103. Cf. Radford's view at this time that "the China area . . . seemed like the best place in the world to try to implement a 'dynamic' and 'positive' policy"; Trachtenberg, "A 'Wasting Asset,'" 46. For a good overview of the Eisenhower administration's implementation of the New Look policy, see Chester J. Pach, Jr., and Elmo Richardson, *The Presidency of Dwight D. Eisenhower* (Lawrence: University Press of Kansas, 1991), chap. 4. Strategists continued to incorporate the uncertainty principle in their concepts of deterrence and coercion forty years later. A recently declassified 1995 study by the U.S. Strategic Command observed: "The very framework of a concept that depends on instilling fear and uncertainty in the minds of opponents was never, nor can it be, strictly rational. Nor has it ever strictly required rational adversaries in order to function"; "Essentials

of Post–Cold War Deterrence," n.d. [probably April 1995], reprinted in Hans M. Kristensen, "Nuclear Futures: Proliferation of Weapons of Mass Destruction and U.S. Nuclear Strategy," BASIC Research Report 98.2. (London and Washington, D.C.: British American Security Information Council, 1998), 31–32.

29. *NYT,* March 13, 1955.

30. Ibid., March 17, 1954.

31. *Time,* July 29, 1985, 50–51.

32. Quoted in *NYT,* March 18, 1955.

33. Michael S. Sherry, *The Rise of American Air Power: The Creation of Armageddon* (New Haven, Conn.: Yale University Press, 1987), 358.

34. *RN,* 155.

35. *NYT,* April 17, 18, and 20, 1954. Cf. *No More Vietnams,* 30: "I made the point in a National Security Council meeting that our choice was to help the French now or be faced with the necessity of taking over the burden of preventing a Communist takeover later."

36. William Conrad Gibbons, *The U.S. Government and the Vietnam War: Executive and Legislative Roles and Relationships, Parts I and II* (Washington, D.C.: GPO, 1984), pt. 1, p. 210.

37. *NYT,* April 20, 1954.

38. Gibbons, *The U.S. Government and the Vietnam War,* pt. 1, p. 210.

39. *RN,* 153.

40. David L. Anderson, *Trapped by Success: The Eisenhower Administration and Vietnam, 1953–1961* (New York: Columbia University Press, 1991), 38.

41. *No More Vietnams,* 31.

42. *FRUS, 1952–1954,* vol. 13, 1270.

43. Ibid., 1141.

44. Gibbons, *The U.S. Government and the Vietnam War,* pt. 1, pp. 258–259.

45. *FRUS, 1952–1954,* vol. 13, pt. 2: 1732.

46. Gary R. Hess, "Redefining the American Position in Southeast Asia: The United States and the Geneva and Manila Conferences," chap. 6 in *Dien Bien Phu and the Crisis of Franco-American Relations, 1954–1955,* 135.

47. *FRUS, 1952–1954,* vol. 6, 1732–1733.

48. Gibbons, *The U.S. Government and the Vietnam War,* pt. 1, pp. 221, 275. Nixon had contributed to SEATO's creation. In January 1954, not long after a goodwill, fact-finding trip to Asia, he supported an idea then circulating among Washington insiders for the formation of an interagency coordinating board that would initiate steps to make possible the delineation of a defensive perimeter against the Communist threat in Asia. Beginning with psychological warfare and paramilitary operations, the board's activities, it was hoped, could grow into an "area" strategy based on indigenous capabilities in the friendly nations of the region. Nixon wanted a politico-military alliance aimed not only at traditional cross-border aggression, like that engaged in by the North Koreans in the recent Korean War, but also at internal Communist "subversion," which was what the American government claimed was the cause of the war between the French and Vietminh. Ambrose, *Nixon,* vol. 1, *The Education of a Politician,* 342. See also *FRUS 1952–1954,* vol. 13, 1270–1272.

49. *FRUS 1952–1954,* vol. 13, 874. Also see Gibbons, *The U.S. Government and the Vietnam War,* pt. 1, p. 253; and *NYT,* April 18, 1954.

50. *FRUS, 1955–1957*, vol. 1, 535–540, 694–695. This document read: "[NSC 5501 (January 6, 1955)] called for highly mobile US forces suitably equipped for local war, including atomic capability, but not dependent on use of atomic weapons for effective action. The Planning Board considered it essential that the US forces should be sufficiently flexible so that a decision to intervene would not automatically mean a decision to employ nuclear weapons. NSC 5602/1 [March 15, 1956] in general reaffirms the necessity for ready mobile units with selective and flexible capability and not inevitably dependent on tactical nuclear weapons." Another study of September 15, 1955, estimated that "*with the use of atomic weapons,* two to four US divisions would be required for a period of a few months to one year 'to check aggression,' with a longer time needed to clear out the Vietminh back to the 17th parallel. . . . Up to eight US divisions would be required . . . to destroy Vietminh forces and take control of North Vietnam." See also Anderson, *Trapped by Success,* 139–140.

51. *RN,* 127.

52. Ibid., 128.

53. *NYT,* April 18, 1954. Rhee, however, was secretive about his stratagem; Nixon was not, and the other side knew he was not.

54. *RN,* 129. Wicker coined the phrase "uncertainty principle" in *One of Us.*

55. *RN,* 122.

56. *NYT,* February 16, 1962.

57. Ibid., October 25, 1963.

58. *No More Vietnams,* 38, 62–73.

59. *NYT,* November 7, 1963. Grateful for Nixon's expression of sympathy, Mme Nhu congratulated him on his election in 1969; Mme Nhu to Mr. and Mrs. Nixon, November 6, 1969, folder: Madame Ngo-dinh Nhu Letter, box 2, NSC: HAKOF, HAKASF, NPM.

60. *RN,* 509, 513–514. See also *No More Vietnams,* 62–73.

61. *RN,* 256–257.

62. See my discussion in chapter 11.

63. This section was based on the following: *NYT,* February 12 , September 6, 13, and 15, November 23 and 29, 1965; January 31, May 1, August 23, September 14, and November 3, 4, 7, 10, 1966; April 8, 15, and 18, 1967. See also "President Nixon's Record on Vietnam, 1954–68," in *Legislative Proposals Relating to the War in Southeast Asia: Hearings Before the Committee on Foreign Relations, United States Senate,* 92nd Cong., 1st sess. (Washington, D.C.: GPO, 1971), 295–299. Nixon recommended increased bombing both when it was not favored by the majority of the public (September 1965 to May 1966) and when it was (July 1966); see John E. Mueller, *War, Presidents, and Public Opinion* (New York: Wiley, 1973), Table 4.2, p. 70. For the Manila conference, see George C. Herring, *LBJ and Vietnam: A Different Kind of War* (Austin: University of Texas Press, 1994), 77, 139.

64. *NYT,* November 5, 1966.

65. Mary Brennan, *Turning Right in the Sixties: The Conservative Capture of the GOP* (Chapel Hill: University of North Carolina Press, 1995), 122–123. See also Jules Witcover, *The Resurrection of Richard Nixon* (New York: Putnam, 1970), chap. 6.

66. *NYT,* September 17, November 3, and December 15, 1967.

67. Garry Wills, *Nixon Agonistes: The Crisis of the Self-Made Man* (Boston: Houghton Mifflin, 1969), 590.

68. Ibid., 406; Wicker, *One of Us,* 440.

69. Abrahamsen, *Nixon vs. Nixon,* (New York: Farrar, Straus and Giroux, 1977), 193–194. Abrahamsen seemed to argue that Nixon's core was nonexistent, because he did not grow psychologically from the child he had been and continued to be. By "hollow" he meant that Nixon had no real values, beliefs, or commitments. This is a fine point. Perhaps Nixon's psychological instincts did not grow or evolve, but he nonetheless did have values, beliefs, and commitments, such as those associated with capitalism, which he practiced and fostered.

70. *NYT,* February 12, 1965.

71. In *Nixon Agonistes* Wills argued that Nixon's philosophy was in the tradition of Wilsonian liberalism. But more than Woodrow Wilson, Nixon's presidential hero was Theodore Roosevelt, another practical conservative. Nixon believed Wilson was a scholar more than a politician, a man of thought and not of action, particularly in his second term; Crowley, *Nixon Off the Record,* 10.

72. *NYT,* October 29, 1967. In contrast, liberal Republican Mark Hatfield, also respected for his loyalty to principles, would virtually withdraw his endorsement of Nixon's Vietnam position in 1968. Ibid., September 29, 1968.

73. Ibid., June 8, 1964, September 13, 1965, August 22, 1967, December 15, 1967. See also Nixon's comment about China as the "common danger" in the Pacific Rim in "Asia After Viet Nam," *Foreign Affairs* 46 (October 1967): 111.

74. Cf. *NYT,* May 1 and September 14, 1966, and August 22, 1967.

75. Ibid., September 13, 1965.

76. Memorandum for the Record by McGeorge Bundy about a discussion between Dean Rusk, Robert McNamara, John McCone, and himself and reported to the president, September 15, 1964, copy held at the Norwegian Nobel Institute, Oslo, Norway. See also Shane Maddock, "LBJ, China, and the Bomb: New Archival Evidence," *Society for Historians of American Foreign Relations Newsletter* 27 (March 1996): 1–5; Raymond L. Garthoff, "A Comment on the Discussion of 'LBJ, China, and the Bomb,'" *Society for Historians of American Foreign Relations Newsletter* 28 (September 1997): 27–31; and Gordon H. Chang, *Friends and Enemies: The United States, China, and the Soviet Union, 1948–1972* (Stanford, Calif.: Stanford University Press, 1990).

77. Dana Crowley Jack, *Silencing the Self: Women and Depression* (Cambridge, Mass.: Harvard University Press, 1991), 8. On gendered language in foreign policy, see Frank Castigliola, "The Nuclear Family: Tropes of Gender and Pathology in the Western Alliance," *Diplomatic History* 21 (Spring 1997): 163–184; Robert D. Dean, "Masculinity as Ideology: John F. Kennedy and the Domestic Politics of Foreign Policy," *Diplomatic History* 22 (Winter 1998): 29–62; Andrew J. Rotter, " Gender Relations, Foreign Relations: The United States and South Asia, 1947–1964," *Journal of American History* 81 (September 1994): 518–542; Emily S. Rosenberg, "Working the Borders," in *Explaining the History of American Foreign Relations,* ed. Michael J. Hogan and Thomas G. Paterson (Cambridge: Cambridge University Press, 1991), 24–35.

78. *RN,* 1088.

79. *In the Arena,* 110.

80. Robert Finch, quoted in Wicker, *One of Us,* 194.

81. Tad Szulc, *The Illusion of Peace: Foreign Policy in the Nixon Years* (New York: Viking Press, 1978), 168; Wicker, *One of Us,* 3–7; Hoff, *Nixon Reconsidered,* 167.

82. On Rebozo, see Safire, *Before the Fall,* 613–616; on Scaife, see the *Washington Post,* March 16, 1997.

83. *RN,* 35.

84. *In the Arena,* 301–305. See also comments in Earl Mazo, *Richard Nixon: A Political and Personal Portrait* (New York: Harper and Brothers, 1959), 283 ff.

85. *RN,* 17.

86. Quoted and paraphrased in *NYT,* September 13, 1967.

87. Wicker, *One of Us,* 132.

88. Quoted in Hoff, *Nixon Reconsidered,* 167.

89. Wicker, *One of Us,* 180; Mazo, *Richard Nixon,* 250, 254.

90. Interview with "Fred" by Tom Wicker, quoted in *One of Us,* 272. On Nixon and "order," see Stanley Hoffmann, *Primacy or World Order: American Foreign Policy Since the Cold War* (New York: McGraw-Hill, 1978), 43–44.

91. Wicker, *One of Us,* 32. On the influence of his pacifist mother's idealism on his foreign policy ideas, see also Leonard Garment, "The Annals of Law," *New Yorker,* April 17, 1989.

92. *NYT,* November 4, 1966.

93. This observation, with additions, is borrowed from George Herring, "Nixon, Kissinger, and Madman Diplomacy in the Far East," unpublished paper, April 1980.

94. Richard Nixon, "To Keep the Peace," CBS Radio Network, October 19, 1968, reprinted in *Nixon Speaks Out,* 230. Cf. Nixon, "Asia After Viet Nam," 111–112; and Lyndon Baines Johnson, *The Vantage Point: Perspectives of the Presidency, 1963–1969* (New York: Holt, Rinehart and Winston, 1971), 529.

95. "Asia After Viet Nam," 111–123. See also "Nixon Sees Asia Helping Itself," *NYT,* September 17, 1967; and Andrew J. Rotter, *The Path to Vietnam: Origins of the American Commitment to Southeast Asia* (Ithaca, N.Y.: Cornell University Press, 1987).

96. *NYT,* April 8, 1967.

97. Ibid.

98. The report was entitled *The Postwar Development of the Republic of Vietnam: Policies and Programs* (New York: Joint Development Group, March 1969); the *Washington Post* story about it was entitled, "Viet Rebuilding Plan Has a Capitalist Blueprint." See these and other examples of Lilienthal–White House correspondence in the file folder: [CF] CO 165, Vietnam 1-1-69 to 6-30-69 in WHSF: CF, SF, [CF] 1969–74, NPM. See also handwritten notes attached to memo, Kissinger to Nixon, July 25, 1972, sub: Meeting with John Hannah, folder: presidential Agenda Briefs/Memos to File [Apr 1971–July 1974], WHSF: SMOF, Peter Flanigan 1969–74, ibid., in which the argument is made that the Agency for International Development is necessary for the development of South Vietnam's markets and natural resources.

3. WINNING ON THE HOME FRONT: 1968

1. *NYT,* October 10, 1968.

2. Ibid., November 5, 1966, and March 6, 1968. Nixon used the word "dominant" during the course of describing Vietnam issues in New Hampshire; *RN,* 298. See also Witcover, *Resurrection of Richard Nixon,* chap. 10.

3. *NYT,* March 6 and 21, 1968.

4. Mueller, *War, Presidents, and Public Opinion,* chap. 3.

5. *WHY,* 272.

6. A statistically significant proportion of white women were more likely to be dovish and less likely to be hawkish than white men; black women were more dovish than black men; and blacks in general were more dovish on the war than whites in general. Persons with more years of formal education, often persons who belonged to a more affluent class, were more likely to support the war than those with fewer years of education; but they also tended to avoid "extreme" solutions more than the less educated, rejecting both dramatic military escalations and de-escalations. Americans under thirty years of age were less likely to support the war than those over thirty. Democrats tended to be more loyal to their wartime leaders, and Republicans even more loyal to theirs. There were also attitudinal differences that transcended these groupings, or at least did not correlate neatly. Conservatives were more hawkish than liberals. "Followers" tended to rally behind presidents during crises and to change their opinions on cue from their leaders. In April 1968, after President Johnson's announcement of a bombing halt, 64 percent of those polled approved the decision; but in March, before the announcement, only 40 percent had voiced support for stopping the bombing. Mueller, *War, Presidents, and Public Opinion,* chaps. 4, 5.

7. Melvin Small, "Influencing the Decision Makers: The Vietnam Experience," *Journal of Peace Research* 24, no. 2 (1987): 185–198; Whalen, *Catch the Falling Flag,* 25, 31.

8. Mueller, *War, Presidents, and Public Opinion,* chap. 4, especially pp. 85–88, 90–91, 105–106. Varying with the question and the time it was asked, 39 to 56 percent of respondents approved the use of atomic weapons during the Korean War.

9. Whalen, *Catch the Falling Flag,* 25, 135.

10. Shortly before his death, Nixon advised presidential aspirant Dole "to move to the political right in the primaries, scoop up endorsements and skip back to the center for the November election"; *NYT,* March 25, 1996.

11. Thomas C. Thayer, *War Without Fronts: The American Experience in Vietnam* (Boulder, Colo.: Westview Press, 1985), 105. For an analysis of public opinion polls on casualties, the economy, and prospects for a long war, see Mueller, *War, Presidents, and Public Opinion,* chap. 3, especially pp. 36, 38, 56.

12. For an insider's reflections on these proposals, see Robert S. McNamara, with Brian VanDeMark, *In Retrospect: The Tragedy and Lessons of Vietnam* (New York: Times Books, 1995), especially pp. 109, 147, 150, 160, 234, 245, 275–276.

13. Herring, *LBJ and Vietnam,* 59.

14. Information for this section is drawn from Thayer, *War Without Fronts,* 37; James William Gibson, *The Perfect War: The War We Couldn't Lose and How We Did* (New York: Atlantic Monthly Press, 1986), pt 3; McNamara, *In Retrospect,* 109, 147, 150, 160, 234, 245, 275–276; Larry Cable, "The Operation Was a Success, but the Patient Died: The Air War in Vietnam," in *An American Dilemma: Vietnam, 1964–1973,* ed. Dennis E. Showalter and John G. Albert (Chicago: Imprint Publications, 1993), 109–158.

15. Charles DeBenedetti, "On the Significance of Peace Activism: America, 1961–1975," *Peace and Change: A Journal of Peace Research* 9, nos. 2/3 (Summer 1983): 14. One of the first authors to call attention to the significance of the movement's impact on the mainstream by the year 1968 was Thomas Powers, *The War at Home: Vietnam and the American People, 1964–1968* (New York: Grossman, 1973).

16. These views can be found in virtually all the published writings of the Vietnamese, but see *Vietnam Documents and Research Notes Series: Translation and Analysis of*

Significant Viet Cong/North Vietnamese Documents; Vo Nguyen Giap: Selected Writings (Hanoi: Foreign Languages Publishing House, 1977); *Ho Chi Minh on Revolution: Selected Writings, 1920–1966*, ed. Bernard Fall (New York: Praeger, 1967); Le Duan, *Letters to the South* (Hanoi: Foreign Languages Press, 1986); and Bui Tin, *Following Ho Chi Minh: The Memoirs of a North Vietnamese Colonel* (Honolulu: University of Hawaii Press, 1995), chap. 3. Cf. *Mao Tse-tung and Lin Piao: Post-Revolutionary Writings*, ed. Kuang Huan Fan (Garden City, N.Y.: Anchor Books, 1972). My comments are also based on conversations with Vietnamese citizens, soldiers, and historians and interviews with former policy makers in 1987, 1988 and 1994, the latter especially with Hoang Tung, Nguyen Co Thach, and Luu Van Loi, September 21, 24, and 26, 1994, Hanoi. For a soldier's view, see Bao Ninh, *The Sorrow of War: A Novel of North Vietnam*, trans. Phan Thanh Hao (New York: Riverhead Books, 1993), especially pp. 192–193. The protagonist in the novel is a disillusioned army veteran with post-traumatic stress syndrome, but during the war his and his comrades' motives were a combination of loyalty to family and fellow soldiers and the pursuit of nationhood, justice, and peace.

17. Cf. Jeffrey J. Clarke, "Vietnamization: The War to Groom an Ally," in *An American Dilemma: Vietnam, 1964–1973*, ed. Dennis E. Showalter and John G. Albert (Chicago: Imprint Publications, 1993), 159–160.

18. People's war theory and practice attained their fullest development during the Communist-led revolutions of China and Vietnam in the twentieth century but had originated in the wars of the American and French revolutions almost two centuries earlier. For an introduction and some references, see John Shy and Thomas W. Collier, "Revolutionary War," in *Makers of Modern Strategy: From Machiavelli to the Nuclear Age*, ed. Peter Paret (Princeton, N.J.: Princeton University Press, 1986), 815–862. General histories include William J. Duiker, *The Communist Road to Power in Vietnam*, 2d ed. (Boulder, Colo.: Westview Press, 1996); Gabriel Kolko, *Anatomy of a War: Vietnam, the United States, and the Modern Historical Experience* (New York: Pantheon Books, 1985); Nguyen Khac Vien, *Contemporary Vietnam, 1858–1980* (Hanoi: Foreign Languages Publishing House, 1981); and Douglas Pike, *Viet Cong: The Organization and Techniques of the National Liberation Front of South Vietnam* (Cambridge, Mass.: MIT Press, 1966). For a critique of Pike's "revisionist" views, see Robert L. Sansom, *The Economics of Insurgency in the Mekong Delta of Vietnam* (Cambridge, Mass.: MIT Press, 1970), chap. 12; and Jeffrey Race, *War Comes to Long An: Revolutionary Conflict in a Vietnamese Province* (Berkeley: University of California Press, 1972).

19. *NYT*, April 18, 1954; *FRUS, 1952–1954*, vol. 13, 949.

20. Nixon: "Meeting the People of Asia," *Department of State Bulletin*, 30, no. 758 (January 4, 1954): 12; "Asia After Viet Nam," 115; *No More Vietnams*, 31–32, 35–37.

21. *FRUS, 1952–1954*, vol. 13, 950–951.

22. Ibid., 954, 1258–1261; Ambrose, *Nixon*, vol. 1, *The Education of a Politician*, 342.

23. Ho Chi Minh was born in south-central Vietnam; Le Duan, the dominant figure, was a southerner; Bui Diem, the South Vietnamese ambassador to Washington, was a northerner, as was Nguyen Cao Ky, the South Vietnamese vice president. These crossover patterns also were found among other political and military leaders.

24. "Viet 3rd Redraft," March 30, 1968, in Whalen, *Catch the Falling Flag*, 284–286.

25. Ibid., 288–289.

26. See, e.g., Ho Chi Minh, "The Path Which Led Me to Leninism," in *Ho Chi Minh on Revolution,* ed. Fall, 6. Also cf. Duiker, *Communist Road to Power,* chap. 2, with Douglas Pike, *Vietnam and the Soviet Union: Anatomy of an Alliance* (Boulder, Colo.: Westview Press, 1987), chap. 1.

27. Quoted in "Viet 3rd Redraft," in Whalen, *Catch the Falling Flag,* 137.

28. Walter Isaacson and Evan Thomas, *The Wise Men: Six Friends and the World They Made: Acheson, Bohlen, Harriman, Kennan, Lovett, McCloy* (New York: Simon and Schuster, 1986), 677.

29. McNamara, *In Retrospect,* chaps. 9, 10; Isaacson and Thomas, *The Wise Men,* 684–685, 690. See also Kent G. Sieg, "W. Averell Harriman, Henry Cabot Lodge, and the Quest for Peace in Vietnam," *Peace and Change: A Journal of Peace Research* 20 (April 1995): 237–249.

30. The 540,000 U.S. military personnel who would be in South Vietnam at the end of 1968, along with the 250,000 in Thailand, Okinawa, Guam, the Philippines, the Seventh Fleet at sea, Taiwan, and Hawaii who were directly involved in war-related activities, constituted 23 percent of active U.S. military personnel worldwide. In 1968 the United States's logistical system also supported 820,000 troops of South Vietnam and 66,000 from South Korea, Australia, New Zealand, the Philippines, and Thailand. The economic costs were commensurately great. The price tag for the war in 1968 was $30 billion, which amounted to 37 percent of total military outlays. Spending on the Vietnam War detrimentally affected the value of the dollar, the balance of payments, and gold reserves, producing a trade and monetary crisis with European and Japanese allies. See *Historical Statistics of the United States: Colonial Times to 1970* (Washington, D.C.: Bureau of the Census, 1975), pt. 2, p. 1141; Shelby L. Stanton, *Vietnam Order of Battle* (Washington, D.C.: U.S. News Books, 1981), 333; and Kolko, *Anatomy of a War,* 288–292, 347–348. See also Thayer, *War Without Fronts,* 23; and *Pentagon Papers,* 4:456–604. Johnson was as deeply concerned as anyone about the general crisis but was also understandably anxious about the dilemmas it created for him. In a morning conference before his luncheon meeting with the group, the president was briefed by Generals Earl Wheeler and Creighton Abrams, who delivered an optimistic assessment of the fighting in Vietnam. (Abrams was soon to replace Westmoreland as commander of MACV.) Although encouraged, Johnson vented his frustrations about the political and economic dilemmas he faced in Vietnam; see Clark Clifford, with Richard Holbrooke, *Counsel to the President: A Memoir* (New York: Random House, 1991), 516.

31. Memorandum for Personal Files, March 27, 1968, box 571, Special Files: Public Service, Kennedy-Johnson Administrations, 1958–71, W. Averell Harriman Papers, MDLC.

32. Quoted in Isaacson and Thomas, *The Wise Men,* 701, 694.

33. Clifford, *Counsel to the President,* 483; Herring, *LBJ and Vietnam,* 155–157.

34. Quotes from Clifford, *Counsel to the President,* 516; and Memorandum for Personal Files, March 27, 1968, box 571, Special Files: Public Service, Kennedy-Johnson Administrations, 1958–71, Harriman Papers, MDLC.

35. Quoted in Clifford, *Counsel to the President,* 517.

36. Proposal by H. C. Lodge for Johnson, March 26, 1968, Papers of Henry Cabot Lodge II, General Correspondence, microfilm, reel 8, Massachusetts Historical Society.

37. Memorandum for the Secretary [of State?], March 29, 1968, box 571, Special Files: Public Service, Kennedy-Johnson Administrations, 1958–71, Harriman Papers, MDLC.

38. Quoted in Whalen, *Catch the Falling Flag*, 26.

39. Ibid., 12, 26.

40. "To Keep the Peace" (CBS Radio Network, October 19, 1968); *Nixon Speaks Out*, 230. On the loss of American nuclear superiority and the attainment of Soviet parity, see the interview of Nixon in *Time*, July 29, 1985, 52.

41. See Nixon's speeches in *Nixon Speaks Out*, 6, 90, 93–100, 103–106, 229–232, 238–244; Nixon, "Asia After Viet Nam"; Whalen, *Catch the Falling Flag*, 12, 25, 28, 29, 31, 76–77, 132–140, 283–294; Franz Schurmann, *The Foreign Politics of Richard Nixon: The Grand Design* (Berkeley: Institute of International Studies, University of California, 1987), introduction and chap. 1; Seyom Brown, *The Crises of Power: An Interpretation of United States Foreign Policy During the Kissinger Years* (New York: Columbia University Press, 1979), chap. 1. For Nixon's economic foreign policies during his presidency, see also Hoff, *Nixon Reconsidered*, pt. 2.

42. Whalen, *Catch the Falling Flag*, 137.

43. See ibid., 135–143; and McNamara, *In Retrospect*, 147, 172–173.

44. Rusk advocated the *partial* bombing halt and did not see it as risky. Herring, *LBJ and Vietnam*, 163.

45. *HRHD*, April 23, 1970.

46. Nixon, quoted in Whalen, *Catch the Falling Flag*, 142.

47. Ibid., 143.

48. Quoted in ibid., 144. Whalen commented: "The maneuver tacitly conveyed a friendlier message to the White House—'You can trust me not to make any trouble for you.' Thus was laid the groundwork for a nonaggression pact between incumbent and challenger that would become increasingly apparent in the months ahead." Concerning bargaining leverage, see *Nixon Speaks Out*, 235; and *NYT*, August 2, 1968.

49. *NYT*, June 30, 1968.

50. See, e.g., Whalen, *Catch the Falling Flag*, 26, 30.

51. Anna Chennault, *The Education of Anna* (New York: Times Books, 1980), 185.

52. *HRHD*, January 12, 1973; Safire, *Before the Fall*, 88; Chennault, *Education of Anna*, 170; Bui Diem with David Chanoff, *In the Jaws of History* (Boston: Houghton Mifflin, 1987), chap. 28; Nguyen Tien Hung and Jerrold L. Schecter, *The Palace File* (New York: Harper and Row, 1986), 23–24; Clifford, *Counsel to the President*, 581–583. Bui Diem was also in touch with Senator John Tower, another Nixon operative. Chennault was Nixon's link to Thieu, either directly or through Thieu's brother, Nguyen Van Kieu, who was the RVN's ambassador in Taipei. She also chaired the Republican Women's Finance Committee and was Chair of Women for Nixon National Advisory Committee. When Nixon needed to make another personal appeal to Thieu in January 1973, he told Haldeman to contact the "dragon lady"; *HRHD*, January 4, 1973.

53. Hung and Schecter, *Palace File*, 23; Chennault, *Education of Anna*, 170–177; Kent G. Sieg, "The 1968 Presidential Election and Peace in Vietnam," *Presidential Studies Quarterly* 26 (Fall 1996): 1068. According to Hung and Schecter, Thieu sent his own messengers to Washington to speak with Chennault and also used his brother as an intermediary.

54. Chennault and Hung and Schecter said that one meeting took place in the winter of 1967; Chennault remembers it to have been snowing. Bui Diem mentions the meeting, or perhaps another meeting, to have taken place in July 1968. Ibid.; Bui Diem, *In the Jaws of History*, 236–237; Sieg, "1968 Presidential Election", 1069.

55. Diem interview in Strober and Strober, *Nixon,* 170.

56. Bui Diem, *In the Jaws of History,* 237.

57. Nguyen Hung and Schecter interviews with Thieu, May 3, 1985, and Hoang Duc Nha, July 23, 1985, in *Palace File,* 21, 29.

58. Drawing on Theodore H. White's account in *The Making of the President, 1968* (New York: Atheneum, 1969), 380–381, Stephen Ambrose, in *Nixon,* vol. 2, *The Triumph of a Politician, 1962–1972* (New York: Simon and Schuster, 1989), 206–217, argued that Chennault had acted in Nixon's name without authorization, but that it did not in any case make a difference, since Thieu would have refused to cooperate with Johnson or Humphrey anyway: "Not that Nixon did not want to [prevent peace in 1968], or try to, but he did not have to" (215). Only "Nixon bashers," he wrote, would suspect something more nefarious. Safire made a similar argument in *Before the Fall,* 88–91; and George Herring offered a comparable disclaimer in *America's Longest War: The United States and Vietnam, 1950–1975,* 3d ed. (New York: McGraw-Hill, 1996), 238, n. 67. It is doubtful, however, that Thieu would have resisted Johnson for as long as he did without Nixon's encouragement. (After the election, for example, Nixon joined Johnson in pressuring Thieu to negotiate, and Thieu relented.) Moreover, the story of the Chennault-Thieu contacts is documented sufficiently to leave little doubt that Nixon was its instigator and that it made a difference, or that if it did not make a difference, he wanted it to. See references above and below, especially Sieg, "1968 Presidential Election," but also *HRHD,* January 8, 11, and 12, 1973; and Nixon's comments in Crowley, *Nixon Off the Record,* 17.

59. Hersh, *Price of Power,* 12–24; Sieg, "1968 Presidential Election," 1069–1070.

60. Memorandum for the President, September 7, 1967, sub: The Kissinger Project, microfiche no. 3594, declassified May 26, 1994, *Declassified Documents Catalog* (Woodbridge, Conn.: Research Publications, 1994), vol. 20, no. 6. For a Vietnamese account, see Luu Van Loi, "The Johnson Episode in the Vietnam War," *Vietnamese Studies* 28, 1 (1992), n.s., no. 33 (103): 28–30. The W. Averell Harriman Papers in the Manuscript Division of the Library of Congress contain a memorandum from Chester L. Cooper, special assistant to Harriman, to Mr. Boudreau, dated August 10, 1967, requesting invitational travel orders for Kissinger, who was going to Paris "with projects of concern to the State Department"; folder: Henry Kissinger, box 481, Special Files: Public Service, Kennedy-Johnson Administrations, 1958–71, Subject File.

61. Letter, Kissinger to Harriman, May 31, 1968, folder: Henry Kissinger, box 481, Harriman Papers, MDLC.

62. Letter, Kissinger to Harriman, August 15, 1968, ibid.

63. *RN,* 345. See also Ilya V. Gaiduk, *The Soviet Union and the Vietnam War* (Chicago: Ivan R. Dee, 1996), chap. 8.

64. These are Nixon's words from *RN,* 323.

65. In his biography of Kissinger, Walter Isaacson argued that Kissinger's information was not crucial, since, as Nixon claimed, Kissinger provided no "details of negotiations," and that in any case Bryce Harlow, a campaign aide, was in touch with a mole in what Nixon called "Johnson's innermost circle"; Isaacson, *Kissinger* (New York: Simon and Schuster, 1992), 129–132. See also *RN,* 323, 326; and Safire, *Before the Fall,* 84. If there was a source in the White House, however, he misinformed Nixon that Johnson was in close touch with Humphrey and acting on his behalf. See White, *The Making of the President,* 353–356; and Clifford, *Counsel to the President,* 593–596. But Nixon, Allen, and Mitchell credited Kissinger with playing a key role; see Hersh, *Price of Power,* 12–24.

Even if he did not provide diplomatic details, he did give the Nixon camp the first news about the possible timing of an announcement regarding a bombing halt, allowing Nixon to speak with informed confidence on the issue during the final stages of the campaign and with the necessary urgency in his secret contacts with Thieu. If nothing else, Kissinger confirmed information that Nixon may have been receiving from others. See also Sieg, "1968 Presidential Election," 1070.

66. *RN,* 324.

67. *NYT,* October 1, 2, and 9, 1968; Hersh, *Price of Power,* 18. See also Sieg, "1968 Presidential Election," 1066–1067. Nixon could accuse Humphrey of lack of clarity because there was press confusion about whether Humphrey's call amounted to a break with Johnson, which it did and did not. The Democratic candidate's position was scarcely different from the president's position in Paris, but publicly, Johnson had not yet committed himself to a halt. Thus, Humphrey was a step ahead publicly. What was slightly new about Humphrey's position was that he said he was willing to stop the bombing even without a formal quid pro quo from Hanoi, but that if Hanoi failed to respond, he would resume the bombing. Yet Humphrey's position was sufficiently similar to Johnson's, i.e., the one he was proposing in Paris, that Hanoi said it all amounted to the same. Meanwhile, Nixon made essentially the same promise. His position was different, however, in its emphasis on strengthening South Vietnamese forces and improving the allied military position before making a deal about a bombing halt. Actually, Nixon was sending mixed signals: he was in favor of a bombing halt under certain conditions, but he accused Humphrey of giving away American advantages when he advocated it. Essentially, Nixon was suggesting, without being specific, that he could get a better deal. Robert Dallek's *Flawed Giant: Lyndon Johnson and His Times, 1961–1973* (New York: Oxford University Press, 1998) includes new information and insights on the Johnson-Nixon-Humphrey relationship, but it was published too late for inclusion in this book.

68. *RN,* 323–324; Clifford, *Counsel to the President,* 576–577; Sieg, "1968 Presidential Election," 1070.

69. *RN,* 327–328; see also Safire, *Before the Fall,* 84–88.

70. *RN,* 327. This is Safire's view as well; *Before the Fall,* 90–91. Nixon and Kissinger would undoubtedly have used the word "treasonous" to describe anyone who would have opposed their government in the manner they opposed Johnson's. Nixon does not discuss his contacts with Thieu in *RN.*

71. Hung and Schecter, *Palace File,* 24; and Bui Diem, *In the Jaws of History,* 244. See also Hersh, *Price of Power,* 21; and Stanley Karnow, *Vietnam: A History* (New York: Knopf, 1983), 585–586.

72. Tom Johnson's notes on the meeting, quoted in Gaiduk, *The Soviet Union and the Vietnam War,* 185.

73. Ibid., 194–197.

74. *RN,* 345.

75. Chennault, *Education of Anna,* 190; Sieg, "1968 Presidential Election," 1070–1071.

76. Safire, *Before the Fall,* 88.

77. The evidence may not have been firm enough by then; see Thomas Powers, *The Man Who Kept the Secrets: Richard Helms and the CIA* (New York: Knopf, 1979), 197–200; cf. Sieg, "1968 Presidential Election," 1070–1072.

78. Memo, Walt W. Rostow to Johnson, October 31, 1968, microfiche no. 3588, declassified December 7, 1992, *Declassified Documents Catalog,* vol. 19, no. 6.

79. Quoted in Clifford, *Counsel to the President,* 593.

80. Additional reasons for Johnson's behavior have been given: his concern about disclosing the surveillance of Diem and Chennault; his concern about appearing to have acted for political motives; his underestimation of the damage Thieu could wreak with his opposition; and his reluctance to expose Chennault, a close friend of Tommy Corcoran, "Mr. Democrat." See pages cited earlier in Hersh, *Price of Power;* Clifford, *Counsel to the President;* and Powers, *The Man Who Kept the Secrets;* Sieg, "1968 Presidential Election."

81. Nixon and his aides regarded Kissinger's role as important, his motives noble, and his efforts to maintain secrecy commendable; *RN,* 323; Hersh, *Price of Power,* 22–24. But Kissinger's motives were hardly noble: he was maneuvering for an appointment to the Nixon administration should Nixon win, believing that he had a good chance to become national security adviser or to play a role in policy planning. Meanwhile, he played to the Humphrey camp, promising Rockefeller's files on Nixon, which he never delivered, and banked on his past services and ties to the Johnson administration. Isaacson, *Kissinger,* 130–134.

82. Gaiduk, *The Soviet Union and the Vietnam War,* 181–193.

83. *WHY,* 52–53.

4. NIXON, KISSINGER, AND THE MADMAN THEORY

1. Quoted in Isaacson, *Kissinger,* 164.

2. There are many books on the Nixon-Kissinger relationship, but see, especially: Hersh, *Price of Power;* Hoff, *Nixon Reconsidered;* Isaacson, *Kissinger;* and Robert D. Schulzinger, *Henry Kissinger: Doctor of Diplomacy* (New York: Columbia University Press, 1989). Hoff's article "A Revisionist View of Nixon's Foreign Policy," *Presidential Studies Quarterly* 26 (Winter 1996): 107–130, is excellent, although I take issue with some of her conclusions in following pages.

3. The Haldeman diaries and notes and the Watergate tapes are peppered with indirect evidence of Nixon's sexual prudishness and anti-Semitism, but both attitudes were mixed up with his political battles, his partisanship, and his dislike of the Left and the Establishment. On anti-Semitism, see "Nixon Library Shelves Plan," *Washington Post,* April 12, 1997, and September 13, 1971, and October 20, 1972, entries in *Abuse of Power,* 31–32, 172. Garment, a Jew himself, offers a defense of Nixon, pointing out that he had many Jewish pals; *Crazy Rhythm,* 199–200. On the question of the role of women, Haldeman summarized Nixon's views as told to Girls Nation, a youth program of the American Legion: "He did a superb job with them, speaking on the role of women in government, and so forth, but then emphasizing that the real role of women is as wives and mothers, and he gave a very eloquent pitch for considering the importance of that role too, as contrasted to women's lib"; *HRHD,* August 6, 1971.

4. Quoted in Oriana Fallaci, *Interview with History,* trans. John Shepley (New York: Liveright, 1976), 42–43. The *Haldeman Diaries* contain several entries that indicate Nixon's public relations concerns about Kissinger's dates and liaisons.

5. Quoted in Nicholas Lemann, "The Decline and Fall of the Eastern Empire," *Vanity Fair,* October 1994, 249.

6. Isaacson, *Kissinger,* 56.

7. On notions of freedom and social stability, he drew from Spinosa; on perspectives on individual will, from Machiavelli and Kant; on views of history's forces and counterforces, from Hegel; on pessimism, from Spengler; and on critiques of bureaucracy, from Weber. See Robert L. Beisner, "History and Henry Kissinger," *Diplomatic History* 14 (Fall 1990): 511–528.

8. Kissinger refers to himself as "the good courtier" in *WHY*, 302. On the restructuring of the NSC, see Memo, Kissinger to Nixon, n.d., sub: A New NSC System, and Memo, Kissinger to Nixon, January 10, 1969, sub: Additional Provisions Concerning the Conduct of National Security Affairs, folders: (4) Memoranda to the President-Elect and (5) Memo to President-Elect, box 2, NSC: HAKOF, HAKASF, NPM.

9. Hoff, *Nixon Reconsidered*, 147–157.

10. See, e.g., *WHY*, 229.

11. Quoted in Fallaci, *Interview with History*, 44.

12. See, e.g., *HRHD*, June 29, 1971.

13. Quoted in Isaacson, *Kissinger*, 100.

14. *HRHD*, January 25, 1969.

15. Kissinger to Nixon, November 7, 1972, folder: Henry Kissinger, box 10 (Kaplow, Herb), 1969–74, WHSF: PPF, NPM.

16. *HRHD*, December 18, 1972.

17. *In the Arena*, 313. Cf. "The people want to believe the best, but nations are motivated by their self-interest, not by love and affection and so forth"; *HRHD*, June 16, 1972.

18. Henry A. Kissinger, *Nuclear Weapons and Foreign Policy* (New York: Harper, 1957), 4.

19. Kissinger made these remarks at a conference for representatives of the military-industrial-scientific-academic-government complex; Kissinger, "The Relation Between Force and Diplomacy," *Military Industrial Conference: Proceedings of the Papers and Discussions*, Chicago, March 14–15, 1957, 17. This publication is filed in Military Industrial Conference, Kenney Collection 168, Air Force Historical Research Agency, Maxwell Air Force Base.

20. Isaacson, *Kissinger*, 283–284.

21. *In the Arena*, 313. After the war Kissinger probably spoke more of victory in Vietnam as an impossible dream than Nixon, but he committed himself to the cause during the war nevertheless. He accused Nixon in at least one postwar comment of belatedly coming to the theory of limits; Kissinger, response to question by the author, Mershon Center, Columbus, Ohio, April 30, 1993. On purported U.S. oscillations in behavior between idealistic over-commitment and isolationist withdrawal, see *WHY*, 57.

22. *HRHD*, April 19, 1969, and May 13, 1971.

23. *Leaders*, 4–5.

24. Beisner, "History and Henry Kissinger," 514. Kissinger told de Gaulle that Bismarck was his favorite; *WHY*, 110.

25. *WHY*, 597.

26. Quoted in Beisner, "History and Henry Kissinger," 514.

27. He followed this remark with, "I also believe that there are limits to the struggle that a man can put up to reach a goal," but his emphasis in this exchange was on the spontaneity of action. Quoted in Oriana Fallaci, "Henry Kissinger," *Interview with History*, trans. John Shepley (New York: Liveright, 1976), 41–42.

28. Ibid., 29.

29. Kissinger, "The Relation Between Force and Diplomacy," 17.

30. *HRHD,* April 19, 1969.

31. Isaacson, *Kissinger,* 88.

32. Kissinger, *Nuclear Weapons and Foreign Policy,* 226.

33. Ibid., 172–173. The debates among defense intellectuals, experts, and policy makers not only represented the theoretical disputes among thinkers but also reflected the nuts-and-bolts debates within the military services and the military-industrial complex about defense policy and where money was to be spent.

34. Other candidates included the strategic thinker Herman Kahn and Edward Teller, the Hungarian refugee physicist who campaigned for the development of the "Super" in the late 1940s and became known as the "father of the H-bomb."

35. For a full account of the origins of arms control among antinuclear activists, policy makers, and leaders of nonaligned nations, see Lawrence S. Wittner, *Resisting the Bomb: A History of the World Nuclear Disarmament Movement, 1954–1970* (Stanford, Calif.: Stanford University Press, 1997).

36. Isaacson, *Kissinger,* 107.

37. See Terry Terriff, *The Nixon Administration and the Making of U.S. Nuclear Strategy* (Ithaca, N.Y.: Cornell University Press, 1995).

38. *WHY,* 231–232, 226.

39. Dana Ward, "Kissinger: A Psychohistory," *History of Childhood Quarterly* 2 (Winter 1975): 288, 302, 324–325.

40. See, e.g., *WHY,* 227, 229.

41. Quoted in Fallaci, "Henry Kissinger," in *Interview with History,* 35.

42. *WHY,* 229–232.

43. Henry A. Kissinger, "The Viet Nam Negotiations," *Foreign Affairs* 47 (January 1969): 212.

44. Ibid., 211–234.

45. Ibid., 218–219; *WHY,* 228. De Gaulle pooh-poohed Kissinger's notions about credibility; ibid., 110.

46. Fallaci, *Interview with History,* 48.

47. Kissinger, "The Viet Nam Negotiations," 217–218, 220, 229, 233–234. Nixon did not see this article until after mid-December; Memo, Kissinger to Nixon, December 13, 1968, folder: Memoranda to the President-Elect, box 2, NSC: HAKOF, HAKASF, NPM.

48. In *RN* Nixon repeated his campaign disavowal, pointing out that he had "never said" he had a "'plan,' much less a 'secret plan' to end the war," for he had recognized "the difficulty of finding a solution" and how "absurd" it would have been at the time to reveal a plan even if he had one: "premature disclosure" would have doomed "even the best-laid plans"; *RN,* 298.

49. *NYT,* August 2, 1968; "Vietnam," in *Nixon Speaks Out,* 234–237.

50. "The All-Volunteer Armed Force," in *Nixon Speaks Out,* 203.

51. "To Keep the Peace," in *Nixon Speaks Out,* 231 ff.

52. Herring, *LBJ and Vietnam,* 58.

53. *NYT,* September 26, 1968.

54. Ibid., August 2, 1968; "Vietnam," in *Nixon Speaks Out,* 234–237.

55. Dale Andradé, *Ashes to Ashes: The Phoenix Program and the Vietnam War* (Lexington, Mass.: Lexington Books, 1990), 71 ff.

56. *NYT,* August 2, 1968; "Vietnam," in *Nixon Speaks Out,* 234–237.

57. *Nixon Speaks Out,* 234.

58. "Viet 3rd Redraft," in Whalen, *Catch the Falling Flag,* 290–292.

59. Herring, *LBJ and Vietnam,* 119.

60. "Viet 3rd Redraft," in Whalen, *Catch the Falling Flag,* 284–286.

61. Ibid.

62. Whalen, *Catch the Falling Flag,* 290 ff.

63. *No More Vietnams,* 103–107.

64. "Viet 3rd Redraft," in Whalen, *Catch the Falling Flag,* 284–286.

65. Quoted in H. R. Haldeman, with Joseph DiMona, *The Ends of Power* (New York: Times Books, 1978), 82–83.

66. Whalen, *Catch the Falling Flag,* 26–27 (italics in original).

67. The most notable are Fred I. Greenstein, "A Journalist's Vendetta," *The New Republic,* August 1, 1983, 29–31; and Joan Hoff, "Richard M. Nixon: The Corporate Presidency," in *Leadership in the Modern Presidency,* ed. Fred I. Greenstein (Cambridge, Mass.: Harvard University Press, 1988), 172, 179. Hoff said that Nixon claimed he never talked to Haldeman about substantive foreign policy matters, but this is not true, as Haldeman's diaries and notes prove. Haldeman may not have worked on foreign policy with Nixon, but he listened to Nixon's and Kissinger's musings and ramblings, and he attended some meetings in which the issue was discussed. He also made his own comments on the subject and weighed in on the advisers' attempts to sway Nixon's decisions. See, e.g., *HRHD,* December 15, 1970.

68. Hoff, "Corporate Presidency."

69. *HRHD,* January 14, 1973.

70. Quoted in Thomas L. Hughes, "Foreign Policy: Men or Measures?" *Atlantic,* October 1974, 56. The president's appointment calendar for this date does show that Nixon had a dinner date with Moorer and Wilson; *HRHD,* December 18, 1972. See also the more well documented account concerning the Jordanian crisis of 1970 in chapter 10.

71. See, e.g., the discussion of Nixon's words during the Jordanian crisis of 1970 in chapter 10.

72. Hoff, "Corporate Presidency," 188; see also Hoff, *Nixon Reconsidered,* 176–178.

73. Journalist Tad Szulc offered an unattributed but similar characterization (good guy-bad guy) of the Nixon-Kissinger diplomatic symbiosis in *Illusion of Peace,* 63.

74. Klein, *Making It Perfectly Clear,* 399.

75. Safire, *Before the Fall,* 48, 368. The account of Safire, who wrote speeches for candidate Nixon and spoke frequently with him about his positions, conforms to the account of Whalen, who was a speechwriter as well, and sat in on the same predraft and postdraft meetings.

76. Winston Lord, interview by author, tape recording, December 5, 1994, Washington, D.C. See also Lord, quoted in Strober and Strober, *Nixon: An Oral History of His Presidency,* 178. In one top secret document, however, Kissinger aides Roger Morris and Anthony Lake described Nixinger strategy in 1969 as consisting of deliberately irrational threats; Memo, Morris and Lake to Kissinger, October 21, 1969, sub: Another Vietnam Option, folder: Tony Lake Chron File (Jun. 1969–May 1970) (1 of 6), box 1047, NSC: SF—LCF, NPM.

77. Quoted in Strober and Strober, *Nixon: An Oral History of His Presidency,* 172.

Also see Daniel Ellsberg's comments on Nixon's plan for bombing and Vietnamization, ibid., 172.

78. Quoted in Isaacson, *Kissinger,* 170.

79. Hersh, *Price of Power,* 53 n. This was probably Kissinger's seminar on Western Europe, which he co-taught, and for which he received $8,000 a year from the Rockefeller Brothers Fund to pay for visiting speakers. Isaacson, *Kissinger,* 99.

80. Copies of all papers provided to the author by Daniel Ellsberg. The terms "anatomy of blackmail" and "sound of blackmail" are to be found in "The Theory and Practice of Blackmail," 363.

81. The book *Fail-Safe* (New York: McGraw-Hill, 1962), by Eugene Burdick and Harvey Wheeler, appeared as a movie in 1964. The character of Walter Grotoschele resembled Kissinger. Based on Peter George's book *Red Alert* (New York: Ace Books, 1958), the movie *Dr. Strangelove or: How I Learned to Stop Worrying and Love the Bomb,* with screenplay by George, Stanley Kubrick, and Terry Southern, was released in 1963. In the movie, the concept of madness is encapsulated in the strategy behind the Doomsday Machine. On American culture during the nuclear age, see Margot A. Henriksen, *Dr. Strangelove's America: Society and Culture in the Atomic Age* (Berkeley: University of California Press, 1997); and Allan M. Winkler, *Life Under a Cloud: American Anxiety About the Bomb* (New York: Oxford University Press, 1995).

82. *Department of Defense Annual Report for Fiscal Year 1965* (Washington, D.C., GPO, 1967), 12; Robert S. McNamara, *The Essence of Security: Reflections in Office* (New York: Harper and Row, 1968), 159–160.

83. Thomas Hobbes, *Leviathan* (1651), chap. 8.

84. Kissinger, *Nuclear Weapons and Foreign Policy,* 225–226

85. Ibid., 224.

86. Henry A. Kissinger, *The Necessity for Choice* (New York: Harper and Brothers, 1961), 89.

87. Quoted in Isaacson, *Kissinger,* 164. In *The Ends of Power,* 97–98, Haldeman wrote: "From the first days in office the brilliant Nixon-Kissinger team was confident they could finish, with honor, the most difficult conflict this nation has ever waged: the Vietnam War. Nixon had conceived the 'Madman Theory' as the way to do it. Henry perfected the theory and carried it to the secret series of Paris peace talks: A threat of egregious military action by an unpredictable U.S. President who hated Communism, coupled with generous offers of financial aid. Henry arrived at the peace negotiations fully expecting this plan to be successful."

88. Haldeman, *Ends of Power,* 83.

89. Historian Nguyen Vu Tung, interview by the author, February 2, 1995, Oslo, Norway.

90. A local newspaper obtained a tape recording of Nixon's private, off-the-record remarks: "What Dick Nixon Told Southern Delegates," *Miami Herald,* August 7, 1968, 1, 22A. Even though Nixon was assured of the nomination at the Miami convention, he was concerned about an "erosion" of delegates, some to Rockefeller and some to Reagan, whom he thought were cooperating to deny him the nomination; *RN,* 309. His speech to these southern conservative delegates was probably partly designed to hold their loyalty. Despite this political purpose, Nixon meant what he said about the applicability of the Korean analogy to Vietnam, and he alluded to this story in public speeches during the campaign and on other occasions after the war. See, e.g., *NYT,* October 8, 1968; *Time,* July 29, 1985, 50.

91. C. Turner Joy, *How Communists Negotiate* (New York: Macmillan, 1955), 161–162.

92. James Shepley, "How Dulles Averted War," *Life*, January 16, 1956, 70–80.

93. Dwight D. Eisenhower, *Mandate for Change, 1953–1956* (Garden City, N.Y.: Doubleday, 1963), 181.

94. Whalen, writing of a conversation with Nixon, said: "The Republican version of recent history claimed that only the threat of nuclear weapons had extricated the U.S. from the Korean War"; *Catch the Falling Flag*, 27.

95. Mark A. Ryan, *Chinese Attitudes Toward Nuclear Weapons: China and the United States During the Korean War* (Armonk, N.Y.: M. E. Sharpe, 1989), 64. Nixon claimed the message was given to Krishna Menon, Indian ambassador to the United Nations. Perhaps he had misremembered or was thinking of other "threats"; *Time*, July 29, 1985, 50.

96. Ryan, *Chinese Attitudes Toward Nuclear Weapons*, 156.

97. Ibid., chaps. 2, 3, 7; Kathryn Weathersby, "New Russian Documents on the Korean War," and Bruce Cumings and Kathryn Weathersby, "An Exchange on Korean War Origins," both in "New Evidence on the Korean War," *Cold War International History Project Bulletin*, Issues 6–7 (Winter 1995/1996): 30–125. Also see Hersh, *Price of Power*, 52; Dingman, "Atomic Diplomacy During the Korean War," 50–91; Keefer, "Eisenhower and the End of the Korean War," 267–268; Daniel Calingaert, "Nuclear Weapons and the Korean War," *Journal of Strategic Studies* 11 (June 1988): 177–202.

98. *Time*, July 29, 1985, 50. Nixon also believed that Rhee's intransigence and unpredictability had added to the credibility of the threat scenario.

99. Ibid.; Whalen, *Catch the Falling Flag*, 27.

100. Oswald Jacoby, *Oswald Jacoby on Poker* (New York: Doubleday, 1947), 1. Statesmen and diplomats during the war often used poker analogies, mixing them with other game metaphors. In July 1968, for example, Johnson's national security adviser, W. W. Rostow, wrote the president concerning recent moves in negotiations with Hanoi and Moscow to bring about a bombing halt and begin talks in Paris: "This is pretty high-risk poker. . . . But the fact is that the Kosygin letter gives us an opening for this gambit." Quoted in Gaiduk, *The Soviet Union and the Vietnam War*, 173.

101. *HRHD*, January 14, 1973. See also *WHY*, 1365.

102. In another of his backhanded threats—in which he typically issued a warning of drastic action by denying his intention to resort to it—Nixon told the press on October 7 that "he had no wish to destroy North Vietnam or conquer it, and that he was, in fact, willing to help rebuild it." Such a "generous peace," he explained, was conditional on their agreement to respect the territorial and political integrity of South Vietnam, which of course was not likely unless he could force them to make this key concession; *NYT*, October 8, 1968.

103. Quoted in Whalen, *Catch the Falling Flag*, 137.

104. *HRHD*, January 14, 1973.

105. Ellsberg, "Political Uses of Madness," p. 17.

106. Kissinger, *Nuclear Weapons and Foreign Policy*, 428.

5. AVOIDING DEFEAT, SEEKING VICTORY: 1968–1969

1. *NYT*, October 8, 1968.

2. *Public Papers of the Presidents of the United States, Richard Nixon: 1969* (Washington, D.C.: GPO, 1971), 1.

3. *RN,* 348. Nixon enumerated additional noble goals in his public statements and postwar books, e.g., obtaining the release of American POWs; see *No More Vietnams,* 100. Other administration officials spoke in principled terms as well. Concerning the protection of the South Vietnamese, self-determination, opposition to aggression, and commitment, President Johnson's defense of U.S. policies presaged Nixon's. In *Vantage Point,* Johnson wrote: "We had kept our word to Southeast Asia. We had opposed and defeated aggression, as we promised we would. We had given 17 million South Vietnamese a chance to build their own country and their own institutions. And we had seen them move well down that road" (529).

4. Quoted in *Time,* July 29, 1985, 49.

5. *No More Vietnams,* 100.

6. The McNaughton memoranda are revealing of how national security advisers and policy makers weigh multiple goals. Nixon's goals and the way he combined them were not very different. McNaughton wrote at least two memoranda in which he ranked America's aims in Vietnam: "Action for South Vietnam," November 6, 1964, and "Annex—Plan for Action for South Vietnam," [appended to memorandum from McNaughton to McNamara], March 24, 1965, *Pentagon Papers,* Senator Gravel edition, vol. 3: 601 and 695.

7. Ibid., 216–217.

8. Briefing, n.d., folder: Vietnam-Rostow, box 16, WHSF: PPF, 1969–74, NPM. Nixon often lectured to his staff about the "whys" of Vietnam; see, e.g., *HRHD,* May 15, 1969.

9. *RN,* 348–349.

10. *HRHD,* July 21, 1969. See also September 5, 1969, regarding the "need to show [the] reestablishment of American leadership around the world."

11. *WHY,* 70, 228–230.

12. Henry A. Kissinger, *Diplomacy* (New York: Simon and Schuster, 1994), 675.

13. Nguyen Tien Hung, Thieu's special assistant, quoted in Hung and Schecter, *Palace File,* 21.

14. Chennault, *Education of Anna,* 197–198. In her conversations with Dirksen, Chennault assured him that she was no longer angry, but said, "I'm going to tell the story some day." Her attitude about the 1968 intrigue was that there had been nothing wrong with it, so convinced was she of its moral correctness. The Nixon camp apparently thought otherwise, and so did the Democrats and the press; ibid., 195.

15. Kissinger, "The Viet Nam Negotiations," 233.

16. On the phrase "game plan," see *HRHD,* October 3, 1969. Nixon used it on this day in the sense of game-planning the alternatives for Vietnam.

17. Haldeman paraphrasing Kissinger; ibid., March 9, 1969.

18. Options Paper, December 27, 1968 (provided to the author by Daniel Ellsberg), [p. 2]. (This document, dubbed "options paper" by the Library of Congress archivist who received it from Ellsberg in 1992, can be found in the March 1998 release by the National Archives of previously classified NSC files in the folder labeled Vietnam—RAND, box 3, NSC: HAKOF, HAKASF, NPM. There it is titled Vietnam Policy Alternatives and is filed with two related documents: The Situation in Vietnam and Sample Questions. In the following notes of this book, the main document, Vietnam Policy Alternatives, is referred to as Ellsberg Options Paper.) Henry Rowen, president of RAND was also present at the first

meeting; Isaacson, *Kissinger,* 162. This definition of victory was also reflected in National Security Study Memorandum 1, which represented the Nixon government's understanding. See Revised Summary of Responses to National Security Study Memorandum 1, March 22, 1969, *Documents of the National Security Council: Second Supplement* (Frederick, Md.: University Publications of America, 1983), microfilm, reel 3, pp. 2, 24, 27, 28.

19. Ellsberg Options Paper, December 27, 1968, n.p. [page following table of contents].

20. Ibid., [p. 1].

21. Ibid., [p. 6].

22. Kissinger quoted in *HRHD,* July 7, 1969.

23. Ellsberg Options Paper, [p. 15].

24. Ibid., [p. 19].

25. Ibid., [p. 18].

26. Quoted in Isaacson, *Kissinger,* 164.

27. NSSM 1, January 21, 1969. Twenty-eight questions were asked of the Department of State and the CIA, twenty-nine of the DOD and JCS.

28. Revised Summary, NSSM 1, March 22, 1969, 1.

29. Ibid., 2.

30. Ibid., 2–3.

31. Jeffrey J. Clarke, *United States Army in Vietnam: Advice and Support: The Final Years, The US Army in Vietnam* (Washington, D.C.: Center of Military History, 1988), 344.

32. Revised Summary, NSSM 1, 15.

33. *WHY,* 238–239. See also Revised Summary, NSSM 1, March 22, 4 ff.

34. Revised Summary, NSSM 1, 16, 26.

35. Ibid., 16, 27.

36. Ibid., 27.

37. Ibid., 27–28.

38. NSSM 1 Directive, January 21, 1969, 5.

39. Clarke, *Advice and Support,* 362.

40. See, e.g., Revised Summary, NSSM 1, 27.

41. Ibid., 30–32.

42. Kissinger claimed in *WHY,* 238, that the summary was prepared by his staff. Isaacson, *Kissinger,* 164, said that Ellsberg, still working as a consultant, collated the responses from February to March.

43. *RN,* 298.

44. *No More Vietnams,* 103–107.

45. *HRHD,* April 23, 1970.

46. See also, *NYT,* May 9, 1969: "The decision to demonstrate to Hanoi that the Nixon administration is different and 'tougher' than the previous administration was reached in January, well-placed sources say, as part of a strategy for ending the war." Joan Hoff argued that "Nixon had no clear idea in 1969 of how to end the war quickly" but pursued those options available to him—secret negotiations and the expansion of the war in Cambodia and Laos; *Nixon Reconsidered,* 210. It is true that these were Nixon's only options, given his commitment to victory (aka ending the war), but to his mind at the beginning of 1969, it was reasonably clear that these options would work, especially when combined with other options.

47. Memorandum of Conversation with H. Kissinger, Dobrynin to A. Gromyko, July 12, 1969, Communist Party of the Soviet Union Central Committee Archive, reprinted in *Cold War International History Project Bulletin,* Issue 3 (Fall 1993): 65.

48. *HRHD,* April 15, 1969.

49. Memo, Kissinger to Nixon, September 10, 1969, sub: Our Present Course on Vietnam, folder: Tony Lake Chron File (Jun. 1969–May 1970) (5 of 6), box 1048, NSC: SF—LCF, NPM. The memo is reprinted in *WHY,* 1480 n. 11.

50. One part of his domestic plan of action was to effect reforms in the Selective Service system, in which the public had lost confidence, and to engage in more vigorous prosecution of draft resisters and evaders. On March 27, 1969, Nixon announced the formation of a commission to look into the creation of an all-volunteer force, and on May 19 he asked Congress to make changes in the Selective Service system that would have the effect of reducing draft calls of men who were twenty years old and older while increasing those for eighteen- and nineteen-year-olds, with the result, presumably, of muting the former's opposition to the war. Nixon's reforms, namely, the lottery (1971) and the all-volunteer system (1973), came at a time when draft calls were declining because troops were being withdrawn from Vietnam, or after the Paris cease-fire agreement, too late to have much effect on protest but early enough to influence the 1972 election.

51. *HRHD,* March 20, 1969.

52. *WHY,* 266–267.

53. Morris, *Uncertain Greatness,* chap. 4 passim.

54. *HRHD,* October 17, 1969, and May 26, 1971.

55. Ibid., passim.

56. Ellsberg quoted in Strober and Strober, *Nixon: An Oral History of His Presidency,* 172.

57. *WHY,* 258.

58. *HRHD,* January 23 and 31, 1969.

59. Ibid., boxed comment, October 8, 1969. Haldeman recalled that on taking office, "there was an absolute conviction on Nixon's part that, by the fall of 1969, he would have Vietnam settled"; quoted in Strober and Strober, *Nixon: An Oral History of His Presidency,* 183. See also, Haldeman, *Ends of Power,* 82; and *NYT,* April 6, 1969.

60. *HRHD,* March 20, 1969.

61. *RN,* 349.

62. Quoted in Marvin Kalb and Bernard Kalb, *Kissinger* (Boston: Little, Brown, 1974), 120. According to the Kalbs, these words were spoken in the "first six months." Hersh, in *Price of Power,* 119, quotes Kissinger as having said "three months" to the Quakers.

63. Quoted in Isaacson, *Kissinger,* 165. In April 1969, however, Lake described the administration's strategy as one of "settlement or 'Vietnamizing' the conflict by 1971/ 72," which suggested that it was considering a decent-interval solution and an extended timetable for ending American intervention; Lake to Richard Sneider, April 17, 1969, folder: W. A. K. Lake File (Apr. 1969), box 1048, NSC: SF—LCF, NPM. But the reference is obscure, and he may have meant that the administration expected to achieve a mutual withdrawal of North Vietnamese and American forces in 1969 or 1970, which would be followed by a struggle between the South Vietnamese belligerents (with Saigon receiving indirect American assistance) that would be settled in Saigon's favor by 1971/72. Or it could have been the case that Lake was not privy to the real Nixinger strategy.

64. *WHY,* 262.

65. Quoted in Haldeman, *Ends of Power,* 81.

66. *HRHD,* October 8, 1969.

67. Memo, Rita Hauser to Nixon, April 29, 1969, folder: Ex 6-1, Paris Peace Talks (sub: Vietnam) [1969–70], WHCF: SF, FO, NPM. Hauser was the American UN representative. See also Memo for the record, Daniel P. Moynihan, March 8, 1969, ibid. For more on Harriman, see Sieg, "W. Averell Harriman, Henry Cabot Lodge," 237–249.

68. *WHY,* 261.

69. Ibid., 284.

6. TALKING WHILE FIGHTING: 1969

1. Nguyen Co Thach, interview by the author, September 24, 1994, Hanoi.

2. For the most part, after the election Nixon's public message was one of cautious optimism: ending the war would be difficult—"tough," as Nixon and Haldeman phrased it—but it could be done. Privately, however, they seemed truly confident; *HRHD,* March 20, 1969.

3. Memo, Nixon to Kissinger, February 1, 1969, folder: Ex 6-1, Paris Peace Talks (sub: Vietnam) [1969–70], box 63, WHCF: SF, FO, NPM. Kissinger phoned Lodge on February 4.

4. *HRHD,* March 20, 1969.

5. *NYT,* April 6, 1969.

6. Ibid.

7. Memo, Nixon to Rogers, Laird, Bunker, Lodge, Kissinger, April 14, 1969, folder: ABM, box 5, WHSF: PPF, Name/Subject File, 1969–74, NPM, with enclosure: Cable, Berger to Rogers, April 11. Wilkinson had helped Nixon during the campaign and was a Republican Party activist.

8. *HRHD,* January 27, 1969.

9. *WHY,* 261.

10. *HRHD,* March 20, 1969.

11. *WHY,* 262–263.

12. See ibid., 260, 284.

13. E.g., Chester Cooper, Harriman's special assistant, recommended the establishment of a direct channel to Hanoi in 1967; Memo, Cooper to Harriman, March 11, 1967, folder: Vietnam, box 520, Special Files: Public Service, Kennedy-Johnson Administrations, 1958–71, Subject File, Harriman Papers, MDLC.

14. The DRV Chronology on Diplomatic Struggle, Hanoi, 1987, January 12, 14, 15–16, February 5, March 8, 22, May 7 and 31, July 18 and 29, 1969. (Portions of this unpublished document are held by the author.)

15. *WHY,* 258.

16. Memo with enclosures, Kissinger to Nixon, January 2, 1969, sub: North Vietnamese Reply to Your Message, folder: Memo to President-Elect, box 2, NSC: HAKOF, HAKASF, NPM.

17. *RN,* 349.

18. Memo with enclosures, Kissinger to Nixon, January 2, 1969, sub: North Vietnamese Reply to Your Message, folder: Memo to President-Elect, box 2, NSC: HAKOF, HAKASF, NPM.

19. *WHY*, 259.

20. *RN*, 349–350.

21. See, e.g., Memo, Kissinger to Nixon, June 24, 1969, folder: [CF], FO-6-1, Paris Peace Talks, box 33, WHSF: CF, NPM.

22. Talking Points for the President's Meeting with Vice President Ky, and Stated to the President, March 2, 1969, Papers of Henry Cabot Lodge II, microfilm, reel 25, MHS.

23. Memorandum of Conversation with President Nixon, February 21, 1969, folder: Nh–Nz, Special Files: Public Service, Kennedy-Johnson Administrations, 1958–71, Subject File, box 494, Harriman Papers, MDLC; Memo, Kissinger to Nixon, June 24, 1969, folder: [CF], FO-6-1, Paris Peace Talks, box 33, WHSF: CF, NPM. See also Allan E. Goodman, *The Lost Peace: America's Search for a Negotiated Settlement of the Vietnam War* (Stanford, Calif.: Hoover Institution Press, 1978), 91–92.

24. DRV Chronology on Diplomatic Struggle, January 14, 1969.

25. Telegram, Rogers to Bunker and Lodge, March 10, 1969, folder: [CF], FO-6-1, Paris Peace Talks, box 33, WHSF: CF, NPM.

26. Telegrams, Rogers to Bunker and Lodge, March 10 and 13, 1969, ibid.; *RN*, 374.

27. Memo, Kissinger to Nixon, Possible Private Talks at the Paris Negotiations, March 1, 1969, folder: Paris Talks—Misc. through Mar 1969 (3), box 3, WH/NSC: POW/MIA, NPM. A General Strategy & Plan for Viet-Nam Negotiations, March 28, 1969, folder: NSC Meeting of March 28, 1969—A General Strategy & Plan for Viet-Nam Negotiations, box 175, NSC: PT/M, NPM. The strategy identified the following as priority objectives: mutual withdrawal; reductions in hostilities; reestablishment of the DMZ as a demilitarized area and of the seventeenth parallel as the boundary between North and South Vietnam; an eventual cease-fire; the release of American POWs; and inspection machinery.

28. Telegrams, Rogers to Bunker and Lodge, March 10 and 13, 1969, folder: [CF], FO-6-1, Paris Peace Talks, box 33, WHSF: CF, NPM.

29. Ibid.; Goodman, *Lost Peace*, 92. Lodge made his public comments in November 1969, not having known that Nixon and Kissinger had been seeking and making their own direct and *secret* contacts both with Hanoi since April and with Moscow since mid-February. On Hanoi's willingness to negotiate privately in this 1968–1969 period, see DOD Memo, n.d., sub: Possible North Vietnam (DRV) negotiating style and patterns, microfiche no. 001378, declassified September 17, 1993, *Declassified Documents Catalog*, vol. 20, no. 3.

30. *WHY*, 263, 173, 194. But he did think it was useful because the Vietnamese indicated concern about the Sino-Soviet split.

31. *Bases for a Settlement of the Viet Nam Problem* (Hanoi: Foreign Languages Publishing House, 1971), 8–9, 25–27; "Text of a Policy Statement by the National Liberation Front of South Vietnam," reprinted in *NYT*, December 15, 1967, 16; *WHY*, 254–258; Memorandum of Conversation with Xuan Thuy and Tran Buu Kiem, Valerian Zorin to Comrade Kozyrev, February 21, 1969, Communist Party of the Soviet Union Central Committee Archive, in *CWIHP Bulletin*, Issue 3 (Fall 1993): 62. On the Johnson administration's negative views of the NLF's four points, see DOD Memo, n.d., sub: Hanoi's four points, microfiche no. 001373, declassified September 17, 1993, *Declassified Documents Catalog*, vol. 20, no. 3. The Johnson administration was aware that Hanoi had indicated it would be flexible on the timing of reunification, the neutrality of South Vietnam, international supervision of elections, and the timing of U.S. withdrawals; DOD Memo, n.d., sub:

Strategies and objectives of North Vietnam regarding peace negotiations, microfiche 001374, ibid. But compare DOD Memo, sub: Thuy's opening and his second statement at the Paris talks analyzed, microfiche 001377, ibid.

32. *WHY,* 258, 262; Revised Summary, NSSM 1, March 22, 1969, pp. 5, 28; Ellsberg Options Paper, [p. 2]; Telegram, Rogers to Bunker and Lodge, March 10 and 13, 1969, folder: [CF], FO-6-1, Paris Peace Talks, box 33, WHSF: CF, NPM; A General Strategy & Plan for Viet-Nam Negotiations, March 28, 1969, folder: NSC Meeting of March 28, 1969—A General Strategy & Plan for Viet-Nam Negotiations, box 175, NSC: PT/M, ibid.

33. Memorandum of Conversation, Zorin to Kozyrev, February 21, 1969, in *CWIHP Bulletin,* 62–63.

34. DRV Chronology on Diplomatic Struggle, March 8 and 22, 1969. Nguyen Van Thieu was president, Nguyen Cao Ky was vice president, and Tran Van Huong was premier. Tran Thien Khiem replaced Tran Van Huong as prime minister of South Vietnam in late 1969.

35. For the ten points see *NYT,* May 9, 1969, and *Bases for a Settlement of the Viet Nam Problem,* 28–33. The Nixon administration initially responded to the ten-point plan suggesting that it offered new "openings" on issues of concern; for example, the NLF delegation's call for the first time for negotiations on prisoner releases, and their hint that Thieu, Ky, and Huong might be allowed to participate in a coalition government. The Paris plenary talks, however, did not subsequently make progress on these or other issues, most probably in large part because of the Nixinger strategy to pursue a hard line in Kissinger's private talks, the administration's assumption that the NLF's conciliatory proposals were evidence of their military decline, and Thieu's opposition to the formation of a coalition government. See Memo, Dean Moor to Richard Sneider, May 12, 1969, sub: Consensus of Views on the NLF's 10 Points, and other intelligence documents in folder: NLF Points May 1969, box 175, NSC: PT/M, NPM, C. M. Cooke, Jr. to Mr. Richardson, May 22, 1969, sub: Last Night's Discussion, folder: W. A. K. Lake File (Apr. 1969), ibid. Continuing American support for Thieu, the man, was an important consideration in the Politburo's thinking, but what was more important was the American determination to maintain an anti-Communist regime in Saigon that was opposed to reunification; Hoang Tung, interview by the author, September 21, 1994, Hanoi. Tung directed Central Committee propaganda during the war.

36. *WHY,* 263.

37. See speech by Gen. Nguyen Van Vinh, April 1966, in Doc. 8, *VDRN,* p. 4.

38. Letter, Duan to Thanh, ca. 1966, Doc. 8, *VDRN,* pp. 3–4.

39. Vinh speech, ibid., p. 4. The Central Office for South Vietnam (COSVN) was an American transliteration of the Central Committee Directorate for the South, which included the southern and central branches of the Lao Dong Party. In 1965, when President Johnson committed American combat troops in large numbers to South Vietnam, many PLAF guerrilla fighters and Vietnamese Workers' Party members had been understandably discouraged, but Party and military leaders such as Le Duan, Le Duc Tho, Nguyen Chi Thanh, Vo Nguyen Giap, and Nguyen Van Vinh had exhorted them to take heart. They argued that in the global arena the United States was no longer as omnipotent as it once was, and in South Vietnam it would have to support a regime that was corrupt and weak, while revolutionary forces were popular and strong. As a result, the United States would be compelled to disperse its troops throughout the countryside in order to defend areas threatened by the resistance; moreover, the great geographic distance it would have to

traverse would make its logistical task difficult, while on its own home front American citizens would question the value of the effort. American forces therefore suffered serious inherent weaknesses. These were accurate predictions, but the effort and costs that would be required to win were underestimated. As events proved after 1965, the great power of the United States was capable of inflicting serious losses and setbacks on resistance forces, which undermined morale and endangered the revolution. Thus even more determination and sacrifice would be required. Duiker, in *Communist Road to Power*, 267–270, 273, suggested that from 1965 to 1967 or so, Thanh's strategy of main force and guerrilla tactics was followed, but stymied.

40. The Soviet Union and China were also rear areas of supply. American leaders complained a great deal about these untouchable rear areas, but the United States had its rear areas, too—in the United States, Thailand, Guam, South Korea, Australia, Canada, and at sea.

41. This resolution of the fighting, however, he said, amounts essentially to a negotiated cease-fire, which requires continued vigilance: "Whether or not the war will resume after the conclusion of agreements depends upon the comparative balance of forces"; Vinh speech, Doc. 8, *VDRN*, p. 4.

42. Letter, Duan to General Nguyen Chi Than, March 1967, ibid., p. 4.

43. *WHY*, 259–260. One of Kissinger's former students made a similar observation in his history of the Washington-Hanoi negotiations: "Americans expect to bargain, and we expect that a military stalemate will cause our adversaries to do the same. . . . This expectation proved unwise and frustrating. Hanoi used negotiations as a tactic of warfare to buy time to strengthen its military capabilities in South Vietnam and weaken the will of those on the side of Saigon. Rather than serving as an alternative to warfare, consequently, the Vietnam negotiations were an extension of it"; Allan E. Goodman, *The Search for a Negotiated Settlement of the Vietnam War* (Berkeley: Institute of East Asian Studies, University of California, 1986), ix. Kissinger's biographer, Walter Isaacson, remarked: "It took some temerity for Kissinger . . . to call the North Vietnamese 'indirect and, by American standards, devious or baffling.' For they must certainly have considered Kissinger's [and Nixon's] supersecret diplomacy and his murky offers to be indirect and, by Vietnamese standards, devious and baffling. What really infuriated Kissinger was . . . that they said the same things in the private, secret talks that they were saying in public— indeed, they stubbornly seemed to mean what they said"; Isaacson, *Kissinger*, 245.

44. *No More Vietnams*, 106. He continued, however: "I had another compelling reason for doing so. I knew it would not be possible to sustain public and congressional support for our military efforts unless we could demonstrate that we were exploring every avenue for ending the war through negotiations."

45. *WHY*, 522.

46. *No More Vietnams*, 103.

47. Quoted in Duiker, *Communist Road to Power*, 288.

48. Duan to Thanh, Doc. 8, *VDRN*, p. 4. See also Memorandum of Conversation, Zorin to Kozyrev, February 21, 1969, in *CWIHP Bulletin*, 63.

49. Duan to Thanh, Doc. 8, *VDRN*, p. 4.

50. Luu Van Loi, "The Johnson Episode in the Vietnam War," 20–21, 31. Privately, American officials used the term as well. For example, in reference to "an intensified bombing effort against Hanoi" in September 1967—after the United States through Kissinger had sent a message offering a bombing cessation in return for Hanoi's assur-

ances to withhold reinforcing forces in the south—one of Johnson's staff wrote in a memo: "North Vietnamese leaders may have viewed this sequence as a not too subtle attempt by the US to apply the carrot-and-stick technique"; Memorandum for the President, The Kissinger Project, September 7, 1967, *Declassified Documents Catalog*. About meetings in Moscow with Soviet leaders in April 1972, Kissinger commented: "My approved instructions for this trip were to use the stick of bombing and carrot of being forthcoming on summit-related matters in order to get mutual de-escalation in Vietnam. So far we have spent two-thirds of our time on Vietnam during which I have gone to the brink with repeated declarations that we will continue military operations"; Memo, Kissinger to Nixon, April 22, 1972, box 74, WHSF: PPF, NPM. American national security intellectuals and academic political scientists more frequently employed other terms, e.g., *blackmail*, or the more esoteric constructions, *compellence* and *coercive diplomacy;* see, e.g., Thomas C. Schelling, *Arms and Influence* (New Haven, Conn.: Yale University Press, 1966); and Alexander George, *Forceful Persuasion: Coercive Diplomacy as an Alternative to War* (Washington, D.C.: United States Institute of Peace, 1991). In the latter book, however, coercive diplomacy is distinguished from blackmail and made out to be benign.

51. Quoted in Hersh, *Price of Power,* 134, from a 1979 interview in Hanoi.

52. On theories of war termination, see Jeffrey Kimball, "How Wars End: The Vietnam War," *Peace and Change: A Journal of Peace Research* 20 (April 1995): 190–191. For American views in 1969 on a cease-fire, see Memo, Kissinger to Nixon, August 28, 1969, sub: Ceasefire in Vietnam, folder: TL Info (Aug. 1969–Jun. 1970) (2 of 2), box 1047, NSC: SF—LCF, NPM.

53. *WHY,* 279.

54. See Gaiduk, *The Soviet Union and the Vietnam War,* 73–74; Duiker, *Communist Road to Power,* 265.

55. COSVN Resolution No. 9, Unnumbered, *VDRN,* pp. 9, 17 (italics in original).

56. Thach, interview with author, September 24, 1994, Hanoi. Thach made a similar point to Seymour Hersh in 1979; *Price of Power,* 134.

57. Memorandum of Conversation with President Nixon, February 21, 1969, folder: Nh–Nz, Special Files: Public Service, Kennedy-Johnson Administrations, 1958–71, Subject File, box 494, Harriman Papers, MDLC.

58. *WHY,* 112–113, 138–139, 144. Apparently, the intention at first was to hold monthly meetings, but Nixon says that "within a short time they were meeting weekly, often over lunch"; *RN,* 369. See also Memorandum of Conversation, Dobrynin to Gromyko, July 12, 1969, *CWIHP Bulletin,* 67.

59. *RN,* 369.

60. Quoted in Fallaci, *Interview with History,* 42.

61. Memorandum of Conversation, Dobrynin to Gromyko, July 12, 1969, in *CWIHP Bulletin,* 67.

62. *WHY,* 142.

63. Ibid., 141, and also see page 527 regarding confusion over who was the Soviet leader in 1969, Kosygin or Brezhnev. Nixon's original intention was to "conduct a series of [summit] meetings, at predetermined intervals, say, once a year" in an unstructured manner, conducting "mutual consultations, an exchange of opinions on potentially explosive situations which could draw both sides into conflict; . . . the sides will better understand each other's motives and not overstep dangerous borders in their actions"; Memorandum of Conversation, Dobrynin to Gromyko, July 12, 1969, in *CWIHP Bulle-*

tin, 64. These periodic, informal summits did not come about. Nixon's views on them seemed to change. When a summit was held, it would be as a capstone to successful negotiations, a reward to the Soviets for their cooperation, and an electoral, political bonanza for the administration. See Memo, V. Andropov to Committee for State Security, April 19, 1971, Communist Party of the Soviet Union Central Committee Archive, reprinted in *CWIHP Bulletin,* Issue 4 (Fall 1994): 70.

64. *WHY,* 112–114; *RN,* 369–370. Regarding Berlin, see also Memorandum of Conversation, Dobrynin to Gromyko, July 12, 1969, in *CWIHP Bulletin,* 64.

65. *RN,* 369–370.

66. *WHY,* 143–144.

67. As Kissinger later understood; see *WHY,* 143–144.

68. Memorandum of Conversation with Ambassador Dobrynin, February 19, 1969, folder: Anatolii Dobrynin, box 455, Special Files: Public Service, Kennedy-Johnson Administrations, 1958–71, Subject File, Harriman Papers, MDLC.

69. Memorandum of Conversation with President Nixon, February 21, 1969, folder: Nh–Nz, box 494, ibid.

70. Memorandum of Conversation with Ambassador Dobrynin, February 23, 1969, folder: Anatolii Dobrynin, box 455, ibid.

71. Terriff, *The Nixon Administration and the Making of U.S. Nuclear Strategy,* 19.

72. Paraphrasing Dobrynin's comments, Harriman wrote: "Soviet leaders were concerned about the talk that they were under pressure to have nuclear restraint because of their economic problems. This made no sense"; Memorandum of Conversation with Ambassador Dobrynin, February 19, 1969, folder: Anatolii Dobrynin, box 455, Special Files: Public Service, Kennedy-Johnson Administrations, 1958–71, Subject File, Harriman Papers, MDLC.

73. *WHY,* 198.

74. Terriff, *The Nixon Administration and the Making of U.S. Nuclear Strategy,* 51–68. See also p. 2 of Strategic Policy Issues, n.d. [probably sometime in 1969], folder: Strategic Policy Issues (TS), box 3, NSC: HAKOF, HAKASF, NPM; and p. 5 of Memo, Lord to Kissinger, January 23, 1970, sub: Issues Raised by the Nixon Doctrine for Asia, folder: TL Info (Aug. 1969–Jun. 1970) (2 of 2), box 1047, NSC: SF—LCF, ibid.

75. Kissinger did *pose* as a messenger, however; he would bring his talking-points memo with Nixon's marginal remarks to the meetings and show them to Dobrynin (*WHY,* 268). Nixon and Kissinger continued to use the carrot-and-stick approach in subsequent meetings with Dobrynin. Kissinger boasted of his technique in *White House Years:* "In all my conversations with Dobrynin I had stressed that a fundamental improvement in US-Soviet relations presupposed Soviet cooperation in settling the war. Dobrynin had always evaded a reply by claiming that Soviet influence in Hanoi was extremely limited. In response, we procrastinated on all the negotiations in which the Soviet Union was interested." The issues Kissinger listed were "strategic arms limitation talks, the Middle East, and expanded economic relations" (266). Kissinger did not put China in this list of issues the Soviets wanted to discuss, but Nixon and Kissinger did bring up China in these early meetings of February and March. See also pp. 263, 268.

76. Memorandum of Conversation, Dobrynin to Gromyko, July 12, 1969, in *CWIHP Bulletin,* 66–67. Dobrynin did not mean that Kissinger dominated Nixon, but that among Nixon's advisers Kissinger was the dominant influence on foreign policy.

77. Ibid., 66.

78. *WHY,* 144.

79. Quoted in Gaiduk, *The Soviet Union and the Vietnam War,* 217.

80. Memorandum of Conversation with President Nixon, February 21, 1969, folder: Nh–Nz, Special Files: Public Service, Kennedy-Johnson Administrations, 1958–71, Subject File, box 494, Harriman Papers, MDLC.

81. Memorandum of Conversation, Zorin to Kozyrev, February 21, 1969, *CWIHP Bulletin,* 62–63, 69. See also Zorin's remarks to Lodge, Memo, Lodge to Kissinger, March 17, 1969, sub: Conversation between Zorin and Lodge, Lodge Papers, reel 9, MHS.

82. Revised Summary, NSSM 1, pp. 6–7.

83. *WHY,* 178.

84. *In the Arena,* 332.

85. *No More Vietnams,* 105.

86. *WHY,* 178.

87. Ibid., 182.

88. Ibid., 169.

89. Ibid., 141–142.

90. Ibid., 179.

91. Ibid., 194.

92. Gaiduk, *The Soviet Union and the Vietnam War,* 215, 59.

93. Figures are from Chen Jiang, "China's Involvement in the Vietnam War, 1964–1969," *China Quarterly,* no. 142 (June 1995): 366–387. See also Duiker, *Communist Road to Power,* passim.

94. Chen Jiang, "China's Involvement in the Vietnam War," 366–387.

95. Quoted in Gaiduk, *The Soviet Union and the Vietnam War,* 112.

96. With tongue in cheek Thach referred to Soviet and Chinese recommendations and pressures as "advice"; interview with the author, September 24, 1994.

97. Quoted in Gaiduk, *The Soviet Union and the Vietnam War,* 215–216.

98. *WHY,* 259; Kissinger, "The Viet Nam Negotiations," 217, 219.

99. Cf. Douglas Pike, *Vietnam and the Soviet Union,* 100–102.

100. Revised Summary, NSSM 1, p. 7.

101. *WHY,* 194.

7. TARGET OF OPPORTUNITY: 1969

1. Filed as "Henry Kissinger Comments" but written in Nixon's handwriting, May 11, 1969, folder: HRH Notes, Jan–Jun 1969, box 40, Handwritten Notes, WHSF: SMOF, HRH, NPM.

2. *WHY,* 239; see also memos, documents, and enclosures in Military Operations in Cambodia and Laos, September 1973 [regarding Kissinger's confirmation hearings in Congress], folder: Cambodia—Cambodian Bombing, box 11, NSC: HAKOF, HAKSF, NPM.

3. *RN,* 380. Kissinger referred to it as Mini-Tet, but this term was used also for Post-Tet January 1968. See also Duiker, *Communist Road to Power,* 303–307.

4. McNamara, *In Retrospect,* 114, 264–270, 275; Hoff, *Nixon Reconsidered,* 210.

5. *NYT,* November 3, 1967.

6. *WHY,* 241. Memos, documents, and enclosures in Military Operations in Cam-

bodia and Laos, September 1973, folder: Cambodia—Cambodian Bombing, box 11, NSC: HAKOF, HAKASF, NPM. See also William M. Hammond, *United States Army in Vietnam: Public Affairs: The Military and the Media, 1968–1973* (Washington, D.C.: Center of Military History, 1996), 63. An excellent account of the military and the media during the Nixon presidency, Hammond's "official" military history also examines policy and draws on classified documents unavailable to other researchers as of 1998.

7. Hersh, *Price of Power,* 54

8. *HRHD,* February 24, 1969.

9. See, e.g., questions 10 and 28/29. No. 10 read: "What are the main channels for military supplies for the NVA/VC forces in SVN (e.g., Cambodia and/or the Laotian panhandle)? What portion of these supplies come in through Sihanoukville?" Question 28 for the DOS and CIA, but 29 for the DOD and JCS, was one having to do with bombing, which elicited recommendations to bomb Cambodia; NSSM 1.

10. JCS and DOD response, NSSM 1.

11. *WHY,* 241

12. Ibid., 239. Cf. Hoff, *Nixon Reconsidered,* 211, who, citing a document, says that Wheeler claimed that everything was being done except the bombing of the Cambodian sanctuaries.

13. *WHY,* 240

14. William Shawcross, *Sideshow: Kissinger, Nixon and the Destruction of Cambodia,* rev. ed. (New York: Simon and Schuster, 1987), 19–20; Hammond, *The Military and the Media,* 64–65.

15. *WHY,* 241.

16. Shawcross, *Sideshow,* 20–21.

17. Isaacson, *Kissinger,* 172; Hammond, *The Military and the Media,* 64–65.

18. *WHY,* 242; see also Hammond, *The Military and the Media,* 64, concerning Bunker's assurances that there were no civilians in the area. But military reconnaissance in fact indicated there were civilians there; Shawcross, *Sideshow,* 28.

19. *WHY,* 242. See also Isaacson, *Kissinger,* 175, regarding Kissinger's memo to Nixon; and Hammond, *The Military and the Media,* 65. In Kissinger's description of this process, he portrays himself as a reasonable diplomat with faith in negotiations and concern for public opinion but surrounded by militarists and an aggressive Nixon, who wanted to attack the enemy. He is finally moved only by enemy provocations and the immorality of their killing of Americans and maintaining sanctuaries in Cambodia.

20. *HRHD,* January 27, 1969. In *RN,* 381, Nixon says that the reason for bombing was to influence negotiations.

21. Memos, documents, and enclosures in Military Operations in Cambodia and Laos, September 1973, folder: Cambodia—Cambodian Bombing, box 11, NSC: HAKOF, HAKASF, NPM; *WHY,* 249; *RN,* 382.

22. In *WHY,* Kissinger says that after Mini-Tet commenced, Nixon ordered the bombing, which implied that plans already existed. He also wrote that he advocated a brief postponement to "go over the military operations once again" (243).

23. Ibid., 242.

24. COSVN Resolution 9, July 1969, Unnumbered, *VDRN,* p. 2.

25. *HRHD,* March 20, 1969. See also Memo, Kissinger to Nixon, September 10, 1969, sub: Our Present Course on Vietnam, folder: Tony Lake Chron File (Jun. 1969–May 1970) (5 of 6), box 1048, NSC: SF—LCF, NPM.

26. Circular, Current Affairs Committee of COSVN, February 12, 1969, Doc. 61, *VDRN*, pp. 5–6.

27. Revised summary of responses to NSSM 1, March 22, 1969, p. 10. Of course, the JCS believed that if it were allowed to resume "full scale hostilities with a relaxation of rules of engagement" and to attack Cambodian sanctuaries, this would turn the tide, resulting "in depletion of the enemy's manpower and war-making resources"; ibid., 11.

28. Study of Directive 81 of 5 Truong Opening of Phase H, Doc. 62, *VDRN*, p. 10; COSVN Resolution 9, Unnumbered, ibid., pp. 16–17. Another COSVN document read: "In short, during the 1969 spring offensive we killed many Americans. The most significant success of the 1969 spring offensive was that it boosted the anti-war movement in the United States, which seriously affected the American plan of aggression. What we should do: for each additional day's stay, the United States must sustain more casualties. . . . They must spend more money and lose more equipment. . . . The American people will adopt a stronger anti-war attitude while there is no hope to consolidate the puppet administration and army; "Enemy Emphasis on Causing U.S. Casualties: A Follow-up," Analysis Report, May 1969, pp. 16–17, quoted in Thayer, *War Without Fronts*, 53. See also Thayer's analysis of the military stalemate, pp. 90–96, 104–105.

29. David Burns Sigler, *Vietnam Battle Chronology: U.S. Army and Marine Corps Combat Operations, 1965–1973* (Jefferson, N.C.: McFarland, 1992), 86–93.

30. Study of Directive 81, Doc. 62, *VDRN*, p. 1; Philip B. Davidson, *Vietnam at War: The History, 1946–1975* (New York: Oxford University Press, 1988), 591. Kissinger wrote that Laird urged delay in early March "to a moment when the provocation would be clearer"; *WHY*, 244.

31. *WHY*, 242; Davidson, *Vietnam at War*, 591. See also Hammond, *The Military and the Media*, 65–67.

32. Circular and Study of Directive 81, Docs. 61 and 62, *VDRN*, pp. 5, 9.

33. COSVN Resolution 9, Unnumbered, ibid., p. 19.

34. Study of Directive 81, Doc. 62, ibid., p. 8; see also COSVN Resolution 9, Unnumbered, ibid., pp. 2, 5.

35. Study of Directive 81, Doc. 62, *VDRN*. See also Duiker, *Communist Road to Power*, 291–230; and William S. Turley, *The Second Indochina War: A Short Political and Military History, 1954–1975* (New York: New American Library, 1987), 100–120.

36. COSVN Resolution 9, Unnumbered, *VDRN*, p. 9.

37. Study of Directive 81, Doc. 62, *VDRN*, p. 9. The formation of the PRG, a "governmental" extension of the NLF, was announced on June 10, 1969. By late summer, local revolutionary councils of the PRG had been organized in 1,268 townships, 124 districts, and three cities; Duiker, *Communist Road to Power*, 308.

38. COSVN Resolution 9, Unnumbered, *VDRN*, p. 10.

39. The exhortation continued: "We must . . . strive to build up our military, political, economic, and financial strength, unceasingly improve the application of precepts and methods in a flexible way which is fitting to the practical reality and through this, to ensure that we are able to fight vigorously and for a sustained period"; ibid., p. 20 (italics in original).

40. Ibid., pp. 12–13.

41. Ibid., p. 13

42. Study of Directive 81, Doc. 62, *VDRN*, pp. 9, 10. Other objectives listed: destroy Saigon security forces; control hamlets day and night; improve political rights; attack lines

of communication and routes leading to province capitals, district seats, and cities. See also COSVN Resolution 9, Unnumbered, *VDRN,* p. 2.

43. COSVN Resolution 9, Unnumbered, *VDRN,* p. 14.

44. *WHY,* 242–243. See Nixon's comment in *RN,* 380, regarding his "immediate instinct."

45. *WHY,* 243.

46. Hoff, *Nixon Reconsidered,* 216, claimed that Kissinger's discussion of this meeting was undocumented (see *WHY,* 243), but it *is* now documented in the full-text CD-ROM version of *HRHD,* February 24, 1969; see also Hersh, *Price of Power,* 60.

47. *WHY,* 243.

48. The scheme had two essential elements. The first was a dual-reporting system designed to bypass normal air force reporting requirements for flight plans, targets struck, fuel consumed, and bomb tonnage dropped. En masse, B-52 crews would receive the standard pre-mission briefing about their targets in South Vietnam, then selected crews would be taken aside and told that shortly before they reached their objective, ground radar stations in South Vietnam would take over their final bombing run. Receiving special instructions by courier from Saigon, the ground radar crews would know that the targets were in Cambodia, and they and their computers would guide the big bombers to their real targets. After the mission, air crews would report routinely to the air force's command and control center about the success or failure of their mission "inside" South Vietnam. The second element had to do with instructions to government press spokesmen in the event that reporters would ask questions about bombs falling and exploding in Cambodia. Spokesmen were to say that targets had routinely been bombed near the border. If the press persisted or the government of Cambodia protested, spokesmen would neither confirm nor deny reports but would say that the matter would be investigated. After replying to any Cambodian protest, the press would be told that the United States had apologized and would be offering compensation. Congressmen (e.g., Russell and Stennis) were told of the first raid, but key congressional oversight committees, the secretary of the air force, and the State Department (except for Rogers) were kept in the dark. See, R. B. Furlong Papers [consisting of reports and papers prepared by the authority of Brig. Gen. R. B. Furlong, USAF, Deputy Asst. Secretary of Defense, regarding "Sensitive Operations in Southeast Asia, 1964–1973" and "Responses to Senator Harold Hughes"], catalogued 168.7122-16 and 168.7122-20, AFHRA; Hersh, *Price of Power,* 61–63; Hoff, *Nixon Reconsidered,* 216–217.

49. *WHY,* 249. See also *RN,* 382, and memos, documents, and enclosures in Military Operations in Cambodia and Laos, September 1973, folder: Cambodia—Cambodian Bombing, box 11, NSC; HAKOF, HAKASF, NPM.

50. Nixon and Kissinger in fact wanted Hanoi to respond, for it would have been a sign that the bombing had made a difference, and when they did not protest, Nixon would order another raid. Why Hanoi did not disclose the bombing of Cambodia remains a mystery. It might have been true, as Kissinger claimed, that they did not want to admit officially they had bases in Cambodia, but it was probably more the case that they did not want to signal Nixon that the bombings had enough of an impact to warrant comment. Moreover, if Nixon had to bomb somewhere, better to bomb Cambodia than North Vietnam. See *WHY,* 247, 250.

51. *RN,* 381–382.

52. See *WHY*, 244. Isaacson observed that "American policy was edging toward what had heretofore been an unfamiliar realm: the use of military power not anchored by concerns about morality and international law"; *Kissinger*, 174. Perhaps it was not so unfamiliar a realm, but nonetheless it was immoral and illegal. For more on Sihanouk's views and also the opinions of Kissinger's former aides about Shawcross's account, see *Sideshow*, appendix.

53. On Sihanouk's ambiguous position and Kissinger's press guidance to Laird, see memos, documents, and enclosures in Military Operations in Cambodia and Laos, September 1973, folder: Cambodia—Cambodian Bombing, box 11, NSC; HAKOF, HAKASF, NPM.

54. *RN*, 382

55. *WHY*, 243.

56. Ibid., 245; Isaacson, *Kissinger*, 173-174.

57. *RN*, 380. Regarding concerns about demonstrations, see *HRHD*, February 24, 1969.

58. *HRHD*, March 1, 1969. Kissinger claimed in *WHY*, 244, that he had advised postponement, because he believed the timing was unfortunate: coming during the president's European sojourn, the bombing might have aroused antiwar demonstrations and dominated press briefings and private leadership meetings. These concerns may explain what Haldeman meant by "risk otherwise too great," yet "K very disappointed" seems to contradict Kissinger's claims for the advice he gave. See also *RN*, 380, and *HRHD*, February, 24, 1969.

59. *Public Papers of the Presidents, Nixon: 1969*, 185-186.

60. Ibid., 185.

61. *HRHD*, March 9, 1969.

62. *Public Papers of the Presidents, Nixon: 1969*, 210.

63. Quoted in *WHY*, 247. Kissinger constantly refers to combined Viet Cong/NVA attacks as "North Vietnamese" attacks. On the Vietnamese offensive and press coverage, see Hammond, *The Military and the Media*, 65-69.

64. *HRHD*, March 10, 1969; *WHY*, 246. The tension between Kissinger and Rogers is an underlying element in Nixon's conduct of foreign policy. Kissinger discusses it frequently in *WHY*; so does Hersh in *Price of Power*, Hoff in *Nixon Reconsidered*, and Isaacson in *Kissinger*—as well as other authors cited previously. I have drawn on these sources for my account but have more frequently cited *The Haldeman Diaries* because it provides new and corroborating evidence, as well as colorful, illustrative anecdotes.

65. Cf. Shawcross, *Sideshow*, 23; and Raphael Littauer and Norman Uphoff, eds., *The Air War in Indochina*, rev. ed. (Boston: Beacon Press, 1972), 25.

66. Truong Nhu Tang, with David Chanoff and Doan Van Toai, *A Vietcong Memoir* (New York: Vintage Books, 1986), 177.

67. *WHY*, 247; *HRHD*, March 17, 1969; Shawcross, *Sideshow*, 26. Kissinger participated in the selection of targets; Hersh, *Price of Power*, 121-122.

68. Shawcross, *Sideshow*, 25.

69. Ibid., 24-26; Daniel Boone operations are reported in Furlong Papers, AFHRA; Cambodia Ground Operations, Military Operations in Cambodia and Laos, September 1973, folder: Cambodia—Cambodian Bombing, box 11, NSC: HAKOF, HAKASF, NPM.

70. Furlong Papers, AFHRA; Map enclosed in Military Operations in Cambodia and Laos, September 1973, folder: Cambodia—Cambodian Bombing, box 11, NSC: HAKOF, HAKASF, NPM. Thayer, *War Without Fronts;* Table 8.5; Shawcross, *Sideshow*, chap. 15.

71. *RN,* 382.

72. Sneider, interview with Hersh, *Price of Power,* 61. Cf. Kissinger's reference to "seriousness" on p. 2 of the Cambodian Bombing Decision, Military Operations in Cambodia and Laos, September 1973, folder: Cambodia—Cambodian Bombing, box 11, NSC: HAKOF, HAKASF, NPM.

73. *NYT,* May 9, 1969.

74. On Beecher's and others' stories, see Hammond, *The Military and the Media,* 74; and Chronology of Publicity on "Menu" Operations, Military Operations in Cambodia and Laos, September 1973, folder: Cambodia—Cambodian Bombing, box 11, NSC: HAKOF, HAKASF, NPM.

75. Furlong Papers, AFHRA, Military Operations in Cambodia and Laos, September 1973, folder: Cambodia—Cambodian Bombing, box 11, NSC: HAKOF, HAKASF, NPM.

76. Ibid.; Thayer, *War Without Fronts,* chap. 8; Hersh, *Price of Power,* 55; Malvern Lumsden, *Anti-personnel Weapons* (London: Taylor and Francis, 1978), 26–27. B-52s were first used to bomb the Plain of Jars in February 1970—discussed in chapter 10.

77. *HRHD,* March 13, 1969.

78. Clarke, *Advice and Support,* 346–348. Laird had arrived in Saigon on March 5.

79. Quoted in ibid., 347.

80. Ibid., 346–348. See also *WHY,* 262.

81. Ellsberg Options Paper, December 27, 1968, n.p. [page following table of contents].

82. *Public Papers of the Presidents, Nixon: 1969,* 215.

83. *WHY,* 271–272.

84. Ibid.

85. Clarke, *Advice and Support,* 348. See also Hammond, *The Military and the Media,* 80–84.

86. Clarke, *Advice and Support,* 348.

87. *WHY,* 263–264. Kissinger, as he was often, was vague and cryptic in his description of the matter.

88. *HRHD,* March 10, 1969.

89. *WHY,* 264. At this moment the DOS, with White House clearance, instructed Bunker to inform Thieu of the imminent commencement of secret, bilateral talks between the United States and the DRV. In the communication to Bunker, the DOS and Rogers faithfully reiterated the Nixinger two-track approach; Rogers to Bunker and Lodge, March 10 and 13, folder: [CF], FO-6-1, Paris Peace Talks, box 33, WHSF: CF, NPM.

90. Kissinger claimed in *WHY* that there was another reason he wanted to bring matters to a head: on April 1 Secretary of Defense Laird announced publicly that for budgetary reasons the Pentagon was reducing B-52 sorties by over 10 percent. Kissinger maintained that "if we were going to de-escalate, it should be as part of a negotiation; the worst way to do it was unilaterally in response to budget pressures." This additional reason seems gratuitous as well as personal, i.e., anti-Laird. While B-52 missions may have been reduced, bombing tonnage was increasing throughout Indochina. Moreover, the origins of Kissinger's new maneuver antedated Laird's announcement; *WHY,* 264–265.

91. Ibid., 268. Kissinger wrote that to bring "matters to a head" he sent a memo on talking points with Dobrynin to Nixon, who made his usual marginal comments.

92. Haldeman added: "Again K surprised he'd take this hard line. K so pleased with his plan, like the earlier one [Breakfast?], that he can't resist telling someone outside his shop, so he goes over it with me"; *HRHD,* April 14, 1969.

93. *WHY,* 265–266.

94. Ibid.

95. Ibid., 144.

96. Ibid., 265–266.

97. Ibid., 267–268.

98. Barry M. Goldwater, *With No Apologies: The Personal and Political Memoirs of United States Senator Barry M. Goldwater* (New York: William Morrow, 1979), 214. Goldwater claimed he met with Nixon on March 5, but Laird had just arrived in Saigon on March 5; he had not "just returned from Saigon." Nixon's appointment calendar for March 5 indicates that Nixon met with a few congressional leaders but not with Goldwater. The first meeting with Goldwater recorded in Nixon's calendar is August 29, 1969. Both Goldwater and the appointment calendar may be in error. My guess is that Goldwater met or spoke with Nixon between mid-March and early April, the period after Laird returned to Washington and when the Cambodian decision was being finalized and the Vance mission was hatched.

99. Quoted in *RN,* 391.

100. *WHY,* 265–268.

101. Ibid., 284.

102. Ibid., 268. Nixon, too, claimed that no response was received; *RN,* 391.

103. Gaiduk, *The Soviet Union and the Vietnam War,* 207–209.

104. *WHY,* 144.

105. See *HRHD,* April 14, 1969.

106. *RN,* 382–383; *WHY,* 312, 316; Hoff, *Nixon Reconsidered,* 174.

107. *HRHD,* April 15, 1969. That they believed an action against one Communist state would be taken by another as retaliation directed against it revealed how fixed they were in their view of the interconnectedness of international communism.

108. Ibid., April 17, 1969.

109. Quoted in *RN,* 384.

110. Quoted in Isaacson, *Kissinger,* 181.

111. This is Haldeman's phrase; *HRHD,* February 24, 1970.

112. Ibid., April 19, 1969.

113. Ibid. (italics in original).

114. Ibid. On the EC-121 affair, see also Hersh, *Price of Power,* 69–77; and Isaacson, *Kissinger,* 180–182. In the end the administration undertook no military or diplomatic action of any consequence against North Korea. Nixon explained his inaction in *RN* as the product of limited options, divided counsel, and domestic political factors. Kissinger made essentially the same argument in *White House Years,* but he was more critical of Nixon's indecisiveness, the Pentagon's obstructionism, and the unwieldiness of the NSC advisory structure at that time. Haldeman's brief, straightforward diary notes generally support both Nixon's and Kissinger's descriptions of the administration's deliberations, but with far less of a self-serving slant.

115. *HRHD,* May 11, 1969.

116. Terriff, *The Nixon Administration and the Making of U.S. Nuclear Strategy,* 52–53. For the public comments of "senior officials" in the Nixon administration on nuclear flexibility, see, e.g., *NYT,* October 20, 1970.

117. Nixon's notes, May 11, 1969, folder: HRH Notes, Jan–Jun 1969, box 40, WHSF: SMOF, HRH, NPM. Each sentence appears on a separate page, but they read as though they are interconnected, one thought following the other.

8. NIXON'S WAR: 1969

1. *HRHD*, October 8, 1969. This diary entry paraphrases comments Nixon made to Haldeman.
2. *WHY*, 270.
3. Ibid.; see also *Bases for a Settlement of the Viet Nam Problem*, 28–33.
4. *RN*, 391.
5. Ibid.; *WHY*, 270–271; *Public Papers of the Presidents, Nixon: 1969*, 371.
6. Memo, Kissinger to Nixon, Assessment of the May 22 Plenary Session on Vietnam, May 23, 1969, folder: Paris Talks, 4/5/69, Memos & Misc/Memcons, Vol. III, 5/3/69, box 3, WH/NSC: POW/MIA, NPM.
7. Quote of Thuy in *WHY*, 271; *Public Papers of the Presidents, Nixon: 1969*, 373.
8. DRV Chronology on Diplomatic Struggle, May 31, 1969.
9. *WHY*, 269.
10. *HRHD*, May 18, 1969.
11. Ibid.
12. Ibid.; see also May 19, 1970.
13. Ibid., May 14 and 15, 1969.
14. Ibid., May 19, 1969.
15. Ibid., July 7, 1969. See Hammond, "The Mood in the United States," in *The Military and the Media*, chap. 7.
16. *HRHD*, February 21, 1969.
17. Ibid., July 7, 1969.
18. Ibid., February 21, 1969.
19. Ibid., May 28, 1969.
20. *WHY*, 255.
21. Curt Smith, *Long Time Gone: The Years of Turmoil Remembered* (South Bend, Ind.: Icarus, 1982), 213–218; Ray Price, *With Nixon* (New York: Viking Press, 1977), 152–156; Melvin Small, *Johnson, Nixon, and the Doves* (New Brunswick, N.J.: Rutgers University Press, 1988), 188.
22. *HRHD*, February 21 and 24, May 15, 1969.
23. *WHY*, 272.
24. Memo, Kissinger to Nixon, June 24, 1969, folder: [CF], FO-6-1, Paris Peace Talks, box 33, WHSF: CF, NPM.
25. Hung and Schecter, *Palace File*, 30–35; Clarke, *Advice and Support*, 348–351.
26. Hung and Schecter, *Palace File*, 32–35.
27. *WHY*, 271.
28. Ibid., 275–276.
29. *Public Papers of the Presidents, Nixon: 1969*, 476.
30. *HRHD*, June 19, 1969. Kissinger's comments to Haldeman were most probably the product of a concern about the strength of his influence with Nixon versus that of Laird and Rogers.
31. Memo, Kissinger to Nixon, June 24, 1969, folder: [CF], FO-6-1, Paris Peace Talks, box 33, WHSF: CF, NPM.
32. *HRHD*, July 7, 1969.
33. Ibid.
34. *WHY* 276. Kissinger claimed that Nixon changed his mind right after the meeting

about altering the mission of U.S. forces, but it was too late, for Laird had already issued orders and leaked to the public. Cf. Clarke, *Advice and Support*, 358–363; and Hammond, *The Military and the Media*, 78–85, 137.

35. See later comments concerning Nixon's visit to Thieu in Saigon on July 30.

36. *HRHD*, July 7, 1969.

37. *RN*, 393.

38. Dobrynin to Gromyko, July 12, 1969, in *CWIHP Bulletin*, 65. In another conversation with Dobrynin on April 14, Kissinger had warned that U.S.-USSR relations were at a "crossroads," linked progress with Vietnam (which was the "major obstacle"), and probably played the China card; *WHY*, 267–268.

39. Dobrynin to Gromyko, July 12, 1969, in *CWIHP Bulletin*, 65–66.

40. Ibid.

41. Ibid., 66.

42. Ibid. Since March 2, 1969, border clashes had taken place on the Ussuri and Amur Rivers; these apparently had been preceded by other "intrusions" and "provocations" since 1967; *WHY* 171–172.

43. Dobrynin to Gromyko, July 12, 1969, in *CWIHP Bulletin*, 66.

44. Reprinted in *Public Papers of the Presidents, Nixon: 1969*, 910. See also *RN*, 394; *WHY*, 278. Kissinger told Xuan Thuy on August 4 that the undated letter had been written three days before delivery, which Nixon claimed in *RN* was July 16. But if the letter was written on July 15, as implied in *WHY* and *RN*, the delivery date, according to Kissinger, would have been July 18 or 19, Paris time; Memorandum of Conversation, August 4, 1969, folder: Tony Lake Chron File (Jun. 1969–May 1970) (6 of 6), box 1048, NSC: SF—LCF, NPM.

45. This warning is not reproduced in *Public Papers of the Presidents, Nixon: 1969*, 910. But Nixon's claim that he made it (*RN*, 394) is confirmed in Memorandum of Conversation, August 4, 1969, folder: Tony Lake Chron File (Jun. 1969–May 1970) (6 of 6) box 1048, NSC: SF—LCF, NPM; and Lodge's notes of meeting with Kissinger, August 4, and Memo, Lodge to Kissinger, August 9, 1969, sub: Your discussion with Xuan Thuy, Lodge Papers, reel 9, MHS.

46. *RN*, 394. Kissinger, *WHY*, 304, claimed that the first he heard of the deadline was when Nixon mentioned it to Sultan Yahya Khan of Pakistan in August. This disclaimer seems to contradict other statements Kissinger made about the threat.

47. *RN*, 394; *WHY*, 278.

48. Quoted in *WHY*, 223–224.

49. On hearing of the incident on July 19, Nixon ordered a White House investigation to make sure that the Kennedy clan didn't "get away" with a cover-up. Haldeman noted on July 26 that Nixon's mind was less on the trip than on Chappaquiddick and his thoughts about shaking up his staff, getting rid of those who "don't carry their load"; *HRHD*, July 19, 21, and 26, 1969.

50. See *WHY*, 224, on making news.

51. *WHY*, 224; Isaacson, *Kissinger*, 241; *HRHD*, July 25, 1969; Memo, Kissinger to Nixon, August 29, 1969, sub: Press Reaction to "Nixon Doctrine," folder: Haldeman File 1969 San Clemente [Part I], box 52, HRH, WHSF: SMOF, NPM.

52. Isaacson, *Kissinger*, 241.

53. *WHY*, 223.

54. See Hoff, *Nixon Reconsidered*, 164, about the absence of documents.

55. Ibid., 164–165. See also *WHY,* 223–225, regarding Kissinger's critics and Cambodia.

56. Memo, Kissinger to Nixon, August 29, 1969, sub: Press Reaction to "Nixon Doctrine," folder: Haldeman File 1969 San Clemente [Part I], box 52, HRH, WHSF: SMOF, NPM.

57. Ibid. (uppercase in original).

58. *WHY,* 225.

59. Memo, Lord to Kissinger, January 23, 1970, sub: Issues Raised by the Nixon Doctrine for Asia, folder: TL Info (Aug. 1969–Jun. 1970) (2 of 2), box 1047, NSC: SF—LCF, NPM.

60. *WHY,* 276–277. See also Clarke, *Advice and Support,* 346–353.

61. *HRHD,* July 30, 1969; see also *WHY,* 276–277.

62. Memo, Kissinger to Nixon, August 29, 1969, sub: Press Reaction to "Nixon Doctrine," folder: Haldeman File 1969 San Clemente [Part I], box 52, HRH, WHSF: SMOF, HRH; see also *HRHD,* August 2, 1969.

63. *HRHD,* August 3, 1969. Ceauşéscu visited Nixon in October 1970; ibid., October 26, 1970.

64. Nixon quoted in *WHY,* 157.

65. *HRHD,* August 3, 1969. See also Isaacson, *Kissinger,* 243; and Raymond Garthoff, *Détente and Confrontation: American-Soviet Relations from Nixon to Reagan,* rev. ed. (Washington, D.C.: Brookings Institution, 1994), 246 ff.; *RN,* 397; Hoff, *Nixon Reconsidered,* 198. The Romanians did open a channel, and on December 10, 1969, when the Chinese agreed to meet at Warsaw, the Romanians were ready to relay the message. On December 10, 1969, e.g., Haldeman noted: "Chinese ready to meet in Warsaw; Rumanians coming in w/ secret msg."; Notes re Chinese, December 10, 1969, folder: Handwritten Notes July–Dec 1969, Part II, box 40, WHSF: SMOF, HRH, NPM.

66. *RN,* 395.

67. *WHY,* 280.

68. Memorandum of Conversation, August 4, 1969, folder: Tony Lake Chron File (Jun. 1969–May 1970) (6 of 6), box 1048, NSC: SF—LCF, NPM; DRV Chronology on Diplomatic Struggle, August 3, 1969. Kissinger's account of the meeting is in *WHY,* 279–282. Nixon appeared to delight in Kissinger's retort concerning "Mr. Nixon's War." Kissinger told Lodge that the president believes there is "no more time," and "is determined to settle this thing" by November 1 through negotiations or turn to "violent action"; Lodge's notes of meeting with Kissinger, August 4, and Memo, Lodge to Kissinger, August 9, 1969, sub: Your discussion with Xuan Thuy, Lodge Papers, reel 9, MHS. Isaacson, in *Kissinger,* 243, 245, suggested that Kissinger recommended a timetable of mutual withdrawal according to a schedule that Lake had been ordered to improvise during the flight to Paris. But the transcript of conversation does not show that a specific timetable was offered.

69. This lecture, Kissinger wrote, was a "ritual" that he had difficulty enduring at this and subsequent meetings; *WHY,* 281–282.

70. Memorandum of Conversation, August 4, 1969, folder: Tony Lake Chron File (Jun. 1969–May 1970) (6 of 6), box 1048, NSC: SF—LCF, NPM. Kissinger characterized Thuy's remarks for Lodge this way: "If the war goes on, or is expanded, they would be forced to continue fighting in order to reach their objectives," but we are "rich in goodwill" and prefer peace; Memo, Lodge to Kissinger, August 9, 1969, sub: Your discussion with Xuan Thuy, Lodge Papers, reel 9, MHS.

71. Memorandum of Conversation, August 4, 1969, folder: Tony Lake Chron File (Jun. 1969–May 1970) (6 of 6), box 1048, NSC: SF—LCF, NPM.

72. *WHY*, 281–282.

73. Szulc, *Illusion of Peace*, 142.

74. DRV Chronology on Diplomatic Struggle, September 2, 1969. Starobin also provided Kissinger with an analysis of the political situation in Hanoi following Ho's death; Letter, Kissinger to Starobin, September 30, 1969, folder: Tony Lake Chron File (Sept. 1969), box 1046, NSC: SF—LCF, NPM.

75. *RN* 397; *WHY* 283. Ho's letter was dated August 25 and is reprinted in *Public Papers of the Presidents, Nixon: 1969*, 910–911; and in Szulc, *Illusion of Peace*, 139.

76. *WHY*, 284.

77. Ibid.

78. Szulc, *Illusion of Peace*, 152. Ducks, of course, are not birds of prey, and if the name Duck Hook had any reference to birds, it was more likely that North Vietnamese targets, and especially the ports, were supposed to be the (sitting) ducks, soon to be pierced, ensnared, blockaded, or destroyed by talons of the hawks, American war planes and ships. Or perhaps the reference was to ducking "the hook," i.e., dodging the cancellation of their forceful plans; or perhaps "getting off the hook" of a dilemma. Perhaps it meant nothing, which is true of many code names.

79. *WHY*, 304, 284–285; *RN* 397–398. Kissinger explained the Duck Hook affair in the context of strategic reassessment, but Nixon explained it in terms of his good-faith efforts to bring about a settlement.

80. *HRHD*, April 14, 1969.

81. Roger Morris, *Haig: The General's Progress* (New York: Playboy Press, 1982), 136; Szulc, *Illusion of Peace*, 152; Hersh, *Price of Power*, 125. Drawing on documents from the Laird Papers and a story from the *Wall Street Journal* of September 12, Hammond (*The Military and the Media*, 149) referred to an air operation code-named Pruning Knife by MACV, designed to damage North Vietnam's air defenses, sow confusion among the population, and demonstrate U.S. ability to escalate the war at will. The plan appears to have been ready by mid-September. One of those plans on the shelf, Pruning Knife, however, does not seem to have been equivalent to what was contemplated in Duck Hook.

82. Szulc, *Illusion of Peace*, 152; Hersh, *Price of Power*, 120–125. Neither Szulc nor Hersh used standard academic citations, but their information nonetheless appears reliable because their informants were former members of Kissinger's staff. Hersh also obtained a partial copy of the plan through the Freedom of Information Act. Szulc argued that "November Option" was the name chosen before October. Hersh said that Watts heard the name Duck Hook mentioned sometime in August. Lake assessed the operation in his memo to Kissinger, September 17, 1969, sub: Initial Comments on Concept of Operations, with enclosure, Concept of Operations, September 16, 1969, folder: Tony Lake Chron File (Jun. 1969–May 1970) (5 of 6), box 1048, NSC: SF—LCF, NPM.

83. *HRHD*, August 28, 1969.

84. Ibid., and October 13, 1969.

85. Ibid., July 21, 1969.

86. Morris, *Haig*, 135.

87. Memo, Kissinger to Nixon, September 10, 1969, sub: Our Present Course on Vietnam, folder: Tony Lake Chron File (Jun. 1969–May 1970) (5 of 6), box 1048, NSC: SF—LCF, NPM. The memo was drafted by Tony Lake three days earlier and marked up

by Kissinger for revision; Memo, Lake to Kissinger, September 7, 1969, ibid. The September 10 memo is reprinted in *WHY*, 1480–1482 n. 11, along with a portion of a September 11 memo from Kissinger to Nixon; ibid., 1482 n. 12. The latter included Kissinger's policy options, which, however, are omitted from the reprint. The text of *WHY*, 234–286, quite clearly indicates that Kissinger recommended his "preference"—Duck Hook.

88. *HRHD*, September 12, 1969. See *RN* and *WHY* on this along with HRH and note that there was an issue about authorized levels and therefore how you count the "withdrawals."

89. See *RN*, 398. See *HRHD*, September 18, 1969.

90. *RN*, 398.

91. Ibid.

92. *WHY*, 284; caption for photographic insert, *HRHD*, September 12, 1969.

93. *HRHD*, September 12, 1969; see *WHY* 264–265.

94. *WHY*, 284. Kissinger says he assembled the special group "in September and October" and implies it was after the September 12 meeting. Isaacson, *Kissinger*, 246, says September. Hersh, *Price of Power*, 125, says that Kissinger assembled the staff in "late August or early September"; Szulc, *Illusion of Peace*, 152, says October 1. Morris, *Haig*, 136, gives the name "September or November" group. The differences may have been the result of different names given by different staff members.

95. Hersh, *Price of Power*, 126–127.

96. Ibid.; Szulc, *Illusion of Peace*, 150.

97. Szulc, *Illusion of Peace*, 151; Hersh, *Price of Power*, 126, 129 (italics added).

98. Hersh, *Price of Power*, 129. Hersh also said that the unnamed aides claimed that at the time they were unaware of Nixon's madman theory.

99. Lord, interview by author, tape recording, December 5, 1994, Washington, D.C.

100. *WHY*, 284–285.

101. Memo, Lake to Kissinger, September 17, 1969, sub: Initial Comments on Concept of Operations, with enclosure, Concept of Operations, September 16, 1969, folder: Tony Lake Chron File (Jun. 1969–May 1970) (5 of 6), box 1048, NSC: SF—LCF, NPM; Szulc, *Illusion of Peace*, 151; Hersh, *Price of Power*, 126–127; Morris, *Haig*, 136.

102. Nixon quoted in *WHY*, 304. Dobrynin and Kissinger quoted in *RN*, 399–400.

103. *RN*, 400. Nixon did not provide a date, but his description of meetings on this day matches a description in *HRHD*, September 27, 1969.

104. Hersh, *Price of Power*, 124–125.

105. *HRHD*, October 9, 1969; Szulc, *Illusion of Peace*, 155.

106. Hersh, *Price of Power*, 124–128; Szulc, *Illusion of Peace*, 153–154; Isaacson, *Kissinger*, 247.

107. *HRHD*, September 15, 1969. Vice President Nguyen Cao Ky had used the figure of 40,000, which included 5,000 troops who had been authorized to be in Vietnam but had not been sent.

108. Ibid., September 18–25, 29, and 30, and October 2, 1969. On the Green Beret affair and Laos, see also Hammond, *The Military and the Media*, 60–61, 138–146, 261–266.

109. *HRHD*, September 27 and 29, 1969.

110. See Small, *Johnson, Nixon, and the Doves*, 188; Charles DeBenedetti and Charles Chatfield, *An American Ordeal: The Antiwar Movement of the Vietnam Era* (Syracuse, N.Y.: Syracuse University Press, 1990), 252; Mueller, *War, Presidents, and Public Opin-*

ion, Fig. 3.2, p. 56; Table 3.3, pp. 54–55; Table 4.6, p. 107. Polls indicated in November that the American public favored troop withdrawals, but only 25 percent wanted an immediate withdrawal; Hammond, *The Military and the Media,* 168 (see p. 101 on general opinion statistics).

111. *HRHD,* September 27 and 29, 1969.

112. Ibid., and September 30, 1969. During the September 29 meeting he also admonished his inner circle for failing to "follow up on his memos" and for losing sight of the "big issues." See also Small, *Johnson, Nixon, and the Doves,* 182–183.

113. *NYT,* January 26, 1969.

114. The POW/MIA issue and the administration's motives are discussed later in the sections on negotiations, which are based on information available in declassified documents. See also H. Bruce Franklin, *M.I.A. or Mythmaking in America* (New Brunswick, N.J.: Rutgers University Press, 1993); and Hoff, *Nixon Reconsidered,* 237–242.

115. Franklin, *M.I.A.,* 49.

116. Perot's unsophisticated albeit successful antics would become a nuisance to the conduct of daily foreign policy business in the Nixon administration; see *HRHD,* passim.

117. *WHY,* 299, 288.

118. Morris, *Uncertain Greatness,* 170.

119. *HRHD,* October 3, 9, 10, 13, 15, and 27, 1969. Concerned that the Kissinger-Rogers squabble was adversely affecting the conduct of foreign policy, Lake and Watts wrote an analysis of the problem; Memo, with enclosures, Lake to Kissinger, November 14, 1969, sub: Relations with the State Department, folder: (T. Lake—Miscellaneous Material) (Sept. 1969–Jan. 1970), box 1047, NSC: SF—LCF, NPM.

120. Ibid., October 9, 1969.

121. Hersh, *Price of Power,* 127–128; Isaacson, *Kissinger,* 247–248. On October 21, Morris and Lake sent a memo to Kissinger in which they labeled as "unrealistic" the current strategy of combining Vietnamization (which was unworkable), with "punishing military action" (Duck Hook). They recommended another option: offering Hanoi terms now that *"they rationally calculate* they'll get by waiting." These terms would be coupled with a willingness to impose on Saigon a settlement that Washington found acceptable and the sending of a signal to the Communist side that Washington cared "so deeply about humiliation" that it would "act irrationally toward the Soviets as well as North Vietnam" in order to prevent it. Except for a better formula for elections in South Vietnam, Lake and Morris did not enumerate the "rational" terms to be proffered, but they unrealistically continued to insist on mutual withdrawal. They also seemed to support a modified madman threat. Kissinger's marginal note reads: "Tony, put pp. 1 and 2 [the critical analysis] into a memo for Pres. Work out other option." On October 30, 1969, Kissinger sent a memo to Nixon containing Lake's criticism of Vietnamization but offering no option other than a study of the problem in order to see what could be done to minimize the dangers. See Memo, Morris and Lake to Kissinger, October 21, 1969, sub: Another Vietnam Option, folder: Tony Lake Chron File (Jun. 1969–May 1970) (1 of 6), box 1047, NSC: SF—LCF, NPM; and Memo, Kissinger to Nixon, October 30, 1969, sub: Assumptions Underlying Vietnamization, folder: (T. Lake—Miscellaneous Material) (Sept. 1969–Jan. 1970), box 1047, ibid. Morris and Lake's advice regarding negotiating terms was not followed, but the day before their October 21 memo was sent to Kissinger, Nixon had brandished carrots and sticks during his meeting with Dobrynin; *WHY,* 305.

122. *HRHD,* October 3, 1969. Nixon was initially pleased with Agnew's performance. He had "now become a really good property and we should keep building and using him"; ibid., November 14. Within weeks, Agnew would become a public relations liability and a loose cannon, and Nixon would take steps to put him on a short leash.

123. Ibid., October 8, 1969.

124. Ibid., October 9, 1969 (italics in original).

125. Ibid.: "K had talked to me earlier, felt maybe we were trying to ease him out, had heard rumors he was leaving and thinks P has decided finally against his plan for Vietnam." See also ibid., October 11, 1969.

126. Ibid., October 9, 1969. Haldeman thought Nixon would explain to the American people that he had done everything he possibly could, accelerate the pace of troop withdrawal, and send a personal envoy to Hanoi to talk if they were willing. If the other side de-escalated, the United States would withdraw; if they did not but escalated dramatically, Nixon would implement a plan similar to Duck Hook in order to get military victory in three to six months.

127. Ibid., October 9, 10, 13, and 15, 1969; *WHY,* 305.

128. *RN,* 401–402. On this day, too, Nixon received a report that Kissinger claimed confirmed "that the other side has leaned heavily on our domestic critics in the exposition of their case"; Memo, Kissinger to Nixon, October 14, 1969, sub: Statements by North Vietnamese and NLF Delegates in Paris on American Domestic Criticism of the War, box 175, NSC: PT/M, NPM.

129. *HRHD,* October 15, 1969.

130. Ibid., October 23, 1969.

131. *RN,* 405.

132. *WHY,* 305. Kissinger also wrote that "Nixon sought to compensate for his unwillingness to face down his old friend" by telling him immediately after the meeting that he, Kissinger, should tell Dobrynin that the president "was out of control" regarding Vietnam. But Kissinger, knowing by this time that Nixon would take no action on his ultimatum, ignored the order.

133. *WHY,* 303–304.

134. *RN,* 398, 414.

135. *No More Vietnams,* 150. Regarding holding the country together, cf. *HRHD,* October 3, 1969.

136. *RN,* 405.

137. Here Nixon is paraphrasing the advice of his confidant, guerrilla warfare specialist Sir Robert Thompson; *RN,* 404. Haldeman wrote in *The Ends of Power:* "The [madman] theory—and Nixon and Kissinger's hopes for peace in Nixon's first year—crumbled. They [Hanoi] wouldn't even negotiate, and the reason was clear. No threat, and no offer could obscure one great fact known to the world at large. The American people had turned against the war" (98).

138. *HRHD,* October 23, 1969.

139. Quoted in Safire, *Before the Fall,* 368.

140. *No More Vietnams,* 149–150.

141. *RN,* 404.

142. *HRHD,* October 9, 1969.

143. *RN,* 404–405. See *HRHD,* April 23, 1969, for ending it in 1970.

144. *RN,* 413. See also my discussion in chapter 9.

145. *Public Papers of the Presidents, Nixon: 1969,* 901–909; *RN,* 409–412. In a 1970 interview Nixon used the term "bloodbath" to describe the Communist massacre that he claimed would follow an American defeat; "A Conversation with the President About Foreign Policy," July 1, 1970, *Public Papers of the Presidents of the United States, Richard Nixon: 1970* (Washington, D.C.: GPO, 1971), 548. See also Memo, Nixon to Kissinger, October 21, 1969, folder: P Memos 1969, box 228, WHSF: SMOF, HRH, NPM, in which he said he wanted a rewrite of the speech for more specific language on bloodbaths and to emphasize the "Silent Majority" message.

146. Hammond, *The Military and the Media,* 157.

147. Nixon, *In the Arena,* 332; and *No More Vietnams,* 115.

148. Memo, Alexander P. Butterfield to Nixon, November 12, 1969, Game Plan for Post-Speech Activities—Second . . . Updating, reproduced in Bruce Oudes, ed., *From the President: Richard Nixon's Secret Files* (New York: Harper and Row, 1989), 65–69.

149. Although Nixon himself only began to wear a flag pin months later, he frequently used it to foster his own purposes; see, *HRHD,* July 10, 1970, September 12, 1972, and February 8, 1973.

150. DeBenedetti and Chatfield, *American Ordeal,* 262; Small, *Johnson, Nixon, and the Doves,* 190.

151. *HRHD,* November 14, 1969.

152. Ibid., October 25, 1969.

153. See analysis in Hammond, *The Military and the Media,* 157–159, 165–169.

154. *HRHD,* November 24 and December 16, 1969.

155. See Hammond's treatment of Nixon's PR offensive during this period in *The Military and the Media,* 159–169.

156. Letter, Cyrus Eaton to Kissinger, November 26, 1969, folder: Ex 6-1, Paris Peace Talks (sub: Vietnam) [1969–70] WHCF, SF, FO, NPM.

157. *HRHD,* November 25 and December 1, 1969; see also Hammond, "My Lai and Other Atrocities," in *The Military and the Media,* chap. 10.

158. *HRHD,* December 16, 1969.

159. *RN,* 413–414.

9. BITING THE BULLET: 1970

1. *HRHD,* May 1, 1970.

2. See, e.g., ibid., November 5, 1969, April 15 and May 9, 1970, July 26, 1971, and February 6, 1973. See also Handwritten Note, April 8, 1970, WHSF: SMOF, HRH, NPM. Perhaps for this reason, Nixon met for an hour on December 1, 1969, with Dr. Arnold Hutschnecker, "the psychiatrist," Haldeman noted, "he was supposed to have consulted years ago." But if the doctor gave the president sound personal advice, he also used the occasion, Haldeman disdainfully remarked, to outline "a plan for world peace, through psychology, or something"; *HRHD,* December 1, 1969. See also Garment, *Crazy Rhythm,* 298–299, who discusses Hutschnecker and Nixon's mood swings, which he described as "nasty," moving "between grandiosity and pettiness."

3. Nixon, *Six Crises,* xiv.

4. *HRHD,* May 9, 1970.

5. *RN,* 403.

424 NIXON'S VIETNAM WAR

6. *HRHD,* March 21, 1970.

7. *WHY,* 482.

8. *HRHD,* February 28, 1970.

9. Memos, Nixon to Haldeman, Ehrlichman, and Kissinger, folder: Presidential Memos 1970, box 229, WHSF: SMOF, HRH, NPM.

10. *HRHD,* January 8, 1970.

11. Ibid., April 15, 1970.

12. Ibid., October 17 and December 3, 1969; Memo, Kissinger to Nixon, December 20, 1969, folder: [CF] CO 165 Vietnam, 11-16-69 to [11-11-70] [1969–70], box 10, WHSF: CF, SF, [CF], 1969–74, NPM; *RN,* 404–405; *WHY,* 436; Neil Sheehan, *A Bright Shining Lie: John Paul Vann and America in Vietnam* (New York: Random House, 1988), 734–736; Robert Thompson, *Peace is Not at Hand* (London: Chatto and Windus, 1974), 71–72.

13. Memo, Kissinger to Nixon, December 20, 1969, folder: [CF] CO 165 Vietnam, 11-16-69 to [11-11-70] [1969–70], box 10, WHSF: CF, SF, [CF], 1969–74, NPM; Memo, Dwight L. Chapin to Kissinger, December 5, 1969, sub: John Vann, folder: Tony Lake Chron File (Sept. 1969), box 1046, NSC: SF—LCF, ibid. Sheehan, *Bright Shining Lie,* 737–738; President's Activities Calendar, *HRHD, December 22, 1969.

14. Kissinger said that he had proposed the VSSG in early September, but its first meeting did not take place until October 20; *WHY,* 434.

15. Ibid., 434–436; Hersh, *Price of Power,* 297–300; Laurence E. Lynn, Jr., and Robert L. Sansom, Report on Trip to Vietnam, January 18–30, 1970, and Vietnam Special Studies Group, The Situation in the Countryside, April 15, 1970, in folders (2 of 2) and (1 of 2) of TL Info (Aug. 1969–Jun. 1970), box 1047, NSC: SF—LCF, NPM; R. L. Sansom, *The Economics of Insurgency in the Mekong Delta of Vietnam,* chap. 12. On the Phoenix program, see Andradé, *Ashes to Ashes.*

16. *WHY,* 476–478; Clarke, *Advice and Support,* 346–359; Hammond, *The Military and the Media,* 85, 90, 109, 111–113, 131–136, 321.

17. See e.g. *WHY,* 434–436; Memo, Kissinger to Nixon, December 20, 1969, folder: [CF] CO 165 Vietnam, 11-16-69 to [11-11-70] [1969–70], box 10, WHSF: CF, SF, [CF], 1969–74, NPM; *HRHD* for 1970 and 1971.

18. *WHY,* 435.

19. See Duiker, *Communist Road to Power,* 305.

20. Speeches by Giap, June and August, 1968, Doc. 68, and "The Party's Military Line," January, 1970, Doc. 70, *VDRN.*

21. Dung, "Under the Party's Banner," Doc. 71, *VDRN.* See also Duiker, *Communist Road to Power,* 305–308; and Kolko, *Anatomy of a War,* 368–373.

22. *WHY,* 435.

23. Speeches by Giap, June and August, 1968, Doc. 68, *VDRN,* p. 9.

24. Quoted in *WHY,* 436.

25. Quoted in ibid.

26. Thayer, *War Without Fronts,* Table 4.6. For Nixon's revisions to the speech, see Speech (draft), December 13, 1969, folder: 1969 Presidential Peace Plan Speech, box 191, WHSF: SMOF, HRH, NPM.

27. *HRHD,* December 15, 1969.

28. *WHY,* 436, 475.

29. *HRHD,* January 15, 1970. See also April 9, 1971.

30. Ibid., April 26, 1971; Thayer, *War Without Fronts,* Table 4.6; cf. *WHY,* 481.

31. *RN,* 404, 413, 445.

32. Quoted in *WHY,* 481.

33. *RN,* 404, 413; Hersh, *Price of Power,* 170. "Neuralgic point" is in Memo, Kissinger to Nixon, January 20, 1970, sub: Conversation with Ambassador Dobrynin, folder: T. Lake Chron—January 1970, box 1046, NSC: SF—NPM.

34. Garthoff, *Détente and Confrontation,* 256.

35. *WHY,* 478–479.

36. See, e.g., *HRHD,* April 23, 1970.

37. *WHY,* 437. Another truism is that the optimum moment to negotiate is when you have to.

38. Memo, Kissinger to Nixon, June 24, 1969, sub.: Appointment with Ambassador Lodge, folder: [CF], FO-6-1, Paris Peace Talks, box 33, WHSF: CF, NPM; Memo, Lodge to Kissinger, March 7, 1969, and Kissinger to Lodge, March 18, and Memo, Lodge to Nixon and Kissinger, May 11, and Lodge's notes of meeting with Kissinger, August 4, and Memo, Lodge to Nixon, August 21, Lodge Papers, reel 9, MHS. See also A General Strategy & Plan for Viet-nam Negotiations, March 28, 1969, folder: NSC Meeting of March 28, 1969—A General Strategy & Plan for Viet-Nam Negotiations, box 175, NSC: PT/M, NPM.

39. Telegram, American Embassy in Rome to Rogers, May 6, 1970, sub: Fanfani's Meeting with Xuan Thuy, folder: [CF], FO-6-1, box 33, WHSF: CF, NPM. Lodge did, however, attend some sessions; his last was on December 4, 1969; Memo, Kissinger to Nixon, the December 4th Paris Plenary Session on Vietnam, box 3, WH/NSC: POW/MIA, ibid.

40. Lodge recommended Habib; Memo, Lodge to Kissinger, n.d. [ca. August 1969], Lodge Papers, reel 9, MHS.

41. *WHY,* 437; Memo, John Holdridge to Kissinger, February 19, and Memo, Kissinger to Nixon, February 25, 1970, sub: Mrs. Binh Replies to Ambassador Habib, folder: Paris Talks, Memos & Misc/Memcoms, Vol. III (#2), box 3, WH/NSC: POW/MIA, NPM.

42. *WHY,* 447.

43. *RN,* 413.

44. Quoted in *WHY,* 438.

45. Available documents bear out Kissinger's admission to optimism; see, e.g., *HRHD,* February 20 and 23, 1970, and passim. Also cf. *WHY,* 437–438, 446–447; and *RN,* 413. On the issue of establishing a record, see also Memo, Kissinger to Nixon, January 30, 1970, sub: Le Duc Tho's Plans and Xuan Thuy's Mood, box 3, WH/NSC: POW/MIA, NPM.

46. *WHY,* 438.

47. Memo, Kissinger to Nixon, January 30, 1970, sub: Le Duc Tho's Plans and Xuan Thuy's Mood, box 3, WH/NSC: POW/MIA, NPM.

48. *HRHD,* February 17 and 20, 1970.

49. *WHY,* 439–440; *HRHD,* February 17, 1970.

50. *WHY,* 442, 438, 279, 1021.

51. Ibid., 443–444; DRV Chronology on Diplomatic Struggle, February 21 and March 20, 1970.

52. Interview by Barnet of Pham Van Dong, cited in Hersh, *Price of Power,* 173. In *WHY,* 445, Kissinger said that the other side demanded that "all anti-Communist leaders" would be barred from a coalition, but the other side's proposal appears to have only barred

the Thieu regime's anti-Communist leaders; DRV Chronology on Diplomatic Struggle, February 21, 1970. Tran Thien Khiem had replaced Tran Van Huong as prime minister of South Vietnam in late 1969.

53. Memo, Kissinger to Nixon, March 16, 1970, with attached Memorandum of Conversation, sub: My Meeting with North Vietnamese on March 16, 1970, folder: Camp David—Sensitive—vol. 3, box 4 (1), WH/NSC: POW/MIA, NPM.

54. WHY, 443.

55. HRHD, February 23 and April 5, 1970.

56. RN, 446. Nixon made similar comments in his marginal notes on Memo, Kissinger to Nixon, May 28, 1971, sub: My May 31 Meeting with the North Vietnamese, folder: Camp David—Sensitive—vol. 6, box 4 (2), WH/NSC: POW/MIA, NPM.

57. Memo, Kissinger to Nixon, May 23, 1969, sub: Assessment of the 22 May Plenary Session on Vietnam, folder: Paris Talks, 4/5/69, Memos & Misc/Memcons, Vol. III, 5/3/69, box 3, WH/NSC: POW/MIA, NPM.

58. See chapter 8.

59. Memo, John Holdridge to Kissinger, February 19, and Memo, Kissinger to Nixon, February 25, 1970, sub: Mrs. Binh Replies to Ambassador Habib, folder: Paris Talks, Memos & Misc/Memcoms, Vol. III (#2), box 3, WH/NSC: POW/MIA, NPM.

60. Memo, Holdridge to Kissinger, March 20, 1970, sub: Ambassador Habib's Presentations in Paris, and Memo, Kissinger to Nixon, March 23, 1970, sub: Ambassador Habib's Presentations in Paris, box 3, WH/NSC: POW/MIA, NPM. The scribbling on the cover sheet to the March 23 memo appears to be in Nixon's handwriting; Kissinger approved the memo as typed by an aide.

61. Memo, Kissinger to Nixon, December 9, 1970, sub: The December 4th Plenary Session on Vietnam, ibid.

62. HRHD, March 13, 1970. Haldeman was referring to their maneuvers in the Middle East.

63. WHY, 448. See also pp. 476–482 for an example of their "bureaucratic chess game" and his discussion of the effect of compartmentalization on Rogers's and Laird's advice. Laird's Vietnamization scheme, for example, was, Kissinger claimed, unacceptable to Le Duc Tho, but since Laird was not included in the making of Nixinger negotiating strategy, he could not know this.

64. Isaacson, Kissinger, 254.

65. Kissinger admits as much in WHY, 448, but of course with a different twist and tone, blaming the final failure of their policies on the bureaucracy and the public.

66. HRHD, March 13, 1970.

67. WHY, 445; DRV Chronology on Diplomatic Struggle, March 20, 1970. See later discussion of Laos and Cambodia.

68. Memo, Kissinger to Nixon, March 16, 1970, with attached Memorandum of Conversation, sub: My Meeting with North Vietnamese on March 16, 1970, folder: Camp David—Sensitive—vol. 3, box 4 (1), WH/NSC: POW/MIA, NPM.

69. HRHD, March 16, 1970.

70. WHY, 445.

71. Thach, interview with the author. This point is discussed more fully in succeeding chapters.

72. Quoted in Hersh, Price of Power, 174.

73. *HRHD*, February 23, April 5 and 13, 1970.

74. Ibid., February 16 and 19, 1970; *WHY*, 452–457; Hersh, *Price of Power*, 168–172; Hammond, *The Military and the Media*, 266–270; Furlong Papers, AFHRA. At the end of March Nixon approved the sending of Thai battalions into Laos.

75. *HRHD*, March 20, 1970; Hammond, *The Military and the Media*, 266–270.

76. *Public Papers of the Presidents, Nixon: 1970*, 244–249. See also Hersh, *Price of Power*, 169.

77. *WHY*, 451–456.

78. *Public Papers of the Presidents, Nixon: 1970*, 244–249; Furlong Papers, AFHRA; Roger Warner, *Back Fire: The CIA's Secret War in Laos and Its Link to the War in Vietnam* (New York: Simon and Schuster, 1995); Littauer and Uphoff, *Air War in Indochina*, chap. 5; John Morrocco and the editors of Boston Publishing Company, *Rain of Fire: Air War, 1969–1973* (Boston: Boston Publishing Company, 1985), 46.

79. Hersh, *Price of Power*, 170.

80. Kissinger made this remark about B-52 symbolism in reference to Cambodia, but it applies equally to his views regarding Laos; *WHY*, 474.

81. *WHY*, 454. See also Hersh, *Price of Power*, 169–171.

82. *WHY*, 452. Nixon, too, wanted the raids to be effective, but although B-52s were more likely than fighter-bombers to have an impact on enemy forces, he wondered on March 2 whether the air force had chosen appropriate targets: "When I heard the bombing program in Laos described I wondered if possibly the Air Force may not just be running these missions for the purpose of building up combat time and getting air medals. I have the feeling that a lot of bombs are dropped on barren territory with knowledge if that is the case. Can you have some discreet checking done on this issue?" Memo, Nixon to Kissinger, March 2, 1970, folder: Presidential Memoranda, box 228, WHSF: SMOF, HRH, NPM.

83. See, e.g., *HRHD*, April 23, 1970.

84. Quoted in *WHY*, 455.

85. *HRHD*, March 24, 1970.

86. Ibid., April 8, 1970. Social psychologists who have studied the phenomenon of exaggerated fear among policy makers have concluded that exaggerated fear about the enemy often leads to irrational behavior, aggressive actions, and a lack of concern about costs; see, e.g., Ralph K. White, *Fearful Warriors: A Psychological Profile of U.S.-Soviet Relations* (New York: Free Press, 1984).

87. *HRHD*, March 13, 1970.

88. Ibid., February 4, 1970.

89. *Public Papers of the Presidents, Nixon: 1970*, 248.

90. *WHY*, 436. See also Hammond, *The Military and the Media*, 272–276; *HRHD*, March 9, 1970, and ff.

91. *HRHD*, March 11, 1970.

92. Ibid., March 9, 1970; see also February 25 and 27, March 2, 3, 4, 10, 11, 13, 20, 21, and 24, 1970. Nixon had been compelled to explain the policy to state governors when he met with them at a governors' conference, answer questions at a scheduled press conference, thrash out the issue in an NSC meeting, suffer episodes of miscommunication between Kissinger and Laird, mediate another bitter dispute between Kissinger and Rogers, and cancel other appointments to work on the March 6 public statement.

93. Ibid., April 1, 1970.

94. See, e.g., ibid., March 10, 1970; Hersh, *Price of Power,* chap. 18; and Kissinger's version of his feud with Rogers in *WHY,* 454, and chap. 10; and *RN,* 478–479.

95. *HRHD,* March 18, 1970.

96. Ibid., April 1, 1970.

97. Ibid., March 30, 1970.

98. Ibid., March 31, 1970.

99. Ibid., April 1, 1970; Morrocco, *Rain of Fire,* 100.

100. See, e.g., *Public Papers of the Presidents, Nixon: 1970,* 1101–1102. Since the reconnaissance aircraft were always accompanied by American fighter planes, it was far from clear whether the North Vietnamese were firing on unarmed reconnaissance planes or protecting themselves against American fighter aircraft.

101. *WHY,* 483.

102. Ibid., 483–484; *RN,* 447–448. See also *HRHD,* April 13–18, 1970.

103. Quoted in *RN,* 448.

104. *HRHD,* April 16, 1970.

105. *WHY,* 483.

106. Shawcross, *Sideshow,* 127. This bare-bones paragraph describing the coup and events leading up to it is based on accounts in ibid.; Hersh, *Price of Power; WHY; RN;* and R. B. Smith, "The International Setting of the Cambodia Crisis, October 1969 to April 1970," unpublished paper, May 1995.

107. Memo, Kissinger to Nixon, April 4, 1970, cited in Isaacson, *Kissinger,* 258. See also *WHY,* 468–469; DRV Chronology on Diplomatic Struggle, March 16, 1970.

108. Handwritten notes, VNLAF security unit, undated [ca. April 25–30], Doc. no. 88, *VDRN.*

109. *WHY,* 463–464; *RN,* 446–447.

110. Quoted in Shawcross, *Sideshow,* 122.

111. Ibid., appendix, p. 409.

112. Hersh, *Price of Power,* 177–183; see also Furlong Papers, AFHRA.

113. Kissinger acknowledges that the enlargement of the sanctuaries was the prime cause of turmoil in Cambodian politics, but he failed to mention the role of Menu in bringing about this enlargement; *WHY,* 475. See also Truong Nhu Tang, *Vietcong Memoir,* 177.

114. Shawcross, *Sideshow,* 122, 130. American intelligence operatives had previously offered aid, American officials had often criticized Sihanouk's tolerance of Communist sanctuaries, and the U.S. government had encouraged South Vietnam and Thailand to press border claims against Sihanouk's Cambodia.

115. *HRHD,* March 30, 1970.

116. Shawcross, *Sideshow,* appendix, p. 403; Herring, *America's Longest War,* 259; *WHY,* 465, 473; Isaacson, *Kissinger,* 258.

117. *WHY,* 488; Hammond, *The Military and the Media,* 287–288, 293; Truong Nhu Tang, *Vietcong Memoir,* 177–178.

118. *WHY,* 475. See also *HRHD,* April 28, 1970: "border raids have been going on for some time."

119. Thach interview in Hersh, *Price of Power,* 186, 201.

120. *HRHD,* April 5, 1970. See also *RN,* 447; Telegram, Am. Embassy in Rome to SecState, May 6, 1970, sub: Fanfani's Meeting with Xuan Thuy, May 5th, folder: [CF], FO-6-1, Paris Peace Talks, box 33, WHSF: CF, NPM.

121. Isaacson, *Kissinger,* 264; Shawcross, *Sideshow,* 130.

122. Report, VNLAF security unit, n.d. [ca. March–April 1970], Doc. 88, *VDRN.* See also Hersh, *Price of Power,* 187; Truong Nhu Tang, *Vietcong Memoir,* chaps. 14, 15.

123. One captured report from a VNLAF special armed political unit that had been written in the latter part of April stated: "Though we do not see all the possibilities yet, the recent coup d'état appears to have given the Revolution a great leap forward, created a revolutionary government, and laid the ground for an anti-American front of the Indochinese peoples." This was a politically exhortative, morale-boosting document, emphasizing positive, though tentative, possibilities in the context of very difficult and complex circumstances. "The American imperialists are very stubborn, and we should beware of their activities"; Unsigned report, April 19, 1970, Document 88, *VDRN.*

124. Handwritten notes, April 29, 1970, sub: Code of Conduct, Document 88, ibid.

125. Memo, Kissinger to Nixon, April 26, 1970, quoted in Shawcross, *Sideshow,* appendix, p. 412. See also *HRHD,* April 26, 1970.

126. Kissinger mentions the options in reference to an NSC meeting of April 22; *WHY,* 490.

127. See Mitchell's Memorandum of Meeting, April 28, 1970, in *WHY,* 1484–1485 n. 10; and Kissinger's comment on his decision, p. 502. See also Hammond, *The Military and the Media,* 292–297.

128. Handwritten Note, April 1970, sub: Chronology, WHSF: SMOF, HRH, NPM.

129. *HRHD,* April 24, 1970. See Davidson, *Vietnam at War,* 626–627.

130. *WHY,* 487. It appears that Nixon would have preferred to meet with only McCain and not the other CINCPAC officers; Handwritten Note, April 17, 1970, WHSF: SMOF, HRH, NPM.

131. President's Activities Calendar, *HRHD,* April 19 and 20, 1970. On McCain, see *WHY,* 480, 487; Shawcross, *Sideshow,* 136–137; Isaacson, *Kissinger,* 259; Hammond, *The Military and the Media,* 284–286, 293. Kissinger dated the original McCain briefing at April 18, but that was Washington time.

132. *HRHD,* April 20, 1970.

133. Ibid.; and Handwritten Note, April 20, 1970, WHSF: SMOF, HRH, NPM.

134. Ibid. See also Hammond, *The Military and the Media,* 288–292.

135. *HRHD,* April 21, 1970.

136. Ibid., April 22, 1970; one of the memoranda is reproduced in *WHY,* 1484 n. 9, and *RN,* 448–449. See also *WHY,* 489–490.

137. *HRHD,* April 22 and 23, 1970.

138. Handwritten Note, April 21, 1970, WHSF: SMOF, HRH, NPM.

139. *WHY,* 491.

140. Ibid., 491–492.

141. Ibid., 483–497. Nixon also spoke of his emotional state in his own account, but he portrayed his attitude as one of courageous decisiveness in the face of great personal and political risk "for me and my administration," and he said nothing about his drinking; *RN,* 449–450.

142. Regarding the pool table, Haldeman wrote: "Absolutely astonishing he could get into trivia on the brink of biggest step he's taken so far"; *HRHD,* April 29, 1970. On *Patton,* see ibid., April 26, May 18, and November 10, 1969, and April 7 and June 12, 1970; *WHY,* 483–489; Isaacson, *Kissinger,* 259; Shawcross, *Sideshow,* 135, 144.

143. *WHY,* 486, 494, 498, 502, 507.

144. *HRHD*, April 22, 1970.

145. After the NSC meeting on April 22, Kissinger told Nixon that "he was great in NSC"; *HRHD*, April 22, 1970.

146. See, e.g., Hersh, *Price of Power*, 188–189.

147. *HRHD*, April 23, 1970.

148. See, e.g., Davidson, *Vietnam at War*, 627.

149. *HRHD*, April 23 and 24, 1970.

150. In *RN*, 450, Nixon says April 26; in *WHY*, 502, Kissinger says the "final decision" was made on April 28.

151. Cf. *WHY*, 490, 494, 502; *HRHD*, April 24, 1970; Handwritten Note, April 20, 1970, WHSF: SMOF, HRH NPM.

152. *WHY*, 494, 502. See also Memorandum of Meeting, April 28, 1970, in ibid., 1484–1485 n. 10.

153. *WHY*, 495, 497.

154. *RN*, 455–456. Cf. *HRHD*, April 23 and 24, 1970.

155. On Agnew, see *HRHD*, passim, for this period from fall 1969 into spring 1970; and also Hammond, *The Military and the Media*, 159–165.

156. *HRHD*, April 23, 1970.

157. *WHY*, 492, 495–496; *HRHD*, April 23, 1970. Kissinger wrote that Nixon approved both WSAG "orders" the next day.

158. *WHY*, 494–495; Isaacson, *Kissinger*, 261–262; *HRHD*, April 24, 1970.

159. *HRHD*, April 24, 1970. Cf. *WHY*, 495–496. Kissinger held in abeyance Nixon's directives to fire personnel until he might cool down and either reissue the orders or not, but he did act to arrange for the delivery of signal equipment to the CIA via military aircraft and prepare papers for the meeting with Helms and Moorer.

160. *HRHD*, April 24, 1970.

161. Ibid., April 23, 24, and 25, 1970. See also Clarke, *Advice and Support*, 420; Isaacson, *Kissinger*, 263.

162. *WHY*, 497, 499.

163. Ibid., 496–497.

164. Ibid., 493–494; Isaacson, *Kissinger*, 263–265; Hersh, *Price of Power*, 188–190.

165. Hersh, *Price of Power*, 188–190, 299. In addition to their "grave reservations" about the invasion, Lake and Morris resigned because of their increasing alienation from the domestic and foreign policies of the administration and their discomfort working in an atmosphere of "suspicion, manipulation, and malice"; Letter, Lake and Morris to Kissinger, April 29, 1970, folder: Tony Lake Chron File (Jun. 1969–May 1970) (1 of 6), NSC: SF—LCF, NPM.

166. Morris, *Haig*, 141, and *Uncertain Greatness*, 147. Watts monitored the call on a dead-key phone.

167. *WHY*, 497–498.

168. *RN*, 455; *WHY*, 498. Kissinger said in his memoirs that he regretted having not gone along with Nixon regarding the go-for-broke approach.

169. Secretary of Defense Laird was aware of contingency planning for the invasion, but, as Kissinger reminded Nixon, he was "not . . . aware of the likelihood of its being approved"; Memo, Kissinger to Nixon, April 26, 1970, quoted in Shawcross, *Sideshow*, 412. Haldeman noted before the meeting that the president "wants to lay groundwork for big moves on Cambodia this week"; *HRHD*, April 26, 1970.

170. *WHY,* 499.

171. *HRHD,* April 27, 1970; *WHY,* 500–501.

172. Handwritten Note, April 27, 1970, WHSF: SMOF, HRH, NPM; *HRHD,* April 27, 1970. The manuscript version has slightly more information. Cf. *WHY,* 500–501.

173. Quoted in Safire, *Before the Fall,* 102–103.

174. Handwritten Note, April 27, 1970, WHSF: SMOF, HRH, NPM. Wheeler had been phoned during the meeting.

175. *RN,* 450–451; *WHY,* 501–502; *HRHD,* April 27 and 28, 1970.

176. *HRHD,* April 28, 1970.

177. Shawcross, *Sideshow,* chap. 15.

178. Davidson, *Vietnam at War,* 625; Sigler, *Vietnam Battle Chronology,* 116; *WHY,* 503, 505–509; Truong Nhu Tang, *Vietcong Memoir,* chap. 15.

179. Handwritten Note, June 21, 1970, WHSF: SMOF, HRH, NPM.

180. *HRHD,* April 29, 1970; the "mystic sessions" phrase is in the October 3, 1969, entry.

181. Ibid., April 30, 1970; *WHY,* 505. On Nixon reading about past presidents, see also *HRHD* June 29 and July 14, 1970.

182. *Public Papers of the Presidents, Nixon: 1970,* 405–410. See also Hammond, *The Military and the Media,* 300–305.

183. *HRHD,* May 1, 2, 3, and 4, 1970. See also Hammond, *The Military and the Media,* 307–318.

10. TRANSITIONS, CONTINUITIES: 1970–1971

1. *HRHD,* December 21, 1970

2. DeBenedetti and Chatfield, *American Ordeal,* 271.

3. Ibid., 270; Kenneth J. Heineman, *Campus Wars: The Peace Movement at American State Universities in the Vietnam Era* (New York: New York University Press, 1993), 245; Small, *Johnson, Nixon, and the Doves,* 201.

4. *HRHD,* March 12, 1970, and April 22, 1971. See also ibid., February 28, September 27, 1970, and July 5, 1971; and Haldeman, *Ends of Power,* 105. His other major accomplishments would be to reduce crime and improve the economy. At the time, July 5, 1971, he was being criticized for his handling of the economy.

5. *HRHD,* October 15, 1970. There were also the occasional protests by students receiving awards at the White House, which "drove him right up the wall"; see ibid., December 3, 1970.

6. Ibid., March 12 and April 29, 1970.

7. This according to an aide quoted in Hersh, *Price of Power,* 191. See also Small, *Johnson, Nixon, and the Doves,* 201.

8. Nixon had said: "You see these bums, you know, blowing up the campuses. Listen, the boys that are on the college campuses today are the luckiest people in the world, going to the greatest universities, and here they are burning up the books, I mean storming around about this issue—I mean you name it—get rid of the war; there will be another one"; *The Nixon Presidential Press Conferences* (New York: Earl M. Coleman Enterprises, 1978), 111 n. 1. For private White House reaction, see *HRHD,* May 6, 1970; for Nixon's published interpretation, see *RN,* 455–456.

9. Heineman, *Campus Wars*, 246–250.

10. Ibid., 249; DeBenedetti and Chatfield, *American Ordeal*, 280; see also Small, *Johnson, Nixon, and the Doves*, 202.

11. *HRHD*, May 3, 4, and 7, 1970; *RN*, 457–458; *Public Papers of the Presidents, Nixon: 1970*, 141.

12. *HRHD*, May 4, 6, and 8, 1970.

13. Small, *Johnson, Nixon, and the Doves*, 203; *WHY*, 515; *HRHD*, May 26, 1970; Isaacson, *Kissinger*, 283–284; *RN*, 457.

14. *HRHD*, May 7, 9, 11, and 14, 1970.

15. They thought he had "zinged the bad guys" in the press, while praising the good guys; he had made all the points he wanted to make; *HRHD*, May 8, 1970.

16. *Public Papers of the Presidents, Nixon: 1970*, 144.

17. DeBenedetti and Chatfield, *American Ordeal*, 279–280.

18. *RN*, 465.

19. *HRHD*, May 9, 1970.

20. Ibid., May 11 and 13, 1970; *RN*, 459–466. The full-text version is in Nixon to Haldeman, May 13, 1970, folder: Presidential Memoranda, box 229, WHSF, NPM. See also *Public Papers of the Presidents, Nixon: 1970*, 423–426.

21. *HRHD*, May 18 and June 2, 1970.

22. Ibid., May 26, 1970. Haldeman also noted: "K pleased because they (*the North Vietnamese*) called Walters in Paris, and said their man would be gone two weeks. K thought they'd call off deal [i.e., plenary Paris talks], but they're keeping it open, sign of real weakness."

23. Ibid., May 18, 20, 21, 27, June 2, 22, 1970.

24. *WHY*, 968.

25. Mueller, *War, Presidents, and Public Opinion*, 55, 56, 95, 115–154, 201, and appendices; *HRHD*, November 22, 1969, January 12, March 13, April 6 and 8, April 20, 1970; DeBenedetti and Chatfield, *American Ordeal*, 271.

26. Regarding Kissinger, see, e.g., *HRHD*, March 13, 1970.

27. Ibid., May 19, 1970.

28. See, e.g., discussion in DeBenedetti and Chatfield, *American Ordeal*, 283 ff.

29. Small, *Johnson, Nixon, and the Doves*, 211. On dissent and morale in the military, see Christian G. Appy, *Working-Class War: American Combat Soldiers and Vietnam* (Chapel Hill: University of North Carolina Press, 1993), chap. 7; David Cortright, *Soldiers in Revolt* (Garden City, N.Y.: Doubleday, 1975); chapters by Terry H. Anderson, David Cortright, Elliott L. Meyrowitz and Kenneth J. Campbell, and William F. Crandell in part 2 of *Give Peace a Chance: Exploring the Vietnam Antiwar Movement*, ed. Melvin Small and William D. Hoover (Syracuse, N.Y.: Syracuse University Press, 1992); Hammond, *The Military and the Media*, chap. 16; and Kolko, *Anatomy of a War*, 363–367.

30. DeBenedetti and Chatfield, *American Ordeal*, 253, 286.

31. *HRHD*, May 12, 15, 18, 19, June 4, 8, 13, 18, 22, 24, 30, July 8, 9, July 13, 14, 1970; Hersh, *Price of Power*, 201; DeBenedetti and Chatfield, *American Ordeal*, 253, 286–287; *Newsweek*, July 6, 1970, 37.

32. "Authority of the President to Permit Incursion into Communist Sanctuaries in the Cambodia-Vietnam Border Area," May 14, 1970, in Oudes, *From the President*, 138. See also Arthur M. Schlesinger, Jr., *The Imperial Presidency* (Boston: Houghton Mifflin, 1973).

33. *WHY,* 513.

34. "We highly appreciate the antiwar movement of the American people during the Vietnam War. This movement represents one of the important elements that led to the end of the American War in Vietnam. Vietnamese people will always be grateful to the American people"; Huong Tung and Nguyen Co Thach, interviews by the author.

35. "Some Characteristics of the Development of the Situation," April 1971, Doc. 92, *VDRN.* See also "The 19th Plenary Session of the Central Committee of the Viet-Nam Workers Party and its Reference Documents," Doc. 91, ibid.

36. "Some Characteristics," Doc. 92, *VDRN.*

37. *WHY,* 970.

38. Ibid., 971.

39. Hoang Tung, Nguyen Co Thach, and Luu Van Loi, interviews by the author.

40. See, e.g., *Bases for a Settlement of the Viet Nam Problem,* 8–10.

41. Clarke, *Advice and Support,* 421.

42. Furlong Papers, AFHRA; Shawcross, *Sideshow,* chap. 15; Hersh, *Price of Power,* 200; *WHY,* 505–506, 517.

43. Quotes in the preceding section are from "Report on the Cambodian Operation," June 30, 1970, *Public Papers of the Presidents, Nixon: 1970,* 540; Nixon provided statistics for the operation on p. 536.

44. Hersh, *Price of Power,* 200.

45. The invasion also delivered a temporary setback to rapprochement between the United States and the PRC. The Chinese canceled a meeting with U.S. representatives in Warsaw that had been scheduled for May 20. On the Warsaw meetings and rapprochement, see Garthoff, *Détente and Confrontation,* 248 ff.

46. Hersh, *Price of Power,* 201; Shawcross, *Sideshow,* 125–127, appendix; Duiker, *Communist Road to Power,* 314.

47. DOD Cable to Abrams, May 6, 1970, microfiche no. 001355, declassified January 23, 1990, *Declassified Documents Catalog,* vol. 20, no. 3.

48. Shawcross, *Sideshow,* appendix, pp. 413–414. For Kissinger's claim of reduced casualties before Congress, see Military Operations in Cambodia and Laos, September 1973, folder: Cambodia—Cambodian Bombing, box 11, NSC: HAKOF, HAKASF, NPM.

49. *RN,* 467; Clarke, *Advice and Support,* 421–422.

50. *Public Papers of the Presidents, Nixon: 1970,* 537.

51. See comments in Garthoff, *Détente and Confrontation,* chap. 7; Kissinger, *WHY,* 968; Kolko, *Anatomy of a War,* pt. 5.

52. Quoted in *WHY,* 969.

53. Garthoff, *Détente and Confrontation,* 448–250, 279.

54. *HRHD,* September 16 and 20, 1970. Regarding the North Vietnamese, Kissinger had been frustrated by a meeting with Xuan Thuy in Paris on September 7.

55. In an Orwellian twist, the original story does not appear in the microfilm records of the *Sun-Times.* My account is pieced together from these sources: Henry Brandon, *The Retreat of American Power* (Garden City, N.Y.: Doubleday, 1973), 134; *Chicago Sun-Times,* September 17 and 18, 1970; Garthoff, *Détente and Confrontation,* 98; Hersh, *Price of Power,* 238–240; *HRHD,* September 16, 17, and 20, 1970; Hughes, "Foreign Policy," 55; Isaacson, *Kissinger,* 294; *RN,* 483; *NYT,* September 18, 1970; *Washington Post,* September 18; *WHY,* 613–615.

56. *WHY,* 979.

57. *HRHD,* July 8, 1970; *WHY,* 969–971, 984–985.

58. Quoted in *WHY,* 969.

59. *HRHD,* July 10 and 25, 1970. On wiretaps, counterintelligence, the public relations campaign, polls, political strategy, and the flag, see ibid., April 17, May 12, 26, June 5, 26, July 4, 7, 11, 13, 23, 25, August 25, and September 15, 16, 22, 27, 1970, April 22, 1972; September 22, 1971 and June 13, 1972 entries in *Abuse of Power,* 37 and 40; DeBenedetti and Chatfield, *American Ordeal,* 225–226, 245, 246, 288; Hammond, *The Military and the Media,* chap. 14; Hersh, *Price of Power,* chap. 7, pp. 209–210, 387; Isaacson, *Kissinger,* chap. 11; Small, *Johnson, Nixon, and the Doves,* 191, 209–212, 223; Theodore H. White, *The Making of the President, 1972* (New York: Atheneum, 1973), chaps. 1, 3.

60. *HRHD,* October 16, September 16, 1970.

61. Ibid., September 11 and October 16, 1970; see also numerous other entries regarding the Scranton Commission and the FBI. On the Kent State investigations and trials, see Heineman, *Campus Wars,* 254 ff.

62. *HRHD,* October 29, 1970. Cf. Bergholz and Wrightson, quoted in Strober and Strober, *Nixon: An Oral History of His Presidency,* 25.

63. *HRHD,* November 4, 5, 6, 1970.

64. Memo, Colson to Nixon, November 6, 1970, reproduced in Oudes, *From the President,* 166–167.

65. *HRHD,* December 3, 9, 24, 30, 1970.

66. *WHY,* 969.

67. Ibid., 979, 969.

68. Ibid., 971–974. Unfortunately, Kissinger does not tell us what these options were.

69. Ibid., 974; *HRHD,* August 18, 1970.

70. See *HRHD,* August 17 and 18, September 21 and 22, November 10 and 16, and December 3, 28, and 29, 1970, February, 11, 1972, and passim. For more on the Kissinger-Rogers feud, see Glad and Link, "Nixon's Inner Circle of Advisers"; Hoff, "Revisionist View of Nixon's Foreign Policy"; Isaacson, *Kissinger,* passim; Hersh, *Price of Power,* passim; Schulzinger, *Henry Kissinger,* passim; *WHY,* passim.

71. *WHY,* 975–976.

72. Ibid., 970.

73. Memo, Kissinger to Nixon, September 17, 1970, sub: New Communist Proposals on Vietnam, folder: Camp David—Sensitive—vol. 7, box 4, WH/NSC: POW/MIA, NPM.

74. *WHY,* 976–977. Kissinger quipped that there was a weird quality to the White House proposal: "They [the North Vietnamese] had better agree to mutual withdrawal now lest we punish them by withdrawing unilaterally later." The proposal was indeed bizarre, but not only for the reason implied in Kissinger's self-effacing remark. Had Hanoi accepted it, they would have received an American commitment to a more rapid withdrawal, but it would still have been a withdrawal at a pace that might have provided time for Vietnamization to take hold. And there were major "loopholes," including the threat of last-minute massive bombing; the release of American POWs before a final settlement; and the oversight of South Vietnamese elections by an "international" body that would serve to legitimate the Saigon regime, which would have remained in power.

75. DRV Chronology on Diplomatic Struggle, September 7, 1970.

76. *Public Papers of the Presidents, Nixon: 1970,* 375.

77. *NYT,* September 18, 1970; and *Bases for a Settlement of the Viet Nam Problem,* 34–39.

78. Memo, Kissinger to Nixon, September 17, 1970, sub: New Communist Proposals on Vietnam, folder: Camp David—Sensitive—vol. 7, box 4, WH/NSC: POW/MIA, NPM.

79. Memo, Kissinger to Nixon, September 22, 1970, sub: A Longer Look at the New Communist Peace Proposal on Vietnam, folder: Paris Talks, July–Sept. 1970, box 3, WH/ NSC: POW/MIA, NPM.

80. Memo, Kissinger to Nixon, September 28, 1970, sub: September 27, 1970 Meeting, folder: Camp David—Sensitive—vol. 6, box 4 (2), WH/NSC: MIA/POW, NPM.

81. Memo, Kissinger to Nixon, September 22, 1970, sub: A Longer Look at the New Communist Peace Proposal on Vietnam, folder: Paris Talks, July–Sept. 1970, box 3, WH/ NSC: POW/MIA, NPM.

82. Safire, *Before the Fall,* 385.

83. *WHY,* 972.

84. Memo, W. Richard Smyser/Winston Lord to Kissinger, September 25, 1970, sub: Revisions in Your Statement for September 27 meeting, folder: Camp David—Sensitive— vol. 7, box 4 (3), and Memo, Kissinger to Nixon, September 28, 1970, sub: September 27, 1970 Meeting, folder: Camp David—Sensitive—vol. 6, box 4 (2), WH/NSC: MIA/ POW, NPM.

85. *Public Papers of the Presidents, Nixon: 1970,* 825–828.

86. *HRHD,* October 7, 1970.

87. Ibid., August 11, 1970. Cf. *WHY,* 972, 974.

88. *HRHD,* October 7, 1970.

89. *WHY,* 972.

90. See, e.g., "Pentagon Wary," *NYT,* October 9, 1970. Haldeman incorrectly summarized the proposal in his diary thus: "P proposed a ceasefire in place throughout Indochina, a negotiated withdrawal of all U.S. troops, and a political settlement which reflected the existing situation in South Vietnam" (October 7, 1970).

91. *WHY,* 980; *HRHD,* October 4, 1970. In Ireland Nixon met with officials, gave speeches, visited the ancestral home of the Milhous clan, and received a pledge from businessman Jack Mulcahy of up to $2 million for the fall campaign.

92. *WHY,* 980.

93. Safire, *Before the Fall,* 384. Safire also wrote that Kissinger resented "being pushed in his negotiations by Ambassador David Bruce's requests and the President's political requirements" (385).

94. See, e.g., *NYT,* October 9, 1970.

95. See Hersh, *Price of Power,* 302 n.

96. *WHY,* 980. But Kissinger continued to obscure the cease-fire–mutual withdrawal connection; see, e.g., ibid, 1493 n. 3.

97. *Public Papers of the Presidents, Nixon: 1970,* 830.

98. Ibid., 826.

99. See *WHY,* 971–973, 986. Concerning the issue of who benefited from a cease-fire, Kissinger argued in his memoirs that on the one hand it would preclude North Vietnamese offensives, but on the other it would erode South Vietnamese gains in the countryside. The latter would be less likely, however, if the NVA withdrew, leaving the NLF to face the RVNAF alone, and this, of course, was the point of continuing to insist on mutual withdrawal.

100. *NYT,* October 9, 1970.

101. DRV Chronology on Diplomatic Struggle, November 17, 1970.

102. The basic book on Son Tay is by Benjamin F. Schemmer, *The Raid* (New York: Harper and Row, 1976), but see also Hersh, *Price of Power,* 304–306, who adds details drawn from interviews with insiders. Hersh wrote that Nixon, Kissinger, Rogers, Laird, and Moorer only discussed the operation on November 18. But *HRHD,* November 18 and 20, 1970, confirms that a decision was made to proceed at the November 18 meeting. Kissinger claimed in *WHY,* 982–983, that there had been an "egregious failure of intelligence," but Hersh's information indicates that Laird and undoubtedly Nixon and Kissinger knew of intelligence doubts about the presence of prisoners in the camp. In a paradoxical statement in *RN,* Nixon skirted the issue of whether he was aware of intelligence indicating that the prisoners were probably not in the camp: "Even if I had known when the operation was being planned that the reports were out of date, I believe I would still have given my approval" (860). Why would he have done so unless there were other purposes behind the operation? See later discussion.

103. *HRHD,* November 20, 1970.

104. *WHY,* 983; Hersh, *Price of Power,* 305.

105. *RN,* 859.

106. *HRHD,* November 23 and 24, 1970.

107. *WHY,* 983; *HRHD,* November 23 and 24, 1970; see also Hersh, *Price of Power,* 304–305. Franklin, in *M.I.A.,* 72, asserted that the administration had intended to conceal the raid. His assessment was based on Laird's denial of the raid, followed by an explanation of the raid, on the day after a Radio Hanoi report. But surely Laird's initial reaction was part of the cover story; see also p. 222 n. 79. See also Hammond, *The Military and the Media,* 359–367, on public relations regarding the war and POWs.

108. "The President's News Conference," December 10, 1970, *Public Papers of the Presidents, Nixon: 1970,* 130.

109. *WHY,* 983.

110. Quoted in Hersh, *Price of Power,* 306; see also *RN,* 860.

111. See *WHY,* 983.

112. *Public Papers of the Presidents, Nixon: 1970,* 1102.

113. *HRHD,* November 20, 1970. Cf. *WHY,* 985.

114. *WHY,* 969. Nixon had threatened to turn to massive bombing in July, as he had threatened previously, but by August he had combined this tactic with the promise of total withdrawal. Actually, "total" withdrawal allowed for American "residual" forces to be left behind—e.g., advisers and, it seems, airpower. See Kissinger's phrase "almost total withdrawal" in ibid., 985, and passim, and his comments on airpower on p. 986.

115. *HRHD,* December 21, 1970. See also December 15 entry.

116. *WHY,* 985.

117. *HRHD,* December 21, 1970.

118. Ibid., December 21, 1970, and January 18, 1971; *WHY,* 986.

119. *WHY,* 986.

120. Interview with Russian historian Ilya Gaiduk concerning information based on the Soviet embassy's end-of-year report.

121. See Davidson, *Vietnam at War,* chap. 23, for a concise American version of the military side of the operation, its planning, and its outcome. The American phase of the

operation was code-named Dewey Canyon II; Sigler, *Vietnam Battle Chronology*, 124.

122. *WHY*, 987. Davidson, *Vietnam at War*, 637, said that "the concept of this offensive sprang from the successful" Cambodian incursion of May 1970, but he gives no source for this claim, except to say that American planners had been persuaded that the Cambodian operation had disrupted enemy logistics in the south, encouraging them to think that another blow farther north against enemy supply lines would have a decisive effect. See also Hammond, *The Military and the Media*, 402–407, who draws on archival material; and Warner, *Back Fire*, 300–303, 326.

123. *WHY*, 987, 989.

124. *HRHD*, December 8, 1970.

125. *WHY*, 989–990.

126. Kissinger described his military reasoning for a thrust into Cambodia in ibid., 990. He did not give a date for Haig's trip to South Vietnam. See also pp. 991–1002 for his description of planning the Laos operation. In *Palace File*, 43, Hung and Schecter leave the impression that neither Thieu nor the South Vietnamese were enthusiastic about such an invasion.

127. *HRHD*, January 26, 1971.

128. *WHY*, 991–992; Davidson, *Vietnam at War*, 642–643; Sigler, *Vietnam Battle Chronology*, 124–125; *HRHD*, December 12, 1971.

129. *HRHD*, February 6 and 12, 1971.

130. Ibid., December 18, 1970.

131. *WHY*, 994–996.

132. Ibid., 994; President's Activities Calendar, *HRHD*, December 22, 1970.

133. *WHY*, 994–996; *HRHD*, January 18, 1971.

134. *WHY*, 1000; *HRHD*, January 21 and 22, 1971. On Rogers see also Hammond, *The Military and the Media*, 402–407.

135. *HRHD*, January 26, 1971; see also, *WHY*, 906, 908–909.

136. *WHY*, 997–1000; Presidential Activities Calendar, *HRHD*, January 27, 1971.

137. *WHY*, 1000–1001; *HRHD*, January 29, February 1, 2, and 3, 1971.

138. *HRHD*, February 3, 4, 1971; *WHY*, 1000–1002. The White House continued to be concerned about congressional, public, and press criticism, however; see, e.g., *HRHD*, February 5 and 7, 1971.

139. Cf. *WHY*, 1004; Hung and Schecter, *Palace File*, 43.

140. Hung and Schecter, *Palace File*, 43; *HRHD*, February 24, 1971; *WHY*, 1003–1007.

141. *Public Papers of the Presidents of the United States, Nixon: 1971* (Washington, D.C.: GPO, 1972), 387.

142. *HRHD*, March 11 and 21, 1971.

143. Thieu, quoted in Hung and Schecter, *Palace File*, 43; see also Davidson, *Vietnam at War*, 645–649; *WHY*, 1003–1009. The same scenario of attack and retreat played out in the Cambodian campaign; Clarke, *Advice and Support*, 472–473.

144. See Davidson, *Vietnam at War*, 650; Hersh, *Price of Power*, 312–313; Sigler, *Vietnam Battle Chronology*, 125. On the operation and South Vietnamese withdrawal see also Clarke, *Advice and Support*, 472–484, 493; and on the operation, withdrawal, and public relations, see Hammond, *The Military and the Media*, 410–492.

145. *Public Papers of the Presidents, Nixon: 1971*, 523–524; Davidson, *Vietnam at War*, 651. On Nixon's development of public relations follow-up to the Laotian operation

even before it worked its course, see *HRHD*, February 8, 9, 1971; Hammond, *The Military and the Media*, chap. 19.

146. *HRHD*, March 21, 23 and May 26, 1971. See also Hammond, *The Military and the Media*, 486–492. Kissinger claimed in *WHY*, 996, 1005, that it was not until February 23 that he and Nixon learned that in 1967 General Westmoreland had thought such an operation would have required two corps, or *four* divisions, of *American* troops. See also *RN*, 499.

147. *RN*, 497–499; *HRHD*, March 23, 1971; *WHY*, 1009–1010.

148. *WHY*, 1010.

149. See Davidson, *Vietnam at War*, 651–654. Davidson was also critical of American planning and command; see pp. 654–659.

150. Hung and Schecter, *Palace File*, 44; Hinh quoted in Hersh, *Price of Power*, 313.

151. Haig quoted in Hung and Schecter, *Palace File*, 44.

152. Vien, *Contemporary Vietnam*, 200; see also Hersh, *Price of Power*, 312 n. 2, on the 1972 exhibit at the National Military Museum in Hanoi (portions of the exhibit were still there when I visited in 1987 and 1994).

153. Van Tien Dung, *Our Great Spring Victory: An Account of the Liberation of South Vietnam*, trans. John Spragens, Jr. (New York: Monthly Review Press, 1977), 124; Bui Tin, *Following Ho Chi Minh*, 70; Truong Nhu Tang, *Vietcong Memoir*, 201.

154. David W. P. Elliott, "NLF-DRV Strategy and the 1972 Spring Offensive," International Relations of East Asia Project, Interim Report No. 4 (Ithaca, N.Y.: Cornell University, 1974), 17–20.

155. Hersh, *Price of Power*, 303, 311–312; also Thach, interview by author.

11. SETTING THE STAGE: 1971

1. *HRHD*, September 19, 1971.

2. DRV Chronology on Diplomatic Struggle, September 7, 1971.

3. *RN*, 497. For a comprehensive history of Nixon's economic policies, see Allen J. Matusow, *Nixon's Economy: Booms, Busts, Dollars, and Votes* (Lawrence: University Press of Kansas, 1998).

4. Quoted in James Olson, ed., *Dictionary of the Vietnam War* (New York: Peter Bedrick Books, 1987), 62. See also DeBenedetti and Chatfield, *American Ordeal*, 308; Hammond, *The Military and the Media*, 230.

5. *HRHD*, March 31, April 1, 2, 3, 1971; and Memo, John Dean to Ehrlichman and Haldeman, April 1, 1971, sub: Presidential Response—Calley Court-Martial Case, box 115, WHSF: SMOF, HRH, NPM. During the next months and years, Nixon successively reduced Calley's sentence to ten years. President Gerald Ford released Calley on parole in November 1975. On the army's and Nixon's reaction to the massacre, see also Hammond, *The Military and the Media*, chap. 10.

6. DeBenedetti and Chatfield, *American Ordeal*, 310.

7. Ibid., 309–310; Nancy Zaroulis and Gerald Sullivan, *Who Spoke Up? American Protest Against the War in Vietnam, 1963–1975* (Garden City, N.Y.: Doubleday, 1984), 355–359.

8. *HRHD*, April 22 and 23, 1971.

9. Ibid., April 24 and 25, 1971. On Nixon's desire to counterattack, see also ibid.,

May 1, 1971, and Hersh's footnote on an Oval Office conversation on May 5, *Price of Power*, 427; Haldeman says in *HRHD* that his tapes for May 5 and May 6 were "garbled." On the demonstration, see DeBenedetti and Chatfield, *American Ordeal*, 304; Zaroulis and Sullivan, *Who Spoke Up?*, 359–365.

10. *HRHD*, May 1, 1971.

11. Ibid., May 5, 1971.

12. For example, on March 8, the day the RVNAF captured Tchepone, the president dictated three audiotapes of memos to Haldeman with instructions on the message he should convey during a dinner meeting that evening, at which senior domestic policy staff were to discuss political campaign strategy. The "whole point" of Nixon's thesis was that they should "emphasize the personal themes, . . . since no one remembers . . . our programs" anyway. There was, however, concern among the staff that one foreign policy program— the administration's handling of the war—was indeed a political "problem," but Haldeman, guided by Nixon, assured the group that it was not and had not been a political issue since the November congressional elections; Transcript, Staff Supper—March 8, 1971, folder: HRH Confidential, box 191, WHSF: SMOF, HRH, NPM. See also *HRHD*, December 30, 1970, January 2, 11, 17, and 18, March 8, April 13 and 14, 1971.

13. The *Times* installments appeared in paperback: *The Pentagon Papers As Published by The New York Times* (New York: Bantam Books, 1971). A fuller compilation was *The Pentagon Papers*, Senator Gravel edition. Historian George Herring edited *The Secret Diplomacy of the Vietnam War: The Negotiating Volumes of the Pentagon Papers* (Austin: University of Texas Press, 1983). For a scholarly analysis of their worth, see George McT. Kahin, "The Pentagon Papers: A Critical Evaluation," *American Political Science Review* 69 (June 1975): 675–684. Ellsberg had come to his decision to turn over the papers in the months after he had advised Kissinger during the presidential transition period of 1968–1969. NSC staffer Morton Halperin had informed him in the late summer of 1969 about the secret B-52 bombing of Cambodia and the threats of military escalation in Vietnam that Kissinger had delivered to the Soviets. Ellsberg had concluded that the Nixon administration was repeating the disastrous pattern of decision making followed by previous administrations, one which the *Pentagon Papers* had so clearly demonstrated to him. He began to speak out publicly against the war, and, believing that Congress should learn the same lesson he had from the DOD study, he photocopied and gave it to the Senate Committee on Foreign Relations chaired by Senator Fulbright. But nothing seemed to develop from this contact; neither Fulbright nor other doves were willing to hold hearings on the *Papers*. After the invasion of Cambodia and by the fall of 1970, Ellsberg determined that the administration's policy would lead to the invasion of Laos and the bombing of Hanoi, which was indeed what Nixon and Kissinger were then contemplating. The Son Tay raid of November 1970 and the invasion of Laos in February 1971 confirmed Ellsberg's view that the administration was determined to expand the bombing. If the war was to be stopped it would be by an informed public and mass antiwar protests. With this in mind, he delivered copies of the *Pentagon Papers* to seventeen newspapers in June 1971; Ellsberg, interview by the author, July 15 and 17, 1992, Washington, D.C. The best account of Ellsberg's story is in Hersh, *Price of Power*, chaps. 24, 28. See also Daniel Ellsberg, *Papers on the War* (New York: Simon and Schuster, 1972); and Jann Wanner, "The Rolling Stone Interview: Dan Ellsberg," *Rolling Stone*, September, 1973, 1–39.

14. *HRHD*, June 13, 1971.

15. Ibid., June 17, 1971.

16. On the Brookings Institution, see June 17 and 30, 1971, transcripts in *Abuse of Power*, 3, 6; Hersh, *Price of Power*, 383, 386–387, 391; *Washington Post*, November 22 and 23, 1996; and *HRHD*, June 14, 1971. On the National Archives, see September 10, 1971, transcript in *Abuse of Power*, 30; and the *San Francisco Examiner*, December 8, 1996. On the origins of the Plumbers, see *HRHD*, June 22, 1971; and July 1, 1971, transcript in *Abuse of Power*, 7–9. The material on Watergate is legion, but see Stanley Kutler, *The Wars of Watergate: The Last Crisis of Richard Nixon* (New York: Knopf, 1990); and Hoff, *Nixon Reconsidered*, pt. 3.

17. See, e.g., Haldeman, *Ends of Power*, 110; Isaacson, *Kissinger*, 327–331; and Hoff, *Nixon Reconsidered*, 294–295. Hersh, who provided one of the fullest and best-informed accounts of the matter in *Price of Power*, chaps. 24, 28, was somewhat ambiguous about the relative roles of the principals, Nixon and Kissinger, but he seemed to argue that while Kissinger was culpable, Nixon was his own man, seizing the opportunity to get back at liberals, Brookings, and Kissinger's former staff, and to identify himself more closely with the new conservative coalition, whose votes he wanted.

18. See, e.g., *HRHD*, January 1 and 20, March 8, November 30, and December 7, 1971.

19. Ibid., June 12 and March 3, 1971.

20. Ibid., June 13, 14, 20, and 16, 1971. In *Abuse of Power*, see the June 23 and July 2, 1971, transcripts, pp. 3–4 and 15–18, regarding the antiwar movement as well as various other entries throughout part 1 regarding Ellsberg.

21. *HRHD*, June 15–20, 1971.

22. Ibid., June 17, 18, 22, and July 1, 1971. See also June 24 and July 27, 1971, transcripts in *Abuse of Power*, 4, 5, 26.

23. *HRHD*, September 18, 1971; *Abuse of Power*, 34–37.

24. *RN*, 509, 513–514, 632–633, 641, 844, 846; Kutler, *Wars of Watergate*, 112, 114, 216, 220–221.

25. *HRHD*, June 20, 1971.

26. Haldeman, *Ends of Power*, 111.

27. *HRHD*, June 29, 1971. See also July 1, 1971, entry.

28. Ibid., June 16, 1971.

29. DeBenedetti and Chatfield, *American Ordeal*, 286–287; Davidson, *Vietnam at War*, 664; Zaroulis and Sullivan, *Who Spoke Up?* 330–332, 338.

30. *HRHD*, June 22 and 23, 1971. Nixon repeated the threat to House Speaker Carl Albert a few days later; ibid., June 28, 1971. See also his remarks in Memorandum for the President's Files, March 26, 1971, folder: Beginning March 21, 1971, box 84, WHSF: POF, NPM.

31. *HRHD*, September 16, 1971. Both the Democrats and the administration were working on an election time line. Although Nixon hoped to end the war in 1971, there were no guarantees, but in any case he intended to close it down, or at least to complete American withdrawals before the 1972 elections; see, e.g., Transcript, Staff Supper—March 8, 1971, folder: HRH Confidential, box 191, WHSF: SMOF, HRH, NPM.

32. See DeBenedetti and Chatfield, *American Ordeal*, chap. 11, for a general treatment of grassroots actions, congressional steps, and the public mood.

33. *HRHD*, February 15 and March 30, 1971.

34. DeBenedetti and Chatfield, *American Ordeal*, 318.

35. *HRHD*, March 30, 1971. Safire expressed a similar impression about the inner circle's mood in *Before the Fall*, 386.

36. *HRHD,* March 30, 1971.

37. Ibid., March 26 and 30, 1971.

38. See, e.g., Hersh, *Price of Power,* 428; Directive No. 26, April 1971, Doc. 92, *VDRN,* pp. 1–11; and Elliott, "NLF-DRV Strategy and the 1972 Spring Offensive," passim; and Bunker's reports to the president, January 30, March 30, and May 9, 1971, reprinted in *The Bunker Papers: Reports to the President from Vietnam, 1967–1973,* vol. 3, ed. Douglas Pike (Berkeley: Institute of East Asian Studies, University of California, 1990), 806–837.

39. Two months later, however, Nixon may have found a reason for his mystic wishfulness about Laos. After pouring over histories of World War I military battles, he thought he saw an analogy between Lam Son 719, which was considered by him and most observers a PAVN victory, and the Marne offensive of March 1918, which, he remarked, "was considered a great German victory, but which turned out to be the turning point in the war and the principal German loss." The aborted campaign in Laos, like the Vietnam War itself, would ultimately yield happy results; *HRHD,* May 26 and 29, 1971; see also March 21 and 23. If he was not wishfully fantasizing, Nixon may have been thinking that Lam Son's failure had reassured the Soviets and the Chinese that the United States would not extend the ground war into Laos or North Vietnam, thereby serving to move détente and rapprochement forward, which in turn could assist his efforts to force a diplomatic concession from Hanoi.

40. *HRHD,* April 26 and May 31, 1971.

41. Memorandum for the President's Files, March 26, 1971, folder: Beginning March 21, 1971, box 84, WHSF: POF, NPM; see also *HRHD,* March 26 and April 26, 1971. In attendance were Laird, Connally, Packard, Moorer, Kissinger, and Haig.

42. *HRHD,* June 2, 1971. See my discussion in chapter 10.

43. *RN,* 404, 413.

44. *HRHD,* October 14, 22, 27 and November 7, 1970.

45. Garthoff, *Détente and Confrontation,* 107–109, 165–167.

46. *HRHD,* January 26, March 26, 30, and April 12, 1971.

47. Haldeman's entry in *HRHD* for August 15, 1970, reads: "Discussion with K about. Soviet-China probabilities; K agrees that something big is stirring. P rather surprised to hear this." Kissinger gave some hint of what events they may have had in mind regarding China in *WHY,* 697–698.

48. Garthoff, *Détente and Confrontation,* 254–257.

49. *HRHD,* April 28, 1971.

50. Garthoff, *Détente and Confrontation,* 260.

51. See *HRHD,* April 15, 1971.

52. Memo, Yuri Andropov to Dimitri Ustinov, April 19, 1971, in *CWIHP Bulletin,* 70.

53. *HRHD,* May 6 and 10, 1971; on the China link to the Soviet Union and Vietnam, see also entries for April 29, July 17, 18, and 19, 1971.

54. *HRHD,* June 2, 1971. At this time, the hole card Nixon thought of playing in November 1971 may have been the one actually played: a series of escalated "protective reaction" strikes in the southern parts of North Vietnam beginning in November 1971 and continuing into the first two months of 1972; see chapter 10. For additional brief accounts, see Hersh, *Price of Power,* 504–505; Mark Clodfelter, *The Limits of Air Power: The American Bombing of North Vietnam* (New York: Free Press, 1989), 147–149; Morrocco,

Rain of Fire, 100–105; *WHY,* 1043; Thayer, *War Without Fronts,* chap. 8. If it was not the play he had been considering, it was the one he settled for at the time.

55. *HRHD,* June 2 and 23, 1971.

56. Nixon paraphrased by Haldeman in ibid., May 26, 1971. See also entry for March 30, 1971: "We've put our ideas into practice, modified some of them and now have a clear idea [of] what we're doing, and see that we're on the road to [a] solution and know how we're gong to get there. With this in mind, we have no great concern about the temporary setback situation, because we realize that is temporary." Cf. a similar remark by Nixon in Memorandum for the President's Files, March 26, 1971, folder: Beginning March 21, 1971, box 84, WHSF: POF, NPM.

57. In *WHY,* 1017, Kissinger cited May 14 as the date of Hanoi's response to his April invitation, but Haldeman recorded that Kissinger received the news in Washington the day before; *HRHD,* May 13, 1971.

58. Memo, Kissinger to Nixon, May 28, 1971, sub: My May 31 Meeting with the North Vietnamese, folder: Camp David—Sensitive—vol. 6, box 4 (2), WH/NSC: POW/MIA, NPM.

59. *HRHD,* May 13, 1971.

60. *WHY,* 1018.

61. Ibid., 1102–1103.

62. Ibid., 1016–1017.

63. Tung, Thach, and Loi, interviews with author. Thieu was not important to them in and of himself; what was important was American support for a Saigon regime.

64. This analysis, by way of introducing the following discussion of the negotiations in 1971, is pieced together from my preceding narrative. See also Elliott, "NLF-DRV Strategy and the 1972 Spring Offensive," passim.

65. *WHY,* 1018. Kissinger also claimed that this was the proposal that "in its essence was accepted sixteen months later by Hanoi." The question turns, however, on what one considers to have been its "essence." The devil was in the critical details.

66. Cover sheet to Memo, Kissinger to Nixon, May 28, 1971, sub: My Meeting with the North Vietnamese, May 31, 1971, folder: Camp David—Sensitive—vol. 7, box 4 (3), WH/NSC: POW/MIA, NPM.

67. The text of the proposal is reprinted in *WHY,* 1488–1489 n.11. See also, Memo, Kissinger to Nixon, May 28, 1971, folder: Camp David—Sensitive—vol. 7, box 4 (3), WH/NSC: POW/MIA, NPM. In *WHY,* 1018, Kissinger wrote that he told Thuy on Nixon's instructions that this was their "final offer," which proved not to be the case. In his May 28 memo, Kissinger used the phrase "last chance for a negotiated settlement." Hersh, *Price of Power,* 429, mistakenly wrote that Kissinger also spoke with Le Duc Tho on May 31 and indicated US acceptance of a coalition government.

68. Memo, Kissinger to Nixon, May 28, 1971, folder: Camp David—Sensitive—vol. 7, box 4 (3), WH/NSC: POW/MIA, NPM. Nixon circled "no infiltration" in Kissinger's text and wrote "negotiate" in the margin.

69. I surmise this from a cryptic remark made by Kissinger in *WHY,* 1018.

70. Thach, interview with Hersh, *Price of Power,* 428–429; Thach and Tung, interview with author. The DRV and its NLF ally may have been doubly skeptical of the sincerity of the American offer, since they were most likely aware through their agents in the Saigon government that Kissinger had not fully and candidly informed Thieu of the no-mutual-withdrawal proviso, expecting that Thieu would oppose a settlement that left PAVN

on his doorstep. Cf. Memo, Kissinger to Nixon, May 28, 1971, folder: Camp David—Sensitive—vol. 7, box 4 (3), WH/NSC: POW/MIA, NPM, with *WHY,* 1018. In the May 28 memo Kissinger said only that Bunker had "informed Thieu of our meeting," telling him "that we will follow up the other side's recent ambiguous public statements in Paris and discuss the relationship between ceasefire, POW's, and the U.S. withdrawals," and reaffirming "that we will not agree to the other side's political demands." In *WHY* he said, "Thieu approved the plan."

71. DRV Chronology on Diplomatic Struggle, May 31, 1971.

72. Tung, interview with author. See also Tho, interview in *NYT,* July 7, 1971.

73. Memo with attachments, Smyser to Kissinger, June 9, 1971, sub: Xuan Thuy's Interview with Chalmers Roberts, folder: Camp David—Sensitive—vol. 8, box 4 (4), WH/NSC: POW/MIA, NPM.

74. Ibid.

75. Memo, Kissinger to Nixon, June 27, 1971, sub: My June 26 Meeting with the North Vietnamese, and Memorandum of Conversation, June 26, 1971, folder: Camp David—Sensitive—vol. 8, box 4 (4), WH/NSC: POW/MIA, NPM; *WHY,* 1021; Smyser, quoted in Hersh, *Price of Power,* 429. In an obvious typo, Hersh incorrectly put the meeting at June 16.

76. Memorandum of Conversation, June 26, 1971, folder: Camp David—Sensitive—vol. 8, box 4 (4), WH/NSC: POW/MIA, NPM.

77. Memo, Kissinger to Nixon, June 27, 1971, sub: My June 26 Meeting with the North Vietnamese, ibid.; DRV Chronology on Diplomatic Struggle, June 26, 1971; *WHY,* 1022.

78. DRV Chronology on Diplomatic Struggle, June 26, 1971.

79. Memo, Kissinger to Nixon, June 27, 1971, sub: My June 26 Meeting with the North Vietnamese, and Memorandum of Conversation, June 26, 1971, folder: Camp David—Sensitive—vol. 8, box 4 (4), WH/NSC: POW/MIA, NPM. Recorded in the transcript, Kissinger's good-natured reply at the meeting was: "George Bernard Shaw once said that, 'I wrote a long letter because I didn't have time to write a short one.' " But in his memoirs he caustically remarked that Thuy's quip was a sign of the North Vietnamese sense of "moral superiority"; *WHY,* 1022–1023.

80. DRV Chronology on Diplomatic Struggle, June 26, 1971; Memo, Kissinger to Nixon, June 27, 1971, sub: My June 26 Meeting with the North Vietnamese, and Memorandum of Conversation, June 26, 1971, folder: Camp David—Sensitive—vol. 8, box 4 (4), WH/NSC: POW/MIA, NPM; *WHY,* 1023; "Seven-Point Program for a Settlement of the South Viet Nam Problem," July 1, 1971, in *Bases for a Settlement of the Viet Nam Problem,* 44.

81. Memo, Kissinger to Nixon, June 27, 1971, sub: My June 26 Meeting with the North Vietnamese, and Memorandum of Conversation, June 26, 1971, folder: Camp David—Sensitive—vol. 8, box 4 (4), WH/NSC: POW/MIA, NPM; *WHY,* 1023–1024. Kissinger's memo listed the positive elements of the DRV plan, but only three were left uncensored in the extant document. He mentions two more in *WHY.* The meeting concluded with an agreement to study each other's plan and to convene again on July 12.

82. *WHY,* 1024.

83. Quoted in ibid., 1026.

84. Ibid., 1026. Kissinger referred to a "counterproposal," but he did not submit a formal plan at the July 12 meeting; instead, the two parties compared the two plans they had previously tabled. Cf. DRV Chronology on Diplomatic Struggle, July 12, 1971.

85. *WHY,* 1025. See also Nixon's comments along these lines in his January 25, 1972, address to the nation, in *Public Papers of the Presidents, Nixon: 1972* (Washington, D.C.: GPO, 1974), 102.

86. Kissinger incorrectly claimed that Binh had altered the cease-fire proposal, setting its commencement to coincide with the formation of a new government, not upon the signing of an agreement; *WHY,* 1025. Cf. "Seven-Point Program for a Settlement of the South Viet Nam Problem," in *Bases for a Settlement of the Viet Nam Problem,* 43; The Provisional Revolutionary Government of the Republic of South Viet-Nam, Part IV: The PRG's Diplomatic Offensive, Doc. 101, *VDRN,* p. 74.

87. *NYT,* July 7, 1971. Tho also said: "Although it is not admitted, not publicly stated, the whole world knows that Thieu had been put in power by the U.S. Administration, and the U.S. will have the decisive voice in the forthcoming elections." He had a point.

88. Memo with attachments, Smyser to HK, June 9, 1971, sub: Xuan Thuy's Interview with Chalmers Roberts, folder: Camp David—Sensitive—vol. 8, box 4 (4), WH/NSC: POW/MIA, NPM. See also later discussion of "option 1," in Kissinger's September 18 memorandum to Nixon.

89. *HRHD,* May 28, 1971.

90. Tho alluded to the *Pentagon Papers* in Lewis's interview on July 6; *NYT,* July 7, 1971. Kissinger compared Thieu and Diem in Memo with attachments, Kissinger to Nixon, July 26, 1971, sub: My Meeting with the North Vietnamese, folder: Camp David—Sensitive—vol. 10, box 4 (5), WH/NSC: POW/MIA, NPM. See also *WHY,* 1029.

91. *HRHD,* June 3 and July 10, 1971.

92. *WHY,* 1019–1020.

93. Ibid., 1027.

94. Ibid., 1028–1029; DRV Chronology on Diplomatic Struggle, July 12, 1971. Tho had encouraged postwar economic aid in the interview with Lewis on July 6; *NYT,* July 7, 1971.

95. Quoted in *WHY,* 1029. A few pages later, Kissinger described Thieu as "the most formidable of the military leaders of South Vietnam, probably the ablest of all political personalities, . . . [who] was also a man of principle; strongly anti-Communist, deeply religious and patriotic, highly intelligent, defending his compatriots with great courage, . . . [and] he did not deserve the obloquy that those who sought excuses for our abdication insisted on visiting on him" (1023–1024).

96. DRV Chronology on Diplomatic Struggle, July 19, 1971; Memorandum of Conversation, July 26, 1971, folder: Camp David—Sensitive—vol. 10, box 4 (5), WH/NSC: POW/MIA, NPM.

97. *WHY,* 1030.

98. Quoted in Hersh, *Price of Power,* 436–437 n.

99. Memo, Kissinger to Nixon, July 26, 1971, sub: My Meeting with the North Vietnamese, folder: Camp David—Sensitive—vol. 10, box 4 (5), WH/NSC: POW/MIA, NPM.

100. Ibid.

101. Ibid.

102. Memorandum of Conversation, July 26, 1971, folder: Camp David—Sensitive—vol. 10, box 4 (5), WH/NSC: POW/MIA, NPM.

103. In *Lost Peace,* Goodman, who followed Nixon's and Kissinger's interpretation, was in error, I think, when he wrote that Hanoi was saying one thing in public and another

in private, and when he described Hanoi's position as one that linked the cease-fire and POW exchange to the "overthrow" of Thieu; pp. 114–115. See also *RN,* 583–584.

104. *HRHD,* July 27, 1971.

105. DRV Chronology on Diplomatic Struggle, July 26, 1971.

106. It may be that Haldeman misunderstood the nuances of Kissinger's oral assessment or that Kissinger slanted his analysis in the direction of skepticism in order to steer a middle course through Nixon's ambivalence. In any event, there are no real contradictions between the fragmentary records of Haldeman's and the DRV Foreign Ministry's notes.

107. Memo, Kissinger to Nixon, August 16, 1971, sub: My Meeting with the North Vietnamese, folder: Camp David—Sensitive—vol. 11, box 4 (6), WH/NSC: POW/ MIA, NPM.

108. DRV Chronology on Diplomatic Struggle, August 16, 1971. Kissinger's account in *WHY,* 1034, is incomplete.

109. Memo, HK to RN, August 16, 1971, sub: My Meeting with the North Vietnamese, and Memorandum of Conversation, August 16, 1971, folder: Camp David—Sensitive—vol. 11, box 4 (6), WH/NSC: POW/MIA, NPM.

110. Quoted in Gareth Porter, *A Peace Denied: The United States, Vietnam, and the Paris Agreement* (Bloomington: Indiana University Press, 1975), 99.

111. Memo, HK to RN, August 16, 1971, sub: My Meeting with the North Vietnamese, and Memorandum of Conversation, August 16, 1971, folder: Camp David—Sensitive—vol. 11, box 4 (6), WH/NSC: POW/MIA, NPM. In the Lewis interview of July 6, cited earlier, Tho had said that an Indochina-wide cease-fire would complicate matters in a withdrawal-for-prisoners deal, but it appears that such a cease-fire would not have been a problem had other issues been resolved, particularly the matter of political power in Saigon. Throughout the negotiations, the two major issues were Thieu and the timing of a total American withdrawal. In *Price of Power,* Hersh errs in his description of and stress upon the cease-fire issue; see, e.g., p. 438.

112. The remaining differences on prisoner releases mainly had to do with Hanoi's call for the release of civilian, political prisoners held by Saigon, but whom Saigon and the Washington regarded as Viet Cong. The relevant passages on this and other POW questions have been deleted by censors from Kissinger's August 16 memo.

113. Memo, HK to RN, August 16, 1971, sub: My Meeting with the North Vietnamese, folder: Camp David—Sensitive—vol. 11, box 4 (6), WH/NSC: POW/MIA, NPM.

114. Quoted in Hersh, *Price of Power,* 438.

115. Cf. *WHY,* 1031–1037, with Hammond, *The Military and the Media,* 518–521; Hersh, *Price of Power,* chap. 31; and "No Ky and a Big Win?" *Newsweek,* August 16, 1971. See also Bunker's report to the president, June 9, 1971, reprinted in *The Bunker Papers,* vol. 3, ed. Pike, 838, 847–848.

116. Frank Snepp, *Decent Interval: An Insider's Account of Saigon's Indecent End Told by the CIA's Chief Strategy Analyst in Vietnam* (New York: Vintage Books, 1978), 11–17; Hammond, *The Military and the Media,* 518–521; Hersh, *Price of Power,* chap. 31; "No Ky and a Big Win?"

117. *Public Papers of the Presidents, Nixon: 1971,* 954.

118. Snepp, *Decent Interval,* 11–17; Hammond, *The Military and the Media,* 518–521; Hersh, *Price of Power,* chap. 31; "No Ky and a Big Win?"

119. *WHY,* 1035.

120. *HRHD*, August 23, 1971.

121. DRV Chronology on Diplomatic Struggle, September 7, 1971.

122. *HRHD*, August 23, 1971. See also September 14, 1971.

123. See Haig's July 10 remarks quoted in *WHY*, 1026; on Nixon's eagerness to cancel the negotiations, see p. 1036.

124. *HRHD*, August 24, 1971.

125. Ibid., August 24, 1971. By "escalating" Haldeman probably meant dragging the war out and continuing in the quagmire, while Nixon wanted to cut his losses, strike hard, and pull out.

126. Ibid., September 8, 1971.

127. DRV Chronology on Diplomatic Struggle, September 13, 1971.

128. *WHY*, 1036.

129. In ibid., 1038, he says that "in this atmosphere" he submitted a long analysis. See also *HRHD*, September 16, 1971, concerning Mansfield.

130. *HRHD*, September 17 and 20, 1971. Kissinger arranged for an "all-out blast at the DMZ" on September 20.

131. Ibid., September 14, 1971.

132. Memo, Kissinger to Nixon, September 18, 1971, sub: Vietnam, box 4, WH/NSC: POW/MIA, NPM. Hammond, *The Military and the Media*, 521 n. 66, who cited a September 17 draft in Haig's NSC files in the Nixon papers, wrote that "it is uncertain whether Kissinger ever sent the memo." The September 18 memo from the NSC/POW files, cited earlier, indicates that he sent it and Nixon read it.

133. Memo, Kissinger to Nixon, September 18, 1971, sub: Vietnam, box 4, WH/NSC: POW/MIA, NPM.

134. *HRHD*, July 31, August 10 and 16, September 13 and 24, and November 5, 1971.

135. Ibid., April 14, 15, 16, 17, and 29, May 6, July 13, 17, 18, 19, and 23, June 28, and August 5, 1971.

136. Memo, Kissinger to Nixon, September 18, 1971, sub: Vietnam, box 4, WH/NSC: POW/MIA, NPM.

137. *HRHD*, September 19, 1971.

138. Regarding fear of failure and Kissinger receiving credit, see, e.g., ibid., September 8 and October 18, 1971. In his summary of the September 18 analysis in *WHY*, 1038–1039, Kissinger did not mention either option 3 or his desire to meet personally with Dong. But in his treatment of a discussion he had with Gromyko on September 30 at the Soviet embassy about the Breshnev-Nixon summit, he wrote that he had broached the subject, whereupon Breshnev passed it on to the Hanoi Politburo. Their reply, which was given by Dobrynin to the White House on October 16, was that they preferred to deal with the United States directly; *WHY*, 839.

139. Kissinger did not specifically discuss the four options in *WHY*, but he did reprint their October proposal, which Nixon approved on September 20; *WHY*, 1039, 1489–1490 n. 12. Point 1 included a provision for the withdrawal of remaining U.S. personnel, the residual force, one month before the South Vietnamese election, a provision that was also encompassed in option 4 of his September 18 memorandum.

140. Memo, Kissinger to Nixon, October 6, 1971, sub: General Haig's Talk with President Thieu, folder: Encore—Sept. 1971—Feb. 15, 1972; Speech of President's—Jan. 25, 1972, box 4 (32), WH/NSC: POW/MIA, NPM.

141. *WHY*, 1040.

142. Ibid., 1040–1041; DRV Chronology on Diplomatic Struggle, November 19, 1971. The plenary talks were also suspended for the rest of November.

143. *WHY*, 1041.

144. Quoted in Hersh, *Price of Power*, 440.

145. DRV Chronology on Diplomatic Struggle, November 11, 1971. John D. Negroponte, a Kissinger aide, seemed to agree that these were Hanoi's motives when he speculated that the cancellation was due both to Nixon's November troop withdrawal announcement, which provided Hanoi with concrete information about Nixon's withdrawal schedule, and to Nixon's "rather strong words"; Memo, Negroponte to Kissinger, March 30, 1972, sub: Next Troop Withdrawal Announcement, folder: HAK Paris Trip—HAK To and Memos to the President, etc., Dec 3–13, 1972, box 5, WH/NSC: POW/MIA, NPM.

146. *Public Papers of the Presidents: Nixon, 1971*, 1034, 1101–1105.

147. *HRHD*, November 12, 1971.

148. See *WHY*, Points 3 and 6 of the October 11 proposal, 1489–1490 n. 12. Kissinger conceded in ibid., 1493 n. 3, that the national frontiers clause was a reference to what was left of the U.S. demand for mutual withdrawal. See also Thach and Tung, interviews with the author. Hersh, *Price of Power*, chap. 11, argued that the major problem with the proposal was its call for an Indochina-wide cease-fire, but the secret history of the negotiations suggests that this was not the case—depending, of course, on whether there was agreement on other provisos.

149. Huong Tung maintained that the United States passed up many opportunities for peace; interview with author.

150. The United States received confirmation of the Soviet invitation on August 11; *HRHD*, August 11, 1971. Nixon accepted on August 17; *WHY*, 838. See also *Public Papers of the Presidents, Nixon: 1971*, 328, for Nixon's statement; and Garthoff, *Détente and Confrontation*, 107–108, for background.

151. *WHY*, 776, 780.

152. Ibid., 840–841.

153. Quoted in Gaiduk, *The Soviet Union and the Vietnam War*, 232.

154. Hersh, *Price of Power*, 365–372, 375–376. See also Garthoff, *Détente and Confrontation*, 261, 288.

155. In *The Soviet Union and the Vietnam War*, 231, Gaiduk claimed that the decision for a spring offensive had been made in May 1971. This is doubtful. The May 1971 Soviet diplomatic report he cited referred to increased bellicosity in the North Vietnamese capital, not a decision to attack: "As the withdrawal of American troops continues, someone in the DRV has his bellicosity up, and ideas of delivering a 'decisive blow' in 1972 and of 'bringing down Nixon' arise. These ideas may cause the war to flare up anew in full force"; see p. 289 n. 30. See also, Morrocco, *Rain of Fire*, for the October date of increased truck movement south.

156. Thach, interview with author. According to former CIA agent Snepp, this was true as well in South Vietnam, where the NLF began a large recruiting drive in August; cited in Hersh, *Price of Power*, p. 438 n.

157. Negroponte seemed to imply this assessment in Memo, Negroponte to Kissinger, March 30, 1972, sub: Next Troop Withdrawal Announcement, folder: HAK Paris Trip—HAK To and Memos to the President, etc., Dec 3–13, 1972, box 5, WH/NSC: POW/MIA, NPM.

158. Gaiduk, *The Soviet Union and the Vietnam War*, 231.

159. Memo, David R. Young to Haldeman, September 18, 1972, enclosure: CIA Intelligence Memorandum, August 1972, box 191, WHSF: SMOF, HRH, NPM. See also CIA Memo, March 4, 1975, enclosure: Communist Military and Economic Aid to North Vietnam, 1970–1974, microfiche no. 000615, declassified October 29, 1993, *Declassified Documents Catalog*, vol. 20, no. 2.

160. DRV/PRG intentions and goals for the Spring Offensive are discussed more fully in the next chapter.

12. FIGHTING, THEN TALKING: 1972

1. Quoted in *HRHD*, September 16, 1972.

2. Ibid., January 1, 1972.

3. See, e.g., *WHY*, 969, 985, 1026, 1036; *HRHD*, December 15 and 21, 1970, and August 24, 1971; Memo, Kissinger to Nixon, September 18, 1971, sub: Vietnam, box 4, WH/NSC: POW/MIA, NPM.

4. *HRHD*, January 1, 1972. See also December 31, 1971, regarding Nixon and the announcement schedule.

5. See, e.g., ibid., July 23 and November 17, 1971, and January 2, 11, and 17, 1972; *RN*, 543. On "Man of the Year," see *Time*, January 3, 1972.

6. Regarding the India-Pakistan conflict and U.S. policy, see Garthoff, *Détente and Confrontation*, 262–288; Hersh, *Price of Power*, chap. 32; Isaacson, *Kissinger*, 371–379; Morris, *Uncertain Greatness*, 214–227; *RN*, 525–531; and *WHY*, 842–918.

7. Hersh, *Price of Power*, 474–479; Isaacson, *Kissinger*, 385–398; *HRHD*, November 30, December 7, 8, 23, and 30, 1971, and January 13, 1972. Quotations are from the last two sources.

8. See, Hersh, *Price of Power*, chap. 33; Isaacson, *Kissinger*, 380–385; *RN*, 531–533; Hammond, *The Military and the Media*, 500–503; and *HRHD*, December 21 and 22, 1971.

9. Safire, *Before the Fall*, 399–408; *HRHD*, December 30, 1971, January 3 and 14, 1972.

10. *HRHD*, December 7, 8, 23, 30, 1971; Hersh, *Price of Power*, 474–479; Isaacson, *Kissinger*, 385–398.

11. *HRHD*, January 3, 1972.

12. *Public Papers of the Presidents, Nixon: 1972*, 30.

13. Thayer, *War Without Fronts*, Table 4.6.

14. Memo, Kissinger to Nixon, September 18, 1971, sub: Vietnam, box 4, WH/NSC: POW/MIA, NPM.

15. *Public Papers of the Presidents, Nixon: 1972*, 100–106.

16. In *RN*, 585, Nixon claimed that he had decided to reveal the secret Paris channel because he feared a leak through the press. Yeoman Radford, who was known to have spoken to columnist Jack Anderson, had had access to the negotiation papers, and Anthony Lake, formerly of Kissinger's staff, was now an adviser to Senator Muskie. A press leak originating from either of these two men would have meant, Nixon argued, that he would have had "political and diplomatic hell to pay." Hersh, *Price of Power*, 483 n., maintained that neither Radford nor Lake leaked news of the negotiations or would have even contemplated such an act, and therefore, Nixon's argument was disingenuous. In fact, Nixon does seem to have been worried about a leak from Radford, but this concern was

only an added incentive, not the real cause of his decision to make the speech. He had long considered exposing the secret channel and going public with his version of the negotiating record, and by mid-January he thought Kissinger's secret channel was "blown anyway"; see *HRHD*, January 14, 1971. The reason he gave in *RN* for going public served to obscure his real motive—namely, that the speech was designed to bolster public support for his continuation of the war.

17. In its seven-point plan, the PRG had only called on the United States to stop supporting Thieu. Now it called for Thieu to resign; DRV Chronology on Diplomatic Struggle for February 2, 1972; and Vien, ed., *Indochina: 1972–73 Turning Point*, Vietnamese Studies, no. 39 (Hanoi: Foreign Languages Publishing House, 1974), 201. Kissinger incorrectly referred to these as clarifications of the DRV nine-point plan; *WHY*, 1045.

18. *Washington Post*, January 27, 1972; Hersh, *Price of Power*, 485; and *HRHD*, January 27, February 2 and 3, 1972.

19. *WHY*, 1044–1046.

20. On these points, see Garthoff, *Détente and Confrontation*, 276.

21. *HRHD*, January 3, 25, and February 11, 1972.

22. Morrocco, *Rain of Fire*, 100–101; Hersh, *Price of Power*, 504–507; Clodfelter, *Limits of Air Power*, 147–149; *WHY*, 1043; see also Thayer, *War Without Fronts*, chap. 8. During this period, Hanoi Radio reported more attacks than claimed by the U.S. government or reported in the American press; Hersh, *Price of Power*, 505.

23. Curiously, while the North Vietnamese refer to the "Spring" Offensive, most American accounts call it the "Easter" Offensive.

24. *RN*, 586; *WHY*, 1045.

25. Hersh, *Price of Power*, 505.

26. *HRHD*, September 17, 1971, and January 25 and February 5, 1972; Transcript, Telecoms with Laird and Moorer, January 25, 1972, folder: Telecom—January 25, 1972, Admiral Moorer, box 191, WHSF: SMOF, HRH, NPM. For a contemporary Pentagon critique of Nixon's management of the December bombings, see *Washington Post*, January 25, 1972.

27. Hersh, *Price of Power*, 507; Morrocco, *Rain of Fire*, 104–105; Furlong Papers, AFHRA. Nixon was unwilling to take public responsibility for his own belligerent policies; see, e.g., *HRHD*, January 25, 1972.

28. Clodfelter, "Nixon and the Air Weapon," in *An American Dilemma: Vietnam, 1964–1973*, ed. Dennis E. Showalter and John G. Albert (Chicago: Imprint Publications, 1993), 169; Davidson provides slightly different figures in *Vietnam at War*, 702. See also *WHY*, 1101, 1109, 1116, and *U.S. News and World Report*, April 24, 1972, 15–17.

29. *WHY*, 1101.

30. *HRHD*, January 25, 1972.

31. *WHY*, 1100.

32. Memo, Nixon to Kissinger, April 23, 1972, folder: April 1972 Kissinger Trip to Moscow, box 74, WHSF: PPF, NPM.

33. *WHY*, 1099–1101.

34. *HRHD*, February 4, 1972.

35. *WHY*, 1105; DRV Chronology on Diplomatic Struggle, February 17, 1972.

36. See, e.g., Hersh, *Price of Power*, 495–496.

37. See, e.g., *RN*, 578–580; *HRHD*, February 29, 1972.

38. *HRHD*, February 17, 1972.

39. *WHY*, 1087.

40. The communiqué is reprinted in *Public Papers of the Presidents, Nixon: 1972*, 376–379, and *WHY*, 1490–1492.

41. *HRHD*, February 29, 1972.

42. This is Kissinger's paraphrase in *WHY*, 1073.

43. *RN*, 569; *WHY*, 1073, 1087.

44. About his meeting with Zhou in January 1972, Haig, for example, told Canadian journalist Michael Maclear years later: "I left that discussion with a very firm conviction that what he was saying was, 'Do not lose in Vietnam, and do not withdraw from Southeast Asia'"; quoted in Hersh, *Price of Power*, 492. Kissinger, however, characterized Zhou's words differently, saying only that Zhou "reiterated his moral support for Hanoi and urged a rapid settlement of the war in order to reduce Soviet influence in Indochina"; *WHY*, 1051.

45. Haldeman's diary entries for this period provide a fascinating, private glimpse into these moods.

46. See Garthoff's comments and citations in *Détente and Confrontation*, 269.

47. *WHY*, 1105–1106; DRV Chronology on Diplomatic Struggle, March 13, 1972.

48. *WHY*, 1106.

49. Ibid., 1105.

50. See citations of classified documents in Hammond, *The Military and the Media*, 538–539 nn 28, 29, 30.

51. *WHY*, 1101–1102; cf. *HRHD*, February 5, 1972. Kissinger did not provide dates for the operation.

52. DRV Chronology on Diplomatic Struggle, March 13 and April 23, 1972; *WHY*, 1106–1108; Hersh, *Price of Power*, 511; *Public Papers of the Presidents, Nixon: 1972*, 488. Kissinger wrote that he disagreed with Nixon's timing. He would have preferred to reap the propaganda benefits of canceling the Paris plenary only after the offensive began.

53. *WHY*, 1108.

54. Memo, Negroponte to Kissinger, March 30, 1972, sub: Your Meeting With Ambassador Porter, 5 p.m., March 1, folder: HAK Paris Trip—HAK To and Memos to the President, etc., Dec 3–13, 1972, [1 of 2], box 5 (23), WH/NSC: POW/MIA, NPM; and Memo, Negroponte to Kissinger, March 30, 1972, sub: Next Troop Withdrawal Announcement, ibid. Negroponte speculated that Hanoi was indicating willingness to talk in April because they expected some gain in leverage from their offensive and that it would also influence Nixon's forthcoming April announcement on troop withdrawals.

55. Memo, Nixon to Kissinger, March 11, 1972, quoted in Oudes, *From the President*, 378–379.

56. Ibid.

57. *Baltimore News-American*, March 17, 1972, quoted in Hammond, *The Military and the Media*, 537.

58. See, e.g., September 18, 1971, Kissinger to Nixon memo; *HRHD*, August 24, 1971; classified memos cited by Hammond, *The Military and the Media*, 539, 557; and *RN*, 587.

59. This section is based on Davidson, *Vietnam at War*, chap. 24; Elliott, "NLF-DRV Strategy and the 1972 Spring Offensive"; Hammond, *The Military and the Media*, chap. 21; and Nguyen Quang Truong, *The Easter Offensive of 1972* (Washington, D.C.: U.S. Army Center of Military History, 1980). On American surprise about the DRV/NLF's shift

from guerrilla to conventional war, see Haig's briefing on May 12, which is summarized in the *HRHD* entry for that date.

60. *HRHD*, April 4, 1972; *WHY*, 1109, 1116. On Nixon's sending additional carriers, see Hersh, *Price of Power*, 508.

61. *HRHD*, April 4, 1972. See also *HRHD*, April 6, 1972; Hammond, *The Military and the Media*, 552.

62. White House tape recording, quoted in Hersh, *Price of Power*, 506.

63. "The enemy" quoted in Hersh, *Price of Power*, 508; but see also *HRHD* for April 25, 1972, when Nixon repeated this sentiment and added "invaders" and "Communist."

64. Quoted in Hersh, *Price of Power*, 508.

65. Quotes paraphrased in *HRHD*, April 4, 1972.

66. Ibid., April 5, 1972.

67. See classified documents cited and summarized by Hammond, *The Military and the Media*, 552–553. On Kissinger's suspicions about Laird's and Rogers's collaborative opposition to the mining and bombing plan, see also *HRHD*, April 13, 1972.

68. *WHY*, 1116.

69. Quotes paraphrased in *HRHD*, April 6, 1972. Haldeman's diary contradicts the version that Nixon later wanted to tell in his memoirs, that Vogt wanted to run the whole war, and it supports Hersh's account in *Price of Power*, 506–507, based on his interview with Vogt.

70. Hersh, *Price of Power*, 507; *WHY*, 1112.

71. *WHY*, 1108–1113. Concerning White House views of the obstructionism of Abrams, Bunker, the bureaucracy, and other individuals in government to the far-north bombing, Haig wrote: They have "long been opposed to the kinds of things that we have been doing. . . . This has been the President's program which he has pushed with great vigor against massive bureaucratic opposition"; Memo, Haig to Haldeman, June 21, 1972, NPM, copy held by the author. The matter triggering the memo had to do with a "knee-jerk" phone call from Frank Shakespeare, a CBS executive on sabbatical, then serving on Nixon's staff. See also *HRHD*, August 19, 1972.

72. Quotes from Haldeman's paraphrases, *HRHD*, April 4, 1972. On the other side's alleged desperation, see also *WHY*, 1113.

73. Quotes from Haldeman's summary in *HRHD*, April 10, 1972. See also ibid., April 8, 1972; *RN*, 588–589; *WHY*, 1116–1117; Safire, *Before the Fall*, 417–420; Nixon's draft speech, April 10, 1974, folder: March 23 to April 25, 1972, box 74, WHSF: PPF, 1969–74, NPM.

74. *WHY*, 1118.

75. Hammond's account, based on classified documents, in *The Military and the Media*, 553. See also *HRHD*, April 15, 1972, for a reference to Abrams's cable.

76. *HRHD*, April 15, 1972; see also Hammond, *The Military and the Media*, 553.

77. *HRHD*, April 15, 1972.

78. *RN*, 587–588; *WHY*, 1113–1114.

79. See Kissinger's comments, *WHY*, 1120–1121.

80. Ibid., 1114–1120.

81. Ibid., 1115, 1119; DRV Chronology on Diplomatic Struggle, April 22, 1972.

82. *WHY*, 1119, 1121, 1122; *HRHD*, April 12, 1972.

83. The record of the talks, which restarted in May, gives no indication of concessions from the DRV or PRG until September.

84. *WHY,* 1120–1121; *RN,* 587.
85. *RN,* 589–591; *WHY,* 1120–1121; *HRHD,* April 15, 1972.
86. *HRHD,* April 15 and 16, 1972; *RN,* 590.
87. *RN,* 591; *WHY,* 1122.
88. *HRHD,* April 17, 1972.
89. *WHY,* 1135–1136; Memo, Kissinger to Nixon, April 22, 1972, folder: Apr 1972 Kissinger Trip to Moscow, box 74, WHSF: PPF, NPM.
90. Memo, Nixon to Kissinger, April 20, 1972, folder: Apr 1972 Kissinger Trip to Moscow, box 74, WHSF: PPF, NPM; *HRHD,* April 19, 1972. See also *WHY,* 1123, 1136–1137.
91. Memo, Kissinger to Haig, April 21, 1972, folder: Apr 1972 Kissinger Trip to Moscow, box 74, WHSF: PPF, NPM. See also *WHY,* 1144–1145.
92. Memo, Kissinger to Nixon, April 22, 1972, folder: Apr 1972 Kissinger Trip to Moscow, box 74, WHSF: PPF, NPM; *WHY,* 1146–1148.
93. Memos, Nixon to Kissinger, April 20 and 23, 1972, folder: Apr 1972, Kissinger Trip to Moscow, box 74, WHSF: PPF, NPM; President's Activities Calendar, *HRHD,* April 19–24, 1972; *WHY,* 1155, 1161.
94. Memos, Kissinger to Nixon, April 20, 22, and 24, and to Haig, April 24, 1972, folder: Apr 1972 Kissinger Trip to Moscow, box 74, WHSF: PPF, NPM; *WHY,* 1160–1161.
95. *WHY,* 1155, 1161.
96. Enclosure in Memo, Situation Room to Kissinger, April 21, 1972, sub: Noon Notes, folder: April 1972, Kissinger Trip to Moscow, box 74, WHSF: PPF, NPM.
97. Memo, Nixon to Kissinger, April 20, 1972, folder: Apr 1972 Kissinger Trip to Moscow, box 74, WHSF: PPF, NPM; *HRHD,* April 19, 1972.
98. Hammond, *The Military and the Media,* 556. Subsequent polls would reveal that public opinion on the fighting and bombing was mixed. Overwhelming numbers wanted American troops home by the end of the year and were willing to sacrifice Thieu for a cease-fire, but there was also strong support for bombing as a means of stopping the Spring Offensive.
99. *HRHD,* April 22 and 23, 1972; Memos, Nixon to Kissinger, April 20 and 23, 1972, folder: Apr 1972, Kissinger Trip to Moscow, box 74, WHSF: PPF, NPM; Haig curried favor with Nixon by supporting his distrust of negotiations and his predilection for military action, but he also defended Kissinger before Nixon and Haldeman; cf. *HRHD,* April 23, 1972, with Isaacson, *Kissinger,* 415, Hersh, *Price of Power,* 519, and *RN,* 600.
100. *HRHD,* April 24, 1972.
101. Memos, Kissinger to Nixon, April 22, and to Haig, April 24, 1972, folder: Apr 1972 Kissinger Trip to Moscow, box 74, WHSF: PPF. NPM; *WHY,* 1160–1163; *RN,* 592.
102. *Public Papers of the Presidents, Nixon: 1972,* 551 (italics added). See also *WHY,* 1166. Nixon's commitment to additional reductions was meant to inspire hope among the people and to signify his confidence in the South Vietnamese, but he also considered the withdrawals politically necessary. The number to be withdrawn was the product of another compromise between Laird, who wanted more, and Kissinger, who wanted fewer; most of the 20,000 would be pulled out toward the end of the two-month period, when the offensive was expected to have run its course.
103. *HRHD,* April 25, 1972.
104. Briefing by Kissinger, April 26, 1972, General Speech Material [II of V], box 44, WHSF, NPM.

105. *HRHD*, April 26 and May 1, 1972.

106. Memo, Nixon to Kissinger, April 30, 1972, quoted in *RN*, 593, 594, and in Hammond, *The Military and the Media*, 562. See also *HRHD*, May 8, 1972, on the Democratic National Convention.

107. *HRHD*, May 1, 1972; *RN*, 594–595.

108. Memo, Nixon to Kissinger, April 30, 1972, quoted in *RN*, 593–594; see also Hammond, *The Military and the Media*, 562, who partially quoted the still-classified document.

109. *HRHD*, May 1, 1972; *RN*, 595.

110. Quote from *RN*, 594; see also, *HRHD*, May 1, 1972; *WHY*, 1168; and Nixon's April 30 memo to Kissinger, partially quoted in Hammond, *The Military and the Media*, 562.

111. *HRHD*, May 1, 1972.

112. The preceding section is based on Memo, Kissinger to Nixon, May 1, 1972, sub: My Opening Statement for the May 2 Meeting, and Memo, Kissinger to Nixon, May 2, 1972, sub: My May 2 Meeting with the North Vietnamese, folder: Camp David—Sensitive—vol. 13, box 4 (7), WH/NSC: POW/MIA, NPM; DRV Chronology on Diplomatic Struggle, May 2 and May 4, 1972; Thach, Tung, and Loi, interviews with author. See also excerpts of the meeting transcript, quoted by Kissinger in *WHY*, 1170–1173, and accounts in Hersh, *Price of Power*, 517.

113. To Haldeman, Kissinger privately complained that he had not been given enough flexibility in Moscow, but, having followed the president's instructions to threaten the Soviets with the bombing of North Vietnam and the cancellation of the summit, the administration could not now turn back; *HRHD*, May 3, 1972.

114. Ibid., May 2 and 3, 1972. Cf. *WHY*, 1174–1176; *RN*, 600–601.

115. *HRHD*, May 4, 1972. Cf. *WHY*, 1176–1179; *RN*, 601–602.

116. *HRHD*, May 4, 1972; *WHY*, 1179; *Public Papers of the Presidents, Nixon: 1972*, 1972, 585.

117. Quotes from classified documents cited in Hammond, *The Military and the Media*, 567–569; *HRHD*, May 4, 1972; *WHY*, 1181.

118. At the NSC meeting on May 8, Connally continued to goad the president to act, while Rogers and Laird objected to the operation, but in any case, Nixon had already made his decision; see preceding analysis and cf. *RN*, 603–604, *WHY*, 1184–1186, and Hersh, *Price of Power*, 524–525.

119. *HRHD*, May 8, 1972.

120. *Public Papers of the Presidents, Nixon: 1972*, 583–587.

121. Memo, Nixon to Kissinger, May 9, 1972, quoted in *RN*, 606–607; *WHY*, 1199; and Hammond, *The Military and the Media*, 571.

122. *WHY*, 1200; see also *HRHD*, May 14, 1972, on propaganda.

123. See, e.g., *HRHD*, May 10, 11, and 19, 1972; *WHY*, 1200.

124. Hammond, *The Military and the Media*, 570–571.

125. The rationale Kissinger gives in *WHY*, 1179–1180, for the decision, "one of the finest hours of Nixon's Presidency," illustrates this point about necessity. He also commented upon inevitability on p. 1200.

126. Alexandrov-Agentov, quoted in Gaiduk, *The Soviet Union and the Vietnam War*, 237–238. For Kissinger's remarks on Soviet responses to American behavior prior to Linebacker, see *WHY*, 1168–1169, 1176, 1181–1182.

127. *HRHD*, May 11 and 20, 1972.

128. Quotes from Alexandrov-Argentov's memoirs, cited in Gaiduk, *The Soviet Union and the Vietnam War*, 239, and *RN*, 613. See also *WHY*, 1224–1228.

129. *RN*, 614; *WHY*, 1228.

130. *HRHD*, May 25, 1972.

131. *WHY*, 1227.

132. *RN*, 618.

133. *WHY*, 1228, 1253.

134. Citing Walt W. Rostow, who relied on information supplied by Kissinger, Clodfelter (*Limits of Air Power*, 167) wrote that for three weeks after the mining began the Chinese refused to ship any goods to Vietnam, and for three months they blocked the transshipment of Soviet supplies across their territory. This claim is not supported by a CIA intelligence memorandum of August 11, 1972, enclosed in Memo, David Young to Haldeman, September 18, 1972, sub: Follow-up Analysis of Rather/Szulc Stories Assessing Mining and Bombing of North Vietnam, box 191, WHSF: SMOF, HRH, NPM, or by Moorer's testimony before Congress; *Hearings Before Subcommittees of the Committee on Appropriations, House of Representatives*, 93rd Cong., 1st sess., Subcommittee on Department of Defense, George H. Mahon, Chairman, Subcommittee on Military Construction, Robert L. F. Sikes, Florida, Chairman (Washington, D.C.: GPO, 1973), 4, 16–17. For the views of a Kissinger aide on Chinese criticism of the United States, see, e.g., Goodman, *Lost Peace*, 122–123. Kissinger acknowledged that the Soviets stood by their public support of Hanoi, albeit "mildly," in the joint communiqué issued after the summit; *WHY*, 1249.

135. Goodman, *Lost Peace*, 124.

136. See Kissinger's comments regarding "domestic turmoil" in *WHY*, 1253.

137. *RN*, 617.

138. Classified Soviet document, cited by Gaiduk, *The Soviet Union and the Vietnam War*, 240. See also Hersh, *Price of Power*, 527.

139. Hersh, *Price of Power*, 527.

140. *WHY*, 1309.

141. Gaiduk, *The Soviet Union and the Vietnam War*, 240; *WHY*, 1303. Podgornyi left Moscow for Hanoi on June 13.

142. Cable, Nguyen Duy Trinh to Xuan Thuy and Le Duc Tho, n.d., summarized for the author by a Vietnamese scholar.

143. Conversation, Erich Honecker and Nguyen Song Tung, July 18, 1972, "Berlin, den 18.7.1972. Vermerk." Sozialistische Einheitspartei Deutschlands (Socialist Unity Party of Germany) B2/20/168, German Federal Archive, Koblenz.

144. See *WHY*, 1196, for the "blinking" comment. In May both sides had sent indirect public and private messages expressing interest in resuming negotiations; see ibid., 1195–1197.

145. DRV Chronology on Diplomatic Struggle, June 11, 20, 26, 1972; *WHY*, 1302–1304. Kissinger wrote that Washington's last reply was on June 23, but that appears to be the date of the decision, Washington time. Nixon and Kissinger seemed to regard Hanoi's interest in the plenaries as nothing more than a desire to use them as a propaganda forum, but it was more likely that the North Vietnamese saw the plenaries as a forum in which the PRG possessed some measure of official recognition as participants in the diplomatic process.

146. Kissinger spent about fifteen minutes of this meeting, if not more, telling Tho not to meet a lawyer for jailed Teamster boss Jimmy Hoffa, who was trying to negotiate with the North Vietnamese to invite Hoffa to Hanoi, where, having been released from prison, he would arrange the release of American POWs. Tho, who seemed amused by Kissinger's concern, said he did not plan on meeting with Hoffa, and that no POWs would be released to him; Memorandum of Conversation, Kissinger to Nixon, July 19, 1972, folder: Camp David—Sensitive—vol. 14, box 4 (8), WH/NSC: POW/MIA, NPM.

147. Ibid., and Memo, Kissinger to Nixon, July 20, sub: My Meeting July 19 with the North Vietnamese, folder: Camp David—Sensitive—vol. 14, box 4 (8), WH/NSC: POW/MIA, NPM. See also Memo, Negroponte to Kissinger, July 14, 1972, sub: Analysis of Recent Public Statement by the Other Side [at the Paris plenary on July 13], folder: HAK Paris Trip—HAKTO & Memos to the President, etc., Dec 3–13, 1972 [1 of 2], box 5 (23), WH/NSC: POW/MIA, NPM. Large portions of these documents are censored.

148. This according to WHY, 1313. Kissinger said that Tho's modification regarding the rest of Saigon's government was new, but this was not so; it had been proposed by Hanoi and the PRG in 1971.

149. Quoted in WHY, 1313.

150. DRV Chronology on Diplomatic Struggle, July 19, 1972.

151. Memo, Kissinger to Nixon, August 3, 1972, sub: My August 1 Meeting with the North Vietnamese, folder: Camp David—1972, May 2–Oct. 7, 1972 (3 of 4), box 4 (36), WH/NSC: POW/MIA, NPM.

152. WHY, 1315–1316.

153. DRV Chronology on Diplomatic Struggle, August 1, 1972.

154. Memorandum of Conversation, August 1, 1972, and Memo, Kissinger to Nixon, August 3, 1972, sub: My August 1 Meeting with the North Vietnamese, folder: Camp David—1972, May 2–Oct. 7, 1972 (3 of 4), box 4 (36), WH/NSC: POW/MIA, NPM. See also Memo, [n.n. to n.n.], [n.d., but ca. August 1, 1972], folder: Jon Howe Vietnam Subject Files/Negroponte Negotiating Files, 1972–73, vol. 1, box 7, ibid. Kissinger may also have brought up the matter of an electoral commission.

155. See analysis below. See also Cable, Haig to Kissinger, August 16, 1972, folder: HAK Paris Trip—HAKTO & Memos to the President, etc., Dec 3–13, 1972 [1 of 2], box 5 (23), WH/NSC: POW/MIA, NPM. It was Kissinger who made the concession, agreeing to abandon the two-track approach.

156. Regarding reparations, Kissinger refused to accept responsibility in a formal negotiating document, but he told the other side that "we are prepared to engage in a substantial reconstruction program for Indochina as a voluntary undertaking." Memorandum of Conversation, August 1, 1972, and Memo, Kissinger to Nixon, August 3, 1972, sub: My August 1 Meeting with the North Vietnamese, folder: Camp David—1972, May 2–Oct. 7, 1972 (3 of 4), box 4 (36), WH/NSC: POW/MIA, NPM; Memo, Negroponte to Kissinger, August 4, 1972, sub: DRV Negotiating Proposal and Where We Go from Here, and Memo, Kissinger to Nixon, August 26, 1972, sub: Further Analysis of DRV August 1 Peace Proposal, folder: Camp David—Sensitive—vol. 16, box 4 (10), ibid.

157. Ibid.

158. U.S. documents, which are partially censored, do not provide information about most political issues discussed, but the DRV Chronology on Diplomatic Struggle entry for August 14 indicates that the North Vietnamese were still using the word "provisional"

in reference to a coalition government. Also, at the 157th plenary session on August 31, Madame Binh talked about a three-element Government of National Concord that would organize free elections; Situation Message, US Delegation to Secretary of State and Embassy Saigon, August 31, 1972, folder: Paris Talks/Meetings/Paris Peace Talks (Computer Files), August 72, box 7, WH/NSC: POW/MIA, NPM.

159. In the interval between the July 19 and August 1 meetings, the United States briefed Thieu, who objected to putting the two-month resignation interval in writing but agreed to presenting it informally if it were tied to the withdrawal of North Vietnamese forces. Kissinger knew and told Thieu that the North Vietnamese would never agree to mutual withdrawal, but he may have raised the two-month resignation question informally at the August 1 meeting; see *WHY*, 1314.

160. DRV Chronology on Diplomatic Struggle, August 1, 1972.

161. On the Conduct of Negotiations, August 14, 1972, folder C[amp] D[avid] Material: U.S.-VN. Exchanges—Aug.–Oct. 1972, box 4, WH/NSC: POW/MIA, NPM; Memo, Kissinger to Nixon, August 19, 1972, sub: My August 14 Meeting with the North Vietnamese, and folder: Files for the President—Vietnam Negotiations, Camp David—1972 [2 of 4], box 7, ibid.; DRV Chronology on Diplomatic Struggle, August 14, 1972; *WHY;* 1318.

162. *WHY,* 1252, 1319.

163. Ibid., 1317–1320.

164. Memorandum of Conversation, August 17, 1972, folder: Jon Howe Vietnam Subject Files, John Negroponte Negotiations Files 1972–73, vol. II, box 7, WH/NSC: POW/MIA, NPM.

165. Memo, Haig to Staff Secretary, August 12, 1972, sub: P-2163—NVA Offensive, copy held at the National Security Archives, Washington, D.C.

166. Elliott, "NLF-DRV Strategy and the 1972 Spring Offensive"; Hersh, *Price of Power,* 561–562; Thach, Tung, and Loi, interviews with author; Duiker, *Communist Road to Power,* 318–325; Dorothy C. Donnelly, "A Settlement of Sorts: Henry Kissinger's Negotiations and America's Extrication from Vietnam," *Peace and Change: A Journal of Peace Research* 9 (Summer 1983): 55–79; Ngoc Tuan, "Development of the Military Situation in 1972," in Vien, *Indochina: 1972–73 Turning Point,* 61–94; Kolko, *Anatomy of a War,* 427–428; Porter, *Peace Denied,* 102–115.

167. Uncoordinated Draft Summary, January 20, 1973, sub: Linebacker I, K712.041–19, AFHRA. The U.S. Air Force lost thirty-eight aircraft in the operation.

168. Clodfelter, *Limits of Air Power,* 161, 166.

169. See, e.g., Clodfelter, *Limits of Air Power,* 166–176; *WHY,* 1195–1201.

170. See, e.g., Hammond, *The Military and the Media,* chap. 21.

171. CIA Intelligence Memorandum, August 11, 1972, enclosed in Memo, David Young to Haldeman, September 18, 1972, sub: Follow-up Analysis of Rather/Szulc Stories Assessing Mining and Bombing of North Vietnam, box 191, WHSF: SMOF, HRH, NPM.

172. *Hearings Before Subcommittees of the Committee on Appropriations House of Representatives,* 93rd Cong., 1st sess., 4, 16–17.

173. Thach, quoted in Hersh, *Price of Power,* 563–564; Thach, interview with author; Letter, Le Duan to the COSVN, 5th Zone and Tri-Thien Zone Party Committee, August 1972, in Le Duan, *Letters to the South,* 175–187; Duiker, *Communist Road to Power,* 318–325.

174. These were their diplomatic options. Kissinger identified three strategic options in *WHY,* 1329, discussed below.

175. Kimball, "How Wars End," 190–197.

176. Kissinger confessed his personal stake in negotiations, but he also explained his bias in terms of realpolitik theory: "I always looked at them as a weapon for seizing the moral and psychological high ground. . . . To me . . . [talking] is [also] a device to improve one's strategic position"; *WHY,* 1302, and see passim, especially pp. 1327–1330. The documentary record of negotiations seems to support Kissinger's claim that he leaned toward settling before the election, and Nixon after the election.

177. Marginal comments on Memo, Kissinger to Nixon, August 3, 1972, sub: My August 1 Meeting with the North Vietnamese, folder: Camp David—1972, May 2–Oct. 7, 1972 (3 of 4), box 4 (36), WH/NSC: POW/MIA, NPM.

178. Nixon's notes on Kissinger's memos, quoted in *WHY,* 1319.

179. See, e.g., *HRHD,* September 28 and October 4, 1972.

180. Quote from Memo, Haig to Kissinger, ca. mid-September 1972, quoted in *WHY,* 1331; on polls, see ibid., and *HRHD,* September 1, 1972.

181. *HRHD,* May 18 and 21, 1972.

182. For example, when on August 16 the *Washington Post* reported on Kissinger's flights from Paris to Switzerland to Saigon, the White House refused to indicate whether a breakthrough was imminent, but Ziegler did say that "we are in a sensitive time now," which, of course, indicated that a breakthrough was possible; quoted in Memo, Situation Room to Kissinger, August 16, 1972, sub: Morning News Summary, folder: HAK's Secret Paris Trip, Aug 13–14, 1972 & Switzerland (#10), box 5 (23), WH/NSC: POW/MIA, NPM.

183. *HRHD,* September 22 and October 2, 1972. The campaign has been widely reported. Numerous entries in *HRHD* for 1972 provide additional insights into Nixon's mood and strategy.

184. See, e.g., ibid., June 17, October 26, 27, and 28, 1972; Memo, Situation Room to Kissinger, August 16, 1972, sub: Morning News Summary, folder: HAK's Secret Paris Trip, Aug 13–14, 1972 & Switzerland (#10), box 5 (23), WH/NSC: POW/MIA, NPM.

185. This point is not mentioned in Kissinger's or Nixon's memoirs, but it becomes apparent in letters Nixon wrote to Thieu. These are discussed and cited below.

186. For Nixon's ambivalence regarding the negotiations, see especially Haldeman's entries for September 28 and October 4. See also, *WHY,* 1329–1331, for Kissinger's analysis of his and Nixon's views about budgetary and electoral factors impinging on the timing of a settlement.

187. These quotes are from Talking Points for Meeting with President Thieu, n.d. [marked "For Aug 17–18 meetings"], folder: Camp David—Sensitive—vol. 17, box 4 (11), WH/NSC: POW/MIA, NPM; but Kissinger's account in *WHY,* 1321–1325, Hung and Schecter's account in *Palace File,* 65–67, and the uncensored parts of the memoranda of conversation indicate that Kissinger did follow his talking points when he met with Thieu; Memoranda of Conversation, August 17 and 18, 1972, folder: Jon Howe Vietnam Subject Files, John Negroponte Negotiations Files, 1972–1973, vol. 2, box 7, WH/NSC: POW/MIA, NPM.

188. Memorandum of Conversation, August 17, 1972, folder: Jon Howe Vietnam Subject Files, John Negroponte Negotiations Files, 1972–1973, vol. 2, box 7, WH/NSC: POW/MIA, NPM.

189. Memoranda of Conversation, August 17 and 18, 1972, ibid.

190. Ibid.; *WHY*, 1321–1329.

191. Memorandum of Conversation, August 18, 1972, folder: Jon Howe Vietnam Subject Files, John Negroponte Negotiations Files, 1972–1973, vol. 2, box 7, WH/NSC: POW/MIA, NPM.

192. *WHY*, 1329.

193. Memorandum of Conversation, August 18, 1972, folder: Jon Howe Vietnam Subject Files, John Negroponte Negotiations Files, 1972–1973, vol. 2, box 7, WH/NSC: POW/MIA, NPM. Hung and Schecter claim that Kissinger recommended a South Vietnamese raid into the North to draw PAVN troops out of South Vietnam; *Palace File*, 67.

194. The letter is reprinted in Hung and Schecter, *Palace File*, 68, and paraphrased in *WHY*, 1327. See *WHY*, 1328, on Kissinger's strategy, and *Palace File*, 68–69, for Thieu's thinking and quotes. See also Memo, Kissinger to Bunker, August 29, 1972, sub: GVN Views on Peace Proposals, folder: Camp David—Sensitive—vol. 16, box 4 (10), WH/NSC: POW/MIA, NPM. The Hawaii meeting is mentioned in *HRHD*, August 31, 1972; *WHY*, 1327; and Memo, Bunker to Kissinger, September 9, 1972, sub: Comments of the Republic of Vietnam on the Revised US Peace Proposal and Procedures for the Conduct of Negotiations, and the Counterproposals by the RVN, folder: Camp David—Sensitive—vol. 17, box 4 (11), WH/NSC: POW/MIA, NPM.

195. *WHY*, 1327–1328.

196. Memorandum of Conversation, September 15, 1972, folder: Camp David—1972, May 2–Oct. 7, 1972 (2 of 4), box 4 (35), WH/NSC: POW/MIA, NPM; Memo, Haig to Nixon, September 15, 1972, sub: Dr. Kissinger's Initial Report on Today's Paris Meeting, box 4 (24), ibid.; DRV Chronology on Diplomatic Struggle, September 11, 1972. Regarding the prisoner release, see Cable, Haig to Kissinger, September 25, 1972, and Cable, Situation Room to Winston Lord, September 25, 1972, and Memo, Haig to Kissinger, September 25, 1972, all in folder: HAK Office Files, HAK Trip Files, HAK's Secret Paris Trip, box 7, WH/NSC: POW/MIA, NPM; Memo, Holdridge to Haig, September 25, 1972, sub: Plans for the September 28 Paris Plenary, folder: Paris Talks, 1972–73, (#6), box 3, ibid.

197. The developing issue on prisoners had to do with political prisoners held by the Saigon government, some of whom had been convicted as "criminals." Saigon and the United States did not want to release them and thus preferred the term "innocent civilians," which could be interpreted to exclude political and "criminal" prisoners. Hanoi and the NLF/PRG wanted all military and civilian personnel of the warring parties released. In the negotiations, the United States tried to postpone and "finesse" the matter; see, e.g., Memo, Negroponte to Kissinger, September 22, 1972, sub: Documents for Forthcoming Meeting, folder: Camp David—Sensitive—vol. 18, box 4 (12), WH/NSC: POW/MIA, NPM.

198. Memorandum of Conversation, September 15, 1972, folder: Camp David—1972, May 2–Oct. 7, 1972 (2 of 4), box 4 (35), WH/NSC: POW/MIA, NPM; Memo, Haig to Nixon, September 15, 1972, sub: Dr. Kissinger's Initial Report on Today's Paris Meeting, box 4 (24), ibid.; DRVN Proposals, September 15, 1972, September 15, 1972, folder: C[amp] D[avid] Material: U.S.-VN. Exchanges—Aug.–Oct. 1972 [2 of 2], box 4, ibid. These partially censored documents are too fragmentary to illuminate the details and nuances of the political questions. Kissinger tried to make it appear in *WHY*, 1332, that Tho was in retreat, but this is not clear from the documents. Tho's proposal for the Gov-

ernment of Concord, for example, was a probe, as well as a statement of principle concerning their position on the "reality" of two governments in South Vietnam. Also, the surviving portions of the transcript reveal that Tho pointed out that there were differences between the two sides on the matter of Thieu's resignation before an election.

199. *WHY,* 1333.

200. Quoted in *HRHD,* September 16, 1972.

201. Memo, Haig to Nixon, September 15, 1972, sub: Dr. Kissinger's Initial Report on Today's Paris Meeting, box 4 (24), folder: Camp David—1972, May 2–Oct. 7, 1972 (2 of 4), WH/NSC: POW/MIA, NPM.

202. *WHY,* 1333.

203. On Kissinger's upbeat reports in relation to North Vietnamese perceptions of Nixon's reelection, see Memo, Haig to Nixon, September 15, 1972, sub: Dr. Kissinger's Initial Report on Today's Paris Meeting, box 4 (24), folder: Camp David—1972, May 2–Oct. 7, 1972 (2 of 4), WH/NSC: POW/MIA, NPM; Kissinger to Nixon memo quoted in *WHY,* 1333; *HRHD,* September 16, 1972. Kissinger and the White House had always assumed that the North Vietnamese would not move toward a settlement until they were sure of Nixon's reelection; Memo, Situation Room to Kissinger, August 1, 1972, sub: Evening Notes, folder: HAK Paris Trip—HAKTO & Memos to the President, etc., Dec 3–13, 1972 [1 of 2], box 5 (23), WH/NSC: POW/MIA, NPM.

204. *WHY,* 1135–1336, 1346; Hung and Schecter, *Palace File,* 71–72.

205. Memo, Negroponte to Kissinger, September 22, 1972, sub: Documents for Forthcoming Meeting, folder: Camp David—Sensitive—vol. 18, box 4 (12), WH/NSC: POW/MIA, NPM; Memo, Kissinger to Nixon, September 28, 1972, sub: My Meetings with the North Vietnamese, September 26–27, 1972, folder: Files for the President—Vietnam Negotiations, Camp David 1972, 9/28/72, box 7, ibid.; Memorandum of Conversation, September 26, 1972, ibid.; *WHY,* 1335, 1337; DRV Chronology on Diplomatic Struggle, September 23, 1972.

206. *WHY,* 1336–1337.

207. Memo, Kissinger to Nixon, September 28, 1972, sub: My Meetings with the North Vietnamese September 26–27, 1972, folder: Files for the President—Vietnam Negotiations, Camp David 1972, 9/28/72, box 7, WH/NSC: POW/MIA, NPM; Memoranda of Conversation, September 26 and 27, 1972, ibid.; Cable, Situation Room to Col. Brown for Haig, September 30, 1972, sub: Responses to Questions, folder: Camp David—Sensitive—vol. 19, box 4 (13), ibid.; Proposal of the Democratic Republic of Vietnam [fragment], September 26, 1972, folder: C[amp] D[avid] Material: U.S.-VN. Exchanges—Aug.–Oct. 1972, ibid.; DRV Chronology on Diplomatic Struggle, September 26, 1972.

208. Cable, Situation Room to Col. Brown for Haig, September 30, 1972, sub: Responses to Questions, folder: Camp David—Sensitive—vol. 19, box 4 (13), WH/NSC: POW/MIA, NPM. Regarding Thieu's ideas for the Committee of National Reconciliation, see *WHY,* 1326, 1494 n.1.

209. Cable, Kissinger to Haig for Bunker, September 27, 1972, folder: HAK's Secret Paris Trip, Sept 25–27, 1972 (#11), box 5, WH/NSC: POW/MIA, NPM.

210. *WHY,* 1338.

211. The message is partially quoted in *WHY,* 1340, and paraphrased in DRV Chronology on Diplomatic Struggle, September 30, 1972.

212. *HRHD,* September 28, 1972.

213. Memo, Thieu to Bunker, September 26, 1972, printed in Hung and Schecter, *Palace File,* appendix B; see also p. 72.

214. DRV Chronology on Diplomatic Struggle, September 30, 1972.

215. *HRHD,* September 28, 1972. The modifications are mentioned in *WHY,* 1338.

216. Memo, Thieu to Nixon, October 4, 1972, printed in Hung and Schecter, *Palace File,* appendix C; see also p. 73, and *WHY,* 1338–1339.

217. *WHY,* 1339, 1342; *RN,* 689; *HRHD,* October 2, 3, and 4, 1972.

218. *HRHD,* October 4, 1972.

219. *WHY,* 1339.

220. Personal Message, Nixon to Thieu, October 6, 1972, printed in Hung and Schecter, *Palace File,* appendix A: Letter 8; see also pp. 73–74.

221. Cable, Situation Room to Col. Brown for Haig, September 30, 1972, sub: Responses to Questions, folder: Camp David—Sensitive—vol. 19, box 4 (13), WH/NSC: POW/MIA, NPM.

13. BANGS AND WHIMPERS: 1972–1973

1. *HRHD,* June 2, 1971.

2. His staff had given him a mixed prognosis of the prospects for a breakthrough in the talks; Cable, Haig to Kissinger [prepared by Negroponte and initialed by Haig, R. T. Kennedy, Jonathan Howe, and Lord], October 4, 1972, sub: Some Thoughts on Where We Stand on Negotiations, folder: Camp David—Sensitive—vol. 19, box 4 (13), WH/NSC Files: POW/MIA, NPM. Nixon was pessimistic about prospects.

3. *WHY,* 1341–1342.

4. Ibid., 1342–1343.

5. Ibid., 1344–1345.

6. Ibid., 1344–1356; Kissinger told Nixon that at the end of the talks, Tho, remarking about four years of negotiating, cried; Notes, October 12, 1972, sub: Vietnam Negotiations, folder: H. Notes Oct–Nov–Dec 1972 Part I, box 46, WHSF: SMOF, HRH, NPM. See also *HRHD,* October 9 and 10, 1972; Agreement on Ending the War and Restoring Peace in Vietnam, United States Proposal [partially censored], October 11, 1972, folder: October Camp David 1972: Originals—HAK (3 of 4), box 4 (27), WH/NSC: POW/MIA, NPM.

7. DRV Chronology on Diplomatic Struggle, October 11–12.

8. On October 9 Nixon had forbade Kissinger from going from Paris to Saigon and then Hanoi to close the deal; *HRHD,* October 9, 1972.

9. Notes, October 12, 1972, sub: Vietnam Negotiations, folder: H. Notes Oct–Nov–Dec 1972 Part I, box 46, WHSF: SMOF, HRH, NPM; *HRHD,* October 12, 1972.

10. *HRHD,* October 9, 12, and 13, 1972; *WHY,* 1360–1361.

11. Memorandum of Conversation, October 13, 1972, October Camp David 1972: Originals—HAK, folder 2 of 4, Box 4 (26), WH/NSC: POW/MIA, NPM. Nixon's message read: "The President accepts the basic draft . . . except for some technical issues to be discussed between Minister Xuan Thuy and Dr. Kissinger on October 17, and subject to the following substantive changes." Much of the document has been blacked out, but several of the changes were about ceasefires and prisoner releases in Laos and Cambodia.

12. Cables between Kissinger and the White House for this hectic period October 17 to 23, 1972, concerning the issues mentioned in this paragraph can be found in box 25, NSC: HAKOF, HAKTF, NPM in the following folders: HAK Paris/Saigon Trip, 16–23 Oct '72 TOHAK [1 of 2] and [2 of 2]; HAK Paris/Saigon Trip, 16–23 Oct '72 HAKTO; and HAK Paris/Saigon Trip, 16–23 Oct '72. See also Memo, Guay to Haig, October 14, 1972, folder: Camp David—Sensitive—vol. 20, box 4 (14), WH/NSC: POW/MIA, NPM; Memo, Haig to Guay, October 14, 1972, ibid.; Memo, Kissinger to Bunker, October 16, 1972, ibid.; DRV Chronology on Diplomatic Struggle, October 16, 1972; Notes, October 14 and 15, 1972, sub: Vietnam Strategy, folder: H. Notes Oct–Nov–Dec 1972 Part I, box 46, WHSF: SMOF, HRH, NPM; *WHY*, 1360–1394; Hersh, *Price of Power*, 586–592; and Porter, *Peace Denied*, 124–130. Haldeman's diary entries in *HRHD* provide illumination.

13. The Politburo had instructed Thuy on October 16 that he should insist on the bipartite signing before the quadripartite signing; DRV Chronology on Diplomatic Struggle, October 16, 1972. It is unclear whether this sequence was agreed to in October. During the signing of the Paris Agreement in January 1973, the quadripartite signing took place first. In box 25, NSC: HAKOF, HAKTF, NPM, see also three cables from Kissinger to Haig dated October 17, 1972, folder: HAK Paris/Saigon Trip, 16–23 Oct '72 HAKTO; Memo, Haig to Nixon, October 17 [regarding message from Kissinger], HAK Paris/Saigon Trip, 16–23 Oct '72; Cable, Haig to Kissinger, October 19, 1972, folder: HAK Paris/Saigon Trip, 16–23 Oct '72 TOHAK [2 of 2]; and Memo, Haig to Nixon, October 20, 1972, sub: Message from North Vietnamese, folder: HAK Paris/Saigon Trip, 16–23 Oct '72.

14. Message from Sung to Guay for Haig to Nixon, October 19, 1972, folder: Camp David—Sensitive—vol. 20, box 4 (14), WH/NSC: POW/MIA; Cable, Quay to Haig, October 21, 1972, sub: [Reply from Prime Min. of DRV to Nixon's msg. of Oct. 20], folder: For the President's Files—Winston Lord, Vietnam Negotiations, ibid.; Cable, Haig to Quay, October 22, 1972, ibid.; Kissinger to Nixon, October 23, 1972, sub: The Draft Agreement with the North Vietnamese, folder: Camp David—Sensitive—vol. 21, box 4 (15), ibid.; Cable, Haig to Kissinger, October 19, 1972, folder; HAK Paris/Saigon Trip, 16–23 Oct '72 TOHAK [2 of 2], box 25, and Memo, Haig to Nixon, October 20, 1972, sub: Message from North Vietnamese, folder: HAK Paris/Saigon Trip, 16–23 Oct '72, box 25, NSC: HAKOF, HAKTF, NPM; *WHY*, 1397.

15. This synopsis of key points is drawn from documents cited earlier and from the draft agreement broadcast in English by Hanoi Radio on October 25, 1972 (reprinted in *NYT*, October 27, 1972), which Kissinger, in *WHY*, 1397, affirmed was an accurate summary, and which is consistent with information in available documents.

16. On Kissinger's meetings with Thieu, see memos from Haig to Nixon, October 18, 19, and 23, 1972, folder: HAK Paris/Saigon Trip 16–23 Oct '72, box 25, NSC: HAKOF, HAKTF, NPM; Notes, October 22, 1972, sub: Vietnam Strategy, folder: H. Notes Oct–Nov–Dec 1972 Part I, box 46, WHSF: SMOF, HRH, NPM. In between these meetings with Thieu, Kissinger flew to Phnom Penh and William Sullivan to Bangkok and Vientiane, where they won the assent of the governments of Laos, Cambodia, and Thailand for the agreement; *WHY*, 1383–1385. On the DMZ, see A General Strategy & Plan for Viet-Nam Negotiations, March 28, 1969, folder: NSC Meeting of March 28, 1969—A General Strategy & Plan for Viet-Nam Negotiations, box 175, NSC: PT/M, NPM.

17. "Exclusive from Hanoi" [de Borchgrave interview of Dong], *Newsweek*, October 30, 1972, 26–27; *WHY*, 1380–1381. The views of Thieu and his supporters are developed

in Hung and Schecter, *Palace File,* chap. 5. The phrase *co cau chinh quyen* was used in the draft to refer to the NCRC; it possessed a stronger implication of "governmental structure" than "administrative structure."

18. In one message Nixon assured Thieu of his continued support—"if you proceed with us"; Cable, Haig to Kissinger, October 22, 1972, folder: HAK Paris/Saigon Trip, 16–23 Oct '72 TOHAK [1 of 2], box 25, NSC: HAKOF, HAKTF, NPM.

19. Annotated News Summaries, October 23, 24, and 27, 1972, WHSF: POF, NPM; Cables, Haig to Kissinger, October 21 and 22, 1972, folder: HAK Paris/Saigon Trip, 16–23 Oct '72 TOHAK [1 of 2], box 25, NSC: HAKOF, HAKTF, NPM; Notes, October 14 and 15, 1972, sub: Vietnam Strategy, folder: H. Notes Oct–Nov–Dec 1972 Part I, box 46, WHSF: SMOF, HRH, NPM; *RN,* 701. See also *HRHD* entries for this period.

20. *HRHD,* October 22, 1972.

21. Cable, Kissinger to Haig for Nixon, October 22, 1972, WHSF: CF, PPF, NPM. In box 25, NSC: HAKOF, HAKTF, NPM, see Cables, Haig to Kissinger, October 22, 22, 23, and 23, 1972, folder: HAK P/ST 16–23 Oct '72 TOHAK [1 of 2]. In WH/NSC: POW/MIA, NPM, see Memo, Kissinger to Nixon, October 23, 1972, and Memo, Negroponte to Kissinger, October 23, 1972, sub: Some Thoughts on Where We Go from Here, folder: Camp David—Sensitive—vol. 21, box 4 (15); Cable, Haig to Quay, October 22, 1972, folder: For the President's Files—Winston Lord, Vietnam Negotiations, box 4; Backchannel Message, Bunker to Haig, October 22, 1972, folder: Backchannel Messages—From Ambassador Bunker—Saigon Sept 1972, box 3. Also see *HRHD,* October 16, 17, 18, 22, 1972. One of the disagreements between Nixon and Kissinger overplayed by commentators was the matter of whether Kissinger should or should not go to Hanoi to finalize the agreement and close the deal. On balance, Kissinger favored such a trip more than Nixon, but Nixon was not opposed until it became clear that Thieu would obstruct an agreement as the American election neared. While in Saigon, Kissinger had thought about Vientiane as an alternative, but Nixon had reservations about the location and the trip. In any case, in the give-and-take between Kissinger and the White House, Kissinger had decided that a trip within the time frame of the original schedule would not be appropriate.

22. Dung quoted in de Borchgrave interview, *Newsweek,* October 30, 1972, 26–27; *NYT* (text of Hanoi's statement and the draft agreement), October 27, 1972; Hung and Schecter, *Palace File,* chap. 5.

23. *WHY,* 1378–1394, 1411; Hersh, *Price of Power,* 592–604; Fallaci, "Nguyen Van Thieu," *Interview with History,* 47–48.

24. Cable, Kissinger to Haig for Nixon, October 22, 1972, WHSF: CF, PPF, NPM; *WHY,* 1388–1392, 1396–1397; Hersh, *Price of Power,* 602; *RN,* 703–704. Kissinger's return, or second, cable to Hanoi was dated October 25, Washington time.

25. *NYT* (text of Hanoi's statement and the draft agreement), October 27, 1972.

26. *HRHD,* October 26, 1972; *WHY,* 1397–1398; *RN,* 704–705. On October 22, worried that Hanoi would "enter into a public polemic" with Washington, Kissinger and the White House tried to enlist Moscow's help in restraining Hanoi by assuring Dobrynin that Nixon would do all he could to salvage the agreement, but also by threatening "to take measures which would be inimical to all the progress that had been made thus far"; Cable, Haig to Kissinger, October 22, 1972, folder: HAK P/ST 16–23 Oct '72 TOHAK [1 of 2], box 25, NSC: HAKOF, HAKTF, NPM.

27. The full text is reprinted in *NYT,* October 27, 1927. See also, *WHY,* 1392–1401.

28. *Public Papers of the Presidents, Nixon: 1972,* 1032, 1037. See *WHY,* 1399, regarding Nixon's approval of Kissinger's remarks. In a November 2 speech to the nation, the Vietnam portions of which were drafted by Kissinger, Nixon again referred to "a major breakthrough toward achieving our goal of peace with honor in Vietnam"; cf. *Public Papers of the Presidents, Nixon: 1972,* 1085–1086, with Talking Points, Kissinger to Nixon, October 30 and 31, 1972, folder: Camp David—Sensitive—vol. 21, box 4 (15), and folder: Paris Talks, 1972–73, (no. 6), WH/NSC: POW/MIA, NPM.

29. See, e.g., *NYT,* October 27, 1972.

30. *RN,* 705.

31. Cable, Haig to Kissinger, October 17, 1972, folder: HAK P/ST 16–23 Oct '72 TOHAK [2 of 2], box 25, NSC: HAKOF, HAKTF, NPM; *HRHD,* October 26, 1972; Hersh, *Price of Power,* 606.

32. Notes, October 14, 1972, sub: Vietnam Strategy, folder: H. Notes Oct–Nov–Dec 1972 Part I, box 46, WHSF: SMOF, HRH, NPM; Cable, Kissinger to Haig, October 18, 1972, folder: HAK P/ST 16–23 Oct '72 HAKTO, box 25, NSC: HAKOF, HAKTF, ibid.; Cable, Haig to Kissinger, October 21, 1972, folder: HAK P/ST 16–23 Oct '72 TOHAK [1 of 2], box 25, NSC: HAKOF, HAKTF, ibid.; Cable, Kissinger to Haig for Nixon, October 22, 1972, WHSF: CF, PPF, ibid.

33. *RN,* 705.

34. *HRHD,* October 26, 1972. See also Annotated News Summaries, October 27, 1972, WHSF: POF, NPM; Hersh, *Price of Power,* 606; and *WHY,* 1399.

35. DRV Chronology on Diplomatic Struggle; Hersh interview with Thach, quoted in *Price of Power,* 602; Kimball interview with Thach.

36. Cable, CINCPAC to CINCPACFLT, CINCPACAF, CINCUSARPAC, September 12, 1972, sub: US Redeployments and Future Force Structure, Message Traffic, May–December 1972, K168.06–229, AFHRA. On Operation Enhance Plus see Arnold R. Isaacs, *Without Honor: Defeat in Vietnam and Cambodia* (New York: Vintage Books, 1984), 47–48; *Washington-Star News,* November 6, 1972; *Washington Post,* January 17, 1972; Porter, *Peace Denied,* 143–144; *WHY,* 1402; Ambrose, *Nixon,* vol. 2, *The Triumph of a Politician,* 644–645; and the following communications in box 25, NSC: HAKOF, HAKTF, NPM: Cable, Haig to Kissinger, October 19, 1972, folder: HAK P/ST 16–23 Oct '72 TOHAK [2 of 2]; Cable, Haig to Kissinger, October 21, 1972, folder: HAK P/ST 16–23 Oct '72 TOHAK [1 of 2], box 25; Memo with enclosures, Laird to Haig, October 21, 1972, folder: HAK P/ST 16–23 Oct '72, box 25. On November 22, Kissinger complained that Department of Defense leaks about the operation were harming his efforts to negotiate with the North Vietnamese; Cable, Haig to Kennedy [Kissinger to the White House], November 22, 1972, folder: HAK Paris Trip 18–25 Nov. 1972 HAKTO, box 26, NSC: HAKOF, HAKTF, NPM.

37. Cable, Kissinger to Haig, October 18, 1972, folder: HAK P/ST 16–23 Oct '72 HAKTO, box 25, NSC: HAKOF, HAKTF, NPM; Cable, Kissinger to Haig for Nixon, October 22, 1972, WHSF: CF, PPF, NPM; *WHY,* 1389–1390.

38. Message, Admiral Noel Gayler, CINCPAC, to Admiral Clarey, General Rosson, and General Clay, October 11, 1972, sub: Management and Control of Air Warfare in SEASIA, Message Traffic, May–December 1972, K168.06–229, AFHRA. Nixon noted in *RN,* 724, that by November 1972 "there were contingency plans for three-day and six-day bombing strikes against North Vietnam." See also, Cable, Haig to Kissinger, October

19, 1972, folder: HAK P/ST 16–23 Oct '72 TOHAK [2 of 2], box 25, NSC: HAKOF, HAKTF, NPM.

39. *RN,* 717.

40. Specifically, the bilateral proposal included the following provisions: a cease-fire; the total withdrawal of US forces in sixty days; the return of POWs within sixty days, with accounting arrangements for MIAs; economic and military aid to Saigon, Congress willing, on one-to-one replacement basis; reconstruction aid to the DRV; the restoration of previous agreements concerning Cambodia and Laos; the release of Communist military prisoners if they are willing to go to the DRV; and, regarding political and military matters in South Vietnam, an exhortation to both parties to cease firing, release prisoners, bring about reconciliation and concord, and agree to a political process, with no provision for international supervision. See, e.g., Memo, Negroponte to Kissinger, Alternate Proposal for Bilateral U.S.-DRV Agreement, November 15, 1972, folder: John Negroponte Negotiations Files, 1972–73, vol. 1, box 5, WH/NSC: POW/MIA, NPM.

41. Cable, Bunker to Kissinger, November 8, 1972, folder: Camp David—Sensitive—vol. 21, box 4 (15), WH/NSC: POW/MIA, NPM.

42. Nixon's letter is reproduced in Hung and Schecter, *Palace File,* 383– 384.

43. Ibid., 121. See also Memo, Kissinger to Haig, November 10, quoted by Hammond, *The Military and the Media,* 597.

44. Letter, Thieu to Nixon, November 11, 1972, folder: Thieu, Nguyen Van, box 16, WHSF: PPF, NPM. The issue of South Vietnamese elections was not as pressing as other issues, since they would be organized by the NCRC, but if they were held, Communists would enter a coalition government.

45. Letters, Nixon to Thieu, November 14 and 18, 1972, ibid. See also, Hung and Schecter, *Palace File,* 385–390.

46. *WHY,* 1400–1402, 1405–1406.

47. *WHY,* 1417; Cables (2), Kissinger to Haig, November 20, 1972, folder: HAK Paris Trip 18–25 Nov. 1972 HAKTO, box 26, NSC: HAKOF, HAKTF, NPM.

48. Porter, *Peace Denied,* 144–149; *WHY,* 1416–1422; *RN,* 720–723; and Goodman, *Lost Peace,* 152–157. Thach, in his interview with the author, commented that Kissinger demanded a partial PAVN withdrawal. Kissinger's reports to the White House seem to confirm these accounts but do not provide a full record of the meeting; Cables (2), Kissinger to Haig, November 20, 1972, folder: HAK Paris Trip 18–25 Nov. 1972 HAKTO, box 26, NSC: HAKOF, HAKTF, NPM; and Memorandum of Conversation, November 20, 1972, folder: Camp David—Minutes of Meetings, Paris—November 20–25, 1972—vol. 21, box 4 (17), WH/NSC Files: POW/MIA, NPM. Regarding elections, one reason that Nixon, Kissinger, and Thieu opposed elections for a Constituent Assembly was that PRG representatives were sure to be elected, making the government a coalition government, even if Thieu were reelected president.

49. DRV Chronology on Diplomatic Struggle, November 20, 1972; Cables (2), Kissinger to Haig, November 20, 1972, folder: HAK Paris Trip 18–25 Nov. 1972 HAKTO, box 26, NSC: HAKOF, HAKTF, NPM.

50. Memo, Kissinger to Bunker, November 20, 1972, folder: Camp David—Sensitive—vol. 21 (2), box 4 (16), WH/NSC: POW/MIA, NPM; Memorandum of Conversation, November 21, 1972, folder: Camp David—Briefings of South Vietnamese, Paris—Nov. 20–25, 1972—vol. 21, box 4 (17A), ibid.

51. Memo, Kennedy to Haldeman, November 21, 1972, and Cables, Kissinger to Haig

and to Bunker, November 21, 1972, folder: HAK Paris Trip 18–25 Nov. 1972 HAKTO, box 26, NSC: HAKOF, HAKTF, NPM; Vien, *Indochina: 1972–73 Turning Point,* 222; Porter, *Peace Denied,* 149; *WHY,* 1417–1418; *HRHD,* November 20 and 21, 1972; *RN,* 720. Concerning the NCRC, it may have been that at some point Tho was willing to use the phrase "administrative organ" but not Thieu's more restrictive "administrative organ in charge of elections." Kissinger is vague on this point. In the end, that is, in the Paris Agreement, there would be no descriptive characterization, such as "administrative" or "governmental," or "organ" or "structure"; the agreement simply defined the NCRC's functions.

52. Cable, Kissinger to Haig, November 22, 1972, folder: HAK Paris Trip 18–25 Nov. 1972 HAKTO, box 26, NSC: HAKOF, HAKTF, NPM; *WHY,* 1418–1419.

53. *RN,* 720.

54. *WHY,* 1418–1419; Memo, Haig to Kennedy [Kissinger to Nixon], November 23, 1972, and Memo, Haig to Kennedy [for Bunker], November 23, 1972, folder: Camp David—Sensitive—vol. 21 (2), box 4 (16), WH/NSC: POW/MIA, NPM.

55. The cable is partially quoted in *WHY,* 1419, and *RN,* 721, and is paraphrased in *HRHD,* November 22, 1972.

56. DRV Chronology on Diplomatic Struggle, November 23, 1972.

57. *WHY,* 1420.

58. Cable, Kissinger to Haig, November 23, 1972, folder: HAK Paris Trip 18–25 Nov. 1972 HAKTO, box 26, NSC: HAKOF, HAKTF, NPM.

59. Cable, Kissinger to Nixon, November 23, 1972, attached to Memo, Kennedy to Military Aide, Camp David, November 23, 1972, folder: HAK Paris Trip 18–25 Nov. 1972 HAKTO, box 26, NSC: HAKOF, HAKTF, NPM; Memo, Haig to Kennedy [Kissinger to Nixon], November 23, 1972, and Memo, Haig to Kennedy [for Bunker], November 23, 1972, folder: Camp David—Sensitive—vol. 21 (2), box 4 (16), WH/NSC: POW/MIA, NPM; *WHY,* 1420; *RN,* 721–722.

60. Cf. *RN,* 721 and *WHY,* 1420.

61. These are summarized or spelled out in NSC: HAKOF, HAKTF, NPM in the following documents: Cables, Kissinger to Nixon and Haig to Kennedy [for Bunker], November 24, 1972, and Memo, Kissinger to Nixon, sub: Changes Obtained in the Draft Agreement, November 25, 1972, with enclosure, Agreement as It Now Stands, folder: HAK Paris Trip 18–25 Nov. 1972 HAKTO, box 26.

62. Cable, Nixon to Kissinger, 1:42 A.M., November 24, 1972, folder: HAK Paris Trip 18–25 Nov. 1972 TOHAK [2 of 2], box 26, NSC: HAKOF, HAKTF, NPM; *HRHD,* November 23, 1972. For Kissinger's and Nixon's accounts, see *WHY,* 1421; *RN,* 722.

63. Cable, Nixon to Kissinger, 6:14 A.M., November 24, 1972, folder: HAK Paris Trip 18–25 Nov. 1972 TOHAK [2 of 2], box 26, NSC: HAKOF, HAKTF, NPM. See also *RN,* 722, and *WHY,* 1421. The record shows that four cables on this subject were sent to Kissinger on November 24. The 1:42 A.M. cable urged a tough-on-Thieu, negotiate-with-Tho approach: the 6:14 A.M. cable urged a tough-on-Tho, bomb–North Vietnam approach; a 10:55 A.M. cable elaborated the tough-on-Thieu approach, and marked another reversal of Nixon's position. In a fourth cable, which appears to have been written in the evening of November 24 and received in Paris at 1:43 A.M., November 25, Nixon instructed Kissinger to recess the talks if necessary, but not to break them off.

64. *HRHD,* November 20, 21, 22, 28, and 29, 1972; Cable, Kennedy to Haig, November 20, 1972 [regarding Fallaci], folder: HAK Paris Trip 18–25 Nov. 1972 TOHAK

[1 of 2], box 26, NSC: HAKOF, HAKTF, NPM. See also, Fallaci, "Henry Kissinger," *Interview with History,* chap. 1; *WHY,* 1406–1410, 1419, 1423–1424.

65. *HRHD,* November 24, 1972; *WHY,* 1421–1422.

66. Memo, Kissinger to Kennedy [for Nixon], November 24, 1972, folder: HAK Paris Trip 18–25 Nov. 1972 HAKTO, box 26, NSC: HAKOF, HAKTF, NPM.

67. This according to Porter, *Peace Denied,* 149–151, who cited North Vietnamese accounts.

68. DRV Chronology on Diplomatic Struggle, November 25, 1972.

69. Cables, Kissinger to Nixon and Haig to Kennedy [for Bunker], November 24, 1972, folder: HAK Paris Trip 18–25 Nov. 1972 HAKTO, box 26, NSC: HAKOF, HAKTF, NPM; Memo, Kissinger to Kennedy [for Nixon], November 24, 1972, and Memo, Kissinger to Nixon, November 25, 1972, sub: Changes Obtained in the Draft Agreement, folder: Camp David—Sensitive—vol. 21 (2), box 4 (16), WH/NSC: POW/MIA.

70. Cable, Kennedy to Haig [Nixon to Kissinger], November 24, 1972 [received 1:43 A.M., Nov. 25], folder: HAK Paris Trip 18–25 Nov. 1972 TOHAK [1 of 2], and Cable, Haig to Kennedy [Kissinger to Nixon], November 25, 1972, folder: HAK Paris Trip 18–25 Nov. 1972 HAKTO, box 26, NSC: HAKOF, HAKTF, NPM. Nixon had urged Kissinger to continue the talks and to recess them only if necessary. In oral comments to the White House, Kissinger claimed that the North Vietnamese were "terrified" by the breaking off of the talks; *HRHD,* November 26, 1972. This hyperbole was no doubt designed to impress Nixon. Kissinger had met with South Vietnamese officials in an equally "electric" meeting on the night of November 24, during which he had delivered a letter from Nixon, urging them to cooperate. Additional documentation on the issues associated with the November round of talks can be found in the two folders labeled HAK Paris Trip 18–25 Nov. 1972 TOHAK [1 of 2] and [2 of 2] of box 26, NSC: HAKOF, HAKTF, NPM.

71. Cable, Haig to Kennedy [Kissinger to Nixon], November 25, 1972, and Memo, Kissinger to Nixon, November 25, 1972, sub: Changes Obtained in the Draft Agreement folder: HAK Paris Trip 18–25 Nov. 1972 HAKTO, box 26, NSC: HAKOF, HAKTF, NPM.

72. *HRHD,* December 20, 1972.

73. Cable, Nixon to Kissinger, 10:55 A.M., November 24, 1972, folder: HAK Paris Trip 18–25 Nov. 1972 TOHAK [2 of 2], box 26, NSC: HAKOF, HAKTF, NPM.

74. Hammond, *The Military and the Media,* 598.

75. Memorandum of Conversation, November 24, 1972, folder: Camp David—Meetings with GVN Advisor Duc—Washington, Nov. 24–Dec. 1, 1972—vol. 22, box 4 (20), and Memorandum of Conversation, November 24, 1972, folder: Camp David—Sensitive—vol. 21 (2), box 4 (16), WH/NSC: POW/MIA, NPM; *WHY,* 1422; *HRHD,* November 25, 1972.

76. Letter, Thieu to Nixon, November 26, 1972, folder: Camp David—Sensitive—vol. 22 (1), box 4 (18), WH/NSC: POW/MIA, NPM. Additional documentation on U.S.-RVN exchanges during October and November can be found in boxes 25 and 26, NSC: HAKOF, HAKTF, NPM.

77. Memorandum of Conversation, November 29, 1972, Camp David—Meetings with GVN Advisor Duc—Washington, Nov. 29–Dec. 1, 1972—vol. 22, box 4 (20), WH/NSC: POW/MIA, NPM; *WHY,* 1426. Nixon promised that the U.S. Seventh Air Force in Thailand would maintain communications with RVNAF, provide targeting information on

PAVN, and launch tactical and B-52 attacks against North Vietnam if it threatened to topple Thieu from power; Nguyen Tien Hung and Schecter, *Palace File*, 136–137.

78. *HRHD*, November 29, 1972; *WHY*, 1426. Nixon claimed, in *RN*, 723–724, that he had been brutal.

79. Documents concerning Thieu's actions and Washington's negotiations with him can be found in the following folders and boxes in WH/NSC: POW/MIA, NPM: folders: Camp David—Sensitive—vol. 22 (1) and (2), box 4 (18) and (19); folder: Backchannel Messages—From Ambassador Bunker—Saigon Sept 1972, box 3; Vietnam Negotiations, Camp David—Memos—1972, box 4 (24). In NSC: HAKOF, HAKTF, NPM, documents regarding Thieu can be found in boxes 27 and 28.

80. Memo, Kissinger to Nixon, November 29, 1972, sub: Talking Points, and Memo, Haig for President's Files, November 30, 1972, sub: The President's Meeting with the Joint Chiefs of Staff, folder: Camp David—Sensitive—vol. 22 (1), box 4 (18), WH/NSC: POW/MIA. See also Hammond, *The Military and the Media*, 598.

81. *HRHD*, December 2, 1972. Concerning similar options in August, see, e.g., the discussion in chapter 12 concerning Kissinger's meeting with Thieu on August 18. Concerning Nixon's instincts about public opinion, see also *RN*, 717 ff., and my discussion of this period in previous paragraphs.

82. See, e.g., my earlier discussion of the November period, but also *HRHD*, November 26 and 27, 1972, and Cable, Haig to Kennedy [Kissinger to Nixon], December 4, 1972, folder: HAK Paris Trip 3–13 Dec. 1972 HAKTO and Memos to Pres., etc. [2 of 2], box 27, NSC: HAKOF, HAKTF, NPM.

83. Memo, Nixon to Kissinger, December 1, 1972, sub: Your Instructions for the December 4 Negotiating Round, folder: HAK Paris Trip 3–13 Dec. 1972 HAKTO and Memos to the Pres., etc. [1 of 2], box 27, NSC: HAKOF, HAKTF, NPM.

84. *HRHD*, November 20, 21, 22, and 29, 1972.

85. Economic Sanctions, n.d., folder: HAK Paris Trip 3–13 Dec. 1972 HAKTO and Memos to the Pres., etc. [1 of 2], box 27, NSC: HAKOF, HAKTF, NPM.

86. *RN*, 719, 724; *WHY*, 1427, 1428.

87. Memo, Nixon to Kissinger, December 1, 1972, sub: Your instructions for the December 4 Negotiating Round, folder: HAK Paris Trip 3–13 Dec. 1972 HAKTO and Memos to the Pres., etc. [1 of 2], box 27, NSC: HAKOF, HAKTF, NPM.

88. *WHY*, 1427.

89. *HRHD*, December 2, 1972.

90. DRV Chronology on Diplomatic Struggle, December 4, 1972; Porter offers a similar but slightly different interpretation in *Peace Denied*, 153. In their memoirs, Nixon and Kissinger gave a quite different spin, emphasizing DRV intransigence, but see Kissinger's comments in *WHY*, 1434, regarding Tho's "concessions."

91. Cables, Kissinger to Nixon, December 4, 5, and 6, folder: HAK Paris Trip 3–13 Dec. 1972 HAKTO and Memos to the Pres., etc. [2 of 2], box 27, NSC: HAKOF, HAKTF, NPM. See also *WHY*, 1428–1429; Porter, *Peace Denied*, 153.

92. Cables, Kissinger to Nixon and Bunker [via aides], December 7, 1972, folder: HAK Paris Trip 3–13 Dec. 1972 HAKTO and Memos to the Pres., etc. [2 of 2], box 27, NSC: HAKOF, HAKTF, NPM; DRV Chronology on Diplomatic Struggle, December 6 and 8, 1972.

93. *WHY*, 1434. Pushed by Haldeman, however, Kissinger agreed that progress had been made by this date; *HRHD*, December 7, 1972.

94. Cables, Kissinger to Nixon [via aides], December 8, 9, 11, 12, and 13, and Mutually Agreed Changes in the Agreement, folders: HAK Paris Trip 3–13 Dec. 1972 HAKTO and Memos to the Pres., etc. [1 of 2] and [2 of 2], box 27; and Haig to Kissinger, December 10, 1972, folder: HAK Paris Trip 3–13 Dec. 1972 TOHAK 100–192 [2 of 2], box 27, NSC: HAKOF, HAKTF, NPM; Cf. Porter, *Peace Denied,* 153–158; *RN,* 724–734; *WHY,* 1426–1446.

95. See, e.g., *HRHD,* December 5–7, 1972; Cables, Kissinger to Nixon [via aides], December 4–7, 1972, folder: HAK Paris Trip 3–13 Dec. 1972 HAKTO and Memos to the Pres., etc. [2 of 2]; and Nixon to Kissinger [via aides], December 4–6, folder: HAK Paris Trip 3–13 Dec. 1972 TOHAK 1–100 [2 of 2], box 27, NSC: HAKOF, HAKTF, NPM. Also see *RN,* 728–730, and *WHY,* 1428–1446.

96. Cables, Kissinger to Nixon, December 12 and 13, 1972, folder: HAK Paris Trip 3–13 Dec. 1972 HAKTO and Memos to the Pres., etc. [2 of 2], box 27, NSC: HAKOF, HAKTF, NPM; *WHY,* 1439; *RN,* 733; Porter, *Peace Denied,* 155.

97. Cable, Kissinger to Nixon, December 13, 1972, folder: HAK Paris Trip 3–13 Dec. 1972 HAKTO and Memos to the Pres., etc. (2 of 2), box 27, NSC: HAKOF, HAKTF, NPM; *RN,* 733.

98. Cables, Kissinger to Nixon [via aides], December 4–7, 1972, folder: HAK Paris Trip 3–13 Dec. 1972 HAKTO and Memos to the Pres., etc. [2 of 2], box 27, NSC: HAKOF, HAKTF, NPM; *HRHD,* December 4 and 5, 1972; *RN,* 725–726; *WHY,* 1429–1430.

99. See *HRHD,* December 4 to 8, 1972.

100. *WHY,* 1440.

101. Cables and memos, Nixon to Kissinger [via aides], December 4, 5, 6, 7, 10, 11, 12, 13, folders: HAK Paris Trip 3–13 Dec. 1972 TOHAK 1–100 and 100–192, box 27, NSC: HAKOF, HAKTF, NPM; *HRHD,* December 4–10, 1972; *RN,* 724–733; *WHY,* 1430–1441. During this period Moscow at first urged Washington to be patient and to avoid making demands for substantive changes. In the end it told Washington that there had been insufficient time for its intercession with Hanoi to have been effective. Beijing, which the administration had also approached, made noncommittal responses to Washington's entreaties to intervene.

102. *WHY,* 1436; *HRHD,* December 4–8, 1972; Memo, Laird to Nixon, n.d. [ca. December 7, 1972], sub: Ceasefire Agreement, folder: Cease Fire 1972, box 7, WH/NSC: POW/MIA, NPM; Memo, Kennedy to Haig, December 7, 1972, folder: HAK Paris Trip 3–13 1972 TOHAK 1–100 [1 of 2], box 27, NSC: HAKOF, HAKTF, NPM. Ehrlichman pointed out that there would already have to be $10 billion in budget cuts across the board; in this situation, getting funds for the continuation of the war and to support Thieu would be very difficult; *HRHD,* December 6, 1972. For Haig's views regarding bombing, see Cable, Haig to Kissinger, December 13, 1972, folder: HAK Paris Trip 3–13 Dec. 1972 TOHAK 100–192 [1 of 2], box 27, NSC: HAKOF, HAKTF, NPM.

103. Cable, Kissinger to Nixon via Haig, December 13, 1972, folder: HAK Paris Trip 3–13 Dec. 1972 HAKTO and Memos to the Pres., etc. [2 of 2], box 27, NSC: HAKOF, HAKTF, NPM. This, like several other cables, can be found in duplicated or summarized memo form in other folders of box 27.

104. *HRHD,* December 13 and 15, 1972; Memo, Haig to Kissinger, December 13, 1972, sub: Items to Discuss with the President's Meeting at 10:00 A.M., December 14, folder:

HAK Paris Trip 3–13 Dec. 1972 HAKTO and Memos to the Pres., etc. [1 of 2], box 27, NSC: HAKOF, HAKTF, NPM.

105. See, e.g., Cables, Kennedy to Guay, December 5, 1972, and Haig to Kissinger, December 11, 1972, folders: HAK Paris Trip 3–13 Dec. 1972 TOHAK 1–100 [1 of 2] and 100–192 [2 of 2], box 27, NSC: HAKOF, HAKTF, NPM.

106. Letter, Nixon to Thieu, December 17, 1972, folder: Thieu, Nguyen Van, box 16, WHSF: PPF, NPM.

107. *RN,* 734.

108. *HRHD,* December 15 and 16, 1972.

109. *RN,* 734–736.

110. Quoted in Hughes, "Foreign Policy," 56.

111. "The plan includes new targets not previously attacked and is designed to accomplish the maximum psychological shock"; Memo, Haig to Kennedy, December 7, 1972, folder: HAK Paris Trip 3–13 Dec. 1972 TOHAK 1–100 [1 of 2], box 27, NSC: HAKOF, HAKTF, NPM. See also Linebacker II USAF Bombing Survey, Pacific Air Forces, April 1973, K717.64, AFHRA. Karl J. Eschmann, *Linebacker: The Untold Story of the Air Raids over North Vietnam* (New York: Ivy Books, 1989), chap. 7, lists B-52s as having flown 742 sorties, fighter-bombers, 640, and tactical air support fighters, 2,066. In *Limits of Air Power,* 194, Clodfelter put the figures for bombs dropped north of the twentieth parallel at 15,237 tons by B-52s and 5,000 tons by fighters.

112. Interviews by the author with Le Mai Phuong, Le Mau Han, Nguyen Van Khanh, and Tran Tuan Mau; Turley, *Second Indochina War,* 152; Porter, *Peace Denied,* 158–161. See also Hammond, *The Military and the Media,* 601–610. The casualty figures given are based on Hanoi's adjustments after bodies were recovered in the rubble. Originally, Hanoi announced 1,318 dead and 1,261 wounded. These lower numbers are the figures usually cited by official U.S. histories.

113. Linebacker II USAF Bombing Survey, p. 37, AFHRA.

114. Eschmann, *Linebacker,* 202–206; *Hearings Before Subcommittees of the Committee on Appropriations House of Representatives,* 93rd Cong., 1st sess., 4, pp. 5, 60; *HRHD,* December 20, 1972. The Vietnamese claimed eighty-one U.S. aircraft, including thirty-four B-52s and five F-111s; Vien, *Indochina: 1972–73 Turning Point,* 82. These figures were no doubt incorrect, but American figures apparently did not include planes lost at sea or those that were damaged and put out of action.

115. Memo, Media Quotes, Larry Higby to Bill Baroody, Jr., February 9, 1973, folder: "Vietnam," Alpha Subject Files: WHSF: SMOF, HRH, NPM. See also Hammond, *The Military and the Media,* 601–610.

116. *HRHD,* January 14, 1973.

117. George H. Gallup, *The Gallup Poll: Public Opinion, 1972–1977,* vol. 1, *1972–75* (Wilmington, Del.: Scholarly Resources, 1978), 79, 87; *RN,* 738.

118. Conversation, Erich Honecker and Vice Prime Minister Le Thanh Nghi, January 9, 1973, "Berlin, den 9.1.1973. Vermerk." Sozialistische Einheitspartei Deutschlands (Socialist Unity Party of Germany) B2/20/168, German Federal Archive; Memorandum of Conversation with Pham Van Dong, December 23, 1972, Daybook of Soviet Ambassador to the DRV, Ilia S. Shcherbakov, fond 5, opis' 66, delo 782, 11.1-6, Storage Center for Contemporary Documentation, Moscow.

119. *HRHD,* December 20, 1972; *RN,* 737–738.

120. Cf. DRV Chronology of Diplomatic Struggle, December 18, 1972, and *WHY,* 1427.

121. *WHY,* 1457–1458.

122. *HRHD,* January 9, 1973; Cables, Kissinger to Kennedy [for Nixon], January 8 and 9, 1973, and Kennedy [for Nixon] to Kissinger, January 9, 1973, folders: HAK Paris Trip 7–14 Jan. 1973 HAKTO 1–48 and TOHAK 1–66, box 28, NSC: HAKOF, HAKTF, NPM; Message, Kissinger to Nixon, January 9, 1973, folder: Kissinger Messages Re Vietnam Peace Negotiations—January, 1973, box 82, WHSF: PPF, NPM.

123. Cables, Kissinger to Kennedy, January 9, 11, and 13, 1973, folder: HAK Paris Trip 7–14 Jan. 1973 HAKTO 1–48, box 28, NSC: HAKOF, HAKTF, NPM; Kissinger to Guay, February 23, 1973, folder: HAK Paris Trip 22–23 January 1973, ibid. Additional and duplicate material on the January talks with Hanoi and Saigon can be found in other folders in box 28.

124. For White House discussions of the Thieu problem, see *HRHD,* December 20, 1972–January 23, 1973. For letters between Nixon and Thieu from December 17, 1972, to January 22, 1973, see folder: Thieu, Nguyen Van, box 16, WHSF: PPF, NPM; and Hung and Schecter, *Palace File,* appendix A.

125. The complete English- and Vietnamese-language texts of the agreement are in *United States Treaties and Other International Agreements,* vol. 24, pt. 1, 1973 (Washington, D.C.: GPO, 1974), 1–224. For partial or complete texts, see also the appendixes in Goodman, *Lost Peace;* Porter, *Peace Denied;* and Vien, *Indochina: 1972–73 Turning Point.*

126. *HRHD,* December 19, 1972.

127. Memo, January 19, 1973, and Marginal revisions by Nixon in Memo, Haldeman to Kissinger [originally from Nixon to Haldeman], January 25, 1973, folder: Vietnam 2 folder: Action Memos, box 112, WHSF: ANF, HRH, NPM.

128. Klein, *Making It Perfectly Clear,* 387–390.

129. Thoughts Regarding the Peace Announcement, n.d. [ca. January 1973], folder: Vietnam, WHSF: ANF, HRH, NPM.

130. Memo, January 19, 1973, and Memo, Ray Price to Haldeman, February 27, 1973, folder: VN Settlement Euphoria folder: Action Memos, box 112, ibid.

131. Key Points to Be Made with Respect to Vietnam Agreement, n.d. [ca. January 1973], folder: Vietnam Peace Reaction, box 178, ibid.

132. Cable, Haig to Kissinger [prepared by Negroponte and initialed by Haig, Kennedy, Howe, and Lord], October 4, 1972, sub: Some Thoughts on Where We Stand on Negotiations, folder: Camp David—Sensitive—vol. 19, box 4 (13), WH/NSC: POW/MIA, NPM. See also Bunker's report to the president, January 26, 1972, reprinted in *The Bunker Papers,* vol. 3, ed. Pike, 848–851.

Bibliography

UNPUBLISHED MATERIAL

Archives

National Security Archive. Washington, D.C.
Nixon Presidential Materials, National Archives and Records Administration. College Park, Maryland.
Papers of Henry Cabot Lodge II, Massachusetts Historical Society. Microfilm.
Socialist Unity Party of Germany, German Federal Archives. Koblenz, Germany.
Storage Center for Contemporary Documentation (former Communist Party Soviet Union Central Committee Archive). Moscow, Russia.
Vietnamese Revolution Museum, Hanoi.
U.S. Air Force Historical Research Agency, Maxwell Air Force Base. Montgomery, Alabama.
W. Averell Harriman Papers, Manuscript Division of the Library of Congress. Washington, D.C.

Documents

The DRV Chronology on Diplomatic Struggle. Hanoi, 1987.
The DRV Foreign Ministry. Fundamental Documents on Vietnam War Negotiations (4/1965–7/1980). Hanoi, January 1981.
Ellsberg, Daniel. Options Paper, December 27, 1968.

Interviews Conducted by the Author

Ellsberg, Daniel. Washington, D.C., July 15 and 17, 1992.
Gaiduk, Ilya V. Oslo, Norway, Spring 1995.
Huong Tung. Hanoi, Vietnam, September 21, 1994.
Le Mai Phuong. Hanoi, Vietnam, September 28, 1994.

Le Mau Han. Hanoi, Vietnam, September 28, 1994.

Lord, Winston. Washington, D.C., December 5, 1994.

Luu Van Loi. Hanoi, Vietnam, September 26, 1994.

Nguyen Co Thach. Ho Chi Minh City, January 17, 1988; Hanoi, Vietnam, September 24, 1994.

Nguyen Van Khanh. Hanoi, Vietnam, September 28,1994.

Nguyen Vu Tung. Oslo, Norway, Spring 1995.

Tran Duc Cuong. Hanoi, Vietnam, September 29, 1994.

Tran Tuan Mau. Ho Chi Minh City, January 18, 1988.

Other

Ellsberg, Daniel. "The Incentives to Preemptive Attack"; "The Political Uses of Madness"; "Presidents as Perfect Detonators"; "The Theory and Practice of Blackmail"; "The Threat of Violence." Lecture transcripts, 1959.

Herring, George C. "Nixon, Kissinger, and Madman Diplomacy in the Far East." Unpublished paper, April 1980.

Kissinger, Henry A. Author notes on Kissinger's lectures and answers to questions, April 29 and 30, 1993, Ohio State University, Mershon Center, Columbus, Ohio.

———. Author notes on Kissinger's lecture and answers to questions, January 13, 1995, Norwegian Nobel Institute, Oslo, Norway.

Smith, R. B. "The International Setting of the Cambodia Crisis, October 1969 to April 1970." Unpublished paper, May 1995.

PUBLISHED MATERIAL

Documents, Diaries, Letters, Reports, Speeches

Abuse of Power: The New Nixon Tapes. Edited by Stanley L. Kutler. New York: Free Press, 1997.

Bases for a Settlement of the Viet Nam Problem. Hanoi: Foreign Languages Publishing House, 1971.

The Bunker Papers: Reports to the President from Vietnam, 1967–1973. Vol. 3. Berkeley: Institute of East Asian Studies, University of California, 1990.

Cold War International History Project Bulletin. [Reprints and analysis of Soviet, East German, and Chinese documents.] Issue 3 (Fall 1993): 62–67; Issue 4 (Fall 1994): 69–70; Issues 6–7 (Winter 1995): 30–126; 186–207; 232–265.

"Congress and the Termination of the Vietnam War." Prepared for the Use of the Committee on Foreign Relations, United States Senate by the Foreign Affairs Division Congressional Research Service, Library of Congress, April 1973. Washington, D.C.: U.S. Government Printing Office, 1973.

Declassified Documents Catalog. Woodbridge, Conn.: Research Publications, 1994.

Department of Defense Annual Report for the Fiscal Year 1965. Washington, D.C., U.S. Government Printing Office, 1967.

Documents of the National Security Council: Second Supplement. Frederick, Md.: University Publications of America, 1983. Microfilm.

Foreign Relations of the United States. Washington, D.C.: U.S. Government Printing Office.

From the President: Richard Nixon's Secret Files. Edited by Bruce Oudes. New York: Harper and Row, 1989.

Gallup, George H. *The Gallup Poll: Public Opinion, 1935–1971.* New York: Random House, 1972.

———. *The Gallup Poll: Public Opinion, 1972–1977.* Wilmington, Del.: Scholarly Resources, 1978.

The Haldeman Diaries: Inside the Nixon White House, the Complete Multimedia Edition. Santa Monica, Calif.: Sony Electronic Publishing, 1994. [The complete text on compact disc, including President's Activities Calendar, photographs, and film clips.]

The Haldeman Diaries: Inside the Nixon White House. New York: Putnam, 1994. [The abridged text in book form.]

Hearings Before Subcommittees of the Committee on Appropriations, House of Representatives. 93rd Cong. 1st sess., Subcommittee on Department of Defense, George H. Mahon, Chairman, Subcommittee on Military Construction, Robert L. F. Sikes, Florida, Chairman. Washington, D.C.: U.S. Government Printing Office, 1973.

Historical Statistics of the United States: Colonial Times to 1970. Washington, D.C.: Bureau of the Census, 1975.

Ho Chi Minh on Revolution: Selected Writings, 1920–1966. Ed. Bernard Fall. New York: Praeger, 1967.

Le Duan. *Letters to the South.* Hanoi: Foreign Languages Press, 1986.

Legislative Proposals Relating to the War in Southeast Asia: Hearings Before the Committee on Foreign Relations, United States Senate. 92nd Cong., 1st sess. Washington, D.C.: U.S. Government Printing Office, 1971.

Mao Tse-tung and Lin Piao: Post-Revolutionary Writings. Edited by Kuang Huan Fan. Garden City, N.Y.: Anchor Books, 1972.

The Nixon Presidential Press Conferences. New York: Earl M. Coleman Enterprises, 1978.

Nixon Speaks Out: Major Speeches and Statements by Richard Nixon in the Presidential Campaign of 1968. New York: Nixon-Agnew Campaign Committee, October 25, 1968.

The Pentagon Papers As Published by The New York Times. New York: Bantam Books, 1971.

The Pentagon Papers: The Defense Department History of United States Decision-making on Vietnam. Senator Gravel Edition. Boston: Beacon Press, 1971.

The Postwar Development of the Republic of Vietnam: Policies and Programs. New York: Joint Development Group, March 1969.

Public Papers of the Presidents of the United States. Washington, D.C.: U.S. Government Printing Office.

Sansom, R. L. *The Economics of Insurgency in the Mekong Delta of Vietnam.* Cambridge, Mass.: MIT Press, 1970.

The Secret Diplomacy of the Vietnam War: The Negotiating Volumes of the Pentagon Papers. Edited by George C. Herring. Austin: University of Texas Press, 1983.

United States Treaties and Other International Agreements. Vol. 24, pt. 1, 1973. Washington: U.S. Government Printing Office, 1974.

Vietnam Documents and Research Notes Series: Translation and Analysis of Significant Viet Cong/North Vietnamese Documents. Bethesda, Md.: University Publications of America, 1991. Microfilm.

Vo Nguyen Giap: Selected Writings. Hanoi: Foreign Languages Publishing House, 1977.

Memoirs, Personal Accounts, Interviews, and Oral Histories

Acheson, Dean. *Present at the Creation: My Years in the State Department*. New York: Norton, 1969.

Bui Diem, with David Chanoff. *In the Jaws of History*. Boston: Houghton Mifflin, 1987.

Bui Tin. *Following Ho Chi Minh: The Memoirs of a North Vietnamese Colonel*. Translated and adapted by Judy Stowe and Do Van. Honolulu: University of Hawaii Press, 1995.

Chennault, Anna. *The Education of Anna*. New York: Times Books, 1980.

Clifford, Clark, with Richard Holbrooke. *Counsel to the President: A Memoir*. New York: Random House, 1991.

Colson, Charles W. *Born Again*. 1976; London: Hodder and Stoughton, 1980.

Crowley, Monica. *Nixon Off the Record*. New York: Random House, 1996.

Dulles, John Foster. "The Evolution of Foreign Policy." *Department of State Bulletin* 30 (January 1954): 107–110.

———. "Policy for Security and Peace." *Foreign Affairs* 32 (April 1954): 353–364.

Eden, Anthony. *Full Circle: Memoirs of Anthony Eden*. Boston: Cassell, 1960.

Ehrlichman, John. *Witness to Power: The Nixon Years*. New York: Simon and Schuster, 1982.

Eisenhower, Dwight D. *Mandate for Change, 1953–1956*. Garden City, N.Y.: Doubleday, 1963.

Ellsberg, Daniel. *Papers on the War*. New York: Simon and Schuster, 1972.

Ely, Paul. *Mémoires: L'Indochine dans la tourmente*. Paris: Librairie Plon, 1964.

Fallaci, Oriana. *Interview with History*. Translated by John Shepley. New York: Liveright, 1976.

Frost, David. *"I Gave Them a Sword": Behind the Scenes of the Nixon Interviews*. New York: William Morrow, 1978.

Garment, Leonard. "The Annals of Law," *New Yorker*, April 17, 1989, 90–110.

———. *Crazy Rhythm*. New York: Random House, 1997.

Goldwater, Barry M. *With No Apologies: The Personal and Political Memoirs of United States Senator Barry M. Goldwater*. New York: William Morrow, 1979.

Haig, Alexander M., Jr. *Inner Circles: How America Changed the World: A Memoir*. New York: Warner Books, 1992.

Haldeman, H. R., with Joseph DiMona. *The Ends of Power*. New York: Times Books, 1978.

Humphrey, Hubert. *The Education of a Public Man: My Life and Politics*. Garden City, N.Y.: Doubleday, 1976.

Johnson, Lyndon Baines. *The Vantage Point: Perspectives of the Presidency, 1963–1969*. New York: Holt, Rinehart and Winston, 1971.

Joy, C. Turner. *How Communists Negotiate*. New York: Macmillan, 1955.

Kissinger, Henry A. *Diplomacy*. New York: Simon and Schuster, 1994.

———. *The Necessity for Choice*. New York: Harper and Brothers, 1961.

————. *Nuclear Weapons and Foreign Policy.* New York: Harper, 1957.

————. "The Relation Between Force and Diplomacy." *Military Industrial Conference: Proceedings of the Papers and Discussions.* Chicago, Illinois, March 14–15, 1957. [Held at the AFHRA.]

————. "The Viet Nam Negotiations." *Foreign Affairs* 47 (January 1969): 211–234.

————. *White House Years.* Boston: Little, Brown, 1979.

————. *Years of Upheaval.* Boston: Little, Brown, 1982.

Klein, Herbert. *Making It Perfectly Clear.* New York: Doubleday, 1980.

————. *The Essence of Security: Reflections in Office.* New York: Harper and Row, 1968.

McNamara, Robert S., with Brian VanDeMark. *In Retrospect: The Tragedy and Lessons of Vietnam.* New York: Times Books, 1995.

Morris, Roger. *Uncertain Greatness: Henry Kissinger and American Foreign Policy.* New York: Harper and Row, 1977.

Nguyen Tien Hung and Jerrold L. Schecter. *The Palace File.* New York: Harper and Row, 1986.

The Nixon Presidency: Twenty-two Intimate Perspectives of Richard M. Nixon. Vol. 6 of *Portraits of American Presidents.* Edited by Kenneth W. Thompson. New York: University Press of America, 1987.

Nixon, Richard. "Asia After Viet Nam." *Foreign Affairs* 46 (October 1967): 109–125.

————. *In the Arena: A Memoir of Victory, Defeat, and Renewal.* New York: Simon and Schuster, 1990.

————. *Leaders.* New York: Simon and Schuster, 1982.

————. "Meeting the People of Asia." *Department of State Bulletin* 30 (January 4, 1954): 10–14.

————. *No More Vietnams.* New York: Arbor House, 1985.

————. *RN: The Memoirs of Richard Nixon.* 1978; New York: Simon and Schuster, 1990.

————. *Six Crises.* New York: Simon and Schuster, 1962.

Price, Ray. *With Nixon.* New York: Viking Press, 1977.

Safire, William. *Before the Fall: An Inside View of the Pre-Watergate White House.* New York: Doubleday, 1975.

Strober, Gerald S., and Deborah H. Strober, eds. *Nixon: An Oral History of His Presidency.* New York: HarperCollins, 1994.

Truong Nhu Tang, with David Chanoff and Doan Van Toai. *A Vietcong Memoir.* New York: Vintage Books, 1986.

Wanner, Jann. "The Rolling Stone Interview: Dan Ellsberg." *Rolling Stone,* September 1973, 1–39.

Whalen, Richard J. *Catch the Falling Flag: A Republican's Challenge to His Party.* Boston: Houghton Mifflin, 1972.

Books

Abrahamsen, David. *Nixon vs. Nixon: An Emotional Tragedy.* New York: Farrar, Straus and Giroux, 1977.

Aitken, Jonathan. *Nixon: A Life.* Washington, D.C.: Regnery, 1993.

Ambrose, Stephen E. *Eisenhower.* Vol. 2, *The President.* New York: Simon and Schuster, 1983.

————. *Nixon*. Vol. 1, *The Education of a Politician, 1913–1962*. New York: Simon and Schuster, 1987.

————. *Nixon*. Vol. 2, *The Triumph of a Politician, 1962–1972*. New York: Simon and Schuster, 1989.

————. *Nixon*. Vol. 3, *Ruin and Recovery, 1973–1990*. New York: Simon and Schuster, 1991.

Anderson, David L., ed. *Shadow on the White House: Presidents and the Vietnam War, 1945–1975*. Lawrence: University Press of Kansas, 1993.

————. *Trapped by Success: The Eisenhower Administration and Vietnam, 1953–1961*. New York: Columbia University Press, 1991.

Andradé, Dale. *Ashes to Ashes: The Phoenix Program and the Vietnam War*. Lexington, Mass.: Lexington Books, 1990.

Appy, Christian G. *Working-Class War: American Combat Soldiers and Vietnam*. Chapel Hill: University of North Carolina Press, 1993.

Bao Ninh. *The Sorrow of War: A Novel of North Vietnam*. Translated by Phan Thanh Hao. New York: Riverhead Books, 1993.

Barber, James David. *The Presidential Character*. Englewood Cliffs, N.J.: Prentice Hall, 1972.

Brandon, Henry. *The Retreat of American Power*. Garden City, N.Y.: Doubleday, 1973.

Brennan, Mary. *Turning Right in the Sixties: The Conservative Capture of the GOP*. Chapel Hill: University of North Carolina Press, 1995.

Brodie, Fawn M. *Richard Nixon: The Shaping of His Character*. New York: Norton, 1981.

Brown, Seyom. *The Crises of Power: An Interpretation of United States Foreign Policy During the Kissinger Years*. New York: Columbia University Press, 1979.

Burdick, Eugene, and Harvey Wheeler. *Fail Safe*. New York: McGraw-Hill, 1962.

Chang, Gordon H. *Friends and Enemies: The United States, China, and the Soviet Union, 1948–1972*. Stanford, Calif.: Stanford University Press, 1990.

Clarke, Jeffrey J. *Advice and Support: The Final Years, The US Army in Vietnam*. Washington, D.C.: Center of Military History, 1988.

Clodfelter, Mark. *The Limits of Air Power: The American Bombing of North Vietnam*. New York: Free Press, 1989.

Cortright, David. *Soldiers in Revolt*. Garden City, N.Y.: Doubleday, 1975.

Davidson, Philip B. *Vietnam at War: The History, 1946–1975*. New York: Oxford University Press, 1988.

DeBenedetti, Charles, and Charles Chatfield, assisting author. *An American Ordeal: The Antiwar Movement of the Vietnam Era*. Syracuse, N.Y.: Syracuse University Press, 1990.

Diagnostic and Statistical Manual of Mental Disorders. 4th. Ed. [*DSM-IV*.] Washington, D.C.: American Psychiatric Association, 1994.

Duiker, William J. *The Communist Road to Power in Vietnam*. 2d ed. Boulder, Colo.: Westview Press, 1996.

Eschmann, Karl J. *Linebacker: The Untold Story of the Air Raids over North Vietnam*. New York: Ivy Books, 1989.

Ewald, William, Jr. *Eisenhower the President: Crucial Days, 1951–1960*. Englewood Cliffs, N.J.: Prentice Hall, 1981.

Franklin, H. Bruce. *M.I.A. or Mythmaking in America*. New Brunswick, N.J.: Rutgers University Press, 1993.

Friedman, Leon, and William F. Levantrosser, eds. *Cold War Patriot and Statesman: Richard M. Nixon.* Westport, Conn.: Greenwood Press, 1993.

Fussell, Paul. *Class: A Guide Through the American Status System.* New York: Summit Books, 1983.

Gaiduk, Ilya V. *The Soviet Union and the Vietnam War.* Chicago: Ivan R. Dee, 1996.

Garthoff, Raymond. *Détente and Confrontation: American-Soviet Relations from Nixon to Reagan.* Rev. ed. Washington, D.C.: Brookings Institution, 1994.

George, Alexander. *Forceful Persuasion: Coercive Diplomacy as an Alternative to War.* Washington, D.C.: United States Institute of Peace, 1991.

George, Peter. *Red Alert.* New York: Ace Books, 1958.

Gibbons, William Conrad. *The U.S. Government and the Vietnam War: Executive and Legislative Roles and Relationships, Parts I & II.* Washington, D.C.: U.S. Government Printing Office, 1984.

Gibson, James William. *The Perfect War: The War We Couldn't Lose and How We Did.* New York: Atlantic Monthly Press, 1986.

Gleick, James. *Chaos: Making a New Science.* New York: Penguin Books, 1987.

Goodman, Allan E. *The Lost Peace: America's Search for a Negotiated Settlement of the Vietnam War.* Stanford, Calif.: Hoover Institution Press, 1978.

———. *The Search for a Negotiated Settlement of the Vietnam War.* Berkeley: Institute of East Asian Studies, University of California, 1986.

Greenstein, Fred I., ed. *Leadership in the Modern Presidency.* Cambridge, Mass.: Harvard University Press, 1988.

Haley, Edward P. *Congress and the Fall of South Vietnam and Cambodia.* Rutherford, N.J.: Fairleigh Dickinson University Press, 1982.

Hammond, William M. *United States Army in Vietnam: Public Affairs: The Military and the Media, 1968–1973.* Washington, D.C.: Center of Military History, 1996.

Heineman, Kenneth J. *Campus Wars: The Peace Movement at American State Universities in the Vietnam Era.* New York: New York University Press, 1993.

Henriksen, Margot A. *Dr. Strangelove's America: Society and Culture in the Atomic Age.* Berkeley: University of California Press, 1997.

Herring, George C. *America's Longest War: The United States and Vietnam, 1950–1975.* 3d ed. New York: McGraw-Hill, 1996.

———. *LBJ and Vietnam: A Different Kind of War.* Austin: University of Texas Press, 1994.

Hersh, Seymour. *The Price of Power: Kissinger in the Nixon White House.* New York: Summit Books, 1983.

Hoff, Joan. *Nixon Reconsidered.* New York: BasicBooks, 1994.

Hoffmann, Stanley. *Primacy or World Order: American Foreign Policy Since the Cold War.* New York: McGraw-Hill, 1978.

Hogan, Michael J., and Thomas G. Paterson, eds. *Explaining the History of American Foreign Relations.* Cambridge: Cambridge University Press, 1991.

Isaacs, Arnold R. *Without Honor: Defeat in Vietnam and Cambodia.* New York: Vintage Books, 1984.

Isaacson, Walter. *Kissinger.* New York: Simon and Schuster, 1992.

Isaacson, Walter, and Evan Thomas. *The Wise Men: Six Friends and the World They Made: Acheson, Bohlen, Harriman, Kennan, Lovett, McCloy.* New York: Simon and Schuster, 1986.

Jack, Dana Crowley. *Silencing the Self: Women and Depression.* Cambridge, Mass.: Harvard University Press, 1991.

Kalb, Marvin. *The Nixon Memo: Political Respectability, Russia, and the Peace.* Chicago: University of Chicago Press, 1994.

Kalb, Marvin, and Bernard Kalb. *Kissinger.* Boston: Little, Brown, 1974.

Kaplan, Lawrence S., Denise Artaud, and Mark R. Rubin, eds. *Dien Bien Phu and the Crisis of Franco-American Relations, 1954–1955.* Wilmington, Del.: Scholarly Resources, 1990.

Karnow, Stanley. *Vietnam: A History.* New York: Knopf, 1983.

Kolko, Gabriel. *Anatomy of a War: Vietnam, the United States, and the Modern Historical Experience.* New York: Pantheon Books, 1985.

Kutler, Stanley. *The Wars of Watergate: The Last Crisis of Richard Nixon.* New York: Knopf, 1990.

Lavalle, A. J. C., ed. *Airpower and the 1972 Spring Invasion.* USAF Southeast Asia Monograph Series, Vol. II, Monograph 3. Washington, D.C.: Office of Air Force History, 1985.

Littauer, Raphael, and Norman Uphoff, eds. *The Air War in Indochina.* Rev. ed. Boston: Beacon Press, 1972.

Lumsden, Malvern. *Anti-personnel Weapons.* London: Taylor and Francis, 1978.

Matusow, Allen J. *Nixon's Economy: Booms, Busts, Dollars, and Votes.* Lawrence: University Press of Kansas, 1998.

Mazo, Earl. *Richard Nixon: A Political and Personal Portrait.* New York: Harper and Brothers, 1959.

McCarthy, James R. *Linebacker II: A View from the Rock.* USAF Southeast Asia Monograph Series, Vol. VI, Monograph 8. Washington, D.C.: Office of Air Force History, 1985.

McCormick, Thomas J. *America's Half-Century: United States Foreign Policy in the Cold War and After.* 2d ed. Baltimore, Md.: Johns Hopkins University Press, 1995.

Morris, Roger. *Haig: The General's Progress.* New York: Playboy Press, 1982.

———. *Richard Milhous Nixon: The Rise of an American Politician.* New York: Henry Holt, 1990.

Morrocco, John, and the Editors of Boston Publishing Company. *Rain of Fire: Air War, 1969–1973.* Boston: Boston Publishing Company, 1985.

Mueller, John E. *War, Presidents, and Public Opinion.* New York: Wiley, 1973.

Nguyen Khac Vien. *Contemporary Vietnam, 1858–1980.* Hanoi: Foreign Languages Publishing House, 1981.

———. ed. *Indochina: 1972–73 Turning Point,* Vietnamese Studies, no. 39. Hanoi: Foreign Languages Publishing House, 1974.

Nguyen Quang Truong. *The Easter Offensive of 1972.* Washington, D.C.: U.S. Army Center of Military History, 1980.

Olson, James, ed. *Dictionary of the Vietnam War.* New York: Peter Bedrick Books, 1987.

Pach, Chester J., Jr., and Elmo Richardson. *The Presidency of Dwight D. Eisenhower.* Lawrence: University Press of Kansas, 1991.

Paret, Peter, ed. *Makers of Modern Strategy: From Machiavelli to the Nuclear Age.* Princeton, N.J.: Princeton University Press, 1986.

Parmet, Herbert S. *Richard Nixon and His America.* Boston: Little, Brown, 1990.

Pike, Douglas. *Viet Cong: The Organization and Techniques of the National Liberation Front of South Vietnam.* Cambridge, Mass.: MIT Press, 1966.

_____. *Vietnam and the Soviet Union: Anatomy of an Alliance.* Boulder, Colo.: Westview Press, 1987.

Porter, Gareth. *A Peace Denied: The United States, Vietnam, and the Paris Agreement.* Bloomington: Indiana University Press, 1975.

Powers, Thomas. *The Man Who Kept the Secrets: Richard Helms and the CIA.* New York: Knopf, 1979.

_____. *The War at Home: Vietnam and the American People, 1964–1968.* New York: Grossman, 1973.

Prados, John. *The Sky Would Fall: Operation Vulture, The Secret U.S. Bombing Mission to Vietnam, 1954.* New York: Dial Press, 1983.

Race, Jeffrey. *War Comes to Long An: Revolutionary Conflict in a Vietnamese Province.* Berkeley: University of California Press, 1972.

Rhodes, Richard. *Dark Sun: The Making of the Hydrogen Bomb.* New York: Simon and Schuster, 1995.

Rotter, Andrew J. *The Path to Vietnam: Origins of the American Commitment to Southeast Asia.* Ithaca, N.Y.: Cornell University Press, 1987.

Ryan, Mark A. *Chinese Attitudes Toward Nuclear Weapons: China and the United States During the Korean War.* Armonk, N.Y.: M. E. Sharpe, 1989.

Safire, William. *Safire's Political Dictionary.* New York: Random House, 1978.

Schell, Jonathan. *The Time of Illusion.* New York: Knopf, 1975.

Schelling, Thomas. *Arms and Influence.* New Haven, Conn.: Yale University Press, 1966.

Schemmer, Benjamin F. *The Raid.* New York: Harper and Row, 1976.

Schlesinger, Arthur M., Jr. *The Imperial Presidency.* Boston: Houghton Mifflin, 1973.

Schulzinger, Robert D. *Henry Kissinger: Doctor of Diplomacy.* New York: Columbia University Press, 1989.

Schurmann, Franz. *The Foreign Politics of Richard Nixon: The Grand Design.* Berkeley: Institute of International Studies, University of California, 1987.

Shawcross, William. *Sideshow: Kissinger, Nixon and the Destruction of Cambodia.* Rev. ed. New York: Simon and Schuster, 1987.

Sheehan, Neil. *A Bright Shining Lie: John Paul Vann and America in Vietnam.* New York: Random House, 1988.

Sherry, Michael S. *The Rise of American Air Power: The Creation of Armageddon.* New Haven, Conn.: Yale University Press, 1987.

Showalter, Dennis E., and John G. Albert, eds. *An American Dilemma: Vietnam, 1964–1973.* Chicago: Imprint Publications, 1993.

Sigler, David Burns. *Vietnam Battle Chronology: U.S. Army and Marine Corps Combat Operations, 1965–1973.* Jefferson, N.C.: McFarland, 1992.

Small, Melvin, *Johnson, Nixon, and the Doves.* New Brunswick, N.J.: Rutgers University Press, 1988.

Small, Melvin, and William D. Hoover, eds. *Give Peace a Chance: Exploring the Vietnam Antiwar Movement.* Syracuse, N.Y.: Syracuse University Press, 1992.

Smith, Curt. *Long Time Gone: The Years of Turmoil Remembered.* South Bend, Ind.: Icarus, 1982.

Snepp, Frank. *Decent Interval: An Insider's Account of Saigon's Indecent End Told by the CIA's Chief Strategy Analyst in Vietnam.* New York: Vintage Books, 1978.

Spector, Ronald H. *United States Army in Vietnam: Advice and Support: The Early Years, 1941–1960.* Washington, D.C., Center of Military History, 1983.

Stanton, Shelby L. *Vietnam Order of Battle.* Washington, D.C.: U.S. News Books, 1981.

Szulc, Tad. *The Illusion of Peace: Foreign Policy in the Nixon Years.* New York: Viking Press, 1978.

Terriff, Terry. *The Nixon Administration and the Making of U.S. Nuclear Strategy.* Ithaca, N.Y.: Cornell University Press, 1995.

Thayer, Thomas C. *War Without Fronts: The American Experience in Vietnam.* Boulder, Colo.: Westview Press, 1985.

Turley, William S. *The Second Indochina War: A Short Political and Military History, 1954–1975.* New York: New American Library, 1987.

Van Tien Dung. *Our Great Spring Victory: An Account of the Liberation of South Vietnam.* Translated by John Spragens, Jr. New York: Monthly Review Press, 1977.

Warner, Roger. *Back Fire: The CIA's Secret War in Laos and Its Link to the War in Vietnam.* New York: Simon and Schuster, 1995.

Weston, Jessie L. *From Ritual to Romance.* Cambridge: Cambridge University Press, 1920.

White, Ralph K. *Fearful Warriors: A Psychological Profile of U.S.-Soviet Relations.* New York: Free Press, 1984.

White, Theodore H. *The Making of the President, 1968.* New York: Atheneum, 1969.

———. *The Making of the President, 1972.* New York: Atheneum, 1973.

Wicker, Tom. *One of Us: Richard Nixon and the American Dream.* New York: Random House, 1991.

Wills, Garry. *Nixon Agonistes: The Crisis of the Self-Made Man.* Boston: Houghton Mifflin, 1969.

Winkler, Allan M. *Life Under a Cloud: American Anxiety About the Bomb.* New York: Oxford University Press, 1995.

Witcover, Jules. *The Resurrection of Richard Nixon.* New York: Putnam, 1970.

Wittner, Lawrence S. *Resisting the Bomb: A History of the World Nuclear Disarmament Movement, 1954–1970.* Stanford, Calif.: Stanford University Press, 1997.

Zaroulis, Nancy, and Gerald Sullivan. *Who Spoke Up? American Protest Against the War in Vietnam, 1963–1975.* Garden City, N.Y.: Doubleday, 1984.

Journal and Magazine Articles

Aitken, Jonathan. "The Nixon Character." *Presidential Studies Quarterly* 26 (Winter 1996): 239–247.

Beisner, Robert L. "History and Henry Kissinger." *Diplomatic History* 14 (Fall 1990): 511–528.

Bernstein, Barton. "The Atomic Bombings Reconsidered." *Foreign Affairs* 74 (January/February 1995): 135–152.

Beschloss, Michael R. "How Nixon Came in from the Cold." *Vanity Fair,* June 1992, 114–119, 148–152.

Brands, H. W. "Fractal History, or Clio and the Chaotics." *Diplomatic History* 16 (Fall 1992): 495–510.

Brinkley, Alan. "Means of Descent." *The New Republic,* October 1, 1990, 28–35.

Calingaert, Daniel. "Nuclear Weapons and the Korean War." *Journal of Strategic Studies* 11 (June 1988): 177–202.

Castigliola, Frank. "The Nuclear Family: Tropes of Gender and Pathology in the Western Alliance." *Diplomatic History* 21 (Spring 1997): 163–184.

Chen Jiang. "China's Involvement in the Vietnam War, 1964–1969." *China Quarterly,* no. 142 (June 1995): 366–387.

Dean, Robert D. "Masculinity as Ideology: John F. Kennedy and the Domestic Politics of Foreign Policy," *Diplomatic History* 22 (Winter 1998): 29–62.

DeBenedetti, Charles, "On the Significance of Peace Activism: America, 1961–1975." *Peace and Change: A Journal of Peace Research* 9, nos. 2/3 (Summer 1983): 6–20.

Dingman, Roger. "Atomic Diplomacy During the Korean War." *International Security* 13 (Winter 1988/89): 50–91.

Donnelly, Dorothy C. "A Settlement of Sorts: Henry Kissinger's Negotiations and America's Extrication from Vietnam." *Peace and Change: A Journal of Peace Research* 9 (Summer 1983): 55–79.

Ellsberg, Daniel. "Call to Mutiny." *Monthly Review* 33, no. 4 (September 1981): 1–26.

Foot, Rosemary J. "Nuclear Coercion and the Ending of the Korean Conflict." *International Security* 13 (Winter 1988/89): 92–112.

Garthoff, Raymond L. "A Comment on the Discussion of 'LBJ, China, and the Bomb.'" *Society for Historians of American Foreign Relations Newsletter* 28 (September 1997): 27–31.

Glad, Betty, and Michael W. Link. "President Nixon's Inner Circle of Advisers." *Presidential Studies Quarterly* 26 (Winter 1996): 13–40.

Greenstein, Fred I. "A Journalist's Vendetta." *New Republic,* August 1, 1983, 29–32.

Herring, George C., and Richard H. Immerman. "Eisenhower, Dulles, and Dienbienphu: 'The Day We Didn't Go to War' Revisited." *Journal of American History* 71 (September 1984): 343–363.

Hoff, Joan. "Researchers' Nightmare: Studying the Nixon Presidency." *Presidential Studies Quarterly* 26 (Winter 1996): 250–266.

———."A Revisionist View of Nixon's Foreign Policy." *Presidential Studies Quarterly* 26 (Winter 1996): 107–130.

Hughes, Thomas L. "Foreign Policy: Men or Measures?" *Atlantic,* October 1974, 48–60.

Kahin, George McT. "The Pentagon Papers: A Critical Evaluation." *American Political Science Review* 69 (June 1975): 675–684.

Keefer, Edward. "President Dwight D. Eisenhower and the End of the Korean War." *Diplomatic History* 10 (Summer 1986): 267–289.

Kimball, Jeffrey. "How Wars End: The Vietnam War." *Peace and Change: A Journal of Peace Research* 20 (April 1995): 181–200.

———."The Stab-in-the-Back Legend and the Vietnam War." *Armed Forces and Society* 14 (Spring 1988): 433–458.

Kopkind, Andrew. "Many Nixons." *The Nation,* May 16, 1994, 651–652.

Lemann, Nicholas. "The Decline and Fall of the Eastern Empire." *Vanity Fair,* October 1994, 242–264.

Luu Van Loi. "The Johnson Episode in the Vietnam War." *Vietnamese Studies* 28, 1 (1992), New Series, no. 33 (103): 19–32.

Maddock, Shane. "LBJ, China, and the Bomb: New Archival Evidence." *Society for Historians of American Foreign Relations Newsletter* 27 (March 1996): 1–5.

McMahon, Robert J. "Credibility and World Power: Exploring the Psychological Dimension in Postwar American Diplomacy." *Diplomatic History* 15 (Fall 1991): 455–472.

Nguyen Ngoc Giao. "Nhen lai [Looking Back]." *Dien Dan Forum*, no. 41 (May 1, 1995): 4–5.

Renshon, Stanley Allen. "Psychological Analysis and Presidential Personality: The Case of Richard Nixon." *History of Childhood Quarterly: The Journal of Psychohistory* 2 (Winter 1975): 415–450.

Rotter, Andrew J. "Gender Relations, Foreign Relations: The United States and South Asia, 1947–1964." *Journal of American History* 81 (September 1994): 518–542.

Shepley, James. "How Dulles Averted War." *Life,* January 16, 1956, 70–80.

Sieg, Kent G. "The 1968 Presidential Election and Peace in Vietnam." *Presidential Studies Quarterly* 26 (Fall 1996): 1062–1080.

——."W. Averell Harriman, Henry Cabot Lodge, and the Quest for Peace in Vietnam." *Peace and Change: A Journal of Peace Research* 20 (April 1995): 237–249.

Small, Melvin. "Influencing the Decision Makers: The Vietnam Experience." *Journal of Peace Research* 24, no. 2 (1987): 185–198.

Stacks, John F. "Oh, They Say, This is the Watergate Man and We're Not Going to Pay Any Attention to Him." *Time,* May 2, 1994, 28–29.

Trachtenberg, Marc. "A 'Wasting Asset': American Strategy and the Shifting Nuclear Balance, 1949–1954." *International Security* 13 (Winter 1988/89): 5–49.

Ward, Dana. "Kissinger: A Psychohistory." *History of Childhood Quarterly* 2 (Winter 1975): 287–348.

Weissenbach, Karl. "Beyond Elvis and the Tapes: Research at the Nixon Presidential Materials Project." *The Record: News from the National Archives and Records Administration* 2 (May 1996): 10–11.

Wicker, Tom, "Richard M. Nixon, 1969–1974." *Presidential Studies Quarterly* 26 (Winter 1996): 249–257.

Other

Elliott, David W. P. "NLF-DRV Strategy and the 1972 Spring Offensive." International Relations of East Asia Project, Interim Report No. 4. Ithaca, N.Y.: Cornell University, 1974.

Kristensen, Hans M. "Nuclear Futures: Proliferation of Weapons of Mass Destruction and U.S. Nuclear Strategy." BASIC Research Report 98.2. London and Washington, D.C.: British American Security Information Council, 1998.

Newspapers and Periodicals

Atlantic
Chicago Sun-Times
Life
Miami Herald
The Nation
New Republic
New York Times

Newsweek
San Francisco Examiner
Time
U.S. News and World Report
Vanity Fair
Wall Street Journal
Washington Post
Washington-Star News

Index